A MAN ATTESTED BY GOD

A MAN ATTESTED BY GOD

The Human Jesus of the Synoptic Gospels

J. R. Daniel Kirk

WILLIAM B. EERDMANS PUBLISHING COMPANY
GRAND RAPIDS, MICHIGAN

Wm. B. Eerdmans Publishing Co.
2140 Oak Industrial Drive N.E., Grand Rapids, Michigan 49505
www.eerdmans.com

Published 2016
Printed in the United States of America

22 21 20 19 18 17 16   1 2 3 4 5 6 7

ISBN 978-0-8028-6795-7

Library of Congress Cataloging-in-Publication Data

A catalog record for this book is available from the Library of Congress

For Laura, Cora Marie, and Eliot

"The others show him as a man: *they gave glory to God who had given such authority to men* (Matt 9:8); but John only says that he is God: *and the Word was God.*"

— Thomas Aquinas, *Commentary on John* 1.67

Contents

Tables	x
Preface	xi
Abbreviations	xiv
Introduction	1
A. Idealized Human Figures	3
B. Methodology: Framework, Hypothesis, and Paradigm Testing	4
C. What This Study Is	9
D. What This Study Is Not	13
E. Recent Proposals for Early High Christology	16
F. Value of the Current Proposal	39
G. The Path Ahead	42
1. Idealized Human Figures in Early Judaism	44
A. Adam as Past and Future	47
B. Moses and the Prophets	77
C. Kings in Worship and Rule	96
D. Priests of Divinity	120
E. The Son of Man	139
F. The Community of the Elect	158
G. Conclusions: Idealized Human Figures and the Identity of God	173

2. Son of God as Human King   177

   A. Son of God as Human King in Mark   179

   B. Son of God, Son of David, Son of Adam in Luke   218

   C. Son of God in Matthew   237

   D. Conclusion: Son of God as Idealized Human King   258

3. Son of Man as the Human One   261

   A. Narrative Unity of the Son of Man Sayings in Mark   263

   B. The Son of Man in Mark's Narrative Arc   269

   C. The Son of Man Outside Mark   339

   D. The Human One: Son of Man as Son of Adam   353

   E. Conclusion: Son of Man as the Human One   356

4. Messiah Born and Raised   359

   A. God with Us: Matthew's Christ in Birth and Resurrection   359

   B. The Son of David: Jesus in Luke's Birth and Resurrection Narratives   387

   C. Conclusion: Messiah Born and Raised   411

5. Lord of All Creation   413

   A. Exorcisms   415

   B. Nature Miracles   433

   C. Healing Hands   460

   D. Conclusions: Human Agent of Divine Power   486

6. Jesus and the Scriptures of Israel   489

   A. Mark   491

   B. Matthew   516

   C. Luke   535

   D. Conclusions: Messianic Hermeneutics   568

Conclusions: A Man Attested by God   570

   A. Jesus as Idealized Human Figure in the Synoptic Gospels   570

   B. The Stories of Jesus in Matthew, Mark, and Luke   573

C. Human Christology and Jesus's Followers   575

D. Locating Jesus in the Biblical Narrative   578

E. Concluding Thoughts   580

Bibliography   583

Author Index   605

Subject Index   609

Ancient Sources Index   619

Tables

Table 1-1 Banners for the Battle in 1QM 170

Table 2-1 Parallels between "Son of God" Declarations in Mark 180

Table 4-1 Announcement, Prophecy, Enactment 368

Table 6-1 Citations in Mark 1:2-3 493

Preface

One of the most popular arguments for the divinity of Jesus comes from the pen of C. S. Lewis in his book *Mere Christianity*. In the final paragraph of a section entitled "The Shocking Alternative," he claims that Jesus can only be understood as "liar, lunatic, or lord."[1] Lord in this case is viewed as equivalent to "Lord and God." As a young Christian I found that this set of alternatives squared well with two things: (1) the understanding of Christianity I had then, that what lies at the center of everything is belief in the divinity of Jesus, and (2) the Jesus whom I met in the pages of John, who often made the sorts of outrageous self-referential claims that I can only imagine are the ones Lewis had in mind.

Where this framework of coming to terms with Jesus left me short, however, was in my encounter with the Jesus who confronted me in the pages of the Synoptic Gospels. This Jesus was not Lewis's despised "moral teacher" (full stop). But neither did he say very many things that left the reader with the choice between "this guy is a lunatic on the level with someone who thinks he is a poached egg" and "this is none other than the Lord God." In short, a divine Jesus whose mission entailed disclosure of a divine identity did not help me make sense of the stories told by Matthew, Mark, or Luke.

The tide began to turn for me at seminary, where a strong tradition of reading the whole Bible diachronically had created a deep sense among the faculty that humanity as represented in Adam, Israel, and David was crucial to the larger biblical narrative. The Jesus story began to take on importance not as demonstrating that Jesus the human was just a better teacher than most, or as showing that the divine had to take on flesh simply so that he could die, but as depicting Jesus playing the part the story had always lacked: a human who fulfilled the purpose of primal humanity to not only rule the world for God, but also to do so as a faithful, obedient son.

1. C. S. Lewis, *Mere Christianity* (New York: Macmillan, 1952), 55-56.

To bring this idea closer to the language of the Synoptic Tradition: I began to see that the kingdom of God comes near not when God rules as such, but when a human king, anointed and empowered by God's spirit, exercises an authority on the earth that by rights belongs to God alone. An article by Dan McCartney entitled "*Ecce Homo*" developed this very theme across various threads of the New Testament and played a seminal role in the formation of a generation of seminary students.[2] Such notions laid the foundation for the following years, in which I read and began to understand the stories of the Synoptic Gospels with very different lenses than the ones I had tried on in my youth: yes, Jesus is the Christ; but no, this does not mean that he is being depicted as divine.

However, just as I was growing into what I had learned and become convinced of it seemed that the tide shifted, and early divine Christology became the word of the day for those readers interested in the theological texture of scripture. Arguments to the effect that, whatever might be the Christological diversity within the New Testament writings, all early Christians showed that they identified Jesus with God or as God left me wondering if the coherence I had found through a human Jesus was going to be swept away. In the face of this shifting tide of scholarship, the current study is an attempt to reassert the centrality of Jesus as a particular kind of human as the operative Christological rubric for the Synoptic Gospels — a reading that has, to my mind, allowed the stories to find a coherence they otherwise lack and to claim their own voices amid the varied New Testament witness to the identity of Jesus.

This book has been a work in process for almost seven years now. No project of such duration could have endured without the encouragement and support of colleagues, family, and friends. I am grateful for Fuller Seminary's generous sabbatical policy, which provided me with two opportunities to be free from teaching responsibilities in order to be devoted to this book. I am thankful also to the students who have endured more "high human Christology" in Gospels class than they bargained for. A number of people read portions of the manuscript, taking on a burden that demonstrates true collegiality and friendship: Michael Bird, Sam Boyd, Craig Carpenter, Justin Dombrowski, Crispin Fletcher-Louis, John Goldingay, Larry Hurtado, Nathan Mastnjak, James McGrath, David Vinson, and Tim Wardle. Special thanks go out to Justin, Stephen, Judy, Mark, Love, David, Jim, Mark, Tim, Keoke, Steve, David, Jer, and countless others who have believed in the value of my work and

2. Dan McCartney, "*Ecce Homo:* The Coming of the Kingdom as the Restoration of Human Vicegerency," *WTJ* 56 (1994): 1-21.

encouraged me along the way. Most of all I am thankful for Laura, Cora Marie, and Eliot, whose love for me and in me allows me to do my work with the freedom that comes from knowing what truly matters most.

Abbreviations

ANCIENT SOURCES

1 En.	*1 Enoch*
11QMelch	11QMelchizedek
2 Apoc. Bar.	*2 Baruch (Syriac Apocalypse)*
3 En.	*3 Enoch*
3 Regn.	Dio Chrysostom, *De regno iii*
Ant.	Josephus, *Antiquities of the Jews*
Bell civ.	Caesar, *Bellum civile*
Hist.	Dio Cassius, *History of Rome*
Ezek. Trag.	Ezekiel the Tragedian
Gen. Rab.	*Genesis Rabbah*
Jub.	*Jubilees*
J.W.	Josephus, *Jewish War*
L.A.E.	*Life of Adam and Eve*
m.	Mishnah
Mos.	Philo, *De vita Mosis*
Opif.	Philo, *De opificio mundi*
Pesiq. Rab.	*Pesiqta Rabbati*
Pesiq. Rab Kah.	*Pesiqta de Rab Kahana*
Praem.	Philo, *De praemiis et poenis*
Pss. Sol.	*Psalms of Solomon*
Prob.	Philo, *Quod omnis probus liber sit*
Rep.	Plato, *Republic*
Rom. Ant.	Dionysius of Halicarnassus, *Roman Antiquities*
Sacr.	Philo, *De sacrificiis Abelis et Caini*
Somn.	Philo, *De somniis*
T. Ab.	*Testament of Abraham*

T. Lev.	*Testament of Levi*
Tg. Ps.-J.	*Targum Pseudo-Jonathan*
Tg. Neof.	*Targum Neofiti*
Frg. Tg.	*Fragmentary Targum*

JOURNALS AND BOOK SERIES

AB	Anchor Bible
ABRL	Anchor Bible Reference Library
ANTC	Abingdon New Testament Commentaries
AYB	Anchor Yale Bible Commentaries
BAR	*Biblical Archaeology Review*
BBR	*Bulletin for Biblical Research*
BDAG	Bauer-Danker-Arndt-Gingrich Greek-English Lexicon of the New Testament
BETL	Bibliotheca Ephemeridum Theologicarum Lovaniensium
BR	*Biblical Research*
BTS	Biblisch-Theologische Studien
BZAW	Beihefte zur Zeitschrift für die alttestamentliche Wissenschaft
BZNW	Beihefte zur Zeitschrift für die neutestamentliche Wissenschaft und die Kunde der ältern Kirche
CBQ	*Catholic Biblical Quarterly*
CBR	*Currents in Biblical Research*
CCSS	Catholic Commentary on Sacred Scripture
CHANE	Culture and History of the Ancient Near East
DR	*The Downside Review*
DSD	*Dead Sea Discoveries*
DSSSE	*The Dead Sea Scrolls Study Edition*
EC	*Early Christianity*
ExpT	*Expository Times*
FRLANT	Forschungen zur Religion und Literatur des Alten und Neuen Testaments
HBS	Herders Biblische Studien
HBT	*Horizons in Biblical Theology*
HTKNT	Herders theologischer Kommentar zum Neuen Testament
HTR	*Harvard Theological Review*
IBS	Irish Biblical Studies

ICC	International Critical Commentary
Interp	*Interpretation: A Journal of Bible and Theology*
ISBE	*International Standard Bible Encyclopedia*
ISFCJ	University of South Florida International Studies in Formative Christianity and Judaism
JBL	*Journal of Biblical Literature*
JCT	Jewish and Christian Texts in Contexts and Related Studies Series
JGRCJ	*Journal of Greco-Roman Christianity and Judaism*
JJS	*Journal of Jewish Studies*
JSJSup	Supplements to Journal for the Study of Judaism
JSNT	*Journal for the Study of the New Testament*
JSNTSup	Journal for the Study of the New Testament Supplement Series
JSP	*Journal for the Study of the Pseudepigrapha*
JSPSup	Journal for the Study of the Pseudepigrapha Supplement Series
JTS	*Journal of Theological Studies*
LCL	Loeb Classical Library
LHBOTS	Library of Hebrew Bible/Old Testament Studies
LHJS	Library of Historical Jesus Studies
LNTS	Library of New Testament Studies
LSTS	Library of Second Temple Studies
NICNT	New International Commentary on the New Testament
NIGTC	New International Greek Testament Commentary
NTOA	Novum Testamentum et Orbis Antiquus
OBO	Orbis Biblicus et Orientalis
OtSt	*Oudtestamentische Studiën*
RB	*Revue Biblique*
RevQ	*Revue de Qumran*
RevScRel	*Revue des sciences religieuses*
SAA	State Archives of Assyria
SBLSCS	Society of Biblical Literature Septuagint and Cognate Studies
SBLTT	Society of Biblical Literature Texts and Translations
SbWGF	*Sitzungsberichte der Wissenschaftlichen Gesellschaft an der Johann Wolfgang Goethe-Universität Frankfurt am Main*
SCS	Septuagint and Cognate Studies
SHR	Studies in the History of Religions
SJS	Studia Judaeoslavica

SNTSMS	Society for New Testament Studies Monograph Series
SSEJC	Studies in Scripture in Early Judaism and Christianity
STDJ	Studies on the Texts of the Desert of Judah
SupNovT	Supplements to Novum Testamentum
SVTP	Studia in Veteris Testamenti Pseudepigrapha
TDNT	*Theological Dictionary of the New Testament*
TLZ	*Theologische Literaturzeitung*
TPINTC	TPI New Testament Commentaries
TynBul	*Tyndale Bulletin*
UNDSPR	University of Notre Dame Studies in the Philosophy of Religion
VT	*Vetus Testamentum*
WBC	Word Biblical Commentary
WMANT	Wissenschaftliche Monographien zum Alten und Neuen Testament
WTJ	*Westminster Theological Journal*
WUNT	Wissenschaftliche Untersuchungen zum Neuen Testament
WUNT2	Wissenschaftliche Untersuchungen zum Neuen Testament, 2nd series
ZTK	*Zeitschrift für Theologie und Kirche*

Introduction

In the first speech in the mouth of a follower of Jesus after receiving the Holy Spirit, the freshly empowered and comprehending Peter refers to "Jesus of Nazareth, a man attested to you by God through miracles, wonders, and signs." This book articulates a paradigm that I call "idealized human figures," by which I intend to show that Peter's depiction is sufficient for understanding the Jesus who meets us in the pages of the Synoptic Gospels.

For those who are not convinced, or entering warily, the approach of this study is conducive to functioning as a thought experiment: what if we were to read the Synoptic Gospels themselves (not some presumed prehistory or reconstructed picture of Jesus) as bearing consistent witness to the fact that Jesus is a particular kind of human being, and to ask all along, what sort of man are we seeing in these texts? So I begin with this invitation: to read and reimagine the identity of Jesus in these texts as an idealized human being.[1] Some who read will be convinced that this is sufficient for explaining Jesus as he appears in the first three Evangelists; I hope that others who read will become more deeply convinced that it is a necessary part of explaining the Jesus who meets us there. I hope that the effect of this study will be to raise awareness of, and appreciation for, the rich Christology entailed in renderings of Jesus as an idealized human figure.

New Testament studies is in the midst of a resurgence of early high Christology, specifically of arguments to the effect that the full compass of early Christian witness to Jesus indicates that the early Christians thought of

---

1. The seed for this project was likely sown by an article written by one of my seminary professors that I read during my seminary training: Dan McCartney, "*Ecce Homo:* The Coming of the Kingdom as the Restoration of Human Vicegerency," *WTJ* 56 (1994): 1-21. In it, McCartney argues that God always reigns; however, God's reign is realized on earth with the rule of a faithful vicegerent. What McCartney argues for the whole of the New Testament I argue here with more focused attention on the Synoptic Gospels.

him, and/or treated him, as divine in what might fairly be called a proto-Chalcedonian sense.[2] Although there are several versions of this argument, many share a common structure. These arguments theorize from the notion that Jews in the first century reserve certain ascriptions, actions, or attributes for Israel's God alone; that the first-century Jews who wrote the New Testament nonetheless apply these very ascriptions, actions, or attributes to Jesus; and that these texts therefore and in these ways treat Jesus as and/or identify him with the God of Israel.[3]

The purpose of this book is, first, to problematize such claims by demonstrating that alongside such singularizing statements in the Jewish biblical and post-biblical corpus are extensive indications that God can share such divine roles and instances in which we see human participation in the divine identity so construed. In Jewish sources, humans play roles that properly belong to God alone, without redefining "Jewish monotheism."[4] Such humans are what I refer to as "idealized human figures." These figures provide an alternative paradigm for assessing the Christology of the Synoptic Tradition. Second, this study tests the sufficiency of the "idealized human figure" hypothesis for explaining even the high Christologies we encounter in the Synoptic Gospels.

2. Most influential are Richard Bauckham, *Jesus and the God of Israel: God Crucified and Other Studies on the New Testament's Christology of Divine Identity* (Grand Rapids, MI: Eerdmans, 2008), and Larry W. Hurtado, *Lord Jesus Christ: Devotion to Jesus in Earliest Christianity* (Grand Rapids, MI: Eerdmans, 2003). Bauckham explicitly says that the "earliest" Christology does not evince movement toward Chalcedon but "is already a fully divine Christology" (x). Hurtado is more cautious in wanting to paint such coalescence as the seed from which the later Chalcedonian Christology was developed, and yet uses "binitarian" in his study (esp. 151-53) in order to capture the heights to which he believes the earliest Christologies attained.

3. The devotion of an entire issue of *Early Christianity* to "Christology from Jewish Roots" (vol. 2:1 in 2011) is an indication of the prominence of the "Jewish context" approach in current scholarship; see especially the editorial by Jörg Frey, "Christology from Jewish Roots," *EC* 2 (2011): 1-3.

4. Students of these matters must take particular care not to assume a uniform "Jewish monotheism," akin to the beliefs of current-day monotheists, across different groups and different times. The diversity of Jewish monotheism and the challenges it presents as an aid to biblical interpretation are captured well by the essays in *Early Jewish and Christian Monotheism* (JSNTSup 263; ed. Loren T. Stuckenbruck and Wendy E. S. North; New York: T&T Clark, 2004). Walter Moberly's essay in that volume, "How Appropriate is 'Monotheism' as a Category for Biblical Interpretation?" (216-34), articulates a number of significant objections to this category serving as a lens for biblical interpretation.

A. IDEALIZED HUMAN FIGURES

The category I posit here, "idealized human figures," refers to non-angelic, non-preexistent human beings, of the past, present, or anticipated future, who are depicted in textual or other artifacts as playing some unique role in representing God to the rest of the created realm, or in representing some aspect of the created realm before God.[5] The object of concern is not the actual historical figures who may stand behind such idealized depictions, but instead the depictions themselves, which interpret the significance of persons through various ascriptions, actions, and attributes. In positing such a categorization, I am seeking to curtail two possible missteps in the interpretation of the historical evidence. First, more limited categories such as "anticipated messiah" might prove too narrow and lead to the wrong conclusion: if Jesus does something that no messiah was thought to do, such as raise the dead, one might conclude in too hasty a fashion that this means Jesus is being depicted as "more than messiah," hinting strongly that he is God. Second, comparing idealized descriptions from early Jewish texts with those in the Synoptic Gospels enables us to compare like with like (i.e., textual depictions of idealized figures). We need not wait for the discovery of an early Jewish sect that worshiped a human alongside God, for instance, to curtail the notion that the early Christians were treating Jesus as God if we do have texts that provide evidence of when such veneration might be acceptable.[6]

The categorization of "idealized human figure" seeks to chart a third way between a "low Christology" that defines Jesus as "a mere human being" and a "high" Christology that depicts Jesus approaching, or attaining to, the status of the God of Israel (what I refer to as "divine Christology").[7] At the same time, I should be quick to add that Jesus as an idealized human figure does not eliminate the possibility that Jesus is (being depicted as) divine. While the

---

5. Although I developed my category of "idealized human figures" independently, an earlier study functions with a similar rubric: John J. Collins and George W. E. Nickelsburg (eds.), *Ideal Figures in Ancient Judaism: Profiles and Paradigms* (SCS 12; Chico, CA: Scholars, 1980).

6. Here I have in mind Larry Hurtado, *One God, One Lord: Early Christian Devotion and Ancient Jewish Monotheism* (New York: T&T Clark, 1988), 38-42, in his dismissals of "literary scenes" as failing to show "precedent in Roman-era Jewish religious practice."

7. Such a dichotomous taxonomy appears, for instance, in Daniel Johannson, "The Identity of Jesus in the Gospel of Mark: Past and Present Proposals," *CBR* 9 (2010): 364-93; the language "a mere human being" is his. Andrew Chester, "High Christology — Whence, When and Why?" *EC* 2 (2011): 22-50, highlights the terminological confusion possible here, especially that "high Christology" need not entail divine Christology (33).

force of my argument is, throughout, to show the sufficiency of the human category for explaining the many Christologies narrated in the Synoptic Tradition, this book should not be read as constituting a claim to the effect that Jesus is not, in fact, God, in the way confessed by many Christian traditions or that idealized human Christologies are incompatible with divine Christologies. Instead, I am arguing for the best way to read these particular books of the New Testament, claiming that the paradigm of idealized human figures makes best sense of the data. Divine and preexistence Christology is attested to in other early Christian literature.

Idealized human Christology is a high, human Christology. I build the case for its plausibility and significance through a wide-ranging study of early Jewish texts. It is a high Christology because such human figures are variously represented as playing roles otherwise belonging to God alone. It is a high Christology, also, because such humans can be depicted as the very embodiment of God, God's visible representation, God's voice, the exhibition of God's rule and majesty. Indeed, one might even say that human Christology can be divine Christology, without imputing inherent divinity to the human in view, because God creates humanity in God's own image and likeness, to exercise God's sovereignty over the earth in God's stead. However, I attempt to restrict the label "divine Christology" to the position that sees Jesus as inherently constitutive of God, rather than contingently entailed in God through special creation or anointing. In Pauline terms, idealized human Christology might at times be something akin to Adam Christology.[8] In the language of Irenaeus of Lyons, idealized human Christology signals recapitulation. In the parlance of the Synoptic Gospels as translated by the Common English Bible, idealized human Christology claims that Jesus is the Human One.

B. METHODOLOGY: FRAMEWORK, HYPOTHESIS, AND PARADIGM TESTING

The methodology entailed in this study is twofold. First, an extensive survey of biblical and post-biblical Jewish literature (chap. 1) provides the raw data for positing the category of "idealized human figures" as a recognizable phenomenon across a sampling of early Judaism that varies widely in time, place, and ideology. Second, my survey of the Synoptic Gospels (chaps. 2–6) is one of testing the hypothesis that the category of "idealized human figures"

---

8. J. R. Daniel Kirk, "Mark's Son of Man and Paul's Second Adam," *HBT* 37 (2015): 170-95.

suffices as an overarching paradigm for explaining the diverse Christological expressions we see there.[9]

The approach, then, entails hypothesis testing, assessing the explanatory capacity of a given paradigm, rather than an attempt to inductively establish at every turn that the Gospel writers are themselves working to create such a category. At many points along the way, I argue that certain Christological indices such as the titles son of God and son of man would have been understood by an author and/or audience as referring to such a human. However, at many other points I make the less direct argument that the paradigm I propose suffices to incorporate the data. This approach commends itself for a couple of different reasons. One reason is that it directly responds to the nature of the early divine Christology arguments; namely, that certain expressions are so tied to the identity of God or other divine figure that they cannot be read as descriptions of a creature. In staking such a claim, the various authors have said that the paradigms of human or angelic figures are insufficient to account for the data, so that recourse to something more akin to divinity is required. This would be tantamount to a paradigm shift in the field of early Jesus research. My assessment of these arguments is that the reason the data did not fit the old paradigms had more to do with insufficiently developed heuristics for assessing Jesus's humanity than the ubiquitous appearance of divine Christology throughout the corpus of earliest Christian writings. Thus, the overall approach of my study is to demonstrate that the data from the varied Gospel narratives fit within the paradigm I propose rather than to argue throughout that the Gospel writers are intending to nod toward such a paradigm with each Jesus story, or to discredit other scholarly views about how each particular passage might signal Jesus's divinity or preexistence.

This takes us to the second reason such an approach commends itself. It is nearly impossible to survey every relevant passage pertaining to the Christology of the Synoptic Gospels, much less to give an in-depth scholarly treatment of all the arguments for various possible interpretations. Many of the passages I deal with come under consideration precisely because they are clear candidates for demonstrating divine or preexistence Christologies, and for this very reason I do not feel the need to relay in detail the scholarly arguments upholding such interpretations. My purpose is not to refute each argument in favor of early divine Christology so much as it is to show that if one assumes

9. The language of "paradigm" and its place in scholarly labors is adapted from Thomas S. Kuhn, *The Structure of Scientific Revolutions* (3rd ed.; Chicago: University of Chicago Press, 1996).

the pervasiveness and prevalence of idealized human figures throughout Jewish religious storytelling, then the Jesus of the Synoptic Gospels is readily interpreted in such a fashion. As I understand it, the question under debate is this: what assumptions about the identity of Jesus make sense of the Gospel stories as told? The early divine Christology proponents have argued that a human or angelic Christology fails to account for the full breadth of the stories told, ascriptions rendered, and the like, and that the explanation for this lies in the fact that the stories narrate the identity of Jesus such that he shares in God's preexistence or in what later theologians would call the divine nature. Such a claim constitutes a call for something closely akin to a paradigm shift in New Testament scholarship, put forward to account for data that did not fit with earlier, developmental views of early Christology.[10] With the category of idealized human figure in place, I aim to demonstrate that, overall, an exalted human paradigm is in fact sufficient to contain the data of the Gospels, and that the appeal to divinity is thus unnecessary for these particular stories.

Endemic to my argument is a shared overall approach with the proponents of early divine Christology, which looks to Judaism, with its commitment to the worship of only one God, as the seedbed for early Christianity and as the most important cultural (including literary) background for making sense of the Gospels as we have them. Issuing this internal critique of recent studies advocating divine Christology serves a couple of purposes. First, it takes the important step of reassessing an argument that many have found compelling on what is essentially its own grounds. In so doing, the reader can reassess with a fresh set of eyes whether the paradigm(s) on offer in the work of my predecessors is truly as compelling an explanation of the data as it appeared at first blush. The presentation of an alternative paradigm (idealized human figure in the place of divine identity) that deals with the same data (depictions of Jesus as found in scriptural accounts) and attempts to make sense of it within the same cultural-religious framework (biblical and post-biblical Judaism with its commitment to the singularity of the creator God) should lend clarity to the options on the table.

Second, this approach enables us to see points at which the early divine Christology arguments themselves stand in need of internal clarification or strengthening. One of the challenges in reading and understanding what these scholars claim is that the conclusions are often vague and amenable to multiple significations. To say, for instance, that Jesus's and God's identities in the

---

10. Though perhaps it is an overstatement to classify this with Kuhn's "scientific revolutions" (*Structure of Scientific Revolutions,* 5-6), a similar dynamic is at work.

Gospel of Luke are inseparable from each other is a faithful assessment of the Third Evangelist. But someone might also rightly say that in various parts of the Bible the identity of Israel and the identity of God are inseparable. The idealized human paradigm provides an alternative to divine Christology for accounting for such data as we find in the Gospels in step with the claims we might make for other idealized Jewish figures. It allows us to see that not only the New Testament data themselves but also the conclusions articulated by other scholars are amenable to various interpretations, including the conclusion that Jesus is depicted as an idealized human figure.

Third, by engaging the same data, and seeing an alternatively construed high Christology (i.e., a high human Christology) in the same (sorts of) passages in which my interlocutors see divine Christology itself, my study demonstrates significant overlap with the work they have done before me. In the end, it is hoped that this study thus has the capacity to enrich the Christological conversation by putting a new piece into play, one that has the capacity to augment the positions of my interlocutors even if they continue holding to their alternative paradigm.

Fourth, a paradigm approach enables me to deal with diverse Christologies without flatting any one into the likeness of another. Paradigms are not singular theories about how something works; they are overarching explanatory grids within which singular theories develop, make sense, and are understood to be coherent. When the paradigm about the earth's shape shifts from flat, stationary mass to spherical, rotating planet, the new paradigm enables us to say opposite things about the lunar and solar orbs that appear to be doing the very same things over our heads: one circles the earth, the earth circles the other, despite the fact that both "rise" and "set" daily across our sky. I argue that Matthew, Mark, and Luke all depict primarily idealized human Christologies, but also recognize ways in which each reflects the peculiar theology of the given writer.

Fifth, and finally, the approach of testing the hypothesis of a paradigm provides room for the study to say that some data might not fit.[11] As I go through the Gospels, it will be Matthew, in particular, whose exalted human Christology at times takes turns that might step beyond the category of idealized human figure. In naming such instances, the study raises the question of how we can clearly frame the reasons for seeing such a transgression of the idealized

---

11. Kuhn, *Structure of Scientific Revolutions*, 17-18: "To be accepted as a paradigm, a theory must seem better than its competitors, but it need not, and in fact never does, explain all the facts with which it can be confronted."

human paradigm. By holding the idealized human paradigm in tension with the divine identity paradigm we can ask whether the data fall within either, or whether anomalous instances of potentially divine Christology are simply outliers that point toward some different paradigm for making sense of Jesus as we encounter him in these pages.

In all, then, I hope that the presentation of an alternative paradigm both enriches the conversation already unfolding and generates new possibilities in our readings of the Gospel texts. By recalibrating the scholarly discussion in light of data that are less often explored in Christology discussions, those pertaining to human figures rather than divine hypostases or angelic figures,[12] I am opening up possibilities for a new family of readings, only some of which are offered in preliminary fashion in the current study.[13] I should underscore here that in discussing the methodology of hypothesis and paradigm I am offering exegetical and hermeneutical suggestions for making sense of the narratives as we have them. The approach of this study is not an abstract application of data to a preconceived paradigm. As much as possible, the chapters that follow seek to honor the developments of the plots of each of the Gospels and the overall stories that they tell, as they narrate those stories in conscious dialogue with Jewish biblical and post-biblical traditions.

As should be evident, then, my work is participating in a particular conversation in New Testament scholarship, in which the Christological question is assessed from within the Jewish frame of reference. I address the question of how these texts signify within the biblical and post-biblical Jewish framework. Each of the Synoptic Gospels offers early indications to its readers that such is the interpretive milieu for understanding the story that unfolds: Matthew begins with a summary of Israel's history from Abraham through David and the exile to Jesus's birth; Mark proclaims that the story begins in accordance with what is written in the prophet Isaiah; Luke says that the life of Jesus consists of the things that have been fulfilled, and weaves his early chapters with themes from Israel's scriptural past.[14] The framework developed here demonstrates promise as a category that explains the exalted depictions of Jesus in a manner

---

12. Hurtado, *One God, One Lord,* 51-70, does explore exalted patriarchs and recognizes the significance such figures play in delimiting what can be said of human agents of God.

13. Again, the analogy with Kuhn's work, *Structure of Scientific Revolutions,* is helpful, as he articulates that paradigms provide starting points for more specific research and discovery (23-24).

14. On Mark in particular, see Heike Omerzu, "Geschichte durch Geschichten. Zur Bedeutung jüdischer Traditionen für die Jesusdarstellung des Markusevangeliums," *EC* 2 (2011): 77-99.

that fits well within early Jewish ideas without the redefinition of monotheism that marks the later Christian tradition.[15] I recognize that with such a singular focus there is a price to be paid. The approach I have taken leaves aside the important, complementary question of how a non-Jewish, Greco-Roman reader would have read the Gospels.[16] Although I take up the perspective of such a reader at a few points in my study, my main intent is to engage the crucial question raised by the proponents of early high Christology: what does it mean for writers who are mostly Jewish themselves, functioning within what we might call the theological parameters of first-century Judaism, to narrate the life of Jesus in the ways we see unfolding in Matthew, Mark, and Luke?

C. WHAT THIS STUDY IS

1. A STUDY OF THE SYNOPTIC GOSPELS

This is a study of the Christology (or, Christologies) of the Synoptic Gospels. As such, it attempts to do justice to the literary features, narrative development, and symbolic worlds created by each story. It is not, then, a study of the historical Jesus and how he presented himself, or a study of the underlying sources. It is a historical study in the sense that it attempts to provide a historically viable reading of the texts from within the first-century Greek-speaking Jewish world in which they were written. This also means that the only diachronic dimension of early Christology that I take up is particular changes introduced by Matthew or Luke into Mark's text. I am not arguing for a developmental theory of early Christology.

Because it is a study of the Synoptic Gospels, it is also not a study that draws firm conclusions about the full Christologies held by the persons who produced them or the communities that first received and read them. It may well be, for instance, that all of the Gospel writers held some sort of divine Christology, and yet told stories that attempted to tell the story of the human Jesus during his time on earth with minimal reference to a divine quality

15. The claim that Paul "redefines" Jewish monotheism is a recurring theme in the work of N. T. Wright, e.g., *The Climax of the Covenant: Christ and the Law in Pauline Theology* (Minneapolis: Fortress, 1993), e.g., 129, and *Paul and the Faithfulness of God* (Minneapolis: Fortress, 2013), 644-90.

16. An important recent work from the Roman perspective is Michael Peppard, *The Son of God in the Roman World: Divine Sonship in Its Social and Political Context* (New York: Oxford University Press, 2011).

that transcended his already transcendent humanity. As an analogy, we might think of the works of Paul, which many hold to contain a stock of verses that indicate preexistence. Throughout his letters, however, the role that Jesus plays in Paul's arguments is almost always one that depicts his idealized humanity, union with and likeness to us, or lordship via resurrection, rather than one that depends on preexistence.

Whatever may be the reason for the depictions of Jesus, the depictions themselves provide their own set of evidence. Difficulties that we might have in determining how these depictions fit within the development of early Christology pose a separate question. The answer may be that Christology did not develop in a straight line, such that "lower" always means "earlier." The answer may be that an author is striving to preserve and present a true portrait of Jesus's earthly ministry. The answer may be that there is a theological point to be made about Jesus as the quintessential human being, the faithful Davidic messiah, the Human One who plays the part of second Adam. Any of these is possible, but the first question to answer is how, in fact, Jesus is depicted in each of the Synoptic Gospels. That is where the current study focuses.

Focusing on three different stories is going to raise some challenges, as it is difficult to honor the respective narratives of each while digging into topics, issues, and themes that stretch across all three. But I endeavor to honor the respective stories even though I do not work through the Gospels book by book. When I study Christological titles (son of God and son of man) I do not examine a title in the abstract and import a given meaning into the Gospels. Instead, I look at how the titles function and develop across the course of the narratives. This provides an inroad into Mark's story in particular. Similarly, studying the birth and resurrection narratives allows Matthew and Luke their own voices in establishing the trajectory and resolution of the Jesus stories they narrate. Throughout, the question is how the Christological signals of any given pericope both find and lend meaning within the developing story.

2. A READING IN CONTINUITY WITH SCRIPTURE AND EARLY JUDAISM

As stated above, the primary frame of reference I am using to read the Gospels is the combination of Israel's scriptural rubric and its development in postbiblical Jewish texts. Of course, any new telling or next chapter of an ongoing story will introduce its novel developments. The question before us is precisely where the Jesus stories introduce those notes of newness. The point of my extensive focus on early Jewish texts is to demonstrate that being identified with God as such is not a novel development that entails a redefinition of monotheism. Or, if it is, then it redefines monotheism in ways analogous to God's earlier self-identification with characters such as Abraham, Moses, and Israel. Because God's identity is known through a narrated story, that story and its characters are always bound up with God's identity, distinguishable if not separable from it.

To say that identification with God itself does not single Jesus out as unique is not, however, to fall off the horse on the other side and claim that the Gospels depict Jesus as just like any other biblical hero. When Jesus exercises powerful control over waters, for instance, there is at least one option between, "Look, Moses is back!" and "Look, God incarnate is among us!" Idealized human figures fall in between the "merely human" and the "divine." In the case of Jesus, the Gospels claim in their own ways that Jesus is the eschatological agent through whom God's promises to visit, redeem, and restore God's people are taking place. Jesus is the expected and uniquely empowered messiah who would share in God's rule over the world and receive the homage of the nations. Jesus is the Human One who exercises God's authority on the earth as God intended for humanity to do at the beginning. Thus, reading in continuity with the scriptures of Israel and with early Judaism is not a claim to Jesus's normalcy, but is a call to understand with greater acuity where, exactly, Jesus's uniqueness lies in these particular stories.

Matthew, Mark, and Luke all invite the readers of their stories to interpret them in conversation with biblical precedents. Luke's Gospel draws to a close with the resurrected Jesus providing provocative suggestions about his whole life being a fulfillment of the law of Moses, the prophets, and the Psalms. These generalities tell us that we cannot understand the Gospels aright unless we are reading them in conversation with the scriptures of Israel. What these generalities do not tell us is what that point of connection might be. For this we must look at the specific exegesis of each passage. The Christological implications will take the whole of each of the Gospels to sort out. I aim to demonstrate that the biblical and Jewish intertexts supply us with tools to recognize a high, human Christology of a man at the turn of the ages who is initiating the restoration of the world's rule to God's appointed human agent(s).

3. LISTENING TO A SURPRISING PERSPECTIVE

Each book of the New Testament, and each author or group of books as well, has the capacity to offer some unique contribution to our understanding of how the early church articulated Jesus's identity. If I have one fear in the midst of the onslaught of "early high Christology" studies it is that an increasing focus on the ways in which Jesus is shown to be divine will lead to an ever-increasing tendency to bypass Jesus's humanity as its own biblically and theologically significant reality. As this study shows in some detail, by "Jesus's humanity" I do not simply mean that Jesus has a body so that he can die. Nor do I simply mean, à la Anselm, that humanity has gotten into such a terrible hole that the only way for God to be paid back is for someone else to get into the terrible hole with us and from there offer restitution to the Divine. Nor, again, do I mean that we need to demythologize the Jesus of the Gospels in order to discover the true Galilean peasant hidden behind. Instead, I am talking about apprehending the stories in the Synoptic Gospels as narratives of "a man attested by God" (Acts 2:22). This is the contribution that the Synoptic Gospels have to make to our understanding of what it means for Jesus to be human.

The Synoptic Gospels offer a rich depiction of idealized, eschatological human agency in the person of Jesus. This is not merely a portico into some deeper mystery of Jesus's identity hidden in the texts, but is its own many-roomed house. Because these texts do not depict Jesus as God, they consistently depict Jesus and God as separate characters: God in charge, Jesus subordinate; God as father, Jesus as son; God as all-knowing, the son as limited in some ways; God remains in heaven, not intervening, while Jesus is crucified on earth below.[17] Because Jesus is an idealized human, he is the demonstration that God is with God's people; he enacts God's own authority to forgive sins; he exercises dominion over even the wind and the waves — as well as the spirits that are hostile to humanity. Through Jesus's hands the creative power of God is at work to feed thousands in the wilderness. Through Jesus's submission to the father, the father brings redemption to Israel. Any reading of the Synoptic Gospels has to do justice to both of these dynamics. Jesus and God (not just "the son and the father") are distinct characters. And Jesus is the human through whom God's authority, and we might even say identity, is being put on display in the world. This is what it means for Jesus to be an idealized human figure. This is the contribution to our understanding of the New Testament picture of Jesus that the Synoptic Gospels uniquely offer.

17. This distinction is important to keep in mind, especially in light of some recent work advocating for early divine Christology. For instance, Michael F. Bird, "Of Gods, Angels, and Men," in *How God Became Jesus* (ed. Michael Bird et al.; Grand Rapids, MI: Zondervan, 2014), 22-40, speaks of "the God of Israel" being revealed "as the Lord Jesus Christ" (28).

D. WHAT THIS STUDY IS NOT

1. NOT A THEORY OF CHRISTIAN ORIGINS

As I have intimated already, this study is not a study of how the Christology of the early church developed. Such motion-picture depictions are important, but this study is, instead, an assessment of three frames. This means that the study raises questions for some readers that it simply does not attempt to answer. For instance, those who see preexistence or other such divine Christology in the genuine Pauline letters might ask how such earlier developments could not be reflected in the later, written Gospels. It is a fair question, one for which there might be any one of several possible answers. But on the other hand, the assumption of a divine Christology in Paul should not be determinative for our reading of the Gospels, and the latter must be allowed, in the scholarly movement from particular data to general theories, to offer their unique claims about Jesus without being forced to fit into preconceptions that are created either by subsequent church history or by larger theories of Christological development.

2. NOT A SUSTAINED CONVERSATION WITH GRECO-ROMAN LITERATURE

Despite the universal recognition in New Testament scholarship that Judaism and its Greco-Roman environment are mutually intertwined, particular studies and even systems of schooling tend to focus on one or the other.[18] In the analysis of early Christology, several recent studies have devoted themselves to bringing Christian claims into conversation with non-Jewish Greco-Roman sources.

David Litwa has pursued such an explanatory field with studies in Paul and in the early Jesus tradition more broadly.[19] In *Iesus Deus,* he lays out the importance of directly engaging the broader Hellenistic milieu rather than following the path of the scholars who are my primary interlocutors. He sees

18. See Martin Hengel, *Judaism and Hellenism: Studies in their Encounter in Palestine During the Early Hellenistic Period* (Philadelphia: Fortress, 1974).

19. M. David Litwa, *We Are Being Transformed: Deification in Paul's Soteriology* (Berlin: De Gruyter, 2012), and Litwa, *Iesus Deus: The Early Christian Depiction of Jesus as a Mediterranean God* (Minneapolis: Fortress, 2014), respectively.

the work of Hurtado, for instance, as betraying the idea that deification would have to be brought into Judaism from without, from a Greco-Roman realm of thought, rather than something that might be an expression of Hellenized Judaism.[20] Because Judaism was already Hellenized, however, Litwa cautions that such an approach will inevitably leave the story unbalanced.[21]

In his study of Jesus as son of God, Michael Peppard deploys a similar grid to a similar end.[22] He aims to get behind Christian commitments entailed in fourth-century confessions in order to help readers better apprehend the connotations of divine sonship in the first century. When it came to being the son of a god, the model of adoption loomed larger in the first-century social reality than disputes about the begetting or making of sons. Divine sons were empowered to rule and to be heirs of their divine adoptive fathers.[23] He critiques the work of Hengel and Hurtado, and to a lesser extent James Dunn, for being insufficiently attuned to the importance of Roman data for understanding Jewish deployments of the term "son of God."[24] Peppard goes on to discuss "son of God" terminology within a Roman rubric in which the distinction between divine and human is not so neatly drawn as it appears to be in the proponents of early divine Christology such as Hurtado and Bauckham, and in which the adopted emperor was the most widespread point of contact for such a title.

Both Litwa and Peppard raise important issues, not just for the study of early Christology, but also for the study of the New Testament across the board. And yet, to return to Litwa's framing of the issue, the argument about the pervasiveness of Hellenization, and its importance for reading the New Testament, is a double-edged sword because it underscores that the Judaism with which scholars are comparing the New Testament is, itself, Hellenized Judaism.[25] This, in turn, raises questions about the value of direct comparisons with non-Jewish Hellenistic elements. The Jewish predecessors with which the New Testament depictions of Jesus are being compared, both in this study and in the studies of my primary conversation partners, are themselves the same Hellenized Judaism within which the early Christian tradition arose. In choosing such a focus, scholars are not eliminating Hellenization from their field of vision, but are homing in on one sprawling set of communities who expressed their religious conviction in ways that were to some degree Helle-

20. Litwa, *Iesus Deus*, 13.
21. Litwa, *Iesus Deus*, 14-15.
22. Peppard, *Son of God*.
23. Peppard, *Son of God*, 3-5.
24. Peppard, *Son of God*, 17-26.
25. As Litwa himself acknowledges (*Iesus Deus*, 19-20).

nized. The choice to focus on Judaism is not a choice to eliminate the Greco-Roman world from consideration, but to focus on one set of data that contains within itself already those Hellenized markers — and which chose at points, whether consciously or unconsciously, ways to assimilate or reject aspects of that culture. Within the Hellenized world, Jewish people were still attempting to live out and to articulate their unique story as told in scripture and lived through various defining rituals and observance of a unique set of laws. Thus, the recent attempts by Hurtado, Bauckham, and Crispin Fletcher-Louis to focus on Jewish texts and practices is not an ignoring of the Hellenization endemic to early Judaism and Christianity; it is an attempt to compare like with like: Hellenized Jewish texts with Hellenized Jewish texts. The apparent strength of Litwa's approach might, in fact, be its weakness. By making direct comparisons between the New Testament and Greco-Roman texts that bear no Jewish markers, connections might be drawn that were consciously or unconsciously eschewed either by the Hellenized Jewish community at large or by the Hellenized Jewish followers of Jesus that rendered the early tellings of his appearance, work, and exaltation.

Both Litwa and Peppard have raised an important caution flag about focusing too singly on the Jewish context of the early Jesus tradition; and both studies offer some measure of important Christological corrective due to their broadening of the field of vision. The current study, however, mines these works for their contributions and debates them where they seem to me to go astray, without attempting the wholesale work of imagining how the Jesus stories might have been heard by the average Roman on the street. The narrative cues to the readers, noted above, direct them from the very first verses of each Gospel to find the significance of the story, and its needful interpretive grid, in the Jewish context. It might thus be argued that in following the advocates of early divine Christology into conversation grounded on biblical and post-biblical texts that this study focuses on the implied authors of the stories rather than on actual readers. It may well be that the discrepancies between my primary conversation partners and the work of Peppard and Litwa mirror discrepancies between what the stories meant to their real authors and what they meant to the first auditors.

3. NOT A FULL-ORBED CHRISTIAN CHRISTOLOGY

This book does not aim to say everything that there is to say about Christology, either the Christology found in the New Testament or the Christology of the

Christian faith. In repeatedly arguing that divine or preexistence Christology is not implied or necessary for making sense of various Gospel texts, I am not thereby arguing either that divine and preexistence Christologies are absent from the New Testament or that they are wrong. Divine and preexistence Christologies can be found in the New Testament, including John's Gospel, the Christ hymn of Colossians 1, and the opening salvo of Hebrews.

My argument, then, is not that these components of Jesus's identity are unattested in the New Testament, but that they are not (significantly) constitutive of the Christologies that empower the narratives of Matthew, Mark, and Luke. A different paradigm is at work. This does have ramifications for the larger Christological posture of Christians. First, the battle for a divine Christ has been so deeply engrained into the collective church psyche that for many Christians it is difficult to imagine a more important thing that could be said about Jesus. Indeed, one wonders if the resurgence in early high Christology is not, at least in part, fueled by the sentiment that to speak of the humanity of Jesus is to engage in a colossal exercise of missing the point. But if we recognize that Jesus in his humanity is the subject matter of these canonical lives of Jesus in ways that profoundly signify the Christology being deployed, then we have to step back and reassess this posture. It might be that the only way to truly make sense of these narrated Christologies is to recognize that in them the human Jesus is precisely the point. It may be that the pious posture of affirming Jesus's divinity is keeping readers from receiving the story that has actually been given.

Second, in my various exposures to Christology in both academic and ecclesiastical settings, the understanding of Jesus's humanity has been thin, and this has been part and parcel with a thin Christian anthropology more generally. Here I hope that my book helps even if the majority are not persuaded by its thesis. That is to say, even if readers are not convinced that idealized human Christology is sufficient to explain who Jesus is, I hope that it will convince most that idealized human Christology is both necessary for understanding his story and a crucial, often missing component in the Christian conceptuality.

E. RECENT PROPOSALS FOR EARLY HIGH CHRISTOLOGY

The purpose of this section is to survey some recent proposals for early high (i.e., divine) Christology. This section is not intended as a review of literature per se, or as a full plotting of the landscape of Christology studies, low and high. Rather than such a broad survey, I have laid out in more detail representative and influential arguments for the family of positions that I aim to offer an alternative to in my own proposal. If there is a resemblance among most of the studies surveyed here, it is in a general methodology that articulates some unique facet of God's identity and then demonstrates how this facet is predicated of Jesus as well. Often, these studies are quite careful to circumscribe particular aspects of the divine identity as being hard lines separating the Deity from all creatures, thus homing in on a particular aspect of Jesus's identity that shows him being placed on the divine side of the creator-creature divide. As I indicate throughout the ensuing engagements, a good part of my argument is devoted to reimagining the relationship between unique divine attributes and others who might bear them.

One challenging dynamic of these studies bears pointing out. While they are engaging the Christological question of Jesus's identity, they are all attempting, at the same time, to be faithful to the historical contexts and content of the texts under consideration. This means that at the same time that they are piling up correlations between God and Jesus, and telling the reader how Jesus is, for instance, "sharing in the divine identity," they are also often careful to not say that Jesus is being depicted as God, or that Jesus is being depicted as divine.[26] The unwillingness to cross such a line is commendable, but it often leaves the reader with a somewhat fuzzy conclusion. Jesus is being depicted as identified with God, but the two characters are consistently distinguished. This is at times said to be the tension that then finds clarification and explanation in the developing God-man Christology of the church. Part of the challenge of these studies, as I read them, is that the rhetorical effect of the arguments is often poised to lead readers to draw the very conclusions that the authors themselves are too careful to make. The Gospel texts are, in fact, full of mystery, luring readers to enter into the story to more fully understand who Jesus is. The following writers, in different ways, suggest that the mystery unfolds as it approaches the paradoxical divinity of Jesus, his sharing in the identity of the God of Israel.

1. RICHARD BAUCKHAM

In many ways, Richard Bauckham is the figure who looms most largely behind the current project. Not only has his particular thesis been widely influential, but also the form of the argument, in which Jesus's identity is understood against a background of strict Jewish monotheism that isolates certain actions,

26. Cf. Chester, "High Christology," 33.

ascriptions, or attributes as pertaining to God alone, has taken on various mutations among other New Testament scholars.

Bauckham claims that the identity of God is known through God's exclusive role as creator and ruler of all things, as recipient of worship, and as bearer of the divine name YHWH.[27] Sharing in the work of creation and rule and the ascription of worship are the three categories that carry the most weight in Bauckham's foundational essay. With the establishment of these categories as the realm of God's unique purview, and articulating these realms as the identifying markers of who God is, Bauckham has created the category of "divine identity." These actions and ascriptions identify God, and any other who is so depicted is being identified with Israel's God. This work has compelled widespread assent. The notion of divine identity, and of Jesus in the New Testament playing roles that are otherwise reserved for God alone, has proven to be fertile soil for explorations of New Testament Christology. The following two scholars whose work I assess, Kavin Rowe and Richard Hays, develop Bauckham's thesis in different ways (though Hays does so more explicitly than Rowe), taking hold of the conceptual framework of "divine identity Christology" and expanding it in more general ways to show how Jesus shares in the divine identity in the Gospels.

When Bauckham turns to a brief discussion of divine identity in the Gospel of Mark, it is notable that the qualifications for "divine identity" become more fluid. The transfiguration is supposed to be a revelation of "Jesus in the glory of his divine identity," but in that scene there is neither application of the divine name, nor affirmation of a place in creation or rule over the cosmos, nor does Jesus receive worship.[28] In Mark 1 Jesus is referred to as "the LORD" from Isaiah 40, but whether this is a signal that he inherently bears the name YHWH is not so clear.

Then, in a footnote, Bauckham lists passages in which Jesus's sharing in the divine identity is supposed to be signaled: the scribes' question of who but God alone can forgive sins (2:7); the disciples' question about who Jesus is because even the wind and sea obey him (4:41); Jesus's self-declaration when walking on water (6:50); Jesus's statement that no one is good but God alone (10:18); Jesus's linking of his authority with the authority given to John the Baptist (11:27-33); Jesus's query about how David can call the Christ his Lord (12:37); and Jesus's claim to be the son of man who will sit at God's right hand (14:62).[29]

---

27. Bauckham, *Jesus and the God of Israel*, 8-13.
28. Bauckham, *Jesus and the God of Israel*, 264.
29. Bauckham, *Jesus and the God of Israel*, 265n40.

Of these, the only two that might fit Bauckham's own rubric for sharing in the "unique divine identity" are the water episodes, which might be ways of indicating that Jesus shares God's unique rule over the cosmos, though they need not be read that way. The last example explicitly falls outside Bauckham's rubric inasmuch as it is sitting on God's own throne, not sitting next to God, which constitutes a violation of monotheistic sovereignty over the cosmos according to his established framework.

I do not doubt that these passages all serve to identify Jesus with God in some manner, but I do question whether they signal an identification after the particular fashion that Bauckham has advanced. My purpose at this juncture is simply to point out that Bauckham himself allows for the general, conceptual framework he has established, that of playing the part of God, to exceed the specific measures he himself has articulated by which we know that such divine identity is depicted. It is therefore all the more important that my study of Old Testament and early Judaism demonstrate not only that numerous Jewish figures share in God's rule and receive worship, while a few others become the subjects of what were originally biblical YHWH texts, but also that the general notion of playing roles otherwise assigned to God is so widespread as to be nearly ubiquitous.

Overall, the argument as Bauckham advances it contains two major problems. First, there is abundant evidence that appears to disprove his case, including some he himself discusses. Bauckham recognizes that the Parables of Enoch depicts the son of man figure as both sitting on God's own throne (what Bauckham sees as the telltale sign that someone is sharing in God's unique sovereignty over the world) and receiving worship.[30] Bauckham discusses this evidence under the somewhat lame rubric of "the exception that proves the rule." It might be better to say that it is the exception that disproves the rule. It is true that this figure does not participate in the work of creation, the other significant marker of divine identity, but the appearance of such an alleged transgression of Jewish monotheism would surely be more shocking than Bauckham lets on were his standards of measure as strong as he claims. Hurtado notes the weakness of Bauckham's framework: "Contra Bauckham's claims, the representation of Christ as participating in God's sovereignty (e.g., sitting on/sharing God's throne) is not unique, and Bauckham's attempts to deny the analogies in ancient Jewish texts (e.g., Moses' enthronement in *The Exagoge of Ezekiel*) are not persuasive."[31] This

---

30. Bauckham, *Jesus and the God of Israel*, 16.
31. Hurtado, *Lord Jesus Christ*, 47n66.

study of early Judaism demonstrates that human beings playing roles otherwise assigned to God alone is a recurring theme in both scripture itself and the writings of its later adherents. Examples of humans receiving worship are expanded to include Adam, Moses, and Solomon, among others. And innumerable instances of humans functioning as co-rulers with God are also on offer.

This brings us to the second and more conceptual weakness of Bauckham's thesis. His explorations of who might be depicted as co-ruler with God or co-recipient of worship focus too narrowly on angelic figures, whereas in the biblical and post-biblical tradition it is humans who are created to share in God's rule over the earth. Humans, created in the image of God, or particular humans standing in for what humanity was meant to be, also function at times like images of other gods: objects the veneration of which signals veneration of the god whose image is represented. There is no one biblical or Jewish theology of humanity that lays out such claims and that commands the adherence of all other biblical and Jewish theologizing about humanity or about particular humans who play special roles for God in heaven or on earth. However, I demonstrate that the case of the son of man in *1 Enoch* is not so anomalous as Bauckham suggests. But we have to be looking in the right place.[32] Rather than focus on angelic or other semi-divine intermediary figures, I look at idealized human figures throughout the Jewish tradition. There we find recurring instances in which a person's (or humanity's) very purpose is to play the role of God, whether in heaven or on earth.

It is impossible to overstate the radical claim that Bauckham is making. Although he, like most of the other authors surveyed here, strives to avoid the ontological language of saying "Jesus is God," what most people would mean by such a phrase is precisely what he offers. In his introduction to *Jesus and the God of Israel*, he says the following:

> The earliest Christology was already the highest Christology. . . . When we think in terms of divine identity, rather than divine essence or nature, which are not the primary categories for Jewish theology, we can see that the so-called divine functions which Jesus exercises are intrinsic to who God is. This Christology of divine identity is not a mere stage on the way to the patristic development of ontological Christology in the context of a Trinitarian theology. It is already a fully divine Christology, maintaining

---

32. Knowing which data are relevant for a given case is a significant component in the establishment of a paradigm as Kuhn discusses it (*Structure of Scientific Revolutions*, e.g., 13-18).

that Jesus Christ is intrinsic to the unique and eternal identity of God. The Fathers did not develop it so much as transpose it into a conceptual framework more concerned with the Greek philosophical categories of essence and nature.[33]

If someone were to say that for Bauckham the very first followers of Jesus always thought that Jesus was God, they might be forgiven for transposing into common ecclesiastical parlance what Bauckham has stated in terms of his own depiction of early Judaism. But while I agree that Jesus performs innumerable divine functions, the burden of my chapter on scripture and early Judaism is to show that Bauckham's exalted claim is unsustainable as proposed. The divine functions that Jesus exercises in the Gospels are also exercised by other humans, some of them within the Gospel narratives themselves. And various other human figures throughout the storied history of biblical and post-biblical Judaism are shown performing similar actions. Indeed, it may well be that creation itself is the only action that is consistently depicted as God's unique purview — except that there one must deal with wisdom (and with the consultation of the divine retinue in the creation of humans in Gen 1:26).

This last point underscores my critique of Bauckham's thesis, my appreciation of his paradigm, and the overall positive goal of my own study. First, as stated, Bauckham's thesis is unsustainable. The thesis argues that early Judaism reserves the action of rule and the ascription of worship to God alone. The evidence he offers shows that this is not a sound conclusion, and I offer more below. As I read the argument and the data, it is a falsifiable thesis that is falsified by the evidence. Second, however, the notion of "divine identity" is a rich one, though it does not mean or prove a person's divinity. Various idealized humans play roles that are otherwise ascribed to God in the biblical tradition; at times they play roles that are reserved for God alone. By recognizing that early reflections on Jesus are developing such a tradition, we are in a position to enrich our understanding of the implications of Jesus's full humanity. This is the positive contribution of the current work, that in recognizing the ways in which Jesus's exalted activity fits the role of an idealized human figure we might better understand Jesus as a human and the fate that the Gospels anticipate lying ahead for other people.

---

33. Bauckham, *Jesus and the God of Israel*, x. A similar claim is found more recently in Sigurd Grindheim, *Christology in the Synoptic Gospels: God or God's Servant?* (New York: T&T Clark, 2012), 149.

2. C. KAVIN ROWE

One of the most careful studies advocating a high Christology through the identification of Jesus with God is Kavin Rowe's *Early Narrative Christology*.[34] Rowe's argument bears marked affinity with my own inasmuch as his work aims to plot the identity of Jesus in Luke's Gospel within the unfolding, dynamic narrative. He concludes that the narrated identity of Jesus as κύριος in Luke's Gospel creates "a coherent pattern of characterization that binds God and Jesus together through the word κύριος such that they finally cannot be separated or abstracted from one another in the story. To apprehend the identity of Jesus in the Gospel of Luke is to include God, and the question, Who is God in Luke?, of necessity places Jesus at the center of its answer."[35] This might be called a Christology of divine identity; however, it does not rest on Bauckham's articulation or measures of such a category. Instead, it depends on detailed exegesis of the relation between God and Jesus, each as κύριος, within Luke's Gospel.

In assessing Rowe's work, in particular, we are confronted with the difficulties of how to parse linguistic possibilities and their Christological implications. For instance, I completely agree with the summary cited above. However, in my work with idealized human figures in early Judaism I see that just such an identification between humans and God is a recurring theme. Because the biblical identity of God is bound to the story of Israel, Israel and its idealized members become the means by which (for better or worse) people (should) know who God is; and, conversely, the identity of God is supposed to be made manifest in the idealized human figures who represent God on the earth.

A further articulation of his conclusions underscores yet again the difficulties inherent in the language describing Jesus in the Gospels. While Luke's κύριος Christology "does not exclude prophetic or agent-like elements in the Lukan text, this κύριος christology is, to use the widespread language of past debates, 'high' rather than 'low.'"[36] The challenge for the reader is that many idealized human anthropologies are quite "high," with some human beings bearing the very glory of God, speaking and acting as God's vicegerents, and sharing in worship and rule. Some prophets, such as Moses, would qualify as "prophetic or agent-like" while being idealized in a God-like manner.

---

34. C. Kavin Rowe, *Early Narrative Christology: The Lord in the Gospel of Luke* (Grand Rapids, MI: Baker Academic, 2009).

35. Rowe, *Early Narrative Christology*, 201.

36. Rowe, *Early Narrative Christology*, 220.

The studies of Bauckham, Rowe, and Hays (see below) all, to varying degrees, claim or imply that to be identified with God is to some degree to be identified as God. The argument that ensues in this study is that identification with God is not sufficient for the consequent claim of Jesus's own inherent (e.g., ontological) divinity or preexistence. Such identification is not, and cannot be, Jesus's simply by virtue of his being a wandering teacher of timeless truths; however, it can be reckoned to him by those who see in Jesus the culmination of God's expectations of and plan for humanity in general, Israel in particular, and Israel's scriptures most specifically.

3. RICHARD B. HAYS

In a short book that serves as a foretaste of a more lengthy study of the Christology of the Gospels, Richard Hays deploys Bauckham's divine identity framework alongside his own trademark literary, intertextual, and theological reading strategy.[37] Indeed, it is in Hays that I have found clearest direct articulation of what seems to me to be hinted at and implied in the rhetorical force of earlier studies. Thus, for instance, he summarizes Mark's Christology with, "Jesus seems to be at the same time — if we may put it crudely — both the God of Israel and a human being not simply identical with the God of Israel."[38] Similarly, he concludes that for Matthew "Jesus *is* the embodied presence of God and that to worship him *is* to worship Yнwн — not merely an agent or a facsimile or intermediary."[39] Of Luke's Jesus Hays claims that "his personal identity is closely bound with God's own being,"[40] and in assessing an allusion to Isaiah 45:15-17 in the Third Evangelist says, "the implicit overtones of the echo also whisper that the κύριος Jesus *is* the God of Israel."[41] Rarely are advocates of early high Christology so bold as to say of the depictions we find in the Gospels, "Jesus is the God of Israel," though as noted above the force of their arguments appears poised to push readers in that direction.

One of the most methodologically significant innovations that Hays makes with respect to Bauckham's paradigm is in greatly expanding the notion of

---

37. Richard B. Hays, *Reading Backwards: Figural Christology and the Fourfold Gospel Witness* (Waco, TX: Baylor University Press, 2014).

38. Hays, *Reading Backwards*, 27.

39. Hays, *Reading Backwards*, 53 (italics original).

40. Hays, *Reading Backwards*, 62.

41. Hays, *Reading Backwards*, 69 (italics original).

"divine identity." No longer is that framework explicative of a carefully defined rubric where only certain attributes, actions, or ascriptions are reserved for God alone. Similar to what we find when Bauckham himself turns to Mark, a wide-ranging set of identifications is canvased in which Jesus plays a role otherwise assigned to God. In Hays's study of intertextuality in the Gospels, the connection occurs most pointedly through casting Jesus in the role of God as God is the agent in various Old Testament passages.

With the broadening of the instances of Jesus being identified with God, Hays also broadens the applicability of my methodological critique of divine identity Christology as a divine Christology as such. As I demonstrate at great length in the following chapter, identification with God, especially through people playing roles that are God's special purview, is a recurring feature of Jewish depictions of idealized human figures. I show that identification with God is not tantamount to identification as God in the ways that other scholars suggest and that Hays explicitly claims. The wide-ranging possibilities of what a Jewish person might say about an idealized human is not something Hays's study shows an awareness of. Because such an alternative reading is not engaged, a great deal more argumentation is needed to establish the sort of divine identity for Jesus that Hays claims to find.

Because I work with a much broader range of possible ramifications for a person being identified with God, most of my disagreements with Hays's work come down to reading the Gospels' identifications of Jesus with God as falling within the range of Jewish precedent rather than that of startling innovation. For instance, where Hays sees a biblical citation casting Jesus in the role of God as God, I more often see the citation carefully changing the divine referent so that it is clear both that this is God's promised work and that God's work is being mediated through another whom the text does not so identify.[42]

It may well be that my differences with Hays come down to one important interpretive choice. In introducing his discussion of Luke, Hays rightfully appeals to the post-resurrection narratives, where Jesus provides a sort of crash course in Christological hermeneutics.[43] However, when interpreting the passage, Hays passes over the actual content of the Christology Jesus articulates, thus slanting the outcome in his favor by somewhat artificial means. He cites Luke 24:25-27: "And he said to them, 'O foolish and slow of heart to trust in all that the prophets spoke! Weren't these things necessary: for the Messiah to suffer and enter into his glory?' And beginning from Moses and from all the

---

42. E.g., the discussion of Mark 1:2-3 in Hays, *Reading Backwards*, 20-22.
43. Hays, *Reading Backwards*, 55-57.

prophets, he thoroughly interpreted for them *the things concerning himself in all the Scriptures*."[44]

After rightly indicating that this speech demands that the reader reread both the Jesus story and Moses and the prophets, Hays asserts that this somehow undermines the notion of "low" Christology in which it is claimed that Luke presents Jesus as "Spirit-anointed prophet, teacher of divine wisdom, and a righteous martyr."[45] He further says that any scholar who denies preexistence and incarnation or Jesus's identification with God is continuing the very failed theology embodied in the Emmaus travelers.

Such rhetoric is not, however, sustained by the words Hays cites. What Jesus has to tell the travelers is never said to be that the Christ is, in fact, divine. What the travelers do not yet understand is that *the messiah must suffer and enter into his glory*. They fail to understand what the disciples throughout the narrative did not grasp: the mighty prophet only fully enters into his messianic kingship along the way of the cross. My critique of Hays's overreading of the passage finds further substantiation later in the chapter (24:36-49). Once again Jesus appears to a group of befuddled disciples. Once again he leads the followers to scripture to have their Christology sorted out: "everything written about me in the law of Moses and the prophets and the psalms must be fulfilled" (24:44b). And once again, the content of those scriptures is specified: "Thus it is written, that the Messiah is to suffer and to rise from the dead on the third day, and that repentance and forgiveness of sins is to be proclaimed in his name to all nations, beginning from Jerusalem" (24:46-47, NRSV).

In both pericopes, the Christological content is specified, and in neither is there warrant for Hays's claim that Jesus invites the readers of the Gospel to discover a divine Christology. The Christological confusion lies in their inability to understand that the messiah must suffer before entering his glory (24:26, 46). Here is warrant, indeed, for discovering a much different Christology in the scriptures than the one Hays generates in conversation with Luke. It is, in fact, the Christology we see articulated in the sermons of the book of Acts, in which Jesus is "a man attested by God" who is killed due to the Jewish people's rejection of him, but whom God raises from the dead.

Conceptually, there is much I agree with in Hays's work. The Gospels do make both explicit and implicit claims to the effect that we must understand the scriptures of Israel if we are to understand the Gospels themselves, and that only by understanding the Jesus who appears in their pages will we be

---

44. Hays's translation, *Reading Backwards*, 56.
45. Hays, *Reading Backwards*, 57.

able to read aright the antecedent scriptures. However, the divine continuity that holds these together is not said to be found in the God of Israel becoming incarnate in the man Jesus of Nazareth, but in the God of Israel anointing (Matthew), sending (Mark), or creating (Luke) Jesus to be the messiah who fulfills the various roles assigned to idealized human figures of Israel's past and hoped-for future.

4. LARRY HURTADO

Across a series of studies marked by the monographs *One God, One Lord* and *Lord Jesus Christ,* Larry Hurtado has made the case that Jesus is treated as divine from very early in the Christian movement.[46] I judge his argument to be similar in form to that of Bauckham, but different in content in two vital ways. In form the argument is similar in that it singles out an ascription or action proper to God alone, in this case worship, and argues that the early Christians' inclusion of Jesus in it signals his being treated in a manner appropriate only to one who abides on the creator side of the creator-creature divide. This veneration did not compete with devotion to the one God but was seen as the way in which the one God would be rightly venerated.[47] Hurtado establishes worship as the heart of Jewish monotheism by demonstrating that no other figures were "treated as rightful recipients of cultic worship in any known Jewish circles of the time."[48] Here we differ on how to weigh the evidence, for I maintain that even without the presence of actual veneration in historical practice, the Jewish biblical and post-biblical documents can (and actually do) provide evidence for the notion that a particular figure might be so venerated should such a figure appear. Evidence in the chapter below on idealized human figures in early Judaism points in this direction. However, in focusing on worship Hurtado's argument stands on more defensible ground than the more wide-ranging argument of Bauckham. It is stronger for one other reason as well.

Hurtado includes a study of exalted human figures in his explorations of early Jewish devotional patterns.[49] While he finds that human heroes are excluded from cultic veneration, he nonetheless recognizes that Jewish reflec-

46. Hurtado, *One God, One Lord*; Hurtado, *Lord Jesus Christ.*
47. Hurtado, *One God, One Lord*, 99-100.
48. Hurtado, *Lord Jesus Christ*, 31.
49. Hurtado, *One God, One Lord*, 50-69.

tion on these heroes from the past "reflect the ability of ancient Judaism to accommodate exalted figures alongside God."[50] This enables him to account for the exalted status and even rule over the world that we see given to Moses or Enoch's son of man. Thus, the bulk of my argument, which focuses on the various ways in which humans can be and are identified with God in early Jewish literature and the application of such explorations to Jesus, falls well within the realm of possibility opened up by Hurtado's study.

For my project on the Synoptic Gospels, it is important that the criterion Hurtado deploys finds little direct expression in the Jesus narratives. His exposition of Q rightly demonstrates that Jesus is of central concern for this stratum of the early church's tradition, and that his role as son of God entails a unique relationship to God. The particular connotations of the "divinelike" role Jesus plays or his "transcendent status" as God's son will be matters of exegetical specification.[51] I do not follow the hints Hurtado lays out that these trails might be followed to a divine Christ; but I also note that the explicit criterion of cultic devotion to Jesus is not argued as the substance of religious life in Q.

Analogously, Hurtado's summaries of the Gospels themselves suggest divine Christology, but by and large avoid arguing that the texts demonstrate cultic devotion to Jesus.[52] In marked and important agreement with what I argue, Hurtado lays out a case for the son of man sayings referring "to him emphatically as human descendant."[53] In tandem, he points out ways that Mark's Jesus appears to be transcendent, such as in his control over the waters, the feeding narratives, and the spiritual beings' recognition of Jesus's divine sonship.[54] I further specify the nature of these moments of exalted Christology as indicating Jesus's status as idealized human figure, but generally I find more

---

50. Hurtado, *One God, One Lord,* 50.

51. Hurtado, *One God, One Lord,* 252, 253.

52. J. Lionel North, "Jesus and Worship, God and Sacrifice," in *Early Jewish and Christian Monotheism* (JSNTSup 263; ed. Loren T. Stuckenbruck and Wendy E. S. North; London: T&T Clark, 2004), 186-202, lays out the case that the New Testament nowhere demonstrates that Jesus was worshiped in the technical sense of the term so as to imply his divinity. North's study includes an examination of the προσκυν- word families and the language of sacrifice that is offered to God (not Christ). James D. G. Dunn, *Did the First Christians Worship Jesus? The New Testament Evidence* (Louisville, KY: Westminster John Knox, 2010), offers a nuanced assessment of the place of Jesus within earliest Christian worship, highlighting both his unique place and even "inclusion," as well as the preponderance of evidence to the effect that Jesus mediates worship that ultimately devolves upon God the Father.

53. Hurtado, *One God, One Lord,* 305.

54. Hurtado, *Lord Jesus Christ,* 285-87.

agreement with Hurtado's summary of Mark than disagreement. There are no clear signs of the line between God and humanity being transgressed by the depiction of Jesus.

Similarly, when Hurtado turns to Matthew and Luke I find myself largely in agreement. He argues that the virgin birth narratives in Matthew and Luke are largely calculated to underscore Jesus's "significance as the true royal heir of David and the fulfillment of royal-messianic hopes."[55] Moreover, I could not agree more with his depiction of Matthew's risen Jesus, who has "august divinelike status," but is "given this authority" by God, so that it "derives from" God and is therefore not, I conclude, Jesus's own intrinsically.[56] Hurtado also highlights three instances in which obeisance to Jesus would likely have been seen by early readers as reflecting the adoration given to Jesus in cultic worship (Matt 14:33; 28:9, 17).[57] In my view, this is inseparable from the previous observation, that Jesus is so revered for something that is bestowed upon him by God.

Hurtado's depiction of Luke is similarly congenial to my own, with a few points of interpretive difference, as he interprets Jesus as both "human hero and also divine Lord."[58] On the latter point, he highlights the extensive use of the title Lord, and that the disciples "worshiped him" (Luke 24:52). He goes on to tie this with Jesus's ascension and exaltation in Luke-Acts, a move with which I am in full agreement. The question that remains is how, precisely, to parse Jesus's being a "figure of divine status/significance," as Hurtado puts it. I interpret Luke-Acts as depicting Jesus attaining to such status as a human enthroned at God's right hand.[59]

A final word is in order about Hurtado's discussion of the Gospels. He highlights that each Synoptic Evangelist embeds his story within the matrix of Israel's scriptural tradition, through explicit citation and extensive allusion. Thus, from the authorial point of view, a strong argument can be made for

55. Hurtado, *Lord Jesus Christ,* 328.
56. Hurtado, *Lord Jesus Christ,* 331.
57. Hurtado, *Lord Jesus Christ,* 338.
58. Hurtado, *Lord Jesus Christ,* 344.
59. Thus I find myself in general agreement with Maurice Casey, "Christology and the Legitimating Use of the Old Testament in the New Testament," in *The Old Testament in the New Testament: Essays in Honour of J. L. North* (JSNTSup 189; ed. Steve Moyise; Sheffield: Sheffield Academic, 2000), 42-64, when he says, "In all cases he fastens on genuinely important evidence of rising Christology, but does not make out his case that Jewish monotheism has been breached" (53). In light of more recent discussions of early Christology, I might also say that he does not make out his case that Jewish monotheism has been "redefined."

focusing on the Jewish religious world for understanding the Christologies developed in each book. This is the path I follow as well.

Perhaps because of the paucity of references to or suggestions of Jesus as an object of cultic devotion found in the Synoptic Gospels, I find that Hurtado's interpretation of Jesus in these texts to be congenial with my own. In large part the greater synergy that obtains between Hurtado's work and mine than between my study and that of Bauckham stems from the former's recognition of the wide-ranging options available to early Jewish writers for depicting what I refer to as idealized human figures.

5. SIMON J. GATHERCOLE

In *The Preexistent Son: Recovering the Christologies of Matthew, Mark, and Luke*, Simon Gathercole covers the same New Testament ground as my project, arguing for the opposite thesis in what can only be described as a detailed, careful, and often insightful study.[60]

A section on Jesus's transcendence in the Synoptic Gospels covers a wide range of indications that Jesus is specially connected with God. By and large, the data Gathercole mines for this section come to support his case as he makes exegetical decisions with which I differ. For instance, the transfiguration recalls the divine sonship attested at the baptism, for sure, but the idea that the baptism indicates preexistent and thus "transcendent" sonship is not likely.[61] If, as he suggests, Jesus is somehow part of a heavenly council by which he sees the eschatological future in which Satan falls like lightning from heaven (Luke 10:18), then he likely is, so it seems to me, in the same manner as the other biblical figure to make such claims, according to Gathercole: the human prophet Daniel.[62] Jesus has authority to forgive, but claims that it is an exercise of the Human One's authority on the earth, not God's heavenly authority.[63] Gathercole's discussion of blasphemy offers evidence that a Jewish person who asserts that an idealized human figure is enthroned at God's right hand, based on Daniel 7, might be accused of blasphemy, thus undermining the notion that such a charge entails a claim to divinity as such.[64] The magi do

---

60. Simon J. Gathercole, *The Preexistent Son: Recovering the Christologies of Matthew, Mark, and Luke* (Grand Rapids, MI: Eerdmans, 2006).

61. Gathercole, *Preexistent Son*, 47-50; see my fuller discussion of the son of God below.

62. Gathercole, *Preexistent Son*, 50-51.

63. Gathercole, *Preexistent Son*, 57-58; see my fuller discussion of the son of man below.

64. Gathercole, *Preexistent Son*, 59-61, esp. 61.

offer obeisance to Jesus, but they do so under the rubric king of the Jews, not God incarnate.[65] Jesus does send prophets, but only after he is raised from the dead — a heavenly continuation of his earthly ministry.[66]

In keeping with the language offered by Bauckham, and with the expansion of that language to include an increasing number of divine actions and attributes, Gathercole concludes that the Synoptic Gospels cannot be wholly explained in terms of a functional Christology, but "include Jesus in the divine identity," showing him as one who transcends the "God-creation divide."[67] I aim to show that human potential for participation in divine functions is much broader than often noted. Indeed, if there is a recurring point at which I find myself disagreeing with all of the studies in favor of divine Christology, it is in their failure to consider the vast number of analogous ways that idealized human figures are rendered in other early Jewish texts.

The heart of Gathercole's study, which he claims to be the strongest evidence for preexistence Christology in the Synoptic Gospels, is a lengthy argument that the "I have come" sayings indicate that the preexistent Jesus was sent from heaven.[68] In particular, Gathercole argues that the phrase followed by a purpose clause is a formula of sorts, indicating that the whole range of Jesus's ministry stands under an antecedent sending from heaven.[69] The idiom, no doubt, regularly carries connotations of having been sent by God. However, the idea that it entails a sending to earth from heaven overreads the evidence. Indicative of the somewhat flexible nature of the expression is Jesus's application of it to John in a context where it sits in immediate and intentional proximity to Jesus himself: "For John came neither eating nor drinking and they say, 'He has a demon!' The son of humanity came eating and drinking and they say, 'Look! A gluttonous person and a drunkard!'" (Matt 11:18-19; par. Luke 7:33-34). Although there is no purpose clause here, this passage confirms that the range of possibilities for the location from which one might be sent by God extends beyond "heaven." It is a way of speaking of someone giving a prophetic mission.[70] Indeed, even John's Gospel, in which it is a clear and

65. Gathercole, *Preexistent Son*, 69.

66. Gathercole, *Preexistent Son*, 71-72.

67. Gathercole, *Preexistent Son*, 76.

68. Gathercole, *Preexistent Son*, 83-189. The claim to the argument's strength is found on p. 83.

69. Gathercole, *Preexistent Son*, 85-86.

70. Cf. Adela Yarbro Collins and John J. Collins, *King and Messiah as Son of God: Divine, Human, and Angelic Messianic Figures in Biblical and Related Literature* (Grand Rapids, MI: Eerdmans, 2008), 124-25.

significant part of the story that Jesus has come "from heaven," the narrator can say, "There was a man sent from God. His name was John" (John 1:6). Being present as one sent by God simply means that one has received a prophetic commission. This is the flip side of the divine query and command in Isaiah 6:8-9, "Who will go to this people?" followed by, "Go! And tell this people. . . ." Similarly, God commands Jeremiah, "You will go to all to whom I send you" (Jer 1:7), and Ezekiel, "Go, speak to the house of Israel," and "Go to the house of Israel" (Ezek 3:1, 4). To claim one has come is a congruous way to indicate that one has been sent on a prophetic mission to "go" to God's people.[71]

As he proceeds to other possible indications of preexistence Christology, Gathercole refrains from playing the part of the "maximalist." I engage some of his other arguments along the way of my own study. Generally, his thesis fails to persuade for much the same reason as other divine Christologies: it does not adequately appreciate the wide-ranging possibilities open for idealized human figures in early Judaism.

6. DANIEL BOYARIN

Daniel Boyarin has taken a lively foray into Gospels Christology with his *Jewish Gospels: The Story of the Jewish Christ*.[72] His overall argument is one that has a good deal of merit: that the early Christian depictions of Jesus are not innovations away from Judaism, but a particular Jewish manner of reflecting on the significance of the life, death, and resurrection of Jesus. Boyarin's strategy is analogous to the one pursued in this book: he looks to the son of God and son of man titles as primary indicators of the Christology deployed in the Synoptic Gospels (especially Mark). Moreover, like the current study Boyarin's work argues that son of God is a title indicating kingship rather than divinity as such.

---

71. The final section of Gathercole's chapter "False Perspectives on the 'I Have Come' Sayings" is an excursus on the Dead Sea Scrolls (*Preexistent Son*, 111-12). This section provides ample evidence that an idealized human figure might be spoken of as coming in the future, for instance: "until the messiah of righteousness arrives" (4Q252 5, 3); "until there shall come the prophet and the messiahs of Aaron and Israel" (1QS 9, 11). Such uses show us that there is no one figure who was expected to "come," but that the language of having come is perfectly congruous to fulfilling the role of a human whom God has commissioned for a particular task. Cf. Collins and Collins, *King and Messiah*, 125-26.

72. Daniel Boyarin, *The Jewish Gospels: The Story of the Jewish Christ* (New York: New Press, 2012).

INTRODUCTION

Boyarin's discussion of the son of man offers some important points of commonality and some sharp points of contrast with my study. First, an important point of commonality is found when Boyarin claims that all son of man sayings have Daniel 7 in view, not just those that allude to the glorious, future coming of that figure.[73] Second, in keeping with an argument that I develop in greater detail below, Boyarin sees Daniel 7, with its reference to the beleaguered people of God, as the primary biblical background even for the Gospel's anticipation that Jesus as son of man must be rejected, suffer, and die prior to entering his glory.[74]

The differences between Boyarin's reading and my own, however, emerge in his exegesis of Daniel 7. He interprets Daniel's "one like a son of man" as a remnant of ancient Canaanite myths in which the ancient god El presides over the investiture of a younger god, Baal.[75] Boyarin maintains that this notion of two gods proved unacceptable to early readers of Daniel, such that it was reinterpreted as a depiction of the exaltation of Israel, as reflected in the current canonical form.[76] Boyarin thus maintains that the Gospels dig into and reflect the earlier layer of a divine son of man: "The theology of the Gospels, far from being a radical innovation within the Israelite religious tradition, is a highly conservative return to the very most ancient moments within that tradition, moments that had been largely suppressed in the meantime — but not entirely."[77]

Historically, Boyarin's proposal is unlikely. It requires that the Gospel writers, or their predecessors in the purveying of the early Christian tradition, read Daniel 7 by stripping off a later redactional layer that interprets the son of man as Israel (the latter is Boyarin's understanding of "holy ones of the Most High" in Dan 7:18, 27). It also requires that the canonical form has influenced the depiction of the son of man inasmuch as what Boyarin sees as the later layer, identifying the beleaguered saints with the son of man, informs the Gospels' depiction of Jesus as son of man who must suffer and die.

The larger question that looms over Boyarin's work, however, is what precisely he means by ascribing divinity to Jesus as son of man. A number of turns of phrase in the book lead readers to conclude that Jesus is what later theologians might call ontologically (or we might say inherently) divine. For

73. E.g., Boyarin, *Jewish Gospels*, 36.

74. Boyarin, *Jewish Gospels*, 141, 144-45.

75. Daniel Boyarin, "Daniel 7, Intertextuality, and the History of Israel's Cult," *HTR* 105 (2012): 139-62.

76. Boyarin, "Daniel 7."

77. Boyarin, *Jewish Gospels*, 47.

instance, Boyarin summarizes his thesis: "The title 'Son of Man' denoted Jesus as a part of God."[78] And he later interprets Jesus's son of man claims to be those of a "Jew claiming that he was God."[79] In another example, he says that Jesus's ability to forgive sins, the prerogative of God alone, "constitutes a direct declaration of a doubleness in the Godhead, which is, of course, later on the very hallmark of Christian theology."[80] And demonstrating that Boyarin interprets this divinity as entailing preexistence and thus (presumably) some sort of heavenly ontology, he says, "the Son of Man is a figure entirely heavenly who becomes a human being."[81]

However, these strong statements appear to find severe qualification in a footnote located in the middle of the son of man discussion. There, Boyarin cites Adela Yarbro Collins's distinction between functional divinity and ontological divinity. In the former, individuals are divine "when they exercise (or are anticipated as exercising) divine activities like ruling over a universal kingdom, sitting on a heavenly throne, judging human beings in the end-time or traveling on clouds."[82] Boyarin claims that it is precisely this sense to which he refers throughout the book. He also claims that the son of man's authority to forgive sins is "obviously delegated by God."[83] The latter claim is easy enough to coalesce with Boyarin's overall argument: Jesus is depicted as the younger, lesser deity who is enthroned at God's right hand in Daniel 7, analogous to what we find in other ancient mythologies. However, the notion that the deity for which he argues is functional rather than ontological cuts against the grain of his entire study. Indeed, it appears that Boyarin's own book bears a redaction parallel to what he claims for Daniel 7: an earlier layer that clearly depicts the son of man as a God, and a second layer that retreats from this claim and assigns the apparently divine role to a human functionary! In fact, I find Collins's depiction of functional divinity to be helpful, and I find it to be true to the content of the Gospels. I argue that such functions are regularly played by idealized human figures, and that Boyarin's concession that Daniel 7, in its final form, conflates the son of man with the people of God is the key to understanding what sort of "divinity" Jesus's character displays in Matthew, Mark, and Luke.

---

78. Boyarin, *Jewish Gospels*, 26.
79. Boyarin, *Jewish Gospels*, 56.
80. Boyarin, *Jewish Gospels*, 58.
81. Boyarin, *Jewish Gospels*, 69.
82. Boyarin, *Jewish Gospels*, 55n.
83. Boyarin, *Jewish Gospels*, 57.

7. CRISPIN FLETCHER-LOUIS

The work of Crispin Fletcher-Louis demonstrates the diverse possibilities available within early high Christology. Although Fletcher-Louis will sometimes use language of "divine" or "epiphany" to discuss depictions of Jesus, the category with which he explores early Christianity and Judaism is "angelomorphism."[84] He locates the category "wherever there are signs that an individual or community possesses specifically angelic characteristics or status, though for whom identity cannot be reduced to that of an angel."[85] The focus on angels allows for two important correctives to be interjected into scholarly conversations about early Christology.

First, attention to angels engages the regular presupposition that there were other divine beings, alongside God, in Israel's vision of the heavenly court. What Fletcher-Louis dubs a "weakly henotheistic" strain of Israel's biblical tradition can refer to other gods in the heavenly sphere who exercise a certain amount of control over the earth.[86] He proceeds to characterize these angelic mediators in exalted terms: "There is a sense in which, not only by agency, but also in identity angels participate in the being of the One God. Some Greek speaking Jews were evidently happy to call angels θεοί, thereby recognising the 'divinity' of the angelic pantheon. Yet angels are clearly distinguished from and subordinate to the One Living God."[87] Here we have a recurrence of the language of identity that I highlighted above in the work of Bauckham, in particular. However, Fletcher-Louis is introducing the notion that divine identity might belong to another creature without inherently redefining God as such, or claiming some sort of direct participation in God's being that sets one on the course toward Nicea.

A second important corrective is that it opens the door to enumerate ways in which humans are treated in exalted terms. Humans might be "angelomorphic, rather than 'angels,' either because they are *less than* fully angelic, (heavenly, immortal, divine, etc. . . .), or because to describe humans as angels would be to *limit* the degree of their divinity."[88] Humans are sometimes depicted as greater than the angels, and thus encroaching on divinity to a

---

84. Crispin H. T. Fletcher-Louis, *Luke-Acts: Angels, Christology and Soteriology* (Tübingen: Mohr Siebeck, 1997); Fletcher-Louis, *All the Glory of Adam: Liturgical Anthropology in the Dead Sea Scrolls* (Leiden: Brill, 2002).

85. Fletcher-Louis, *Luke-Acts,* 14-15 (italics original).

86. Fletcher-Louis, *Luke-Acts,* 3-4.

87. Fletcher-Louis, *Luke-Acts,* 3-4.

88. Fletcher-Louis, *Luke-Acts,* 15 (italics original).

greater degree than even these heavenly creatures. And yet, such exaltation often takes root in rather mundane fidelity to God. Those who are exalted with such "heroic idealisation" are nonetheless "paragons of ordinary Israelite virtue within the context of their (covenantal) relationship as humans to the creator God."[89] In this sense, what Fletcher-Louis depicts as angelomorphic humans might well be one particular manifestation of my larger category of idealized human figures. The lack of preexistence or other such heavenly origin does not limit their capacity either to attain to an exalted, heavenly state after death, or to have a story about their lives told in such a fashion that transcendent attributes or even embodiments of the identity of God might be predicated of their lives on earth.

In *All the Glory of Adam*, Fletcher-Louis lays out most fully his justification for the notion of angelomorphic humans in early Judaism. He summarizes the exaltation of Moses in biblical and post-biblical tradition, including the Dead Sea Scrolls, before briefly laying out similar evidence surrounding kingship.[90] Priesthood becomes a special focus of angelomorphic representation, as this will be one of the more significant lines of development in the Dead Sea Scrolls.[91] Primeval humanity comes in for its own examination, as depictions of Adamic glory reflect not only the past with creation in God's image but also likely the present or anticipated future in which the Qumran community sees itself participating.[92] The extensive nature of the material is underscored as Fletcher-Louis continues with a survey of Enoch as a Heavenly High Priest; Israel as an angelic, possibly preexistent, person; *Joseph and Aseneth* as a conduit of the "angelomorphism of the righteous"; and the *Testament of Moses* as expecting an eschatological angelomorphic priest.[93] In all, it is an impressive catalog that prepares the way for an extensive deepening and strengthening of the category in the subsequent study.

Fletcher-Louis's study of Luke-Acts uses angelomorphic categories to explain data that are claimed as high Christology by other scholars on other grounds. The application of scriptural texts to Jesus such that "the LORD" refers to Jesus is highlighted as an indication that Jesus is identified with YHWH.[94] Jesus receives worship and is exalted.[95] Claims to forgive sins, ability to calm

---

89. Fletcher-Louis, *Luke-Acts*, 17.
90. Fletcher-Louis, *All the Glory of Adam*, 6-11.
91. Fletcher-Louis, *All the Glory of Adam*, 13-17.
92. Fletcher-Louis, *All the Glory of Adam*, 17-19.
93. Fletcher-Louis, *All the Glory of Adam*, 20-32.
94. Fletcher-Louis, *Luke-Acts*, 21.
95. Fletcher-Louis, *Luke-Acts*, 22-23.

storms, and possibly drawing the rich man to see that Jesus is good all suggest for Fletcher-Louis Jesus's possible "inclusion in the divinity."[96]

Such an assessment of Luke's Christology raises a host of questions. It seems that Fletcher-Louis is reading Luke's narrative as providing a sort of divine Christology that is roughly analogous to what we see in the work of Bauckham, Hurtado, and Gathercole. The indices of exalted Christology are seen as ways in which Jesus is "included in the divinity." However, the larger category of angelomorphic humans, which he develops more fully in his later book on the Dead Sea Scrolls, provides a category for explaining all these data without recourse to the sort of divine identity Christology that the others sometimes work with. The question that looms over his work is whether the category that had originally sufficed to depict "angelic" humans, including those who look like angels, bear divine glory, have YHWH texts applied to them, enter into the heavenly company, and share God's sovereignty over the earth, now must be seen as only a step on the way to a higher Christology in Luke-Acts, or whether Jesus there is being depicted in terms that are, in fact, analogous to what came before. In the latter case, the possible implications of phrases such as "inclusion in the divinity" seem to stand in need of some curtailing so that the difference between Jesus as idealized angelic human and Jesus as manifestation of God's own unique identity in a proto-Chalcedonian sense might be more readily apprehended.

Notwithstanding this concern, my approach aligns with that of Fletcher-Louis on many points. First, there is a broad range of exalted human figures, and communities, whose glorified descriptions provide important backdrop to the sorts of things that the New Testament writers say of Jesus. Second, this idealization of various human figures entails a participation in divine identity — but in a sense different from how Bauckham means such phrases. People are made like God and even stand in for God, but are not divine with the same ontology as the one God of Israel, nor is the understanding of God's identity transformed in any ontological manner by such human participation in divinity. As I said above, in instances where a person is rightly said to bear the form of an angel, such a rendering is consistent with the idealization of humanity I argue for in my own thesis.

A few other concerns linger, however. First, it seems to me that a clearer line needs to be drawn between "angelization" and "divinization." If these are roughly equivalent terms, then what is the equivalence, and in what position does it leave the exalted person with regard to the one God? Second, as indi-

96. Fletcher-Louis, *Luke-Acts*, 25.

cated above in the summary of Fletcher-Louis's study, the term "angelomorphic" might be misleading inasmuch as it might limit one's conception of what is being said of a human who is, in fact, depicted as superior to the angels. Thus, 4Q381 appears to distinguish humanity from angels based on the fact that the latter are created to serve while the former are created to rule.

Third, Genesis 1 sometimes looms in the background of idealized human figures. The *Life of Adam and Eve* depicts angels being commanded to bow before Adam because he bears the image of God. In this case, the glory of Adam is not angelic, but properly divine. Similarly, 4Q504 speaks of Adam being fashioned after the image of God's glory. There is no angelic mediator in such cases, but an unmediated approximation of the divinity. Evoking Adam, in turn, creates a further difficulty in assessing the material: is the reader to see such glory as humanity participating in an angelic reality? Or is this a restoration of what it means to be truly human? Might there, in fact, be a notion of an idealized anthropomorphic humanity that is more exalted than angelic counterparts? All the glory of Adam might, at least at points, exceed the glory of the angels. In such instances, the notion of a glorious, idealized human might better represent the data than the rubric of angelomorphic humanity.

8. THE CONCEPTUAL QUANDARY OF EARLY HIGH CHRISTOLOGY

One of the problems that besets attempts at articulating an early, high, divine Christology is to articulate clearly what the evidence has shown. Because the New Testament material itself does not say "Jesus is the God of Israel," and because it carefully distinguishes Jesus and God as characters in the stories, commentators are left with a significant challenge when it comes to saying what, precisely, early high Christology entails. Bauckham, for instance, says that Jesus is identified with God, but seems careful to avoid saying that Jesus is identified as God. Similarly, Hurtado sees cultic worship as the line that definitively separates what is appropriate for the creator from what is appropriate for created beings. But he is not willing to say that Jesus is thus being depicted as the creator. Instead, he wants to remain content with the notion that what we see in the veneration of Jesus is a mutation in monotheistic practice that constitutes the decisive, novel reality that accounts for Jesus's uniqueness in early Christian worship. To hold such a line indefinitely is clearly not sustainable. For this reason, the authors of the studies will often say that these are the very data that lead to later articulations of the divinity of Christ such as what we see in the creeds. However, this response cannot cover all the relevant material.

When Bauckham denies substantive Christological development in any way other than the reframing of Jewish ways of speaking for Greek philosophical modes, he is saying what his readers might have fairly inferred previously: Bauckham's divine identity Christology demonstrates that Jesus is being identified as (not simply with) the God of Israel.

But scholars are often aware that too bald assertions of Jesus's divinity push beyond what the evidence can sustain. An example of this is Darrell Bock's discussion of the son of man in Luke 21:27, where the allusion to Daniel 7 is strong. Bock states, "His coming with the clouds seems to be another suggestion that Jesus as the Son of Man is a person who possesses more than human authority or honour. Again, Messiah is not an adequate category for him."[97] What is this "more" of which Bock speaks? If "messiah" is not adequate, what category is adequate? A nod toward divinity is left undeveloped. He goes on in a subsequent discussion: "Luke 21.27 says that ultimately he returns in a divine manner with power and great glory. . . . In this picture, the Messiah is revealed to have both victory and all authority in a return that takes on a 'suprahuman' character."[98] The language of "suprahuman" is Bock's own, a pointer in the direction of deity aided by the phrase "divine manner." The problem with the vagueness is not simply that it leaves the reader uncertain. The problem is that it beckons the reader to draw a conclusion that the responsible scholar himself cannot clearly make. In the conclusions of his work, Bock articulates what has been hinted at elsewhere: "Luke in his presentation of OT Christology consciously takes us from a consideration of Jesus as the Messiah-Servant to the declaration that he is Lord of all in the fullest divine sense."[99] Importantly, Bock never explains how the Christ is divine, as he understands it, while the Lukan narratives consistently depict the character of "God" who acts as an agent distinguishable from Jesus throughout. Within the narrative world, it appears that only God (the father) is divine "in the fullest possible sense." A better, and clearer, explanation of the relationship between the two characters is needed. Such precision is desirable across many of the studies in early high Christology. What does it mean to argue that Jesus and God share an identity if they are different characters in the identity-forming story? What does it mean that Jesus is divine or possesses divine sonship given, for instance, that the New Testament regularly depicts all Christians as being God's daughters and sons?

97. Darrell L. Bock, *Proclamation from Prophecy and Pattern: Lucan Old Testament Christology* (JSNTSup 12; Sheffield: JSOT, 1987), 136.

98. Bock, *Proclamation*, 137.

99. Bock, *Proclamation*, 270.

F. VALUE OF THE CURRENT PROPOSAL

1. A BETTER PARADIGM FOR READING THE SYNOPTIC GOSPELS

My primary purpose for writing this book is to offer what I believe to be a better, more coherent reading of the Synoptic Gospels than those in which Jesus's divine identity is part of the mystery being disclosed by the narrative. Despite the arguments that have recently developed about Jesus as a divine figure in even the Synoptic Tradition, I continue to find that the narratives cohere better if their point is to demonstrate Jesus as messiah and Lord than if their point is to draw the reader to conclude that Jesus is preexistent or otherwise divine.

To take one example, the great mystery of Mark's Gospel that swirls around Jesus's identity is how it is that he can be authoritative Lord, son of God, and son of humanity, and at the same time have a destiny that leads him to the cross. What befuddles the disciples is not that Jesus might be the messiah — Peter gets this part right — but that the messiah might be one who has to suffer, die, and be raised. This is the mystery that is finally apprehended, if through blindness, by the centurion, who calls Jesus son of God only when he sees how Jesus expires. This is the mystery that allows the cry of dereliction to be completely coherent with the antecedent narrative: the father is the God of Israel, and the God of Jesus, and there is no blurring of this distinction in the narrative, even as Jesus speaks and acts for God, enacting the dominion of God that he proclaims.

Jesus as idealized human makes the narratives coherent. This is so even if the writers themselves believed Jesus was divine but muted that belief for various reasons. The payoff this study is looking for is not to question the theological significance of Jesus as divine. But it is to suggest that like any one-size-fits-all theological grid it is of limited usefulness, depending on which portion of scripture we are trying to understand. This book guides us through a reading that I have found to be more historically and exegetically plausible as well as more narratively satisfying. These are not stories of God coming into the world from without in order to save it through an act of incarnation. These are stories of God's commitment to well up a resolution to the story from within, to save it through the presence and person of an empowered, obedient human agent.

2. CHRISTOLOGICAL ANTHROPOLOGY

The more we attribute of Jesus's actions to his divinity, the less material we have to work with when it comes to discussing the significance of Jesus as a human. Hebrews will point to Jesus's sharing in our weakness, suffering, and temptation as a significant point of contact. When Anselm answered the question of why the divine became human it was to claim solidarity and participation with those who owed God an unspeakable debt of honor. Modern pop theology will point to the fact that Jesus had to be human in order to die. None of these accounts for Jesus the man who walks around Galilee teaching, eating, healing, touching, exorcising, feeding, disputing.

The first step toward developing a more robust theology of Jesus's humanity is recognizing the biblical datasets that apply. The Synoptic Gospels, I am suggesting, provide just such a dataset. They thereby demonstrate humanity, in Jesus as representative, as the Human One, ruling the world on God's behalf, as originally intended according to Genesis 1:26-28. They demonstrate this rule extending to spirits and bodies, to nature and society, to speaking for God and hearing God speak. The Gospels disclose a human that is other than the rest not because of ontological distinction but because the rest stand in need of the empowering spirit and fidelity to God that color the entirety of Jesus's ministry, and because Jesus plays a unique role in the eschatological drama of salvation. In the Synoptic Gospels, Christian theology can find rich fodder to develop and improve on Irenaeus's often-neglected theme of recapitulation.

Exploration of this theme is not the focus of the current book in any great degree. The theological ramifications will have to be explored in other studies — my own, perhaps, and hopefully those of others. But this book provides an indispensible first step. As I see the relationship between Christian theology and biblical interpretation, biblical studies must always begin with historical-critical readings of the texts. In this case, that means a study of the final form of the Synoptic Gospels. This provides the primary set of data that biblical scholars have to offer to Christian theology. It is not the job of biblical scholars to provide readings of texts that conform to, or fully articulate, statements of faith. Those statements might provide perspective for a second reading of the text that fleshes out and/or reinterprets the text in light of broader theological commitments. But that is always a second step, and always runs the risk of muting the voice of the text we actually have. If this study contributes to Christological anthropology it does so because such is the topic of the New Testament books under review. If it avoids discussion of the manifestations of Jesus's divinity or preexistence, or even denies them, it does so because this is what is required by the texts under review. In the conclusion, I offer some further reflections on reading the Synoptic Gospels in light of a fuller Christian confessional stance. But this book is a "first reading," a reading that strives as much as possible to read the text as it was meant to be read by the author,

---

Value of the Current Proposal

and/or as it was likely to be heard by the audience. As it takes this approach, it returns again and again to aspects of Jesus's ministry that show him to be an idealized human figure.

3. JESUS AND DISCIPLES

One of the more important dynamics in play in the Synoptic Gospels is the interrelatedness of Jesus's ministry and what is expected of Jesus's followers. Jesus gathers people whose job it will be to gather people (Mark 1:17). Jesus preaches, exorcises, and heals; he calls his disciples for the purpose of preaching and exorcising (3:15); and when Jesus eventually sends them, they preach and exorcise and heal (6:12-13). Jesus feeds the multitudes, but only through the hands of the disciples whom he had commanded to do the deed (6:37, 41). Jesus will go to a fate of rejection, suffering, and death on a cross, and he demands that any who would follow him similarly deny themselves and take up the cross and walk after him (8:31, 34). This is one of the crucial narrative threads of the Synoptic Gospels that begins to unravel once we read these as stories designed to narrate a divine Christ. If Jesus performs his actions due to his divinity, then there is precious little compulsion, or even capacity, for those who are merely human to act in kind.

With the issue of Jesus and discipleship, we are at a critical conjunction of exegesis and Christian practice. Once again, the focus of this book is on exegesis, rather than the contemporary implications of it. However, the two come hand in hand. If our exegesis of the Synoptic Gospels depicts a Jesus whose power derives from his divinity, then this will both blind us to the connection between Jesus's actions and those of his followers and sever human players from all possibility of enacting anything like the script that Jesus enacts. Conversely, if we recognize that Jesus acts as an empowered, idealized human figure, then the expectations that devolve upon his followers are both understandable and immense. As Jesus is empowered and directed by the spirit, so too might Jesus's followers be. The imperatives of making known the reign of God through indications of its in-breaking at the hands of human agents become comprehensible within the narratives themselves (including Luke's extension of it into the early church in the book of Acts).

The contemporary church, in turn, must confront the question of how such a story summons contemporary followers of Jesus along similar paths. Once again, this aspect of the question will have to be left largely to other studies, but my work here helps enable it, and gives it exegetical grounding for its task.

41

G. THE PATH AHEAD

The most important leg of this project is the first chapter, in which I sketch the wide-ranging occurrence of idealized human figures in scripture and early Judaism. This is the development of the paradigm that, I hypothesize, provides the comprehensive framework within which each of the Synoptic Gospels can be understood. The chapter functions on two levels. First, it specifically demonstrates that various actions that some have argued pertain to God alone (such as sitting on God's throne or receiving worship) can be asserted of human figures in early Judaism without compromising or transforming the inherent identity of God. Second, it shows more generally that being identified with God, sharing in God's work or God's attributes, is a regular feature of Jewish depictions of human persons and peoples. Together, the numerous examples of idealized human figures demonstrate the capacity for associating people closely with God. In this way it also shows why being associated closely with God in the earliest Christian tradition cannot be read as a way to make claims about Jesus's divinity, without further ado. The chapter thus functions both positively and negatively in the creation of the paradigm I propose and as a rebuttal to the paradigmatic claims on offer in studies of divine identity Christology and other early high Christologies.

The subsequent chapters (chaps. 2–6) turn to the Synoptic Gospels to test the hypothesis that divine identity Christology is a paradigm capable of providing an interpretive lens for the stories. Throughout, I attempt to honor the narrative dynamics and unique story of each while demonstrating that "idealized human figure" is a sufficient category for understanding Jesus. The first two chapters focus on titles, but do not take the titles in isolation as fixed expressions that might be plugged into any context with predetermined meaning. I study son of God in chapter 2 and son of man in chapter 3 with an eye toward how the deployment of each title in the Gospel of Mark enables the reader to build a coherent understanding of the narrative that is unfolding. In each chapter, I then turn to the deployments of the titles in Matthew and Luke, where we see how other uses enrich the respective son of God and son of man Christologies for the other Evangelists.

Chapter 4, "Messiah Born and Raised," tests my hypothesis against some of the strongest evidence for divine Christology: the birth and resurrection narratives. In so doing, it also provides Matthew and Luke their chance to set the reading agenda, as it studies the Christological indications in portions of the story absent from Mark. This chapter is not an exhaustive study of the framing chapters of Matthew and Luke, but focuses on the identity of Jesus as disclosed in them. The importance of beginnings and endings cannot be overstated when it comes to interpreting the narrative that falls in between.

This chapter is thus a crucial component in the argument for idealized human Christology in Matthew and Luke.

I explore exorcisms, nature miracles, and healings in chapter 5, "Lord of All Creation." These constitute some of the most significant enactments of high Christology in the Synoptic Gospels. In the exorcisms, Jesus demonstrates his authority over malevolent spirits; they in turn identify him in various ways, including eschatological nemesis. In the nature miracles, Jesus performs actions typical of God in scriptural precedent, especially in stilling a storm and walking on water. Healings show Jesus's authority over both physical and spiritual realities. Comparisons with prophets and other idealized humans help sustain the idealized human figure hypothesis.

A final investigation concerns intertextuality in chapter 6, "Jesus and the Scriptures of Israel." The question that looms over this segment of the study is, What does the use of scripture in each Gospel contribute to that Gospel's depiction of the identity of Jesus? The study of Luke in this chapter also encompasses a good deal of material from Acts, where the conjunction between scripture and Christology becomes much more apparent. As with other chapters, the preponderance of evidence points toward a representational, idealized human Christology, while possible outliers that might signal divinity are shown to have precedence in other early Jewish texts that use scripture in similar ways to talk about other human figures.

The method outlined above, then, aims to create a series of representative tests to see how much explanatory power is found in the idealized humanity paradigm. The specific examples and narratologically sensitive engagements aim to honor the specific stories and survey the preponderance of important evidence. I do not claim to have examined every piece of evidence. Nor do I claim to have read every study and engaged every alternative reading. Indeed, I often engage a passage with the assumption that many readers will read the claim as one signaling a divine Christology, and proceed to offer my reading as an alternative. However, the expectation is that once we have established the major narrative outlines and how those coincide with crucial Christological titles, examined the Christologies of opening and closing chapters, studied the activities of Jesus and how scriptural citations speak to Jesus's identity, we will have established a sufficiently thorough framework for describing the identity of Jesus that any evidence that might come from passages I bypassed would present itself in a context in which a strong presupposition in favor of idealized human Christology has already been established. The establishment of such a presumed paradigm must begin by demonstrating its plausibility within the world of religious thought that produced it. To this I now turn.

1 Idealized Human Figures in Early Judaism

The conversation in which I am participating with this book is located in the world of early Judaism. Each of the Gospel writers signals to his readers in the opening verses that the story of Jesus somehow connects with, or fulfills, the scriptures of Israel. Without prejudicing the question of how each author sees the relationship between those scriptures and the story of Jesus, it is fair to say that from the start each of the Synoptic Gospel cues the reader toward a scriptural matrix for understanding the connotations of the plots that unfold in their pages. Such scriptures, however, do not come into the Gospels unmediated, but within a Jewish tradition of interpretation and what might be called theological development. These realities have led to the sorts of arguments I outlined in the introduction, arguments to the effect that the uniqueness of God as articulated at various points in Israel's scriptures generated a Jewish monotheism in the Second Temple period that, in turn, limited what might be said about other beings, angelic or human. Scholars whose work has been attuned to the strongly monotheistic conviction of early Judaism (visible, as they will often point out, in the perhaps daily recitation of the *shema*) have thus turned to the New Testament and asked what the implications might be for a Jewish writer, committed to monotheism, who depicts Jesus in the various ways visible in the early Christian writings.[1]

The purpose of this chapter is not to deny that "divine functions which Jesus exercises are intrinsic to who God is."[2] Instead, I wish to argue that prior to Jesus, innumerable people, what I am calling "idealized human figures,"

1. As Shaye J. D. Cohen, *From the Maccabees to the Mishna* (Philadelphia: Westminster, 1987), 81-85, points out, the recitation of the *shema* did not in and of itself create clearly defined "monotheism," but may have arisen at the very time that the heavenly realm was increasing its population in the Jewish imagination.

2. Richard Bauckham, *Jesus and the God of Israel: God Crucified and Other Studies on the New Testament Christology of Divine Identity* (Grand Rapids, MI: Eerdmans, 2008), x.

are also depicted as performing such functions in Jewish literature. Thus, the framework developed here demonstrates that the exalted depictions of Jesus found in the Synoptic Gospels fit well within early Jewish ideas without redefining God as such.[3] Whereas Bauckham seeks to establish the absolute uniqueness of some functions by analyzing texts descriptive of angelic activities and finding (almost) no instances in which God's intrinsic functions are impinged, this chapter demonstrates that attribution of such unique functions of God to other figures happens remarkably often once we turn our gaze from the heavenly host to humanity. Jewish literature in the biblical and Second Temple periods repeatedly assigns to human figures the roles and attributes that are typically seen as being reserved uniquely for God alone. By focusing on this facet of early Jewish writings, we discover that Jesus's identity markers are of a piece with this rich Jewish tradition.

The category I posit here, "idealized human figure," refers to non-angelic, non-preexistent human beings, of the past, present, or anticipated future, who are depicted in textual or other artifacts as playing some unique role in representing God to the rest of the created realm, or in representing some aspect of the created realm before God.[4] In a weak sense, this category might simply refer to a person or people who fill a particular role, without necessarily commenting on whether they are uniquely powerful or pious. There is a stronger sense, however, in which such idealization entails the very sorts of sharing in the (otherwise) unique prerogatives of God that New Testament scholars might point to as signaling a divine Christology. Both types of figures are surveyed below, though the latter subset will prove more enlightening for demonstrating the broad range of possibilities open to early "monotheistic" Jews for describing a person as playing the role of God without impinging on their "monotheistic" commitments. As I discussed in the introduction, the construction of the category of idealized human figure in this chapter then provides a paradigm whose explanatory power I test in extensive conversation with the New Testament writings.

Scholars have deployed such a category before in their studies of early

---

3. The claim that Paul "redefines" Jewish monotheism is a recurring theme in the work of N. T. Wright, e.g., *The Climax of the Covenant: Christ and the Law in Pauline Theology* (Minneapolis: Fortress, 1993), 129, and *Paul and the Faithfulness of God* (Minneapolis: Fortress, 2013), 644-90.

4. By "non-preexistent" I mean that the human in view had no heavenly existence prior to a first appearance on earth. Elijah, for instance, might still be an idealized human figure according to my definition, due to his earthly origins, even though he might be treated as one who is preexistent prior to some second appearance on earth.

Judaism. A 1980 volume edited by John Collins and George Nickelsburg explores "ideal figures" in early Judaism.[5] The essays in their volume came into being through a process of realization that heroes in early Jewish literature were not simply celebrated for reasons such as faithful Torah keeping, but for virtues such as leadership, strength, righteousness (variously defined), or faithful embodying of a touchstone vocation such as prophet, priest, or king. They categorized the figures in three ways. First are those "drawn from the ancient past."[6] Initially, these appeared in the "history-like" literature of Israel, but their significance blossoms in ways that are often "distinct from their role in the unfolding history of the people."[7] Second are figures of the anticipated future. Messiahs and "son of man" figures fit here.[8] Third are the character types: visionaries, wise men, martyrs, charismatics, zealots, the righteous.[9] An important dynamic that runs across all three types is that the various depictions of the characters depend more on the "circumstances, purposes, and ideals of the authors" than on historical antecedent, biblical precedent, or abstract ideal.[10] Tradition and social setting play off each other to generate figures who help convey the message that a given author is striving for.

The object of concern here is not the actual historical figures who may stand behind such idealized depictions, but instead the depictions themselves, which interpret the significance of the person through various ascriptions, actions, and attributes. In positing such a categorization, I am seeking to curtail two possible missteps in the interpretation of the historical evidence. First, more limited categories such as "anticipated messiah" might prove too narrow and lead to the wrong conclusion: if Jesus does something that no messiah was thought to do, such as raise the dead, one might conclude in too hasty a fashion that this means Jesus is being depicted as "more than messiah," hinting strongly that he is God. Second, comparing idealized descriptions from early Jewish texts with those in the Synoptic Gospels enables us to compare like with like (i.e., textual depictions of idealized figures). Here, I am engaging the work of Larry Hurtado, who suggests in defense of his own thesis that what would be required to demonstrate that the early Christians were not treating Jesus as God would be nothing less than another historical, Jewish community

5. John J. Collins and George W. E. Nickelsburg (eds.), *Ideal Figures in Ancient Judaism: Profiles and Paradigms* (SCS 12; Chico, CA: Scholars, 1980).

6. Collins and Nickelsburg, *Ideal Figures*, 4.

7. Collins and Nickelsburg, *Ideal Figures*, 4.

8. Collins and Nickelsburg, *Ideal Figures*, 4-5.

9. Collins and Nickelsburg, *Ideal Figures*, 5.

10. Collins and Nickelsburg, *Ideal Figures*, 5-6.

worshiping their founder alongside Israel's God.[11] Such a measure is unduly high. If textual evidence indicates that an idealized human figure, should such a figure appear, would be included in the worship of God's people, then this may well explain the actions of the earliest Christians, echoed in the texts we now possess.

The category of "idealized human figure" seeks to chart a third way between "low Christology" that defines Jesus as "a mere human being," and a "high" Christology that depicts Jesus as the God of Israel.[12] To claim that someone is an "idealized human" is to open up a broad range of potentially exalted descriptions. From the shady hints of Genesis 1, an idealized human might be depicted as ruling not only the earth, but even the heavens and the angels.[13] Growing out of the suggestive language of "image and likeness," an idealized human might be seen as physically bearing the divine likeness through a glory that cows the nations. Royal theology might be elaborated with the notion that the king sits on God's own throne and even shares in the worship that God is due. An idealized human might be imagined as a priest who actually enters the heavenly court in his duties, who completes the work of creation, or whose word is the very word of God itself. An idealized eschatological redeemer might even play the part assigned to Yʜᴡʜ in a prophetic text about a coming visitation. We see all of this and more in biblical and post-biblical Judaism. I turn now to demonstrate the wide-ranging presence of idealized human figures in early Jewish religious texts.

A. ADAM AS PAST AND FUTURE

When probing the question of how it comes to be that early Christians depicted Jesus as performing actions or receiving ascriptions or possessing attributes typically reserved for God alone, a tendency within scholarship has been

---

11. E.g., Larry Hurtado, *Lord Jesus Christ: Devotion to Jesus in Earliest Christianity* (Grand Rapids, MI: Eerdmans, 2003), 38-42, argues that "literary scenes" fail to show "precedent in Roman-era Jewish religious practice."

12. Such a dichotomous taxonomy appears, for instance, in Daniel Johannson, "The Identity of Jesus in the Gospel of Mark: Past and Present Proposals," *CBR* 9 (2010): 364-93; the language "a mere human being" is his.

13. The place of humanity as necessary rulers for the fullness of God's kingdom to be in play, and that as a framework for understanding Jesus as human king, is laid out in brief by Dan McCartney, "*Ecce Homo*: The Coming of the Kingdom as the Restoration of Human Vicegerency," *WTJ* 56 (1994): 1-21.

to look to angels, Wisdom, Logos, and other heavenly figures. My contention, however, is that within the Jewish scriptures the first intimation of humanity's purpose is none other than playing the role of God on the earth. Without claiming that there was one, broadly deployed Adam theology in biblical and early Judaism, we can see that both the creation narratives of Genesis 1 and 2–3 themselves and the reuse of those traditions, create an important set of possible identifications between God and idealized human figures.[14]

1. GENESIS

The creation stories deploy models of God's engagement with creation that recur elsewhere in Israel's scriptures as well. One particular model that resonates broadly with the current project is what Mark Smith calls the "divine power" model.[15] In this model, "the deity is viewed primarily as a warrior-king and power is the primary idea in this divine reality."[16] This royal language of "warrior-king" signals how such a view of God at times finds its earthly touchstone in the person of the human king. The human king's power comes from the divine king, so that "it is through the human king that divine power is made manifest in the world."[17] Within this model of God's unique work of creation and sovereignty, there are certain idealized human figures whose role is nothing less than being assigned a share in that very sovereignty that is God's by right of creation.

In Genesis 1 humanity itself fits such a description. It is often asserted that Christian interpretation has made a bit too much of the protoplasts; however, we do well to remember that stories of origins are never told simply for their own sake. They are told to locate the tellers within (and often at the center of) a cosmic narrative.[18] Genesis 1 is no different on this score. The depiction of humanity in this narrative is no less significant for having been well worn by generations of Christian theologizing:

14. On the diversity of Adam speculation in early Judaism, see John R. Levison, *Portraits of Adam in Early Judaism: From Sirach to 2 Baruch* (JSPSup 1; Sheffield: JSOT, 1988).
15. Mark S. Smith, *The Priestly Vision of Genesis 1* (Minneapolis: Fortress, 2010), 12-13.
16. Smith, *Priestly Vision*, 13.
17. Smith, *Priestly Vision*, 13.
18. To much the same effect is the assertion with which Gary Anderson begins *The Genesis of Perfection: Adam and Eve in Jewish and Christian Imagination* (Louisville, KY: Westminster John Knox, 2001), 1, saying that Jews and Christians "do not so much read [Genesis] as it stands as re-read it in light of its proper end or goal."

Then God said, "Let us make humanity in our image, according to our likeness, and let them rule the fish of the sea and the birds of the sky and the beasts and the whole earth." So God created humanity in his own image; in the image of God he created it, male and female he created them. Then God blessed them and God said to them, "Be fruitful and multiply and fill the earth and subdue it. And rule over the fish of the sea and the birds of the sky, and all the living things that creep on the earth." (Gen 1:26-28)

Four aspects of this description point to the way in which the first humans are being idealized in the text: (1) the function of rule, (2) bearing God's likeness, (3) the possibility that they are being described as God's children, and (4) the blessing of fruitfulness and multiplication.[19]

The Priestly creation story in Genesis 1 not only puts on display God's own sovereign rule through God's creating order out of chaos but also depicts God sharing that sovereign rule with the creations. First, the sun and moon and stars are created to rule (משל) the lights (Gen 1:18). Later, humanity is created to rule (רדה) the creatures and to subdue (כבש) the earth (Gen 1:28). The notion of a deity sharing its creative power with a human agent was a fairly common trope in the ancient Near East: creation occurred through conflict, and the primordial conflict and victory were emblematic of the nation's conflict and (hoped for) victory on earth.[20] Genesis 1 democratizes this picture by depicting primal humanity, not just Israel's kings, as those who are entrusted with rule over the earth.[21] Moreover, this rule is part of what makes humanity

19. Such multiple layering in the notion of divine image is also articulated in Stephen L. Herring, *Divine Substitution: Humanity as the Manifestation of Deity in the Hebrew Bible and the Ancient Near East* (FRLANT 247; Göttingen: Vandenhoeck & Ruprecht, 2013), 95: "The Priestly conception of humanity as divine image is more than mere function, more than a raised status, but concerns the manifestation of divine presence as well."

20. J. Richard Middleton, *The Liberating Image: The Imago Dei in Genesis 1* (Grand Rapids, MI: Brazos, 2005). Cf. Smith, *Priestly Vision,* 19. Smith cites a letter from a prophet from Aleppo, Nur-Sin, to a king, Zimri-Lim, of Mari, in which the storm god says to the king, "I brought you back to the throne of your father, and I handed you the weapons with which I battled the sea." The power of the god's victory is handed over to the earthly king. Smith's overall thesis is that the royal, divine-power model is subverted by the Priestly presentation of Genesis 1; however, this makes it all the more striking that such royal elements are present and even prominent in the depictions of humanity.

21. John Goldingay, *Old Testament Theology,* vol. 1, *Israel's Gospel* (Downers Grove, IL: InterVarsity, 2003), 99-100; J. G. McConville, *God and Earthly Power: An Old Testament Political Theology* (LHBOTS 454; Edinburgh: T&T Clark, 2006), 35.

God-like.[22] Thus, John Goldingay draws the following conclusion about Genesis 1: "It has implicitly described God as a king who fulfills the king's vocation of exercising sovereignty in such a way as to bring life to his people. In being created in God's image, humanity is to fulfill this royal role in the world on God's own behalf."[23] Taking up the role of God's sovereignty over creation is part of the biblical picture of humanity's idealized vocation.

The objection that the Priestly source has little to no interest in royal theology need not detract from this line of argument, though it may introduce a surprising turn. The argument has been made that Moses himself is "shaped according to the model of the Israelite king."[24] Such a rendering is clear in the subsequent history of interpretation, including texts from Philo and the Exagogue of Ezekiel that I discuss below.

We turn now, second, to the connection between God and humanity connoted by the language of "image [צֶלֶם] and likeness [דְמוּת]" (Gen 1:26, 27). Each word appears to denote that humanity in some way is a visible embodiment of the God who created it.[25] The word צלם captures this notion of "visible embodiment" because it is regularly used to denote statues, visible depictions of gods, the likes of which Israel's aniconic tradition rejects (e.g., Num 33:52; 2 Kgs 11:18; Ezek 7:20; Amos 5:26).[26] The word דמות is a more general word of comparison. However, it is taken up in Ezekiel repeatedly in order to describe ways in which heavenly beings resemble humans, in particular, or other earthly phenomena (1:5, 10, 13, 16, 22, 26, 28; 8:2; 10:1, 10, 21, 22). Mark Smith draws attention to the way that Ezekiel 1:26-28 uses the language of likeness to indicate how God resembles humanity, seated on the throne as one with "a likeness that was of human appearance."[27] Summing up the Priestly picture of humanity as God's image and likeness, Smith concludes: "Genesis 1 provides a vision of the human person that leads back

22. Goldingay, *Israel's Gospel*, 111.

23. Goldingay, *Israel's Gospel*, 114.

24. William Horbury, *Jewish Messianism and the Cult of Christ* (London: SCM, 1998), 31, following J. R. Porter, *Moses and Monarchy* (Oxford: Blackwell, 1963).

25. Cf. Goldingay, *Israel's Gospel*, 102-3. I use "embodiment" here rather than "representation" as an attempt to take on board the warning of Zainab Bahrani, *The Graven Image: Representation in Babylonia and Assyria* (Philadelphia: University of Pennsylvania Press, 2011), esp. 121-48. "Embodiment" attempts to articulate and maintain that the image itself is part of the constitutive reality it represents, not a representation of some other thing that is more truly what is real. See also Herring, *Divine Substitution*.

26. Cf. Walter Brueggemann, *Theology of the Old Testament: Testimony, Dispute, Advocacy* (Minneapolis: Fortress, 1997), 452.

27. Smith, *Priestly Vision*, 101.

to the Creator. The creation of the human person is a sign on earth of the reality of God the Creator. Humanity is not only the representation of God on earth; the human person is the living representation pointing to a living and real God, perhaps unlike the lifeless images of other deities made by human hands."[28]

Even this, however, might put too great a distance between God and people. Zainab Bahrani's work on *ṣalmu* in Assyro-Babylonian antiquity suggests that images in at least some ancient Near Eastern contexts were viewed as constitutive of the reality that they represented, rather than representing a true reality on some other plane (in what we might call a Platonic understanding of reality).[29] Similarly, Stephen Herring concludes, "*Ṣalmu* is not a replica but is more like a repetition or an extension of the referent's very presence."[30] The correspondence between God and humanity in the biblical texts approaches this level of confluence, such that Randall Garr suggests that humanity itself is "(like) a theophany."[31] His reading of the דמות language in Ezekiel, which shares Priestly sensibilities with Genesis 1, is that it is theophanic throughout.[32] The notion that humanity is created to be a sort of theophany greatly complicates the exegetical judgments we have to make about the Christology of the Synoptic Gospels. Noting correspondence, for instance, between the water-walking episode and biblical precedents of divine disclosure opens up not only the possibility that Jesus is being disclosed to be God, in some sense, but also the possibility that he is being revealed to be the idealized human who can truly disclose the God whom he represents.

The likelihood that physical resemblance between God and humanity is involved in Genesis 1:26-28 provides a clue to how other early Jews depicted primeval humanity.[33] As I discuss below, Psalm 8:6 speaks of humanity being crowned with glory and honor, which is a divine investiture. The recurring phrase from the Dead Sea Scrolls, "all the glory of Adam," betrays a similar sensibility (see below). Glory is a native divine property that is often identified with physical luminosity. It may well be that both Psalm 8 and the Qumran covenanters are reading the language of either image or likeness, or both, as

---

28. Smith, *Priestly Vision*, 101.

29. Bahrani, *Graven Image*, e.g., 140-42.

30. Herring, *Divine Substitution*, 47.

31. W. Randall Garr, *In His Own Image and Likeness: Humanity, Divinity, and Monotheism* (CHANE 15; Leiden: Brill, 2003), 117.

32. Garr, *In His Own Image*, 122-23. See also his parallel thoughts on צלם as theophanic language on p. 144.

33. See Herring, *Divine Substitution*, 113.

indicating that primeval humanity bore the physical likeness of God in being endowed with resplendent glory.

Beyond physical affinity, however, the content of both Genesis 1:26-28 and older ancient Near Eastern parallels suggests that the connotations of being God's image-bearing likeness revolve largely around the task of rule that Genesis 1:26, 28, placed on humanity.[34] An inscription from Tell Fakhariyeh contains Aramaic cognates of the Hebrew words צלם and דמות (צלמה and דמותא), each referring to the statue of the governor on which they are carved.[35] The statue was placed in front of the god Hadad, and the inscription includes persuasive appeals for the god to grant petitions.[36] The likeness thus has a function of cultic embodiment of the people.

Analogously, Garr draws attention to Akkadian inscriptions in which priests and kings are said to be the image of the god.[37] To be the king of the world is to be the image of Marduk, which makes the king a conduit of the god's anger and mercy, and of the god's needful presence, but also binds the king to act as the god himself is thought to act.[38] Garr finds a pervasive pattern in which the god's image, in some human person, embodies and enacts divine attributes. In the ninth-century Tell Fakhariyeh inscription, the צלם is a physical representation of a king being depicted as one who enacts sovereign power over food, plague, and even gods.[39] Perhaps somewhat closer to Genesis 1 in both time and connotation, we find a seventh-century Neo-Assyrian letter proclaiming that the king "is the [ima]ge of Marduk. The word of [the king], my lord, [is] just as [final] as that of the gods."[40] The king, as image of god, speaks with the definitive authority of the god himself. Such expression of rule finds parallel expression in Genesis 1, "as 'image,' the human race will embody and assert the power of its referent [i.e., God] over the natural world."[41] The connotations of the image language encompass the function humanity plays. The coherence between God and humanity means that the function is not merely to rule, but

---

34. Cf. Middleton, *Liberating Image*, 15-42; Goldingay, *Israel's Gospel*, 109; Adela Yarbro Collins, "The Apocalyptic Son of Man Sayings," in *The Future of Early Christianity* (ed. Birger A. Pearson; Minneapolis: Fortress, 1991), 220-28, here 222.

35. Garr, *In His Own Image*, 121.

36. Garr, *In His Own Image*, 121-22.

37. Garr, *In His Own Image*, 144-45.

38. Garr, *In His Own Image*, 145-46.

39. Garr, *In His Own Image*, 151.

40. From Steven W. Cole and Peter Machinist (eds.), *Letters from Priests to the Kings Esarhaddon and Assurbanipal* (SAA 13; Helsinki: Helsinki University Press, 1998), 43; cited in Middleton, *Liberating Image*, 113.

41. Garr, *In His Own Image*, 156.

also to exercise God's own power of rule over the world.[42] Such a coalescence between God and humanity means that the identity of God itself, and likeness to God, will govern any application of what it looks like to bear divinely given power. Genesis 1 idealizes primordial humanity by depicting it being delegated the power of God by which God creates. The creative acts themselves, possibly to be read as intentionally free from cosmic violence, provide the connotations requisite for understanding what it looks like for humans to embody and implement divine rule. This gives specific content to the conclusions of Garr: "Through its 'image,' the human race will ultimately represent divine rule. The human race will be the vessel, or personification, of divine lordship on earth."[43]

This brings us back to the point made above, that an image was not merely a representation, but was seen as an embodiment of the thing signified. "The *ṣalmu* went beyond merely expressing its referent. It actually made manifest the presence of its referent; becoming what it presented. It functioned as a valid substitute of the referent when the referent was not physically present. Therefore, the image did not merely symbolize power or dominion; it was actually empowered to accomplish tasks."[44] The stated purpose in the act of creation, of humanity ruling the world, likely inheres in the language of "image" itself. Herring concludes: "Thus, Genesis 1:26 is primarily indicating humanity's purpose in the world: it is to serve *as* God's 'image.' Humanity manifests the presence and power of אלהים in his (physical) absence."[45]

A third line of interpretation that is worth pursuing for our purposes is that Genesis 1:26-28 describes humanity as divine offspring.[46] We have already seen that what these verses ascribe to humanity other ancient Near Eastern texts tend to restrict to kings and priests. It should therefore not be surprising to discover that the parent-child relationship that the Hebrew Bible itself ascribes to Israel's kings (e.g., Ps 2:7; 2 Sam 7:14) is also predicated of the royal humanity depicted in Genesis 1. The evidence for this interpretation comes from Genesis 5:1-3.[47] There, we find the "generations of אדם" (תולדת אדם), a genealogy that begins with God's creation of אדם, when אדם was made in

---

42. Smith, *Priestly Vision*, 134-35. I see this as a conceptual problem for Bauckham's claim that sovereignty over the world is one area completely reserved for God alone in early Jewish texts (*Jesus and the God of Israel*, 7-11).

43. Garr, *In His Own Image*, 157-58.

44. Herring, *Divine Substitution*, 117.

45. Herring, *Divine Substitution*, 118 (italics original).

46. Cf. Herring, *Divine Substitution*, 121-23.

47. Cf. Carly L. Crouch, "Genesis 1:26-27 as a Statement of Humanity's Divine Parentage," *JTS* 61 (2010): 1-15.

the divine likeness (בדמות אלהים), and reiterates that אדם was male and female and blessed by God on the day of its creation (vv. 1-2). The placement of this summation of Genesis 1:26-28 at the beginning of a genealogy is, itself, a first piece of evidence that the creation of אדם is being interpreted as the creation of divine offspring. Confirming this, the genealogy redeploys the terms "image" and "likeness" to describe Adam's begetting of Seth: "he begot in his likeness and according to his image" (ויולד בדמותו כצלמו, Gen 5:3).[48] One reason that the language of image and likeness is reiterated might be found in the passing on of the divine likeness through the human race (as perhaps Gen 9:6 indicates).[49] More basically, however, the parallels between Genesis 1:26-28; 5:1-2 and Genesis 5:3 suggest that Adam is to God as Seth is to Adam, that is, a son. Garr reaches the same conclusion: "In effect, then, the referent of P(T)'s 'image' is a parent of the child."[50]

For the purposes of my overall study of the Christology of the Synoptic Gospels, the interpretation of this genealogy by later readers is as important, and perhaps more important, than whether the interpretation I have suggested was intended by the implied author or understood by first readers. In fact, this appears to be precisely Luke's interpretation of the verses, as the final entry into his genealogy of Jesus is "Adam, the son of God" (Luke 3:38).[51] Both the genealogy in Genesis 5:1-3 itself and the reception of it in Luke's Gospel contribute to the somewhat broad canvas of the conceptuality of "son of God" in early Judaism and Christianity on which such divine children are idealized human figures. Here, the idealized "son of God" is primeval humanity.

In discussing the "likeness" of God and Adam in their generation of children, Garr sees not only correlation but also the very point of likeness. He suggests that likeness is so tied to reproduction that the ability to produce other human creatures is, itself, what makes people "a theophany. Specifically, Adam, Seth, and his descendants share the God-given ability/capability to generate תולדות and populate the world with human beings."[52] Again, Garr's

---

48. Cf. Herring, *Divine Substitution*, 113-14.

49. That this passage indicates a continuation of humanity in the divine image seems to be the majority view of modern scholarship: Brueggemann, *Old Testament Theology*, 452; Middleton, *Liberating Image*, 213; Gordon J. Wenham, *Genesis 1–15* (WBC 1; Waco, TX: Word, 1987), 127. However, Goldingay expresses some ambivalence: "they have offspring who resemble their parents, not the creator" (*Israel's Gospel*, 159).

50. Garr, *In His Own Image*, 154.

51. I. Howard Marshall, *The Gospel of Luke* (NIGTC; Grand Rapids, MI: Eerdmans, 1978), 165.

52. Garr, *In His Own Image*, 132.

language of "theophany" is immensely helpful because it demonstrates that part of the ongoing function of humanity, as expected by this creation story, is to put God on display for the world. Such "sonship" is inseparable from the vocation of ruling the world for God. The combination of sonship and idealized humanity is found elsewhere in the Jewish biblical tradition, in reference to both Israel as a whole (e.g., Exod 4:22-23) and especially to the Davidic king (Pss 2:7; 89:26; 2 Sam 7:14).

The fourth area to explore is the blessing of fruitfulness and multiplication (Gen 1:28). The blessing had been spoken over the birds and fish (Gen 1:20) before being reiterated over humanity. In the case of humanity, the call to fill the earth is expanded with a command to subdue it and exercise dominion. This suggests that fecundity in humans is one further aspect of the purpose articulated for them in being created to rule the earth. Moreover, if Garr is correct in the connection between bearing the divine likeness and the ability to generate humans, then the proliferation of God-likeness is twice accomplished in reproduction: the reproduction itself demonstrates that humanity is like God, and the product of the reproduction is another God-like human.[53]

The centrality of fruitfulness and multiplication for idealized humanity comes into sharper focus once we recognize that this primordial blessing/command is not only repeated in the restarting of creation after the flood (Gen 8:17; 9:1, 7), but also becomes a promise that devolves upon Israel's patriarchs (Gen 17:6, 20; 28:3; 35:11).[54] This promise is fulfilled, at least in part, by the end of Genesis and beginning of Exodus (Gen 47:27; Exod 1:7). The promises to the patriarchs in the Priestly literature include another allusion to Genesis 1:26-28 as well. In both Genesis 17:6 and Genesis 35:11 the promise of abundant offspring includes, more specifically, a promise that kings will come from the patriarch.[55] In the latter instance, this royal promise comes as God changes Jacob's name to Israel, thereby signaling that the nation of Israel will be the special locus for the fulfillment of both the creational blessing of fecundity and the creational purpose of humanity to exercise royal rule over the earth. According to Joel Baden, this national flavor is very much to the point and is also in play when the promise of kings is made to Abraham only after his name has been changed from Abram.[56] These promises signal a political future for the

---

53. Cf. Smith, *Priestly Vision*, 102.

54. Cf. Wright, *Climax*, 21-23.

55. This is highlighted in the short note by Daniel S. Diffey, "The Royal Promise in Genesis: The Often Underestimated Importance of Genesis 17:6, 17:16, and 35:11," *TynBul* 62 (2011): 313-16.

56. Joel Baden, *The Promise to the Patriarchs* (Oxford: Oxford University Press, 2013),

descendants of Abraham and Isaac beyond life as tribes. "The easiest way that Jacob's descendants could be understood as nations, plural, is if the promise refers to the northern and southern kingdoms of Israel and Judah."[57] In this light, P is referring to the Israelite kings of both kingdoms.[58] Baden concludes in terms that resonate deeply with the concerns of this section of my study: "Although Israel and Judah are political entities, *gôyīm*, just like the other nations surrounding them, they are different. They alone, both corporately and as embodied in their kings, are the living representation of God's will, vivid demonstrations of God's power on earth."[59] Given the close connection that exists in Genesis 1 and other ancient Near Eastern literature between God's creative/defeating power and the empowering of human kings, it comes as no surprise to discover that the later royal promises in the Priestly material of Genesis hearken back to creation, through the repetition of the language of fruitfulness and multiplication, in the same context in which they promise royal offspring. Israel will be the beneficiaries of the delegated creation-power of God in the person of the king.

This reiteration of Genesis 1 in the articulations of God's promise to the patriarchs demonstrates how the creation story is an idealization of humanity. The male and female אדם created in Genesis 1 provide a mold in which Israel itself subsequently will be cast. Conversely, the role that Israel, and its kings, play on the earth is a reiteration of the role that, according to Genesis 1, God created all humanity to play.[60] In this way, אדם, Israel, and Israel's kings each play the part of idealized human figures. Israel and its king aspire to the idealized place occupied by first humanity. Conversely, Israel and its king are idealized as the embodiment of what God created in the beginning. To use the language of Garr, this means that Israel and Israel's king, no less than first humanity, is a living theophany.

Recognition of the close relationship between God and humanity in cre-

---

110-11. He argues that the promise of kings, unique to P, is part of a larger complex of themes that highlight P's concern to distinguish Israel from other peoples and articulate "the formation of an Israelite national identity" (104).

57. Baden, *Promise to the Patriarchs*, 110.

58. Baden, *Promise to the Patriarchs*, 110.

59. Baden, *Promise to the Patriarchs*, 111.

60. There is a challenge to this reading inasmuch as royal theology is not typically considered a hallmark of the Priestly writer. However, the notion that humanity is the image of God, analogous to a cult-statue, and that such images embody the real presence of God in the places where they are located (as Garr and Herring so thoroughly argue) may provide a way forward. The cult image, as the presence of God, includes the embodiment of God's power to rule.

ation and shared sovereignty is crucial in pinpointing a place where Richard Bauckham's work closes off a critical way in which someone might play the part of God without being identified as divine. Bauckham rightly recognizes that the two facets of God's work of creation and sovereignty are mutually intertwined.[61] We have seen from the ancient Near Eastern parallels and even Genesis 1 itself that the work of creation is often depicted as an act of great might that subdues all enemies and leaves the creator God in charge. Lacking in his analysis, however, is that in both the broader ancient Near Eastern stories and Genesis, this exclusive sovereignty of God, including a share in God's creative power, is depicted for the purpose of upholding the claims of sovereign people. Bauckham claims that "they are the features which most readily distinguish God absolutely from all other reality."[62] The distinction is not so absolute as he claims. The power resides with God, but rather than relegating such power to God as God's own in an incommunicable, absolute sense, the ancient stories bolster the claims of certain God-empowered humans in their exercise of power on the earth.

Bauckham is surely correct when he explains that in early Judaism any other would-be ruler must still be acknowledged to be subject to divine authority. Yet he wishes to push his case further, and so he assesses the creatures he thinks provide the best possible counterexample: angels. He concludes that the depictions of angels as servants, as standing rather than seated as though enthroned, creates a picture in which "participation of other beings in God's unique supremacy over all things is ruled out . . . by placing them in strict subordination as servants, excluding any possibility of interpreting their role as co-rulers."[63]

From what we have seen, however, the generalization of this claim finds much of its strength from not engaging the data that provide the greatest challenge to the theory. In the Genesis 1 account, and in the reception of Adam stories in later Judaism as we will see below, it is not angels but rather humans who were created to share in God's sovereignty over the world. This is not to deny a distinction between the creative power of God and, for instance, the begetting power of humanity; however, conceptually there is a force to Bauckham's argument that fails in the first chapter of the Jewish scriptures as humanity is given a creative, God-like blessing.[64] It is, in fact, quite possible

---

61. Bauckham, *Jesus and the God of Israel*, 8-11.
62. Bauckham, *Jesus and the God of Israel*, 9.
63. Bauckham, *Jesus and the God of Israel*, 10-11.
64. Smith, *Priestly Vision*, 135.

for a Jewish writer who believes in the unique divinity of God to depict other beings, idealized human figures, as theophanies by ascribing to them a share in nothing less than the creative and sovereign powers of God, or, in Smith's words, to by portraying them as a "living representation pointing to a living and real God."[65] Describing a human in such terms is not to indicate that the one God has somehow become personally incarnate in such a figure, but is instead an indication that the human is idealized precisely through possession of an ascription, action, or attribute typically reserved for God alone, but which God has chosen to share.

2. PSALM 8

Psalm 8 shares much of the view of humanity and its place in the created order found in Genesis 1.[66] Importantly, Psalm 8 indicates that God's own lordship over the earth is prerequisite to humanity's sharing in it. YHWH is described as "our Lord" (אֲדֹנֵינוּ) and as one who silences his enemies (v. 2). The fact that the psalm moves immediately from the notion of silencing enemies to the direct lauding of God's work in creation indicates that the psalm is drawing on a "divine power" model of creation in which God conquers enemies in order to bring creation to fruition.[67]

Humanity, in turn, is but little lower than God (or, "the gods," v. 6), and is royally crowned (v. 6) as it executes its reign over the earth.[68] God's sovereignty is mediated through humanity.[69] More than this, however, the bestowal of "majesty and glory" is an investiture of divine qualities. Generally, הדר is a quality of YHWH (e.g., 1 Chron 16:27; Pss 29:4; 90:16; 96:6; 104:1; 145:12),[70] particularly as the deity is in view as the creator or one who defeats his enemies — two ideas that come hand in hand as we have seen in reference both to Genesis 1 and to Psalm 8. However, it is also a characteristic bestowed upon others, especially royal figures (Pss 21:5; 45:4, 5; cf. Deut 33:16-17).[71] The combination of kingship and military victory, along with divine bestowal of majesty, is captured in Psalm 21:5: "His glory is great through your help; splendor and

65. Smith, *Priestly Vision*, 101.
66. Smith, *Priestly Vision*, 27-32.
67. Smith, *Priestly Vision*, 29.
68. Cf. Collins, "Apocalyptic Son of Man," 222-23.
69. Cf. Garr, *In His Own Image*, 221.
70. Smith, *Priestly Vision*, 31.
71. Smith, *Priestly Vision*, 31.

majesty you bestow upon him." In Psalm 8 we see humans being described not only as royal, ruling figures, but also as kings who bear a special endowment of God's own glory. As Smith points out, Job 40:9-10 signals that such investiture is impossible for a human to attain on her own: "Do you have an arm like God? . . . Adorn yourself with majesty and dignity! Clothe yourself with glory and splendor!" (NRSV, alt.).

What is impossible for a person to do for himself, God does through the powerful act of creation, endowing humanity with a portion of what is properly God's. "These are God's characteristics, and humanity is graced with these divine qualities in Psalm 8:6."[72] It is possible that such a sharing in God's splendor is a reflection of the notion of humanity being created in God's image and likeness.[73] Whether or not this is the case, Psalm 8 provides us with an idealized portrait of first humanity, one that not only shows humanity little lower than God, but also indicates that this proximity entails a sharing in God's attributes of glory and actions of rule. As the psalm is framed with a repeated line, praising the grandeur of YHWH's name in all the earth, it becomes clear that this idealized portrait of humanity ruling God's creation does not diminish but instead enlarges the glory of Israel's God.[74]

3. EZEKIEL 28

The notion of first humanity prior to transgression as living in an idealized state finds expression in Ezekiel 28.[75] The king of Tyre is described as the first formed human, full of beauty, "in Eden, the garden of God" (v. 13). The prophet describes him as having a divine position on God's mountain, alongside an angelic being (v. 14). Indeed, two verses later, judgment is pronounced on this king's sin, and there he himself is the cherub, expelled from God's

---

72. Smith, *Priestly Vision*, 31.

73. So Garr, *In His Own Image*, 219-22.

74. We have already seen enough participation of idealized humanity in God's rule of the earth to problematize Bauckham's claim that God as sole ruler over the created realm is a clear marker of divine identity (*God Crucified*, 9). While this may be true in and of itself, the attendant situation in creation and in God's relationships with Israel's kings is that God shares this rule with other, human agents. It bears repeating that Bauckham's misstep is in looking to angels rather than idealized humans as God's potential co-rulers (10).

75. See Lester L. Grabbe, "'Better Watch Your Back, Adam': Another Adam and Eve Tradition in Second Temple Judaism," in *New Perspectives on 2 Enoch: No Longer Slavonic Only* (SJS 4; ed. Andrei A. Orlov and Gabriele Boccaccini; Leiden: Brill, 2012), 273-82.

mountain (v. 16), and the original reading of verse 14 might have so identified him as well.[76] The conclusion of Lester Grabbe appears to be apt: "The
figure in this passage looks like more than an ordinary man but is a mortal
capable of sin nevertheless."[77] This captures the both/and of primal humanity as an idealized human figure: idealized in the glory possessed, but with
the idealized character lost through transgression. From what we saw above
concerning the link between God and humanity in Ezekiel, such a glorified
depiction of an Adam figure is unsurprising. Grabbe goes on to suggest that
such a glorified depiction of first humanity may well lie behind other idealizations of Adam in Second Temple Judaism, such as those discussed below,
or at very least be representative of the sorts of glorified depictions that arise
across the tradition.[78]

4. WISDOM OF SOLOMON

In post-biblical Jewish texts Adam continues to function as an idealized figure.
In Wisdom of Solomon, Wisdom rescues the "first-formed father" of the world
and gives him strength to rule over everything (10:1-2).[79] Adam here is not only
protoplast, but also paradigmatic for any who would flourish and, especially,
rule on the earth.[80] In two brief verses Adam becomes the paradigm for Solomon, whose legendary wisdom provides the premise for the book of Wisdom.[81]

In another instance as well the Wisdom of Solomon draws on the royal
dynamic of the creation narrative, using humanity's mandate to rule as a
paradigm for Solomon's role as king. In a prayer in chapter 9, Solomon connects his job as king with the purpose for which God created humanity at
the beginning: "You created humanity by your wisdom, to have dominion
over the creatures you made and to rule the world in holiness and righteousness. . . . Give to me the wisdom that sits beside you on your throne" (vv.
2-4). The juxtaposition between creation and kingship likely connotes that

76. Grabbe, "Better Watch Your Back," 274-75.
77. Grabbe, "Better Watch Your Back," 275.
78. Grabbe, "Better Watch Your Back," 281-82.
79. We also find idealization of Adam, but with little commentary, in Sirach 49:16: ὑπὲρ πᾶν
ζῷον ἐν τῇ κτίσει Αδαμ. On this passage, see Levison, *Portraits of Adam*, 44-45, 47.
80. An interpretation shared by Levison, *Portraits of Adam*, 58-59.
81. Such a retrospective idealization of Adam fits exactly with the paradigm suggested by
Anderson in *Genesis of Perfection*: reread in light of a story whose goal is the wise Solomon
(cf. p. 1), the Adam story is told so as to describe the origin of human perfection (cf. p. 8).

Solomon sees himself taking on the Adamic role.[82] Together, these allusions to first humanity in Wisdom 9 and 10 verify that at least some early Jewish readers of Genesis 1:26-28 saw the creational purpose of rule as a template for Israel and/or its kings. More can be said as well. John Levison compares the language deployed to speak of human rule in 9:1-3 with the language used to speak of God's rule in 12:15-18. In both instances, and only these instances, the verbs διέπειν and δεσπόζειν are used.[83] Moreover, the words ὁσιότης, δικαιοσύνη, and κρίσις are used in reference to the king in 9:3, 5, and of God in 5:17-20. Levison roots this idea in "Greek categories," but we have seen enough of Genesis 1 in its ancient Near Eastern context to know that such a human embodiment of divine qualities is equally at home in the categories of biblical Judaism.[84]

5. DEAD SEA SCROLLS

The notion that Adam as a glorious, royal ancestor anticipates the future glory of Israel finds regular iteration in the Dead Sea Scrolls. The Dead Sea Scrolls are replete with reflections on creation — both God's original act and anticipations that the first creation establishes expectations that should be fulfilled in the age to come. At times it is difficult to discern whether a text should be discussed as a new creation text per se, or whether it is better suited to reflections on fulfillment of the Davidic kingship (see below). This difficulty itself underscores one thread of this chapter's argument: the stories of Israel are told in light of one another, such that the calling of Israel and its kings are told in terms of fulfilling the vocation of Adam; or, in the words of the scrolls, inheriting "all the glory of Adam." The source of this glory is none other than Israel's God, who has chosen first humanity in general and then Israel in particular to share in the sovereign rule of the cosmos.[85]

82. Cf. Levison, *Portraits of Adam*, 55-56.
83. Levison, *Portraits of Adam*, 56.
84. Levison, *Portraits of Adam*, 56.
85. As discussed in the introduction, my approach has many similarities to that of Crispin Fletcher-Louis, and his work, *All the Glory of Adam: Liturgical Anthropology in the Dead Sea Scrolls* (Leiden: Brill, 2002), will be a regular conversation partner here. The important difference is that Fletcher-Louis sees the idealization of humanity as evidence of angelomorphic renderings, whereas I see the glorified theological anthropology as, more often, an expression of the close proximity with God that is the life for which humanity itself was created. Insofar as this is a "divinization," it is a recapturing of the primal investiture of God-likeness.

a. The Community Rule (1QS)

Some of the exalted language, or glorious depictions, that the New Testament uses of Jesus find parallels in the scrolls' description of the community in terms of Adam. The Community Rule is important in this regard. 1QS IV, 20-26, depicts the future of the righteous, when they will be exalted with "all the glory of Adam" (1QS IV, 23). This state of glory is inaugurated by an outpouring of God's spirit that is likened to cleansing waters (1QS IV, 21), all of which is both "the end" and the beginning of "the new creation" (1QS IV, 25). This new creation context provides a crucial piece of evidence that the language of "all the glory of Adam" is not an angelomorphic expectation but is, instead, a profoundly anthropomorphic expectation. Adam, in his created state, is an idealization of what humanity was, is intended to be, and can be again.[86] This protological glory, then, is the interpretive context within which to read the prior line, in which the fate of the righteous is described as "everlasting blessings, eternal enjoyment with endless life, and a crown of glory with majestic raiment in eternal light" (1QS IV, 7-8). In fact, that line may well reflect an assimilation of Psalm 8 with the notions of Adam's creation in glory: "You have made them a little lower than God and crowned them with glory and honor" (Ps 8:5, NRSV). Importantly, such depictions of Adam are tied to the community's future: the idealized human of the past provides a template for how the faithful community will be glorified in the future.[87] Idealized human figures provide one signal of what a particular religious community might expect in some eschatological future — a point of no little significance when assessing the Gospels' eschatologically charged depictions of Jesus.

b. Hodayot (1QH^a)

Within the community's songs of praise we catch glimpses of where humanity, especially as represented in the community, stands with relation both to God and to the rest of creation. 1QHodayot[a] anticipates that the future in store for God's faithful people entails a restoration of "all the glory of Adam [and] numerous days" (בכול כבוד אדם [ו]רוב ימים, 1QH[a] IV, 15). The next psalm takes up the theme of humanity's glory, the reward God has in store for those

---

86. On the new creation context, cf. Émile Puech, "Immortality and Life after Death," in *The Dead Sea Scrolls Fifty Years after Their Discovery* (ed. L. H. Schiffman et al.; Jerusalem: Israel Exploration Society, 2000), 512-20, here 517.

87. Fletcher-Louis, *All the Glory of Adam*, 96-97.

who are faithful (1QH^a V, 8-12). As the song unfolds, it becomes increasingly clear that the glory awaiting humanity is none other than God's own glory.[88] Sharing in God's glory, glorified (Adamic) humanity makes known the glory of God: "For you have established them before the centuries . . . so that they can recount your glory throughout all your dominion. . . . In the mysteries of your insight [you] have apportioned all these things, to make your glory known" (1QH^a V, 16-17, 19; cf. 1QH^a XI, 3; XII, 5).[89] The glory of eschatological humanity comes to acquitted people who are embellished with God's own splendor (1QH^a V, 23). This line of thinking provides one significant hint as to the conjunction between God and humanity as it gets worked out at Qumran. The God who will not give his glory to another (Isa 48:11) gives his glory to faithful humanity so that all the world may know God's glory.

Imagery of a restored Eden recurs in this hymnic material. Column 14, in particular, provides a snapshot of humanity's location in an idealized cosmos. Within humanity ("the sons of Adam"), the faithful council of God's people receives God's glory, "together with the angels of the face, without there being a mediator between" (1QH^a XIV, 11-13). This congregation, mingling with heavenly creatures, represents a restored humanity, as becomes clear in the subsequent lines. Those in the council are said to be God's princes — echoes of Adam and perhaps, also, of the Hebrew Bible's sometimes title for David (2 Sam 6:21; 7:8; Ezek 34:24; 37:25; cf. 1 Chr 29:22). The council is then described as a tree that will cover the whole world and be watered by the streams of Eden (1QH^a XIV, 15-16; cf. XVI, 4). We see in this song that though "sons of Adam" is, on the one hand, a general depiction of humanity, it also evokes primeval humanity and the garden of Eden as establishing a trajectory for faithful humanity's eschatological future.[90] Ruling for and representing God in an Edenic paradise continues to be the people's hope.[91]

Balancing the idealistic vision of coming glory is a sober pessimism about

88. Peter Schäfer, *The Jewish Jesus: How Judaism and Christianity Shaped Each Other* (Princeton, NJ: Princeton University Press, 2012), 197-213, indicates various ways that later Jewish traditions continued to wrestle with the notion that Adam as "image of God" meant a glory that might even lead to confusion between the two.

89. Florentino García Martínez and Eibert J. C. Tigchelaar, *DSSSE* (2 vols.; Grand Rapids, MI: Eerdmans, 1998), 1:151.

90. Puech, "Immortality and Life after Death," 518.

91. As with the biblical material in Genesis 1 itself, so here also there is a danger that in focusing on passages where "rule" comes to the fore, we might leave the mistaken impression that Davidic kingship is as important as, or even more important than, the priestly role. The latter appears to be more significant for the constitution and hopes of the Dead Sea Scrolls community.

humanity's ability to walk justly before God. In contrast to God's ways of justice, humans are defined by "iniquity and deeds of deception" (1QH^a IX, 27).[92] There is hope for the "sons of Adam," however, in the spirit of God bringing the perfecting power required for them to walk in God's paths of justice (1QH^a XII, 30-32). Humans enact the works of God as they are strengthened by God's spirit. This opens up one possible avenue for pursuing why the Gospels might say what they say about Jesus, inasmuch as the ministry of Jesus begins with his reception of God's spirit at baptism.

Adam is depicted as an idealized human figure in this hymn material, an idealization that includes bearing God's glory, mingling with angelic hosts, and representing the future for which God's faithful people might hope. Such exaltation can be called "divinization" only in the sense that God creates humanity to be like God. Thus, I want to nuance the conclusion of Fletcher-Louis. He concludes that "it is not simply a human 'honour' or 'dignity' that is in view, but a Glory which is God's own. The Qumran community believed then, that it was their vocation to fulfil the responsibility originally given to Adam to embody God's own glory."[93] I would want to change the phrase, "it is not *simply* a human honor" to "it is not a *generalized* human honor." The language of "simply a human honor" might create the impression that humanity as such is inherently deficient, whereas the creation stories as engaged here suggest that humanity at the present is, generally speaking, deficient, but an idealized original humanity was, we might say, more fully human for its bearing of the divine glory. The honor entailed in being invested with God's own glory is the honor that describes an idealized human and idealized persons who later come to embody the protoplast's native endowment.

c. Jubilees (4Q216)

Jubilees is among the manuscripts found at Qumran, and it contains an interesting piece of corroborating evidence for the reading of the biblical story provided here. I argued above that the creation narrative depicts humanity as God's children. The language of image and likeness carries the dual royal connotations of rule and sonship. In *Jubilees* 2 (4Q216 VII, 11) the creation narrative is overlaid with God's intention to call the people of Israel: "And he chose the descendants of Jacob among [all those I saw. And I registered them for me as the firstborn son and consecrated them to me] for ever and ever.

---

92. Martínez and Tigchelaar, *DSSE*, 1:161.
93. Fletcher-Louis, *All the Glory of Adam*, 97.

The [seventh] day [I will teach them so that they can keep the Sabbath on it above all]."[94] As the creation story itself moves from the creation of humanity to Sabbath, *Jubilees* anticipates the election of Jacob for the purpose of keeping Sabbath. Israel thus becomes the reembodiment of אדם, set apart to fulfill what *Jubilees* sees as humanity's primal vocation.

d. Blessings (4Q287)

The "blessings" text 4Q287 points toward a time in the future when the role of Adam will be taken up by God's faithful people such that the blessing of Abraham might come to all the nations of the earth as anticipated in Genesis 12:3. Though the text is fragmentary and the arrangement of the fragments is debatable, several important points can still be taken away.

First, fragments 3 and 4 draw on the creation narrative of Genesis 1. Fragment 3 speaks of animals, birds, reptiles, and fish as those whom God has created in order to bless God's name. Fragment 4, in turn, echoes the creation narrative, or perhaps its retelling in Psalm 8, as it states that God gave dominion to humanity (ותמשל את האדם). The text appears to be looking to humanity as an active agent in bringing about the blessing of God for which all creatures were made.[95]

In the subsequent fragment, the blessing text seems to progress from creation to the Abraham narrative. Fragment 5 speaks of a time of coming exaltation (perhaps the coming of God's kingdom itself)[96] when the nations will be drawn into the sphere of God's blessing. The final line speaks of the families of the earth (משפחות האדמה), a phrase found in the Hebrew Bible in Genesis 12:3 and 28:14 (4Q287 5, 13). In both of those biblical precedents, the writer is looking to a time in the future when the nations will, as promised, be blessed by Abraham's family. The conjunction of the creation imagery from fragments 3 and 4 with the Abraham allusion in fragment 5 might suggest that Jews in the post-biblical period understood their calling as the seed of Abraham as the means by which the purposes of creation would be fulfilled. The fragment, however, is too sparse to speak with any confidence on this particular point.

One more aspect of this scroll is worthy of note, though its significance is also somewhat speculative, given the document's fragmentary nature. If the fragments have been correctly grouped and ordered, then the blessings of

---

94. Martínez and Tigchelaar, *DSSSE*, 1:463.
95. See also 4Q301 3, 5-8.
96. Cf. Martínez and Tigchelaar, *DSSSE*, 2:651.

God begin with a survey of heavenly glory (frags. 1-2) before descending to the blessings of creation (frags. 3-5). Heavenly dwelling places are described as well as angelic inhabitants. The angels are depicted as holy servants (2, 9) who seem to attend to the holy festivals of God's people (2, 7). These servants either attend to God or themselves dwell in heavenly palaces. The juxtaposition of the heavenly and earthly realms is striking in that though the angels are depicted as bedecked in glory and splendor, dwelling in the presence of God and God's righteousness, yet they are also deemed servants (2, 9). In contrast, when humanity comes into view in the subsequent blessings, humans are viewed, as in Genesis 1, as those upon whom dominion has been bestowed. Angelic beings are faithful to God in ministering in the heavens; humans are faithful to God in ruling on the earth (frag. 4). Here is yet another indication that surveying angelic functions might introduce a category mistake when attempting to explain the Christologies of the New Testament.

e. Noncanonical Psalms (4Q381)

The first song in the "noncanonical psalms" scroll 4Q381 is a psalm of praise that recounts the wisdom made known in creation. Speaking of humans, it highlights their assignment to rule the world — a task bestowed upon humanity by God's spirit (4Q381 1, 8). The final line of this fragment indicates that the purpose of some agent of God's creation sent to earth, likely some member of the angelic host, was "to serve man and to wait on him" (4Q381 1, 11). Humanity is placed on the earth to rule and to be served — a function that tends to stands in contrast with that of not only other creatures but also heavenly agents, which are servants. Such contrasting roles, in which humans rule and heavenly beings are sent to serve them, underscores the importance of distinguishing idealized human figures from angelic beings. The idealization of humanity at creation makes it possible, a possibility realized in some early Jewish literature, to depict humanity at creation as higher in the celestial pecking order than the angelic host, both because of its likeness to God per se (see the *Life of Adam and Eve* on this score) and because it is created to rule, while angels are often depicted as bearing a function of service.[97]

Evidence such as this points to a possibility that is widely ignored in recent claims about early high Christology. Isolation of certain types of figures, such as angelic beings or "messiahs" per se, has prevented scholarship from wrestling with the breadth of possibility available to a Jewish monotheist who

97. A point made also by Fletcher-Louis, *All the Glory of Adam*, 98-103.

took seriously, and further developed, the portrayal of humanity we find in Genesis 1:26-28. Humanity was created to depict God to the world. It is a failure to consider these latter points that keeps Bauckham's argument about the place of angels from sustaining his overall point about what is wholly unique to God.[98] His claims that angelic beings serve rather than rule may all be true without his yet having demonstrated that any being depicted as ruling the cosmos is playing the part of God as God. There might be another creature in creation, in this case humanity, that was created for a purpose that transcends the angelic role of service. This contrast is exploited in at least some of the literature at Qumran, and appears to be part of a broader tendency to idealize first humanity.

Later, the scroll provides evidence of the people of Israel as a whole (or a purified representative remnant) playing the role set out for Adam and the Davidic kings of ruling the world on God's behalf: "He has chosen you [. . .] [. . . from among] [m]any [peoples] and from among great nations so that you will be a people for him, to rule over all [. . .] [. . . heav]en and earth, and to (be) the most high of all the nations of the earth" (4Q381 76-77, 14-16). The purpose of Israel here matches the outline of the biblical story I traced above: to fulfill the vocation originally assigned to humanity as a whole of ruling the world on God's behalf. The fragmentary nature of line 16 makes it impossible to know for sure whether this song envisions humanity ruling with God over the heavens as well, though in this context it seems plausible.

f. Words of the Luminaries (4Q504)

This scroll offers an important piece of validation for the notion that the glorification of primal humanity we see at Qumran is not rooted in claims of angelic humanity, but is instead an articulation of humanity's native possession due to its being created in the likeness of God. In fragment 8, recto, the author recounts the creation of humanity: "[. . . Adam] our [fat]her, you fashioned in the likeness of [your] glory [. . .] [. . . the breath of life] you [b]lew into his nostril, and intelligence and knowledge [. . .] [. . . in the gar]den of Eden, which you had planted. You made [him] govern [. . .] [. . .] and so that he would walk in a glorious land."[99] This fragment conflates the two creation stories of

---

98. Bauckham, *Jesus and the God of Israel*, 10-11.

99. Martínez and Tigchelaar, *DSSSE*, 2:1009, alt. I have rendered בדמות "likeness" rather than "image," to keep the parallel with Genesis 1:26 more exact. Cf. George H. van Kooten, *Paul's Anthropology in Context: The Image of God, Assimilation to God, and Tripartite Man in*

Genesis 1 and 2, and develops them in ways germane to the question of how idealized human figures are represented at Qumran.

First, the text deviates slightly from the language of "image and likeness" (בצלמנו כדמותנו, Gen 1:26), instead reading "likeness of your glory" (בדמות [. . . כה]כבוד). This may well be interpreting the language of likeness as a sort of physical resemblance, in which God's luminous brightness is bestowed upon humanity at its creation. The "likeness of the Lord's glory" (דמות כבוד־יהוה) is a phrase the book of Ezekiel uses at the end of its opening vision of God, to summarize what the prophet has seen.[100] As noted above in our exploration of Genesis 1, Ezekiel itself is part of the Priestly tradition and interacts heavily with Genesis 1.[101] Together, the biblical texts and the Qumran manuscript all create a picture in which God's appearance can be given physical approximation, which is referred to using the language of "glory," and humanity in its pristine state can rightly be said to reflect that likeness.

Second, the idealization of primal humanity includes gifts of wisdom and knowledge, which, in the words of Crispin Fletcher-Louis, makes it similar "to the sapiential anthropological doxography" that one finds in Sirach.[102] In other words, Adam is depicted as someone who not only shines with God's glory, but also endowed to act in a righteous manner as that manner is defined by the wisdom traditions of Israel. Moreover, this gift may be connected with the gift of God's spirit, as it is signaled immediately after reporting that God blew into the man's nostril (line 5).

Third, the depiction of humanity at creation combines Genesis 1 with Genesis 2–3 by expressing God's purpose that humanity rule alongside its place walking "in a glorious land." In the reiteration of the word "glory" (כבוד), we see the inflation of both the human being and the space he was created to occupy. The Qumran community is actively engaging the creation stories, not only recognizing the idealization of humanity within them, but also cultivating that idealization so that their depictions of first humanity more clearly indicate proximity with God and embodiment of divine characteristics.

Fletcher-Louis rightly points out that this idealization of humanity sets the stage for a later depiction of Israel (or the Qumran covenanters as the righteous remnant of Israel) in 4Q504 fragment 1-2, column 3.[103] Reflecting

Ancient Judaism, Ancient Philosophy, and Early Christianity (WUNT 232; Tübingen: Mohr Siebeck, 2008), 15-27.

100. Fletcher-Louis, *All the Glory of Adam*, 93.
101. See also van Kooten, *Paul's Anthropology*, 16.
102. Fletcher-Louis, *All the Glory of Adam*, 93; cf. van Kooten, *Paul's Anthropology*, 16.
103. Fletcher-Louis, *All the Glory of Adam*, 93.

the primordial deep, the nations are "as chaos" (כ[תהו]; cf. Gen 1:2; Isa 40:17, 23). In contrast, Israel is created for God's glory and as God's children. Here again we see the language of glory, and God's glory, specifically, as a human possession. This underscores that the idealization of first-created humanity is tied to the present, idealized identity of the Qumran community.[104] In step with the notion that idealized humanity is a "theophany" of God, this scroll goes on to say that God's presence in the midst of Israel means that all nations have seen God's glory (4Q504 frag. 1-2, col. iv). God is identified with idealized humanity in the Qumran scrolls.

g. *The Covenant of Damascus (CD-A)*

The Covenant of Damascus repeats the imagery of the Hodayot by saying that the future of the elect from within Israel entails "all the glory of Adam" (CD-A III, 20). Interestingly, this future life is tied to an identification of the members of the community with the priests, Levites, and sons of Zadok from a prophecy in Ezekiel: "But the levitical priests, the descendants of Zadok, who kept the charge of my sanctuary when the people of Israel went astray from me, shall come near to me to minister to me; and they shall attend me to offer me the fat and the blood, says the Lord GOD" (Ezek 44:15, NRSV). The reestablishment of Adamic glory comes to those who function as priests before God by ministering in God's presence because they kept the law (CD-A III, 18- IV, 4).

h. *Conclusions: Qumran*

The notion that Adam as a glorious, royal ancestor anticipates the future glory of Israel finds regular iteration in the Dead Sea Scrolls. The future new creation entails not only endless life but also "a crown of glory with majestic raiment in eternal light" (1QS IV, 7-8), in which the righteous are exalted with "all the glory of Adam" (1QS IV, 23).[105] In the hymnic material in 1QH[a] this theme is enriched, as the glory is further delineated as God's own glory (e.g., 1QH[a] V, 16-17, 19; XIV, 11-13). Idealized, faithful humanity lives into the "glory of Adam" as it possesses and walks by God's spirit en route to receiving God's own glory and restoration to the place of exercising reign over the world on God's behalf. As a final example, the "blessings" text 4Q287 intersperses allusions to creation with references to Abraham as well as the heavenly court. While the angelic

---

104. Cf. van Kooten, *Paul's Anthropology,* 18.
105. Cited from Martínez and Tigchelaar, *DSSSE,* 1:77, 79.

figures are, for all their glory, deemed servants (2, 9), humanity is faithful to God by ruling on the earth (frag. 4).

Such passages point out the flaw in Bauckham's approach, in which depicting someone as sharing in God's rule is to depict the person as divine. Bauckham made this claim in arguing against an angelomorphic Christology; it is my contention that he looked in the wrong place.[106] An explanation for these data is not far to seek. The Qumran scrolls demonstrate a reading of the creation accounts in which sharing God's reign is not what angels are created to do; in the scriptures of Israel it is what humans are created to do. A figure "sharing in the reign of God" is as likely to be putting on display an anthropomorphic Christology as a divine Christology, if the latter means anything more than humanity bearing the divine marks with which Genesis intimates it was created at the beginning.

Moreover, the data I have briefly surveyed here signal an important distinction between humanity and angels. Thus, I am wary of pushing the language of "angelomorphic" humanity because not only is human glory said to be directly derivative from God, but there are also instances in which the divine likeness distinguishes humans from the angels. The Qumran scrolls idealize the first humans in order to demonstrate humanity's potential God-likeness and to mark out the eschatological future in store for the faithful of the community. These are the sorts of moves that, I argue, make best sense of the exalted depictions of Jesus we discover in the Synoptic Tradition: a human who is glorified because he is the eschatological agent who is fulfilling the vocation to be the human who represents God to the world.

6. PHILO

Philo's depiction of humanity in his exposition of the Genesis 1 creation story, *On the Creation of the World* (*De opificio mundi*), includes an extended picture of humanity ruling the world like kings (*Opif.* 83-88). As part of a larger series of defenses of humanity being created last, Philo asserts that the sudden appearance of humanity would strike fear into the other animals.[107] "For," he continues, "it was fitting that they, as soon as they first saw him, should admire and worship him, as their natural ruler and master" (τεθηπέναι καὶ

---

106. Bauckham, *Jesus and the God of Israel,* 14-16.

107. On humanity's rule over the created world, but not the heavenly, in *De opificio mundi,* see Levison, *Portraits of Adam,* 67-68.

προσκυνεπεῖν ὡς ἂν ἡγεμόνα φύσει καὶ δεσπότην; *Opif.* 83). The other crea-tures worship the first humans.

As the paragraph unfolds, Philo paints a vivid picture of human sover-eignty over the animal world, expanding broadly on the notion of human rule through use of metaphors such as slave-master and subject-sovereign. The obeisance that Philo envisions being rendered to humanity is appropriate for the creatures of the earth to offer because of the function of rule God en-trusted to people. Human rule, moreover, is not simply a newly created realm of power, a vacuum into which humanity is placed. Instead, Philo asserts that the rule humanity exercises is a delegation of God's own.[108] Combining the imagery of a ship and that of a chariot, Philo says that humanity functions like a pilot or driver over everything (ἐφ᾽ ἅπασιν), having been so commissioned in order to serve as a viceroy (ὕπαρχος) under the first and great King (*Opif.* 88). Idealized humanity exercises God's reign over the earth in God's stead.

Philo may be the Jewish author who comes closest to consciously working with a category akin to the idea of the idealized human figure that I have posited. For his Middle Platonic philosophy finds a ready source for its expres-sion in the differing stories of Genesis 1 and Genesis 2. He describes the first humanity, depicted in Genesis 1, not only as androgynous but also as only an idea perceptible to the mind (*Opif.* 134). Conversely, the man made from the clay (Gen 2:7) is corporeal and perceptible to the external senses (*Opif.* 134). And yet, Philo idealizes the corporeal human as well, in the sense that I use the term throughout my work, affirming that the original man was excellent in both body and soul, truly beautiful and good (καλὸς κἀγαθός, *Opif.* 136; cf. *Opif.* 140).

In a similar manner, Philo depicts primeval humanity as practitioners of virtue, thereby making Adam a portrait of humanity's potential telos (*Leg.* 1.88-89). Adam not only demonstrates the unique human capacity for reason and virtue; in these very respects he demonstrates how idealized humanity fulfills its God-like character.[109] Philo's vision of the idealized future includes not only humanity being restored to a state of virtue but also, in echo of the situation in paradise, of rule over the beasts (*Praem.* 89-91).[110] Idealized figures of the past serve as a mold for casting the idealized people of the future, as Philo not only describes Adam in such a way as to correspond to the hoped-for destiny

---

108. Per Jarle Bekken, *The Word Is Near You: A Study of Deuteronomy 30:12-14 in Paul's Letter to the Romans in a Jewish Context* (BZNW 144; Berlin: De Gruyter, 2007), 124-27.

109. Cf. Levison, *Portraits of Adam*, 71-72.

110. Bekken, *The Word Is Near You*, 124-27.

of people in general, but of the Jewish people in particular: Israel will rule the nations (e.g., *Praem.* 125).[111]

Adam theology shapes Philo's portrayal of the earth after the flood. He depicts the situation as a sort of new creation, in which the earth and the universe are restored to the way they were when first created (*Mos* 2.64).[112] Noah and his family thus occupy the place originally given to Adam as rulers (ἡγεμόνες) of the earth in its regeneration (παλιγγενεσίας). This rulership over the creatures of the earth, in turn, devolves upon humanity as it also is bestowed with a power like God's own (ἀντίμιμον γεγονὸς θεοῦ δυνάμεως, 2.65). The human likeness to God is further explained as Philo uses and expands on the idea of humanity being God's image (εἰκών), "the manifest image of the invisible, eternal nature" (εἰκὼν τῆς ἀοράτου φύσεως ἐμφανής, ἀιδίου γενητή, 2.65).[113] Noah thus represents what Adam, too, was to represent: humanity as representative embodiments of the divine nature and the divine rule on the earth.

7. ANIMAL VISIONS (1 ENOCH)

An Adam figure comes on the scene as the third in a series of three idealizations that are depicted toward the end of the Animal Visions story that runs from creation through consummation (*1 Enoch* 85–90). After a messiah figure and Israel itself are depicted as standing in the place of God in rule, worship, and even prayer (see discussions below when I take up the Animal Visions under "The Community of the Elect"), a third and final instance of a human representative of God comes in a second Adam figure — a snow-white cow (*1 En.* 90:37; cf. 85:3). This one takes on the role that had been more generally assigned to the sheep: the one who is feared and to whom petitions are made (*1 En.* 90:37). The advent of this Adam figure begins the final leg in the creation of a new humanity, as the sheep are transformed into snow-white cows as well, thus returning to the primeval form of Adam and Eve (*1 En.* 90:37; cf. 85:3).[114]

111. Bekken, *The Word Is Near You,* 136; Levison, *Portraits of Adam,* 86. In between Adam and Israel, Noah, too, plays this role in Philo's work (*Mos.* 2.59-65); cf. Levison, *Portraits of Adam,* 78-79.

112. Cf. Levison, *Portraits of Adam,* 78-79.

113. Perhaps it is not superfluous to draw the reader's attention to the correspondence between Philo's εἰκὼν τῆς ἀοράτου φύσεως and the claim in Colossians that Jesus is εἰκὼν τοῦ θεοῦ τοῦ ἀοράτου (1:15).

114. Cf. George W. E. Nickelsburg, *1 Enoch: A Commentary on the Book of 1 Enoch, Chapters 1–36; 81–108* (Hermeneia; Minneapolis: Fortress, 2001), 406-7.

This episode highlights several possibilities for early Jewish interpreters. First, it shows how speculation about Adam not only reflects eschatological expectations, but can also be used to idealize (Davidic) rulers and Israel itself.[115] Second, it shows that idealized human figures can become the ones in whom the destinies of other people are represented. Third, it shows how a figure can mediate between God and humanity such that attaining to God's eschatological (/protological) blessing can be tied to how a person treats God's representative agent. He is thus a stand-in for God not only in executing God's will or judgment on the earth, but also in being the earthly embodiment of the one to whom a person must be faithful if that person is to be judged as being faithful to God.

8. *LIFE OF ADAM AND EVE*

The *Life of Adam and Eve* provides some of the clearest evidence of an idealized anthropology derivative of humanity's creation in God's image, and at the same time demonstrates that the place of such idealized humans in the cosmic hierarchy is both distinct from and superior to the place assigned to angels. Humanity's bearing of the divine image provides such an identification with God that the angels themselves are called to bow down and worship before Adam (*L.A.E.* [Vita] 13:1-3; 14:1-2). The idealization of humanity in this text is derivative of humanity's relationship to God, and yet that derivation, precisely because it is of divine origin, places humanity at such an exalted point in the cosmic hierarchy that they are recipients of worship — not merely from other earthly creatures, but even from the heavenly angels.[116]

Significantly, part of the devil's resistance to Michael's command that the angels worship is that he is prior and superior to the human (*L.A.E.* [Vita] 14:3). This line of resistance reflects the notion that in the hierarchy of the cosmos angelic figures are a little lower than God. Such a celestial ranking scheme is operative also in much modern scholarship, particularly when we

115. There is no direct indication that this final figure is Davidic; cf. the discussion in Nickelsburg, *1 Enoch*, 406-7.

116. Schäfer, *Jewish Jesus*, 197-213, shows that the God-like condition of Adam's creation is resolved in the opposite way in rabbinic sources. There the angels' temptation to worship Adam must be undone through some divine diminishment of the protoplast. Such stories reinforce the tradition of the God-like state of primal humanity while at the same time reinforcing what would become more normative theological positions about the exclusive place of God in the worship of Israel.

look to "angelomorphic" figures to help explain the glorification of God's faithful people in general ("all the glory of Adam" at Qumran, for instance) or of Jesus in particular. This is the line that Bauckham suggests cannot be toed when it comes to early Judaism: angels do not sit on God's throne or receive God's worship.[117] But we see time and again that it is completely possible within a Jewish context to so depict idealized human figures. Here, as in some of the Qumran texts as well, the creation story is read to signal that it is not angels who are next to God in prominence, honor, power, and glory, but it is idealized and faithful humanity who occupies this role. Humans are the image of God, and as such can even rightly share in the worship that otherwise is due to God alone.

The centrality of human identity as those bearing the image of God continues when Seth is bitten by a serpent (Vita 37–38; Apocalypse 10–11). In the Apocalypse version, Eve asks, "How did you not remember your subjection, for you were once subjected to the image of God?" (*L.A.E.* [Apocalypse] 10:3).[118] The failure of current reality to live up to the idealized picture of the past that the *Life of Adam and Eve* depicts derives, in part, from the rule that once was humanity's being ceded to the beasts due to humanity's sin. The serpent says to Eve, "The rule of the beasts has happened because of you" (*L.A.E.* [Apocalypse] 11:1).[119] The loss of human rule, and subsequent disorder on the earth, are reiterated when Eve tells the story of God issuing judgment after their transgression (*L.A.E.* [Apocalypse] 24:4).

When the Apocalypse proceeds to predict a coming resurrection, it indicates that Adam's resumption of dominion over the earth will entail a displacing of Satan, the usurper. Adam will once again rule the earth on a glorious throne, and this is a restoration of humanity to the place from which it was displaced when it disobeyed God's command (*L.A.E.* [Apocalypse] 39:2-3; cf. [Vita] 47:3).[120] This is a clear instance of the mutual interdependence of protological and eschatological visions. The hope for the future is a restoration of the rule that was humanity's in the beginning. Someone working with a cosmological map akin to the one laid out in the *Life of Adam and Eve* could

---

117. Bauckham, *Jesus and the God of Israel,* esp. 7-17.

118. M. D. Johnson, trans., "Life of Adam and Eve," in *The Old Testament Pseudepigrapha,* vol. 2, *Expansions of the "Old Testament" and Legends, Wisdom, and Philosophical Literature, Prayers, Psalms, and Odes, Fragments of Lost Judeo-Hellenistic Works* (ed. James H. Charlesworth; New York: Doubleday, 1985), 273.

119. Johnson, "Life of Adam and Eve," 2:275.

120. As Levison notes, *Portraits of Adam,* 167, this restoration of dominion is a clear signal that currently humanity does not possess its primeval gift of rule.

very easily depict eschatological humanity receiving worship from other creatures, even angels, precisely because it is an idealized humanity remade after the likeness of the idealized protoplasts.

The *Life of Adam and Eve* appears to have been popular with early Christians, and may have been written in the Christian era. It is thus not a text to which we can appeal as "background" for the New Testament. However, background is not exactly what this chapter seeks to establish. It is assessing ways in which Jews with "monotheistic" commitments might depict idealized humans.[121] Such information is valuable even if it postdates the Gospels. Moreover, if the *Life of Adam and Eve* is judged to be a Christian composition, then its depictions of humanity's relationship to the angelic host simply affirm that other early Christians understood the idealized place of humanity in the cosmos along the lines of what I argue for the human Jesus of the Synoptic Gospels.

9. TESTAMENT OF ABRAHAM

In the *Testament of Abraham,* Abraham sees a vision of ancestors whose depictions join them in close proximity with God. His vision of Adam is one in which Adam sits on a golden throne, beholding the fate of humanity (*T. Ab.* 11). In addition to sitting enthroned, Adam is said to be "terrifying," with an appearance like "the Lord's" (*T. Ab.* 11:4), and he is also described as being "in glory" (*T. Ab.* 11:9). Here we apparently have a rendering of Adam that reflects the creation narrative of Genesis 1:26-28, in which humanity is created to rule (embodied in the golden throne) and is made in the image and likeness of God (embodied in a glorious appearance like the Lord's). While Adam is not said to perform any particular divine functions in this story, the imagery reflects the idealized condition of the created protoplast in looking like God and in having a seat that signifies share in God's rule. Reading this passage with my larger project in view, the notion of physical appearance is important: idealized human figures can be depicted as looking like God, particularly "in glory." Such a notion is reflected in Daniel's expectation that the resurrected righteous will shine like the stars of heaven (Dan 12:3), and perhaps also in Jesus's statement that those resurrected will be like angels (Mark 12:25 and pars.). Physical appearance that embodies heavenly luminosity (e.g., in the transfiguration story, Mark 9:2-8) is no indication that a figure is either divine per se or angelic. It

121. Once again, Schäfer, *Jewish Jesus,* 197-213, is relevant.

may be, instead, an indication that a human has been restored to the glory that properly belongs to humans as those created in God's image.[122]

Similarly, in the following scene Abraham sees Abel superintending the antepenultimate judgment (T. Ab. 12–13). He is described, similarly, as sitting on a throne (Abel's being of crystal and fire, T. Ab. 12:4). And his appearance is wondrous, like the sun, like a son of God (T. Ab. 12:5). The physical description is a restatement of the depiction of Adam in different terms: looking like God and being like God's son, shining in glory, make equivalent claims. Once again, this is likely reading the language of "image and likeness" as an indication of physical resemblance. And such a connection between God and the firstborn human child is made without any suggestion of a change in the identity of God. The appellation "son of God" can be made of someone, or suggested of someone, without any hint of preexistence or divinity as such, and may in fact be a signal that the person is regaining what was humanity's native endowment as human creatures.

In this particular scene, moreover, the human identity of Abel is central to the role he plays. He acts as first judge because God has determined that every human must be judged by a human (T. Ab. 13:3, 5). Sitting in judgment, Abel is a representative human figure, idealized not only in his appearance but also by the role he plays as righteous judge. Abraham's guide, Michael, also tells him (somewhat anachronistically) that the penultimate judgment will occur at the hands of the twelve tribes of Israel (T. Ab. 13:6), which becomes another instance of idealized, representative human figures participating in God's activity of judging the world. Finally, the ultimate judgment is rendered by God himself (T. Ab. 13:7).

10. CONCLUSIONS: ADAM AS IDEALIZED FIRST HUMANITY

This survey of early Jewish reflections on Adam represents diversity within a shared range of possibilities. In general, it may be said of the material surveyed that the suggestions inherent in Genesis 1 of a humanity that stands in closest proximity to God, "theophanies" to use the language of Garr, was variously explored and developed by ancient interpreters who depicted Adam as an idealized human. In various texts with sundry *Tendenzen*, the God who is sovereign (Pss

---

122. Even in the *Testament of Abraham*, angelic figures can also reflect heavenly glory (e.g., the archangel Dokiel; T. Ab. 13:10). What we learn from the story, however, is that such a depiction is not a sufficient condition to designate someone or something as "angelic" or "divine" because it may apply to idealized human beings as well.

22:28; 47:2) shares sovereign rule with humanity, especially idealized human figures.[123] In Wisdom and some Qumran scrolls, such ruling comes with an endowment of divine wisdom; in Philo, this means manifesting divine virtue. Idealized human figures represent God to the world by sharing in various divine actions (such as rule), attributes (such as glory), and even ascriptions (such as worship), but are not thereby depicted as instantiations of Israel's God; instead, they are fulfilling what it means to be an ideal human. Moreover, this idealization is not, generally speaking, an angelic exaltation, inasmuch as it is directly derivative of God (in step with the divine endowment that is usually understood to be in play in Genesis 1) and can at times depict humans as higher than the angelic host in the cosmic hierarchy. These depictions are also not given merely for their own sakes, but to establish an expectation, often eschatological, for those humans who faithfully follow God. Both biblical and post-biblical Jewish reflections on primal humanity so link idealized humanity with God as to demand that any reader who comes across a would-be divine being in Jewish literature stop to consider whether the dynamics in play might be those in which protological glory is being restored through an idealized human agent.

B. MOSES AND THE PROPHETS

1. MOSES AS GOD AND KING

Moses occupies a central place in the story of Israel as God's agent in perhaps the greatest act of salvation (the exodus from Egypt) and in receiving the most centrally defining aspect of Jewish practice and identity (the Torah). Both within

---

123. Later Jewish traditions continue to develop such themes. The targumic expansions on Jacob's ladder, for instance, speak of Jacob's image on God's throne of glory (*Tg. Ps.-J.*, *Tg. Neof.*, *Frg. Tg.*). Jarl E. Fossum, *Image of the Invisible God: Essays on the Influence of Jewish Mysticism on Early Christology* (NTOA 30; Göttingen: Vandenhoeck & Ruprecht, 1995), 140, follows Christopher Rowland, "John 1.51, Jewish Apocalyptic and the Targumic Tradition," *NTS* 30 (1984): 498-507, here 504, in suggesting that Jacob's image is not so much "engraved" on the throne as Jacob's image is, itself, a manifestation of God's glory. Here we see significant development of the notion that Adam was created in God's image and for the purpose of ruling the world, such that an idealized patriarch is said to have his image as part of the divine glory in the place of heavenly sovereignty over the earth. Although the Targums cannot be used as "background" influence for study of the New Testament, they demonstrate the extent to which Jewish writers can fuse an idealized human figure with God, God's image, God's glory, God's throne, and God's sovereignty without in any way "redefining" monotheism by "including in the identity of God" this other human figure.

the biblical tradition itself and in later Jewish reflection, we see Moses ascribed the role of God in his relationship to foreign nations and to the Israelites.

a. Moses in the Bible

In Exodus, Moses plays the role of God as God himself assigns this role to Moses. First, in response to Moses imploring that he not be sent to speak, God allows Aaron to serve as Moses's surrogate, saying, "You will speak to him and put words in his mouth . . . and he will be a mouth for you, and you will be God for him" (תהיה־לו אלהים, 4:15, 16). When the idea recurs in 7:1, Moses is said to be God not for Aaron but for Pharaoh (נתתיך אלהים לפרעה), while Aaron plays the role of Moses's own prophet. Modern translations tend to soften the divine declaration that Moses will be God for Aaron or Pharaoh, saying instead that Moses will be "like" God (7:1, NRSV, NIV, ESV; contrast KJV: "I have made you a God to Pharaoh"). These statements, however, are clear pointers to the function Moses will play in the story: he will, as primeval humanity itself was intended, act for God, bringing God's rule to bear on the earth. In this case, the act of ordering creation with which Moses is entrusted is the deliverance of Israel from servitude to Pharaoh. In *Human Agents of Cosmic Power*, Mary Mills comments on the role Moses here takes up: "Moses now becomes the human being in whom cosmic power resides and the source of that power's practical working out. Moses is to use Aaron as his prophet to Pharaoh. . . . We might see in this set of relationships the basic definition of the role of the king in Israel. The human agent is the site for the earthly dwelling of the divine energy."[124] These comments signal the importance of human representation, the close conjoining of the divine and the human agent in some miraculous displays, and the basic pattern of divine representation through embodiment of various divine characteristics that span not only Israel's prophets but also its idealized kings.

A crucial component in the theology of Moses's leadership in Exodus is that God himself is at work in the actions of Moses. As Walter Brueggemann comments, "Yahweh still has one active verb: 'I will send.' But it is Moses who will go. . . . We notice that Yahweh's 'mighty acts,' as attested in Israel's core testimony, are considerably changed by the centrality of a human agent and actor, in this case Moses. . . . Yahweh's commitment and engagement are complete, but now they are mediated."[125] God's actions converge with the actions of

---

124. Mary E. Mills, *Human Agents of Cosmic Power in Hellenistic Judaism and the Synoptic Tradition* (JSNTSup 41; Sheffield: JSOT, 1990), 34.

125. Brueggemann, *Theology of the Old Testament*, 364.

Moses such that the same events are attributed to both of them. Yнwн is the one who bestows upon Moses the power (4:21) and the words (4:12); Yнwн performs the wonders (3:20) and delivers Israel (3:8, 21; 6:7). And yet Moses and Aaron are entrusted with the tasks of bringing Israel out of Egypt (6:26) and of speaking with Pharaoh (6:27). Throughout the plagues themselves, God and Moses and Aaron work together. Jeffrey Stackert comments on this phenomenon in the J source specifically:

> J at several points equates and even conflates Yнwн and Moses. For example, in the plague of blood, J's first plague, Moses strikes the Nile water with his staff to enact the wonder (Exod 7:17, 20b). Yet Exod 7:25 states unequivocally that it was Yнwн who struck the Nile, an assertion that emphasizes Moses' role as an intermediary that, in light of vv. 17 and 20b, introduces an equivalence between Moses and Yнwн.[126]

Similarly, when at Moses's command Aaron's striking the dust creates a plague of gnats (8:16), Pharaoh recognizes in it "the finger of God" at work (8:19, NRSV). As mediator of Israel's God, Moses's role extends beyond the effecting of God's will on the earth. It works the other way as well. Moses brings the requests of people before God and thereby affects the actions of God themselves. For example, Moses both commands Aaron so as to bring about the plague of frogs (8:5-6) and also prays on Pharaoh's behalf that Yнwн take away the frogs — a prayer Yнwн hears and responds to (8:8, 12-13). In this two-way interchange, Moses is an ideal prophet.

The synergy that develops between God and Moses continues in the crossing of the Red Sea itself. When Moses tells the people to take courage because "Yнwн will fight for you" (14:14), the divine response is to have Moses lift up his staff and divide the sea (14:16). When Moses complies, it is God who divides the sea (14:21). After the Egyptians have been eliminated, the narrative takes one final opportunity to draw our attention to the inseparability of Yнwн from Moses: "Israel saw the great work that Yнwн did against the Egyptians. So the people feared Yнwн and believed in Yнwн *and in his servant Moses*" (14:31; NRSV, alt.).[127] The story of the exodus itself identifies Moses with God in the strongest possible terms, not only assigning Moses to play the role of

126. Jeffrey Stackert, "Mosaic Prophecy and the Deuteronomistic Source of the Torah," in *Deuteronomy in the Pentateuch, Hexateuch, and the Deuteronomistic History* (ed. Konrad Schmid and Raymond F. Person Jr.; Tübingen: Mohr Siebeck, 2012), 47-63, here 51.
127. Stackert, "Mosaic Prophecy," 51, makes the same observation.

God and demonstrating how God is at work in Moses, but also making both together the object of the people's trust.

The exodus story also provides some hints that God's actions are exertions of the divine creative power. Gordon McConville draws attention to the themes of divine conquest of the forces of chaos, and as we saw above, such themes are often articulated in service of establishing a human agent on earth as the embodiment on earth of the creator God's creative power.

> But here as elsewhere the creative act is also a political-historical one. Yahweh's overcoming of Chaos now takes the form of his defeat of Pharaoh. The deliverance of Israel, with its correlative in the gift of the land of Canaan, is an assertion of his cosmic rule, and a step toward the redemption of the political sphere. The rival claims of Pharaoh and Yahweh upon the life and allegiance of Israel both are portrayed as "king." At stake then, is the true nature of ultimate royal authority and how it relates to the condition of the people.[128]

With such a cosmic-political battle under way (God executes judgment on all the gods of Egypt, 12:12), Moses's mediation of the acts of YHWH takes on the royal overtones assigned to humanity in Genesis 1. YHWH is the king of the cosmos, but Moses is the one executing that rule on the earth. (In this sense, one might say that Moses is a new Adam.) Just such an exalted interpretation of Moses is found in several early Jewish interpretations.

In light of both the depictions of Adam that we explored above and the transfiguration scene that will occupy our attention when we come to the Gospels, Moses's shining face is of some importance (34:29-35).[129] Moses's face shines when he comes down from speaking with God (v. 29), such that the radiance is understood to be the reflection of God's own glory. This radiance makes Moses the visible representation of God as Moses relays God's words to the people. Herring establishes an argument that builds on the notion that humanity as God's image takes the place of statuary embodiments of the deity in other religions. In the larger story that runs through Exodus 32–34, God rejects the calf as an image of God, only to favor Moses with the role of materially representing the divine.[130] The story begins with such hints, as Moses's

---

128. McConville, *God and Earthly Power*, 55.

129. As Herring, *Divine Substitution*, 127-64, argues, this correlation between Adam and Moses is all the more significant if we recognize that Exodus 34 belongs to the Priestly tradition of the Pentateuch.

130. Herring, *Divine Substitution*, esp. 145-57.

absence is spoken of as creating a need for a god (32:1), and continues with YHWH telling Moses to go to the people whom Moses had brought up from Egypt (32:7).[131] When Moses descends from the mountain the second time, and his face is shining, the people respond with the same fear (34:30) with which they responded to the original Sinai theophany (20:18-19).[132] Importantly, both upon his descent from the mountain and in subsequent addresses to the people, Moses does not apply the veil before he has spoken the words that he had been commanded (34:33-35). This bearing of God's likeness thus upholds Moses's position as the person who speaks God's words, demonstrating the extent to which Moses plays the role of God in his function of lawgiver. More than merely upholding a position, however, Moses through this bearing of the divine glory becomes the visible manifestation of God for Israel.[133] The fact that the word for "light," קרן, can also mean "horn," only augments this suggestion, as the notion of Moses sprouting horns would likely associate him with deity, and perhaps as a replacement to the golden calf, in particular.[134]

All told, Herring concludes that the various indications of Moses's sharing in the divine identity across the story of Exodus, together with other narrative cues as to the necessity of a physical embodiment of God's presence, demonstrate that he bears the divine image, a "divinization" that comes through playing the part of God in his service of Israel.

In addition, Moses's face shining on the people provides a twofold realization of the Aaronic benediction (Num 6:23-26). There, the blessing is for God's face to shine on the people, as God's countenance is lifted up on the people. Moses not only has received such a blessing, but also is the agent of this blessing to the people of Israel. Through him, the light of God's face shines on the congregation.

Finally, the Deuteronomic tradition creates its own line of reflection on Moses as idealized human figure. In Deuteronomy 18:15 Moses prophesies of a prophet like himself whom God will raise up from among the people. This is perhaps the most direct disclosure of the idea that Moses is an ideal figure, as he becomes a type for future leaders of the people. Within the Deuteronomistic history, this role is played first by Joshua (cf. Num 27:18-23), who is very much a second Moses figure as he, too, leads people through waters on dry ground (cf. Josh 4:14). The threat that attends not listening to the Moses-like prophet — that God will demand recompense for such heedlessness from the

---

131. Herring, *Divine Substitution*, 150.
132. Herring, *Divine Substitution*, 152.
133. Herring, *Divine Substitution*, 153.
134. Cf. Seth L. Sanders, "Old Light on Moses' Shining Face," *VT* 52 (2002): 400-406.

person who is guilty — is made good in the later history of the kings, as is the promise that any prophet whose word comes true is, in fact, an emissary of the Lord (e.g., 2 Kgs 9:7; 17:13, 23; 21:10; 24:2). Beyond this, however, the notion of a Moses-like prophet becomes one aspect of Israel's expectations for its ideal future — both the eschatological figure as we see reflected in John 1:21 and the more mundane future as in 1 Maccabees 4:46; 14:41.

b. Philo's Moses

Such lofty depictions of Moses proved rich fodder for later interpreters, especially Philo.[135] Philo's depictions of Moses are notable for their full-scale renderings of the great prophet as a king to whom God had entrusted the world in its entirety.[136] In his *Life of Moses*, we read that God gave to Moses the entirety of the riches of the world, including a share of those elements that God had allotted as God's own as to an heir (*Mos.* 1.155). In return, each of these elements obeyed Moses as master (*Mos.* 1.156). The primal vocation to rule the entirety of the world on God's behalf is being depicted as conveyed upon Moses as God's specially endowed agent who shares God's own portion of and sovereignty over the earth.

Philo's depictions of Moses are complex. It is quite possible that they extend beyond the sort of Adamic idealization we saw above into divinization. And yet, even such depictions do not entail a transformation of God by the person of Moses or signal that Moses is the incarnation of a preexistent deity. Thus, "divinization" of the sort we see in Philo itself provides an alternative paradigm to the notion that Jewish monotheism requires a reconfiguration of our understanding of the inherent identity of God once another creature has been assigned certain divine characteristics. Here, then, are some of the salient claims Philo makes concerning Moses.

A clear example of Philo's exalted depiction of Moses comes in his exposition of Exodus 4:16 and 7:1, in which God says he will make Moses God to Aaron and Pharaoh, respectively. In *Life of Moses* 1.158 he says that God not only made Moses God to Pharaoh, but to the nation of Israel as well: "He was named god and king of the whole nation" (ὀνομάσθη γὰρ ὅλου τοῦ ἔθνους

---

135. See Wayne A. Meeks, "Moses as God and King," in *Religions in Antiquity: Essays in Memory of Erwin Ramsdell Goodenough* (SHR 14; ed. Jacob Neusner; Leiden: Brill, 1968), 354-71.

136. Cf. Eric Eve, *The Jewish Context of Jesus' Miracles* (JSNTSup 231; New York: Sheffield Academic, 2002), 66-72. This idealization as king and also as lawgiver, prophet, and priest, not only includes exalted titles and descriptions, but also the ability to work miracles.

θεὸς καὶ βασιλεύς).[137] One way that Philo elaborates on human capacity for divinity is through the path of virtue. In Philo's philosophy, a person who faithfully loves God can be described as no longer human, but God, in a sense, being "a god of people" (ἀνθρώπων μέντοι θεόν, *Prob.* 43). The mark of divinity is superiority to, and apparently authority over, other humans.

Moses's proximity to God during his time on earth foretells something of a postmortem deification as well. Philo articulates this in the midst of a discussion of those who attend to good doctrine and attain to the number of "the people of God" (*Sacr.* 5). Abel's attainment of such immortality is said to make him like the angels (ἴσος ἀγγέλοις, *Sacr.* 5). This angel-likeness contains three elements: (1) they are God's army (στρατός); (2) they are bodiless (ἀσώματοι); and (3) they are blessed souls (εὐδαίμονες ψύχαι). In this sense, the future in store for those who are faithful to divine instruction might be called an angelomorphic state. A similar, though more vague assessment of Isaac's attainments says that he migrated to the immortal and perfect race (ἄφθαρτον καὶ τελεώτατον γένος). Coming to Moses, however, Philo appears to say more. He stakes his claim on God's words to Moses in Deuteronomy 5:31: "For there are some whom he has led up, preparing them to soar above every genus and species. He has established them close to himself, as he says to Moses, 'But you, stand here with me' [Deut 5:31]" (*Sacr.* 8). In common with the previous heroes Philo discussed, this example also is proof for him that "the mind is immortal" (*Sacr.* 8). Moses, however, is not added to a class of idealized beings like the others, but is instead raised up by God's own word in order that he might be seen as equal with the world itself (ἰσότομον κόσμῳ, *Sacr.* 8). Moses's translation is then depicted as a sort of divinization; however, the process was likely one that was already under way during Moses's lifetime (ἅτε κατ᾽ ἐκεῖνον τὸν χρόνον ἐπιθειάζουσαν, *Sacr.* 10).

One more possible piece of evidence is worth mentioning at this point. Erwin Goodenough has argued that at one point Philo slips into a prayer to Moses, addressing a petition to ἱεροφάντης (*Somn.* 164-65).[138] This is a title that Philo uses almost exclusively for Moses, and never for God or a divine power.[139] If the

---

137. Meeks, "Moses as God and King," compiles a number of examples of this conjunction from later rabbinic exegesis and Samaritan sources, thus demonstrating that such an exalted depiction of Moses as somehow sharing in divinity is not isolated, either temporally or geographically.

138. Erwin R. Goodenough, *By Light, Light: The Mystic Gospel of Hellenistic Judaism* (New Haven, CT: Yale University Press, 1935), 233.

139. John Lierman, *The New Testament Moses: Christian Perceptions of Moses and Israel in the Setting of Jewish Religion* (WUNT2 173; Tübingen: Mohr Siebeck, 2004), 193-94.

identification is correct, then Moses is at very least depicted as an active agent at work in those who study Torah in a manner that transcends the influence he has as the one who wrote the words of the text. Of course, Moses's playing such a role does not transform the identity of God as such. John Lierman's conclusion appears apt: "Philo is careful to avoid giving the impression that Moses was a being of the same order of God. . . . But at the same time he clearly thinks of Moses as a mortal of a different order than other mortals."[140]

From even this brief look at Philo's Moses, we see a complex picture emerging in which Moses during his time on earth, through his faithfulness to God, is empowered and transformed in ways that anticipate his final divinization. Thus, heavenly exaltation is the final installment of a life in which Moses has not only been made to play the part of God and king in a functional way, but has also been transformed from within into the divine likeness. In these ways, Philo's Moses both transcends the category of "idealized human figure" that I am developing in this chapter and blurs the exclusivity of claims to divinity that can sometimes be made on behalf of Jewish monotheism. Philo is not "radically redefining monotheism" around Moses, though he includes him in the sovereignty of God, ascribes the appellation "god" to him, and allows Moses to participate in God's very nature. Instead of Mosaic monotheism, Philo variously depicts Moses in terms of an idealized human figure, identified with God through his virtue, representing God to the world in a reappropriation of the Adamic vocation to rule, at times in his deification, and being held up as an illustration of what God's virtue looks like when embodied in a faithful human agent.[141]

c. The Exagogue of Ezekiel the Tragedian

The Exagogue of Ezekiel the Tragedian contains similar motifs and may have influenced Philo.[142] Likely written in the second or first century BC, it provides another witness of the heights to which idealized human figures might obtain in early Jewish religious texts without substantially modifying Jewish "monotheism."[143] This text includes an enthronement scene that Moses sees in a vision

140. Lierman, *New Testament Moses*, 194.

141. Cf. Meeks, "Moses as God and King," 361-65; see also Mills, *Human Agents*, 44-45.

142. See Pierluigi Lanfranchi, "Reminiscences of Ezekiel's *Exagoge* in Philo's *De vita Mosis*," in *Moses in Biblical and Extra-Biblical Traditions* (BZAW 372; ed. A. Graupner and M. Wolter; Berlin: De Gruyter, 2007), 144-50.

143. On the date of Ezekiel, see Pierluigi Lanfranchi, *L'exagoge d'Ezéchiel le Tragique* (Leiden: Brill, 2006), 10; also the introduction to Ezekiel the Tragedian in Carl R. Holladay,

(lines 70-82). In it, a nobleman summons Moses, vacates his throne in favor of Moses's own session, and hands Moses his scepter and royal crown. Once enthroned, Moses surveys all creation and a great number of stars kneel before him (line 81). Moses's father-in-law interprets the dream as indicating that Moses will establish a throne, and will himself judge and lead humanity (lines 85-86). This vision demonstrates the close correlation between a human being, whom God chooses, ruling the world on God's behalf, and God's own sovereign rule over the world. Moses's "establishing a throne" (line 85) is depicted pictorially as God giving over to Moses God's own place of rule over the cosmos.

The imagery is, as Bauckham has argued, heavenly imagery depicting Moses's earthly rule.[144] He downplays the impact that the pairing of the heavenly imagery with Moses's earthly rule has on his own thesis, as indeed he must, because he has placed a good number of eggs in the basket of God not sharing God's throne:

> The most exalted angels serve God; they do not participate in his rule. Two features, among others, make this clear. In the first place: they never sit with God on his heavenly throne, the obvious symbol which Jewish writers could have used in their depictions of the heavens, to portray a viceroy or co-ruler. On the contrary, they stand, in the posture of servants. Secondly, not only are they never worshipped, but they explicitly reject worship.[145]

In the vision, not only does Moses sit on God's throne, but he also receives the obeisance of the stars — an honor that the angelic host typically reject, but which is rightly received in this instance. In my judgment, these apparent infringements on God's unique prerogatives cannot be eliminated from consideration simply because they are part of a dream. The dream is not declared blasphemous, but is instead thought to reflect an earthly reality. It is not simply that Moses is given a throne, but that the throne he occupies is the very throne of God. This point of connection provides the dream with its signification: Moses is king because God has given Moses a share in the royal power that God himself exercises over the cosmos. And Moses receives the obeisance

---

Fragments from Hellenistic Jewish Authors, vol. 2, *Poets* (SBLTT 30; Atlanta: Scholars, 1989), 301-37.

144. Richard Bauckham, "The Throne of God and the Worship of Jesus," in *The Jewish Roots of Christological Monotheism* (JSJSup 63; ed. Carey C. Newman et al.; Leiden: Brill, 1999), 42-69.

145. Bauckham, *Jesus and the God of Israel*, 15.

of the stars because God himself is due the worship of the nations. As in the creation myths we surveyed above, the human ruler on earth becomes a sort of theophany of the God whose power he represents.[146] Ezekiel the Tragedian's Moses fits the category of idealized human figure perfectly: here is a human of an idealized past being described in such a way that ascriptions, actions, and attributes typically reserved for God are shared with him.

d. Moses at Qumran

Both Philo and Ezekiel the Tragedian have possible ties to Alexandria. But exaltation of Moses is not limited to this region, as the Qumran scrolls also attest. The hands behind the Qumran scrolls did not hesitate to embrace the striking language of Exodus to the effect that Moses stands before Pharaoh as God (Exod 7:1; cited in 4Q374 2 II, 6).[147] Crispin Fletcher-Louis has argued that this passage places Moses in the role of God, not only by recalling that God made Moses's face to shine before the Israelites (line 8) but also then by applying divine warrior language to Moses as well (lines 9-10).[148] If Fletcher-Louis is correct, then we have yet another instance of God's power as heavenly conqueror being embodied in a human representative. He also interprets this instance of Moses's shining face in the same way that I developed it above: "there is perhaps a deliberate allusion to the Aaronic blessing. . . . This would mean that in this text Moses' shining face is an embodiment of God's own shining face for the blessing of Israel: God's face is now mirrored in Moses' face."[149]

---

146. Such biblical precedent makes unnecessary the thesis at the other extreme, namely, that the vision represents Moses's deification (unless that deification is taken to be one of function rather than substance); thus Pieter W. van der Horst, "Moses' Throne Vision in Ezekiel the Dramatist," *JJS* 34 (1983): 21-29. But, if deification is in fact in view, then the implications are that an idealized human figure has become divine in some sense without God's own identity being transformed in the process.

147. Martínez and Tigchelaar, *DSSSE*, 1:741, altered.

148. Crispin Fletcher-Louis, "4Q374: A Discourse on the Sinai Tradition: The Deification of Moses and Early Christology," *DSD* 3 (1996): 236-52. His claims are contested by Phoebe Makiello, "Was Moses Considered to Be an Angel by Those at Qumran?" in *Moses in Biblical and Extra-Biblical Traditions* (BZAW 372; ed. A. Graupner and M. Wolter; New York: De Gruyter, 2007), 115-27. Many of Makiello's objections amount to claiming that elsewhere God is the subject of such verbs and descriptions as those Fletcher-Louis wants to ascribe to Moses; however, such arguments are question-begging when the point at issue is whether Moses is being depicted in divine terms. My idealized human category allows for such ascriptions without demanding either a literal deification or angelomorphosis for the human character involved.

149. Fletcher-Louis, *All the Glory of Adam*, 140.

e. Conclusions: Moses as Idealized Human Figure

Exodus depicts Moses as playing the role of God in two particular relationships: those with Aaron and Pharaoh. Moreover, the story joins the actions of God and the actions of Moses so that it becomes clear that God is made known and is at work through the activities of Moses. The same actions are ascribed to each, underscoring the inseparability of the two distinct characters in the story. Later, Moses even bears the divine likeness in the radiance of his face. These hints about Moses's peculiar relationship with God are worked out in Philo and the Exagogue of Ezekiel, and might also be hinted at in Qumran. Moses is an idealized human figure, one who stands in for God at a crucial juncture in Israel's story and in this role is depicted as more than a "mere" human. The ascription of the title God, the actions of conquering hostile, even cosmic powers, sitting on God's throne, and receiving celestial adoration — all of these place Moses in a unique standing vis-à-vis God, yet without transforming the identity of God in any other way than binding God's identity to the identity of this human agent through whom God has chosen to act.

2. PROPHETS PAST AND FUTURE

a. Elijah in the Jewish Scriptures

Elijah the Tishbite looms large as an idealized prophetic figure in the biblical and post-biblical tradition. His importance stems from the presentation of him in the historical narratives, his assumption into heaven, the expectations of his return, and, for my purposes, his mentions and literal appearance in the Gospel narratives.

The first appearance of Elijah in scripture has him confronting King Ahab with the claim that he can control dewfall and rainfall by his own word (1 Kgs 17:1). As the narrator tells the reader in the immediately subsequent verse that the word of YHWH came to Elijah, telling him where to find water, and promising that ravens would provide food, it is clear that Elijah's power to execute his nature miracle is a mediated authority, coming from God. After assuring a widow of a miraculous provision of grain and oil, Elijah mediates a resuscitation of her dead son. The story highlights how this action demonstrates Elijah's role as one who mediates God's presence in the world: "Now I know that you are a man of God and that the word of YHWH in your mouth is truth" (1 Kgs 17:24, NRSV, alt.). Throughout the story, the role of Elijah as he performs various miracles is to attest to the fact that the God whom he serves is the true God. Or, perhaps, we might invert this way of putting it and say that Elijah was a man attested by God, as the actions performed at his hands, or through his command, demonstrated that his call of the people to return to the worship of Yhwh was a call issued by none other than the one true God. In addition to the widow's confession, so too the episode with the prophets of Baal on Mount Carmel has as its conclusion that Elijah's is the true God (1 Kgs 18:24). The mutually proving nature of the exercise is underscored in Elijah's prayer on Mount Carmel, as he entreats a divine response so that the people will know both that Yhwh is God and that Elijah is his servant (1 Kgs 18:36). Similar validation is entailed, later, when Elijah asks for fire from heaven to confirm that he is a man of God (2 Kgs 1:10, 12). In all this, Elijah is an idealized human figure. When he acts in his capacity as prophet, his words and actions are the words and actions of God on the earth.

Importantly, the conjunction between Elijah and God is in the arena of what we might call nature miracles, evincing control over elements that are typically the unique purview of God. In her seminal study of Elijah, Brenda Shaver summarizes the situation thus:

> There are few human beings in the biblical texts besides Elijah who are said to be capable of sending and withholding rain, or bringing down fire from heaven and raising the dead to life. Throughout the ancient Near East, these powers were typically associated with figures of the heavenly and not the earthly realm. Although Elijah is sometimes called a "man of God" (איש אלהים) or "the servant of YHWH" (עבד יהוה) in these miracle stories, he is still a human being. The reader is well aware that the prophet acts as the deity's messenger and that YHWH is the ultimate source of the prophet's special powers. Yet the miracles associated with Elijah (and his successor Elisha) are unique because they are performed through the words and actions of an entirely human character, who, nevertheless, seems to possess divine capabilities.[150]

This is a perfect representation of an idealized human figure. Not only is Elijah elevated as a quintessentially faithful follower and prophet of Yhwh; he is also empowered to control aspects of the world that are typically the purview of God alone. Elijah's control over the storms and the attendant fertility of the

150. Brenda J. Shaver, "The Prophet Elijah in the Literature of the Second Temple Period: The Growth of a Tradition" (PhD diss., University of Chicago, 2001), 41.

earth serves well the polemic of the tale: "By taking this awesome and miraculous power out of the hands of the god [Baal] and placing it in the hands of Elijah, the biblical writer has created a rather forceful and scathing criticism of Baal worship."[151] The demonstration that Elijah, rather than Baal, has authority over the storms is not in the end an indication that Elijah is divine, but a way of demonstrating that the God who empowers Elijah is the true Divinity. Elijah's power over nature (repeated to a great degree in the Elisha cycle) is a potent reminder of the capacity of a human being in Israel's biblical tradition to play various roles typically reserved for God alone when God chooses to distribute those parts.[152]

Elijah's position as idealized prophetic figure is augmented by two ways in which his story echoes the story of Moses.[153] A cluster of similar themes runs through the stories of the two prophets, including flight from a king, lodging with foreigners, confronting the king of the home country, a Horeb theophany, and setting up twelve stones as a sign of God's commitment to Israel.[154] Two aspects are worth exploring in more detail.[155] First, Elijah has an experience on Mount Horeb that echoes the experience of Moses (whose encounters with God were on Mount Horeb in the Deuteronomic tradition). Elijah's arrival at the mountain is preceded by forty days of fasting (1 Kgs 19:8), while Moses's experience on the mountain itself entailed a forty-day fast (Deut 9:9). Significantly, God reveals Godself, perhaps in surprising ways, to each prophet in this locale. God appears to Moses while Moses is stationed in a cleft of the rock (Exod 33:22), while Elijah receives his divine visitation outside a cave (1 Kgs 19:9, 11, 13). Each responds with an act of humble obeisance, Moses with bowed head and worship (Exod 34:8-9), Elijah with a covered face (1 Kgs 19:13). The parallels between the passages are not so strong as to say that the Elijah story is simply a rewriting of the Moses story; however, there are sufficient points of narrative contact to suggest that Elijah is, in his own story, reliving the experiences of Moses, and that each is wrestling with God in the face of Israel's faithlessness.

A second way in which Elijah's story echoes the Moses story is in his di-

---

151. Shaver, "Prophet Elijah," 44.

152. Shaver goes on to demonstrate how Elijah's ability to call down fire from heaven is a continuation in the same vein, in which Elijah's work demonstrates that Yhwh truly has dominion over those areas that Baal would claim for himself ("Prophet Elijah," 45-47).

153. The connections with Moses have been noted at least since the work of Hermann Gunkel, *Elijas, Jahve und Baal* (Tübingen: Mohr, 1906); cf. Shaver, "Prophet Elijah," 58-62.

154. J. T. Walsh, "Elijah," *ABD* 2:464; Shaver, "Prophet Elijah," 58.

155. Cf. Shaver, "Prophet Elijah," 59-60.

viding the waters of the Jordan en route to his heavenward chariot. Like his Mosaic predecessor, Elijah splits waters in two in order to have dry passage, in this case, across the Jordan (2 Kgs 2:8).[156] Authority over waters is a sign par excellence of divine, cosmic power at work. And the water-crossing traditions indicate that such power over creation is held, at times, by prophetic figures. The analogue to Jesus's authority over chaotic waters should not be missed. The Elijah story may also depict the prophet in Mosaic hues by having him be removed from the earth on the far side of the Jordan River. Crossing to the eastern shore, Elijah comes to the side of the Jordan where Moses died and was buried, not being allowed to cross the Jordan into the Promised Land (Deuteronomy 34). That Elijah is a "prophet like Moses" is another way in which the narrative signals that he is an idealized, exemplary figure.[157]

Elijah's miraculous removal from the earth is another peculiar experience afforded him as an idealized human figure. Like the mysterious disappearance of Enoch, it appears to be the reward for a faithful person, in this case a prophet, living a righteous life. Moreover, there is some possibility of an echo of a Moses tradition, as Moses's burial by God's hand raised the possibility to some interpreters that he had been taken to heaven (cf. Josephus, *Ant.* 4.326 — the protest would seem to indicate someone holding the view; also Philo, *Sacr.* 10).[158] Although the development of resurrection expectations during the Second Temple period provides the most important line of development for understanding claims associated with Jesus's resurrection, such biblical precedents (and/or their interpretive traditions) attest to the possibility of human figures being taken to heaven as the conclusion of a faithful life well lived on the earth.[159]

Finally, the idea that Elijah ascended into heaven without dying left open the possibility that he might return in a similar fashion. Such a possibility is realized in what we might call the eschatological expectations of the book of Malachi: "Lo, I will send you the prophet Elijah before the great and terrible

156. Joshua's execution of the same feat with this same body of water was itself a recapitulation of Moses's action intended to demonstrate God's presence with Joshua in the same way that God was present with Moses (Josh 3:7-17; 4:14).

157. Shaver, "Prophet Elijah," 61-62. This is so even if the traditions of Elijah predate Deuteronomy 18:15.

158. James L. Kugel, *Traditions of the Bible: A Guide to the Bible as It Was at the Start of the Common Era* (Cambridge, MA: Harvard University Press, 1998), 861-63.

159. Shaver, "Prophet Elijah," 52-54, also explores the possibility that Elijah joins God's heavenly, angelic forces after his assumption, perhaps laying out another possible parallel for the Gospels' depictions of the exalted Jesus.

day of the LORD comes. He will turn the hearts of parents to their children and the hearts of children to their parents, so that I will not come and strike the land with a curse" (4:5-6, NRSV). Elijah plays a restorative role, one at which he was not entirely successful during his first life on earth. At least some of the people will, at his future appearing, heed his warnings and stave off another disaster for the land of Israel (cf. 3:1).[160] Looking back further into Israel's story, Malachi associates the prophet Elijah with the prophet Moses by suggesting that the teaching Moses gave Israel on Horeb (4:4) is the content of Elijah's future instruction.[161] Malachi's depiction of Elijah sets up an important marker in the history of Israel's interpretive tradition as that tradition touches on idealized human figures. Here we see the viability of the notion that a human who had lived on earth might not only be taken up into the heavenly realm, but also be sent back down as a participant in eschatological deliverance. Shaver has demonstrated that the viability of such a claim comes from the coupling of the notion that as one who ascended, Elijah was part of God's heavenly retinue, and the expectation that a revival of prophecy would accompany the eschatological restoration of God's people (an application to the prophet of Exod 23:20 as well as, e.g., Deut 18:18 and Joel 3:1-2).[162] Such a pattern will recur, as I argue below, in *1 Enoch,* as well as in the expectations of the Gospels, especially as they center on the eschatological son of man.

b. Elisha: Elijah's Great Successor

We return to Elijah below, and explore the reception of his legend in Judaism of the Second Temple period. Before leaving the biblical text, however, it is worth looking at the depiction of Elisha. Elisha is introduced in 1 Kings 19:15-21 as Elijah's successor, and his story begins in earnest with the transporting of Elijah in 2 Kings 2. The story is at pains to point out that Elisha is not only Elijah's successor (1 Kgs 19:16), but that he is also the continuing earthly embodiment of the same spirit of power that invested his predecessor. Elisha requests that when Elijah is gone he might have a double portion of Elijah's spirit (ברוחך, 2 Kgs 2:9) — a request whose condition ("if you see me," v. 10) is met ("And Elisha saw," v. 12). Elisha then employs Elijah's mantle to enact the dividing of the Jordan River, after which a group of prophets proclaims that Elijah's spirit

160. The messenger in Malachi 3:1 is anonymous. It is widely held that the prophecy about Elijah specifically was added later, and perhaps serves to specify the identity of that messenger.

161. On the conjunction between Moses and Elijah here, and the possibility that the latter legitimates the former, see Shaver, "Prophet Elijah," 106-7.

162. Shaver, "Prophet Elijah," 108-9.

rests upon him (2 Kgs 2:14-15). Thus the Elisha cycle begins both with an ideal-izing of Elijah such that his spirit and power are enabled to pass on to another, and with an idealization of Elisha as the one who possesses his great master's power. This passing of the spirit from a prophetic hero to his successor finds precedent in the Moses stories (Num 11:16-29; 27:18-23), and will recur in the Jesus narratives (perhaps between John and Jesus in Luke's telling; cf. Luke 1:15; 3:22; between Jesus and the disciples, John 20:22) and in Acts (2:1-39). Sharing in the spirit, power, and ministry of an idealized prophet is exceptional within the biblical traditions of early Judaism, but it occurs in the succession of the very two prophets with whom Jesus is most directly associated in the Synoptic Tradition: Moses and Elijah (Mark 9:2-8 and pars.).

Elisha's own acts of power cover a similarly broad swath as those executed by Elijah. The later prophet purifies a well, exercising power over the quality of the water under the earth (2 Kgs 2:19-22); destroys those who mock his prophetic connection with his master (2 Kgs 2:23-25); mediates the filling of a wadi with water (2 Kgs 3:11-20); enables a self-filling jar of oil (2 Kgs 4:1-7); raises the dead son of a Shunammite woman (2 Kgs 4:8-37); unpoisons a pot of stew (2 Kgs 4:38-41); and feeds one hundred people on twenty barley loaves and some ears of grain (2 Kgs 4:42-44). This is a wide-ranging array of what might be called nature miracles, several of which find some measure of reiter-ation in the ministry of Jesus. The purification of the well and the appearance of water in the wadis together with the dividing of the Jordan River are of particular significance for their demonstration of the prophet's participation in God's rule over the waters, which is a sign of God's unique authority. The miraculous provision of oil and raising of a dead son both look back to Elijah's care for the widow of Zarephath (1 Kgs 17:9-24), indications that Elijah was a man of God in whose mouth was YHWH's word (1 Kgs 17:24). The raising of the only son of a widow also echoes in Jesus's ministry in Luke 7:12-16, a story that ends with the proclamation that "a great prophet has risen among us" and "God has visited his people." The Elisha cycle underscores the massive breadth of possibilities open to human agents empowered as prophets in the Jewish tradition, and the particular connections with the Jesus stories signal that "great prophet" is a primary category for interpreting the work of Jesus we see in the Synoptic Gospels.

The story of Elisha's healing of Naaman the Syrian's leprosy provides a further pair of surprising actions available to him as an idealized prophet. First is the healing itself: he mediates the erasure of Naaman's skin disease. The conjunction between Elisha and God is established as the narrator says that Naaman washes "according to the word of the man of God" (2 Kgs 5:14,

NRSV), followed immediately by Naaman confessing, "There is no God in all the earth except in Israel" (2 Kgs 5:15, NRSV). Elisha's word is heeded, but his word is inseparable from the God he serves. Second, when Elisha's servant Gehazi goes after Naaman in hopes of securing for himself the gift that Elisha had refused, Elisha confronts him by saying, "Did my heart not go [with you] when the man turned from his chariot to greet you?" (2 Kgs 5:26). Elisha has the capability of some sort of personal presence with his servant when his servant is at some physical remove from himself — something the apostle Paul, as well, will later claim (1 Cor 5:3-4; cf. Col 2:5). Supernatural perception, and even something that can be called presence with distant friends or followers (e.g., Matt 28:20), need not be a signal of divinity in early Jewish literature.

Elisha's supernatural powers are again exerted to overcome what we might call "laws of nature" when he causes an ax-head to float (2 Kgs 6:1-7). He is accompanied by a legion of heavenly forces to protect him in a scene that depicts him having God's ear for the power of giving and taking away both natural and supernatural sight (2 Kgs 6:14-23). So great is his power that a dead man coming in contact with Elisha's bones is restored to life (2 Kgs 13:21). Thus the richly developed tale of Elisha provides a thick depiction of an idealized prophet. He possesses a wide-ranging authority to control the world in the name and power of God. Not only does he speak for God in matters pertaining to their standing before God and geopolitical events, but he also exercises authority over food and drink, over flowing waters and wells, over sight literal and spiritual. He can be present "in heart" with a somewhat distant companion. He is also an agent and messenger of divine judgment. Although Elisha will not loom as large as Elijah in the history of interpretation, due especially to the latter's prophesied return in Malachi, he augments substantially the picture of what might be fit into the prophetic mold in the biblical Jewish tradition. Such a mold goes a long way toward explaining the cast of Jesus in the Synoptic Gospels, as we will see especially in chapter 5 below, "Lord of All Creation."

c. Elijah in Sirach

We return now to Elijah. The tantalizing conclusion to his life created a world of possibilities for his future that was not typically open to a people who had not yet fully developed a notion of life after death in general or resurrection in particular. Like Enoch, the idea that Elijah might still be alive in a heavenly realm not only stood as a signal of his extraordinary piety, but also opened up possibilities for a return to earth. The latter possibility is first articulated in Malachi 4:5 (Eng.; 3:23, MT). Both facets are fodder for later reflection on the prophet.

Sirach 48 celebrates Elijah's power, his piety, and his coming future.[163] It credits Elijah with bringing famine on the people (v. 2) and with employing the word of the Lord to withhold rain (v. 3). In this, Sirach reflects the biblical source material, assigning to Elijah agency in the control over the natural world while also indicating that it is the Lord's word that works as Elijah's instrument. A similar conjunction of God's word and Elijah's deed comes in Sirach's celebration of Elijah raising the dead: "You raised a corpse from death and from Hades, by the word of the Most High" (v. 5, NRSV).[164] This sharing of the divine prerogative of authoritative speech might help explain the interjection of praise that comes between the two assertions: "How glorious you were, Elijah, in your wondrous deeds! Whose glory is equal to yours?" (v. 4, NRSV). In these verses we see that the role of the prophet Elijah included an agency through which Elijah's works are identified with the simultaneous role being played by God, and that the upshot is possession of incomparable glory. Later, the Gospels will reflect such idealization of prophetic characters through their depiction of Jesus's authoritative speech (e.g., Mark 1:21-27; Matt 7:28-29) and incomparable glory (Mark 9:2-7; Matt 19:28; 24:30). Sirach also anticipates that Elijah will return to restore Israel so that God's wrath does not break out unchecked on the people (48:10). The language of Sirach 48:10 echoes not only Malachi's Elijah but also the servant of Isaiah 49:6. Sirach anticipates that Elijah will restore the "tribes of Jacob," a description of Israel that occurs elsewhere in the Hebrew Bible only in Isaiah 49:6.[165] There is here a possible identification of the work of the future, eschatological Elijah with the servant, another idealized, if fraught, character in the biblical tradition. Sirach is a book that otherwise has little concern for eschatological matters, so that the expectation of an eschatological appearance for Elijah is all the more striking as a testimony to the breadth and acceptance of possibilities open to idealized human figures in early Judaism.

d. The Prophet (Elijah) at Qumran

The traditions surrounding Elijah have left their mark on the Dead Sea Scrolls. Not only is Elijah mentioned by name, but the roles he plays on earth also appear to have influenced the expectations of how future eschatological figures might act.

163. In both 1 Maccabees 2:58 and Sirach 48:2 Elijah is described as one having "zeal" (ζῆλος). The further mentioning of Elijah in a list of heroes from Israel's past is worth mentioning, but will not be pursued further here.
164. Cf. Shaver, "Prophet Elijah," 139-40.
165. Shaver, "Prophet Elijah," 145-47.

i. Aramaic Vision (4Q558)

The Aramaic Vision papyrus (4Q558) mentions Elijah, but in a scroll so fragmentary it is difficult to know much of the context in which he appears. After Elijah is named (line 4) there appears to be a reference to cosmic portents of judgment (line 5).[166] The scroll provides important evidence that Malachi's expectation of a return of Elijah became part of the eschatological expectations of at least one other early Jewish community besides the early Christians. It appears to uphold the expectation that the idealized human prophet will play a role as forerunner in a coming visitation from God.

ii. Messianic Apocalypse (4Q521)

I deal with the so-called Messianic Apocalypse in greater detail below, in my discussion of royal messianic figures at Qumran. It is not my intention to argue for either the prophetic or the royal interpretation of the scroll per se. Here, then, I note some of the facets of the anointed figure in 4Q521 that suggest its depiction has been shaped by Elijah. John Collins offers two arguments in favor of such an identification. First, the scroll indicates that either God or God's agent will heal, raise the dead, and proclaim the good news to the poor (4Q521 2 II 11-12). While "raising the dead" in eschatological scenarios is typically a task reserved for God, it is peculiar to say that God is the one who preaches good news.[167] Inasmuch as the scroll echoes Isaiah 61 at this point, the notion of an anointed prophet as the agent of such proclamation and healing is not far from the surface.[168] The anticipated anointed one, then, may be a prophetic figure who, like Elijah and Elisha, raises the dead.[169] A second significant argument in favor of this hypothesis is that fragment 2 III states, "the fathers will return to the sons," a citation of Malachi 4:6 (3:24, MT) that articulates such a turn as the purpose of Elijah's coming before the day of the Lord.[170] However we choose to classify this figure (prophet, priest, or king), he stands as a significant piece of evidence for the expectation that a yet-to-come

---

166. John J. Collins, *The Scepter and the Star: Messianism in Light of the Dead Sea Scrolls* (2nd ed.; Grand Rapids, MI: Eerdmans, 2010), 128-30. A review of the scholarly arguments about the possible interpretations and significance of the fragment can be found in Shaver, "Prophet Elijah," 164-68.

167. Collins, *Scepter and the Star,* 132.

168. Collins, *Scepter and the Star,* 132-33; cf. Shaver, "Prophet Elijah," 174.

169. Collins, *Scepter and the Star,* 134-35.

170. Collins, *Scepter and the Star,* 136; Shaver, "Prophet Elijah," 179-80.

idealized human figure will share in the divine prerogatives of sovereignty over heaven and earth, perhaps to the extent of even being God's agent in the final resurrection of the dead.

3. CONCLUSIONS: PROPHETS AND THE PRESENCE OF GOD

Moses, Elijah, and Elisha stand out as prophets whose characters are developed across some breadth of biblical and extra-biblical literature. Together, the depictions allow us to accumulate a striking reservoir of affiliations between God and human agents tasked to play the role of God on earth. Prophets can play God's part by giving words to another speaker. They can be the embodiment of God's powerful presence on the earth, standing for God especially in conflict with the enemies of God and/or God's people. This connection between the prophet and the divinity can be depicted as a human exercising God's own power over the destructive forces of chaos, which is itself a sharing in God's creation power. Moses may well play the part of divine warrior himself. Such allotment of the divine power bleeds into the realm of nature miracles, where prophets control the waters, exercise power over life and death, and mediate miraculous provisions of food. As God's intimates, they can bear the physical likeness of God through radiated glory. And idealizations of the prophets can include enthronement on God's own throne and receipt of the obeisance of the nations. A faithful prophet might be assumed into heaven, from which preexistent state he might be expected to return in tandem with an eschatological deliverance and/or judgment from God. A prophet might be able to be personally present with someone who is physically distant, and may also have his own empowering spirit bestowed upon a successor. Indeed, the idealization of these prophets attains to such exalted heights that one would be hard pressed to generate a list of any length of stories in the Synoptic Gospels that could not be explained as casting Jesus in such a mold.

C. KINGS IN WORSHIP AND RULE

1. DAVID AND SOLOMON IN BIBLICAL TEXTS

David and Solomon each occupy places of idealized human figures in different strands of Israel's tradition. As I showed above, the Priestly history echoes creation in the covenant promise to Abraham that kings will come from him (Gen

1:26-28; 17:6, 16). This ex post facto anticipation of Israel's royal narrative indicates that at least some early Jews were reading Israel's later history, and time of monarchy in particular, as a fulfillment of sorts of the creation narrative.[171]

a. David in Historical Texts

Israel's historical narratives hint at the idealization of David as a type for future kings. His connection with God is established not only by God's choice of him, but also by the indications that David is a man after God's own heart (1 Sam 13:14) and by his reception of God's spirit (1 Sam 16:13). Moreover, David's endowment with God's spirit is immediately coupled with stories of his power to exorcise an evil spirit that takes hold of Saul (1 Sam 16:14-23). This precedent of a king who becomes capable of exorcism after receiving God's spirit in his anointing to the kingship forms a key biblical intertext for interpreting the deeds of power in which we find Jesus engaged in the Synoptic Gospels.

Despite subsequent missteps that mar the kingship of David in 2 Samuel, he is still the standard by which subsequent kings in his line are measured (1 Kgs 3:14; 11:6; 15:11; 2 Kgs 14:3; 16:2; 18:3).[172] Perhaps the most important moment for developing Davidic kingship as an idealized human category, however, comes from God promising David an unbroken line of descendants to sit on the throne (2 Samuel 7, esp. vv. 11-16).[173] That passage not only promises a kingship that lasts forever; it also reflects the royal theology in which the Davidic king is the son of God on earth (v. 14).

The son of God theology behind Israelite kingship is reflected in other places as well (esp. Pss 2, 45, 89; Isa 9:6-7). However, as John Collins notes, the notion of "begetting" is absent from this particular passage, and the liability

171. Other indications of this, from a different strain of biblical tradition, can be found in 2 Samuel and 1 Kings. In the former, a woman describes David being like an angel of God, knowing good and evil (2 Sam 14:17), which strongly echoes Genesis 3:22. Such discernment between good and evil is the content of Solomon's prayer for wisdom (1 Kgs 3:9). Moreover, the J/E covenant promise of being as numerous as the sand of the sea (כחול אשר על־שפת הים, Gen 22:17; 32:12) echoes in the statement of 1 Kings 4:20 that Israel and Judah were as numerous as the sand by the sea. Cf. Peter Leithart, *1 & 2 Kings* (Brazos Theological Commentary on Scripture; Grand Rapids, MI: Brazos, 2006), 44, 46.

172. Indeed, David's rise to power itself is marked with ambiguity, as is kingship more generally, throughout the narrative of 1–2 Samuel. Recognition of ways that the text idealizes him, and/or provides fodder for later idealizations, is not a claim for David being a thoroughgoing idealized figure throughout the stories of his life in Samuel or Chronicles.

173. Even this, however, is tinged with a note of disapproval, as David himself is not allowed to build Yhwh a house. Cf. McConville, *God and Earthly Power*, 142-43.

of David's seed to corrective blows shows that the kings are not considered perfect (2 Sam 7:14).[174] He sees this as possibly a "demythologization, or accentuation of the human element," entailed in the king's divine sonship.[175] The theology of Davidic kingship is thus a microcosm of the spectrum of possibilities available in the idealizing of human figures in Israelite traditions, and those attendant to the son of God tradition in particular.

One more piece of evidence sheds light on the notions available for Israelites reflecting on the connection between God and Davidic kingship. The final word of Nathan to David in 2 Samuel 7 includes the promise, "Your house and your kingship will be confirmed forever" (v. 16). The Chronicler, however, changes this so that the house and the kingship are not David's but YHWH's: "I will set him in my house and my kingdom forever" (1 Chr 17:14). The language of Chronicles elevates the identity of the kingdom of Israel, such that it is identified as the kingdom of God. However, the king of this kingdom is not therefore God and God alone, but the human agent whom God has promised to establish over it.

b. Psalm 2

The divine sonship of the Davidic kings provides an entry point into the Psalter's enshrining of royal theology within the worship of Israel.[176] Psalm 2 reflects a royal theology in which the king is "begotten" at his enthronement (v. 7; cf. 2 Sam 7:14 as well as the discussion of Gen 1:26-28 above).[177] This familial union creates an identification between God and the king such that how the nations respond to the king on earth is how they are responding to

174. Adela Yarbro Collins and John J. Collins, *King and Messiah as Son of God: Divine, Human, and Angelic Messianic Figures in Biblical and Related Literature* (Grand Rapids, MI: Eerdmans, 2008), 27-28.

175. Collins and Collins, *King and Messiah*, 28.

176. On the conjunction between the Davidic king and YHWH in biblical texts, and the Psalms in particular, see Antti Laato, *A Star Is Rising: The Historical Developments of the Old Testament Royal Ideology and the Rise of the Jewish Messianic Expectations* (ISFCJ 5; Atlanta: Scholars, 1997), esp. 81-95.

177. Collins and Collins, *King and Messiah*, 10-15, argue that the Judahite understanding of kingship has been influenced by the Egyptian model such that the enthronement ceremony is one of divine begetting and the king is addressed as "my son" by the deity. See also the seminal article by Gerhard Von Rad, "Das judäische Königsritual," *TLZ* 73 (1947): 211-16. J. J. M. Roberts, "Whose Child Is This? Reflections on the Speaking Voice in Isaiah 9:5," *HTR* 90 (1997): 115-29, cautions against using the language of "adoption," arguing instead that God's "begetting" the king better coheres with Psalm 2, the ancient Near Eastern parallels, and other biblical expressions of divine fatherhood (e.g., Deut 32:18).

God himself: standing against God and God's anointed are one and the same (v. 2); God enthrones (vv. 5-6) while the king is enthroned and given a promise by God that the nations are his possession (vv. 7-9); and in the end, fear of the Lord is expressed in reverence toward the son (vv. 10-12).[178] Such a tight connection between the king and Israel's God might be called a kingship of divine identity, where for all intents and purposes the idealized royal figure represents God to the nations and represents those nations before God and where none of this indicates that Israel had to rethink the inherent identity of God or ascribe ontological divinity to the king. It seems, rather, to be a refocusing of the Adamic identity from Genesis 1:26-28 on Israel's king: a son of God who rules the world on God's behalf.[179]

c. Psalm 45

Psalm 45 opens up further avenues for understanding the roles that the king, as an idealized human figure, might play in Israel's theology and worship. This song stands as counter-testimony to the theological ideal on which Hurtado's project depends. For Hurtado, Israel's "monotheism" plays itself out in the specific activity of worship, such that inclusion of any other in Israel's worship is tantamount to equating that other with God.[180] Psalm 45 stands as evidence that the idealized human figure that was Israel's (or Judah's) king might well be included in Israel's worship, were such a figure believed to have appeared. Unlike some other royal psalms whose subject is kingship, in this psalm the king himself is the object of praise. Presumably, this means that it was at some point sung as part of the worship of Israel even if the particular setting was, like enthronement songs, the royal court.

The king is celebrated as the embodiment of virtues that would identify him with Israel's God (truth, humility, righteousness, v. 4, CEB) and is commended to victory over his enemies (vv. 4, 5). Most significantly, the writer addresses the king as "God" in verse 6: "Your throne, O God, endures forever and ever" (NRSV); however, this direct identification did not lead to a wholesale reimagination of monotheism. In the words of John Collins, "The king is still subject to the Most High, but he is an *elohim,* not just a man."[181] Such daring naming of the king occurs one other time in the Hebrew Bible, in Isaiah 9:6, which I

---

178. Cf. Peter C. Craigie, *Psalms 1-50* (WBC 19; Waco, TX: Word, 1983), 64.
179. See above on the connotations of sonship in Genesis 1:26-28.
180. Hurtado, *Lord Jesus Christ,* e.g., 31.
181. Collins and Collins, *King and Messiah,* 15.

discuss below. The king is not only the representative, but also the very embodiment of God on earth, and that relationship to God is tied to the office rather than the ontological status of the king himself. The relationship accounts for the exaltation of the king: "In the royal worldview, the king could be exalted as a minor divinity (*'elohim*) because of his relationship to God."[182] The God-making of Moses, discussed above, is somewhat analogous. The king's close identification with God as God's agent on the earth thus enables the psalmist to write a hymn of praise in which the king is praised in worship for the ways in which he and his reign are upheld by and reflect Israel's God.

d. Psalm 72

Most royal psalms are subtler in their identification of the king with God, and yet the idealization of the king is no less present for this subtlety. Psalm 72 is another instance of God's rule over creation being manifest through the reign of the king. It may also be, like Psalm 2, a coronation psalm.[183] Gordon McConville summarizes the significance thus: "Kingship guarantees this cosmic order (as in Ps 72), and prophets proclaim it. Creation is not in one category while history, politics and salvation are in another. Rather, salvation is restoration of how things ought to be."[184]

The psalm begins with a request for God to give the king God's own justice and righteousness: the king is to be the embodiment of God's just rule on the earth (vv. 1-2).[185] Such petitions are mingled with prayers for the mountains and hills to bring such attributes to bear, and for the king to play the role of rain showers that water the earth (vv. 6-7). Such metaphors are not as directly indicative of the king having personal authority over the created order as we find in Psalm 89, and yet they demonstrate, as McConville states above, that God's sovereignty over the earth and the king's sovereignty over the earth are woven together, shared expressions of the same reality.

In subsequent verses, the psalm depicts the adequate human response to the king's sovereignty. Both the "desert dwellers" (v. 9, CEB) and the kings are to do obeisance before him (vv. 9, 11). The word "desert dwellers" (צִיִּים) typically means wild or desert creatures (cf. Isa 13:21; Jer 50:39). This suggests that the NRSV's "foes" and the NASB's "nomads" or NIV's "desert tribes" are

---

182. Smith, *Priestly Vision*, 31.
183. Marvin E. Tate, *Psalms 51–100* (WBC 20; Waco, TX: Word, 1990), 222.
184. McConville, *God and Earthly Power*, 32.
185. Tate, *Psalms 51–100*, 223.

an unnecessary anthropomorphizing of the extent of the king's rule. The clause that contains this word is set in parallel with one that speaks of the king's "enemies" (אֹיְבָיו); however, the parallel construction need not indicate numerical identity between the first opponent and the second. Throughout the psalm, the parallelism employed has consistently been progressive, such that the second line adds to the thought of the first. And so the psalm that has depicted the king's rule in terms of the interdependence of the king and the created order is making a direct statement, now, about the king's reign extending to the wild creatures. Rule over the wild beasts has obvious resonance with the creation of humanity to rule over the beasts (Gen 1:26-28), and may also find a point of contact with Mark's laconic statement that Jesus was with the beasts during his wilderness temptation (1:13; cf. Isaiah 11).

In Psalm 72 wild creatures and enemies, kings and nations, all bow down and serve the king (vv. 9-11). The pairing of the roots חוה and עבד in verse 11 is precisely the pairing of words that one finds in the commandment forbidding the adoration of idols (Exod 20:5; Deut 5:9). Thus, while it is possible to separate cultic worship from courtly obeisance, we have begun to seen enough of the confluence of idealized human figures and actions and ascriptions typically reserved for God to keep us from being able to rule out "worship and service" of the king as a rite appropriate even for Israel's monolatrous belief and practice. The Priestly creation story has already opened up the possibility that idealized, original humanity stands as the image of God that grounds the prohibition of images made by human hands. It is no great leap from such a creational theology of idealized human figures to such a figure playing precisely the role of God's proxy in worship and service, such that what is forbidden to images made by human hands is allowed to the image formed by God. The idea would be that God is worshiped through this service because God stands behind this king.[186]

In the succeeding verses, the king is deemed worthy of such adoration because he is deliverer (v. 12), savior (v. 13), and redeemer (v. 14). And so the king's name, like God's own glory, is celebrated as something that should last forever (v. 17). "The psalm seems to hold out the possibility that a king might be granted life to a fuller and greater extent than an ordinary human being. Here again, the Judahite conception of divine kingship is less explicit and exalted than what we find in Egypt . . . but it still has a mythical dimension that

---

186. Though Tate, *Psalms 51–100*, does not take the same strong view of the words "worship" and "serve" as I do, the logic he sees in the verse is very much to my point: "His [the king's] power has the effect of drawing together the rest of the world to serve him (v. 11). Since he serves God, by implication he brings the nations to Yahweh's service as well" (224).

goes beyond the common human condition."[187] Even beyond this, the petition that the king's name flourish "before the sun" (לפני שמש, v. 17) became an opening for the idea that the name of the king existed before the sun.[188] James Kugel maintains that this was a source of hope for those who were awaiting the messiah, to know that his name was known to God from eternity past.[189] Collins suggests that this might provide hints of a preexistent messiah, though he does not offer strong evidence for it.[190]

e. Psalm 89

After echoing 2 Samuel 7 in its promise of an unbroken line of David in its first four verses, Psalm 89 turns to a celebration of God's cosmic rule (vv. 5-18), moves into a lengthy section of praise for David's sharing in that rule (vv. 19-37), and then turns to lament the apparent failure of God's promise, as Jerusalem stands in ruins (vv. 38-42). The correlations between the praise of God and the promises made to David demonstrate the idealization of the Davidic line.[191] The last thing said about God before David is reintroduced is that God is Israel's king (v. 18). Thus, in the idealization of Israel's kingship (contrary to the initiation of it as depicted in 1 Sam 8:4-9) the king is for Israel on earth what God is for Israel "in heaven" (cf. Ezek 34:11-16, 24). Moreover, the final section of the psalm, in which the lack of Davidic kingship is a source of lament and petition, indicates that the psalm is looking forward to an idealized fulfillment of God's promise.

The psalm draws on imagery of God as cosmic warrior, and hence creator, moving from God's power over the seas to God's victory over primordial chaos to a generalized celebration of God's victory over enemies (vv. 6-13). We see here the development of what Mark Smith calls the "divine power" model of creation, one that often upholds the rule of a nation's king.[192] This cosmic warrior motif embeds itself in the celebration of Davidic kingship that follows. In the transition verses, God makes the people strong (v. 17), specifically through the king who is described as Israel's shield (v. 18). God protects Israel by making the king the agent of God's own strength and cosmic victory. This is precisely the sort of combination of divine might over creation with the up-

---

187. Collins and Collins, *King and Messiah*, 23.

188. Kugel, *Traditions of the Bible*, 59-60.

189. Kugel, *Traditions of the Bible*, 59-60.

190. Collins and Collins, *King and Messiah*, 58.

191. Cf. Jon D. Levenson, *Creation and the Persistence of Evil: The Jewish Drama of Divine Omnipotence* (Princeton, NJ: Princeton University Press, 1994), 22-23.

192. Smith, *Priestly Vision*, 17-23.

holding of a nation's royal claimant that Smith draws attention to as prevalent throughout the ancient Near East. Thus, for example, the God whose own arm is powerful and whose own hand is strong (v. 13) is the God whose arm will strengthen the king (v. 22). The God who crushed Rahab (v. 10) is the one who will pulverize the king's enemies (v. 23). When God is enthroned, love and faithfulness (חסד ואמת) stand before God (v. 14), and the king's confidence comes from God's promise of the same (v. 24).

Finally, the divine power of controlling the seas and waves (v. 9) is extended to the king: "I will set his hand on the sea and his right hand on the rivers" (v. 25). As Smith comments, "Here God invests the king with power capable of mastery over the cosmic enemies, Sea and River, which are elsewhere titles of God's cosmic enemy."[193] This demonstrates that there is not only a parallel between God and the human king, but also that the human king's rule comes from an extension of God's own power to the monarch.[194] This verse epitomizes the difficulty of saying that a particular sphere of sovereignty belongs so peculiarly to the divine that any character wielding such power should be understood to be none other than the creator God. The conjunction of divine power over sea and waves is in fact unique; however, Psalm 89 demonstrates that God can also extend this unique power to idealized human agents as God so chooses.

This psalm's Davidic Christology demonstrates that playing the role of God on earth is precisely the prerogative of Israel's king. Conceptually, this sort of correlation is what Bauckham refers to as a Christology of "divine identity." However, what it means to be identified with God is not the divine Christology of Bauckham's thesis but instead the idealized human representative of God on the earth.[195] The notion that Israel's king shares God's authority over "sea" and "rivers" looks back to earlier heroes such as Moses (Exod 14:16, 27) and Joshua (Josh 3:7–4:19), who mediated God's power over the Red Sea and Jordan River, respectively.

In the first century, the would-be revolutionary Theudas expected that he would recapitulate these earlier extensions of power by parting the Jordan River at his own command, so he could lead his band of rebels on a reconquest of Israel: "He stated that he was a prophet and that by a command he would divide [σχίσας] the river" (Josephus, *Ant.* 20.97). This is one indication that a

---

193. Smith, *Priestly Vision*, 21; Collins and Collins, *King and Messiah*, 31.

194. Compare the deployment of Psalm 89 in 4Q381 fragment 15.

195. See J. R. Daniel Kirk and Stephen L. Young, "'I Will Set His Hand to the Sea': The Relevance of Ps 88:26 to Debates about Christology in Mark," *JBL* 133 (2014): 333-40.

first-century would-be messiah took with utmost seriousness and literalness the idea of God's chosen agent being able to exercise control over "rivers" (Ps 89:25). Later rabbinic exegesis of the verse indicates that such replication of the work of Moses and Joshua would be a hallmark of the coming messiah. *Pesiqta Rabbati* reads, "The Holy One, blessed be He, will reply, 'He is the Messiah, and his name is Ephraim, My true Messiah. . . . And even the seas and rivers will stop flowing,' as it is said, 'I will set his hand also on the sea, and his right hand on the rivers'" (36:1). For the purposes of exploring the Christology implicit in the storm-stilling and water-walking Jesus of the Synoptic Tradition, we have a significant piece of evidence that idealized humans could not only be described as controlling the waters, but also that such control was actually something expected of God's idealized, messianic agent, by at least some Jews, including some of the first century in Palestine.[196]

Psalm 89 also fills out the picture of idealized human figures, in this case Davidic kings, as sons of God, as it reflects the adoption/begetting of the king into God's family: "He shall cry to me, 'You are my Father, my God, the Rock of my salvation!' I will make him the firstborn, the highest of the kings of the earth" (vv. 26-27, NRSV). In themselves, these verses augment the royal son of God theology we catch glimpses of in Psalms 2 and 45, as well as in 2 Samuel 7. Indeed, verses 30-33 echo the dynastic promise of the latter passage, indicating that wandering descendants will be chastised and scourged but not ultimately rejected. In the broader context of the creation through conflict motif, the sonship of God's king also echoes the creation of first humanity in Genesis 1, as discussed above. The conjunction of creation and kingship receives a final nod in the psalm as God promises that David's throne will "endure before me like the sun. It shall be established forever like the moon" (vv. 36-37).

f. Solomon's Throne and Worship in 1 Chronicles

At least one other passage in Israel's biblical tradition suggests that idealized royal figures might be incorporated into Israel's worship. As 1 Chronicles 29 tells the story of David's passing the reins of the kingdom to his son Solomon, David commands the assembly to worship Yhwh: "And all the assembly blessed Yhwh, God of their ancestors, and bowed their heads and worshiped Yhwh and the king" (ויקדו וישתחוו ליהוה ולמלך) (v. 20, NRSV, alt.).[197] Three

---

196. Kirk and Young, "I Will Set His Hand."

197. James McGrath, *The Only True God: Early Christian Monotheism in Its Jewish Context* (Urbana: University of Illinois Press, 2009), 19.

verses later, the Chronicler tells us that "Solomon sat on the throne of Yhwh as king, in place of his father David" (v. 23). The throne of Israel's king is Yhwh's throne, likely signifying that it is the earthly counterpart and instantiation of the heavenly reality. Margaret Barker aptly summarizes the action:

> The people worship the Lord and the king. Any possible ambiguity is removed a few lines later when we are told: "Solomon sat on the throne of the Lord as king" (1 Chron 29:20, 23). In other words, the Chronicler says that Solomon was worshipped when the assembly worshipped the Lord and that the king sat on the throne of the Lord. The form of the words is important: "They bowed down to the Lord and to the king." There is one verb but two direct objects, for the Lord and then the human king. . . . The king was the visible presence of the Lord in the temple ritual and Solomon's enthronement was his apotheosis.[198]

Such a depiction of Solomon directly involves this idealized king in two realities that, according to Bauckham, are the strict purview of God alone in early Judean belief: sovereignty over the world, expressed by sitting on God's throne, and receipt of worship.[199]

g. Isaiah 9

Idealization of Davidic kingship appears at several key junctures in the prophetic writings, including the celebration of the king in Isaiah 9:6-7. The setting in which this exalted depiction finds its context and meaning is debated; however, the idea that it refers to a Davidic king such as Hezekiah is ubiquitous in scholarship, and the view of Gerhard von Rad and his teacher Albrecht Alt that it refers to a coronation modeled on Egyptian ceremonies has been vigorously reasserted by J. J. M. Roberts.[200]

The verses read, "For a child has been born for us, a son given to us; authority rests upon his shoulders; and he is named Wonderful Counselor, Mighty

---

198. Margaret Barker, "The High Priest and the Worship of Jesus," in *The Jewish Roots of Christological Monotheism: Papers from the St. Andrews Conference on the Historical Origins of the Worship of Jesus* (JSJSup 63; ed. Carey C. Newman et al.; Leiden: Brill, 1999), 93-111, here 94-95.

199. E.g., Bauckham, *Jesus and the God of Israel*, 8-9, 132-81. In the Christian tradition, Revelation 3:9-21 is an important development of this same idea; cf. McGrath, *Only True God*, 78-79.

200. Roberts, "Whose Child Is This?"

God, Everlasting Father, Prince of Peace. His authority shall grow continually, and there shall be endless peace for the throne of David and his kingdom. He will establish and uphold it with justice and with righteousness from this time onward and forevermore. The zeal of the LORD of hosts will do this" (vv. 6-7, NRSV). Importantly, these specific appellations come as the culminating explanation for a proclamation of an age of liberty, notable for its expressions of military victory. Thus, we have intimations of the combination of divine warrior and royal ascension motifs that have cropped up on several occasions in this study. The idealized king will be the means by which the divine warrior brings peace to God's people.

This child is the one who will see peace established for his kingdom and the Davidic line (v. 7). The names recited in celebration of this king are shocking for their conjoining of him to God: "he is named wonderful counselor, mighty God, everlasting father, prince of peace" (v. 6, NRSV, alt.). Von Rad argued that such identification of the king and God is evidence of a divinization that takes place, or is celebrated, at the king's enthronement (though a celebration of birth is also possible). The passage celebrates God begetting the Judahite king in a manner analogous to Psalm 2. The king enters into possession of these titles as he is enthroned to rule on God's behalf.[201] This begetting enables the king to be addressed here, as in Psalm 45, as God. These verses depict the king (perhaps Hezekiah) as sharing in the divine identity, both in name and in enacting a reign that embodies God's own reign over the earth, demonstrating the coherence between God and God's idealized human representatives that might be anticipated in Jewish religion and politics.[202] Collins and Collins summarize the evidence from Isaiah 9 in a manner that recognizes its depiction as an idealization of Davidic kingship: "Isaiah 9 was allowed to stand, without any hint of criticism. This strongly suggests that Isaiah accepted the ideology of the Davidic house as an ideal, even if historical kings failed to live up to it."[203]

h. Ezekiel 34

Ezekiel 34 uses the extended metaphor of shepherding sheep to describe the failure of Israel's leadership, God's judgment on those leaders, and the resto-

---

201. Cf. Roberts, "Whose Child Is This?" 127-29.

202. For a summary of the argument in favor of a reference to Hezekiah, see Collins and Collins, *King and Messiah*, 40-41.

203. Collins and Collins, *King and Messiah*, 42.

ration of the people. Throughout my study of idealized human figures, I have been noting the manifold ways that human beings play the role of God. In something of an inversion of this theme, in Ezekiel 34 God plays the role that was originally assigned to the shepherds. Verse 4 delineates the failures of the shepherds as failing to strengthen, heal, bind up, bring back, and seek. In a nearly perfect inversion of this, God promises in verse 16 to seek, bring back, bind up, and strengthen. God's rescue is from the shepherds who will no longer shepherd the flock (v. 10). Instead, God plays the part of shepherd in gathering, feeding, and caring for the sheep (vv. 11-16). However, verse 23 indicates that the tending and feeding will not be God's sole direct prerogative. Instead, David will feed the sheep and be the shepherd. The role of shepherd who feeds the sheep shifts in this passage from those who played the part poorly, to God's remanding of the prerogative to himself, to the redistribution of it to a Davidic prince. This is another indication of the rich interplay between divine prerogatives and representative human figures to whom these have been entrusted.

Another theme that has loomed large over this chapter of my study appears in Ezekiel 34 as well. We find a reiteration of the complex of themes that includes God's sovereignty over creation, the nation's victory over its enemies, and the establishment of royal authority. The era of restoration that is described by God's voice in the first person includes more than gathering the people to their land. It entails promises of terrestrial fecundity: the land will be fertile, the people will be fed on good, green pastures (vv. 13-15). After promising a coming Davidide, the view of creation returns. Wild animals will be driven from the land so that people can be secure in either desert or forest (v. 25). This addresses the same problem of threatening wild animals, particularly desert animals, that I argued Psalm 72 to be addressing; however, rather than animal subservience Ezekiel 34 depicts animal eviction. As in Psalm 72, these beasts are paired with hostile nations as enemies that are subdued: "The nations will not longer prey on them, and wild animals will no longer devour them" (Ezek. 34:28). God's sovereignty over the animal kingdom is not the only facet of God's rule over creation that is paired with removal of geopolitical threats. In verses 26-27 God promises blessings of rain and fruit-bearing trees, "and they will know that I am the LORD when I break the bars of their yoke and deliver them from those who enslaved them" (CEB). God's sovereignty receives a double expression in which the "natural world" is inseparably tied to the need of the people for God to deliver them from the rule of hostile worldly powers. This paradisiacal picture of Israel's life, secure on the fruitful land, sits alongside God's promise of David to be the people's shepherd and prince (vv. 23-24). Ezekiel 34 thus stands as another witness to the inherent interconnectedness between God's sovereignty over creation, Israel's geopolitical peace and power, and the authority of Israel's king. By playing the part of sheep-feeding shepherd, David plays the role of human counterpart to the God who is shepherding the people by feeding them on a fertile land.

i. Micah 5

The prophet Micah anticipates a child born in Bethlehem (5:2). He describes the child in almost mythical language as one "whose origins are of old, from long ago [מוצאתיו מקדם מימי עולם]." Reginald Fuller captures the nuances of this passage well: "Here the affinity of the ideal king with Yahweh is expressed in terms of ancient origin (v. 2 . . .). This means no more than that he will come of the ancient Davidic family. . . . But despite the highly coloured charismatic endowments of the ideal king, the Messiah (who is not yet so called) is still an earthly figure in all of these pre-exilic prophecies."[204] The possibility of an identification with God extends beyond the hoary origins of the coming king. The prophesied ruler will come forth on God's behalf (לי).

In a later verse, the prophecy makes clear that not only is the king "for God," but God is also for the king as he stands to feed and shepherd God's people. Specifically, God bestows upon the ruler God's strength and even the loftiness (בגאון, MT; δόξῃ, LXX) of God's own name (v. 4, Eng.; v. 3, MT, LXX). The theme of the ruler's shepherding as an expression of God's authority is one that we have seen frequently. Especially striking here is God's bestowal of the majesty of God's own name. This unique identifier of God is invoked to demonstrate the power of the God who stands behind the king. Equally important here are that the name is unique and that it is extended so as to cover or include the human ruler.

This is a figure of an idealized future, and yet it must be doubted that the figure is here being depicted as a peculiar, surprising hypostasis of the one true God. The issue of God's name being bestowed upon Jesus becomes a point of direct significance for New Testament Christology in the Christ hymn of Philippians (2:9) and in the "name of the Lord" who must be confessed in Acts 2:21, 25, 34, 36, 39, and Romans 10:9, 13. In Micah, we see an idealized messianic figure of the future functioning with the imprimatur of the divine name, within a prophetic "story" in which the figures of God and the human ruler are clearly distinct.

---

204. Reginald H. Fuller, *Foundations of New Testament Christology* (New York: Charles Scribner's Sons, 1965), 25.

j. Zechariah 12

Zechariah 12 tells of a day when the fortunes of Judah and Jerusalem will be restored through some sort of final battle. The promised victory will bring glory to all the people, not only the line of David and the Jerusalemites, but also those who live more broadly in Judah (v. 7). The subsequent verse spells out the glory that will come to the former: "On that day Yʜwʜ will protect the inhabitants of Jerusalem so that the feeblest among them shall be like David on that day, and the house of David shall be like God, like the angel of Yʜwʜ before them" (v. 8).

Zechariah 12 provides another angle of vision for seeing the divine warrior motif in conjunction with idealized kingship. Here, Yʜwʜ fights the earthly opponents of the people, not mythological forces of anti-creation. The language of Yʜwʜ as shield or protector sounds at first blush as though the people will not be fighting at all. Verse 9 has God taking ownership of the battle and claiming, "I will seek to destroy all the nations that come against Jerusalem" (NRSV). Within this scene, the Davidic king, and perhaps the people as a whole, are given to anticipate God-like glory: "David shall be like God, like the angel of Yʜwʜ before them." Generally, we can say that Zechariah 12:8 participates in the strand of tradition that so affiliates the king with God that his idealization entails a sort of identification with the divine. Since the explicit nature of this glorification is not made clear, we do well to leave this as a general piece of evidence to the effect that what might be called the "divinization" of idealized royal figures was quite at home in post-exilic Judaism. There is some sense in which a glorification of the human king on the earth entails his becoming "like God," more specifically, "the angel of the Lord," in the sight of the people.

k. Conclusions: Idealized Kings in Scripture

Within the biblical tradition itself, David and Solomon are developed as idealized types of Israel's royal theology. The kings are God's sons, those who are enthroned at God's right hand. At times, they are even depicted as sitting on God's own throne, for the purpose of enacting God's reign on the earth. This reign is far-reaching, inasmuch as it is an expression of God's own reign over all the chaotic forces that threaten creation, human life in general, and Israel in particular, and thus it reaches not only to persons and nations but also to the created elements themselves and to oppressive spirits. This identification with God bleeds into Israel's worship in several respects, including not only the celebration of God for God's choice and enthronement of the king, but also incorporation of the king himself as an object of worship. In the idealization of its royal figures, the biblical Israelite tradition depicts Israel's kings in precisely the ways that some New Testament scholars have argued to be signals that a being is none other than God. As the evidence for idealized human figures continues to mount in both biblical and post-biblical traditions, it becomes increasingly clear that much of the approach of the recent early high Christology movement is off course. It demonstrates that many early Jewish writers were developing depictions of certain types of human figures, describing their appearance, functions, and location in the cosmos, without the least concern that the exalted depictions might infringe on some realm supposedly reserved for God alone. In other words, it is not simply the case that New Testament scholars have failed to pinpoint the correct criterion, the application of which to any being would signal that this person is none other than God, but that such a way of approaching the question of a uniquely divine Christology is conceptually flawed. It may, of course, be equally true that some writers (e.g., a Deuteronomistic historian) felt that such exalted representations were inappropriate infringements and sought to counter or bury such elements. However, the presence of such a counter-voice does not mute the other. Although some Jews perhaps thought that the divine prerogative was wrongly infringed by such exalted depictions of royal figures, other Jews not only penned such notions across various periods of the biblical history, but also continued to develop them in the interpretations of the biblical tradition that continued throughout the Second Temple period.

2. IDEALIZED KINGS IN POST-BIBLICAL JUDAISM

a. Psalms of Solomon

The final two psalms in *Psalms of Solomon* express some of the clearest expectations of a coming Davidic messiah in early Judaism. *Psalms of Solomon* 17, in particular, is replete with indications that the function of the Davidic king is to play the role of God on earth, specifically, over Israel.[205] The role of king itself is one that properly belongs to God. The first line reads, "Lord,

---

205. Cf. Gene Davenport, "The 'Anointed of the Lord' in Psalms of Solomon 17," in *Ideal Figures in Ancient Judaism: Profiles and Paradigms* (SBLSCS 12; ed. John J. Collins and George W. E. Nickelsburg; Chico, CA: Scholars, 1980), 87-92.

you are our king forevermore" (v. 1). This is mirrored in verse 4 when David is mentioned for the first time with the affirmation, "You chose David to be king over Israel" (v. 4). Thus, as John Collins argues, "The kingship of God . . . is implemented through human kingship."[206] Moreover, the psalm celebrates God's kingdom (ἡ βασιλεία τοῦ θεοῦ) as going on forever (v. 3), and then articulates God's promise that David's royal house (βασίλειον αὐτοῦ) will not fail (v. 4). After recounting the people's exile and various rulers of Jerusalem (vv. 5-20), the psalm pleads with God to raise up a Davidic king. Gene Davenport summarizes the relationship between God and the king found in the psalm:

> The use of the appositive your servant (vs. 21) further reminds us that ultimately the people are not subjects of the earthly monarch, but of God. Their subjection to the earthly king is the means of their subjection to God, and, conversely, by their rejection of the Davidic dynasty the usurpers have rejected God's kingship. . . . Consequently, the one who will sit upon the restored Davidic throne will be one who is not merely triumphant in human power politics, but one in whom the Lord's own kingship once again is made concrete.[207]

The idealized king described in *Psalms of Solomon* 17 reflects his close connection with God through his holiness, his knowledge and wisdom, his rule over the nations, and his care for the people. Much of this is summed up in verses 22-25, where the king is anticipated as one who will drive Gentiles from Jerusalem and fulfill the prerogative articulated in Psalm 2:9 of shattering the nations with an iron rod (*Pss. Sol.* 17:24). The theme of the king's righteousness, particularly in judgment, runs throughout the psalm (vv. 23, 26, 27, 29, 32, 37, 40). Indeed, the psalm even goes so far as to say that the king will be free from sin (v. 36). His righteousness, in turn, creates a holy and righteous Jerusalem, where the people of God can thrive (vv. 26-27, 30, 40-41, 43-45). In this vein, the psalm hints at a preternatural ability to read the hearts of people, proclaiming, "he will condemn sinners by the thoughts of their hearts" (v. 25). Not only is the righteous quality of the reign an indication of the divine leaking through the human, so too is its extent. The king will rule not only over Israel, but over all (or at least many) nations (e.g., vv. 29-31).[208]

The means by which this king comes into his righteousness and wisdom

---

206. Collins, *Scepter and the Star,* 54.
207. Davenport, "Anointed of the Lord," 72 (underscore original).
208. Davenport, "Anointed of the Lord," 75.

signal his close relationship with God. First, the psalm juxtaposes the king's righteousness with the claim that the king will be "taught by God" (v. 32). Later, it declares that the source of his strength will be God's holy spirit (v. 37). This latter claim echoes both the historical narrative in which David receives God's spirit when he is anointed king (1 Sam 16:13) and similar reflections elsewhere (e.g., Ps 51:11).

Within such a richly textured articulation of the Davidic king's representation of God in righteousness and rule, three particular dynamics stand out as indicating that the psalm depicts the king as one who plays the role of God on the earth. First, in verses 29-32 there is an echo of Isaiah 66:18-21, but in the psalm the king plays the role of master of the nations that was the direct prerogative of God in the prophet.[209] Isaiah 66:18 says that God knows the thoughts of the people, something ascribed to the king in *Psalms of Solomon* 17:25.[210] The prophet in that same verse declares that the nations will come and see "my glory," whereas the coming nations see the glory of the king in *Psalms of Solomon* 17:31, in addition to the glory of God. In the psalm, the Davidic king is the means by which the nations are subjected to God and the one through whom they express their subjection to God. This is a mediatorial relationship in the strongest possible sense, as the king plays God's role as ruler over the earth, and represents God to the nations, also, in the homage that they pay to the God who rules over them.[211]

Second, the psalm depicts the king as bearing God's glory.[212] The nations come "to see his [the king's] glory . . . and to see the glory of the Lord with which God has glorified her" (*Pss. Sol.* 17:31). The God who will not share his glory with another (Isa 42:8) has no problem sharing his glory with his own representative on the earth and the city that God has chosen. At a number of points throughout this chapter we see God's glory being reflected or embodied by idealized human figures. It is one way in which their peculiar relationship with God is signaled in early Jewish texts, and it tells us that the writers of such texts see such people playing the role of God and dressing the part. This should

---

209. Davenport, "Anointed of the Lord," 75.

210. The psalm depicts the Davidic king as fulfilling other scriptures as well, including Isaiah 11:2-4 and Psalm 2; see Collins, *Scepter and the Star,* 58.

211. Cf. Davenport, "Anointed of the Lord," 75.

212. The masculine singular pronoun makes it clear that in the extant Greek version the reference is to the glory of the king. Jerusalem is referred to using feminine pronouns throughout. Also, the masculine and feminine third-person singular endings are not readily confused in either Hebrew or Greek, making the reference to the king likely in both the original and the Greek translation.

give us great caution when studying early Christian texts such as the story of the transfiguration (Mark 9:2-8 and pars.), that we not jump too quickly to the conclusion that such a bearing of God's glory is a signal of some inherent or preexistent divinity.

Third, the psalm asserts both that God is king and that David's heir, also, is the people's king. The correlation is peculiar for its directness. Throughout much of the literature on kingship such a shared sovereignty is intimated in various degrees, but the assigning of the same title to both figures in one locale is unusual. The psalm is bookended by declarations that God is king. Verse 1 states, "Lord, you are our king forevermore," whereas the final phrase is, "The Lord himself is our king forevermore" (v. 46). The Davidic king, in turn, is tightly connected with God: God chose David to be king (v. 4), and it is in God's hands to restore the broken line (v. 21).

The title king is used at several junctures as the psalm articulates the intimate connection between God and the king as the basis of the king's righteousness and of the holiness of the people. Verse 32 captures this: because of God's instruction the king is righteous, and the people are holy as they live under a king whom God himself has anointed. Here we see that sharing of kingship over the people entails not only playing a common role, but also sharing in God's moral quality. Similarly, verse 42 concludes a description of the king's righteousness leading to the righteousness of the people by saying, "This is the beauty of the king of Israel which God knew." The hoped-for leader is called king in a context of God's own knowledge and instruction. In between verses 32 and 42 we find the royal appellation applied to God as God stands in relationship to the king: "The Lord himself is his king" (v. 34). This underscores both that the king is playing the role over the people that God is playing over him, and that the reason for the human king's successful reign is that he has been given the role of the true, heavenly king to play on the earth, and is faithfully doing so. Not only the role, but also its power and its holy quality are given by God to the Davidic king and typify the latter's reign.

With this intimate connection established, it is not surprising to find that as the anticipated king bears the righteousness and holiness of God, so too does the people bear the righteousness and holiness embodied in its human king.[213] This interrelation runs throughout the psalm, but is perhaps best captured in verse 32: "And he will be a righteous king over them, taught by God. There will be no unrighteousness among them in his days, for all shall be holy, and their king shall be the Lord Messiah" (Wright trans.). The people's holiness is

---

213. Cf. Davenport, "Anointed of the Lord," 76-77.

at least in part dependent on the holiness of the king, as this verse indicates, and also derives from the king's purge of sinners from the city and gathering of the holy people (e.g., vv. 22, 26, 27, 30).[214] The king thus stands in an analogous position vis-à-vis the people as God stands in relationship to the king, as the source of righteousness and holiness.

b. Animal Visions (1 Enoch)

The Animal Visions depict the biblical story from creation through consummation. These visions anticipate a turning point at which Israel's story swings from one of death and destruction to one of life and restoration. The advent of a messiah-figure is the turning point in the story.[215] A champion arises among the sheep, who represent Israel, in a sheep who sprouts a large horn (1 En. 90:9). This sheep not only fights for the people but is also the instrument of their healing. Perhaps in echo of Isaiah 42:6-7 (cf. Isa 42:19), he opens the eyes of blind Israel (1 En. 90:10). He then gathers the sheep to himself. After the Lord comes to the sheep's aid, this horned sheep is enthroned. The language of his enthronement is telling: "a throne was erected in a pleasant land, and he sat upon it for the Lord of the sheep" (1 En. 90:20). Sitting on the throne of Israel is playing the role of God as the ruler and judge of the people.

Moreover, this champion of Israel, enthroned in the beautiful land, has the authority to open the sealed books on the basis of which judgment is rendered (1 En. 90:20). The Animal Visions offer other evidence for idealized human figures as well. As I discuss below, the entire community becomes the object of veneration from the nations who come to worship and make supplication of the "sheep" who are Israel.

c. Anointed King at Qumran

The purpose of this section is not to give a fulsome overview of messianic expectations at Qumran. This ground has been more than adequately covered by John Collins in *The Scepter and the Star*. This foray into the Dead Sea Scrolls focuses on the few indications of the ways that a coming, eschatological king was idealized by the community.[216]

214. Davenport, "Anointed of the Lord," 75, says that the king is "the one who will sanctify the city," a role he takes to be a signal of the king's priestly function.

215. Nickelsburg, *1 Enoch*, 400, suggests that this figure represents Judas Maccabeus.

216. I thus bypass some scrolls that mention a coming Davidic king but do not substantively contribute to our understanding of David as an idealized human figure (e.g., 1QM XI; 4Q161;

i. Son of God in 4QAramaic Apocalypse (4Q246)

The identity of the "son of God" in the text is much mooted: "He will be called son of God, and they will call him son of the Most High" (4Q246 II, 1). Collins has laid out a compelling case for the figure being not only a positive figure, but also a human messiah, in the vein of the Davidic "son of God" passages in Psalm 2 and 2 Samuel 7.[217] The overall force of his argument is that speculation that "son of God" carries negative connotations depends too much on an assumption that the text moves in a linear fashion from negative figures to a positive redeemer — something that does not hold true for much apocalyptic literature. Moreover, the title son of God was not used of Seleucid kings.[218] To add a further dimension in favor of the son of God as a positive figure, there is a shift in pronoun to the third-person plural in the immediate context. Not only do we read, "they will call him son of the Most High," which may refer to either his loyal subjects or his opponents, but we then read immediately, "Like the sparks that you saw, so will their kingdom be; they will rule several year[s] over the earth and crush everything" (4Q246 II, 1-3). The juxtaposition of "he" and "they" in the first few lines is best explained a shift between the expected eschatological king and the nations whom he will defeat. On this interpretation of the scroll, son of God is a messianic title at Qumran.[219]

Even if this reading is rejected, however, the ensuing description of God's coming kingdom in lines 4-9 signals a messianic age in which the king's attributes and actions are merged in various ways with God's own. In addition to the identification with God that comes through this appellation of sonship, actions ascribed to God are also assigned to the king within short compass. In line 4 God acts to bring an end to warfare; in line 5 the king judges the earth and makes peace. This is because God acts for the king: "he will wage war for him" (4Q246 II, 8). God is at war, and the king is as well. The actions of the king on earth are none other than the manifestation of the actions of God in heaven.

The conjunction of divine action and the king's rule of the world echo what

---

4Q252). Cf. Lawrence H. Schiffman, "Messianic Figures and Ideas in the Qumran Scrolls," in *The Messiah: Developments in Earliest Judaism and Christianity* (ed. James H. Charlesworth; Minneapolis: Fortress, 1992), 116-29.

217. Collins, *Scepter and the Star*, 171-86.

218. Collins, *Scepter and the Star*, 174, 178.

219. The text finds a striking parallel in Luke 1:31-35. See Joseph A. Fitzmyer, *The Gospel according to Luke I–IX: Introduction, Translation, and Notes* (AB 28; New York: Doubleday, 1981), 347-48.

we saw above in Psalm 89. Thus, for the king to perform God's function of judging the earth is no infringement on the divine prerogative. In the scroll, God is the strength of the king and the one who wages war for him (lines 7-8). This appears to link the expected king with the eschatological war (e.g., 4Q285 5, 3-4). Finally, this royal figure is said to reign with an eternal rule (שׁלטן עלם).

ii. Branch of David in 4QFlorilegium

A Davidic messiah makes a brief appearance in 4QFlorilegium. The prophecy is clearly eschatological ("the last days," 4Q174 1 I, 2). Though somewhat vague, the passage ascribes to the Davidic king a measure of agency in the deliverance of the faithful from their enemies (lines 7-9). Confirmation for this can be found in the exposition of Amos 9:11, in which the raising up of the Davidic "hut" is for the purpose of saving Israel (להושיע את ישראל, line 13). In this scroll, the Davidic king plays an important role, perhaps as a leading agent in the eschatological war by which (the redefined/"elect of") Israel is saved. The mingling of divine action with the ascription of salvation to the human king underscores yet again how the role of the idealized human agent is often to play the role of God on the earth.

iii. Messianic Apocalypse (4Q521)

In dealing with 4Q521 under the rubric of Anointed King, I do not intend to make a strong case for a particularly Davidic or royal messianism in this text. For my purposes, the nondescript "anointed" can be conveniently located here, inasmuch as my goal is not to define ancient Davidic messianism as such, but to illustrate the wide-ranging possibilities for depicting idealized human figures. The messiah figure of 4Q521 certainly qualifies.

Fragment 2 depicts the messiah as God's executive, ruling over both the heavens and the earth: "[for the heav]ens and the earth will listen to his anointed one" (4Q521 2 II, 1).[220] This demonstrates that an idealized messiah might possess an authority to command not only the humans of the earth but also the natural order, assuming that "the heavens" here refers to the ability to control rainfall (cf. Elijah in 1 Kgs 17:1-7).[221] The exalted nature of this future

---

220. Martínez and Tigchelaar, *DSSSE,* 2:1045. Cf. Michael O. Wise and James D. Tabor, "The Messiah at Qumran," *BAR* 18 (1992): 60-65.

221. Collins, *Scepter and the Star,* 135, points to Sirach 48:3 as celebrating this tradition, and to the two prophets of Revelation 11 exercising a similar function.

anointed ruler is underscored by the parallelism between the statement that heavens and earth will obey the anointed one and the following line that reads, "[and all th]at is in them will not turn away from the precepts of the holy ones" (4Q521 2 II, 2).[222] "Holy ones" most often means angels in the scrolls, signaling "that the anointed one enjoys a status that is comparable to that of the angels."[223] Idealization of human rulers can serve a broader purpose than legitimating rule over hostile nations; it can also be a means of ascribing to a person a share in God's rule over the natural world. That is to say, nature miracles can be the purview of idealized human figures of the future as well as the biblical prophets.

The era of restoration and prosperity one finds depicted in the scrolls is ascribed to the Lord's direct action. The Lord enthrones the חסידים, frees prisoners, gives sight to the blind, straightens the twisted, and also heals the wounded, raises the dead, and proclaims the good news (4Q521 2 II, 7, 11-12; echoing Isa 42:7; 61:1-2). The unlikelihood that God would directly proclaim the good news, however, together with the Isaiah 61 background in which an anointed prophet proclaims good news and restores God's people, has led John Collins to argue that the actions ascribed to the Lord in 4Q521 are mediated by an anointed human agent.[224] As he also points out, and as we will see in greater detail below, in 11QMelchizedek "the year of the Lord's favor" from that same passage, Isaiah 61:1, is rendered "the Lord of Melchizedek's favor."[225] This provides another angle on the possibility that God's actions are being ascribed to a human agent in 4Q521. Although the idea of an anointed figure raising the dead appears to uniquely ascribe to a human agent a purview reserved for God, it may be that such an association is simply rendering a historical narrative in an eschatological key. In 1 Kings 17:17-24 Elijah raises the dead son of the widow of Zarephath. In 2 Kings 4:11-37 Elisha raises the dead son of the Shunammite woman. Also, in 2 Kings 13:20-21 we read of a man who is resuscitated after his body touches Elisha's bones. And so the rabbis invoke these prophets as anticipating God's work of raising the dead: "Everything that the Holy One will do, he has already anticipated by the hands of the righteous in this world, the resurrection of the dead by Elijah and Elisha" (*Pesiq. Rab*

---

222. Martínez and Tigchelaar, *DSSSE*, 2:1045.

223. Shaver, "Prophet Elijah," 172.

224. Collins, *Scepter and the Star*, 133-35. Wise and Tabor, "Messiah at Qumran," 63, say that "proclaiming the good news" is never used of God in the Hebrew Bible, thus indicating that the lines in question probably refer to the messiah as the agent of resurrection, healing, and proclamation. See also the discussion in Eve, *Jewish Context*, 189-96.

225. Collins, *Scepter and the Star*, 133.

Kah. 76a).[226] If one follows Collins in this reading, the anointed of 4Q521 is so tightly entailed in the activities of God that they are ascribed to the Lord, despite the use of human agency.

Beyond the fact that the proclamation of good news is inherently more likely to be ascribed to a human than to God, further evidence that a human is intended as the mediator of such divine action might be found in column 3. There, the voice has shifted to the first person, and the speaker claims to be the one who will set people free (4Q521 2 III, 1), echoing the action that is ascribed to God in column 2 (line 8). Here, I disagree with Collins's suggestion that God is the speaker.[227] The previous sentence refers to "the law of your favor," such that the second-person pronoun, rather than the first-person pronoun, seems to be referring to God at this juncture.

One more aspect of the text is worthy of attention. In a phrase evocative of the spirit's work at creation, the spirit is said to hover upon the poor (ועל), ורוח אלהים מרחפת על פני המים :cf. Gen 1:2 ;7 ,II 2 4Q521 ,עניים רוחו תרחף), after which renewal the pious ones (חסידים) are said to be given the throne of an eternal kingdom (2 II, 7). The enthronement of God's messiah and God's people more generally is clear in this text; and the extent of the reign implied as over heaven and earth is likely tied to the echoes of new creation. And so Émile Puech comments, "The Essene eschatology recaptures the original state of Eden (protology), as the just wait for entry into paradise lost. The Essene expected the restoration of the just to the state of humanity before the original fall."[228] People are restored, through this faithful community, to their role of ruling the world on God's behalf. This is an idealized human eschatology, one in which the idealized humanity of the past provides the contours for the community's expectations for what life will be like in the eschatological future.

3. CONCLUSIONS: IDEALIZED KINGS IN ANCIENT ISRAEL

Idealized kings in biblical and post-biblical Judaism shared in God's sovereignty over the earth, sitting on God's throne, ruling the nations, governing God's people, manifesting God's wisdom and righteousness. Their rule could extend beyond the earth to include the heavens; and their rule of the earth

226. Collins, *Scepter and the Star,* 134; Émile Puech, "Une apocalypse messianique (4Q521)," *RevQ* 15 (1992): 475-522, here 492.

227. Collins, *Scepter and the Star,* 136-37.

228. On the evocations of new creation, see also Puech, "Immortality and Life after Death," 516.

could include a share in God's control over the chaos of the waters. These figures are included in Israel's worship through their adoration in psalms, and through their pairing with God as the objects of the people's and nations' adoration. Kings share in God's glory, manifesting that glory to the world, and they make the nation holy as God acts through them as agents of purification and of war. The king is king by virtue of sharing in God's kingship, and is said to be like YHWH. As son of God, the king not only bears a special relationship to God, but also has a unique capacity to make God known in his own person: to be the son of God is to be the human representation of God on earth, such that how a person treats the king is how a person treats Israel's God. No doubt some complex of such themes lies behind the willingness of Isaiah 9 to use such epithets as "mighty God" and "everlasting father" in its depiction of a newly born and/or enthroned royal figure.

No one text, or community or stream of theological reflection for that matter, includes all of these notions of idealized Davidic kingship. But it is precisely the impressive array of options that were available to early Jews wishing to depict a unique agent of God that calls into doubt theses about divine Christology that depend on Jewish monotheism as a limiting factor. Simply put, the standards put forward in recent New Testament scholarship, which have tried to preserve ground that is ceded to God alone, are taken down repeatedly by early Jewish writers who all too willingly depict their own Jewish heroes as occupying just such space. We have seen enough already, and will continue to see as this chapter unfolds, to suggest that the whole project of attempting to preserve one or two actions, ascriptions, or attributes for God alone, such that the reckoning of them to another is, itself, an indication of binitarian theology falls regularly before the evidence of early Judaism.[229] Such evidence indicates that there are numerous Jewish writers who simply do not function with such a conscious set of limiting factors created by their monotheistic commitments. While some early Jewish renderings of monotheism can be rightly read as demanding such strictures, a vast amount of evidence indicates that the authors of such strictures did not exercise anything like a controlling voice over the various textual manifestations of early Judaism.

When it comes to kings in particular, it appears that the very purpose of the king was, for many writers and to varying degrees, to be on earth a human

---

229. The one exception for the material I am most concerned with — that touching on idealized human figures — might be the work of creation. But even here there are important considerations concerning both Wisdom and the heavenly court (e.g., Gen 1:26) that might give us pause. Moreover, priests were at times depicted as enacting creation (see below).

manifestation of the divine. This conjunction of identity is something that we will see Jesus fitting into in the Synoptic Gospels, not something that is a new creation of the early Christian communities. Indeed, part of the persuasive power of Bauckham's thesis lies in the fact that Jesus is, in fact, someone depicted as sharing in the divine identity. However, what has been too much overlooked is that bearing of divine identity on the earth is a role frequently assigned to idealized human agents. Kings show such adoption of the divine identity by being called God, receiving worship, being God's stand-in in rule, bearing God's spirit, executing God's judgments, fulfilling scriptures of which God is the subject, and standing in filial relationship to God.

D. PRIESTS OF DIVINITY

1. MELCHIZEDEK

a. Melchizedek in Scripture

The Hebrew scriptures refer to Melchizedek twice. The first time is in a brief note upon Abram's return from a battle in which he had rescued looted people and goods. "King Melchizedek of Salem" is also called "priest of God most high" (כהן לאל עליון, Gen 14:18). This priest blesses Abram, and Abram's God, and in return Abram gives a tenth of his plunder to the priest. This figure is enigmatic (how does it come to be that a non-Israelite king is also a priest that Abram honors with the spoils of war?),[230] and serves as a priest, but the character receives no further development, and hardly qualifies as an idealized figure except in his function of priest.

The second mention of Melchizedek is in Psalm 110:4, a verse that appears to give validation to the ways in which the Davidic king served as priest despite his lack of Levite descent (2 Sam 6:12-14 [cf. Exod 28:6]; 2 Sam 8:18, "The sons of David were priests," ובני דוד כהנים היו).[231] It remains a peculiar interjection, however, into a psalm whose primary motif appears to be that of

---

230. Whether the "Most High God" is supposed to be Abram's God or a reference to the high God of the Ugaritic pantheon (a likelihood pointed out to me by Sam Boyd) is a question that need not detain us here, though its interpretation in Hebrews leans heavily in the former direction.

231. See Israel Knohl, "Melchizedek: Union of Kingship and Priesthood," in *Text, Thought, and Practice in Qumran and Early Christianity* (STDJ 84; ed. Ruth C. Clements and Daniel R. Schwartz; Leiden: Brill, 2009), 255-66, esp. 256-58.

YHWH the divine warrior conquering the enemies of Israel's king.[232] The verse reads, "The LORD has sworn and will not change his mind, 'You are a priest forever, according to the order of Melchizedek'" (NRSV). This declaration sits in parallel with the opening of the psalm in which YHWH speaks to the king and says, "Sit at my right hand until I make your enemies your footstool" (NRSV).[233] The notion that the people will offer themselves to the king might evoke Abram's free offering of his winnings to Melchizedek. This psalm is, as a whole, a picture of an idealized priestly king.[234] He is enthroned at God's right hand, and God's own activity on the earth is executed through the wars the human king leads. The allusion to Melchizedek aids in the idealization inasmuch as it establishes the royal figure in a priestly office, grounds this separation for service in a divine decree, and claims that the appointment is "forever." These tantalizing hints, in conjunction with a "lord" enthroned at God's right hand, provide rich fodder for later interpreters, both in the New Testament book of Hebrews and at Qumran.[235]

b. Melchizedek at Qumran

The identity of Melchizedek in 11QMelchizedek (11Q13) is a much-mooted question. As we explore here, the figure is equated with God in numerous ways in the scroll, including having his name replace the Tetragrammaton in a citation of Isaiah 61:2.[236] For this reason, Melchizedek is often read as an angelic figure in this text, perhaps most regularly as the archangel Michael.[237] Without downplaying the humanity of Melchizedek, Fletcher-Louis makes the compelling case that he should not be regarded as entirely "suprahuman," but instead as a "divine human."[238] The most obvious piece of evidence for this view is the name Melchizedek itself, which points back to a human, if mysterious, priest in Genesis 14 and Psalm 110.[239] Fletcher-Louis also argues

232. Cf. Leslie C. Allen, *Psalms 101–150* (WBC 21; Waco, TX: Word, 1983), 84-85, 86.
233. Allen, *Psalms 101–150*, 84, 85.
234. Knohl, "Melchizedek," 257-58.
235. Cf. Kugel, *Traditions of the Bible*, 275-93.
236. Fletcher-Louis, *All the Glory of Adam*, 216.
237. This follows the early suggestions of A. S. van der Woude, "Melchisedech als himmlische Erlösergestalt in den neugefundenen eschatologischen Midraschim aus Qumran Höle XI," *OtSt* 14 (1965): 354-73; and J. T. Milik, "*Melkî-Ṣedeq et Melkî-Reša'* dans les anciens éscrits juifs et chrétiens (I)," *JJS* 23 (1972): 95-144.
238. Fletcher-Louis, *All the Glory of Adam*, 216-18.
239. Cf. David Flusser, "Melchizedek and the Son of Man," in *Judaism and the Origins of Christianity* (Jerusalem: Magnes, 1988), 186-92.

that the divine Melchizedek of 2 *Enoch* 71 has "weak maternal parentage," but is "nevertheless, *human* and the one who rightfully occupies the priestly office."[240] Finally, we find an exaltation of Melchizedek also in the New Testament book of Hebrews, where the biblical priest becomes a model for Jesus's own priesthood; however, the book is also adamant about Jesus's being greater than the angels.[241] In Hebrews, we see clearly the possibility of a "divine human" occupying a different, even higher place in the cosmic order than the angels. Such an approach makes best sense of the data of the scrolls as well: Melchizedek is a heavenly figure, but has not been dissociated with the human figure who appears in the biblical narrative — he is an exalted and idealized human figure.[242]

The scroll indicates that Melchizedek will proclaim the year of jubilee and will, himself, cause the return of people to their land (11Q13 II, 6). The proclamation of liberty (וקרא להמה דרור, line 6), particularly as an indication of what happens in the "first jubilee," appears to be an allusion to Isaiah 61:1 (לקרא לשבוים דרור). This possibility is heightened by another allusion to Isaiah 61 shortly after. In line 9 we see a paraphrase of Isaiah 61:2; however, instead of the "year of YHWH's favor" (שנת־רצון ליהוה), the Melchizedek scroll reads "year of Melchizedek's favor" (לשנת הרצון למלכי צדק). Whether Melchizedek is a glorified human figure or an angel, the displacement of YHWH in favor of this other figure is striking. The blending of the identities extends also to the armies, which seem to be both those of God and those of Melchizedek.[243]

The identification of Melchizedek with God is not accidental. The scroll states that he is the one about whom the psalm of David speaks (עליו בשירי דויד אשר אמר) when it says, "God will stand in the assembly of the gods, in the midst of the gods he judges" (Ps 82:1). God's role of judge is here ascribed to Melchizedek, as it is in the following passage cited, Psalm 7:8-9. That the writer of this scroll intends for Melchizedek, and not God himself, to occupy

240. Fletcher-Louis, *All the Glory of Adam*, 217 (italics original). See also Knohl, "Melchizedek," 260-61.

241. Fletcher-Louis, *All the Glory of Adam*, 217-18.

242. As I read this text, then, it is a peculiar but generally supportive piece of evidence that idealized human figures can occupy the place of God in sundry ways in early Jewish texts. However, for those who maintain an angelic reading (e.g., angel, otherworldly and eschatological priesthood), Melchizedek in 11Q13 offers evidence of an angelic figure who plays the role of God, even standing in for God in the interpretation of Isaiah 61:2. It thereby offers further evidence against the sort of exclusivist depiction of Jewish monotheism on which studies such as that by Bauckham is built, whether or not the particular alternative I am proposing for the Gospels is upheld by this particular scroll.

243. Carl Judson Davis, *The Name and Way of the Lord: Old Testament Themes, New Testament Christology* (JSNTSup 129; Sheffield: Sheffield Academic, 1996), 42.

this role of judge, is confirmed when he goes on to say, "Melchizedek will carry out the vengeance of Go[d's] judgments" (11Q13 II, 13).[244] This day of judgment is also the day of freedom for God's people, the fulfillment of the prophecy of Isaiah 52:7. It has also been argued that II, 23-24 interprets "your God" of Isaiah 52:7 as Melchizedek.[245] That prophecy indicates a coming messenger, whom the scroll identifies with the anointed prince of Daniel 9:25.

Paul Rainbow argues that the allusion to Daniel 9:25, as well as the allusion to Isaiah 61, tells of a human, messianic identity for Melchizedek since both passages speak of God's anointed.[246] Taking on the exalted language of divinity in the scroll, he maintains that the limits of human messiahship have not been breached: "Even granting the premise that 11QMelchizedek takes the 'God' of the Psalm quotations to be Melchizedek, the conclusion [that he is an angel such as Michael] would not follow. For in certain ceremonial contexts the human king of Israel too could be called 'God' (Ps 45:7 MT; cf. Isa 9:5) by virtue of his official exaltation to share in unique prerogatives of Yahweh (Ps 110:1; 1 Chr 28:5, 29:23)."[247] Based on the confluence of the subsequent descriptions of the activity of this anointed one with the previous discussion of Melchizedek, it appears that Melchizedek in this scroll plays the role of savior, conqueror on the cosmic stage, occupying the place of God in judgment and battle throughout the scroll. We do well to remember that such themes of conquest pervade Psalm 110, in which the promise of an eternal priesthood after Melchizedek's order is made. It may well be that the heavenly enthronement with which that psalm begins provides a framework for an exalted human to play the role of God as depicted in this scroll.[248]

Israel Knohl argues that the link between Melchizedek, whose name means "king of righteousness," and his identification with YHWH is Jeremiah 23:56. There, a messianic prophecy says that the shoot of David will be called by the name "YHWH is our righteousness."[249] When describing a messianic figure as Melchizedek, "king of righteousness," Jeremiah 23:56 opens the door for applying the Tetragrammaton in order to identify him with God as the shoot of David was said to be so identified.

In parallel with the exalted, heavenly human figures one finds in the Self-Glorification Hymn (see below) and other early Jewish literature, David

244. Martínez and Tigchelaar, *DSSSE*, 2:1207.
245. Cf. Davis, *Name and Way of the Lord*, 40.
246. Paul Rainbow, "Melchizedek as a Messiah at Qumran," *BBR* 7 (1997): 179-94, here 188-90.
247. Rainbow, "Melchizedek as Messiah," 182.
248. Rainbow, "Melchizedek as Messiah," 184, points out that only Genesis 14 and Psalm 110 were, as far as we know, available precursors for generating such reflection about Melchizedek.
249. Knohl, "Melchizedek," 261.

Flusser suggests that the "eschatological heavenly judge" of the Melchizedek scroll "is at the same time the biblical Melchizedek."[250] Like Fletcher-Louis, he contrasts his view, in particular, with the notion that the figure represents the archangel Michael. The both/and of an exalted, divine figure and human identity provides a startling portrait of an idealized figure who crosses the porous boundary between the one true God and other beings, but without any indication that the identity of God as such has been transformed or that Jewish monotheism has been given up.

Melchizedek may also appear in 4Q401, Songs of the Sabbath Sacrifice. Fragment 11, line 3, reads "[. . . Melchi]zedek, priest in the assem[bly of God]." The notion of heavenly assembly supports an exalted divine or even angelic figure; however, his role of priest is also maintained from the biblical tradition, underscoring the unity of the biblical character with at least some of his appearances at Qumran.

2. PRIESTS IN SIRACH

Sirach attests to the exaltation of priests in the Second Temple period. Aaron's glory is mostly attributed to his priestly vestments (45:7-8), through which he is said to be clothed with complete splendor (v. 8). Less restrained are the lines in praise of the high priest Simon, son of Onias, in chapter 50. The paean includes these lines: "How glorious he was, surrounded by the people, as he came out of the house of the curtain. Like the morning star among the clouds, like the full moon at the festal season; like the sun shining on the temple of the Most High, like the rainbow gleaming in splendid clouds. . . . When he put on his glorious robe and clothed himself in perfect splendor, when he went up to the holy altar, he made the court of the sanctuary glorious" (vv. 5-7, 11, NRSV).

The imagery is no less striking for being presented in a series of similes. The glory of Simon is described in terms evocative of other texts' descriptions of glorified humans or heavenly agents who shine like heavenly lights. The reference to morning stars may be evocative of those who were present at creation (cf. Job 38:7);[251] and the rainbow in the clouds appears to echo the divine appearance in Ezekiel 1:28. In verse 11 the splendor is attributed to the robe he wears and the language echoes that of 45:8.

---

250. Flusser, "Resurrection and Angels," 568. Knohl, "Melchizedek," 266, makes a similar connection between 11QMelchizedek and the Self-Glorification Hymn.

251. Cf. Barker, "High Priest," 101-2.

Perhaps the most striking dynamic of this depiction of Simon is that it is the priest himself, rather than God directly, whose glory makes the sanctuary glorious. This would appear to signal that Simon is, in some way, reflecting heavenly glory, analogous to the manner in which Moses reflected the divine glory after entering into the presence of God. And it may be reflective of the glory of Adam, who is described immediately before the introduction of Simon (49:16). In the Hebrew text, Adam is praised for a beauty (תפארת) above that of every living thing and in the subsequent verse Simon is praised as the greatest of the beauty (תפארת) of his people (50:1).[252]

Fletcher-Louis, following the earlier suggestion of Robert Hayward, develops the connections of Simon with both Adam and God in striking detail.[253] With a series of observations and arguments, he builds the case that the depiction of Simon is one in which the high priest plays the role of God in a dramatic telling and completing of the creation narrative through the temple liturgy.[254] In an extended argument, he shows how Sirach 24 and 50 both show evidence of knowing the sevenfold parallel between the P creation narrative in Genesis 1:1–2:4 and the giving of the law in Exodus 25–31. A sevenfold structure is suggested for Sirach 50, in which Simon plays the role of God in creation through his appearance and actions. Language of making firm the sanctuary echoes God's creation of the firmament and sealing off waters above from waters below on the second day of creation.[255] The third day of creation, with its establishment of dry land and holding back of the sea, finds its enactment in the creation of the bronze sea and preservation of the people against enemies (50:3-4).[256] With the conjunction of enemy subjugation and power over the waters, Simon acts "as the creator fulfilling the role of the divine warrior's restraint of the chaotic waters."[257] What Psalm 89 anticipates for a future Davidide, Sirach 50 ascribes to an idealized high priest. Simon himself then embodies the glory of the heavenly orbs in parallel with creation day four (50:5-8).[258] Here, the

252. Crispin H. T. Fletcher-Louis, "The Cosmology of P and Theological Anthropology in the Wisdom of Jesus ben Sira," in *Of Scribes and Sages: Early Jewish Interpretation and Transmission of Scripture*, vol. 1, *Ancient Versions and Traditions* (SSEJC 9/LSTS 50; ed. Craig A. Evans; New York: T&T Clark International, 2004), 69-113, here 95.

253. Fletcher-Louis, *All the Glory of Adam*, 74-75; C. T. R. Hayward, *The Jewish Temple: A Non-Biblical Sourcebook* (London: Routledge, 1996), 78-80.

254. Fletcher-Louis, *All the Glory of Adam*, 72-84.

255. Fletcher-Louis, "Cosmology of P," 97-100.

256. Fletcher-Louis, "Cosmology of P," 100-103.

257. Fletcher-Louis, "Cosmology of P," 102.

258. Fletcher-Louis, "Cosmology of P," 103-4.

correlation between divine glory and that of the heavenly host coalesces upon the priest. In describing Simon as "like the rainbow which appears in the cloud" (50:7b), the author applies the high priest Ezekiel's description of the likeness of YHWH's glory in Ezekiel 1:28: "like the bow in a cloud on a rainy day."[259] The high priest is glorifying the temple with God's glory. This is an embodiment of idealized humanity as theophany that I discussed above in relationship to Adam in the Priestly literature. The fifth unit (50:9-10) corresponds more directly to Exodus 30, the fifth speech in the giving of the law, than creation itself.

The creation of humanity as the embodiment of God and as co-rulers echoes through Sirach 50:11-13. In this portion, Simon moves out from the temple itself into the presence of the altar in the courtyard. The language of being clothed with glory insinuates divine likeness. Like Psalm 8 in its echoes of Genesis 1:26-28, Sirach 50:12 speaks of Simon being crowned.[260] Moreover, as noted above, it is Simon whose radiance makes the court of the sanctuary glorious. In this way he is standing in for God within the cosmos that is the temple, even as Adam stood in for God in original creation. Elsewhere, Fletcher-Louis cites and bolsters the case of Margaret Barker regarding one more way that Simon is playing the role of God as he enacts his temple service in the courtyard: he is playing the part of "the divine warrior coming out of his heavenly habitation."[261] Fletcher-Louis strengthens Barker's argument considerably by demonstrating how Sirach draws on biblical descriptions of Aaron playing the role of divine warrior, thus closing the gap between Simon's emergence from the temple and the scriptural precedent of God emerging from God's sanctuary.[262]

A seventh unit (50:14-21) evokes the completion of creation and Sabbath rest. Here, the mediating passage from Exodus 39–40 is important, as the completion of the tabernacle first recapitulated the completion of creation, and then Simon's completion of the temple work recapitulates both.[263] Both Moses and Simon bless the people upon the completion of the work as well. Thus, Fletcher-Louis concludes, "Just as Moses participates in God's 'being,' by virtue of his recapitulation of cosmic creativity and blessing, so also here Simon 'is beautified/boasts' in the Name of the LORD, which of course he both utters and wears on his turban."[264] Additionally, Simon, who has been identified

259. Fletcher-Louis, *All the Glory of Adam*, 72-73.
260. Fletcher-Louis, "Cosmology of P," 105-7.
261. Barker, "High Priest," 101-3; Fletcher-Louis, *All the Glory of Adam*, 81.
262. Fletcher-Louis, *All the Glory of Adam*, 81-83.
263. Fletcher-Louis, "Cosmology of P," 108-9.
264. Fletcher-Louis, "Cosmology of P," 109.

with Wisdom, comes to the end of the Tamid and the people pray, according to the Greek version, ἕως συντελεσθῇ κόσμος κυρίου καὶ τὴν λειτουργίαν αὐτοῦ ἐτελείωσαν ("until the order/cosmos of the Lord is completed, and his worship has been accomplished," 50:19). Hayward suggests that the Greek translator has here created an allusion to Genesis 2:1 LXX, which reads, καὶ συνετελέσθησαν ὁ οὐρανὸς καὶ ἡ γῆ καὶ πᾶς ὁ κόσμος αὐτῶν, and concludes that "we may understand that ben Sira's grandson looked on the Tamid as the final adornment of the world created by the universal and almighty king."[265]

In addition to what I have here presented in this focused discussion of Sirach 50, Robert Hayward has demonstrated that the praise of Wisdom found in Sirach 24 is the source of much of the language used to describe Simon in Sirach 50 (e.g., cedar in Lebanon, 24:13; 50:12; cypress, 24:13; 50:10; olive tree, 24:14; 50:10).[266] Wisdom itself has been depicted in terms that echo the Priestly creation narrative and the giving of the law in Exodus. In this way Sirach depicts Wisdom as an agent in creation. By recapitulating that language and structure in the description of Simon, the book provides even stronger indications that the high priest "actualizes the presence of wisdom,"[267] and thus of God as well.

In Sirach 50 we see an idealized human figure in the strong sense: the high priest Simon plays the role of God in a dramatic scene in which God's work is the work of creation. Moreover, Simon plays the role of God as creator, a function that clearly separates the divine from the human, a role that Bauckham singles out as one that no person can share in and that thus distinguishes the one God absolutely from all creatures. At the same time, however, the uniqueness of God is maintained. Playing God's role in this dramatic reenactment is not a blasphemous encroachment on the divine prerogative of creation because, presumably, God is the one who has established the temple as microcosm and assigned the role of creation completion to the high priest. God is the one who not only shares God's glory with the human agent, but also cedes the role of creator in the dramatic enactment of creation that unfolds. As Fletcher-Louis puts it, "the high priest not only embodies Wisdom, he also acts as co-creator in as much as the temple service is itself symmetrical with God's (original) creative action."[268]

<hr/>

265. Hayward, *Jewish Temple*, 79.
266. C. T. R. Hayward, "Sacrifice and World Order: Some Observations on Ben Sira's Attitude to the Temple Service," in *Sacrifice and Redemption* (ed. Stephen W. Sykes; New York: Cambridge University Press, 1991), 22-34.
267. Fletcher-Louis, *All the Glory of Adam*, 74.
268. Fletcher-Louis, *All the Glory of Adam*, 75. He goes on to strengthen the notion of

Simon is an idealized human figure both in the sense of his being depicted as the quintessential high priest, and in the sense of his being described with ascriptions, actions, and attributes that are otherwise reserved for God alone. Fletcher-Louis even suggests that the people bow down and worship before the priest as the bearer of the divine name (Sir 50:21).[269] In Sirach 50 we thus see another way that a type of idealized human figure, in this case a priest, can play roles otherwise reserved for God alone. "Simon, the ideal high priest, imitates the creator in following in all its essential details the order of creation. And yet, simultaneously, as a creature — as the true human being — he embodies the perfect order of creation, the sun, the moon, and stars, and panoply of nature in all its beauty and creative energy."[270]

3. TESTAMENT OF LEVI

The eighteenth chapter of the *Testament of Levi* anticipates an eschatological, idealized priest. With a likely allusion to the prophecy of Numbers 24:17, we read, "And his star shall rise in heaven like a king, kindling the light of knowledge as day is illuminated by the sun" (v. 3).[271] The imagery of light continues in verse 4 as he is described as shining like the sun, taking away darkness from all the places under heaven. Numerous biblical traditions appear to be reflected here, including Moses's reflection of the glory light of God (Exod 34:29-35) and Zion's shining with the advent of God in Third Isaiah (60:1). The light that people see is God's own glory, but as reflected in an earthly agent. The effects of this priest's rule not only flow "downward," bringing peace and joy to the earth, but also "upward," causing the heavens to rejoice and making glad the angels of the presence (*T. Lev.* 18:5).

There is no doubt that the *Testament of Levi* has received some editing at Christian hands (e.g., 16:3-5), and so it may be with 18:6-7 as well. The scene depicted is one of heavenly anointing and sanctification, and the means by which the eschatological priest receives his share in the divine glory: "The heavens will be opened, and from the temple of glory sanctification will come

---

Simon's participation in creation by demonstrating that Sirach is aware of an intertextual relationship between Genesis 1 and Exodus 25–31, and builds on this in its description of Wisdom and then Simon.

269. Fletcher-Louis, "Cosmology of P," 109.

270. Fletcher-Louis, "Cosmology of P," 112.

271. The translation is that of H. C. Kee, *The Old Testament Pseudepigrapha*, vol. 1, *Apocalyptic Literature and Testaments* (ed. James H. Charlesworth; New York: Doubleday, 1983).

upon him, with a fatherly voice, as from Abraham to Isaac. And the glory of the Most High shall burst forth upon him. And the spirit of understanding and sanctification shall rest upon him [in the water]." This priest receives his sanctifying (anointing?) from the heavenly sanctuary, and appears to serve in his capacity as one who is son of God. The notion that the eschatological agent is to God as Isaac is to Abraham is one that I discuss as a crucial component of the Synoptic Gospels' son of God Christology; in their case, it implies the coming death of Jesus.[272] Importantly, the *Testament of Levi*'s priest bears the divine glory not only for his own exaltation but also in order to bestow God's majesty upon his own sons — priests, perhaps, but the verse insists that there will be no successors (18:8).

This eschatological priest opens the way for humanity's return to its protological state, disarming the guardian of Eden and opening its gates so that the holy ones might eat the fruit of the tree of life (18:10). This eschatological restoration includes both the priest and the people exercising dominion over demonic enemies: "And Beliar shall be bound by him, and he shall grant to his children the authority to trample on wicked spirits" (18:12). The binding of Beliar is an exercise of dominion that would most commonly be associated with angelic or divine forces; yet here the power and authority for such a conquest is embodied in a human, priestly agent, and extended to his "children."

As I indicated above, the *Testament of Levi* bears some marks of Christian redaction. Chapter 18 itself might well echo, rather than anticipate, an Abrahamic designation of Jesus as God's son at his baptism with the reception of God's spirit, as well as the notion of binding Satan and extending power over Satan's minions to the idealized agent's people. If so, it is all the more striking, in light of early Christian developments of divine Christologies, that the *Testament of Levi* 18 articulates these expectations as befalling a human priest-king, with no hint of preexistence or ontological divinity.

4. JUBILEES

Isaac's blessing of Levi in *Jubilees* 31 demonstrates a theology of priestly sanctification analogous to what we find in the *Testament of Levi*. The blessing reads in part, "May he draw you and your seed near to him from all flesh

272. See Leroy A. Huizenga, *The New Isaac: Tradition and Intertextuality in the Gospel of Matthew* (SupNovT 131; Leiden: Brill, 2009).

to serve in his sanctuary as the angels of the presence and the holy ones. May your sons' seed be like them with respect to honor and greatness and sanctification" (*Jub.* 31:14).[273] From the *Testament of Levi* 3:3-8 we learn that the angels of the presence are immediately in the presence of God, offering sacrifices in the heavenly holy of holies, apparently also sitting upon thrones and offering praises, while another, lower rank of angels mediates answers to them. This helps fill in the picture of the glorious function being played by idealized priestly figures in *Jubilees*. The priests perform on earth the functions that the angels of the presence perform in heaven. This includes the implied function of rule, as the blessing of Levi goes on to promise that Levi's descendants will become "judges and rulers for all of the seed of the sons of Jacob" (*Jub.* 31:15). This priestly exaltation is well labeled an "angelomorphic" exaltation, inasmuch as the human figures are offered participation in angelic status. Moreover, the priestly concerns of *Jubilees* do not shape the Adam and Eve narrative such that the role of priest as such can be seen as a recapturing of a primeval human vocation. This particular idealization, like the vast majority of others this chapter attends to, is not, however, an ontological transformation of the priests into angelic beings, or otherwise a divinization in the strict sense. If there is any ontological transformation, as Fletcher-Louis suggests, it is a transformation into humans who, like Moses before them, bear the divine glory.[274] Particular human agents share in the role and function of a heavenly counterpart. The priests play the role on earth that is played by the angels of the presence in heaven. Such a parallelism paves the way for more exalted depictions of priestly and perhaps royal figures entering into the heavenly sanctuary itself, standing among the angels of the presence as exalted and thereby idealized humans.

5. PRIESTS AT QUMRAN

It is well known that the eschatological expectations of the Qumran community included an Aaronic high priest in addition to a royal messiah (1QS IX, 11; CD XII, 23; XX, 1; 1QSa II, 11-22). The Rule of the Congregation (1QSa) provides strong indications that the high priestly figure is of higher rank in the community than the messiah (1QSa II, 11-22). What follows is a discussion

273. Translations from *Jubilees* are all from O. S. Wintermute, "Jubilees," in *Expansions of the "Old Testament" and Legends*.
274. Fletcher-Louis, *All the Glory of Adam*, 16.

of texts in which such a figure might be depicted in idealized categories that signal his close proximity to the divine.[275]

a. 1QRule of Benedictions (1Q28b)

A priest receives a blessing in 1QSb that idealizes his role as one in which he occupies both sides of the heaven-earth divide. First, it is hoped that the priest will be able to enter into the very presence of God, "like an angel of the face" (פנים כמלאך, 1Q28b IV, 25), much like the expectation of *Jubilees,* discussed above. Union with the angelic host is actualized in the priest's service in the temple, as he identifies with both the angels who dwell immediately in God's presence and the council of the community. The blessing anticipates a priest who will shine with a heavenly light, and whose face illuminates the congregation (1Q28b IV, 27). There are obvious connections here with Moses's shining face as a result from his meetings with God. But whereas Moses covered his face, the purpose of the Qumran priest's luminous glory is to shine the light of God on the people. This is a striking transformation of the Aaronic benediction, where the blessing offered is that YHWH will make his own face shine on the people (Num 6:23-27). The priest is standing in the place of Israel's God as the source of luminous glory that illuminates the faces of those who come into his presence. Moreover, the exalted status of this figure is such that he brings glory to God (lines 25, 28). The priest is angel-like in his access to the divine presence, and God-like in his mediation of that presence back to the community. The scroll reworks Israel's tradition about God so that it applies to a human. Such a reworking happens without any indication that the priest is in any sense divine. The priest is like an angel, to be sure, but still fully human.

b. Songs of the Sabbath Sacrifice (4Q400)

Analogous to what we saw above with respect to 1Q28b, Songs of the Sabbath Sacrifice (4Q400) speaks of the priests serving in the inner sanctuary as though they are swept up into the eternal throne room of God itself and thus made members of the divine retinue. The "most holy ones," that is, the priests, are among (perhaps established among) "the eternal holy ones," (1 I, 3). This entrance into the assembly of all the gods (כול אלי) enables humans to know

275. See Joseph L. Angel, *Otherworldly and Eschatological Priesthood in the Dead Sea Scrolls* (STDJ 86; Leiden: Brill, 2010).

the wisdom that flows from God's glory (1 I, 6).[276] The imagery of the temple, depicting an entrance into the divine throne room, is literalized in this text such that the priests are envisioned as ascending into the heavenly throne room itself through their temple service. Their exaltation to God's presence, in turn, accounts for Israel's possession of the wisdom of God. Moreover, as God's agents they not only guard the sanctity of the temple but also become the agents through whom the holy people are sanctified as well (1 I, 15).

c. 4QInstruction[d] (4Q418)

At one point in 4QInstruction[d] (4Q418) an individual is described who may be either a king, high priest, or other ruler of the people (frag. 81). Crispin Fletcher-Louis argues that the figure is a priest, and draws attention to the way that Numbers 18:20 is applied to the addressee in the scroll.[277] The Numbers text reads, "Then the LORD said to Aaron . . . I am your portion and your inheritance among the sons of Israel" (אני חלקך ונחלתך בתוך בני ישראל). The scroll, in turn, says, "he is your portion and your inheritance among the sons of Adam" (והוא חלקכה ונחלתכה בתוך בני אדם, line 3).[278] The instruction employs language of temple and tabernacle when it calls the addressee a "holy of holies [over all] the earth" (line 4).[279] The phrase "holy of holies," which in the scroll is written לקדוש קודשים, is evocative of the phrase that in the Hebrew Bible can refer not only to the holiest place within the temple or tabernacle (e.g., Exod 26:33; 1 Kgs 6:16; 2 Chr 4:22; Ezek 41:4), in which case the definite article is typically employed (קדש הקדשים), but also the sanctified implements associated with the temple such as the altar and the incense altar (e.g., Exod 29:37; 30:10), in which case the definite article is not used. An additional consideration, however, when discerning the implications of

276. The confluence of human and angelic priests in this scroll makes confusing who is under discussion at various junctures and underscores the exalted nature to which human priests attain in the estimation of the author of this scroll. Cf. Angel, *Otherworldly and Eschatological Priesthood*, 87-97. He calls humanity's approximation of the angelic a "semblance of ontological participation" (97).

277. Fletcher-Louis, *All the Glory of Adam*, 176-87. Torleif Elgvin, "Priestly Sages? The Milieus of Origin of 4QMysteries and 4QInstruction," in *Sapiential Perspectives: Wisdom Literature in Light of the Dead Sea Scrolls* (STDJ 51; ed. J. J. Collins and G. Sterling; Leiden: Brill, 2004), 67-87, argues conversely that the priestly language is applied to someone as a description of the benefits of his elect status. The precise rubric for interpreting the addressee's status is not as important for my argument as the benefits of that status as described by the scroll.

278. Fletcher-Louis, *All the Glory of Adam*, 178.

279. Martínez and Tigchelaar, *DSSSE*, 2:871.

this ascription is that the following and apparently parallel phrase reads, "and among the [g]o[ds] he has cast your lot" (lines 4-5). The connotations of the holy of holies as a place where a person enters into the place where God dwells appears to be shaping the imagery. As the "most holy one over all the earth," this person's (likely, priest's) place straddles the human and divine spheres. This is an inflating and transformation of the role played by priests in the biblical texts, whose job it was to enter into the most holy place, where God was enthroned above the cherubim, once a year. In the instructional scroll, the priest himself is designated most holy, and appears to have more regular concourse with heavenly beings. It is in this light that line 1 should be interpreted: "your lips he has opened, a spring to bless the holy ones" (לברך קדשים) (*DSSE*). Though Fletcher-Louis argues for a reference, here, to the sanctified community in general, the language of holy ones more often applies to angelic beings in the scrolls and such a heavenly referent coheres better with the lot among the gods that the scroll goes on to describe in lines 4-5.[280]

The exaltation of the addressee in this fragment of 4Q418 includes being set up as God's firstborn and having his glory exceedingly multiplied (line 5). We have seen above that the imagery of glory adheres to conceptions of idealized human figures in Qumran, including both Adam and the eschatological people of Israel (1QS IV). The language of firstborn might apply to Adam, or it might instead be picking up the descriptions of Israel as God's firstborn (e.g., Exod 4:23; *Jub.* 2:20 = 4Q216 VII, 11) or the Levites as the redemption price of Israel's own firstborn (Num 3:12-13).

In light of all we have seen thus far, not only in the Qumran scrolls but on the broader canvas of early Judaism, and in light also of how vague language pointing toward divinity is sometimes deployed in New Testament scholarship, I want to be circumspect in delineating what it might mean to say, in Fletcher-Louis's language, that we see here a "transcendent ontology."[281] The notion of glorification and even the ability to stand in the divine presence and among the heavenly retinue certainly signal participation in divine traits and entry into divine spaces. But what, precisely, is the ontological claim for this "real priest," as Fletcher-Louis calls him? The language used echoes that employed to speak of idealized humanity in 1QS; the depictions of the actions entailed are an expansion on the role enacted by the priest who would enter the divine

280. Fletcher-Louis, *All the Glory of Adam*, 177-79. The possibility that there is also royal language throughout the scroll (Angel, *Otherworldly and Eschatological Priesthood*, 67-68) does not detract from the priesthood thesis, inasmuch as priests are sometimes depicted as royal rulers as well.

281. Fletcher-Louis, *All the Glory of Adam*, 177.

presence by entering the holy of holies. The priestly figure perhaps becomes the meeting place (holy of holies) between humanity and divine. In all these things, the exaltation of the figure is firmly within the realm of human ontology; however, it is a glorified human ontology that recalls the lost splendor of the first parent, a splendor that makes its appearance at times in Israel's story, such as when it is reflected on the face of Moses. If this is what is meant by "transcendent ontology," then the phrase is not objectionable. But we must also bear in mind that such priestly humans bear "transcendent ontology" when we come to the New Testament and attempt to sort out the significance of such depictions of Jesus.

The early lines of the fragment speak of the addressee blessing the holy ones (line 1) and receiving an inheritance among the sons of Adam (line 3). These themes recur in lines 11-14: "Before you take your inheritance from his hand, honour his holy ones, and be[fore . . .] begin [with] a song (for) all the holy ones. And everyone who is called by his name (will be) holy [. . .] during all times his splendour, his beauty for the eter[nal] plantation [. . .] . . . world. In it will walk all who inherit the earth" (4Q418 81, 11-14).[282] If I am correct and "holy ones" refers to the angelic host rather than the community itself, then the instructions indicate either that the angels receive a song of worship or that the person sings to God for the sake of, and perhaps to lead, the angelic beings.[283] In either case, the bleeding of the human and divine realms works both ways, as the human figure participates in some sort of heavenly chorus, and the holiness that marks the holy ones finds additional resting space upon all those who are called by the divine name. The glory that is bestowed upon the addressee appears to be the divine splendor that is given to all the members of the community God has established.

As the instructions unfold, the role played by this figure is more and more shown to be a priestly role, whether or not that role is being democratized to some degree. The person is bestowed with "priestly" benefits, and the benefits entail an exalted position in the presence of divine beings for some human, thus signaling a peculiar level of exaltation of one person. This exaltation is not an ontological transformation into something superhuman, but an idealizing glorification of a human who is allowed to transgress the supposed boundaries of humanity and the divine host. Summarizing the similarities between 4QInstruction and the Hodayot, Matthew Goff comments, "In different ways the two texts describe the elect as a symbolic re-establishment of the prelapsarian

---

282. Martínez and Tigchelaar, *DSSSE*, 2:873.
283. Cf. Angel, *Otherworldly and Eschatological Priesthood,* 73-76.

bliss enjoyed in the garden of Eden. Both also relate the elect to the angels."[284] In fragment 81 in particular this conjunction is seen, as an idealized human figure plays a role among the gods, glorified with the glory of God's firstborn son.

d. Self-Glorification Hymn (4Q471b, 4Q491c)

It is uncertain what role in the community is played by the singer of the Self-Glorification Hymn (4Q471b, 4Q491c; cf. 4Q427).[285] More certain, however, is the identification of the person, in the words of Esther Eshel, as "a human being, seated in heaven, and sharing the lot of the angels."[286] In a short essay exploring the similarities between this figure, angels, and early Christology, David Flusser continually refers to his state as "deified."[287] The terminology is not defended, and I would say that "glorified" is a more accurate label. There is a sense in which "deification" may be accurate, but if this piece is consistent with the glorification anthropology of Qumran, then that sense is derivative: the figure is more like God because God's glory was imparted to first humanity, and the destiny of idealized humanity is "all the glory of Adam" and a transcending of the thin veil between "the house of Israel/the holy ones on earth" and "the angels [who are] the holy ones above, in heaven."[288] Flusser helpfully suggests that such heavenly exaltation must be reckoned with as a notion of exaltation that precedes the historical Jesus in its appearance in early Jewish literature, opening up new avenues for understanding the possibilities that were available within Judaism itself to express the earliest Christologies of Christian communities.

The text indicates that the singer is not the king himself, but instead "friend of the king," and thus "companion of the holy one(s)" (4Q471b 1-3, 7; cf. 4Q421 7 I, 10-12).[289] This exalted status garners for the singer a place of greater ex-

284. Matthew Goff, "Reading Wisdom at Qumran: 4QInstruction and the Hodayot," *DSD* 11 (2004): 263-88, here 264.

285. However, the role of "eschatological priest" carries a great deal of merit. Cf. Esther Eshel, "4Q471B: A Self-Glorification Hymn," *RevQ* 17 (1996): 175-203. For a discussion of the speaker's identity, see Angel, *Otherworldly and Eschatological Priesthood*, 137-41.

286. Eshel, "4Q471B," 189. Eshel's article also helpfully contravenes an earlier suggestion that the speaker is an angel.

287. David Flusser, "Resurrection and Angels in Rabbinic Judaism, Early Christianity, and Qumran," in *The Dead Sea Scrolls Fifty Years after Their Discovery* (ed. L. H. Schiffman et al.; Jerusalem: Israel Exploration Society, 2000), 568-72.

288. Flusser, "Resurrection and Angels," 569.

289. Eshel, "4Q471B," 182, suggests that the king in view here is God, not a human king; however, the idealized human framework that I propose calls such a conclusion into question. A divine king is not necessary to articulate such an exalted place for the king's friend.

altation than the angels: "who is like me among the angels?" (4Q471b 5; cf. 4Q421 7 I, 11-12).[290] Eshel suggests that the phraseology is derived from Exodus 15:11, "Who is like you, LORD, among the angels?" but changed to refer to the speaker rather than God.[291] If so, then we have here a striking example of a phenomenon seen a couple of times already in this study and evident also in the Gospels, where references to an idealized human figure replace references to God in a biblical citation or allusion.

This place of glory and exaltation seems tied to the role of the singer in giving instruction (4Q471b 4). Moreover, to be so exalted is to both take a seat in the divine assembly (4Q491c) and to be enthroned above the "kings of the East" (4Q491c 1, 5). And because of this exalted status, the singer possesses an incomparable glory (4Q491c 1, 8; cf. 4Q421 7 I, 11). This fits with the pattern for which I am arguing here that the roles assigned to humanity indicate that they are more exalted than the heavenly beings not because they are somehow heavenly creatures but precisely because they are humans given a task that is greater than the tasks assigned to the heavenly retinue. Eshel also points out that such a notion of glorification is condemned in other Jewish literature: the king of Babylon's boast in Isaiah 14:13-14 and Antiochus IV Epiphanes's self-aggrandizement in 2 Maccabees 9:8-10, but that the singer of the Qumran hymn is in no way castigated for his claims but rather embodies them in his exalted state.[292]

Here we have an example of the importance of attending to the particular texts that demonstrate possibilities within Judaism that other texts might create strong presuppositions against. The theological anthropologies of the sorts laid out above in conversation with the creation narratives of Genesis 1–2 provide handholds for those who want to depict God working in and through a person in a way that transcends the normal course of human affairs. Humans entrusted with God's instruction are envisioned as heavenly beings without in any way exploding the limits of their humanness: they are glorious and enthroned in the heavens because God has exalted them above the gods and above the kings of the earth.[293] If this is so for the king's companion, how much more should we not expect early Jews to say such things about the messiah himself if they believed that such a messiah had come and been exalted to God's right hand?

290. Eshel, "4Q471B," points out that the scrolls use אלים only for angels, and not for God.
291. Eshel, "4Q471B," 180.
292. Eshel, "4Q471B," 195.
293. Angel, *Otherworldly and Eschatological Priesthood*, 142-46, makes a strong case for this figure being a present figure rather than one anticipated in the future.

e. 4QApocryphon of Levi (4Q540-41)

The depiction of the eschatological, human high priest in 4Q541 describes his work in terms of a teacher,[294] yet one whose work is also reminiscent of creation. Fletcher-Louis summarizes the description of the priest and his work in terms that fit well with my category of idealized human figure. He refers to the song's subject as "a priest with a heavenly and cosmic identity."[295] He continues: "That he is a priest is certain because he makes expiation in line 2. There is no doubt that this is a *human* priest because the phrase 'for all the sons of his generation' and the language of suffering is hardly appropriate for a priestly angel."[296]

The description of this priest's work in fragment 9 takes on cosmogonic overtones: "His word is like the word of the heavens, and his teaching, according to the will of God. His eternal sun will shine and its fire will burn in all the ends of the earth; above the darkness it will shine. Then, darkness will vanish [fr]om the earth, and gloom from the dry land" (4Q541 9 I, 3-5).[297] Genesis 1 echoes in the imagery of a heavenly word and the appearance of sunlight that lights the whole earth, and in the language of "dry land" (יבישתא, line 5; cf. יבשה in Gen 1:9). Without suggesting that the high priest is co-creator in the beginning, he "recapitulates God's creative work," in a manner akin to what we see in Sirach 50.[298] Across a broad spectrum of Jewish traditions, God alone creates the world and therefore has sovereign authority over it. In these depictions of idealized high priests, we see a striking example of the assignment of God's unique prerogative to a human. The priest is identified with God through his recapitulation of God's role in creation; moreover, this comes without any indication that the priest is being identified as God or as some other divine being.

f. Replacing YHWH in Biblical Citations

In New Testament studies on early Christology, much is sometimes made of the fact that biblical passages that originally spoke of YHWH are, in their New Testament context, applied to Jesus (e.g., Joel 2:32 in Acts 2:21; Rom 10:13). The argument is that such an application entails an identification of Jesus with Israel's God that recognizes them as, in some sense, one and the same. However,

---

294. Collins, *Scepter and the Star*, 127.
295. Fletcher-Louis, *All the Glory of Adam*, 190.
296. Fletcher-Louis, *All the Glory of Adam*, 190 (italics original).
297. Martínez and Tigchelaar, *DSSSE*, 2:1081.
298. Fletcher-Louis, *All the Glory of Adam*, 191.

there are at least two instances of biblical citation in the extant scrolls from Qumran, in addition to 4Q471b and 11QMelchizedek discussed above, in which a biblical text referring to YHWH has been reinterpreted as referring to a priest. In 1QpHab, the commentary on Habukkuk 2:4b (וצדיק באמונתו יחיה) shifts the object of faith(fulness) from God to the Teacher of Righteousness.[299] The comment reads, "Its interpretation concerns all observing the Law in the House of Judah, whom God will free from the house of judgment on account of their toil and of their loyalty to the Teacher of Righteousness" (ואמנתם במורה הצדק, 1QpHab VIII, 1-3).[300] Here, the switch from God to the Teacher of Righteousness is conceptual; which is to say, there is not a name or title of God that is identified with the Teacher, but the implied object of fidelity has been shifted. Nonetheless, in a manner somewhat akin to what we see with Matthew's Jesus in the Sermon on the Mount, the standard for righteousness has been shifted from God's word spoken to Moses directly in the Torah to an interpreter of that law — the person himself no less than the words he teaches.

A more direct replacement of YHWH by a priestly figure is found in 4Q167, in its commentary on Hosea 5:14: "For I will be like a lio[n to E]ph[ra]im [and like a lion cub to the House of Judah. Its interpretation con]cerns the last priest who will stretch out his hand to strike Ephraim" (4Q167 frag. 2, 2).[301] Hosea 5 presents a string of judgments spoken by YHWH in the first person. The interpretation here thus applies to the "last priest" in a verse that originally speaks of YHWH stretching out his hand.[302] For this one aspect of the judgments pronounced by God in Hosea 5, the writer of the scroll depicts the last priest as an eschatological agent who plays the role that the biblical *Vorlage* reserved for God himself. Such human agency in an eschatological scenario, in which God's actions are deployed through human agents who are identified with God, recurs in the War Scroll as well (see below).

6. CONCLUSIONS: PRIESTS AND THE PRESENCE OF GOD

Summing up his study of priestly figures, Fletcher-Louis writes, "Texts such as Sirach 50, *Aristeas* 99 and Jubilees 31:14 all testify to the widespread opinion

299. Davis, *Name and Way of the Lord*, 47-48; following Maurice Casey, "Chronology and the Development of Pauline Christology," in *Paul and Paulinism: Essays in Honour of C. K. Barrett* (ed. M. D. Hooker and S. G. Wilson; London: SPCK, 1982), 124-34, here 128.

300. Martínez and Tigchelaar, *DSSSE*, 1:17.

301. Martínez and Tigchelaar, *DSSSE*, 1:333.

302. Davis, *Name and Way of the Lord*, 47-48.

that Israel's serving priest — not some eschatological future redeemer — is glorious, heavenly and the bearer of God's creative power and presence within history."[303] His own work has tended toward acknowledging an ontological transformation of the priests in some works. I have found instead that the exaltation of priests as "bearers of God's creative power and presence within history" is an idealization and glorification of human figures without loss of their true humanity. Exalted human priests bear in themselves the glory of God, pass this on to others, reenact God's work of creation through their priestly service, slide between the divine and human realms, participate in the worship offered in each, embody the creative wisdom of God, and have applied to them scriptures that originally spoke of YHWH. Idealized priests provide another lens through which to see that early Jewish monotheism plays little role in limiting how Jewish writers can depict (human) figures whom they or their communities recognize as being specially endowed for some task or function. Indeed, an opposite inclination seems to be at work: it is precisely through depicting some human figure through ascriptions, actions, or attributes otherwise indicative of the identity of God that early Jewish writers signal that God has given these humans crucial roles to play in the past, present, or idealized future.

E. THE SON OF MAN

1. ONE LIKE A HUMAN BEING IN DANIEL

Perhaps no idealized human figure in early Judaism is more directly apropos for the study of Jesus in the Synoptic Gospels than the "one like a son of a human" (כבר אנש) in Daniel 7. I make two important arguments about this passage. First, at the level of its imagery, Daniel 7 leans on anti-creation/restored creation imagery. Within this framework, rightly ordered creation is a world in which humans rule the beasts rather than vice versa. Second, at the level of the vision's meaning I argue that the text as we have it tells of Israelite exaltation over the nations rather than the exaltation of Israel's angelic deliverer. With such a reading in place, Daniel 7 is the vision of an idealized human figure, with the literal humans of which it speaks being the corporate people of God.

---

303. Fletcher-Louis, *All the Glory of Adam*, 192.

a. An Anti-creation Narrative

Turning to the imagery of Daniel's vision, a good deal of its horror depends on its depiction of creation gone awry. This is reflected both in the mixing of types of animal creatures and, more specifically, in the ways that the beasts are acting like humans. As to the first point, John Goldingay comments, "The portrayal of the nations as hybrids, which transgress nature's laws and threaten nature's harmony, and as predators who are as such unclean, has part of its background in the Torah's categorization of the animal world and its concern with preserving distinctions between the species."[304] This categorization and distinction between species, largely the concern of the Priestly writer, finds its first articulation in the Priestly creation narrative. There, the commands and the results of the heavenly voice are for a world in which plants, trees, fruit, and seed (Gen 1:11-12); sea animals, swarming things, and birds (Gen 1:21); livestock, creeping things, and wild beasts (Gen 1:24-25) are all created "according to [their] kinds" (לְמִין).

The significance of these discrete "kinds" is found both in their participation in the general theme of dividing unlike things that runs through Genesis 1, and in the later distinctions between clean and unclean animals. The latter are regularly recognizable through their transgression of the established kinds. Chewing cud must always go with split hooves, or else the animal is unclean (Lev 11:3-8). Sea creatures must have both fins and scales (Lev 11:9-12). The unclean sea creatures are those whose bodies are admixtures of land animal and sea animal.[305] Mary Douglas has demonstrated that a vital aspect of holiness was "keeping distinct the categories of creation."[306] Seeds should not be mixed in the field, and cattle should only be allowed to breed with their own kind (Lev 19:19). In establishing her case for a holistic understanding of the taboos of Jewish cleanliness law, Douglas notes of the biblical precepts that "observing them draws down prosperity, infringing them brings danger. We are thus entitled to treat them in the same way as we treat primitive ritual avoidances whose breach unleashes danger to men."[307] In Daniel, the mixed nature of the beasts is itself a symbol of a dangerous disintegration of created order, as the first three beasts in particular mix animal and bird kind. Further distancing these beasts from a whole and safe world, these land-bird admixtures arise

304. John E. Goldingay, *Daniel* (WBC 30; Dallas: Word, 1989), 149.
305. Cf. Mary Douglas, *Purity and Danger: An Analysis of the Concepts of Pollution and Taboo* (New York: Routledge, 1966), 55-57.
306. Douglas, *Purity and Danger*, 54-55.
307. Douglas, *Purity and Danger*, 51.

from the sea, so that the sea is not giving rise to sea creatures but to animals of land and air. The sea itself, of course, plays its role of chaotic enemy whose ways must be overcome if Israel's God, and thus God's people, are going to flourish. In describing Daniel 7 as an anti-creation narrative, we can see how at the level of the symbolism of the vision the creatures are sources of danger by the mere fact of their existence. They are fantastic violations of the laws of animal kinds and thus of the holiness that preserves Israel and promises it prosperity. Israel is not directly responsible for the intermingling of animal kinds in the grotesque beasts that rule the world, but they are nonetheless victims of the danger that ensues (vv. 21, 25).

Once we have noticed the anti-creation dynamics of the intermingled animal-kind beasts that populate Daniel's vision, we are poised to recognize one more way in which the vision trades on a dissolution of creation's order, particularly as established in Genesis 1. Not only are the beasts composed of various animal kinds, but they also take on human likeness. This might provide the most terrifying dynamic of the vision. The lion with eagle's wings "was lifted up from the ground and made to stand on two feet like a human being; and a human mind was given to it" (Dan 7:4, NRSV). The fourth beast, which appears to be much of human making with its iron teeth and bronze claws, has "eyes like human eyes" in one of its horns (v. 8, NRSV). Once we recognize that the vision's thematic traction is found in its anti-creation motifs, we can then see that the leopard being given dominion (v. 6) is also a description of a beast who acts like a human being. At the level of the vision, as will be clarified in its interpretation, this is the epitome of the problem that the Ancient One solves: beasts are acting like humans by ruling over the earth. By exercising dominion over the world on God's behalf, beasts are playing the role that humans were created to play, thus making their usurpation of humanity's place the culminating horror of the vision. This bestial usurpation of human vicegerency, then, provides the matrix within which the climactic scene finds its purchase: one who is like a human being comes onto the scene and is given humanity's rightful place as agent who rules the world on God's behalf. God takes away the dominion of the beasts (v. 12) in order to give dominion into the hands of one like a human being (vv. 13-14). In the vision itself, the arrival of one like a human being is the arrival of God's agent whom God establishes as the ruler over the world on God's behalf.

The specific ways in which, I have argued, the dynamics of Genesis 1 are undone and then reestablished in the vision sequence of Daniel 7 affirm the more general suggestion that Daniel 7 is best understood when read against the background of ancient Near Eastern *Chaoskampf* stories and their representations across the Hebrew Bible.[308] As I discussed above, Genesis 1 draws on such depictions of God defeating enemies of chaos, including not least the watery depths. The Bible's first creation story is a particularization of these themes, shared broadly across ancient Near Eastern literature. By depicting an anti-creation vision that draws on and exploits the ideals of Genesis 1 (cf. Psalm 8), Daniel 7 also deploys themes that have a broader range of resonance with similarly themed depictions of God's creative work.

b. The Humanlike Figure as God's Faithful People

Within the vision itself, the humanlike being plays the part of idealized human figure. Like the first humans created in Genesis 1:26-28, this being is given dominion by God, even over what remains of the beasts and their realms. The likely implication of the setting up of thrones (plural) before the entrance of the Ancient One in 7:9 is that one like a son of humanity will be enthroned next to God. At the level of the vision (leaving aside for the moment the question of its interpretation), the humanlike being is given a reign appropriate to a human, as his kingship is over the inhabited earth (peoples, nations, languages, v. 14, NRSV). The question that we must now turn to is whether, in the interpretation of the vision, the one like a son of a human represents an angelic being or human beings (specifically, the people of Israel).[309]

At first blush, the argument for human beings appears to be the clear implication of the text. The vision is interpreted twice (vv. 17-18, 23-27). In the first interpretation, the beasts are interpreted as kings who "arise out of the earth" (v. 17). Here, "king" appears to function as a metonymy for "kingdom." Be that as it may, the real-life parallel to what Daniel sees in his dream is kingship that plays out within the human realm as these powers "arise out of the earth." In other words, these particular beasts do not represent spiritual powers that lie behind the earthly reality, but represent the earthly reality itself. Thus, when the one like a son of a human is interpreted, a parallel reality would presumably be in view: "But the holy ones of the Most High shall receive the kingdom

308. So, e.g., Goldingay, *Daniel*, 149-50.

309. I interpret this passage as a unified whole, though it bears clear signs of development and redaction. The purpose of my study of Daniel 7 is to investigate how the one like a son of a human functions within the text that we have, which was fully compiled by the first century. As I discuss in conversation with Boyarin's work below, I do not find plausible the notion that writers of the Synoptic Gospels, or other early Christians, in alluding to Daniel, would be alluding to an earlier strand that presents a different message once various interpretive cues from the final text have been peeled away.

and possess the kingdom forever — forever and ever" (v. 18, NRSV). If the figures are parallel, then the "holy ones" should represent an earthly rather than a heavenly reality; which is to say, they should represent the people of God.

The need to correlate the sphere occupied by the beasts with that occupied by the humanlike figure is reinforced when Daniel retells the portion of the vision concerning the fourth beast. It reads in part, "As I looked, this horn made war with the holy ones and was prevailing over them, until the Ancient One came; then judgment was given for the holy ones of the Most High" (vv. 21-22, NRSV). The beast operates in the same sphere as the holy ones of the Most High. Thus, if the beast represents a king, then the holy ones of the Most High most likely describe people who are oppressed by this king. The interpretation of this more detailed version of the vision reinforces the point. One king arises who has "put down three kings" (v. 24, NRSV). The reference is to one particular king on earth. The interpretation continues: "He shall speak words against the Most High, shall wear out the holy ones of the Most High, and shall attempt to change the sacred seasons and the law; and they shall be given into his power for a time, two times, and half a time" (v. 25, NRSV). The war with the holy ones includes a heavenly dimension, but that is found in speaking words against God. The "holy ones" are subject to his attempts to change the law of God, and are given over into this king's power. The interpretation of the vision still more pointedly indicates that the holy ones are subject to the human king who is taking divine prerogatives to himself, particularly by Israel's not being able to keep the law. As is widely recognized, this exposition is a thinly veiled reference to Antiochus IV Epiphanes, whose name itself ("God made manifest") might be taken as a word spoken against the Most High, and whose attempt to exert control over the Jewish people included forbidding them to keep Sabbath, punishing them cruelly for circumcising their children, and compelling them to eat unclean foods (cf. Josephus, *J. W.* 1.1.2; *Ant.* 12.5.4). The real-world correspondence between the horn's war with the holy ones and the interpretation of the holy ones being subject to the king's power is the Jewish people's endurance of persecution under the reign of Antiochus.

The final interpretation of the appearance of the one like a human being reinforces the notion that he represents the human people of God. After judgment is set and the king destroyed, "The kingship and dominion and the greatness of the kingdoms under the whole heaven shall be given to the people of the holy ones of the Most High" (v. 27, NRSV). The expression "people of the holy ones" (עַם־קַדִּישִׁין; cf. 8:24) provides one final clue that the identity of the one like a human being is representative of the people of God as such rather than a reference to a heavenly protector. This is not to deny that the book of Daniel views a heavenly component to God's delivery of the people from Antiochus (cf. 12:1), but it is to say that the hope articulated in the passage appears to be best understood as a vindication of Israel through its being given its rightful place in representing God's rule over the earth. Thus the preliminary conclusion I offer is that the vision's depiction of a rightly ordered cosmos, in which a human resumes dominion over the earth after its subjugation to destructive beasts, translates into a rightly ordered creation in which Israel plays the role of God's ruler over the earth after its enslaving enemies have been destroyed.

This interpretation, however, is not uncontested. In particular, John Collins has mounted a strong argument in favor of the notion that the one like a human being is representative of an angelic deliverer of God's people.[310] He works his argument backward from Daniel 11–12, where the fate of Antiochus is depicted in non-visionary terms. A brief note indicates the end of his life and reign: "Yet he shall come to his end, with no one to help him" (11:45, NRSV), after which we read of Michael arising, a time of anguish, and the deliverance of the people. This becomes a model for Collins, demonstrating that angelic hosts are entailed in the conflict between God's people and Antiochus, and further showing that at the climactic moment of Antiochus's defeat (roughly the same place where the one like a human being appears in the vision in chap. 7), an angelic deliverer arises on the scene.[311] Collins argues also that the text depicts Antiochus warring not merely against people but also against heavenly beings in 11:36, and notes that chapter 12 does not depict an eschatological kingdom.

I am more cautious about Collins's readings and their implications than he is. First, while I do not disagree that an angelic figure appears as a decisive agent in chapter 12, it is also the case that whereas chapter 12 does not mention the eschatological kingdom that is the particular point at issue in chapter 7, it is also true that chapter 7 does not mention an eschatological battle fought by heavenly forces. In other words, the precise point of correlation needed to draw a firm conclusion about the identity of the one like a son of a human is missing. Additionally, I do not read chapter 11 as indicating that Antiochus's

---

310. John J. Collins, "Son of Man and the Saints of the Most High in the Book of Daniel," *JBL* 93 (1974): 50-66. The argument is carried over into his more recent commentary, *Daniel: A Commentary on the Book of Daniel* (Hermeneia; Minneapolis: Fortress, 1993). See also Stefan Beyerle, "'Der mit den Wolken des Himmels kommt': Untersuchungen zum Traditionsgefüge 'Menschensohn,'" in *Gottessohn und Menschensohn: Exegetische Studien zu zwei Paradigmen biblischer Intertextualität* (BTS 67; ed. Dieter Sänger; Neukirchen-Vluyn: Neukirchener, 2004), 1-52, esp. 15-16.

311. Collins, "Son of Man," 57-58.

war rises to the level of heavenly combat. The verse in question is Daniel 11:36: "He shall exalt himself and magnify himself above every god, and he shall speak astonishing things against the God of gods" (RSV; ויתרומם ויתגדל על־כל־אל ועל אל אלים, MT). To my mind, Collins overreads this as "direct conflict with the heavenly host and with God himself," attacks in which Antiochus is "successful."[312] Antiochus's claiming to be Θεὸς Ἐπιφανής is sufficient exalting of himself to the place of God to reflect the "exalting himself and magnifying himself above every god" that we read of in 11:36; indeed, that verse speaks of the arrogance of Antiochus in much the same fashion as 7:8 and 21 but does not mention a heavenly battle. Thus, the depiction of Antiochus, his rule, and his ultimate downfall do not create quite the synergy with Collins's interpretation of chapter 7 that he leads the reader to expect.

Collins next steps back to Daniel 8, where there is another vision that recounts the story of Antiochus's rise to power over God's people. Here he draws special attention to the depiction of Antiochus in verses 9-12. In this section of the vision we read that a horn "grew as high as the host of heaven. It threw down to the earth some of the host and some of the stars, and trampled on them. Even against the price of the host it acted arrogantly; it took the regular burnt offering away from him and overthrew the place of his sanctuary. Because of wickedness, the host was given over to it together with the regular burnt offering; it cast truth to the ground, and kept prospering in what it did" (vv. 10-12, NRSV). The time of prospering here certainly aligns with the time of success expressed in Daniel 11:36. Is this constellation of verses, then, evidence that Antiochus's battle reaches to the heaven, even to the point of throwing down heavenly forces? It certainly seems that way. Collins says, "The parallelism of the stars here with the host of heaven makes quite explicit that supernatural heavenly angelic beings are referred to. It appears then that here, as in Daniel 11, Antiochus IV Epiphanes passes over from the purely human domain and launches an attack on the heavenly host. This is precisely parallel to Dan 11:36."[313] Although I contest the notion that this is precisely parallel to Daniel 11:36, Collins's reading is in line with standard depictions of the heavenly hosts as both stars and angelic beings. Moreover, it squares with the depiction of Michael as prince in 12:1.

However, the notion that the earthly realities have heavenly counterparts is a double-edged sword. The following chapter of Daniel speaks of an anointed prince who restores the sanctuary, only to have his line cut off

312. Collins, "Son of Man," 57.
313. Collins, "Son of Man," 58.

sixty-two weeks later (9:25-26). In chapter 8 the overthrow of the prince is correlated with the cessation of the burnt offering and the conquest of the sanctuary. One of the challenges in interpreting the vision(s) is that they are, in fact visions. As such, it might thus very well be that the celestial symbolism of the vision intends to depict earthly realities. In this case, the interpretation of the vision is less decisive in Collins's favor than we might expect. The "growing high as heaven" (v. 10) is interpreted as "in his own mind he shall be great" (v. 25, NRSV). Thus, as we saw before, the image of heavenly exaltation is nothing else than a depiction of Antiochus's arrogance. The interpretation does not signal that his self-exaltation entails a war in the heavenly places. Moreover, "prince" is a title for the first in a line of human priestly caretakers of the temple in chapter 9. Thus, Antiochus's war against the "prince of princes" (8:25) might well be a stand against a priestly foe. Indeed, the interpretation of the vision rendered in 8:25 suggests such an earthly referent. The final clause says that he will be destroyed, but not by human power. Here, the implication seems to be that the one who will destroy Antiochus is of a different order than the prince he opposes. Rather than saying, "The prince will destroy him," the vision progresses from the prince who was opposed to the non-human power that will destroy the king. In conclusion, I would say that the vision of Daniel 8 maintains the perspective that Antiochus's war afflicts the human agents of God and their worship on the earth. The notion that the "prince" on earth will be finally delivered by the heavenly prince of God's armies is a composite picture that is drawn only when we combine the hints of chapter 8 with the clear articulation of chapter 12. When Daniel 8 speaks of Antiochus destroying "both the mighty and the people of the holy ones," the distinction is likely between two classes of humans, and the question of whether "people of the holy ones" refers to "holy people" (e.g., TNIV) or to people who are under the watchful care of holy angels is left open.

Collins turns last of all to the most opaque of the depictions of Antiochus's reign: the vision of Daniel 7 and its interpretation. When he does, he highlights that Antiochus is said to make war on the holy ones (v. 21).[314] Having previously argued that Antiochus's war extended to the heavenly realms, Collins is in a position to conclude that here, too, holy ones refers to the angelic host against which Antiochus has arrayed himself. However, I have shown that the claims for a heavenly war are far less certain, and likely absent from the latter two readings. Thus, I draw the opposite conclusion: Daniel 7:21 speaks

314. Collins, "Son of Man," 61-62.

The Son of Man

of Antiochus's defeat of the people of God, the earthly counterpart to what Collins sees as a heavenly battle.

Importantly, in his understanding of the "holy ones" as the angels, Collins recognizes that the final interpretation of the vision includes the people of God as recipients of the kingdom.[315] Here it is crucial that we recognize the portion of Daniel's vision that is being interpreted. The verses in question read: "Then the court shall sit in judgment, and his dominion shall be taken away, to be consumed and totally destroyed. The kingship and dominion and the greatness of the kingdoms under the whole heaven shall be given to the people of the holy ones of the Most High; their kingdom shall be an everlasting kingdom, and all dominions shall serve and obey them" (vv. 26-27, NRSV). The first phrase, about the court sitting in judgment, corresponds to verses 9-10, when the thrones are set up and the court sits in judgment. The second phrase, about his dominion being taken away and totally destroyed, corresponds to verse 11(-12), where the fourth beast is put to death, destroyed, and burned with fire. The second sentence, then, corresponds to the giving of dominion and kingship to the one like a son of humanity in verses 13-14.

Perhaps most importantly, Collins claims that verse 27 is simply an earthly analogue to a more comprehensive heavenly reality, inasmuch as the people of the holy ones are given the kingdoms "under heaven." However, there is a precise analogue between "under heaven" and the vision's statement that the human one's rule is over "peoples, nations, and tongues" (v. 14). In the final interpretation, it is the people who clearly receive the kingdom and who, therefore, correspond to the one like a son of humanity in the original vision.[316] The best conclusion as to the identity of the one like a human being is that he represents the people of God whom God exalts to a place of everlasting kingship over the nations of the earth. This means that the one like a human being from Daniel 7 represents an idealized human figure in the form of God's people: a beleaguered and defeated people whom God exalts to exercise rule over the world on God's behalf.

My argument, outlined here in conversation with Collins, stands also against the more recent proposal of Daniel Boyarin. In *The Jewish Gospels: The Story of the Jewish Christ*, Boyarin maintains that it is precisely through

315. Collins, "Son of Man," 62; Collins, *Daniel*, 322.

316. See also Matthew Black, "The Messianism of the Parables of Enoch: Their Date and Contribution to Christological Origins," in *The Messiah: Developments in Earliest Judaism and Christianity* (ed. James H. Charlesworth; Minneapolis: Fortress, 1992), 145-68; Black, *The Book of Enoch or 1 Enoch: A New English Edition: With Commentary and Textual Notes* (SVTP 7; Leiden: Brill, 1985).

the son of man title that the early Jewish Christians expressed their belief in Jesus's divinity.[317] This claim builds on Boyarin's reading of Daniel 7 that sees in Daniel's "one like a son of man" echoes, or perhaps the rewriting, of ancient Canaanite myths in which the ancient god El presides over the investiture of a younger god, Baal.[318] Boyarin maintains that this notion of two gods proved unacceptable to early readers of Daniel, such that it was reinterpreted as a depiction of the exaltation of Israel, reflected in the current canonical form.[319] Boyarin thus maintains, "The theology of the Gospels, far from being a radical innovation within the Israelite religious tradition, is a highly conservative return to the very most ancient moments within that tradition, moments that had been largely suppressed in the meantime — but not entirely."[320]

Of course, "the theology of the Gospels" to which Boyarin here refers is not the theology of the Gospels as the current study understands it. At least, it does not seem so on first blush. In a peculiar footnote that appears in the heart of his discussion of son of man as a divine title for Jesus, Boyarin quotes Adela Yarbro Collins's description of functional divinity as something distinct from ontological divinity. The former refers to exercising "divine activities" such as "ruling over a universal kingdom, sitting on a heavenly throne, judging human beings in the end-time or traveling on the clouds."[321] Boyarin says that it is this functional sense of divinity that he has in mind throughout his work.[322] It seems to me, however, that such a claim undermines the force of his larger argument. The claim that there are two divinities in heaven, and that Jesus is one of those deities, stakes out ground in notions of preexistence and some sort of heavenly ontology. It is difficult to imagine how one is supposed to hear that the son of man in the Gospels is a recovery of an ancient myth of two divinities in a heavenly court and not imagine that a divine ontology is entailed in some way that extends beyond "functional" divinity.

Be that as it may, the more important factor at this point in the study is

317. Daniel Boyarin, *The Jewish Gospels: The Story of the Jewish Christ* (New York: New Press, 2012), esp. 25-70.

318. Daniel Boyarin, "Daniel 7, Intertextuality, and the History of Israel's Cult," *HTR* 105 (2012): 139-62; cf. the discussion in Collins, *Daniel*, 289-91.

319. Boyarin, "Daniel 7."

320. Boyarin, *Jewish Gospels*, 47.

321. Adela Yarbro Collins, "'How on Earth Did Jesus Become God?' A Reply," in *Israel's God and Rebecca's Children: Christology and Community in Early Judaism and Christianity: Essays in Honor of Larry Hurtado and Alan F. Segal* (ed. David B. Capes et al.; Waco, TX: Baylor University Press, 2007), 55-66, here 57.

322. Boyarin, *Jewish Gospels*, 55n.

Boyarin's recognition that Daniel 7, as it stands, depicts the exaltation of Israel rather than a second divine power in heaven. I take this as proof of my point, that Daniel 7 itself, whatever its precursors, refers to the exaltation of Israel to its rightful place of rule over the other nations. I find it highly unlikely that the Synoptic Gospels would draw on a pre-canonical message of Daniel 7, occluded by the message of its canonical form, in order to encode a divine Christology in their narratives. I address the particular issues pertaining to the Gospels below. For now it suffices to say that Boyarin's reading of Daniel 7, if unwittingly, confirms the interpretation of the chapter offered here.

c. Rule of the Vindicated Sufferer

With the claim that the one like the son of a human being refers to Israel now in place, we can return to the overall dynamics of Daniel's vision and its interpretation. In the first part of my discussion of Daniel, I laid out the vision as functioning with an anti-creation, restored creation motif. Central to this claim is the notion that humanity is being restored to its rightful place of rule over the created order, a set of symbols that signifies Israel's rule over the world. The climactic, eschatological scene is then one in which Israel is the means by which God exercises God's rule over the earth. The cohesion between God's rule and the rule of the one like a human being is signaled, first of all, by the plural "thrones" being set up as the judgment scene begins. The implication seems to be that the one who comes into God's presence will sit on this second throne.

The viability of a human figure, as a metonymy for Israel, sitting enthroned in God's heavenly court is established in Psalm 110, which itself speaks of a royal figure enthroned at God's right hand (v. 1), makes clear that this image has its tangible reality in the world of people (v. 2), coalesces the royal enthronement with a priestly identity (v. 4), and claims that the session is eternal (v. 4). Moreover, Psalm 110 anticipates that the divine power and presence connected to this priestly kingship will find expression in judgment on and destruction of hostile kings (vv. 5-6).

In Daniel, the vision indicates that the rule received will be an eternal kingship and dominion. This point is reiterated at three separate points. In the original vision, the one like a son of a human is given authority over all peoples and nations, an everlasting dominion and kingship (Dan 7:14). In the interpretation of the vision, Daniel hears that the holy ones will receive "the kingdom" and possess it forever (v. 18). In the summary reiteration of the vision, Daniel says "the time arrived when the holy ones gained possession of the kingdom" (v. 22, NRSV). And in the second interpretation of the vision the angel tells Daniel that every realm under heaven will be given to the people of the holy ones and that "their kingdom shall be an everlasting kingdom, and all dominions shall serve and obey them" (v. 27, NRSV). Eternal kingship is predicated of this human agent of God. Moreover, it is notable that verses 18 and 22 use the absolute, מלכותא ("the kingdom"), suggesting perhaps that the kingdom over which they rule is none other than the one kingdom of God. The eternality of the dominion and kingship is derivative of the God for whom the human kingship is ruling.

One final piece remains to be put in place, namely, that the exalted king is also the vindicated sufferer. In the second iteration of the vision, Daniel says, "As I looked, this horn made war with the holy ones and was prevailing over them" (v. 21, NRSV). As I argued above, Daniel consistently locates the wars of Antiochus within the human realm, making this an indication that the people of God are being beleaguered through the martial machinations of Antiochus. In this vision, the tide reverses itself when the Ancient One gives judgment for the holy ones and they gain the kingdom. Because the one like a human is representative of a corporate people, there is a possibility here of using language of defeat that would appear to imply death while at the same time arguing for this same figure to be vindicated and enthroned. The second explanation speaks somewhat vaguely about the defeat of the holy ones, saying that the horn will "wear out the holy ones" as he attempts to change the law (v. 25). These worn out, defeated foes of Antiochus are the ones who then receive kingship and dominion. This movement from defeat, and even death, at the hands of the geopolitical enemies of God's people, followed by enthronement to an eternal kingship, is a corporate claim that the Synoptic Gospels will rework into their narratives about Jesus as the son of man.

d. Conclusion: Daniel's Idealized Humanlike Figure

Daniel draws on a primeval depiction of idealized humans ruling the world on God's behalf in order to tell a story of hope in which God's people will be given such a role through divine and angelic intervention. Daniel's idealized human figure is depicted as a single, exalted being, but stands for a corporate entity. God's people in this text are idealized in terms of the role they will play in an anticipated future. That future is one in which they share in God's rule over the world as God has given that rule to them. This rule, in turn, is the way that the world will be rightly ordered. The imagery of Genesis 1 suggests that Israel's rule over the nations is the means by which God's primeval intention to have people rule the world on God's behalf is going to come to find eschatological realization. The hoped-for future of Daniel 7 is one in which humans faithfully rule the nations, under God.

2. ENOCHIC LITERATURE

a. 1 Enoch

The Enochic literature opens up numerous vistas on the diversity of Jewish expression that was possible without signaling a wholesale transformation in the identity of God. In keeping with the overarching thesis of this chapter, we find the son of man figure in the Parables of Enoch playing several roles that identify him with God. This messiah figure (e.g., *1 En.* 48:10; 52:4) will, among other things, receive the worship of all who live on the earth, and the rulers of the nations in particular (48:5; 62:9).[323] He is endowed with eternal glory and might (49:2), and he can judge secret things (49:3). In such ascriptions, *1 Enoch* depicts the humanlike figure as embodying traits in a derivative fashion from "the Lord of Spirits,"[324] clearly juxtaposing the son of man with God as it ascribes to the former various honors typically reserved for the latter. When the son of man is worshiped in 48:5, hymns are sung to the Lord of Spirits. Denial of the one is denial of the other (48:10).

Similarly, it is due to the Lord of Spirits giving the Chosen One a seat on the Lord's throne that this representative figure has wisdom and glory (51:3).[325] Sitting on God's throne also entails a sovereignty that extends beyond the day of judgment and into the age to come. In a scene replete with indications that the dead have arisen (chap. 51) we read, "In those days, (the Elect One) shall sit on my throne, and from the conscience of his mouth shall come out all the

---

323. As James C. VanderKam notes, "Righteous One, Messiah, Chosen One, and Son of Man in 1 Enoch 37–71," in *The Messiah: Developments in Earliest Judaism and Christianity* (ed. James H. Charlesworth; Minneapolis: Fortress, 1992), 169-91, here 171, 1 Enoch 52:4 likely echoes Psalm 2:2. This highlights the significance of the biblical idealization of kingship, including the king's co-regency with God and receipt of worship, for some later Jews' descriptions of divine representatives.

324. Citations of are taken from George W. E. Nickelsburg and James C. VanderKam, *1 Enoch: The Hermeneia Translation* (Minneapolis: Fortress, 2012).

325. Black, "Messianism of the Parables," 163, notes the significance of sitting on the divine throne as both a striking development in the son of man tradition and an important precedent for the parallel language deployed in Matthew 19:18; 25:31.

secrets of wisdom, for the Lord of the Spirits has given them to him and glorified him. In those days, mountains shall dance like rams; and the hills shall leap like kids satiated with milk. And the faces of all the angels in heaven shall glow with joy, because on that day the Elect One has arisen" (vv. 3-4). Sitting on the throne is, not surprisingly, combined with the kingly theme of wisdom. This conjunction also enables the Chosen One to execute the final judgment (61:8-9). Moreover, the glorification of this Human One leads to the enlightening and joy of even the heavenly angels. Perhaps even more importantly, the Elect One judges the "holy ones in heaven above" (61:8), an apparent reference to the angelic beings (61:10).

Here we catch a glimpse of the exalted Human One doing for the heavenly host, as well as the heavens and the earth, what those angelic beings themselves were not charged to do: bear God's name and represent God's reign to the earth. The imagery of glowing faces also places the Elect One in the place of God. The faces of the angels glow because the Elect One has arisen as one whose face was made to shine by the Lord of Spirits. The Elect One becomes for the heavenly host what God was for Moses: the source of a reflected heavenly glory (cf. Exod 34:29-34; Num 6:25). We have here a cluster of ascriptions, actions, and attributes that weigh heavily against the notion that God's unique prerogatives cannot be shared without transforming one's understanding of who God is as such.

It is not merely that the son of man acts on God's behalf, but that this figure stands in the place of God both as the executor of God's action and as the recipient of what is due to God himself. When the kings of the earth are judged, it is because "they do not extol and glorify" or obey the son of Man (1 En. 46:5). In the following verse, we are told that they lack hope, not because they do not extol the son of man but because "they do not extol the name of the Lord of the Spirits," that is, God (v. 6). In so juxtaposing the extolling of God's human representative and God himself, the Similitudes are participating in the biblical tradition, reflected clearly in Psalm 2, that the king is so identified with Israel's God that to reject the king is to reject God, and, conversely, to honor and even worship the king is to honor and worship God (cf. 1 En. 48:10).

First Enoch appears to use imagery of worship in the strong sense of cultic adoration, as it says that people are gathered before "the son of Man sitting on the throne of his glory" (62:5). The rulers of the earth "bless, glorify, extol him who rules over everything. . . . On that day, all the kings, the governors, the high officials, and those who rule the earth shall fall down before him on their faces, and worship and raise their hopes in that son of Man; they shall beg and plead for mercy at his feet" (62:6, 9).

It might be argued that these examples are not germane to the current thesis, in which I am arguing for a particular set of actions suitable for idealized human, rather than heavenly, beings. Three lines of response are in order. First, the argument advanced by a number of advocates of early divine Christology is that the way a Jew would demonstrate that a character in the story is a manifestation of the one God is by having that character play roles that are restricted to God alone. *First Enoch* undermines that thesis. But as Larry Hurtado rightly observes, "The meaning of this is not that the figure rivals God or becomes a second god but rather that he is seen as performing the eschatological functions associated with God and is therefore God's chief agent, linked with God's work to a specially intense degree."[326]

Second, at least one early Jewish writer interpreted *1 Enoch*'s son of man as an idealized human figure: the writer responsible for *1 Enoch* 71. Whether this portion of the Parables is original, as James VanderKam argues, or whether it is a later addition, these chapters identify the son of man with Enoch the seer (*1 En.* 71:14).[327] This move in effect transforms the "preexistence" of this exalted figure from some sort of pretemporal mode of life in heaven to the existence of Enoch as translated to heaven before returning to the earth as messiah and judge.[328] For the author or redactor of the final chapters of *1 Enoch,* the glorification of the son of man, his receipt of worship, his session on God's throne, and his judgment of the world are all predicated of an idealized human figure exalted to heaven.[329] Third, it may not, in fact, be the case that *1 Enoch* claims that the son of man exists before time. This conclusion is drawn from *1 Enoch* 48:2-3, which speaks of the son of man being given a name by God before time, before all creation. However, James Kugel points out that this might be a development of a particular tradition of interpretation that grew up around Psalm 72:17.[330] As

---

326. Larry W. Hurtado, *One God, One Lord: Early Christian Devotion and Ancient Jewish Monotheism* (2nd ed.; New York: Continuum, 1998), 55-56.

327. VanderKam, "Righteous One," 176-86. See also Daniel C. Olson, "'Enoch and the Son of Man' Revisited: Further Reflections on the Text and Translation of *1 Enoch* 70.1-2," *JSP* 18 (2009): 233-40. Christfried Böttrich, "Konturen des 'Menschensohnes' in äthHen 37–71," in *Gottessohn und Menschensohn: Exegetische Studien zu zwei Paradigmen biblischer Intertextualität* (BTS 67; ed. Dieter Sägner; Neukirchen-Vluyn: Neukirchener, 2004), 53–90, argues that the transcendence and eternal preexistence of the son of man renders such an identification impossible (85-86). However, this conclusion depends on both downplaying the likely transcendence of a human who was translated to heaven, and reading his name's existence prior to the heavenly bodies as an indication of personal preexistence. Both are debatable.

328. See also the discussion in Black, "Messianism of the Parables," 165-66; Black, *Book of Enoch,* 189.

329. Cf. Hurtado, *One God, One Lord,* 53-54.

330. Kugel, *Traditions of the Bible,* 59-60.

Kugel translates the verse it reads, "May his name be forever; his name bursts forth before the sun (לְפְנֵי שֶׁמֶשׁ)." In this tradition, the messiah himself is not in heaven awaiting orders to go down to earth, but those on earth can take comfort in the fact that God has known the name since before the creation of the world.[331]

It might well be, then, that the son of man figure in *1 Enoch* is one whose identity maintains the meaning of "son of man," which is, simply, "human being." This suggestion is bolstered by the fact that there is no one, fixed phrase in the Ethiopic that expresses the identity of the central figure as "son of man."[332] First there is a rather literal "that/this son of Man" (*zeku/zentu walda sab'*) at 46:2, 3, 4; 48:2, and the application of *walda sab'* and without the demonstrative adjective when Enoch is addressed in 60:10.[333] Second, and most frequent, is, "that/this son of the offspring of the mother of the living" (*zeku/we'etu walda 'eguāla 'emma ḥeyāw*), found in 62:7, 9, 14; 63:11; 69:26, 27; 70:1; 71:17, without the demonstrative adjective in 62:7; 69:27.[334] Third, *we'etu walda be'si*, "this son of man," appears a few times, depending on the manuscript consulted (62:5; 69:29, 71:14), and has variations that include *walda be'sit* ("son of woman," 62:5) and, in 71:14, *walda be'si* without the demonstrative adjective.[335] Based on the Ethiopic renderings of the Hebrew בְּנִי־אָדָם and the Greek ὁ υἱὸς τοῦ ἀνθρώπου in the biblical texts, as well as a few other points of data, Black argues that all three renderings reflect a common original בֶּן־הָאָדָם.[336] The widespread agreement in translating all three phrases into English as "son of man" appears to demonstrate something of a consensus on Black's position. However, the diversity of expressions should not be entirely set aside as it suggests two potentially important conclusions. First, as Hurtado has argued, it appears that for the translators, at any rate, son of man was not a fixed title.[337] Second, and more important for my purposes, the variety of expression in general, and the phrase "son of the offspring of the mother of the living" in particular, show that the connotation of "son of man" as it means "human being"

---

331. Kugel, *Traditions of the Bible*, 60.

332. Black, *Book of Enoch*, 206-7. Hurtado, *Lord Jesus Christ*, 296n90, challenges Black's assumption that these various forms go back to a common, fixed Hebrew expression. See also Ulrich B. Müller, "Jesus als der 'Menschensohn,'" in *Gottessohn und Menschensohn: Exegetische Studien zu zwei Paradigmen biblischer Intertextualität* (BTS 67; ed. Dieter Sägner; Neukirchen-Vluyn: Neukirchener, 2004), 91-129, here 94.

333. Black, *Book of Enoch*, 206.

334. Black, *Book of Enoch*, 206.

335. Black, *Book of Enoch*, 206.

336. Black, *Book of Enoch*, 206.

337. Hurtado, *Lord Jesus Christ*, 296.

was not lost through allusion to Daniel's heavenly figure. Quite the contrary, *1 Enoch* most often uses a phrase that further underscores that the identity of this heavenly figure is determined by his birth from those who descended from Eve. If such a phrase were always used to translate "son of man," one might argue that it, too, is a fixed form, such that the connotation "human" has been lost through connotative usage. However, given the variation of terms, the Ethiopic version of *1 Enoch*, at any rate, makes clear that the identity of the Chosen One is that of an idealized human being.

b. Evidence from 3 Enoch

A further piece of evidence that Enoch's god-like son of man might be interpreted as the exalted human Enoch is found in *3 Enoch*. In this later Enochic tradition, the angelic being Metatron is none other than Enoch the son of Jared (*3 En.* 4). His exaltation is of such a height that the seer, R. Ishmael, is driven to ask, "Why are you called by the name of your Creator with seventy names? You are greater than all the princes, more exalted than all the angels, more beloved than all the ministers, more honored than all the hosts, and elevated over all potentates in sovereignty, greatness, and glory."[338] This later mystical tradition not only affirms Enoch's exaltation as entailing a position of sovereign rule, but also asserts that Enoch became a sharer in the divine name itself. One might claim that this is the epitome of participation in the divine identity, without any claim that God's own nature is thereby more clearly disclosed.

c. 4QPrayer of Enosh (4Q369)

Although it does not directly address the question of the son of man, the so-called Prayer of Enosh (4Q369) provides another angle on the exalted status of Enoch in the Judaism of the Second Temple period. God's special possession on the earth is here referred to as Enoch's inheritance (frag. 1 II, 1). It is the place where God's own glory will appear (frag. 1 II, 3). Enoch is then described as God's firstborn son and prince and ruler over the inhabited world (frag. 1 II, 7). As God's firstborn son, Enoch is glorified with the crown of heaven and the glory of the clouds, while tantalizing fragments toward the end suggest a father-son relationship that enables Enoch to rule over those upon whom God has bestowed God's glory.

---

338. P. Alexander, trans., "3 (Hebrew Apocalypse of) Enoch," in Charlesworth, *Apocalyptic Literature and Testaments*, 223-302.

In contrast to these humans who share in God's glory and rule, the angel of peace is present in the congregation, but seemingly as a help to the people rather than the direct manifestation of God's glory that is true of the people. Here we find further evidence that in order to understand the heights of early Jewish Christology we do better to look at what early Jews expected for God's ideal people rather than what they say about angels.

The cosmic depiction of Enoch's rule, analogous in many respects to that of the son of man in *1 Enoch,* is predicated upon his exaltation and adoption rather than eternal preexistence. He is an idealized human figure. Moreover, such idealized anthropology here depicts a human as being more like God in sharing God's glory and rule than his angelic counterparts.

d. Conclusions: Enoch's Son of Man

The interpretation of *1 Enoch* offered here creates a telling antecedent for the Synoptic Gospels' son of man traditions. There, too, the son of man enthroned in heavenly glory is preexistent in the sense of having been a human on earth before being translated into heaven due to his fidelity to God. Each text has developed the Danielic antecedent by interpreting "the one like a son of a human" in an individual rather than corporate fashion. However, at the same time each maintains the movement of Daniel 7 in which this human figure is exalted into the presence of God only after life on earth. In itself, the form of *1 Enoch* we currently have (Ethiopic, and including chap. 71) provides further demonstration of the extent to which idealized human figures can be identified with God in early Judaism.

3. 4 EZRA

Fourth Ezra offers a variation on the theme of human identification with God that we have been surveying in early Jewish literature. Ezra's son of man appears to be one and the same with the messiah, the son of God (*4 Ezra* 7:28). But as with the son of man in *1 Enoch,* this Davidic and thus human messiah (12:32) also seems to exist in heaven with God before coming to earth. This son is reserved where none can see him (13:52), but Ezra is about to go to live with him (14:9). Thus, there is evidence in early Judaism (though in this case, likely later than the advent of Christian speculation on the preexistence of Jesus) of a preexistent messiah.

In terms of shedding light on the Gospels, there are two significant points to be made. First, this messiah dies after a reign of primeval proportions (four hundred years; 7:28-29) and then his role in the unfolding of Ezra's eschatological vision ceases. Thus, despite his preexistence, this figure is not eternal.[339]

In light of this first consideration, the second gains in significance: the messiah is identified with God in acting for God, but without any implication that this messiah is God in the sense that later Christians would ascribe to Jesus.[340] The messiah plays the part of God in Israel's drama without creating what later theologians would call a "high Christology," and the work thus offers further evidence against the notion that identifying a figure "with God" is tantamount to identifying the figure "as God."

The particular instance of divine identification comes in the eschatological war in which the son of man brings deliverance. In Ezra's vision, a human defeats an onrushing multitude without weapons of war, but only with a stream of fire from his mouth (13:8-12). After this, the people are gathered to him (vv. 12-13). In the interpretation of the vision, the lack of martial weaponry is interpreted as a direct intervention of the Most High: "Behold the days are coming when the Most High will deliver those who are on the earth . . . then my son will be revealed" (vv. 29, 32). God acts to deliver through the son. The son taking his place and standing in the battle is requisite, but God is the one who works. The son plays the role of judge, judging and destroying the nations by the fire that is the law (v. 38). Participating in the divine identity is not to be God, but to faithfully stand in for God and to act for God on the earth.

4. CONCLUSIONS: SON OF MAN AND IDEALIZED HUMANS

Against the arguments of John Collins and of Daniel Boyarin, I have laid out the case for Daniel's "one like a son of a human" to be not a preexistent divinity but, instead, a symbol for the people of God on earth. Indirectly, Boyarin helps my case, as he recognizes that the interpretation of Daniel's vision, which he sees as a later addition to Daniel 7, describes the figure in terms of the people of God. Such recognition is important, as it cuts against the argument advanced by John Collins that the interpretation itself refers primarily to an angelic representative of Israel. I have made the case that shows that Boyarin's reading of the interpretation of the vision is correct, and that the canonical form of Daniel's vision thus depicts "the one like a human being" in order to speak

---

339. Collins and Collins, *King and Messiah*, 97.
340. Cf. Collins and Collins, *King and Messiah*, 98.

of the human beings who make up the faithful people of Israel. The biblical antecedent for Jesus's claims to be son of man, echoing Daniel 7:14, is thus an idealized human figure.

Similarly, I have argued that the heavenly son of man in *1 Enoch* is an exalted human, at least in the form of the book that has come down to us. At very least, the Ethiopic text that includes chapter 71 demonstrates an interpretive tradition in which the son of man is described in various ways so as to underscore his birth from a human woman. And Enoch, who is referred to as a son of man (60:10), is told in the end that he is the son of man whom he had seen in the vision (71:14). *First Enoch's* son of man thus provides further examples of the ways in which an idealized human figure can be identified with God without suggesting that the person is being identified as God, as a rival to God, or transforming the divine identity as such.

Fourth Ezra's son of man pushes the argument in a different direction, indicating that a preexistent angelic figure might be imagined as playing a messianic son of man role — but, once again, without divinity as such being imputed to him or God's own divinity experiencing transformation. It is not an example of what I am calling an idealized human figure, as it depicts an angelic being as a preexistent messiah that it identifies with Daniel's humanlike figure. It will be up to my exegesis of the Synoptic Gospels to demonstrate that their rendering of Jesus is closer to Daniel and *1 Enoch* than to the depiction of *4 Ezra*.

F. THE COMMUNITY OF THE ELECT

In my investigation of Daniel's "one like a son of a human," the idealized human figure is actually an idealized human people, that is, faithful Israel. This brings up the final category of idealized human figures that I wish to highlight: the community of the faithful.

1. ISRAEL IN SCRIPTURE

a. Israel as Son of God

Above I have shown that Adam and Davidic kings stood in a filial relationship to God in sundry strands of the biblical tradition. In between these two representative figures stands corporate Israel as a whole, which also occupies such a place.

Israel's identity as son of God finds a center of gravity in the exodus narrative and later traditions about it. First, there are God's final words to Moses prior to his return to Egypt: "When you go back to Egypt, see that you perform before Pharaoh all the wonders that I have put in your power; but I will harden his heart, so that he will not let the people go. Then you shall say to Pharaoh, 'Thus says the LORD: Israel is my firstborn son. I said to you, "Let my son go that he may worship me." But you refused to let him go; now I will kill your firstborn son'" (Exod 4:21-23, NRSV). Thus, the ensuing story of Moses's confrontations with Pharaoh is overshadowed by the expectation of the Passover deliverance. As God contends with Pharaoh for the right to Israel's service, the claim Pharaoh makes on Israel is couched in such a way that God's claim on Pharaoh will be rendered in kind: for trying to take God's firstborn son, God will in turn take Pharaoh's firstborn son. In this case, the idealization of Israel is not based on Israel's fidelity to God but on God's fidelity to the covenant he made with Abraham, Isaac, and Jacob (e.g., Exod 2:24-25). Here, then, to be son of God entails a special claim on God by which God is obligated to care for and rescue the people.

Deuteronomy 32:6 echoes this notion that God is father to Israel: "Is he not your father, who created you, who made you and established you?" (NRSV). As in the Hosea text discussed below, in Deuteronomy 32 the father-son relation is fraught. The disobedience of Israel leads Moses to say, "They are not his children" (לא בניו, v. 5). The sonship is focused on God's election: "the LORD's own portion was his people" (v. 9, NRSV). The claim that God sustained the people in the desert and guided them (vv. 10-11) alludes to the exodus. The verses go on to describe God's protection and provision of fine food (vv. 13-14). In response, Israel rebelled (vv. 15-17). In a shift of the metaphor, verse 18 depicts God as mother: "You were unmindful of the Rock that bore you; you forgot the God who gave you birth" (NRSV). The important point here is that Israel stands in an idealized position as God's chosen, even begotten people, despite their failure to reciprocate fidelity toward God. Moreover, there is a promise in this chapter of faithless Israel not only being disciplined through exile, but also of being ultimately restored (vv. 36-42). The nature of the relationship is such that God has bound Godself to Israel. This means that God's own reputation rises and falls with the vicissitudes of God's people (v. 27). God's identity is formed through this relation because God has chosen to have Israel be God's people on the earth. In this specific way, the divine identity is shaped through the filial relationship established between God and Israel.

Later prophetic reflections on the exodus also depict Israel as God's son.

Hosea 11:1 articulates this relation as an expression of God's love: "When Israel was a child, I loved him, and out of Egypt I called my son" (NRSV). Here, the relationship is not defined merely in terms of rescue but as one in which God enacts special loving care and nourishment toward the people, teaching them to walk, healing them, leading them, bending down to feed them (11:3-4). However, if there are echoes of God's covenant faithfulness here, it stands in sharp antithesis to Israel's infidelity (11:2). It is thus even more clear in Hosea that the idealization of Israel as "son of God" is not based on Israel acting in an idealized fashion, but is instead based on God's election of Israel as a people. Thus, Israel is "idealized" here not in the strong sense of having divine actions, attributes, or ascriptions predicated of it, except insofar as "son of God" entails a special relationship with God that in some sense indicates an aspect of the character of God.

We find similar dynamics in Jeremiah. In Jeremiah 3 addressing God as father forms both the ideal of Israel's fidelity to God (v. 19) and the display of its hypocrisy as the people pray for deliverance while engaging in every manner of evil (v. 4). But the latter idea that God should deliver precisely because God is father, with its echoes of the exodus, also becomes the standard to which God promises to be faithful: "With weeping they shall come, and with consolations I will lead them back, I will let them walk by brooks of water, in a straight path in which they shall not stumble; for I have become a father to Israel, and Ephraim is my firstborn" (Jer 31:9, NRSV). God acts as father in faithfully delivering Israel from its enemies; Israel's part in the relationship is to be a loyal son, honoring its father (cf. Mal 1:6).

The idea that God as father creates an obligation to act on Israel's behalf is redeployed in Third Isaiah as well. Isaiah 63 recalls the God who rescued Israel by the hand of Moses (vv. 11-14) and turns to ask God to act in this manner again: "Look down from heaven and see, from your holy and glorious habitation. Where are your zeal and your might? The yearning of your heart and your compassion? They are withheld from me. For you are our father, though Abraham does not know us and Israel does not acknowledge us; you, O LORD, are our father; our Redeemer from of old is your name" (vv. 15-16, NRSV). The exodus provides the narratological framework within which the connotations are developed in Isaiah 63, cultivating a call for deliverance that parallels the cry of the Davidic king in Psalm 89. In the act of redemption and deliverance God acts as father of the people. A later plaintive address to God as father calls for God to cease disciplining the people and to restore them (64:8-12). As Marianne Meye Thompson summarizes, "the prophets point to a future hope, a hope for restoration, and do so by calling upon God's mercy and forgiveness as a Father."[341] God as father is the deliverer of God's people.

Perhaps the most significant aspect of Israel's unique sonship is that it indicates a position occupied vis-à-vis God without establishing any inherent claim to a particular character of the people. Claiming God as father nods to the relationship created by the exodus and evokes covenantal obligations. But even for a people who have been less than entirely faithful, such a relation can be called on in order to summon God to act as rescuer of God's people.

b. God on Display in Israel

When discussing the biblical and ancient Near Eastern connotations of humanity as bearing God's image, we saw evidence of the idea that idealized humanity is to function as a theophany. In an analogous way, Israel as an idealized people is to represent God through their actions in the world and interactions with other peoples.

A hint of this is found in the beginning of the Abram narrative. The posture of people toward the patriarch becomes a mirror for God's posture toward them: "I will bless those who bless you, and those who curse you I will curse" (Gen 12:3). Abram stands as intermediary in a manner analogous to what we saw of the Davidic king in Psalm 2: he stands in the place of God to such an extent that one's posture toward him is tantamount to one's posture toward God. The conclusion of verse 3 adds to the picture by indicating the expected results of Abram's mediation: "all the families of the earth will be blessed in you." I take it that these expectations are spoken to Abram with a view toward their fulfillment through the people of Israel. The patriarchal narratives are origin stories, depicting where Israel came from for the purpose of aiding the later people in locating themselves as part of God's activity and promises. The very beginning of the story of Israel as a particular people, in Genesis 12, shows them as standing in a unique, idealized relation between God and the world.

The Torah itself was to be a manifestation of God within Israel and a sign to the nations. As Moses admonishes the people to keep the commandments in the beginning of Deuteronomy he says, "You must observe them diligently, for this will show your wisdom and discernment to the peoples, who, when they hear all these statutes, will say, 'Surely this great nation is a wise and

---

341. Marianne Meye Thompson, *The Promise of the Father: Jesus and God in the New Testament* (Louisville, KY: Westminster John Knox, 2000), 33.

discerning people!' For what other nation has a god so near to it as Yhwh our God is whenever we call to him?" (4:6-7). The content of the law itself, as well as Israel's keeping of it, are signs of Israel's unique status as those to whom God has drawn near. The idealized status of the people is not based on their own inherent identity, but on the relation established between God and them. As Moses continues this speech, he cites the unique experiences of Israel hearing God speak from fire and being taken out from within another nation (4:32-38). These unique experiences ("Has any people ever heard . . . has any god ever attempted . . . ?") place Israel in a unique position based, once again, not on what they have done but on God's actions on their behalf, God's choice of them, and God's love for the ancestors in particular (4:7). Thus, what God has uniquely displayed to Israel (God's proximity, power, and wisdom), Israel is to put on display to the world through its single-hearted devotion to God through its keeping the law. We see here multiple layers of interconnection, as God has bound Godself to this people through the patriarchal covenants, as God has acted on behalf of this people as the one who fights their wars, as God has given the people laws that reflect God's own wisdom. Here we have hints of Israel's identification with God, as God has chosen to be identified with Israel.

This identification is articulated more fully in the prophet Ezekiel. In his work, the connection between God and the people is understood in such a way that God's identification with Israel makes it incumbent upon God to protect and deliver Israel; God's reputation on the earth is inseparable from the occurrences in the life of Israel. Ezekiel 20 rehearses the exodus. The story it tells is one in which Israel in Egypt refused to stop worshiping Egyptian idols (vv. 7-8). Ezekiel's telling shows God's posture toward the people standing on the edge of a knife, on the one side lying God's desire to pour out his wrath on the people in the midst of Egypt (v. 8), on the other lying God's decision to rescue the people (v. 9). The latter option is chosen, according to Ezekiel, not because of love for the people or the ancestors, but "for the sake of my name, that it should not be profaned in the sight of the nations among whom they lived" (v. 9). Although God's covenant with the patriarchs might lie behind God's association with Israel, fidelity to the covenant is not highlighted as the impetus of God's blessing here. Instead, the fact that Israel is identified with God means that God must walk warily in choosing to discipline the people because it will appear to the world that Israel's God is weak or capricious if Israel does not flourish on the earth. Similarly, Ezekiel depicts Israel's rebellion in the wilderness bringing it to the point of destruction at Yhwh's hand, only to have it stayed due to God's concern for God's own name among the nations

(vv. 14, 22). God is so identified with Israel that God's reputation on the earth is inseparable from Israel's fate.

Ezekiel reiterates his theology of identification as the impetus for God to deliver the people from exile. "But when they came to the nations, wherever they came, they profaned my holy name, in that it was said of them, 'These are the people of the YHWH, and yet they had to go out of his land'" (36:20, NRSV, alt.). The failure of YHWH's people to occupy the land affronts YHWH's reputation. The implication would seem to be that the exile of Israel is an indication that Israel's God does not have the power to protect his own people. In such identifications of God and God's people as we see in Ezekiel, we discover a different dynamic at play in what is otherwise a common identification of God with humans. The common element is the identification itself, as we have seen throughout this lengthy survey of early Judaism. The unique dynamic is that the truly idealized figures whom we have studied by and large represent God's strength, majesty, authority, power, sovereignty, glory, and the like. In this case, the identification of God with the people means that God is identified with Israel's failure, weakness, defeat, and exile.

The identification of God with Israel finds a brighter articulation in Third Isaiah, where the presence of God in the midst of Zion is demonstrated by Zion's glory, and the nations' being drawn to Zion's glory (55:5) is their coming to serve YHWH (56:4-7). Such a vision is for an idealized future, as Isaiah 56:8–59:21 makes clear — Israel is not yet that glorified nation, and stands in need of God's redemption (59:20). Isaiah 60 reiterates the theme of God's glory becoming Israel's, such that the nations drawn to God's glory are drawn to the people themselves: "Arise, shine, for your light has come, and the glory of YHWH has risen upon you. . . . YHWH will rise upon you, and his glory appear over you. Nations will come to your light and to the brightness of your dawn" (vv. 1-3, NRSV, alt.). The glory is simultaneously YHWH's own and, derivatively, that of the people. The nation is so identified with YHWH that people flock to the latter and glorify his name by streaming to the former. The nations will "proclaim the name of YHWH" (v. 6), and they will be servants of Israel (vv. 12, 14). The obeisance the nations render to Zion is due entirely to Zion's identification with YHWH: "they shall call you the city of YHWH, the Zion of the Holy One of Israel" (v. 14). Such an identification of the people with God is evocative of the role played, for example, by the king in Psalm 2. There, the king and YHWH are so conjoined that to avert the wrath of God subservience to the king is requisite, and such honoring of the king is the means by which the nations will be subject to Israel's God. Isaiah 60, as well as Isaiah 61, entail similar dynamics but with Zion as a whole playing the role of God's embodiment on the earth.

c. Conclusions: Israel and Divine Identity

This brief survey of the Jewish scriptures is sufficient to demonstrate that divine identification was not limited to persons but could also be a way of imagining the people as a whole. The Isaiah texts come closest to an idealized character in the strong sense of someone whose ascriptions or attributes are said to be those typically reserved for God. Moreover, this idealization is of such a kind as to create a strong identification between the two, so that Zion on the earth serves as a proxy for God vis-à-vis the nations. The other instances show that in lesser ways as well God's identity is often bound up with the people of Israel, they representing God to the world or the world to God, or else standing as a proxy for the glory or shame of God among the nations.

2. JUBILEES

Jubilees makes a few contributions to our understanding of idealized human figures in early Judaism. First, an early depiction of idealized Israel contributes to our bank of figures to whom the title son of God is applied. In the first chapter of the book, God reviews for Moses the future of Israel, a future of rebellion, idolatry, and forsaking the law, for all of which God will hand the people over to destruction and exile followed by a restoration (vv. 7-18). After Moses prays for God to "create for them an upright spirit" God describes how God will transform the people in language evocative of Deuteronomy 10:16 and 30:6: "I will cut off the foreskin of their heart and the foreskin of the heart of their descendants" (v. 23).[342] This inward transformation is otherwise described as creating a "holy spirit" for them, and purifying the people (v. 23), with the result that the people will obey God (v. 24).

With regard to this transformed people, God says, "And I shall be a father to them and they shall be sons to me. And they will all be called 'sons of the living God.' And every angel and spirit will know and acknowledge that they are my sons and I am their father in uprightness and righteousness. And I shall love them" (vv. 24-25). The first phrase, "I shall be a father to them and they shall be sons to me," appears to echo the promise God makes to David concerning his son in 2 Samuel 7:14, but democratizing it such that the language that applied to the Davidic king now applies to an idealized,

---

342. Unless otherwise noted, all translations of *Jubilees* are by O. S. Wintermute in Charlesworth, *Expansions of the "Old Testament" and Legends*, 35-142.

transformed Israel of the future. The subsequent phrase, "And they will all be called 'sons of the living God,'" echoes Hosea 1:10 (2:1, MT) in its prediction of a restored Israel who are named God's children (בני אל־חי) after the exile. The father-child relationship envisioned in *Jubilees* is between God and idealized humans. They are "idealized" inasmuch as the relationship is predicated of people who have been transformed by God's doing (circumcision of the heart, provision of a pure spirit) so as to act uprightly in a manner that actual Israel had not been able to attain to. This idealization, moreover, is anticipated in the future, signaling some sort of eschatological expectation, a time when the identity of Israel is rightly captured by the phrase "son of God" because the people live up to a certain standard and are therefore in a peculiar relationship with God.

The "son of God" status that is Israel's eschatological future is, also, the root from which it sprang. *Jubilees* 2:17-20 depicts God forecasting the selection of Israel from the moment when creation had culminated in the Sabbath: "I have chosen the seed of Jacob from among all that I have seen. And I have recorded him as my firstborn son, and have sanctified him for myself forever and ever" (v. 20). In this strand of tradition, Jacob (Israel) is the original "son" who holds the identity that the later "sons of God" will have to reacquire. One reason for this familial conjunction between God and humanity is that humanity is sharing in a heavenly practice when it keeps Sabbath. The angels themselves keep Sabbath along with God both in heaven and on earth (v. 18), and the selection of a family in Jacob is so that they might keep the Sabbath along with the heavenly host (vv. 21, 31). The relationship with God that makes Israel an idealized nation thus includes an embodiment on the earth of the defining heavenly activity of Sabbath keeping (cf. vv. 28, 30).

Jubilees does not focus on humanity's vocation to rule the world on God's behalf. But the dynamics of rule that come to the fore in the creation narrative of the Hebrew Bible are echoed in *Jubilees*'s rendering of the Noah and Abraham stories. Just before the death of Noah we are told that one-tenth of the evil spirits are left on the earth in order to be subject to Mastema, or Satan, and that the upright angelic host entrust the remedies for these spirits' ills to Noah (10:7-14). Thus, *Jubilees* depicts the people of God as possessing the antidote to stand against the effects of the evil spirits who have been given some dominion on the earth — and that dominion is particularly exercised over people (12:20).

In addition to depicting ideals for the people of God as a community, *Jubilees* also idealizes the ancestors of Israel. The portrait of a battle between humanity and evil spirits is developed when *Jubilees* introduces us to Abram

(11:14-24). His devotion to the creator enables him to overcome the wiles of Mastema, who had sent crows to consume the crops of the people. Abram's overcoming of the seed-eating crows entails both a commanding authority that drives the crows away (11:18-22) and the wisdom to create sowing implements that would immediately bury the seed in the ground (11:23-24). Abram's devotion to the creator enables him to overcome the evil spirit by subjecting nature to himself through the commanding of the crows. The result of his protection from the avian menace was that the people had enough food. Thus, providing for the people's need for food, overcoming opposing spiritual powers, and commanding of nature are all integrated in the authority Abram possessed because he forsook his father's idols and worshiped the creator. The exodus story places Abram's ability to thwart the plots of Mastema in sharper relief. In the later narrative, it is the heavenly host and God himself who overcome the plot and powers of Satan that threaten to destroy God's people (48:9-19).

In the blessing of Jacob, Isaac depicts his heir occupying the role of ruler: one to whom both the nations and his own family will bow (26:23-24). And in Isaac's blessing of Judah, the ancestor of Israel's kings is said to be the help and salvation of Israel (31:19). The blessings of kingship take on hues of divinity as the kings receive reverence of bowing subjects and bring about God's promised salvation.

3. WISDOM OF SOLOMON

The Wisdom of Solomon helps round out the picture of Israel functioning collectively as God's idealized agents on the earth. The prayer in chapter 9 refers to Israel as God's sons and daughters (υἱῶν σου καὶ θυγατέρων, v. 7). Such an idea of the whole people being God's children reflects scriptural precedents (e.g., Exod 4:22-23; Hos 11:1), and is an important reminder that "son of God" is a category with a broad range of connotations that often encompasses humans or specially selected humans in its number. The idea that the righteous are God's children runs right through Wisdom, as it forms a claim that is mocked by the foolish (2:18), and becomes especially prominent as a description of God's people who went through the exodus (16:10, 26; 18:4, 13). In Wisdom, the "sons" or "sons and daughters" of God are God's chosen people.

Another way in which Israel is named in Wisdom provides an important reference point for titles that might be given to representative human figures. Israel is dubbed "the holy ones" (ὁσίοις, 10:17; τῶν ὁσίων, 18:5) or "God's/his holy ones" (τοῖς ὁσίοις αὐτοῦ, 4:15; τοῖς ὁσίοις σου, 18:1). Such an appellation for God's chosen people should be borne in mind when we attempt to discern the connotations of the "holy ones of the Most High" (ἅγιοι ὑψίστου) in Daniel 7:18, and the demonic identification of Jesus as "the holy one of God" (ὁ ἅγιος τοῦ θεοῦ) in Mark 1:24.

4. DEAD SEA SCROLLS

The covenanters at Qumran saw their community as uniquely faithful in its understanding and execution of the ordinances of God. The scrolls reflect a group of people whose self-identity is that of the idealized people of God. In at least one set of reflections, the War Scroll, this idealization entails identification with God as well. Here we will take just a few soundings into the scrolls to show how its community is depicted, as a whole, as occupying this unique location.

a. The Community in 1QS

Throughout the Community Rule we find both explicit and implicit expectations that the community in the desert plays a peculiar role in embodying the holiness of God. This is reflected in the discussion of a man who refuses to enter the covenant in columns II-III. By being excluded, "He shall not be justified [לוא יצדק].... In the source of the perfect he shall not be counted. He will not come clean by the acts of atonement, nor shall he be purified by the cleansing waters.... For it is by the spirit of the true counsel of God that are atoned the paths of man.... And it is by the holy spirit of the community, in its truth, that he is cleansed of all his iniquities" (1QS III, 3-8).[343] The community itself is the location of God's atoning work, the source of purifying holiness. The cleansing agent, the holy spirit, is identified with the community in lines 7-8. The community thus performs the roles of purification that rightly belong to God alone. The discussion of the outsider concludes in the hope that he will turn to walk in the way God has appointed. "In this way he will be admitted by means of atonement pleasing to God, and for him it will be the covenant of an everlasting Community" (1QS III, 11-12).[344] The community is now identified as the substance of God's saving, atoning covenant.

The notion of the community as the saving covenant finds further elabora-

343. Martínez and Tigchelaar, *DSSSE*, 1:75.
344. Martínez and Tigchelaar, *DSSSE*, 1:75.

tion in column V. Fidelity to the standards outlined in the scroll lays "a foundation of truth for Israel, for the Community of the eternal covenant" (1QS V, 5-6).[345] Here we see an identification of this representative community with/as Israel itself. Moreover, this people is seen as the substance of God's covenant. As God's unique, representative people on the earth, the members are privy to the revelations about the law of Moses God has made to the priests within the sect (line 9). Those who reject this community and its embodiment of the covenant are subject to the covenant curses, including eternal destruction (lines 12-13). The community and its leadership thus become the proxy of God on the earth through their determination of who is truly part of God's people, led by the Prince of Lights, and who are the people of wickedness, led by the Angel of Darkness (cf. 1QS III, 20-22).

A final way in which the Community Rule idealizes the community is by depicting it as the meeting place between heaven and earth. The inheritance of the elect is "in the lot of the holy ones. He unites their assembly to the sons of the heavens in order (to form) the council of the Community and a foundation of the building of holiness to be an everlasting plantation throughout all future ages" (1QS XI, 7-9).[346] Though the community itself is not composed of divine beings, its temple-like proximity to the divine realm makes its gatherings the meeting place between heaven and earth. The assembly provides the way for humans to have contact with the angelic and divine.

b. Identification with God in the War Scroll (1QM)

Throughout this chapter I have argued that identification with God is something applicable to many types of humans, such that the evidence of early Judaism makes unsustainable the notion that identification with God is in any way tantamount to identification as God. The muster of the armies as outlined in columns III and IV of the War Scroll depict another such identification. The banners name the army of the covenanters and its various parts as nothing less than the embodiment of God on the field of battle. Throughout columns III and IV the people are commanded to label the army (see Table 1-1 on pp. 170–71).

345. Martínez and Tigchelaar, DSSSE, 1:81.

346. Martínez and Tigchelaar, DSSSE, 1:97. John J. Collins, "Qumran, Apocalypticism, and the New Testament," in The Dead Sea Scrolls Fifty Years after Their Discovery: Proceedings of the Jerusalem Congress, July 20-25, 1997 (ed. L. H. Schiffman et al.; Jerusalem: Old City, 2000), 133-38, points to this conjunction of heaven and earth as an indication of an inaugurated eschatology within the community.

The banners are wide-ranging. In all, they communicate that God is with this army and fighting for it. More than that, however, a number of the banners clearly indicate that the army is itself the manifestation of God on the earth. God's own truth and justice are known in the army that goes out for battle. God's fury is made known in the fury of their weapons. The might of the army is, in actuality, the might of God. The banners make clear that the humans one might behold with their eyes do not tell half the story.

Crispin Fletcher-Louis argues for an additional dynamic of the community's identification with God. In column X Israel is described as being "uniquely like God and privy to the secrets and order of creation."[347] The juxtaposition of "Who is like you, God of Israel?" with "Who is like your people Israel?" does not merely invite a repeated answer of "No one," but prompts the reader to recognize that no one is like Israel precisely because of the ways that Israel is like God (1QM X, 8-9). As Fletcher-Louis points out, God's incomparability is articulated with the question, "Who is like you . . . to do according to your great works and mighty strength?" whereas Israel has previously been described as those strengthened in the might of God (1QM X, 5-6).[348] No one is like Israel precisely because Israel as an idealized people uniquely embodies the identity of God. Another layer of this identification may well be found in the community's observance of the festival calendar, which functions as a repetition within the community of God's own acts of creation.[349]

Later, the "chosen ones of the holy people" "are described as seated with God and the angels in the holy dwelling" (1QM XII, 1).[350] The description of God's exalted people provides a bit more evidence for the thin veil between heavenly beings and idealized humans with which the Qumran sectarians operated.[351] This group of humans is tantamount to a theophany. By looking at their deeds, one sees the deeds of God himself. This is an ecclesiology of divine identity, in which the assembly is identified with God in God's unique, eschatological judgment of the earth. In 1QM, Israel, represented by the community,

347. Fletcher-Louis, *All the Glory of Adam,* 403-4.
348. Fletcher-Louis, *All the Glory of Adam,* 406.
349. Fletcher-Louis, *All the Glory of Adam,* 407-8.
350. Eshel, "4Q471B," 196.
351. This is not to say that the evidence from Qumran is univocal about the relationship between humanity and the angelic forces as one in which humans have not only a unique access to the likeness of God but also a position of rule over the angels. Some of the scrolls testify to the notion that angelic forces themselves rule over God's people in particular or humanity in general (e.g., 1QS, *Visions of Amram,* 4Q543, 4Q544, 4Q545, 4Q546, 4Q547, 4Q548).

Table 1-1 Banners for the Battle in 1QM (translations from *DSSSE*)

Aspect of the Army or Battle	Label
Trumpets of Muster	Mustered by God
Trumpets of Commanders	Princes of God
Trumpets for Enlisting	Rule of God
Chiefs in the Meeting House	God's directives for the holy council
Trumpets of the Camps	Peace of God in the camps of his holy ones
Trumpets Pulling Them Out	God's mighty deeds to scatter the enemy and force all those who hate justice to flee Withdrawal of mercy from those who hate God
Trumpets of Battle Formations	God's battle formations for avenging his wrath against all the sons of darkness
Trumpets of the Muster of the Infantry-men when Gates Open	Memorial of revenge at the moment appointed by God
Trumpets of the Slain	God's mighty hand in the battle to fell all the slain of unfaithfulness
Trumpets of Ambush	God's mysteries to destroy wickedness
Trumpets of Pursuit	God has struck all the sons of darkness, he shall not cause his wrath to return, until they are exterminated
Trumpets of Retreat	God has re-assembled
Trumpets of the Path of Return from Battle	Exaltations of God in peaceful return
Head of the Nation	God's nation
Banner of the Tribe	God's flag
Banner of the Thousand	God's fury unleashed against Belial and against all the men of his lot so that there is no remnant
Banner of the Hundred	From God is the hand of battle against all degenerate flesh
Banner of the Fifty	No longer do the wicked rise, [due to] God's might
Banner of the Ten	Songs of jubilation of God on the ten-string lyre

Aspect of the Army or Battle	Label
Banners for going into battle	God's truth
	God's justice
	God's glory
	God's judgment
Banners for approaching battle	God's right hand
	Time appointed by God
	God's confusion
	God's slaughter
Banners for retreat from battle	God's glorification
	God's greatness
	God's praise
	God's glory
First banner going out into battle	God's congregation
Second banner going out into battle	God's camps
Third banner going out into battle	God's tribes
Fourth banner going out into battle	God's families
Fifth banner going out into battle	God's battalions
Sixth banner going out into battle	God's Assembly
Seventh banner going out into battle	Summoned by God
Eighth banner going out into battle	God's armies
Banners for approaching battle	God's battle
	God's revenge
	God's lawsuit
	God's reward
	God's might
	God's prize
	God's power
	God's destruction of every futile people
Banners for retreat from battle	God's acts of salvation
	God's victory
	God's help
	God's support
	God's joy
	God's thanksgiving
	God's praise
	God's peace

is an idealized people in the strong sense, in its being depicted with actions, ascriptions, and attributes otherwise reserved for God alone.

5. ANIMAL VISIONS (1 ENOCH)

After the Animal Visions depict the rise of a king who rules the world for God, imagery depicting people standing in the place of God is democratized. After the judgment, the animals who survived, representative of the Gentile nations, bow down and worship the sheep (90:30), perhaps in echo of Daniel 7:27.[352] The posture of the nations toward Israel is one of submission as the sheep are specially identified with God. Not only do they bow, but they also make petitions of them (pray to them?) and obey them.[353] The sheep of Israel are the sovereign recipients of worship and petition.[354] This role is then focused on an Adam figure who appears in the form of a snow-white bull (90:37; cf. 85:3, as discussed above). The narrative tells us that these figures are identified with the Lord, playing his sovereign role in the presence of the nations. In ruling for God, receiving the worship, prayer, and obedience due to God, they play out roles that God has reserved for himself — and for those whom God chooses to act on God's behalf. There is a "divine identity" here, and it does set apart one person and one nation as specially exalted in the sight of God. But this special exaltation and identity do not imply either preexistence or ontological divinity.

The appearance of the Adam figure, after idealized depictions of a king and of Israel itself, affirms the move made in my own study of the biblical tradition to place idealized representation of God within the larger framework of the story of creation. What the kings and Israel do as representatives of God is to be a fulfillment of God's original creative purpose. God's representative humans not only stand in for God such that the rest of humanity must see God in them, but the representatives also represent humanity before God such that

352. If this does, in fact, echo the homage of the nations before the holy ones (יפלחון) in Daniel 7:27, we have evidence of the influence of Daniel 7 outside the Similitudes.

353. Darrell L. Bock, *Proclamation from Prophecy and Pattern: Lucan Old Testament Christology* (JSNTSup 12; Sheffield: JSOT, 1987), 134, comments on Daniel 7:27 that the notion of the nations worshiping before Israel "was never part of Israel's theology," such that its presence in Daniel 7:27 would be "unique, if not heretical." The worship and supplication of the nations demonstrates that Bock has overstated his case.

354. Nickelsburg, *1 Enoch*, 405: "In contrast to the sheep, who are at home within Jerusalem, the animals and birds of heaven are reduced to a position of great inferiority — worshipping, petitioning, and obeying the sheep."

those whom they represent eventually share in their fate. In this instance, the final human Adam figure comes as one whose primeval form is shared in by all who submit to him.

G. CONCLUSIONS: IDEALIZED HUMAN FIGURES AND THE IDENTITY OF GOD

The breadth and content of this survey of early Judaism parallels the breadth discovered by Maurice Casey, who concluded:

> The variety and extensive elaboration of these figures is remarkable: the Davidic king, an eschatological High Priest, an eschatological prophet, Abel, Elijah, Enoch, Melchizedek, Michael, Moses, Wisdom, all these were held by some Jews in this period to be of unusually elevated status and to have performed or to be about to perform some function of evident significance. The ascription of significant new functions to these figures ... [is] of greater importance than the static parallels already discussed, because they testify to the existence of a developmental process whose variability shows that when another intermediary figure is elaborated we should not expect it to conform to any existing figure.[355]

As Casey rightly notes, there is rich variety in the sorts of figures who can stand in for God, and an equally rich variety in the types of work that they might perform. In addition, Casey points out the significant freedom Jewish authors exercised in describing the nature and functions of such figures, a freedom that will be important to bear in mind as we turn to the Synoptic Gospels. In terms of the breadth of possibilities we find in early Judaism, my own investigation allows for the following conclusions:

1. Idealized human figures are a widespread and wide-ranging reality in the literature of early Judaism. This is so both in the soft sense of persons or communities who are depicted as chosen by God or ideally pious, and in the stronger sense of human beings of the past, present, or idealized future who are depicted with actions, ascriptions, or attributes that are typically reserved for God alone. The textual data of early Judaism provide overwhelming evidence

---

355. Casey, "Chronology and Development," 128; cf. idem, *From Jewish Prophet to Gentile God: The Origins and Development of New Testament Christology* (Cambridge: J. Clarke & Co., 1991), 81-82.

against the notion that a theological commitment to monotheism placed significant restrictions on how a faithful Jew might depict a human hero.

2. Although there are angelic figures who play such roles as well, early Judaism maintained a special role for humans as God's idealized agents. In focusing on human figures rather than angelic beings or divine hypostases, this chapter has opened up a significant new vista for interpreting the work of Jesus as it is depicted across early Christianity, including the Synoptic Gospels. This book is not intended to function as a holistic account of the Christological development of earliest Christianity; however, it has demonstrated that a good deal of what is often taken to be "high Christology" in the sense of divine Christology actually has antecedents in idealized human figures, and thus is a high, *human* Christology. The widespread phenomena of idealized human figures suggest both that many scholars have jumped too quickly to the assumption that divinity of some sort is entailed in some of the earliest depictions of Jesus, and that the quest for parallels among angelic or other celestial figures might be less fruitful than has often been hoped. Specifically at this point I return to the arguments of Richard Bauckham, who looked for parallels to his "divine identity Christology" among angels, but found that they, for instance, serve rather than rule. In the final analysis, his argument fails to prove his case not only because the data directly contradict it (as he himself notices with regard to *1 Enoch*) but also because he tried to prove the point from the wrong set of data. It is more often idealized human figures, not angels, who bear the divine identity through actions, ascriptions, or attributes otherwise reserved for God alone.

3. Idealized human figures are identified with God in various ways in early Judaism, including sharing in God's sovereignty and receiving worship. This shows us that being identified *with* God is not the same as being identified *as* God. Such is the claim of Bauckham in his denial of Christological development, and his claim that all Christian Christology depicts a Jesus who is fully divine in what will only be framed in different categories in Chalcedonian orthodoxy.[356] Instead, we find in early Jewish literature wide-ranging claims for various human figures sharing in the divine identity, without any sense that this puts pressure on the inherent identity of God, demanding its reconfiguration.

4. Despite the assertions of some early Jewish writers, we discover a notable absence of anxiety about applying divine attributes to people in both biblical and post-biblical Judaism. This is a crucial point in parsing many of the ar-

---

356. Bauckham, *Jesus and the God of Israel*, x.

guments about biblical Christology, particularly those that lean on a divine identity Christology or some variation of it. The theological conviction about Israel's one God is, of course, important to Israel's daily piety and practice. That such a conviction is firmly rooted is undeniable. The significance of this conviction in delimiting what can or cannot be said about other creatures, however, can only be known through a study of early Jewish representations of these others. This chapter demonstrates that for many Jewish writers across a wide span of years and of Jewish conviction, the confession of God's one-ness sat easily alongside the identification of their own heroes with this God. Although it lies outside the scope of my work, one suspects that the rhetorical effect of delimiting particular ascriptions, actions, or attributes to God in early Jewish texts is to distinguish the group's theology from that of outsiders, rather than to serve as a control over what might be said about the group's own heroes, divine or human.

The conclusions articulated in points 3 and 4 above resonate with the work previously done by Casey. He summarizes his study of early mediator figures by saying, "In particular, there was no bar against taking over features of God. For example, at Wis. 10–11 the major events of Salvation History are attributed to Wisdom, rather than to God, while in the *Similitudes of Enoch* God's function as the eschatological judge has been taken over by Enoch. It is this massive flexibility within a framework of commitment to Jewish monotheism which explains how devotion to Jesus could be expressed with genuinely unique features, without the perception that Jewish monotheism was breached."[357] Similarly, John Collins observes, "The sharp distinction between heaven and earth that was characteristic of the Deuteronomic tradition and of much of the Hebrew Bible was not so strongly maintained in the Hellenistic age, even in the Hebrew- and Aramaic-speaking Judaism presented by the Dead Sea Scrolls."[358] The conclusion I draw above based on the idealization of priests is equally apt as a conclusion for this chapter as a whole: Jewish monotheism plays little role in limiting how Jewish writers can depict (human) figures whom they or their communities recognize as being specially endowed for some task or function. Indeed, an opposite inclination seems to be at work: *it is precisely through depicting some human figure through ascriptions, actions, or attributes otherwise*

---

357. Maurice Casey, "Christology and the Legitimating Use of the Old Testament in the New Testament," in *The Old Testament in the New Testament: Essays in Honour of J. L. North* (JSNTSup 189; ed. Steve Moyise; Sheffield: Sheffield Academic, 2000), 42-64, here 54.

358. Collins, *Scepter and the Star,* 164.

indicative of the identity of God that early Jewish writers signal that God has given these humans crucial roles to play in the past, present, or idealized future.

Of the categories put forward by recent advocates for early high Christology that would connote Jesus as a divine figure per se, the two that might remain important are preexistence (as explored and defended by Simon Gathercole) and/or participation in creation (as argued by Bauckham). When either of these is in play, then we have to ask the question of what sort of heavenly being we are dealing with. Even here, however, we must take caution, as the example of *1 Enoch* makes clear. It is possible that a heavenly figure is heavenly only because his humanity has been exalted and glorified.

Early Jewish texts provide a great deal of material substantiating the broad category of "idealized human figures" who share in ascriptions, actions, and attributes otherwise reserved for God alone. What I have been arguing based on pre-rabbinic Jewish sources is captured perfectly in the later midrash *Tanḥuma Bemidbar* 3:15: "Our rabbis teach us that no king of flesh and blood rides on God's steed or puts on his robes or uses his crown or sits on his throne, but the Holy One, blessed be He, apportions all these to those who fear him, and gives them to them."[359] To pair with another being an action that is God's exclusive purview does not function as an indicator for early Jews that such a being is essentially divine; rather, it demonstrates that the being is a specially chosen agent with whom God has chosen to share it. It remains now to turn to the Synoptic Gospels and assess how far such a category takes us in interpreting the Jesus we meet in their pages.

---

359. As cited by Wayne A. Meeks, *The Prophet King: Moses Traditions and Johannine Christology* (Leiden: Brill, 1967), 193; cf. Hans Bietenhard, *Midrasch Tanḥuma B: R. Tanḥuma über die Tora, genannt Midrasch Jelammedenu* (2 vols.; Bern: Peter Lang, 1982), 2:263-64.

2 *Son of God as Human King*

If there is one phrase that carries the weight of divine Christology in the popular imagination, it is "son of God." The reason for this is not far to seek, as the Gospel of John uses such an identification of Jesus for the express purpose of articulating unique claims for Jesus's preexistence and divinity. One thinks, for instance, of how the Sabbath controversy in John 5 pointedly embodies John's Christology. Jesus's claim, "My father is working until now, and I also am working" (ὁ πατήρ μου ἕως ἄρτι ἐργάζεται κἀγὼ ἐργάζομαι, v. 17), is met with vigorous opposition from the Jewish leaders that the narrator interprets thus: "For this reason, therefore, the Jews were seeking to kill him even more, because . . . he said God was his own father, making himself equal to God" (διὰ τοῦτο οὖν μᾶλλον ἐζήτουν αὐτὸν οἱ Ἰουδαῖοι ἀποκτεῖναι, ὅτι . . . πατέρα ἴδιον ἔλεγον τὸν θεὸν ἴσον ἑαυτὸν ποιῶν τῷ θεῷ, v. 18). Although John's Jesus quickly qualifies this equality as derivative (the son only does what he sees the father doing), the thrust of the story is clear: Jesus's claims to sonship are somehow blasphemous for their infringements on divinity. This conflict unfolds, for the reader of the canonical Gospel of John, under the umbrella of John 1:1, where the son has been called θεός, and in a narrative that repeatedly calls attention to Jesus's sonship as something he has prior to coming to earth on his saving mission. For John, then, the son of God is preexistent and, in some sense, divine.

But such a distinctive, ontologically divine sense of "son of God" is not what we find in the majority of early Christian texts. Whereas John is generally careful to distinguish Jesus as God's υἱός from other children as τέκνα (1:12; 11:52), Paul is equally careful to speak of Christians as God's children using identical verbiage for the very purpose of making it clear that Jesus's sonship marks him as the first "son" among many "sons and daughters" who are God's new family. For Paul, Jesus is son of God in a manner that other humans can participate in (cf., e.g., Gal 3:26-27), instead of being son of God in a manner that completely distinguishes him from other persons as preexistent divinity. The fact that other persons are υἱοὶ θεοῦ in earliest Christianity should make us cautious in the extreme about using the singular form as an indication of divine Christology when it is applied to Christ. As the reference to Paul makes clear, others' participation in that designation does not make Christ's sonship any less representative or special, but it is Christological in the sense that this Christ is the first ("firstfruits," 1 Cor 15:20, 23) to attain to a destiny and to play a role that is assigned to God's people as a whole (cf. Rom 8:29). Others come to bear that same name as they are joined to the work of Christ.

In this, our first foray into the Gospels themselves, I seek to establish that the paradigm of idealized human figure accounts for the "son of God" data across all three Synoptic Gospels. In keeping with this, the argument of the current chapter is that in the Synoptic Gospels the title son of God reflects the notion of representative Christology that we find in the earliest extant Christian texts (i.e., Paul's letters) more closely than it does the later book of John with its higher Christology. The Synoptic Gospels thereby draw on the son of God theology that we saw reflected in the Adam and David ideals from the biblical and post-biblical tradition. In contrast to an earlier generation's view of son of God language reflecting a Greek God-man tradition, I have shown in the previous chapter how son of God language appears in reference to Israel and to Israel's idealized heroes of the past, as well as in reference to messianic hopes and a coming kingdom for God's people (e.g., 4QAramaic Apocalypse). This son of God tradition, that of the idealized and therefore God-attested human agent, is a key component to the Jewish idealized human figure paradigm, and here we will see that it provides the framework for understanding the use of the phrase across the Synoptic Tradition.

In the Synoptic Gospels we discover that son of God is a Christological title that indicates Jesus is king of the kingdom of God that he is proclaiming and enacting. Moreover, the route to his enthronement is the way of the cross. In Mark, we will see that Jesus as son of God structures the story such that Jesus is and fulfills his identity to be the Christ, son of God, in his particular calling of going to the cross. A threefold indication of Jesus's sonship structures the narrative on its way to the cross, within which we also find a few other indications that Jesus's sonship is tied to functions of ruling and judging the world on God's behalf. After studying Mark's story, we will look at Jesus as son of God in Luke and Matthew. In Luke, in particular, we see a clear development of Jesus as son of God within an intertwined royal Christology and Adam Christology. In light of our study of the Jewish scriptures and of early Judaism, this connection is not surprising, nor is its application to a messiah figure. In Matthew, the notion of sonship is expanded so that Jesus's followers are more frequently the daughters and sons of God, and so that Jesus receives obeisance because of his own unique messianic and filial identity and embodies in himself the identity of God's faithful and redeemed people.

A. SON OF GOD AS HUMAN KING IN MARK

1. SON OF GOD AND MARK'S NARRATIVE

Rudolf Bultmann summarized the transition between Jesus and the early church with the neat aphorism *"the proclaimer became the proclaimed."*[1] Jesus who had come announcing the reign of God was swept up into the church's proclamation as the messiah and agent of that kingdom. But in the Gospel narratives themselves, even as Jesus dedicates himself to proclaiming and enacting the kingdom of God, an even more important character proclaims Jesus within the story, for the reader to overhear — that character is God. Twice in Mark's Gospel the divine voice breaks in from above, once at the baptism (1:11) and once at the transfiguration (9:7). Each time, the voice declares that Jesus is God's son. The first time this voice speaks to Jesus; the second time, to the disciples on the mount of transfiguration. Then, after Jesus's messianic identity has been publicly proclaimed at his Jewish hearing, we hear the proclamation of Jesus's divine sonship on the lips of a human for the first time upon Jesus's death (15:39).[2] Here, I follow the arguments of those who have made the case that these three declarations are related, structuring the story of Jesus as divine son such that this divine sonship is shown to carry connotations of a messiah who suffers and dies — a rendering that thus fits within idealized human Christology without requiring additional connotations of divine ontology.[3]

---

1. Rudolf Bultmann, *Theology of the New Testament* (2 vols.; trans. K. Grobel; Waco, TX: Baylor University Press, 2007), 1:33 (italics original).

2. On Mark as a structured narrative, and the significance of Christology and the son of God title in particular in that structure, see Eugene Boring, "Mark 1:1-15 and the Beginning of the Gospel," *Semeia* 52 (1990): 43-81.

3. This framework, and several of its key components, builds on the work of Donald H. Juel, e.g., "The Origin of Mark's Christology," in *The Messiah: Developments in Earliest Judaism and Christianity* (ed. J. H. Charlesworth; Minneapolis: Fortress, 1992), 449-60. The idea that the last of these declarations provides the key to the Christology of Mark's Gospel has been argued by Philip G. Davis, "Mark's Christological Paradox," *JSNT* 35 (1989): 3-15. One important

The persuasiveness of viewing each of the three scenes as in conversation with the other two will have to come from detailed exegesis; however, there are a few considerations that I outline here in order to establish the initial plausibility that Mark's readers should so see them. In suggesting that son of God language is a structuring device, and that its literary signals are sufficiently clear to an ideal reader, I am arguing that Mark's narrative as a whole intends to demonstrate what this son of God title entails. Further, I am arguing that the narrative discloses that Jesus as son of God is the king who must suffer in order to fully come into his kingship.

Table 2-1 Parallels between "Son of God" Declarations in Mark

	Baptism	Transfiguration	Crucifixion
Son of God	God: σὺ εἶ ὁ υἱός μου ὁ ἀγαπητός, ἐν σοὶ εὐδόκησα (1:11)	God: οὗτός ἐστιν ὁ υἱός μου ὁ ἀγαπητός, ἀκούετε αὐτοῦ (9:7)	Centurion: οὗτος ὁ ἄνθρωπος υἱὸς θεοῦ ἦν (15:39)
Elijah	John the Baptizer (1:6; cf. 9:12)	Elijah with Moses (9:4; cf. Ἡλίας μὲν ἐλθὼν πρῶτον, 9:12)	ἴδωμεν εἰ ἔρχεται Ἡλίας (15:36; cf. 15:35)
Rent [Heavens]	σχιζομένους τοὺς οὐρανούς (1:10)	[ἐγένετο νεφέλη ἐπισκιάζουσα αὐτοῖς, καὶ ἐγένετο φωνὴ ἐκ τῆς νεφέλης (9:7)]	τὸ καταπέτασμα τοῦ ναοῦ ἐσχίσθη εἰς δύο ἀπ᾽ ἄνωθεν ἕως κάτω (15:38)
Spirit	τὸ πνεῦμα . . . καταβαῖνον εἰς αὐτόν (1:10)	[luminous whiteness]	Ἰησους . . . ἐξέπνευσεν (15:27; cf. 15:39)
Death	Baptism (cf. 10:38)	Suffering son of man (8:31, 9:12), "listen to him" (9:7)	Crucifixion, death
Kingship?	"stronger one who comes" (1:7); served by angels (1:13); proclaiming kingdom (1:15)	Peter's confession (8:29), glorified son of man (8:38)	ὁ βασιλεὺς τῶν Ἰουδαίων (15:26); ὁ χριστὸς ὁ βασιλεὺς Ἰσραήλ (15:32)

takeaway from Davis's study is that attention to the son of God title in Mark is not an attempt to simplistically understand Mark's Christology by attention to titles, but is, in fact, honoring the text and its narrative developments.

To begin, table 2-1 lists parallels among the scenes. The extensive parallels exist on both verbal and conceptual levels. In support of the claim for the interrelatedness of these passages, we should note first of all that the son of God scenes sketched in table 2-1 follow the gradual revelation of Jesus's identity that unfolds within the story world of Mark's Gospel (the reader, of course, knows of Jesus's identity from 1:1). The first declaration that Jesus is son of God is made solely to Jesus himself (σὺ εἶ, 1:11). The divine revelation to the disciples that Jesus is God's son (οὗτός ἐστιν) is made only after Peter has made his confession that Jesus is the Christ (8:29) and Jesus has refracted the Christological title in favor of a predication of the suffering son of man (which Peter, in turn, rejects) (8:31-33).[4] Then, the only confession of Jesus as son of God by a human being is made after Jesus himself has openly affirmed that he is the Christ, the son of the Blessed, during his Jewish hearing (15:61-62). The Christological reality encompassed in the phrase "son of God" comes, then, in approbation of Jesus at his baptism, in rebuke to the disciples who have, in Peter, rejected suffering as Jesus's messianic vocation, and in proclamation by a man who sees in the way that Jesus breathes his last that Jesus was son of God. As I demonstrate in greater detail below, this is a movement from death symbolized (in baptism) through death prophesied to death actualized. The title son of God thus anchors a narratological and thematic development about Jesus as suffering Christ.

Moreover, the verb σχίζω appears in both chapter 1 with respect to the heavens and in chapter 15 with regard to the temple veil. These are the only two uses of the verb in the book. This invites a connection between the stories, as the heavenly realm where God lives is breached at Jesus's baptism for the purpose of his spirit anointing, and as the image of that space between the divine dwelling in heaven and human dwelling on earth is breached with Jesus's death. In addition, the presence of God in the cloud on the mountain indicates a conjoining of the typically separated realms of earth and heaven. If those who see in the use of the verb σχίζω an allusion to Isaiah 64:1 are correct ("O that you would rend the heavens and come down," Isa 63:19 in the LXX and MT),[5]

4. The language of "refraction" as well as "deflection," used here and throughout the discussion of Mark, builds on the deployment of the term by Elizabeth Struthers Malbon in *Mark's Jesus: Characterization as Narrative Christology* (Waco, TX: Baylor University Press, 2009). "Deflected Christology" is what Jesus says in response to others' claims about him; "refracted Christology" is what Jesus says instead. In the case of the son of humanity sayings, the line is somewhat blurry, inasmuch as these are often what Jesus says both in response to what others say and what Jesus says instead.

5. The LXX contains the verb ἀνοίγω rather than Mark's σχίζω for the Hebrew קרעת; how-

then this presence of God in the cloud is connected to the first and last son of God sayings by its scriptural antecedent: God comes down.

There is, then, sufficient preliminary grounds for associating these three passages that we can proceed with the more detailed exegesis to discover how each functions in the narrative as well as their interactions. Thus will we discover whether the connections made are fruitful for our interpretation of what Mark means to signify by identifying Jesus as son of God at the beginning, middle, and end of the story. I maintain that Mark is showing the readers that son of God means precisely what one hears from the mouth of the high priest when he questions Jesus by placing the title in apposition to Christ (14:61). To be the son of the Blessed is to be nothing other than messiah, a royal title that is paradoxically claimed, in Mark, by going to the cross, and without any allusions to eternal sonship, preexistence, incarnation, or divine intervention into Jesus's birth.[6]

a. Baptized Son of God

The reader of Mark's Gospel first meets Jesus in the baptism scene, but has been given a preliminary framework for interpreting what happens there. First, the opening lines of the book indicate that Jesus's title is Christ or messiah (1:1).[7] Then, a litany of Old Testament texts, introduced under the rubric of what is written in Isaiah, indicates that God has sent John the Baptizer ahead of Jesus. We return to a fuller discussion of the verses cited in chapter 7 below, but for now it is important to note that the author of Mark has replaced possible divine references in the Old Testament texts with references to Jesus.

The previous chapter identified the phenomenon of replacing the divine name or God as the subject of a given text with another idealized figure in other early Jewish texts (Melchizedek's replacement of the Yhwh in 11QMelchizedek II, 6; the Teacher's replacement of Yhwh as object of fidelity in 1QpHab VIII, 1-3; the priest playing the role of Yhwh from Habakkuk 5:14 in 4Q167 frag. 2, 2). In Mark, rather than having the divine voice say, in keeping with Malachi 3:1, that the messenger prepares the way "before me" (πρὸ προσώπου μου), Mark reads instead that the messenger prepares the way "before you"

---

ever, Mark does not appear to follow any extant version of the LXX in his biblical allusions, so the lack of verbal agreement is no definitive argument against an allusion here.

6. Adela Yarbro Collins, "Mark and His Readers: The Son of God Among Jews," *HTR* 92 (1999): 393-408, here 403.

7. It seems best to presume that "son of God" in 1:1 is not original, given the shakiness of its textual basis.

(πρὸ προσώπου σου). Similarly, rather than maintaining the divine identity between the one for whom the way is prepared and Jesus, Mark reads, "make his paths straight" (εὐθείας ποιεῖτε τὰς τρίβους αὐτοῦ) in place of Isaiah's "make the paths of our God [τοῦ θεοῦ ἡμῶν] straight" (Isa 40:3). Whereas in their original scriptural settings these verses speak of a messenger who comes before God as such, Mark has introduced a distance between God and the Lord who appears in the story. God is still identified as the sender of the messenger (Mark 1:2; Mal 3:1), but the messenger precedes one whom the divine voice addresses in the second person.[8] The messenger in this story is sent before a κύριος (Mark 1:3) who is distinct from God as such. Pursuing a similar line of argument, Joel Marcus concludes, "Mark thus establishes the identity between the two ways, that of Jesus and that of the Lord, without simply identifying Jesus with God, for the distinction between them is maintained in that Jesus's apparent defeat is the occasion for God's victory" (cf. 15:33-39).[9]

The opening pericopes tie John and Jesus closely together while also making clear to the reader that Jesus is the main character in the story. The introductory salvo of biblical citations creates just such a connection: God has sent John in preparation for the main character who will then come on the scene. John also characterizes their ministries as typified by distinct baptisms. John's is a baptism with water, indicating repentance and offering forgiveness of sins (1:4; 8). He contrasts this water baptism with Jesus as one who will baptize with the spirit (1:8). With Mark's rapid-fire indications of a preparatory ministry that would be superseded by a greater one, the reader is poised to recognize Jesus's appearance as the arrival of the "Lord" and the "greater one" whose way John has prepared. The baptism scene itself serves as the transition from the one to the other as Jesus participates in John's baptism of repentance for forgiveness of sins only to receive the same spirit that would mark Jesus's own baptismal ministry. The initial parity between Jesus's baptism and that of the others who come to John is striking (and seems to have caused Matthew no little consternation! — see Matt 3:14). Jesus comes from Galilee, but otherwise the report of his baptism prior to his coming out of the water is remarkable only for its similarity with other people's. Jesus, from Galilee (Mark 1:9), joins the crowds from Jerusalem and Judea (1:5) by being baptized by John in the Jordan River (1:9; 1:5). This parity is significant for highlighting the momen-

8. So also R. T. France, *The Gospel of Mark* (NIGTC; Grand Rapids, MI: Eerdmans, 2002), 63-64.

9. Joel Marcus, *The Way of the Lord: Christological Exegesis of the Old Testament in the Gospel of Mark* (Louisville, KY: Westminster John Knox, 1992), 40-41.

tous import of the post-baptismal scene in which the heavens open. Despite the anticipation of the appearance of a greater one, Jesus is not marked out as this greater one simply by the appearance of his character in the story for the first time, but only by the divine response to his solidarity with the rest of the Jewish people in the baptism of John.

When Jesus comes out of the water, the readers of Mark's Gospel are privy to a scene that only Jesus can see (εἶδεν): the heavens ripped apart and the spirit descending into (εἰς) Jesus like a dove (1:10). That Jesus is the only one who apprehends the scene is confirmed in the voice addressing him directly, σὺ εἶ ὁ υἱός μου ὁ ἀγαπητός, ἐν σοὶ εὐδόκησα ("You are my beloved son, in you I am well pleased," 1:11). These two heavenly events, the descent of God's spirit and the declaration of sonship, are interrelated and mutually interpreting. In Mark, the spirit itself is not a native possession of Jesus by virtue of either divine identity or even conception and birth, but is received for the first time at this baptismal event. Receiving God's spirit, in the biblical (i.e., Old Testament) world that Mark has signaled his readers is to be the interpretive grid for his story (in 1:2-3), is amenable to several interpretations. It is the endowment from God for wisdom and insight to accomplish specific tasks (Gen 41:38; Exod 28:3; 31:3; Wis 7:7), the enabler of specific acts of prophecy (e.g., Num 23:7; Mic 3:8; Joel 3:1), the bestowal that enables people to function as prophets and judges of the people (e.g., Num 11:16-30; 27:18; Judg 3:10; 6:34), and the marker of kingship that includes prophecy and even exorcism (1 Sam 10:1-10; 16:13-16, 23; Isaiah 11).[10] The servant of Isaiah 41:1 seems to play an amalgam of such roles as he receives the spirit. The one interpretive key that Mark has already provided for making sense of this bestowal of the spirit comes in 1:1, where Jesus is called Christ, which leads to the preliminary assessment that this is a royal anointing (which, as we see in 1 Samuel 16 and Isaiah 11, as well as other scriptural precedents, is simultaneously an endowment to act on God's behalf in a number of ways).

The voice from heaven confirms that this is a royal anointing.[11] As we have seen in our survey of Israel's scriptures, sonship was predicated of Adam, Israel, and Davidic kings, among others. In this case, the words "you are my son" allude to Psalm 2, which in turn draws from a broader reservoir of Israel's royal theology in which the king is elevated to the role of "son of God" upon his

10. Cf. Adela Yarbro Collins and John J. Collins, *King and Messiah as Son of God: Divine, Human, and Angelic Messianic Figures in Biblical and Related Literature* (Grand Rapids, MI: Eerdmans, 2008), 127.

11. Collins and Collins, *King and Messiah*, 127.

ascension to the throne.[12] In that psalm, the divine voice speaks to the nations, telling them of the enthronement of Israel's king in Zion (v. 6). Then, the royal voice speaks: "I will tell of the decree of YHWH: He said to me, 'You are my son; today I have begotten you'" (v. 7; υἱός μου εἶ σύ, LXX). Moreover, the king in Psalm 2 is king over a kingdom as a subordinate to YHWH, who sits enthroned in the heavens.[13] Robert Rowe thus concludes, "By this allusion to Psalm 2 at the beginning of Mark's gospel, Jesus's messiahship/Sonship is shown to be both subordinate to God's kingdom, and the primary means whereby that kingdom is to be manifested on earth."[14] The verbal parallel, in which God is addressing the regent, compels the conclusion that the reception of the spirit and the divine voice together amount to a royal anointing. Donald Juel connects the opening line of the story with the divine voice in 1:11 and comments, "For those who know the psalm, the association of Jesus with messianic promises appropriately confirms what has been stated by the narrator."[15] Moreover, Joel Marcus has documented the pervasive presence of Psalm 2 giving shape to messianic expectations in early Judaism.[16] The two dynamics of receiving the spirit and the divine proclamation are twin endowments, each of which is necessary for Jesus to enact the royal sonship with which he is bestowed. A true change takes place for Jesus in this scene, inasmuch as he is not only given an "office" but is also endowed with the power necessary to be the agent who opposes and defeats God's enemies.[17]

A brief reference to some material from the Dead Sea Scrolls will confirm that son of God language in early Judaism could be used of an expected coming king. In a passage that slides easily between the son of God and the people of God whom he rules (or, better, who rule with him) we find considerable overlap with the Christology of the Synoptic Gospels: "He will be called son of God, and they will call him son of the Most High. . . . Until the people of God arises and makes everyone rest from the sword. His kingdom will be an

12. Cf. Donald Juel, *Messianic Exegesis: Christological Interpretation of the Old Testament in Early Christianity* (Philadelphia: Fortress, 1988), 59-79; Sam Janse, *"You Are My Son": The Reception History of Psalm 2 in Early Judaism and the Early Church* (Leuven: Peeters, 2009), 105-19.

13. Cf. Stephen P. Ahearne-Kroll, "The Scripturally Complex Presentation of Jesus in the Gospel of Mark," in *Portraits of Jesus: Studies in Christology* (WUNT2 321; ed. Susan E. Meyers; Tübingen: Mohr Siebeck, 2012), 45-68, here 48-49.

14. Robert D. Rowe, *God's Kingdom and God's Son: The Background to Mark's Christology from Concepts of Kingship in the Psalms* (Leiden: Brill, 2002), 242.

15. Donald Juel, *A Master of Surprise: Mark Interpreted* (Minneapolis: Fortress, 1994), 37.

16. Marcus, *Way of the Lord,* 59-66.

17. Marcus, *Way of the Lord,* 48-79.

eternal kingdom, and all his paths in truth. He will jud[ge] the earth in truth and all will make peace. . . . His rule will be an eternal rule" (4Q246 II, 1-5).[18] In addition, 4QFlorilegium provides an amalgam of biblical texts interpreted as prophecies of the coming Davidic messiah. These include the promise to David in 2 Samuel 7:14 that God will be a father to David's son, interpreted as a reference to "the branch of David" (4Q174 *frag.* 1, I, 10-11). This David figure is the one through whom God is going to "save Israel" (line 13). Moreover, the fragment includes the beginnings of a messianic reading of Psalm 2. Together, these are important indications that the biblical notion of king as son of God might carry messianic overtones for a Jewish community using the title of one whom they believed to be the messiah, that Mark's son of God Christology might well fit within the early Jewish idealized human Christology sketched in the previous chapter.

The royal overtones of the baptismal anointing, including the empowerment by the spirit, give the reader a knot of related connotations that provide an interpretive grid for the ensuing narrative: Jesus as one who acts as the spirit directs and empowers him, as one who possesses unique divine authority, and as one who not only announces but also enacts the reign of God, are mutually interdependent.[19] As Christ (Mark 1:1, 11), Jesus is depicted as king of the kingdom he announces.[20] Thus, in keeping with the expectations created by Psalm 2 and developed in early Judaism, Jesus's first act as spirit-endowed king is to confront the enemy of God's people.[21] In the narrative of Mark, however, that enemy is not the kings of the earth but Satan (who stands behind them?): "And immediately the spirit drove him out into the wilderness, and he was in the wilderness forty days being tempted by Satan" (1:12-13). Then, after John's arrest, Jesus proclaims the good news by saying that the reign of God has drawn near (ἤγγικεν ἡ βασιλεία τοῦ θεοῦ, 1:15). Thus, from anointing and confrontation of God's enemies, Jesus turns immediately to proclaim that God's reign is near. The preliminary indications, confirmed throughout, are that Jesus is the king of this kingdom.

Interestingly, though Mark tells his readers that Jesus went around proclaiming this kingdom, he does not immediately provide any extended teach-

18. Florentino García Martínez and Eibert J. C. Tigchelaar, *DSSSE* (2 vols.; Grand Rapids, MI: Eerdmans, 1998), 1:495.

19. Rowe, *God's Kingdom*, 60, includes in his summary of kingship in the Psalter the significance of the spirit as the agent of the king's anointing, extending other divine characteristics such as universal rule and glory to the king.

20. Cf. Janse, *"You Are My Son,"* 113-14.

21. Cf. Marcus, *Way of the Lord*, 66.

ing; instead, Mark's Jesus demonstrates through the actions of the subsequent narrative what the advent of that kingdom looks like. It consists in gathering people to himself (1:16-20; 2:13-17; 3:7-8, 13-19, 31-35), healing (1:29-34, 40-45; 2:1-12; 3:1-6, 10), and casting out demons (1:21-28, 32-34, 39; 3:11). These three preliminary activities are demonstrative of the same reality: Jesus is establishing a new reign of God, and in the process overthrowing the powers that stand opposed to the holistic well-being that marks God's rule. Thus, Mark interposes the Beelzebul controversy within the narrative of Jesus's redefinition of family. To be his mother, sister, and brother is to be one of those who, by sitting at Jesus's feet, identify themselves as those who do the will of God (3:34-35). This story sandwiches the debate over whose kingdom it is that Jesus serves through his casting out of demonic powers (3:22-30). The answer there is that the spirit of God is the power and thus makes known whose reign Jesus enacts and whose reign Jesus opposes. Jesus marks the coming of the reign of God by his own exercise of rule, by the spirit, over the demons, thus freeing people from the reign of Beelzebul so that they might participate in the kingdom whose kingship he holds.

Once again, Davidic parallels are apt, as Jesus's Old Testament type not only was endowed by the spirit but also served as an exorcist (1 Sam 16:23) and, during the period during which Saul was still on the throne, gathered a growing group of loyal followers to himself (e.g., 1 Sam 22:2). In the late first century, Josephus reflects a tradition in which God enabled Solomon to learn the arts of exorcism (*Ant.* 8.45). In this biblical and post-biblical tradition, power to exorcise fits within a royal framework.[22] Thus, the story about the coming of the kingdom as the good news of God, as it unfolds over the early chapters of Mark, provides further support to the notion that Jesus's baptism is a royal anointing.[23]

This first pass at the significance of the baptismal scene as a royal anointing has not yet taken full account of why the baptism scene per se is the context for Jesus's messianic endowment. The answer is bound up with the larger theme of the messianic secret in Mark's Gospel. Jesus's identity as messiah is only

---

22. For a more extensive discussion of the interconnections between exorcism and royal power, see below, chapter 5, "Lord of Heaven and Earth."

23. Oscar Cullmann, *Christology of the New Testament* (rev. ed.; trans. S. C. Guthrie and C. A. M. Hall; Philadelphia: Westminster, 1963), 284, avoids the language of kingship, choosing a unique relationship of "oneness" with the father, instead. Though I agree with Cullmann's insistence that suffering is the outworking of Jesus's unique identity as "son of God," it seems to me that he goes astray in dissociating the son of God language from messianic and/or royal ideas.

gradually revealed. When Peter tells Jesus that he is the Christ, Jesus refracts Peter's answer through the lens of the suffering son of man (8:27-33).[24] When Jesus openly confesses his messianic status at the Jewish hearing, it leads immediately to calls for his death (14:60-64).[25] And it is only by witnessing Jesus's death that a human being in the story is ever brought to the point of confessing that Jesus is God's son (15:39). The revelation of Jesus's messiahship is made in conjunction with the revelation that in order to be messiah, Jesus must die. Baptismal imagery participates in this theme.

Not only was baptism associated with Jesus's death in our earliest extant body of Christian literature (Paul's letters; e.g., Rom 6:3-5), Mark's Gospel itself draws on baptism as an image of death. Significantly, the question of baptism, and of Jesus's baptism in particular, recurs when James and John are asking for exalted thrones at Jesus's right and left hands in Jesus's glory (10:37). The latter passage itself participates in the larger motif of a messiahship made incomprehensible to the disciples precisely because Jesus's story, as the Christ, is heading inexorably toward the cross. In response to their request, Jesus asks about their ability to participate in his death by using two metaphors: being baptized and drinking a cup. For the reader, the implication is clear. Three times Jesus has predicted his death, to the befuddlement of his followers. The first time, this prediction was for the purpose of reframing Peter's confession of Jesus as Christ — a reframing that Peter rejected. And in each of the subsequent passion-resurrection predictions, we find the disciples thinking about their own greatness rather than recognizing the significance of Jesus's cruciform redefinition of his, and their, calling.

The connection to Jesus's looming death also becomes clear as Mark moves immediately into another engagement of Jesus with his disciples, in which Jesus has to deal with the ten other disciples' disgruntlement with James and John (10:41-45). In that subsequent text he attempts to reorient them toward a different view of greatness, one in which service and laying down one's life mark the way to being first of all. As Mark's reader approaches the passion narrative, the connection between Jesus's response to James and John and his own death becomes stronger still: the "cup" is the cup of Jesus's blood, and it is also the cup of his looming death that he prays might be taken away during his anguished lament in the garden (14:24, 36). Finally, the reader will discover that the request of James and John to sit at Jesus's right and left hands finds a dark echo in the crucifixion scene when those crucified alongside him occupy

24. Cf. Rowe, God's Kingdom, 230-31.

25. For further exploration of both scenes, see the following chapter on the son of man.

the places at Jesus's right and left hands (15:27). When Jesus talks to his disciples about his baptism he is talking to them about his death. This later light shines backward on the original baptism scene itself, showing the reader that the earlier scene conceals Mark's messianic secret in plain sight: death looms ahead of Jesus, but it is precisely in going to this death that Jesus fulfills his calling to be the son of God, which is to be the Christ who reigns over the world on God's behalf.

Recently, Leroy Huizenga has offered another line of inquiry that bolsters the notion that Jesus's baptism and the heavenly voice that attends it indicate that Jesus's destiny is death.[26] Although his argument is focused on the Gospel of Matthew, which carries additional weight in favor of his thesis, the basic argument applies to Mark as well. In short, the argument is that the "beloved son" in the Jewish tradition comprised an allusion to Isaac, and to Abraham's offering of Isaac in particular.[27] The first important factor in drawing the Isaac connection is the phrase ὁ υἱός μου ὁ ἀγαπητός (Mark 1:11), a phrase that finds striking similarity in the occurrence of the five words in the same sequence in Genesis 22: τὸν υἱὸν σου τὸν ἀγαπητόν (v. 2, LXX) and τοῦ υἱοῦ σου τοῦ ἀγαπητοῦ (vv. 12, 16, LXX).[28] Huizenga notes, further, that each story indicates divine intervention into the earthly sphere from heaven (ἐκ τῶν οὐρανῶν, Mark 1:11; Matt 3:17; ἐκ τοῦ οὐρανοῦ, Gen 22:11, 15, LXX). This is a striking set of correspondences that invites the reader to understand God as the father who will not spare his own son even as Abraham did not spare Isaac (οὐκ ἐφείσω, Gen 22:12; cf. Rom 8:32, οὐκ ἐφείσατο).

Thomas Hatina has developed the argument with respect to Mark itself.[29]

---

26. The argument below follows Leroy Huizenga, but a parallel argument is offered with a focus on Mark's Gospel by Matthew S. Rindge, "Reconfiguring the Akedah and Recasting God: Lament and Divine Abandonment in Mark," *JBL* 130 (2011): 755-74, here 762-71. He demonstrates the pervasiveness of the theme of a lamenting Jesus forsaken by God, a crucial set of considerations to keep on the table as we parse the relationship between the two characters in Mark's telling of the story.

27. Leroy A. Huizenga, *The New Isaac: Tradition and Intertextuality in the Gospel of Matthew* (SupNovT 131; Leiden: Brill, 2009). The argument had been taken up previously, with specific regard to the Gospel of Mark, by William R. Stegner, "The Baptism of Jesus: A Story Modeled on the Binding of Isaac," *BR* 1 (1985): 36-46; however, Stegner's argument leans too heavily on potentially late targumic material as necessary antecedents to Mark and also too much on vague correspondences between the two stories to be entirely compelling.

28. Huizenga, *New Isaac*, 153.

29. Thomas R. Hatina, "Embedded Scripture Texts and the Plurality of Meaning," in *Biblical Interpretation in Early Christian Gospels*, vol. 1, *The Gospel of Mark* (LNTS 304; ed. T. R. Hatina; New York: T&T Clark, 2006), 81-99, here 88-93.

Hatina not only highlights the connections between the voice from heaven and that which addressed Abraham, but also teases out a couple of important Jewish co-texts to be read alongside the baptism scene. *Testament of Levi* 18:6-7 is remarkable, even if laced with Christian interpolations. If the elements corresponding to Mark 1 are later Christian additions, then it simply indicates that early readers of Mark recognized the allusion to Genesis 22. The portion cited by Hatina includes the opening of the heavens, "a fatherly voice, as from Abraham to Isaac," the glory of the most high descending on the chosen one, and "the spirit of understanding and sanctification" remaining on him.[30] Hatina also cites Philo's calling Isaac υἱὸς θεοῦ and Josephus's depiction of Isaac as a willing and pious victim, a rendering that puts Josephus's account in a stream of interpretation that sees Isaac's sacrifice as that of an ideal martyr, effective for the nation.[31] In light of the active place that Isaac played in the imagination of early Jewish idealized martyr figures, the allusive force of the voice from heaven seems to disclose, to the attentive reader, that the Christological title secretly bestowed upon Jesus entails as well a particular task of submitting to death.

As I read the options, one need not choose between an allusion to royal enthronement as described in Psalm 2 and an allusion to the binding of Isaac as described in Genesis 22.[32] Instead, the David and Isaac references function in tandem, introducing the two-pronged messianic identity that it will take the duration of the story to fully disclose: Jesus is Christ, but his particular calling as Christ is to be rejected, suffer, die, and rise again.[33] The baptism scene provides a coalescence of this theme from various angles: the imagery of baptism itself, the language of sonship, the allusions to Psalm 2 and Genesis 22, the repetition of the royal and suffering and son of God themes at the end, and the modulation of Peter's confession by Jesus's destiny. Each of these larger narrative dynamics underscores that for Mark's Gospel (and, as Huizenga's work begins to indicate for us, Matthew's as well) son of God is a title of suffering royalty rather than preexistent divinity.[34]

---

30. Hatina, "Embedded Scripture," 89.

31. Hatina, "Embedded Scripture," 89-90.

32. Cf. the plural possibilities suggested in Hatina, "Embedded Scriptures."

33. Malbon, *Mark's Jesus*, 76-78, sees in the scene that Jesus is designated as someone being set apart for a special relationship to God through which God will be at work in the world (assuming the person's faithfulness), and also possible hints of looming death. Focusing on the literary development of Mark per se, she leaves these possibilities open for what will follow in the narrative.

34. Edwin K. Broadhead, *Naming Jesus: Titular Christology in the Gospel of Mark* (JSNT-Sup 175; Sheffield: Sheffield Academic, 1999), 121, comes to a similar conclusion, though he

b. Transfigured Son of God

The second time that God directly enters the story it is, substantively, to re-iterate the first divine speech. At the transfiguration scene, the divine voice breaks out from the overshadowing cloud to proclaim Jesus's sonship. This time, however, the disciples, who have been brought in on the messianic secret through Peter's confession and Jesus's son of man interpretation of the Christ title, are the objects of the divine address: οὗτός ἐστιν ὁ υἱός μου ὁ ἀγαπητός, ἀκούετε αὐτοῦ (Mark 9:7).

This is a crucial moment in the narrative. It serves as the culmination of the transitional scene that begins with Peter's confession. Mark has tied together the various pericopes from 8:27–9:13 by various means. The pericope of the confession itself (8:27-30) is tied to the first passion prediction (8:31-33) as Jesus's instruction redefines the nature of Peter's "Christ" under Jesus's rubric of the son of man (discussed fully in the following chapter). This, in turn, runs immediately into sayings material in which Jesus conjoins his upcoming martyrological destiny with the nature of discipleship (8:34–9:1), material that culminates in a second son of man saying, one that links willingness to follow Jesus to death with eschatological recognition before God. Through his narrative progression Mark has linked the messianic title with a particular way of life for both Jesus and the disciples, and in Peter's reproof the disciples have rejected the cross as Jesus's way to eschatological glory. The transfiguration scene not only follows this previous narrative unit, but also is tied to it as the following scene in a coherently developing story. Mark makes this tie by using a rare temporal marker to introduce the transfiguration pericope: "after six days" (καὶ μετὰ ἡμέρας ἕξ, 9:2). Thus, Mark ties together the transfiguration story and its climactic, divine declaration that Jesus is God's son with Peter's Christological confession, Jesus's cruciform destiny, and the glory that awaits both Jesus and those who are willing to follow him on the way of the cross.[35]

---

skirts the particular claim of kingship: "the narrative associates sonship terminology with two contrasting images: authority and submissive suffering." It is difficult to know how similar or dissimilar the position I hold is to that of Marcus, *Way of the Lord*. While agreeing that a true transformation and empowering takes place in the baptism scene, I am unclear how Jesus can both be said to participate in "God's very power and being" and also be "distinct from God" (72). If this means that Jesus fulfills the Adam Christology in which Israel's king becomes the idealized humanity that is the image and likeness of God, I concur. If it pushes beyond a high human Christology into some sort of ontological transformation, I demur.

35. Rowe, *God's Kingdom and God's Son*, 259-60, also makes note of the transfiguration as a culmination of Jesus's cruciform reorientation of Peter's Christological confession.

A final indication that Mark intends a literary unity across these stories comes from the conversation that unfolds as the disciples and Jesus descend the mount. Jesus warns the disciples not to mention what they have seen until the son of man has been raised from the dead (9:9) — a coming reality to which both the reader and the disciples have been alerted in the passion-resurrection prediction in 8:31. When the disciples ask, in turn, about the need for Elijah to come first, Jesus again alludes to his son of man passion-resurrection prediction, asking how it is written that the son of man must suffer and be despised (9:12). Sandwiched between these son of man sayings, the transfiguration serves as a divine approbation of Jesus's delineation of his messianic calling in terms of the suffering and then glorified son of man.[36]

As indicated above, this larger discourse unit is also evocative of the opening scenes of Mark's Gospel. Not only is this the second appearance of the divine voice in the story, making the same proclamation about Jesus's identity, but a host of other narrative cues also take the reader back to the beginning of the Gospel. Taking into account the entire unit of 8:27–9:13, we note the following:

1. Peter's confession is only the second time that the word χριστός has appeared in the text, the first being in 1:1.

2. For those readers of the Gospel whose manuscripts contained υἱοῦ θεοῦ in 1:1, the confession-transfiguration unit corresponds to, and lends substance and explanation to, the opening line of the book.

3. John the Baptist is present as an Elijah figure in both passages (1:4-6; 9:4, 11-13).

4. In the baptism scene, the heavens are torn open and God's spirit descends (1:10); in the transfiguration, God descends in the cloud (9:7).

5. The implications of baptism as indicating a martyrological end for Jesus are affirmed in the son of man passion prediction.

6. Not only is Jesus called "son" in each text, but also the particular appellation ὁ υἱός μου ὁ ἀγαπητός is spoken by the divine voice (1:11; 9:7).

7. In the baptism, after the divine voice affirms Jesus's baptismal vocation of death, Satan tempts Jesus (1:13); after the first passion prediction, Satan tempts Jesus a second time in Peter's attempted dissuasion (8:33).[37]

---

36. Cf. James D. G. Dunn, *Christology in the Making: A New Testament Inquiry into the Origins of the Doctrine of the Incarnation* (2nd ed.; Grand Rapids, MI: Eerdmans, 1996), 47.

37. The character of Satan is mentioned in the Beelzebul controversy (3:23, 26) and in the interpretation of the parable of the sower as well (4:15). Otherwise, this is the only other

8. God becomes present in each, through the dove at the baptism and the
    shekinah cloud at the transfiguration.

Thus, the connections between the two divine declarations of Jesus as son of
God go far beyond the words themselves. The reader who attends to the larger
dynamics of the first story is enlightened about the second, and vice versa.[38]
The royal connotations of son of God that I argued for in the baptism, as well
as their peculiar cruciform overtones, provide the basic framework for understanding the phrase in the transfiguration as well.[39]

The particular question that this passage raises for my study is this: is the
transfiguration a disclosure of divine identity as such, or is it, instead, a revelation of glorified messianic identity? Adela Yarbro Collins has argued for
the possibility of the former, suggesting that Greek readers would have read
the scene as an indication of Jesus's own divinity. She suggests that readers
familiar with the Greek canon would know the tradition of gods going about
disguised in human form. Collins cites the example of Demeter who so conceals her divinity, only to later reveal herself in all her divine glory to her em-
ployer.[40] The strongest point of comparison is in the gleaming brightness that
attends both Jesus and Demeter. The dissimilarities are more compelling than
the similarities, however. Importantly, Jesus does not disclose his own divine
identity, but it is revealed, instead, by a heavenly voice. Also, in the Jesus story
in Mark, there is no indication of a prior possession of divine glory that Jesus
is disclosing (John's Gospel might provide stronger points of comparison). As
Collins also points out, Demeter's revelation leads to the building of an altar
and temple, while Peter's lesser proposal is dismissed.[41]

More importantly, however, this reading lacks purchase for a reason that I

---

naming of Satan in the story, perhaps a final failure to tempt Jesus away from a martyrological
interpretation of his son of God/Christological identity.

38. I see Simon Gathercole going astray here in *The Preexistent Son: Recovering the Christologies of Matthew, Mark, and Luke* (Grand Rapids, MI: Eerdmans, 2006), 49-50. He rightly
claims that the readers of the Gospels know that Jesus is son of God throughout, but assumes
that this title indicates some sort of heavenly divinity that, as this chapter shows, is foreign to
Mark and Luke especially, and highly unlikely for Matthew as well. My argument is that the title
has less to do with a divine ontology than with executing a divinely appointed function. There
is true development of Jesus's character in the Synoptic Gospels. Jesus attains to a glory that was
not previously his own because he is the faithful son of God to the point of death on the cross.

39. Cf. Collins and Collins, *King and Messiah*, 131.

40. Adela Yarbro Collins, "Mark and His Readers: The Son of God among Greeks and
Romans," *HTR* 93 (2000): 91.

41. Collins, "Mark and His Readers: The Son of God among Greeks and Romans," 91-92.

give in her own words: "The whole complex from Mark 8:27 to the end of the transfiguration suggests that the heart of Jesus's teaching, the message to which the disciples should listen, is that the messiah, the Son of God, must suffer."[42] The identity of Mark's Jesus as son of God revolves around the actions he must perform, and God's appointment and empowering of Jesus to this task. The "Greek and Roman" reading demands that these broader narrative cues be muted in favor of something more akin to an ontological divinity. As I discuss more fully in the following chapter, Mark develops a theology of Jesus's glory, and it is a future endowment with the father's glory that awaits Jesus precisely because he is the son of God who is also the son of man who obediently goes to death on a cross.

Based on both the internal logic of Mark's narrative and the broader compass of early Jewish and biblical antecedents, the better reading is of Jesus as an idealized and glorified human figure. With the climactic intrusion of the divine voice, the transfiguration scene shows itself to be a scene of disclosure in which the characters within the story come to see and hear the nature of Jesus's identity. For grasping the nature of that identity, it is crucial to recognize that Jesus has disclosed already that his messianic status entails a future glory. In response to Peter's Christological confession, Jesus not only prophesies rejection and death but also future resurrection life (8:31). Even more important, Jesus depicts a future coming of the son of man in the glory of his father (8:38) immediately prior to the story moving to the transfiguration pericope.

Thus, the larger narrative scope has prepared the reader for the transfiguration on two counts: (1) Jesus's Christological mission is cruciform, but it proceeds from the cross through to a subsequent heavenly glory; and (2) the glory with which Jesus will be endowed is not his own native glory but instead the reflected glory of his father. When we read then of Jesus in shining glory and a voice affirming Jesus as the beloved son, we have imagery that confirms before the eyes of the disciples that Jesus participates, or will participate, in the glory of God as messianic son of the heavenly father. Tying such an expectation into the broader Jewish expectation of a glorious existence of the resurrected righteous, Barry Blackburn concludes, "It is probable that the Transfiguration is to be interpreted as a proleptic view of Christ's heavenly glory received upon his resurrection and session at God's right hand and to be revealed publicly in his parousia."[43]

---

42. Collins, "Mark and His Readers: The Son of God among Greeks and Romans," 401.

43. Barry Blackburn, *Theios Anēr and the Markan Miracle Traditions: A Critique of the Theios Anēr Concept as an Interpretive Background of the Miracle Traditions Used by Mark* (WUNT2 40; Tübingen: Mohr Siebeck, 1991), 120.

A recurring theme around the passion predictions is that the disciples anticipate that Jesus's earthly ministry, his way to enthroned glory, is anything but the way of death. As readers of Mark's story, we must not allow the relentless movement toward Golgotha to obscure the anticipation that messianic glory also awaits Jesus, but through this peculiar means. The story of a crucified and then glorified messiah accounts for the nature of the glory that the disciples see in the transfigured Jesus.[44] I referred above to the transfiguration as an anticipatory display of Jesus's glory. Here, I agree with the instinct of Rudolf Bultmann that we are seeing a preview of the resurrected Christ,[45] though I disagree with his form-critical analysis that this is a misplaced resurrection appearance as such.[46] As is evident in Daniel, later Jewish tradition, and even the disciples themselves in the Synoptic Tradition (cf. Matt 13:41), raised people shine with glory.[47] The glory being disclosed is the glory of Jesus as he will appear after his resurrection and at his return (cf. 13:26; 14:62 — as we will see throughout this and the following chapter, the two titles son of God and son of man are mutually interpreting in Mark).

Such a reading is confirmed by the instructions that Jesus gives as he and the disciples descend the mountain: they are not to tell what they have seen until the son of man is raised from the dead (9:9).[48] Now, apparently, is not the time for messianic glory. The three insiders, and the readers, have been given a glimpse of the future in order to demonstrate for them that the way of the cross is, in fact, Jesus's messianic path to glory. The conclusion we may draw for the purposes of my thesis is this: the glory revealed to the disciples is a glory that will come fully to Jesus at a future moment in time. In the temporal sequence of Mark's Jesus, unlike John's, this is not a disclosure of some divine glory that was Jesus's prior to his incarnation, but instead is a disclosure of divine glory into which Jesus will come as a reward for his faithfulness to his messianic mission. Such a future orientation coincides with the other indications of Jesus's glory in Mark, and there are no indications that it was Jesus's prior to his appearance on the earth.

---

44. So, also, Collins and Collins, *King and Messiah,* 131.

45. He, in turn, was building off others, in Rudolf Bultmann, *The History of the Synoptic Tradition* (trans. John Marsh; Oxford: Blackwell, 1968), 259.

46. Such a claim is rendered problematic by any number of missing features, not least of which are initial lack of knowledge about who the resurrected Jesus is and a sending of the disciples. Cf. Joel Marcus, *Mark 8–16: A New Translation with Introduction and Commentary* (AYB 27A; New Haven, CT: Yale University Press, 2009), 637.

47. Cf. Blackburn, *Theios Anēr,* 119-21.

48. Marcus, *Way of the Lord,* 85-87.

Not only is the glory a part of Jesus's future in the sense just discussed, but it is also a reflection of God's own glory and not a native possession of Jesus. Two pieces of evidence point decisively in this direction. First, as I mentioned above, the glory that Mark's Jesus has already spoken of with regard to his own future as coming son of man is the glory of the father (8:38). Second, the story is rich with allusions to the story of Moses, whose own face shone after entering the presence of God on the mountain (Exod 34:29-30).[49] The various possible Mosaic connections include the ascent taking place after six days (Mark 9:2), a possible echo of Moses being called up to the mountain after the cloud had been present for six days (Exod 24:16); the presence of God in a cloud (Mark 9:7; Exod 24:16), as well as the mountain itself; and the accompaniment of three named companions (Peter, James, and John in Mark 9:2; Aaron, Nadab, and Abihu in Exod 24:1).[50] Then, of course, there is the presence of Moses himself, accompanied by Elijah, at the moment of Jesus's transfiguration (Mark 9:4). The Moses story provides further confirmation of Jesus's claim in Mark 8:38 that a human being who has been exalted into the presence of God might embody the divine glory without that human being transgressing the bounds of divinity in himself.[51] It is also not superfluous to mention, in light of the likely overtones of resurrection that this passage contains, that shining radiance is a common characteristic of resurrected humans (e.g., Dan 12:3). Thus, Simon Gathercole draws, I would say, precisely the wrong conclusion from the presence of these other exalted humans.[52] He follows Rudolf Pesch in concluding that the appearance of these now heavenly figures indicates that Jesus belongs to their heavenly world.[53] The similarity between Jesus and these other figures does, indeed, seem to be a significant component of the scene. What Gathercole does not adequately weigh, in my judgment, is that these are idealized human figures who, in the biblical and some later Jewish traditions (especially the latter in Moses's case), are human beings who were exalted to heaven. If Jesus is one of them,

---

49. Dunn, *Christology in the Making,* 47-48.

50. Marcus, *Mark 8–16,* 631-37; idem, *Way of the Lord,* 80-84; Blackburn, *Theios Anēr,* 118-19.

51. Ahearne-Kroll, "Scripturally Complex Presentation," 53-54, suggests that the heavenly prophets show us that Jesus is a "heavenly being." However, he does not attend to the fact that the two prophets are depicted as heavenly agents after their earthly lives, not as preexistent beings. Jesus is like them as glorified prophet meeting God on a mountain (as Aherane-Kroll goes on to state as well, pp. 53-57). His heavenly exaltation awaits his post-ministry future, as did theirs.

52. Gathercole, *Preexistent Son,* 49-50.

53. Gathercole, *Preexistent Son,* 49.

it is indicative of Jesus's idealized humanity, not some sort of preexistent or ontological divinity.

The divine voice that intervenes not only repeats the filial affirmation of the baptism scene, but also directly addresses the bystanders with the imperative, ἀκούετε αὐτοῦ (Mark 9:7). Marcus sees this command as a further echo of the Moses narratives, this time the admonition that Israel must listen when God raises up a prophet like him (ἀκούσεσθε, Deut 18:15).[54] If so, the possible double entendre of God raising up (ἀναστήσει, Deut 18:15, LXX) such a person as an allusion to resurrection is tantalizing. However that may be, the story Mark tells underscores the superiority of Jesus, so that the category of one like Moses, like the category of rabbi that Peter invokes (9:5), is ultimately insufficient. The divine voice declares that the one to whom the disciples are to listen is none other than Jesus who is God's anointed son. As we explored with reference to the baptism, the language of sonship itself, and of being a beloved son in particular, contains a Christological affirmation, and possibly also an indication that Jesus must be offered up much like Abraham's own beloved son. Such a holistic understanding of what is contained in the divinely acknowledged appellation is discernible as we inquire more thoroughly into what, precisely, the disciples are to "listen to."[55] As I demonstrated above, the transfiguration scene is joined with the confession and passion prediction pericopes of chapter 8. Though Peter's confession truly names Jesus as messiah, the more significant disclosure of Jesus's identity for the readers of the story is Jesus's reframing of his destiny in terms of the suffering and rising son of man. Thus, between Peter's articulation of a title and Jesus's reinterpretation of it in light of his particular destiny, the confession-disclosure scene of 8:27-33 articulates the same suffering messiah Christology that I argued was the Christology of the baptism scene. Moreover, it is just this notion of a Christ who suffers before entering into glory that Peter had refused to hear. Throughout the second half of Mark's narrative, the plainly spoken (παρρησίᾳ, 8:32) destiny of Jesus falls on deaf ears. The divine voice, then, is not simply articulating a principle that one must listen to God's agent, but is also siding with Jesus on the disputed question of what Jesus's being the Christ entails. The disciples must listen to Jesus because he knows what it means to be the Christ, the son of God; it means going to the cross as God's beloved son.[56]

If the imagery of the scene is suffused with Mosaic allusions, how then does

---

54. Marcus, *Mark 8–16*, 634, 640, 1114; also Collins, "Mark and His Readers," 400-401.
55. Cf. Dunn, *Christology in the Making*, 48.
56. Cf. Collins and Collins, *King and Messiah*, 131.

a divine indication of Jesus's role as messianic suffering king fit the stories told about Moses? Early Jewish interpreters of Moses did not shrink back from recognizing and elaborating on the exalted role given to Moses as God's representative on earth. As I noted in a previous chapter, the Qumran scrolls embrace the striking language of Exodus to the effect that Moses stands before Pharaoh as God (7:1): "He made him as God (יתננו לאלוהים[ו]) over the powerful ones, and a cause of reel[ing] (?) for Pharaoh" (4Q374 2 II, 6).[57] Even more striking is the royal imagery with which Ezekiel the Tragedian depicts Moses:

> On Sinai's peak I saw what seemed a throne
> so great in size it touched the clouds of heaven.
> Upon it sat a man of noble mien,
> becrowned, and with a scepter in one hand
> while with the other he did beckon me.
> I made approach and stood before the throne.
> He handed o'er the scepter and he bade
> me mount the throne, and gave to me the crown;
> then he himself withdrew from off the throne.
>
> (Ezek. Trag. 68-76)

Moses's mountainous ascent becomes an entry into God's heavenly throne room, where Israel's quintessential prophet is enthroned as king in God's stead.[58] This scene not only duly illustrates the plausibility of my thesis that an exalted human being can rule the world on God's behalf without claiming divinity as such; it also provides a bridge between the Mosaic and the royal connotations of Jesus's transfiguration. Moses could be depicted in messianic terms, and a would-be messiah might attempt to enact Moses-like feats in order to demonstrate his divine anointing (cf. Theudas as described by Josephus in *Ant.* 20.97). Modulated through such Second Temple depictions of a Mosaic king, the coalescence of Mosaic imagery with the divine predication of Jesus as beloved son form a unified Christology in which Jesus is depicted as messiah in his coming glory.[59]

Here the rich background of exalted humans in early Judaism, surveyed

57. Martínez and Tigchelaar, *DSSSE*, 1:741, altered.

58. Marcus, *Way of the Lord*, 84-85, also draws attention to this parallel text. Marcus also highlights Philo, *Life of Moses* 1.155-58, where Moses is "named God and king of the whole nation," a passage that we explored in the previous chapter as an indication of the heights to which humans might attain within the "monotheistic" reflections of ancient Israel.

59. Cf. Marcus, *Way of the Lord*, 85-87.

in the previous chapter, finds renewed significance. Not only Moses but David also is depicted as "a light like the light of the sun" (11Q5 27, 2),[60] a theme repeated in the Prayer of Enosh (4Q369) with possible Adamic overtones as well. Moreover, it seems that in each case the Qumran community is applying to particular persons the recovery of what was lost with Adam's fall — and what will be restored to the community as a whole (1QS IV, 7-26). Embodying the divine glory in such a context is not a signal of a person's surprising divinity, but of a person's restoration to true humanness. Thus, Marcus's conclusion regarding the transfiguration story is apt: "In the transfiguration, then, the Markan audience has been shown a vision of Jesus in his Adamic, messianic glory."[61]

c. Crucified Son of God

The passion narrative provides some of the clearest evidence that for Mark son of God is a royal rather than divine title as such. The primary reason for inclusion of the crucifixion scene in discussion with the baptism and transfiguration scenes is that the centurion's response to Jesus's death (15:39) is the third occurrence in which a non-demon refers to Jesus as God's son.[62] The moment of Jesus's death is also when we find the rending of the temple curtain (ἐσχίσθη, 15:38) in echo of the baptism's rent heavens (σχιζομένους, 1:10). This is also the scene that, for all its death, contains the most extensive and overt royal imagery found in the Gospel.

The passion narrative, from the trial scenes on, drips with dramatic irony as the participants of the story mock Jesus as one who foolishly and wrongly thinks himself king, while the reader knows that the words and acts that the characters perform in sarcastic derision are, in fact, true. Thus, for the reader of the story, when the centurion makes his proclamation, he shows himself to be the first person to recognize not only that Jesus is, truly, king, but also that the divine sonship therein entailed is realized through suffering and death.[63] In fact, the first time divine sonship comes up in this extended

---

60. Martínez and Tigchelaar, *DSSSE*, 2:1179.

61. Marcus, *Mark 8–16*, 640.

62. Davis, "Mark's Christological Paradox," 4-5, neatly demonstrates that the centurion's proclamation is the climax of the passion narrative, such that interrogating it as a key to the narrative's Christology honors Mark's narrative development. However, his arguments for an intrinsic divine Christology are not strong, and depend on interpretations of verses (1:11) that are given better readings throughout this study.

63. The woman who anoints Jesus with oil (Mark 14:3-9) might well precede the centurion

dramatic act it is at Jesus's trial. There, the high priest asks, by way of hendiadys, "Are you the Christ, the son of the Blessed?" (σὺ εἶ ὁ χριστὸς ὁ υἱὸς τοῦ εὐλογητοῦ, 14:61). This verbal yoking would seem to confirm that, in the mouth of the high priest at any rate, the titles Christ and son of God are equivalent: the two expressions are part of a single, royal concept.[64] That the reader should accept such an equation is signaled by Jesus's unmitigated acceptance of the dual title: ἐγώ εἰμι (14:62). However, as he does when Peter uses the title Christ, so here also Jesus refracts the messianic appellation by use of the phrase "son of man." As we will see in greater depth in the following chapter, son of God and son of man are mutually interpretive, marking out Jesus as a particular kind of messianic king — one who suffers and dies as his path to resurrection and glory. The brief interchange between Jesus and the high priest provides another piece of evidence that son of God is a Christological rather than divine title in Mark's Gospel.

Jesus as "king" comes increasingly to the fore as the scene shifts to the trial before Pilate. Pilate refers to Jesus as ὁ βασιλεὺς τῶν Ἰουδαίων three times (15:2, 9, 12). The mockery that ensues prior to Jesus's crucifixion proper reinforces the royal charge for which Jesus had to answer: purple robe, mocking crown of thorns, and mock obeisance (χαῖρε, βασιλεῦ τῶν Ἰουδαίων, 15:18). The phrase is repeated again as the charge over Jesus's head (15:26). The mockery of the Jewish contingent at the foot of the cross recalls the titles Jesus accepted at his trial, as the scribes and high priests address Jesus saying, ὁ χριστός ὁ βασιλεὺς Ἰσραὴλ καταβάτω νῦν ἀπὸ τοῦ σταυροῦ, ἵνα ἴδωμεν καὶ πιστεύσωμεν ("Let the messiah, the king of Israel, come down now from the cross in order that we might see and believe!" 15:31-32). Thus, from both Jewish and Roman characters, Jesus is mockingly hailed in royal terms, the former including the term "Christ," a title under which the entire story has developed for the readers, occurring as it does in the first verse. Moreover, the readers know that the surprising content of Jesus's messianic vocation is that it finds its glorious fulfillment only through Jesus's rejection, suffering, and death.[65] Thus, the scene of Jesus's crucifixion is suffused with dramatic irony as the readers know that it is precisely in the rejection and mockery by

in the recognition of this combination of messiahship and suffering; however, this happens without direct reference to Jesus as son of God.

64. Cf. Juel, *Master of Surprise*, 99.

65. As I explore in more detail in the following chapter, the "son of man" phrase shapes the reader's understanding of who Jesus is as son of God, such that the latter more clearly becomes a title of suffering and vindication and eschatological glory. Cf. John R. Donahue, "Jesus as the Parable of God in the Gospel of Mark," *Interp* 32 (1978): 369-86, here 378.

which the characters think that they are conclusively demonstrating that Jesus is not, and cannot be, Christ the king that they are ensuring Jesus's heavenly enthronement and glorious return.

The dissonance between the meaning of the mockery for the characters within the story and the significance for the readers is crucial for understanding the connotations of the centurion's confession within Mark's narrative. Returning to the jeering of the high priests and scribes, they not only address Jesus with the equated terms of "Christ" and "King," but they also tell him that they will believe if they see him come down. This taunt picks up Jesus's own expansion on the high priest's question of whether Jesus is the Christ, the son of the Blessed. Jesus tells them that he is, and that they will see (ὄψεσθε) the son of man at God's right hand and coming with the clouds (14:62). The taunt at the cross, then, is for Jesus to make good on his own prediction of displaying himself to them by coming down before their eyes. Similarly, when Jesus's cry of dereliction is misunderstood as an invocation of Elijah, a bystander says, "Leave it, let's see if Elijah comes and takes him down!" (ἄφετε, ἴδωμεν εἰ ἔρχεται Ἠλίας καθελεῖν αὐτόν, 15:36). In the narrative Jesus has been constructing for his disciples in Mark, Elijah comes before Jesus, not as one descended from heaven in order to pave the way for the messiah's glorious return, but as one who is first killed, even as the messianic son of man must suffer and die (9:11-13). In the rich tapestry of Mark's narrative, the blindness of Jesus's opponents continually hides from them the thanatological nature of Jesus's messianic mission and identity.

And so, while the bystanders hurl insults at Jesus about Elijah coming to rescue him from death, and about Jesus coming down to demonstrate that he is the glorious son of man, the readers know that Elijah has already come and paved the way, and that Jesus is rightly following his way to glory even in the moment of his abandonment by God. The way prepared for the Lord Jesus, by John the Baptist, ends up being the way to the cross (cf. 1:2-4).[66] Throughout the scene at Golgotha, Mark deploys the literary device of dramatic irony such that readers who remember what the narrator and Jesus have indicated earlier know that things are not as they seem to the characters in the narrative: Jesus's staying on the cross is not a defeat of his messianic claims, but their very fulfillment.[67] And so, when the narrator introduces the centurion's words, "Truly this man [ὁ ἄνθρωπος!] was son of God" (ἀληθῶς οὗτος ὁ ἄνθρωπος υἱὸς θεοῦ ἦν), with "Seeing that he thus breathed his last" (Ἰδὼν . . . ὅτι οὕτως

66. Cf. Marcus, *Way of the Lord*, 12-47.
67. Juel, *Master of Surprise*, 96-97.

ἐξέπνευσεν), he is signaling to the informed reader that these words truly summarize what the other characters have missed. Son of God here is not given a new connotation of preexistent divinity within the narrative; instead, it is a confirmation that Jesus, as Christ, as king of Israel, is "the son of the Blessed," as demonstrated in his death.

For readers who have made the connections between this scene and the prior scenes that use similar imagery and language, the connections between Jesus as son of God and Jesus as crucified Christ or king are even stronger. Immediately before the centurion's confession we find in quick succession the allusion to Elijah (15:36), the reference to Jesus expiring (15:37), and the second use of the word σχίζω along with the indication that the torn temple veil was ripped from top to bottom as if by divine fiat (15:38). The divinely sanctioned connotations between Jesus's death and his Christological anointing, hinted at in the baptism and transfiguration scenes, are now fulfilled as Jesus's death enables one lone human being in the book to recognize that Jesus, precisely as a human who died by crucifixion, is God's royal son.

Thus far, I have largely pursued the question of connotation from the angles of Jewish scriptural resonance and an author-focused narrative criticism. Another approach to the question is to turn to the readers (or auditors) and ask how the son of God language would likely have resonated with their cultural cues. For both the baptism and the crucifixion the possible Greek and Roman overtones resonate much more harmoniously with the overall narrative of Mark than those discussed above in reference to the transfiguration. Collins highlights how both cosmic portents and phraseology including "son of God" (θεοῦ υἱός) were indicative of transitions into and out of imperial power.[68] She draws attention to Plutarch's description of the death of the idealized founder of Rome as being attended with darkness, deafening thunder, and torrential rains.[69] The same historian cites the death of Caesar being accompanied by the sun being blocked.[70] It was this Caesar's death that led to the practice of divinization that resulted in later Caesars being named sons of God.[71]

In a much more thoroughgoing manner, Michael Peppard has explored the considerable evidence about the connotations that might be carried by the

---

68. Collins, "Mark and His Readers: The Son of God among Greeks and Romans," 93-96.

69. Collins, "Mark and His Readers: The Son of God among Greeks and Romans," 94; citing Plutarch, *Romulus* 27 6-7.

70. Collins, "Mark and His Readers: The Son of God among Greeks and Romans," 94; citing Plutarch, *Caesar* 69.3-5 and a parallel account in Virgil.

71. Collins, "Mark and His Readers: The Son of God among Greeks and Romans," 94-95.

phrase "son of God" in the Roman world.[72] "Son of God" was not only a Jewish way of describing the ruler who had been adopted to rule the world on God's behalf, it was also a title claimed by the Roman emperor.[73] The crucial points for Peppard's argument, and for the considerations of Christology that my own work is exploring, are that the Roman emperor was son of God by adoption and through exercise of power.[74] He appeals to recent work on divinity in the Roman world that argues that "divinity in the Roman world was not an essence or a nature, but a concept of *status* and *power* in a cosmic spectrum that had no absolute dividing lines."[75] To be son of god was most often a claim to a place in the lineage of imperial rule — a place that was more frequently secured by adoption into the family line than it was by natural birth.[76] Peppard goes on to explore how adoption of a son into the imperial family mapped onto the larger cultural place of the father, and the political ideology that grew up in the first century that placed the emperor as *paterfamilias* over the "the largest family on earth," namely, all of Rome.[77] With this, the so-called religious, the political, and the familial were bound together. Without claiming ontological distinction (even the ontological distinction of being of the same physical, flesh and blood line of the previous emperor) or preexistence, the Roman imperial ideology became a royal son of god theology that built on its own, often fictive kinship in order to provide an ideological support for Caesar's rule.

When Peppard turns to explore the Gospel of Mark with this set of cultural lenses, it comes as no surprise that he discovers there a story that would resound to Roman ears very much like the story resounds to Jewish ears according to the argument I have already made. Turning to the baptism scene, he argues that God's declaration that Jesus is "well pleasing" (ἐν σοὶ εὐδόκησα) contains more than simply a statement of pleasure; it carries connotations of election: God is "pleased to choose" Jesus.[78] He argues that the spirit is akin to the *genius* and the *numen* (those aspects of the Roman emperor that were worshiped and/or prayed for) in the function it plays as "unifying life-force of a family."[79] Finally, he suggests that the dove functions as a kind of anti-eagle,

72. Michael Peppard, *The Son of God in the Roman World: Divine Sonship in Its Social and Political Context* (New York: Oxford University Press, 2011).

73. Peppard, *Son of God*, 28.

74. Peppard, *Son of God*, 31-85.

75. Peppard, *Son of God*, 31 (italics original).

76. Peppard, *Son of God*, 46-49.

77. Peppard, *Son of God*, 61.

78. Peppard, *Son of God*, 106-12.

79. Peppard, *Son of God*, 114.

a symbol of gentleness and peace emblematic of the ways that Jesus's ministry will subvert the expectations even, apparently, of his closest followers.[80] The baptism scene, then, is tantamount to Jesus's adoption: his entry into the family of the father God in whose power and name Jesus will exercise his own rule. He thus concludes in terms that strongly resonate with my own thesis: "Mark's Christology was as high as humanly possible."[81]

I am crafting my own argument for this point from within the narrative of Israel's scriptures and early Judaism; Peppard makes an identical point from a different set of data: "The Roman emperor, the most powerful person in the world, gained his sonship by adoption. If Mark was crafting a narrative that presents Jesus to Roman listeners as a counter-emperor, the authoritative son of God, then adoption was the most effective method of portraying his divine sonship."[82] Without overreading such signals as means by which Mark was attempting to subvert Roman imperial authority or claim Jesus for its replacement, the Roman reading complements the overall narrative thrust of son of God being a royal title indicating that Jesus's ministry is a kind of kingship that ironically finds the path to death as the path to coronation. The confluence of the biblical, post-biblical Jewish, Roman, and narratival approaches issue a common set of connotations, namely, that Jesus is son of God in the sense of exalted human ruler representing the power of God on earth. This lends a broad base of plausibility to the thesis of this chapter (and the book as a whole).

The three scenes of baptism, transfiguration, and crucifixion work together to structure the book around Jesus's identity as son of God. In each, the connotations of the phrase revolve around the peculiar messianic status and calling of Jesus as one who must enter his glory by way of rejection, suffering, death, and resurrection. Son of God as a royal title of divine status and power takes on added significance once its role in the overall story is recognized. It is not simply that Mark has used a title that happens to not contain divine connotations in a few scenes, but also that he has chosen to place this non-divine, but rather royal title upon Jesus at the beginning, middle, and end of the story, including the first and the final appearances of Jesus. If, as we might rightly claim, the Gospel intends to indicate through its story the identity of Jesus, such a positioning of the non-divine title bears considerable weight and sets the presumption strongly in favor of an exalted human, rather than divine, Christology at work throughout the story.

80. Peppard, *Son of God*, 115-23.
81. Peppard, *Son of God*, 131.
82. Peppard, *Son of God*, 131.

2. "SON OF GOD" FROM OTHERS WHO KNOW

Though the three instances discussed above are critical for understanding Mark's son of God Christology, due to their placement and their divine and human sources, there are two other character types who know that Jesus is son of God and speak or allude to such a relationship: unclean spirits and Jesus himself.

a. Unclean Spirits

Throughout Mark, the unclean spirits recognize Jesus, and know that he occupies the place of God's agent who has authority over them (1:24; 3:11; 5:6-7). In Mark, Jesus's first encounter with such a spirit is related in 1:21-28. The exorcism itself is sandwiched between two statements in which the crowds express astonishment over Jesus's teaching authority — teaching authority that is authoritative even to the extent of exercising power over demons (διδαχὴ καινὴ κατ᾽ ἐξουσίαν· καὶ τοῖς πνεύμασι τοῖς ἀκαθάρτοις ἐπιτάσσει, καὶ ὑπακούουσιν αὐτῷ, 1:27; cf. 1:22). This provides an interpretive framework for the exorcism scene: the authority to exorcise, and the expression of it in the title with which the demons name Jesus, is of a piece with the authority Jesus exercises as teacher.

The spirits' knowledge of Jesus includes his name and his standing vis-à-vis God: "What is it between us and you, Jesus the Nazarene? Have you come to destroy us? I know who you are, the Holy One of God!" (τί ἡμῖν καὶ σοί, Ἰησοῦ Ναζαρηνέ; ἦλθες ἀπολέσαι ἡμᾶς; οἶδά σε τίς εἶ, ὁ ἅγιος τοῦ θεοῦ, 1:24). Naming Jesus rightly seems to be part of the power play in which the spirit attempts to grasp the upper hand through the power of naming the other. Here, Jesus is not referred to as "son of God," but "Holy One of God." The title is more vague, and may or may not carry royal overtones. The closest biblical precedent seems to be found in Psalm 16:10 (15:10, LXX), a verse picked up in Acts, in which the Davidic speaker expresses confidence that God will not allow "your holy one" to see the pit (חסיד, MT) or decay (διαφοράν, LXX). The match is not exact, however, as the LXX reads ὅσιον whereas Mark uses the word ἅγιος. Previously, the adjectival use of ἅγιος defined the spirit with whom Jesus would baptize (1:8), presumably the same spirit Jesus received at his baptism (1:12). So the correlation between Jesus as God's holy one and Jesus as the one who received the holy spirit within him might be the most we can say here: "holy one" indicates one who has been given God's spirit.[83]

---

83. A conclusion reached also by Blackburn, *Theios Anēr*, 110.

As holy one, Jesus exercises authority, to the point where the demonic brood is afraid Jesus might destroy them. The various strands of this story coalesce nicely with the later Beelzebul controversy, in which it becomes clear that Jesus exercises authority over demons due to his possession of the Holy Spirit. Thus, the knowledge that these demons have about Jesus is that he plays the role of exercising divine authority on earth. This fits squarely within an idealized human paradigm.

One other aspect of the demons' naming of Jesus calls for our attention: their knowledge of who Jesus is is not expressed simply in terms of a spiritual reality that they might recognize, for instance, from the time before Jesus came to earth. They name him first of all according to his human name, Jesus the Nazarene. As in Acts with the spirit's knowledge of not only Jesus but also Paul (19:15), so here the opposing spirits know the human identities of those who are God's agents engaging them in conflict. Because the spirits' knowledge includes both the natural, human identity of Jesus and his secret status with respect to God, we cannot conclude from their recognition of him that they are identifying someone whom they know from a preexistent past. If a preexistence paradigm were in play in the writing of this Gospel then one might argue that such recognition is a likely or necessary component of the demons' knowledge; but such knowledge of Jesus is not sufficient to indicate the presence of such a framework. The demons know the human (as well).

The words of unclean spirits are next reported as part of a summary statement in chapter 3.[84] After relating that people who had maladies were "falling upon" (ἐπιπίπτειν, 3:10) Jesus in hopes of touching him and finding healing, Mark plays on the πίπτω root in telling the readers of the response of the unclean spirits to Jesus's presence: "The unclean spirits, when they saw him, were falling before [προσέπιπτον] him and crying out, saying, 'You are the son of God!'" (τὰ πνεύματα τὰ ἀκάθαρτα, ὅταν αὐτὸν ἐθεώρουν, προσέπιπτον αὐτῷ καὶ ἔκραζον λέγοντες ὅτι σὺ εἶ ὁ υἱὸς τοῦ θεοῦ, 3:11). Jesus's response to the spirits makes this a classic instance of Mark's messianic secret motif: "He rebuked them greatly that they not make him known" (πολλὰ ἐπετίμα αὐτοῖς ἵνα μὴ αὐτὸν φανερὸν ποιήσωσιν, 3:12). What the spirits "know" is what the reader knows, and what has been disclosed to Jesus at his baptism: that he is the son of God. The reader is thereby informed that the demons are aware of what God, Jesus, and the readers also know. The demons' experience and

84. Given the summary nature of this section, the unclean spirits' address of Jesus as son of God may be intended to interpret for the reader the "holy one of God" statement that preceded in chapter 1.

recognition of Jesus as a man endowed with unique divine authority suffices to explain their knowledge and Jesus's silencing rebuke. Corroborating evidence that this is in fact a messianic secret rather than a divine secret can be found in the story of Peter's confession. It comes by way of a verbal parallel, especially the repetition of the verb ἐπιτιμάω (rebuke), in Jesus's injunction to the disciples after Peter confesses Jesus to be the Christ (ἐπιτίμησεν αὐτοῖς ἵνα μηδενὶ λέγωσιν περὶ αὐτοῦ, 8:30). Jesus silences those who know his title, while he (and the entire Gospel) will proceed to redefine the nature of his messianic vocation.

The short description of Jesus's demonic encounters includes the further detail that they fell before Jesus, which connotes in this context an act of obeisance. This action is appropriate for someone (a spirit, in this case) that finds itself in the presence of a king. As I demonstrated in the survey of early Judaism, spirits bowing down before someone need not indicate divinity. In the *Life of Adam and Eve*, for instance, the exalted status of Adam was such that all the heavenly host were commanded to bow in worship before him (*L.A.E.* [Vita] 13:1-3; 14:1-2). Gathercole's claim that such knowledge of Jesus and obeisance indicates both preexistence and sharing in God's being loses its force once we recognize that idealized human figures were presented as reigning over the entire earth, including angelic forces, and that as such an idealized human might well be anointed to restore such a reign.[85]

Adam is not the only figure standing behind Mark's Gospel offering an interpretive option for understanding Jesus the exorcist. John Donahue has drawn attention to the fact that not only David but also Solomon was viewed as an exorcist in whose name exorcisms were performed (Josephus, *Ant.* 8.45).[86] He concludes, "Therefore when the demons address Jesus as Son of God and as Son of the Most High God (3:11; 5:7), he is announced as King whose Kingdom (1:14-15) spells the downfall of the kingdom of evil."[87] Both as "royalty" more generally conceived and as someone who, as king of Israel and imbued with God's spirit, plays the role of an idealized human being, ruling the world on God's behalf, Jesus would rightly receive the humble obeisance of the demons without any necessary indication that its cause is ontological divinity. In the story, the point of the exorcisms is authority (cf. 1:22, 27). The paradigm of idealized human figure provides a grid for understanding the exalted supremacy

85. Gathercole, *Preexistent Son*, 274-75.

86. John R. Donahue, "Temple, Trial, and Royal Christology," in *The Passion in Mark* (ed. Werner H. Kelber; Philadelphia: Fortress, 1976), 61-78, here 73. See also Collins, "Mark and His Readers," 399, esp. the references in note 40.

87. Donahue, "Temple, Trial, and Royal Christology," 73-74.

Jesus exercises. As human king, and rightful ruler of, first, Israel and then the cosmos on God's behalf, Jesus (like David in the biblical tradition and Solomon in the larger Jewish tradition before him) acts by the power of the spirit in order to displace Satan, under whose authority these unclean spirits work, freeing those who had been enslaved (3:22-30; cf. 1:12-13; 4:15; 8:33).

The important conversation between Jesus and the scribes, in which Jesus describes his work as binding the strong man (τὸν ἰσχυρὸν δήσῃ, 3:27), provides a backdrop for the following story in which unclean spirits address Jesus, this time through the mouth of a man whom they had made so powerful that no one was able to bind him (οὐδεὶς ἴσχυεν αὐτὸν δαμάσαι, 5:4). The pattern articulated in 3:11 repeats itself in 5:6-7, as the demoniac runs up to Jesus, falling before him and addressing him as son of God (τί ἐμοὶ καὶ σοί, Ἰησοῦ υἱὲ τοῦ θεοῦ τοῦ ὑψίστου, v. 7). Here, Mark uses the word προσκυνέω rather than προσπίπτω as he did in chapter 3. The former appears only one other time in the Gospel, when the Romans are bowing before Jesus in mock regal homage (15:19). Within the narrative world of Mark's Gospel, messianic authority seems to be in view.

The close proximity between God and Jesus as God's agent is likely indicated toward the end of the story, when there is a possible interchange of "the Lord" as a reference for God and "Jesus" as the agent of God's work. When Jesus refuses the request of the healed demoniac to join his troop of disciples, he sends the man, instead, to return to his people and proclaim to them "what the Lord has done for you and how he has shown mercy to you" (ὅσα ὁ κύριος σοι πεποίηκεν καὶ ἠλέησέν σε, 5:19). The referent of ὁ κύριος here is ambiguous, but most likely refers to God. When the man goes out into the Decapolis, however, he proclaims what Jesus has done for him (ὁ ἐποίησεν αὐτῷ ὁ Ἰησοῦς, 5:20). Such interplay precisely captures the close proximity between God and idealized divine agents on the earth. Unlike the scribes in the Beelzebul controversy, this man recognizes that God's is the power through which Jesus is at work in exercising such authority over demons. Within the paradigm of an idealized human Christology that we are testing as an explanatory hypothesis, such an oscillation finds ready precedent in figures such as Moses, who was the human agent of divine power throughout the exodus.

A further fact that must not be overlooked is that Jesus has called his twelve disciples for the express purpose of sharing in his power over demons (3:15; 6:7, 13). The first indication of such a calling for Jesus's followers (i.e., 3:15) comes immediately after the summary statement in which we learn of the demons falling before Jesus and calling him son of God (3:11-12) and just before the Beelzebul controversy in which we learn that he casts out demons by the power of the spirit he received at baptism (3:20-30). Such a succession of stories demonstrates that the authority Jesus has can be shared with other human beings. I take this to be decisive evidence against the notion that Jesus's authority over demons demonstrates his unique divinity. If the disciples are included in a certain range of activity, then such activity is insufficient to demonstrate Jesus's unique divinity, and more likely identifies him as a particular kind of human. When Jesus succeeds in an exorcism in the face of the disciples' failure in Mark 9, the explanation is not that Jesus possesses some ontologically superior status, or even that he is messiah, but that fasting and prayer are demanded for that particular kind of confrontation (vv. 14-29). This does not mean that Jesus is simply doing what anyone else might do if a person had realized the power was at his disposal. Mark's disciples derive their authority from Jesus (6:7). Jesus is the king, and the other agents of his kingdom can act in the king's name, extending the king's reign (cf. 9:38-39). Jesus's identity as son of God in Mark carries messianic connotations, indicative of a reign even over the unclean spirits.

b. Jesus

Jesus himself alludes to his identity as son of God on three notable occasions not yet discussed (the ἐγώ εἰμι in response to the high priest, 14:62, being another important affirmation from Jesus about this particular way of framing his identity). In each, Jesus places himself in a category in which he is distinguished from God as a different character in the story, even while claiming a unique place in God's climactic engagement with Israel and the world.

i. Parable of the Vineyard

The parable of the vineyard (12:1-12) is set within a context of escalating tensions. After the temple-clearing incident, the high priests and scribes had gone out to plot Jesus's destruction (11:18), and upon Jesus's return to Jerusalem they are joined by the elders in questioning the source of Jesus's authority (11:27-28). Authority has been the point at issue throughout the Gospel, as Jesus has demonstrated his authority in such a way that the people have recognized him as greater than the scribes (1:22, 27), as Jesus's claim to authority is his response to the accusation of blasphemy leveled by the scribes (2:6-10, see the following chapter), and as the source of Jesus's power is the point at issue for the scribes in the Beelzebul controversy (3:22-30, though the term ἐξουσία is not used). The parable of the vineyard, then, not only is spoken "against them," that is to say, against the Jewish leaders (12:12), but it is also told about Jesus as the one whose rejection brings about God's judgment. And within this parable, Jesus plays the role of beloved son.[88]

Two indications of the beloved son's identity must be held together in this parable. First, he is like the others who came for the fruit of the vineyard in that he was "sent" by the vineyard owner. Since all of the people are "sent," being "sent" by the vineyard owner cannot possibly indicate a special preexistence for Jesus that is not shared by the innumerable other servants who came before.[89] Second, the son is distinguished from those who preceded inasmuch as they are referred to as servants (δοῦλος), and the final figure is referred to as the beloved son (υἱὸν ἀγαπητόν, 12:6). Thus, the final emissary stands in a unique relationship to the vineyard owner as beloved son.

For illumination on the significance of this difference, Simon Gathercole rightly directs us to interpret the parable in light of the larger context of Mark's narrative.[90] In the Gospel story, Jesus has been referred to as God's beloved son on two previous occasions (the baptism and transfiguration scenes discussed above). Moreover, the parable is clearly about the role Jesus plays as the rejected son, as indicated in the passion predictions and the broader context of this pericope. It is precisely because I agree with Gathercole that the larger context of Mark must determine the significance of "beloved son" at this juncture in the story that I disagree with his conclusion that this is revelatory of a heavenly/preexistent divine identity.[91]

As beloved son, Jesus is the adopted, messianic son of God, specially chosen to represent God's reign to the world and to take his throne along the way of rejection, death, and resurrection. This, as I argued above, is the significance of the threefold son of God designation that structures the Gospel through baptism, transfiguration, and crucifixion. The parable itself confirms that Jesus's identity as suffering messiah is the particular connotation of "beloved son" at this point in Mark's story. The rejection of the beloved son, followed by judgment on the caretakers, finds its interpretation in Psalm 118: "The stone which the builders rejected [ἀποδοκίμασαν], this one has become the chief cornerstone. This has come from the Lord and it is amazing in our sight" (Mark 12:10-11). "Rejection" is a key component to how Jesus defines the "son of man's" destiny in the first passion prediction — one that cites the very

---

88. Cf. Klyne Snodgrass, *Stories with Intent: A Comprehensive Guide to the Parables of Jesus* (Grand Rapids, MI: Eerdmans, 2008), 292-95.

89. A point well acknowledged by Gathercole, *Preexistent Son,* 187-88.

90. Gathercole, *Preexistent Son,* 188.

91. See also Snodgrass, *Stories with Intent,* 294.

groups currently opposing Jesus as those who will reject him: "It is necessary . . . to suffer many things and to be rejected [ἀποδοκιμασθῆναι] by the elders and the chief priests and the scribes and to be killed and after three days to rise" (8:31). Rejection and killing at the hands of the "vineyard keepers" is parabolic language by which Mark's Jesus restates the nature of his destiny as Christ, which he had previously refracted by use of the "son of man" terminology (see the following chapter on this latter phrase). Thus, maintaining the messianic sense of "beloved son," particularly as Jesus's Christological vocation is depicted in terms of suffering followed by resurrection glory, makes best sense of the parable. Here we catch a small glimpse of what will be explored more extensively in the following chapter, that son of God and son of man are mutually interpreting titles in Mark's Gospel. While the former indicates a royal position, the latter becomes the grid through which Jesus reinterprets "messiah" in terms of suffering followed by glory rather than a glorious and/ or military victory during Jesus's life on earth.

ii. The Unknowing Son

The second significant self-identification of Jesus as God's son occurs in 13:32. Once again, Gathercole indicates that this is an affirmation of a "heavenly identity," but it occurs in a text that demonstrates the clear subordination and differentiation of the son from God.[92] In a verse that poses no end of consternation to Christian interpreters, Jesus claims filial ignorance concerning the timing of the eschatological prophecies he himself has made: "No one knows, neither the angels in heaven nor the son but only the father" (13:32). In addition to the professed ignorance of the son that distinguishes him from the father, Mark distinguishes the angels and the son by noting that the former are "in heaven," while not making any such heavenly qualification of the latter. This raises significant questions about Gathercole's claim that this indicates a "heavenly" identity for Mark's son of God. Jesus has claimed a unique prophetic authority for his words (13:30-31), and readers will recognize that his depiction of the coming son of man marks Jesus out as a decisive agent in the coming eschatological assize (13:26-27). But as I discuss in greater detail in the following chapter, this coming son of man is preexistent in Mark's Gospel only in the sense that he had a life on earth and was raised to glory before appearing a second time. When Jesus identifies himself as son of God, he does so as one whose current status is the messiah heading toward his death, but who is

92. Gathercole, *Preexistent Son*, 188.

looking forward to an existence and return in resurrected glory. The notion that Jesus is an idealized human being in Mark's Gospel allows us to accent both sides of the phrase. As idealized, he is God's special agent, God's son, God's spirit-empowered messiah, God's child who is willing to be obedient to the point of death in order to ransom the many. But as human, he is not preexistent, or omniscient, or in any other sense divine. In particular, he must face, embrace, and endure the greatest human evils of rejection and death in order to fulfill his particular calling. Whatever problems 13:32 may pose for later Christian theology, it fits perfectly within Mark's story of the idealized, representative human being who is Jesus the Christ.

iii. Abba, Father

In his prayer in the garden of Gethsemane, Mark's Jesus directly addresses God as father for the only time in the book. This cry has its own infamous story, as the twentieth century saw it celebrated by Gerhard Kittel and Joachim Jeremias as a unique, unprecedented, and shockingly intimate address to God, claims defeated by James Barr's hard-striking "Abba Isn't 'Daddy.'"[93] Jesus's struggle in the garden is an enacted moment of the father-son relationship with which Mark has punctuated his narrative. What, if anything, do we learn of Mark's Christology from this scene?

A first piece of evidence that we should bear in mind is that the "*abba, father*" prayer occurs on two other occasions in the New Testament: Galatians 4:6 and Romans 8:15. In both instances, the speaker is the Christ follower crying out to God as father by the inspiration of the spirit. Thus, in the Christian tradition that precedes the writing of Mark's Gospel, the utterance of this prayer was not an indication of preexistence or divinity but of participation in the divine family through the spirit and, significantly, through suffering (esp. Rom 8:15, but also, arguably, Gal 4:6).

Second, and more important, is the story within which the prayer is spoken. The context within which Jesus addresses God as father is in wrestling with, and finally submitting to, the vocation to die that he has received from God. In 14:34 Mark's Jesus alludes to Psalm 42:5, 11, saying, "My soul is sorrowful" (λυπός ἐστιν ἡ ψυχή μου; 41:6, 12, LXX). The quote is not exact, but Adela Yarbro Collins suggests that in taking up a psalmic lament, Jesus might be seen as

---

93. Gerhard Kittel, ἀββᾶ, *TDNT* 1:6; Joachim Jeremias, *Abba: Studien zur neutestamentlichen Theologie und Zeitgeschichte* (Göttingen: Vandenhoeck & Ruprecht, 1966), esp. 59-67; James Barr, "'Abbā Isn't 'Daddy,'" *JTS* 39 (1988): 28-47.

"speaking in the voice of David, the lamenting prototypical king."[94] Mark's Jesus significantly qualifies this sorrow as a sorrow "unto death" (ἕως θανάτου). Thus, the ensuing scene unfolds under the rubric of the looming death of Jesus. Further, the command to the disciples to stay awake (γρηγορεῖτε, 14:34) echoes the apocalyptic discourse from the prior chapter, signaling to the reader that the eschatological assize, at whose center lies the son of man, is finding some anticipation in the events unfolding in the passion narrative.[95] The eschatological conditioning of the passage continues as Jesus prays for the "hour" to be taken from him (14:35).[96] As Dale Allison has shown, this "eschatological hour" is itself the arrival of Jesus's death.[97]

The prayer related in Jesus's own voice uses different language to communicate the same reality: Jesus is praying to God to keep him from having to die: "*abba,* father. All things are possible for you. Take away this cup from me — but not what I want, but what you want" (14:36). Despite Barr's decisive rebuttal of Jeremias, commentators and theologians still claim to discover in this prayer a "unique intimacy" with God, and at times an existential uniqueness of Jesus's relationship with God.[98] But we have already put enough pieces of the puzzle in place to see a different picture emerging. Mark's Jesus addresses God as father, thus indicating his role as God's son, in a context of filial obedience

94. Adela Yarbro Collins, *Mark: A Commentary* (Hermeneia; Minneapolis: Fortress, 2007), 677.

95. Cf. Dale Allison, *The End of the Ages Has Come* (Philadelphia: Fortress, 1985), 36-38.

96. Cf. Brant Pitre, *Jesus, the Tribulation, and the End of the Exile* (Tübingen: Mohr Siebeck, 2005), 481-82.

97. Allison, *End of the Ages,* 36-38.

98. David E. Aune, "*abba,*" in *ISBE* (4 vols.; ed. Geoffrey W. Bromiley; Grand Rapids, MI: Eerdmans, 1979), 1:3-4; C. Clifton Black, *Mark* (ANTC; Nashville: Abingdon, 2011), 293; Craig Blomberg, *Jesus and the Gospels: An Introduction and Survey* (2nd ed.; Nashville: B & H Academic, 2009), 293, 393; W. D. Davies and Dale C. Allison, *Matthew 1–7* (ICC; Edinburgh: T&T Clark, 1988), 602; James D. G. Dunn, *Jesus and the Spirit: A Study of the Religious and Charismatic Experience of Jesus and the First Christians as Reflected in the New Testament* (Grand Rapids, MI: Eerdmans, 1997), 23; Dunn, *Romans 1–8* (WBC 38a; Dallas: Word, 1988), 461; R. T. France, *The Gospel of Mark* (NIGTC; Grand Rapids, MI: Eerdmans, 2002), 584; Mary Healy, *The Gospel of Mark* (CCSS; Grand Rapids, MI: Baker Academic, 2008), 292; Craig S. Keener, *The Gospel of Matthew: A Socio-rhetorical Commentary* (Grand Rapids, MI: Eerdmans, 2009), 638; Edgar Krentz, "God in the New Testament," in *Our Naming of God* (ed. Carl E. Braaten; Minneapolis: Fortress, 1989), 88; Aquila H. I. Lee, *From Messiah to Pre-existent Son: Jesus's Self-Consciousness and Early Christian Exegesis of Messianic Psalms* (WUNT 192; Tübingen: Mohr Siebeck, 2005), 126; Donald K. McKim, *Westminster Dictionary of Theological Terms* (Louisville, KY: Westminster John Knox, 2000), 1; William L. Portier, *Tradition and Incarnation: Foundations of Christian Theology* (New York: Paulist, 1994), 238, 278.

as messianic, representative, and eschatological suffering. Here is Jesus taking the part of idealized Davidic king, as represented in psalms such as Psalm 42, suffering at the hands of enemies and praying to God as the one with whom Jesus stands in relationship as a son precisely because of that messianic role. The strongest narratival cues for how to interpret this passage align squarely with the larger son of God theology in Mark's Gospel: Jesus is son of God because he is the messiah who is also the suffering son of man.

3. SON OF GOD AND SONS OF GOD

In pursuing the question of whether Jesus as "son of God" carries connotations of divinity or preexistence, it is important to ask whether there are other characters in the narrative that bear the same title. Although God as "father" of earthly "sons" who are Jesus's followers is not a major theme in Mark's Gospel, it does appear in a couple of locations.

First, there is the inclusion of the disciples as those to whom God is related as father in 11:25: "When you stand praying, forgive if you have anything against anyone, in order that your father [ὁ πατὴρ ὑμῶν] who is in the heavens might also forgive you your transgressions." Without in any way diminishing the unique role that Jesus plays in the story, the inclusion of other persons within the filial relationship to God stands as a caution against overreading son of God language as indicative of divinity. Before Jesus, Adam, Israel, and Davidic kings all were spoken of as standing in such a relation; and, importantly, throughout the New Testament those who follow Jesus are said to share in just this identity marker (cf. Rom 8:29). Moreover, as I have argued elsewhere, whatever the literary or oral prehistory of this saying about forgiveness, its function in the Markan pericope is to locate the divine work of forgiveness within the community of Jesus's followers.[99] The disciples are going to be the fulfillment of the temple's purpose of being a house of prayer for all people, in the wake of Jesus's judgment and condemnation of it. They will be the place, also, where forgiveness is found. The embodying of forgiveness within the community of those children of God who are Jesus's followers places them in an analogous role to that which Jesus plays in the healing of the paralytic (discussed in greater depth in the following chapter). Whereas the scribes ask who can forgive sins but God alone, Jesus claims that as the son of man he

---

99. J. R. Daniel Kirk, "Time for Figs, Temple Destruction, and Houses of Prayer in Mark 11:12-25," *CBQ* 74 (2012): 510-28.

has that authority, and in 11:25 indicates that analogous authority is located in the community of his followers (cf. John 20:23). Being a son of God indicates a special place on the earth, representing and enacting the reign of God, but it need not indicate divinity per se.

The disciples' ability to forgive (and their other son-of-God-like activities) derives from their participation in the family of God that Jesus is renewing and redefining around himself. In Mark 3 sandwiching the Beelzebul controversy is Jesus's controversy with his family members who think he has lost his mind (vv. 20-21, 31-35). In the latter portion of this pericope Jesus redefines his family from biological consanguinity to what we might call spiritual affinity. Here we discover the requisites for being numbered a sibling of Jesus, which would be to share in God's fatherhood. Jesus asks the rhetorical question, "Who are my mother and my siblings?" (v. 33) and gives a two-pronged answer. First, the narrator tells us that he looks at those seated around him (τοὺς περὶ αὐτὸν κύκλῳ καθημένους) and says, "Behold my mother and my siblings" (v. 34). Thus, the first leg of Jesus's answer is that he himself is the determining factor for this redefined familial relationship. The summons issued to the first disciples to follow (1:17-18, reiterated in cruciform terms in 8:34) begins to work its way through the story as the means by which the family of God is known: they are the sons of God who are formed around Jesus, the son of God.

The second prong of this redefinition of the family of God might not seem like much of a redefinition were it not for the first. Jesus says, "Whoever does the will of God, this person is my brother and sister and mother" (3:35). However, in light of the first statement, when Jesus looks at those sitting around him and identifies them as children of God, in this context "doing the will of God" has been redefined precisely in terms of discipleship of Jesus. Jesus has brought about a moment of eschatological differentiation in his own person and work. Those who recognize him as God's agent and respond accordingly demonstrate themselves to be part of God's faithful family. In this way, the ability of the many to call themselves sons of God is derivative of Jesus's primary claim to that title. He is the messianic king, and they are the royal family due to their loyalty to that king. But precisely because they are all siblings and thus are children of God their father, the title does not differentiate Jesus as ontologically distinct from them as one who is preexistent or divine as such.

Indeed, there are numerous indications throughout the Gospel of Mark that discipleship is inherently connected with Jesus's messiahship. The very markers of the coming reign of God in its proclamation and Jesus's astounding powers to heal and exorcise are the exact purposes for which the disciples are called (3:13-15) and the very mission on which the disciples are successfully sent (6:7, 12-13). Jesus is inaugurator of the kingdom of God as its king, but the disciples are called to continue and extend this reign. Suzanne Watts Henderson has demonstrated how such a vision for God's entrusting of the coming kingdom into human hands becomes a crucial theme of the Gospel. With regard to the summoning of the twelve in Mark 3 she comments, "If Jesus has emerged in the second gospel as God's specially designated emissary, in this passage he explicitly extends his power and authority to the Twelve who surround him."[100] She summarizes the parable chapter with an indication that God is entrusting the mystery of the kingdom, not only in deed but also in word, to these fallible humans:

> Jesus's parabolic teaching in Mk. 4:1-34 further develops the evangelist's emphasis on the disciples' participation in the dawning rule of God, which features Jesus as its prototypical embodiment. Central to Jesus's exposition of that reign ("the kingdom of God") is a symbiotic effort in which a vulnerable God entrusts humanity with the task of sowing the seeds even while a sovereign God ultimately ensures victory over evil and the abundant harvest that victory promises.[101]

Jesus is the prototype, but the disciples are subsequent embodiments of that type, continuing the ministry that Jesus does as king of the kingdom. Proceeding to Mark's discussion of the disciples' mission in Mark 6, Henderson continues, "As it recounts Jesus's sending out of the Twelve, Mk. 6:7-13 only continues, and etches more indelibly, the lines of continuity between Jesus's and the disciples' display of the 'gospel,' which is God's encroaching dominion."[102]

The point of drawing out the deep narratival connections between Jesus's inauguration of the kingdom of God and the disciples' participation therein is to underscore the plausibility that for Mark Jesus's mission as messiah, which I have argued is his mission as son of God, is a quintessentially human mission. Jesus is the idealized representative human being, who performs the messianic task of bringing God's reign to bear on the earth. And Jesus is forming a people who will continue that task in his absence. As we will see at other points of this study, the disciples' role in continuing Jesus's ministry in his absence becomes most clear in Matthew's Great Commission, where the eleven are called to teach

---

100. Suzanne Watts Henderson, *Christology and Discipleship in the Gospel of Mark* (SNTSMS 135; Cambridge: Cambridge University Press, 2006), 66.

101. Henderson, *Christology and Discipleship,* 98.

102. Henderson, *Christology and Discipleship,* 136.

what Jesus has already taught (28:12), and in Luke's depiction of Pentecost where the disciples receive the same spirit Jesus received (Acts 2:4). Across all three Synoptic Gospels, even the most unique and unrepeatable aspect of Jesus's messianic task and the pinnacle of his embodiment of divine sonship, that is, dying on the cross, forms an integral component to the call to discipleship Jesus issues.

The profound integration of Jesus's messianic task and the tasks to which his disciples are called illustrate for us the significance, for Mark, of Jesus's fulfilling his own task as a human being. The paradigm of idealized human Christology suggests that Jesus is enacting a role that he can perform because he is the idealized human representative of God on earth, and that other humans can therefore be called to enact in order to continue the ministry of Jesus.[103]

To sharpen the point a bit: if we read Mark as depicting Jesus as issuing his proclamations, enacting his authority, exorcising demons, feeding the multitudes, and so on, on the basis of some preexistent divinity, we cut the ground out from underneath the feet of the larger, narratologically depicted argument that the humans who follow Jesus are called to enact these very same instantiations of the coming reign of God. What idealized human Christology cogently accounts for is left oddly incongruent on the basis of an inherently divine Christology. Stating this the other way around, the summons to continue, embody, and extend the ministry of Jesus is only possible among Jesus's human followers if Jesus himself does these things because he, too, is human. Using such means to argue for Jesus's divinity becomes a de facto argument that the disciples, too, are ontologically divine.

4. CONCLUSION: SON OF GOD AS MESSIANIC KING IN MARK

Mark's son of God theology can find no better summary than the one offered by John Donahue, whose reading of Mark coheres with what is presented above:

> In Mk Jesus is anointed King at his baptism, and proclaimed so at his transfiguration; his ministry brings about the arrival of the Kingdom, but an arrival which precipitates a struggle to obtain full possession. For Mk the final assumption of total power and the handing on of the royal authority will take place when Jesus returns as Son of Man. Mk uses Son of Man as an interpretative symbol for these royal traditions as he does for others.[104]

103. Henderson, *Christology and Discipleship*, 136.
104. Donahue, "Temple, Trial, and Royal Christology," 77.

Mark's is a messianic and royal Christology in which Jesus is anointed and proclaimed king by God, and recognized as king by demonic powers and by a lone human being. This quasi-royal messianism is refracted through the particular vocation of Jesus to suffer in order to enter into his glory. Though Mark employs language that points toward a royal son of God Christology, it is the story of Mark itself that demonstrates to us the peculiar, suffering nature of that dynamic of Mark's messianism.[105] Such a reading of Mark constitutes a unique contribution to the Jewish panoply of idealized human figures in early Judaism, but fits well within it. Mark's Jesus functions and is identified in the narrative as an idealized human figure, and his life demarcates for his followers what their lives, as the heirs of the kingdom, are also to look like.

B. SON OF GOD, SON OF DAVID, SON OF ADAM IN LUKE

Luke offers several additional glimpses and interpretations of the son of God title. I look at not only unique uses of the title, such as those in the birth narrative and genealogy, but also those shared with Matthew and, in a couple of places, those shared with Mark. The instances shared with Mark provide a particularly interesting window into Luke's son of God Christology inasmuch as he takes the opportunity to clarify and/or reaffirm that son of God connotes messiah.[106] The uniquely Lukan material is significant inasmuch as it demonstrates that for Luke "son of God" functions much like it did in the scriptures of Israel as a reference to idealized, representative humanity in the persons of Adam and David in particular.

1. CONCEPTION, BIRTH, AND CHILDHOOD

The birth narrative more generally will occupy our attention in a subsequent chapter. For now, I focus on the announcement to Mary with its two indications that Jesus will be called God's son (υἱὸς ὑψίστου, 1:32; υἱὸς θεοῦ, 1:35). The first indication that Luke's Jesus is God's son comes in the word of the

---

105. Cf. Broadhead, *Naming Jesus*, 122-23.
106. I thus find myself in general agreement with the assessment of Hans Conzelmann, in *The Theology of St. Luke* (trans. G. Buswell; New York: Harper & Row, 1961), 174: "All three principal Christological titles, Christ, Lord and Son, signify in this respect the same facts. Whichever of them is used to express Jesus's position, his office appears as something conferred on him by God."

angel that Jesus will be called υἱὸς ὑψίστου (1:32), and is followed by multiple indications that it is a royal title. The larger context reads:

οὗτος ἔσται μέγας καὶ υἱὸς ὑψίστου κληθήσεται καὶ δώσει αὐτῷ κύριος ὁ θεὸς τὸν θρόνον Δαυὶδ τοῦ πατρὸς αὐτοῦ, καὶ βασιλεύσει ἐπὶ τὸν οἶκον Ἰακὼβ εἰς τοὺς αἰῶνας καὶ τῆς βασιλείας αὐτοῦ οὐκ ἔσται τέλος.

And this one will be great and will be called son of the Most High and the Lord God will give to him the throne of his father David, and he will reign over the house of Jacob forever and of his kingdom there will be no end. (Luke 1:32-33)

It would be difficult to imagine a stronger set of indications that Luke wants his readers to interpret "son of the Most High" as a royal title than those provided in these verses.[107] Moreover, this pericope occupies a signal position in Luke's Gospel. As Mark Strauss rightly points out, "the first thing the narrator tells the reader about Jesus — the main character in his story — is that *through him God will fulfill his promises to David.*"[108] The announcement draws not only on the idea that the enthroned king is adopted as God's son (e.g., Psalm 2) but also that David's son in particular has God as his father (2 Sam 7:12-16). Indeed, Luke's promise that Jesus will be son of God reads as something close to a point-by-point fulfillment of the promise made to David in 2 Samuel 7. There, God promises that God will raise up David's seed (2 Sam 7:12; Luke 1:32), that this offspring will sit on a throne (2 Sam 7:13; Luke 1:32), that God will be a father to him and he will be God's son (2 Sam 7:14; Luke 1:32), and that the kingdom will endure forever (2 Sam 7:12, 16; Luke 1:33).[109] Here we see none of Mark's reticence in associating Jesus's messiahship with Davidic kingship, as David and the promises made to him are invoked both explicitly and implicitly. Υἱὸς ὑψίστου in this passage clearly functions within the antecedent scriptural framework within which being king of Israel made a man son of God. Moreover, the Davidic king ruling for God correlates with the presence of Yʜwʜ's own rule.[110] This is a clear instance of idealized human Christology.

107. Collins and Collins, *King and Messiah*, 143-44.
108. Mark L. Strauss, *The Davidic Messiah in Luke-Acts: The Promise and Its Fulfillment in Lukan Christology* (JSNTSup 110; Sheffield: Sheffield Academic, 1995), 89 (italics original).
109. Cf. Joel B. Green, *The Gospel of Luke* (NICNT; Grand Rapids, MI: Eerdmans, 1997), 88; Strauss, *Davidic Messiah*, 88-89.
110. Green, *Gospel of Luke*, 88, highlights this with particular focus on the eschatological context and the expectation of the "everlasting dominion of Yahweh."

The second usage of "son of God" terminology comes almost immediately afterward, in the angel's response to Mary's query about how this could be, given her virgin state (Luke 1:34). The birth is attributed to the activity of the spirit of God, and this is given as an additional reason for the child's being called "son of God": πνεῦμα ἅγιον ἐπελεύσεται ἐπὶ σὲ καὶ δύναμις ὑψίστου ἐπισκιάσει σοι· διὸ καὶ τὸ γεννώμενον ἅγιον κληθήσεται υἱὸς θεοῦ ("[The] holy spirit will come upon you and the power of the most high will overshadow you; therefore, also, the begotten holy one will be called son of God"). Here God clearly stands in the place of an earthly father in the process of Jesus's physical generation.[111] Thus, there is a clear sense in which God is father to the earthly Jesus in a way that God was not father to David or Solomon. However, we must decide whether the thrust of the prophecy is creational rather than incarnational. The passage does not tell us, for instance, that the child will descend into Mary's womb from above, but that God's power will be at work within her by means of the spirit. The verb ἐπισκιάζω appears twice more in Luke's corpus. First, Luke follows Mark in using the verb to speak of the cloud of divine presence on the mount of transfiguration. Second, he uses the verb in Acts to depict how Peter's healing power came to those whom Peter passed by. The people would lie out the sick on beds and mats, ἵνα ἐρχομένου Πέτρου κἂν ἡ σκιὰ ἐπισκιάσῃ τινὶ αὐτῶν (5:15). Overshadowing is a means for the power of God to be at work in re-creation. Analogously, the idea of the spirit coming upon people (πνεῦμα ἐπέρχομαι) recurs in Acts 1:8 as the language Jesus uses of the disciples' yet-to-come experience on Pentecost. In light of this, the language of spiritual conception should not be pressed into an incarnational framework as though it is the means by which a preexistent son comes to take up human residence in Mary's womb.

Two options, then, present themselves. First, this could be an indication that a new divine being is formed, analogous to the half-gods of Greek mythology, by this divine-human union. The second is that the work of the spirit and the power of God in view here should be seen as an act of new creation. If the former, Luke would be creating a story in which a Hellenistic trope is being employed as a further indication of how it is that this particular being comes to occupy the throne of an eternal kingdom, that is, by being the semi-divine offspring of one divine parent.[112] If the latter, Luke is drawing deeply

111. Collins and Collins, *King and Messiah*, 145.

112. The idea that this indicates a "metaphysical" differentiation of Jesus is suggested in I. Howard Marshall, *Luke: Historian and Theologian* (Grand Rapids, MI: Baker Academic, 1989), 168.

on Adamic categories for explicating and enriching the idea of the Davidic rule into which Jesus is being inaugurated. Either is possible at this point in the story; however, the baptism and genealogy in Luke lead me toward the second view, so I turn to those below.

For now, I simply wish to register the importance of pursuing the Adamic interpretation of this son of God reference. Strauss notes the significance of the spirit as a creative agent in scripture and Jewish tradition, including the creation of both the cosmos (Gen 1:2; Ps 33:6) and individuals (Job 33:4; Ps 104:30; 2 *Apoc. Bar.* 21:4; Jdt 16:14).[113] But he does not see such spiritual activity conjoined with divine sonship. Given that Luke uses son of God language not only of David, as here, but also of Adam in 3:38, it appears that Luke's own contribution to son of God theology is not in moving toward a metaphysically different type of human being, but toward integrating the son of God titles as he received them from different places in scripture and tradition. The Adam reference becomes all the more important if, as Strauss maintains, Luke is building off of a tradition similar to the one found in Romans 1:3-4, in which Jesus is of Davidic descent, but enthroned as king when the spirit, in its power, raises him from the dead.[114] For Paul, this is an Adamic moment, the creation of new humanity, not the disclosure of divine ontology. Given Luke's subsequent claim that Adam, too, is son of God (Luke 3:38), such a route toward understanding Luke's son of God Christology seems more apposite to the universe of the narrative.

One story nearer to hand, however, demands attention first. Jesus refers to God as his father when, as a youth, he stays behind in Jerusalem talking Torah with the temple leadership (2:41-51): οὐκ ᾔδειτε ὅτι ἐν τοῖς τοῦ πατρός μου δεῖ εἶναί με; ("Did you not know that it was necessary for me to be in the matters concerning my father?" 2:49). Significant for interpreting this text is that the passage repeatedly refers to Jesus's parents (γονεῖς, plural, vv. 41, 43; μήτηρ and πατήρ, v. 48). As Joel Green comments, the juxtaposition of the narrator's and mother's voice with Jesus's claim to be about his father's business (or in his father's house) makes the overall effect of the pericope one in which ultimate family allegiance is in question.[115] The business with which Jesus has occupied himself is the business of learning Torah. If one approaches this passage with a divine Christology paradigm in play, the scene is readily enough integrated: Jesus knows even at this tender age that God is his true father, perhaps not only

---

113. Strauss, *Davidic Messiah*, 91.
114. Strauss, *Davidic Messiah*, 92.
115. Green, *Gospel of Luke*, 156-57.

as Jesus is God the son but also as Jesus is king in waiting, as suggested by the "son of the Most High" prediction articulated to Mary. But with an idealized human Christology in play, the latter element sustains the passage, and does not leave the reader with any awkward remaining material not made sense of.

The notion that Jesus as king in waiting needs to attend to the Torah draws on both the biblical hope that any king of Israel would know and be governed by the law (Deut 17:18-20) and the later Jewish hope that the king would lead the people in faithfulness to Torah, even if tutored in it by another (e.g., Covenant of Damascus). A passage that demonstrates Jesus's supernatural apprehension of Torah indicates that this is an early manifestation of a vocation that will pull his loyalty completely in the direction of the God who is related to him, specially, as father, and away from those who could otherwise be recognized as his father and mother. While this passage, as the others that mention Jesus's sonship to God, indicates his peculiar role, it does not argue for or demonstrate a peculiar ontology or preexistence.

2. BAPTISM AND GENEALOGY

The baptism scene is the location of one of the notorious Mark-Q overlaps. But Luke, being constrained neither by Mark nor by his sayings source, has provided a unique clue for interpreting the identity of Jesus as disclosed in the baptism. While all three Synoptic Gospels include John the Baptist's assurances that one who is stronger and greater will succeed him, a greatness embodied in spirit versus water baptism (Mark 1:7-8; Matt 3:11-12; Luke 3:16), and while both Luke and Matthew include the imagery of eschatological judgment by way of a winnowing fork to separate wheat from chaff, only Luke includes an introductory musing by the crowds that these assertions answer. In Luke 3:15-16 we learn that the people are wondering about John's identity: προδοκῶντος δὲ τοῦ λαοῦ καὶ διαλογιζομένων πάντων ἐν ταῖς καρδίαις αὐτῶν περὶ τοῦ Ἰωάννου, μήποτε αὐτὸς εἴη ὁ χριστός, ἀπεκρίνατο λέγων πᾶσιν ὁ Ἰωάννης . . . ("While the people were waiting expectantly, and all were reasoning in their hearts about John, whether he might be the Christ, John answered saying to all . . .").

Two dimensions of the verse in question are worthy of note. First, and most important, John's statement about the stronger and greater one is in direct response to the people's wondering whether or not he is the messiah (χριστός). The deflection that follows, in which John calls attention to the coming one who will baptize with the spirit and perform the function of eschatological judge, answers the people's question of who, in fact, the messiah is. Thus, the entire baptism scene stands under the rubric of messiah as the Christological disclosure that occurs.[116] The people wonder about John's being the messiah (3:15), John indicates instead that the coming one is the messiah (3:15-17), and the divine voice indicates that Jesus is this messiah when he is anointed son of God and receives the spirit (3:22).[117] Jesus is the coming one, the messiah who serves as God's human agent. The son of God title bestowed at baptism is thus Christological, not ontological.

The second dimension deserves briefer notice. It is simply this: John responds directly to the thoughts that people do not voice out loud (3:15-16). Thus, when Jesus later responds to the reasoning of people's hearts (e.g., 5:22; 9:47), it is no indication of a unique ontological status that differentiates him from John by being identified with or as God in any sort of proto-Chalcedonian sense.[118] Otherwise, the baptism itself in Luke adds little to the particular question I am investigating. It is interesting to note that Jesus comes out to be baptized at the same time as all the people (ἅπαντα τὸν λαόν), a potential indication that solidarity with all Israel is an important component of his messianic status, but this is far from conclusive.

After the baptism, Luke goes further in demonstrating that Jesus, as son of God, is an idealized human figure rather than ontologically divine.[119] Immediately subsequent to the divine declaration of Jesus as God's son at the baptism, Luke provides a genealogy of Jesus. The genealogy in 3:23-38 traces Jesus's ancestry back to the very beginnings of Israel's primordial history. Concluding with the ancestors listed in Genesis 5, Luke follows the implications of that first biblical genealogy by ending, τοῦ Ἀδὰμ τοῦ θεοῦ. This indicates that Jesus is son of God as Adam was son of God. As I argued in my investigation of Israel's scriptures, against the idea that a genealogy with God at its head is absent in the Jewish writings,[120] the language of image and likeness is sonship language: Seth is the image (Heb דמות; Gr εἰκών) of Adam as Adam is the image (Heb דמות; Gr εἰκών) of God (Gen 5:1-3). Each is the son of the other. By inserting such a reading of the genealogy immediately

---

116. Cf. Strauss, *Davidic Messiah,* 200-201.

117. As Strauss points out, the subsequent claim of Jesus that he is anointed as one possessing the spirit (Luke 4:18; citing Isa 61:1-2) confirms that this scene, with the reception of the spirit, is an anointing (*Davidic Messiah,* 202).

118. *Pace* Gathercole, *Preexistent Son,* 70-71.

119. On the baptism of Jesus in Luke as a royal anointing, echoing Psalm 2:7, as I argued above in the case of Mark, see Green, *Gospel of Luke,* 185-87.

120. So, e.g., Strauss, *Davidic Messiah,* 211.

after the baptism, it becomes a commentary on the declaration of Jesus as son of God made by the divine voice. Son of God is not only the language of Davidic royalty, as we saw that it was in the announcement to Mary, and as I argue it is in the baptism based both on what we saw in Mark and in the crowd's question about John as messiah in Luke, it is also the language of Adam, the first royal son of God.

My study of Israel's scriptures and of early Judaism has prepared us for such a dual Adam-David idea of Jesus as son of God. It reflects the ways in which Adamic categories and Davidic categories are developed in light of one another in both the biblical and post-biblical traditions. The Adam story is a story of one who was created son of God in order to rule the world on God's behalf. And that very language of ruling the world on God's behalf prepares for a story in which kings will arise within the covenant people of God (Gen 17:6, 16; 35:11), thus making the heirs of Abraham the fulfillment of the idealized humanity depicted in Genesis 1. Luke provides a richly textured theology of the son of God that encompasses both the specifically Davidic dynamics of the royal son of God and also the more general Adamic dynamics of the primal, reigning son of God. That Luke does so fits well within his theological concern of demonstrating that in Jesus the God of Israel is now making known to the nations that Israel's is, in fact, the only true God, who calls all people to repent before the final judgment (e.g., Acts 17:29-31). If David represents the specificity of God's election of Israel and a promised line of kingship, Adam represents the generality of God's claims on, and purposes for, all humanity. Perhaps more specifically, Adam Christology means that God rules over the Gentiles, not through one who is "other," because Jewish, but through one who is the same because he is human. In both instances, of course, Jesus is distinguished by the role he plays as God's anointed king, but in both instances he is also ontologically and/or sociologically the same.

This conjunction of Davidic and Adamic motifs around the language of son of God takes us back to the question I left unanswered at the end of the previous section. Although Luke does not have to work with a consistent Adam-David duality throughout his writings, the fact that such a duality explicates the son of God language at the baptism provides important evidence for an Adamic reading of Luke 1:34. The language of the spirit's creation of Jesus in the womb of Mary is well accounted for by analogies found in the brooding spirit of Genesis 1:2 and perhaps even the breath of God enlivening the Adam of Gen 2:7. Jesus is conceived son of God as he is a new Adam, and he is anointed son of God in this Adamic sense with his reception of the spirit at his baptism.

3. TEMPTATION NARRATIVE

It is precisely Jesus's identity as son of God that is put to the test in the temptation narrative that follows Luke's genealogy (as well as the parallel account in Matthew).[121] In Luke's ordering of the three temptations, they begin and end with the challenge from the devil, "If you are son of God" (εἰ υἱὸς εἶ τοῦ θεοῦ, 4:3, 9). Parsing these temptations with our particular Christological question in mind yields a tremendous amount of insight into the nature of the temptations Jesus is facing. The temptations allow us to pose the question of what paradigm is being tested. Do they confront Jesus in such a way as to cause him to doubt or betray a preexistent, divine ontology or in such a way as to cause him to doubt or betray his role as idealized human being?[122] The temptation narrative itself is rife with echoes of Israel's wilderness wanderings, through its location, the forty-day duration, Jesus's being led by the spirit, and the citations from Deuteronomy.[123] This provides prima facie evidence that Jesus is fulfilling Israel's vocation or story rather than demonstrating a special divinity.[124]

The first temptation is for Jesus to enact or prove his divine sonship by speaking to a stone such that it becomes bread: "If you are son of God, say to this stone that it become bread" (εἰ υἱὸς εἶ τοῦ θεοῦ, εἰπὲ τῷ λίθῳ τούτῳ ἵνα γένηται ἄρτος, 4:3). The temptation to exercise such power might, indeed, be a means of demonstrating that he shares in the divine nature in some way that has not been true of any other person. Jesus, however, sides with faithful

---

121. See also Birger Gerhardsson, *The Testing of God's Son (Matt 4:1-11 & Par.): An Analysis of an Early Christian Midrash* (trans. J. Toy; Lund: Gleerup, 1966), 19-20. In both Matthew and Luke, the son of God Christology articulated in the baptism provides a crucial backdrop to the temptation narrative, as Hans-Christian Kammler notes in "Sohn Gottes und Kreuz: Die Versuchungsgeschichte Mt 4,1-11 im Kontext des Matthausevangeliums," *ZTK* 100 (23): 163-86, here 170. He suggests that the point of both stories in tandem is to show the cruciform nature of Jesus's ministry (171).

122. Gerhardsson, *Testing of God's Son,* 25-28, suggests that πειράζειν is close to a technical term, indicating that the terms of a covenantal relationship are being tried, either positively by God or negatively by God's people. Though I am wary of pushing the notion of a technical term too far, this lends support to the idea that it is a relationship between Jesus and God rather than a native divine possession that is being put to the test in the pericope.

123. Robert L. Brawley, *Text to Text Pours Forth Speech: Voices of Scripture in Luke-Acts* (Bloomington: Indiana University Press, 1995), 17.

124. Gerhardsson, *Testing of God's Son,* 20-22, demonstrates how a number of son of God texts that refer to Israel bearing such an identity are found in "the desert wandering texts, not least in Deuteronomy," from which several key scriptural references are taken in this scene.

humanity (ὁ ἄνθρωπος) as the means by which his divine sonship is made known: "It is written, 'Not by bread alone does the human live'" (γέγραπται ὅτι οὐκ ἐπ᾽ ἄρτῳ μόνῳ ζήσεται ὁ ἄνθρωπος, 4:4). Jesus cites Deuteronomy 8:3, a verse that speaks of God testing Israel with hunger and feeding the people. Jesus's forty days of testing in the wilderness parallel Israel's own forty years. Significantly, the concluding remarks of the pericope in Deuteronomy 8 are these: "So, know in your heart that just as a man disciplines his son, Yhwh your God disciplines you" (v. 5). The passage to which Jesus alludes not only speaks of true humanity being composed of those who know that its sustenance is not to be found only in bread, but it also envelops Israel's experience of testing in the wilderness as proof that Israel is related to God as a son to a father.[125] Jesus is highlighting a fidelity to God in which he makes good on the filial devotion that was supposed to typify Israel, itself a people who were to stand in the place of Adam, the son of God, as God's idealized humanity. The language of discipline is repeated both in Deuteronomy 8:5 and in the Deuteronomistic history's promise of a Davidic heir who is himself to be son of God (2 Sam 7:14). The first temptation is well read as Jesus's claim to being son of God in the sense of idealized human being by drawing on Israel's place in the Adam-Israel-David complex that punctuates the scriptures of Israel.

The second temptation does not use son of God language, but it does provide Jesus with an alternative method of attaining to worldwide reign (depicted in son of God language in Luke 1:32-33) through worship of the devil.[126] As Robert Brawley provocatively puts it, "By promising to give Jesus authority over all the kingdoms of the world the devil claims in essence to be the restorer of the Davidic covenant and mediator of the Abraham covenant . . . the temptation is for Jesus to worship the devil as an intermediary — God's broker."[127] Jesus's response once again alludes to Deuteronomy, this time 6:13 or 10:20: γέγραπται· κύριον τὸν θεόν σου προσκυνήσεις καὶ αὐτῷ μόνῳ λατρεύσεις ("It is written, 'You shall worship the Lord your God and him alone shall you serve,'" 4:8). Though the match is not exact, the likely allusion to Deuteronomy 6 fills in, further, the means by which Jesus is making good on the fidelity to God that was to be embodied in Israel. This passage speaks not only of the Israelites needing to reserve worship for God alone, but also of their remembering such obeisance when coming into the inheritance

125. Cf. Gerhardsson, *Testing of God's Son,* 43-48.
126. Cf. Strauss, *Davidic Messiah,* 216-17.
127. Brawley, *Text to Text,* 21.

of cities that they did not build and cisterns they did not dig (vv. 10-12). The offer that the devil has just made provides Jesus not only with an alternative power to worship, but also with an alternative source for his inheritance of an inhabited, developed world (Luke 4:5). Jesus is trusting God for provision of an inherited kingdom and glory by maintaining fidelity in worshiping God alone.[128]

The third temptation directly focuses on Jesus's sonship. The devil tests Jesus's assuredness about his sonship by taking him to a high point and suggesting he experience the promised provision of Psalm 91 (MT and Eng.; Psalm 90, LXX). With such an allusion, it becomes even clearer that the tests have to do with Jesus as an idealized human as that person is related to God. Psalm 91 is neither Davidic nor Adamic, nor is it demonstrative of Israel's calling as a people, particularly. It speaks of the person who has faithfully clung to God, trusting God to be deliverer. Jesus, however, once again invokes the lessons that Israel was to have learned in the wilderness, and recognizes that such is a test not of Jesus's sonship but of his confidence in God: "It is said, 'You shall not test the Lord your God'" (εἴρηται· οὐκ ἐκπειράσεις κύριον τὸν θεόν σου, Luke 4:12; citing Deut 6:16). The quoted verse is notable for what Jesus does not include: Deuteronomy 6:16's remembrance that Israel did, in fact, put God to the test at the waters of Massah. Whereas the devil would have Jesus prove his sonship by a successful test, Jesus's citation of Deuteronomy 6:16 indicates that it is precisely in refusing to put God to the test that he shows himself to be a faithful son.

Throughout the temptation narrative, the allusive force of the setting, the verbiage, and the scriptural citations take the reader back to Israel's years of infidelity in the wilderness as a stark contrast to Jesus's own faithfulness.[129] With such an allusive framework, we see Luke enriching his "son of God" category by adding another category of idealized humans who bore such a filial title in the scriptures of Israel, namely, Israel itself. Green summarizes well the temptation narrative: "Unlike Israel, Jesus proved his fidelity in the wilderness and so is '. . . presented as the true Son of God, in whom the destiny of Israel was recapitulated and the divine purpose accomplished in that he renders to God the obedience and trust that Israel failed to give.' Now Jesus

---

128. Cf. Gerhardsson, *Testing of God's Son*, 62-66.

129. Thus, in commenting on the Matthean version, Terence L. Donaldson, "The Vindicated Son: A Narrative Approach to Matthean Christology," in *Contours of Christology in the New Testament* (ed. R. N. Longenecker; Grand Rapids, MI: Eerdmans, 2005), 100-121, argues that while the tempter depicts the son of God "in terms of royal sovereignty," itself a scriptural category, Jesus "understands the term against the background of Israel's calling" (117).

is ready to engage in his public ministry in the service of God's redemptive program."[130] The truth of Jesus's sonship is made known not in a display of ontological dissimilarity from humanity but in a display of ideal human faithfulness. Using the language of vice-regency, Darrell Bock argues in a similar vein: "The theme of the temptations is the issue of vice-regency and who Jesus will serve. . . . Jesus is not only representative of Israel but a worthy, faithful vice-regent of all humanity."[131] In withstanding the temptations, Jesus refuses to use the power concomitant with his anointing of the spirit "apart from the fulfillment of his specific commission as the Son," a vocation of obedient suffering.[132]

4. DEMONS

Luke follows Mark's early sequence of a Sabbath day on which Jesus exorcises a demon in a synagogue (Luke 4:33-37; par. Mark 1:23-28) and heals Peter's mother-in-law (Luke 4:38-39; par. Mark 1:29-31) before the multitudes gather for healing after sunset (Luke 4:40-41; par. Mark 1:32-34). This third pericope contains a narrative summary of Jesus's interactions with the demons. As we saw in Mark, so also in Luke Jesus silences the demons because of their supernatural knowledge of his identity. However, Luke fills in the gaps such that the reader knows more precisely what the demonic insight entails. The demonic cry is, σὺ εἶ ὁ υἱὸς τοῦ θεοῦ ("You are the son of God," 4:41 — surely the precise echo of the satanic temptation from earlier in the chapter is not accidental). Thus, we are again confronted with the question of what Luke's son of God Christology entails, a question that the narrator answers for us in explaining Jesus's command to silence. He did not allow them to speak, ὅτι ᾔδεισαν τὸν χριστὸν αὐτὸν εἶναι ("because they knew that he was the Christ," 4:41). The concern of Luke's Jesus is not that they will disclose his unique ontological status as preexistent divine being, but that they will disclose his Christological status as such — that he is the messiah.[133]

---

130. Green, *Gospel of Luke,* 193; citing C. F. Evans, *Saint Luke* (TPINTC; London: SCM, 1990), 256 (italics original).

131. Darrell L. Bock, "Proclamation from Prophecy and Pattern: Luke's Use of the Old Testament for Christology and Mission," in *The Gospels and the Scriptures of Israel* (JSNTSup 104/SSEJC 3; ed. C. A. Evans and W. R. Stegner; Sheffield: Sheffield Academic, 1994), 280-307, here 289.

132. Cullmann, *Christology,* 277.

133. Cf. Strauss, *Davidic Messiah,* 94.

5. TRANSFIGURATION, MOSES, AND EXODUS

A detailed exposition of Luke's telling of the transfiguration story would be fruitful, but unduly repetitive.[134] Therefore, I only wish to highlight a couple of peculiarities of Luke's telling of the story, each of which helps to place the accent of the story on Jesus's similarity to, rather than ontological difference from, his Mosaic predecessor as one who shines in the divine glory.[135] This, then, enriches the context in which Jesus is addressed as God's son and provides an interpretive framework for the particularities of that address itself.

First, Luke changes the time designation. Whereas both Mark and Matthew indicate a span of six days between Jesus's prophecy about some not tasting death before they see the kingdom, Luke indicates instead a span of eight days (9:28). There are several possible allusions, including the general idea that an eighth day might be a "second week" after the seven days of creation, an idea that would comport nicely with a second Adam Christology. However, the more common use of the language about the eighth day revolves around dedication to God of Israel's firstborn males. For human males, the rite of circumcision on the eighth day, first introduced in the patriarchal narratives (Gen 17:12), comes to be coordinated with the offering up of firstborn males of all animal species (Exod 22:29-31). In the final form of Exodus, this command is embedded in the larger exodus narrative, in which Israel is God's firstborn son, all of Egypt loses its firstborn sons in order for Israel to be redeemed, and thus Israel must recognize that all firstborn sons belong to God and either offer them in sacrifice or redeem them (13:11-16). The offering and redeeming of firstborn sons on the eighth day was to be a perpetual reminder that Yhwh had redeemed Israel from slavery through the exodus (13:16). Thus, while Luke's change of day from the sixth to the eighth likely maintains an allusion to Exodus, it may well be creating a context within which Jesus as God's son has a more specific point of contact as God's own possession, the one who is redeemed from the enslaving power of the enemy of God's people.

Second, Luke draws attention, specifically, to the transformation in Jesus's face. While Mark tells us that Jesus was transformed and his clothes began to shine, Luke says that the appearance of Jesus's face was changed while he was

---

134. Strauss, *Davidic Messiah*, 263-72, covers several points with special reference to Luke that I took up as I focused on Mark's transfiguration account above, including the connections with the baptismal anointing as son of God.

135. Similar to Mark is Luke's connection of the story with the confession of Peter, and thus the overall context of Jesus's vocation and its relationship to what faithful following entails (cf. Green, *Gospel of Luke*, 379-80).

praying in addition to his clothes shining (ἐγένετο ἐν τῷ προσεύχεσθαι αὐτὸν τὸ εἶδος τοῦ προσώπου αὐτοῦ ἕτερον καὶ ὁ ἱματισμὸς αὐτοῦ λευκὸς ἐξαστρά- πων, 9:29). This strengthens the Mosaic allusions in the story. Immediately thereafter, Luke tells the reader that Moses and Elijah were speaking with Jesus. The mention of Moses directly after the comment about Jesus's transformed face and shining clothing helps associate Jesus with Moses, and substantiates the notion that Jesus is another human who has entered into the divine presence and is now reflecting the glory of God. Moreover, Luke's indication that Jesus was praying upon his transformation picks up on the ongoing renewal of Moses's shining face that would happen whenever he went in to speak to Yʜwʜ (Exod 34:34). Additionally, Luke goes on to describe Moses and Elijah; he says that they appear in glory (οἱ ὀφθέντες ἐν δόξῃ, 9:31), likely echoing the LXX in its description of Moses's face (e.g., δεδόξασται, Exod 34:29; cf. 34:30, 35). With this network of more specific allusions to the Moses story, Luke again reinforces the significance of the exodus narrative for interpreting the pericope, demonstrates that such glorification as Jesus reflects is appropriate to idealized human figures like the quintessential prophets of the biblical tradition, and thereby aids the reader in locating the son of God declaration on such a biblical map.[136]

Luke's allusive instrument becomes blunter, still, with his description of the conversation that unfolds between Jesus and his two visitors. "They spoke of Jesus's exodus, which he was about to fulfill in Jerusalem" (ἔλεγον τὴν ἔξοδον αὐτοῦ ἥν ἤμελλεν πληροῦν ἐν Ἰερουσαλήμ, 9:31). The allusion to the first exodus in the forthcoming death of Jesus is strengthened by the language of fulfillment (πληρόω), a word Luke uses elsewhere to speak of fulfillment of divine promise (1:20) and scripture (4:21; 24:44), as well as the Passover itself (22:16). This latter point is of particular significance, inasmuch as both the transfiguration scene and the Last Supper scene are looking forward to a fulfillment of the exodus story specifically in Jesus's death. In this third way, also, Luke invokes the exodus as a co-text for interpreting the transfiguration scene. Looking to a future exodus, Luke's crafting of the story agrees with the reading of the scene given for Mark, above, to the effect that this story discloses the destiny toward which Jesus is headed as son of God rather than disclosing the past and present reality of Jesus as preexistent son of God.[137]

Finally, there is the exact verbiage of Luke's divine declaration in 9:35.

---

136. Strauss, *Davidic Messiah*, 270, agrees that what we see in these two prophets is indicative of Jesus's future, though to his mind this mutes somewhat the significance of Sinai as background for understanding the scene.

137. Strauss, *Davidic Messiah*, 271-72.

Rather than repeating the language of beloved son, Luke's God says, οὗτός ἐστιν ὁ υἱός μοῦ ὁ ἐκλελεγμένος ("this is my son, the elect one"). On a general level, this language of election indicates that the kind of sonship in view is one of vocation rather than ontology. Although there is no clear biblical antecedent, the Deuteronomic historian does refer to David as the one whom God has chosen (in contrast to his brothers, 1 Sam 16:8-10; when David contrasts himself to Saul, 2 Sam 6:21; in contrast to Absalom, 2 Sam 16:18; and as God's affirmation of David's role, 1 Kgs 8:16).[138] The Greek translations of Deuteronomy also use the verb ἐκλέγω to speak of God's choice of Israel (e.g., 4:37; 7:7; 10:15; 14:12). If either biblical precedent lies behind the use of the terminology of election, Jesus as son of God is the chosen human being who represents the people of God by embodying the deliverance of Israel in himself. Joined together with the exodus terminology, Luke's "son of God" phraseology takes on dimensions of corporate representation, as Jesus represents Israel from within, as one of its number, rather than as one who has come to it from beyond the earthly sphere.

The language of "the elect" is also pervasive across various sections of *1 Enoch* (e.g., 1:1, 8; 5:7-8; 25:5; 38:2-3; 45:5; 58:1-3; 70:4; 93:1). Most often, this refers to the people of God. *First Enoch* 38 describes the final judgment. There, we read that the mighty and exalted "will not be able to look at the face of the holy, for the light of the Lord of Spirits will have appeared on the face of the holy, righteous, and chosen" (v. 4).[139] Here is a further democratization of the shining faces of the people of God, realized at the final judgment. As I argued in the section on *1 Enoch* in the previous chapter, the messianic figure of the book is most often identified in ways that show his participation in the identity of the faithful people of God. "Elect One" is one title that encapsulates this. Thus we read, for example, in *1 Enoch* 39:6, "And in that place my eyes saw the Chosen One of righteousness and faith, and righteous will be his days, and the righteous and chosen will be without number before him forever and ever." The repetitive language of "chosen," as well as "righteousness," indicates solidarity between this representative figure and the people of God. This, too, fits well with Luke's overall Christology as seen thus far, in which Jesus represents all humanity in his fidelity to God, Israel's king as Davidic son of God, the king of all peoples as Adamic son of God, and faithful, obedient people as Israelite son of God. Although Enoch's Elect One is preexistent, at least in having been human before exercising his

138. Cf. Strauss, *Davidic Messiah,* 265-67.

139. Translation from George W. E. Nickelsburg and James C. VanderKam, *1 Enoch: The Hermeneia Translation* (Minneapolis: Fortress, 2012), 51.

apocalyptic reign, the context of Luke 9 shows evidence of possibly picking up on representation of God's people, but not on the dynamic of preexistence.

Luke's telling of the transfiguration story more deeply entrenches that story in the grooves of the exodus narrative. It does not reduce Jesus's identity to one character in that story — likely depicting him as the one who leads the people out, as the people itself, and possibly even the representative firstborn who is the cost of that deliverance. Within this framework, the son of God declaration does not draw the eyes of the audience to Jesus's heavenly past, but instead to his cruciform and then glorious future.

6. UNIQUELY KNOWING SON AND FATHER

Luke 10:21-24 contains the Third Evangelist's version of the "bolt from the Johannine blue." Here, Jesus rejoices and celebrates that God has both hidden and revealed "these things" (ταῦτα, v. 21) from the wise and revealed them to babies. It then moves into the third person ("No one knows who the son is except the father," v. 22b), at which point Jesus declares that all things have been given to him by his father, that the father has unique knowledge of the son's identity, that the son has unique knowledge of the father's identity, and that this latter knowledge of the father is only given to those to whom the son wishes to reveal it (v. 22). This statement about the father's and son's unique knowledge of one another, with its clear parallels from John's Gospel, might be read as indicating a nascent preexistence Christology analogous to that of the Fourth Evangelist. However, we must not allow the Johannine parallel (or even the Matthean) to overly influence our interpretation of Luke. The unique knowledge of heavenly father and messianic son fits well within the high human Christology of sonship that Luke has established through the pericopes we have already discussed.

The father's knowledge of the son of which this passage speaks is the knowledge of his identity in some sense, rather than personal knowledge as such. Luke's version of the sayings makes this clear as he says, οὐδεὶς γινώσκει τίς ἐστιν ὁ υἱὸς εἰ μὴ ὁ πατήρ (10:22). The τίς ἐστιν helps locate this discussion securely under the understanding of knowledge in the sense of the German *wissen* (expressing knowledge of facts) rather than *kennen* (expressing knowledge of a person). With this on the table, it is important to note that the notion of a hidden identity of Jesus, known only to God, fits quite well within the messianic secret motif that Luke carries over from Mark. As in Mark, the divine voice at the baptism is directed to Jesus alone (Luke 3:22). Moreover, the idea that the identity of Jesus is hidden from everyone is only partially correct, as other spiritual agents know that Jesus is the Christ, the son of God, as discussed above. Further, in the transfiguration scene just discussed, the father's voice comes to the disciples to make the identity of Jesus known. Also, in Luke's version of the parable chapter, his Jesus picks up on the notion that teachings come in parables to outsiders so that they might see without seeing and hear without understanding. Finally, the theme of Jesus's hiddenness continues through the crucifixion and early appearances, such that recognition of him and knowledge of his mission must finally be disclosed by the resurrected Christ himself (24:16, 30, 38-43). Thus Cullmann rightly concludes that the passage "is connected with the specific view that the relationship of Jesus with the father is his exclusive secret, the perception of which demands a supernatural knowledge which can only be given to a man from outside himself — either from the Father, as in the case of Peter (Matt. 16.17); or from Satan, as in the confession of those possessed by demons (Mark 3.11; 5.7)."[140]

In sum, there is nothing peculiarly Johannine in the notion that God the father has insight into Jesus as messianic son that must be made known by divine revelation. None of the data demands that the secret of Jesus's identity is that he is God, and all is well accounted for under the notion that Jesus's identity is well understood as messiah, once that category has been reconfigured around Jesus's particular mission.

Thus far, my engagement with the passage has focused on the father's knowledge of the son. The son's knowledge of the father is also something that can be accounted for under a messianic, rather than divine, rubric. Special knowledge of God is a messianic endowment that we find, for instance, in *Psalms of Solomon*: "He will be a righteous king over them, taught by God" (17:32).[141] The idea of knowing God and making God known that we read in Luke 10 reflects the expectation that the messiah will be specially taught by God and wise. As Luke's Jesus celebrates this mutual knowledge "in the Holy Spirit" (ἐν τῷ πνεύματι τῷ ἁγίῳ, 10:21), so the *Psalms of Solomon* sees the messiah acting "in the fear of his God, in the wisdom of spirit, and of righteousness and of strength, to direct people in righteous acts, in the fear of God" (18:7-8). It may even be that *Psalms of Solomon* envisions this king speaking special heavenly knowledge, as it says, "His words will be as the words of the holy ones, among sanctified peoples" (17:43, where "holy ones" may well refer

---

140. Cullman, *New Testament Christology*, 278.

141. All citations of *Psalms of Solomon* are from R. B. Wright's translation in *The Old Testament Pseudepigrapha*, vol. 2, *Expansions of the "Old Testament" and Legends, Wisdom, and Philosophical Literature, Prayers, Psalms, and Odes, Fragments of Lost Judeo-Hellenistic Works* (ed. James H. Charlesworth; New York: Doubleday, 1985), 639-70.

to angels). In the Qumran material surveyed in the previous chapter, the king played the role of God's agent through mirroring the activity of God. Idealized humans occupied a special place even in the heavenly cosmos (e.g., 1QH^a XIV, 11-13). Adamic motifs of ruling, being son of God, and possessing wisdom from God by the spirit are blended in psalms that anticipate a reiteration of such a conjunction in Israel (4Q381 1, 8). And priests who enter specially into God's presence receive heavenly knowledge that is tantamount to divine wisdom (4QShirShabb^a 1 I, 6). The point of parallel is that idealized human figures are often admitted into the divine council, and they are given the special wisdom of God, without being rendered divine in and of themselves.

Jesus's teaching ministry discloses who God is and thus what it means to be a faithful child of God. God is the one who is kind to the ungrateful and evil (Luke 6:35), thus those who are his children must be the same. The father is the one who, precisely as father, gives the Holy Spirit to his children (11:13) — a possession that prompts this very speech that Jesus gives (10:21). God is the father who embraces the wayward son as alive from the dead, and demands that the self-styled slave son celebrate the finding of the one who was lost (15:11-32).

This passage in Luke leaves lingering the question, what are "these things" that are hidden from the wise but revealed to the babies? The antecedent in Luke's narrative is the authority of the seventy and their names written in the heavens. The subjugation of the demons is a demonstration of the advent of the reign of God — the disciples are exercising the authority of God by acting in the name of Jesus (10:17). This is part and parcel of the throwing down of Satan from his perch of ruling over the cosmos (10:18). The strong man has, in fact, been bound (11:21). Jesus has given his authority to his followers (10:19). And those who follow are part of the "heavenly" family of God. Thus, the narrative cues leading up to Jesus's moment of celebration are not about the secret of Jesus's divinity, but about the advent of the kingdom of God and Jesus as its authoritative king.

Narratologically, both Luke and Acts end by underscoring that people need to have specially disclosed to them the messianic identity of Jesus. As I discuss in chapter 6, Luke ends with Jesus's followers needing to have revealed to them that the messiah must suffer before entering his glory (24:25-26, 46). Acts, in turn, ends with Paul claiming the applicability of Isaiah 6:9-10 to the Jews who came to hear his message: they lack the ability to see, hear, and understand. The content of his message was the kingdom of God, and Jesus — whom he proclaimed from the law and the prophets (Acts 28:23-28). The kingdom of God, and Jesus's place within it, constitute the material that stands in need of disclosure in Luke's two-part composition, especially as it is openly hidden in Israel's scripture.

The notion that Jesus's words have to do with the advent of his kingship and the disclosure of God as father to this particular kind of Davidic messiah finds further confirmation in the Lukan pericope. Jesus turns to his disciples alone and calls them blessed for what their eyes have seen — visions that many kings and prophets wanted to see, words that they had wanted to hear. The blessing the disciples are enjoying to this point in the story is the eschatological advent of the spirit-anointed messenger of God. In following Jesus, hearing his words, watching his actions, and extending his ministry they are witnesses to the "today" of prophetic fulfillment that arrives in the person of Jesus as messiah (Luke 4:18-21). For Luke, the prophets of old spoke of the messiah in terms of the acts of the messiah and their consequences: death, resurrection, and future mission (e.g., 24:26-27, 44-48). The great disclosure is the revelation of a humble and then crucified and subsequently resurrected Christ as the son of the heavenly father. Although the words of Luke's Jesus are compatible with a preexistent, and thus divine, son of God as we find in John, nothing in the text demands such a reading, and the context both immediate and broad points in the direction of messianism as such rather than divinity as the best reading in its Lukan context.

7. THE HEARING BEFORE THE COUNCIL

Luke's unique rendition of Jesus's hearing before the Jewish authorities provides a final confirmation that his son of God theology is a statement about Jesus as messiah, not about Jesus as inherently or ontologically divine. The hearing is discussed in more detail in the following chapter, as Jesus's claim to be "son of man" occupies the heart of his self-assessment, yet Luke's editing of the Markan text is significant for the son of God question. I intentionally use the word "hearing" because Luke contains no Jewish trial: there are no witnesses, no accusations, no charges, and no proclamation of guilt. Whereas Mark's story demonstrates that Jesus is condemned to death under Jewish law for blasphemy before a separate charge is brought to Pilate, in Luke's Gospel the sole purpose of the Jewish hearing is to establish a charge by which Jesus would be worthy of death before the Gentiles. Luke's concern that Jesus be a righteous man is preserved to the point of not even depicting a kangaroo court declaring Jesus guilty. Thus, we see in Luke 22:66-71 that the Jewish leadership has one purpose: to affix a political claim to Jesus that would merit his death at Roman hands.

The question that the assembly puts to Jesus, then, is whether or not he is the messiah (εἰ σὺ εἶ ὁ χριστός, εἰπὸν ἡμῖν, 22:67). Jesus provides a somewhat complex answer that concludes with a claim that he will soon be sitting at God's right hand. His questioners then follow with, "Then you are the son of God?" (σὺ οὖν εἶ ὁ υἱὸς τοῦ θεοῦ; 22:70). After Jesus's somewhat affirmative answer, they determine that they need no witnesses because they have what they need. Then, before Pilate, they lay out their accusation: he forbids people from paying taxes to Caesar and claims that he is Christ — a king (λέγοντα ἑαυτὸν χριστὸν βασιλέα εἶναι, 23:2). In the questioning, Christ and son of God are parallel queries, meaning the same thing. The affirmation that Jesus is son of God does not bring a charge of blasphemy, but surfaces in the charge to Pilate that he claims to be Christ, which is a claim to kingship. Lest we think that this train of connections between Christ, king, one sitting at God's right hand, and sonship is a matter of misinterpretation by the leading antagonists of Luke's story, the claim recurs in Peter's speech in Acts 2. Davidic kingship is marked out by the one sitting at God's right hand being a fulfillment of God's promise, an exaltation that shows that God has made the crucified Jesus both Lord and Christ. To be the Christ is to be the heir of David, God's appointed king. Son of God stands in parallel to such claims, indicating that Jesus is the son of God in the sense of God's appointed king.

8. CONCLUSION: LUKE'S ROYAL SON OF GOD

Luke is more overt than Mark in his celebration of Davidic frameworks for interpreting Jesus's ministry. Such a royal motif provides the earliest indications of how to understand Luke's son of God Christology. The son of God theme is enriched throughout the Gospel as both Adamic and Israelite dimensions are added. However, there is no indication that Luke understands such sonship to indicate ontological difference from other human beings except, perhaps, as a newly created Adam. Jesus possesses the spirit as God's anointed, he occupies a special place in the eschatological plan of God, and he even has special access to God and the authority to grant such access to others as he chooses. In all such ways, the high Christology of Luke fits within the paradigm of Jesus as an idealized human figure who takes up the primordial call to rule the entirety of the created order on God's behalf. Such messianism is not unique within the literature of early Judaism, as references above to 1 Enoch and Psalms of Solomon make clear. Indeed, this faithful submission and service under God points toward a picture of sonship that fits like a glove within Luke's ancient context. As Joel Green summarizes:

The term "son" (υἱός) as it circulated in antiquity would already have suggested certain nuances. These included the son's obedience to the father, the father's role as primary educator of his son, and the son's service as his father's agent, his surrogate. In fact, Luke builds his perspective on Jesus on the foundation of these ways of understanding sonship. For him, Jesus's role as God's Son was characterized by his allegiance to God's purpose and his service as God's envoy.[142]

What Luke "builds" on such a foundation is found in the deep biblical roots of God's own human sons whose calling it was to faithfully represent their father God to the world.

C. SON OF GOD IN MATTHEW

Matthew maintains the Markan triumvirate of son of God designations at Jesus's baptism, transfiguration, and crucifixion. With Luke, Matthew contains some sayings material in which Jesus indicates his own filial relationship to God. But what stands out most in terms of Matthew's use of father-son terminology is its application not to Jesus himself but to the entire community of those who seek to serve God by following Jesus and Jesus's teachings. While son of God is a Christological title in Matthew, and thus specially applicable to Jesus in this sense, it is also a designation of those to whom God reveals that Jesus is the Christ. Thus, our study of Matthew will show that "son of God" is a relational category that does not distinguish Jesus as ontologically distinct from other people, but as bearing a relationship as messiah into whose kingdom and into whose family others may enter as they come under the yoke of his teaching.[143]

1. BIRTH AND BAPTISM: JESUS AS REPRESENTATIVE ISRAEL

The first time Jesus is directly called God's son in Matthew's Gospel is in the formula citation of Hosea 11:1 in Matthew 2:15, "Out of Egypt I called my son" (ἐξ Αἰγύπτου ἐκάλεσα τὸν υἱόν μου).[144] Three points merit attention for the

142. Joel B. Green, *The Theology of the Gospel of Luke*, New Testament Theology (Cambridge: Cambridge University Press, 1995), 50.

143. I discuss the conception in the chapter below on birth and resurrection narratives.

144. The formula citations stand out in Matthew's Gospel as a unique indication of his

current study. First, Matthew does not, like Luke, take advantage of the virgin birth scene to declare directly that Jesus is son of God.[145] Second, in Hosea the "son" in view is Israel. Third, throughout Matthew's Gospel in general and in the scriptural citations in particular, a thoroughgoing typological approach to Jesus's ministry is employed in which Jesus embodies in himself faithful Israel, significant moments from Israel's story, and/or heroes of Israel's past.[146] In assigning to Jesus a sonship label that was previously employed of Israel, Matthew's first depiction of Jesus as son of God draws the reader to understand such a title as the title of God's elect people rather than a title of ontological distinction.

Matthew's unique elaboration on the baptism scene functions in a similar manner. There, the discomforting notion that Jesus participates in a baptism of repentance (3:2, 6, 11) finds voice in John the Baptist, who protests that he should be baptized by Jesus and not vice versa (3:14). Jesus's answer is somewhat strange in its reconfiguration of the significance of "righteousness": "Permit it for now, for in this way it is fitting for us to fulfill all righteousness" (ἄφες ἄρτι, οὕτως γὰρ πρέπον ἐστὶν ἡμῖν πληρῶσαι πᾶσαν δικαιοσύνην, 3:15). As with the formula citation that I discussed briefly in the previous paragraph, so here and subsequently in the Sermon on the Mount, the language of "fulfillment" (Gr πληρόω) simultaneously designates an affirmation of the biblical and Jewish standards while reinscribing their particular content around the person and work of Jesus. To understand the both/and of affirmation and reinscription of the content of "righteousness," we need to recognize the divergent reactions of John the Baptist to Jesus and the religious leaders within the larger context of the baptism narrative. In contrast to the Pharisees and Sadducees, whose arrival provokes John to accuse and question, "You brood of vipers, who showed you that you needed to flee from the coming wrath?" Jesus's arrival is met with a query indicating that he has no need to flee from

---

Christology and of his understanding of the relationship between Jesus and the scriptures of Israel. I address them in greater detail below. Throughout, there is a complex both/and relationship in which Jesus to some degree conforms to the biblical pattern, and yet is providing new substance to the words through his own life experience. Cf. J. R. Daniel Kirk, "Conceptualising Fulfilment in Matthew," *TynBul* 29 (2008): 77-98.

145. See Donald J. Verseput, "The Role and Meaning of the 'Son of God' Title in Matthew's Gospel," *NTS* 33 (1987): 532-66.

146. Matthew is arguably the best place to discover the kind of "Jesus as ideal Israel" theology that pervades, e.g., N. T. Wright's depictions of Jesus in *Jesus and the Victory of God* (Christian Origins and the Question of God 2; Minneapolis: Fortress, 1996); cf. Dunn, *Christology in the Making*, 4; Collins and Collins, *King and Messiah*, 140.

the coming wrath — largely because John knows that Jesus himself is the wrath bringer (3:11-12)! Jesus's definition of righteousness entails his own affiliation with the Jews as they are called to repentance.[147] Jesus is part of the people whom he has been marked out to save (1:21). His baptism is an expression of solidarity with them in their sinfulness, in their standing under the looming judgment of God, and in God's deliverance of them.

The first mention of Jesus as son, in which he is so described using a biblical text that originally had redeemed Israel in view, works together with the second mention of Jesus as son at the baptism, in which Jesus has just identified himself completely with Israel, even in its current need for repentance and salvation. Matthew is the Gospel that provided the basis for Huizenga's argument that, at the baptism, the Gospels depict Jesus so as to evoke Isaac, the sacrificed son of Abraham.[148] Not only does the Abraham narrative provide verbal repetition of the language of beloved son (ὁ υἱός μου ὁ ἀγαπητός, 3:17; cf. Gen 22:2, 12) and of a voice coming from heaven,[149] but it also provides a quintessential demonstration of what it looks like to fulfill righteousness.[150] Thus, Huizenga summarizes: "Jesus's fulfilling of all righteousness at the baptism involves doing the total will of God and will result in his death, the unrighteous fruit of a human conspiracy."[151] The juxtaposition of wrath-fleeing vipers and fulfiller of all righteousness is made complete when the former fulfill their serpenthood through their participation in Jesus's death and as Jesus fulfills his role in submitting to the divine necessity of his own death for the sake of Israel's salvation.[152] Thus, the early indications of Jesus as son of God in Matthew pertain to Jesus as a human who occupies the role of fulfilling the story of Israel through typological correspondence to defining figures and stories of the past.[153] Jesus is the son who fulfills the exodus of the son who is Israel. Jesus is the son who fulfills the offering of the son who is Isaac.

147. Cf. Jack Dean Kingsbury, *Matthew as Story* (2nd ed.; Minneapolis: Fortress, 1988), 51.

148. Huizenga, *New Isaac*, 153-88. The polyvalent allusions to Psalm 2:7, perhaps Isaiah 42:1, and also to Genesis 22:2 are noted as well by Kingsbury, *Matthew as Story*, 52, though he draws conclusions from this with a bit more reserve, claiming that Jesus is depicted as uniquely chosen eschatological messiah in the line of David.

149. Huizenga, *New Isaac*, 153-54.

150. Huizenga, *New Isaac*, 173.

151. Huizenga, *New Isaac*, 173.

152. Huizenga, *New Isaac*, 172-73.

153. Kingsbury, *Matthew as Story*, 53-55, says a good deal about Jesus as unique son and savior in Matthew's Gospel, but does not specify the precise Christology entailed. There is a uniqueness to Jesus's sonship, but Kingsbury leaves the precise nature of that uniqueness, the topic of my work here, somewhat vague.

In so doing, Jesus is the son who fulfills the righteousness that the offering of the beloved son brings about, a righteousness that is not only for Israel's great patriarch but also for all who are truly sons of Abraham (1:1; cf. 3:8).[154]

2. FATHER AND SON(S) IN THE SERMON ON THE MOUNT

I forgo another pass at the temptation narrative, noting only that the reader who comes to the first major teaching unit in Matthew, the Sermon on the Mount in chapters 5–7, has through this additional story had reinforced the notion of Jesus as "son of God" being one who stands in the place of Israel and fulfills its duty to single-minded fidelity to God.[155] Jesus's embodiment of the corporate identity of Israel, alluded to in the citation of Hosea (2:15), and affirmed from heaven at the baptism (3:17), is put to the test in the temptation narrative (4:3, 6). In the sermon itself, we hear words that are directed to Jesus's followers who come to him on the hilltop (5:1), a people whom he identifies in the beatitudes not simply by their experiences of suffering and sorrow, but ultimately by their participation in his Christological mission (5:11-12). And we learn that these very people, gathered around Jesus, also stand in filial relationship to God.[156]

The sermon contains more than a dozen indications that God is father of those to whom the sermon is addressed, the first coming in 5:9, "Blessed are the peacemakers, for they shall be called sons of God [υἱοὶ θεοῦ]." The sermon then proceeds under the assumption that those gathered around Jesus qualify for the label. Their good works will cause other people to glorify their heavenly father (5:16). By doing such good works toward all, including enemies, such sonship is put on display (5:45, 48). And the three great acts of piety (alms, prayer, and fasting) are all to be done for the sake of the father, who can see and reward what is done in secret (6:1, 4, 6, 18). The instructions governing prayer indicate that God's identity as father is tied up with the twin notions of provision for earthly needs and of forgiveness of sins (6:8, 9, 11, 13, 14, 15). Earthly provision comes particularly into view when God as father is the ob-

---

154. Kammler, "Sohn Gottes und Kreuz," gives a reading of the baptism and transfiguration that leans much more heavily toward a divine Christology as such. This, in turn, is tied to his reading of the birth and childhood narratives, so I address his arguments in the chapter below on the Matthean and Lukan birth and resurrection narratives.

155. Cf. Brandon D. Crowe, *The Obedient Son: Deuteronomy and Christology in the Gospel of Matthew* (BZNW 188; Berlin: De Gruyter, 2012), 158-66; Kingsbury, *Matthew as Story*, 55-57.

156. Cf. Crowe, *Obedient Son*, 169-70.

ject of the trust to whom Jesus commends his hearers in the passage against worry (6:25-34, esp. vv. 26, 32), with similar instructions to ask in faith of God's paternal provision given in 7:7-11. Thus, throughout the sermon we see that the category of "son of God" is one that applies to Jesus's followers, and that within the narrative of Matthew "son of God" indicates the distinct identity of those who, because they follow Jesus, are part of the community of faithful disciples on the earth. Discipleship is its own category of idealized humanity.

The final mention of God as father in the sermon specifies God as father of Jesus in particular rather than of all who are hearing his words. The person who will enter the kingdom of heaven is "the one who does the will of my father who is in the heavens" (ὁ ποιῶν τὸ θέλημα τοῦ πατρός μου τοῦ ἐν τοῖς οὐρανοῖς, 7:21). Even here, where Matthew's Jesus denies the sufficiency of referring to Jesus as κύριος for final salvation (7:21), there is a Christological qualification to the identity of the people of God. Confronting those who claim to have prophesied, exorcised, and enacted miracles in his name, Jesus rejects them as workers of lawlessness (7:23). But even as he does so, he maintains his own place in the assessment of their participation in the family of God: "I have never known you" (οὐδέποτε ἔγνων ὑμᾶς, 7:23). The subsequent paragraph elaborates on what it means to do the will of God when Jesus says, "Therefore, whoever hears these words of mine and does them" (πᾶς οὖν ὅστις ἀκούει μου τοὺς λόγους τούτους καὶ ποιεῖ αὐτούς, 7:24).[157] Thus, the conclusion of the sermon affirms the implication of the final beatitude, that participation in the family of God as Jesus describes it in chapters 5–7 is derivative of Jesus's own position as one who faithfully embodies in practice and delineates in words what it is to be a faithful son of God.[158] Thus, being "son of God" is not simply about being human, nor is it the identity of the people of God as defined by Torah or Abrahamic descent. For Matthew it is the identity of the people of God as defined first by Jesus himself and inclusive of those who follow the way of Jesus in obedience to his teaching. By so integrating the identities of Jesus and the people of God under the rubric son of God, Matthew indicates that such a title is a designation not of one who is ontologically distinct, but instead of a people who are distinct for their fidelity to God and for the representation to the world of what the heavenly father is like in love and generosity (e.g., 5:43-48), in goodness (5:16), and in forgiveness (6:14-15).

---

157. This is consistent with the mandate of the so-called Great Commission, in which Jesus sends out his disciples to teach the nations to obey everything Jesus has commanded (Matt 28:20).

158. Crowe, *Obedient Son*, 166-75, makes a similar point.

3. SON-KNOWING FATHER, FATHER-REVEALING SON

Two pericopes in Matthew's Gospel underscore that God the father uniquely knows the identity of Jesus as son of God, and discloses it to whomever God will. One of these is Matthew's version of the bolt from the Johannine blue, and the other is the confession of Peter at Caesarea Philippi.

Matthew's version of the bolt from the Johannine blue differs from Luke's in one important respect. Where Luke has οὐδεὶς γινώσκει τίς ἐστιν ὁ υἱὸς ... καὶ τίς ἐστιν ὁ πατήρ ("No one knows who the son is ... and who the father is," 10:22), Matthew has οὐδεὶς ἐπιγινώσκει τὸν υἱὸν εἰ μὴ ὁ πατήρ οὐδὲ τὸν πατέρα τις ἐπιγινώσκει ("No one knows the son except the father nor does anyone know the father," 11:27). It is thus possible that the type of knowledge Matthew intends here is *kennen*-type knowledge as opposed to the *wissen* knowledge that I suggested was Luke's point. The Matthean story, however, need not be read as bursting an idealized human paradigm in favor of one of preexistence.[159]

First, Matthew's narrative (like Mark's before it) ties together the divine knowledge of Jesus's sonship with Jesus's messianic calling to suffer as those are put on display in the baptism. What is known about Jesus, and what is disclosed by the heavenly agents who reveal God's knowledge to people (e.g., the angel who appears to Joseph), is that Jesus has a role to play in the salvation of the people. There is no inherent reason why the knowledge shared between father and son must be derivative of ontological unity (something questionable even in a Johannine scheme), or preexistence in heaven, rather than the special knowledge of God that kings and prophets are sometimes thought to have, together with an exclusive divine knowledge about Jesus's hidden identity that pervades the Synoptic Tradition.

The chapter within which the pericope at hand is contained creates a context where this latter theme comes to the fore. This is the second important point for consideration: throughout this section of the Gospel the question of people's ability to recognize God's agents pervades. John the Baptist is unsure about Jesus's identity, in all likelihood because he is not seeing what he anticipated (11:2-6). Jesus, in turn, underscores the aspects of his ministry that demonstrate him to be the agent of the eschatological restoration anticipated in Isaiah (11:4-5). The question has to do with whether or not the time of escha-

---

159. Cf. Collins and Collins, *King and Messiah*, 140-42. There, Sirach 51:23-27 is highlighted as a parallel text in which a person invites others to acquire a yoke and labor that ultimately give rest.

tological arrival has come: is Jesus the coming one, or must another be awaited (11:3)? Jesus then challenges the crowds about John's identity, suggesting that he is the great prophet who arrives in anticipation of the kingdom of God — Elijah who was to come (11:7-15). Once again, the time of arrival is paramount, as Jesus claims that a new era, the era of fulfillment rather than anticipation, has dawned with his proclamation of the kingdom.

In the comparison of Jesus's generation to children who are not followed as they lead with joyous or mournful music, Jesus links the failure of the people to recognize John and the time of his work to their failure to recognize Jesus and the time of his work (11:16-19). The difficulties in knowing the prophet of God are therefore not something that Matthew limits to Jesus but extends to John as well. Jesus and John are at work in an eschatological moment, the significance of which is being largely missed by the fickle generation.

In the final pericope before the so-called bolt from the Johannine blue, Jesus rebukes the cities in which he had done his miracles. Whereas the things Jesus does cause John to question whether or not he has Jesus's identity correct (11:2), such that Jesus must provide a richly allusive response demonstrating the biblical nature of his work, Chorazin, Bethsaida, and Capernaum have failed to apprehend the nature of Jesus's identity, to their own greater judgment. The conjunction of John's baptismal ministry of warning, and Jesus as the one who fulfills that word, comes together in this chapter, highlighting for the reader that Jesus is, in fact, the agent of whom John spoke.

The beginning of the pericope about John's questioning is more specific. It tells us that John sends his messengers when he hears about the works of the messiah (τὰ ἔργα τοῦ χριστοῦ, 11:2). Moving backward from this pericope, Matthew's Jesus sent out his twelve disciples to extend his ministry after he saw the people like sheep without a shepherd (9:36). Shepherding is a royal or else prophetic motif, picking up on either the Moses typology that pervades the early chapters of the book or the claim that Jesus is the son of David in 1:1. The works that the cities of Chorazin, Bethsaida, and Capernaum have failed to recognize, in Matthew's Gospel, are the works of the royal shepherd and powerful teacher who is now on the scene as God's eschatological deliverer and will soon be on the scene as eschatological judge. Within the story as it has so far unfolded, we might recognize that the Sermon on the Mount, with all its talk about God as father, is in fact the way in which Jesus as God's son has made God known. Jesus as the embodiment of eschatological Torah, rather than Jesus as embodiment of preexistent Godhead, would be a way to parse Jesus as the one who reveals the father that does greater justice to the larger sweep of Matthew's story. Such a line of interpretation finds further confirmation in the subsequent pericope, where Jesus claims for himself what his Jewish compatriots would claim for Torah, inviting his hearers to take his yoke upon themselves and thereby find rest. Thus, I suggest that the best reading of this text is that the father knows and reveals the Christology that one might rightly discern from Jesus's ministry, while Jesus as Christ makes known the God who is the father of those who follow him, the God whose identity is disclosed to the world through the disciples' faithful embodiment of good works (cf. 5:16).

A third argument concerns the possibility that Jesus is here reflecting his place in the heavenly council.[160] Once again, the false either/or of heavenly being or earthly human has led interpreters to see a claim to be admitted to such a sphere as an indication of preexistence and/or divinity. However, both the biblical precedent and the Qumran scrolls provide some indications that representative humans might be admitted into such heavenly space. First, there is the notion that Moses's ascent of Sinai was an entry into the heavenly courts themselves (cf. Heb 8:5). Second, we see in Isaiah 6 a human standing in God's court by virtue of being at the juncture of heaven and earth in the temple (a passage that is of no little importance in the Synoptic Tradition). Third, Zechariah's visions take him into the court (Zechariah 3). Fourth, there is an allusion to the conjunction of human and divine courts in Psalm 82. Finally, we might remember the Self-Glorification Hymn (4Q471b, 4Q491c; cf. 4Q427), in which the singer takes an exalted place among the gods, standing, as it were, with one foot in the heavenly realm and one in the earthly. With such an impressive array of possibilities for a human having access to the divine realm, and with Matthew's Jesus playing the role of the idealized, faithful people of God (and several of its representative roles and/or heroes), participation in the divine council (if such a claim is indicated here) becomes a much less compelling argument for preexistence. Idealized human Christology opens up several other avenues for understanding Jesus standing in the tradition of Israel's exalted heroes.

4. PETER'S CONFESSION: SON OF THE LIVING GOD

The notion that the father's revelation of the son as "son of God" is Christological, that is, messianic, rather than ontological finds confirmation in the confession of Peter in Matthew 16:15-17. Peter's confession is a uniquely Matthean

160. Gathercole, *Preexistent Son*, 279-80.

son of God text. Rather than "You are the Christ," Matthew's Peter says, "You are the Christ, the son of the living God" (σὺ εἶ ὁ χριστὸς ὁ υἱὸς τοῦ θεοῦ τοῦ ζῶντος, 16:16). The phrases ὁ χριστός and ὁ υἱὸς τοῦ θεοῦ τοῦ ζῶντος sit in apposition to one another, locating in the mouth of Jesus's disciple the equation between messiah and son of God that Mark, for instance, leaves to Jesus's high priestly opponent (14:61).[161] This Christological understanding of son of God language finds added significance for our understanding of Matthew's Christology due to Jesus's response to the confession. He praises Peter: "because flesh and blood did not reveal this to you but my father in heaven (did)" (ὅτι σὰρξ καὶ αἷμα οὐκ ἀπεκάλυψέν σοι ἀλλ᾽ ὁ πατήρ μου ὁ ἐν τοῖς οὐρανοῖς, 16:17). With the addition of "son of God" in the confession itself, and Jesus's praising of Peter, this passage becomes a demonstration of the revelation of Jesus as son of God of which Jesus speaks in chapter 11.[162] What is revealed here is not an ontological identity of Jesus as preexistent son, but a messianic identity of Jesus as Christ.

In an important article on this text, Mark Goodwin has argued that the description of Jesus as son, not simply of God, but of the living God, is an allusion to Hosea 2:1 (LXX; 1:10, MT and Eng.).[163] This passage identifies Israel as God's children upon its restoration from the scattering of exile. Matthew includes three other references to Hosea not included in any other Gospel (Hos 6:6 in Matt 9:13; 12:7; and Hos 11:1 in Matt 2:15). The reference to Hosea 11:1 is relevant inasmuch as it identifies Jesus as the son of God that is Israel in the book of Hosea.[164] Thus, Matthew has signaled that his ideal readers are familiar with the writings of Hosea (or, at very least, that he as author finds in Hosea indications both of Israel's failings, realized afresh in the ministry of Jesus, and of Jesus's sonship as it fulfills that of Israel). The confession of Peter, then, would identify Jesus as "the son of the living God" who fulfills the destiny of the "sons of the living God" spoken of in Hosea 2:1. Those sons are the restored and redeemed Israel after their time of exile. Such an allusion comports with Matthew's concern to demonstrate Jesus's ministry as the culmination of Israel's time of exile (1:11, 12, 17) and as the embodiment of the story of ideal/faithful Israel.[165] Goodwin concludes, "Peter's confession indicates that with Jesus comes the fulfillment of Hosea's promise that the living God is acting

---

161. Collins and Collins, *King and Messiah*, 142.

162. Cf. Cullmann, *Christology of the New Testament*, as cited above.

163. Mark J. Goodwin, "Hosea and 'the Son of the Living God' in Matthew 16:16b," *CBQ* 67 (2005): 265-83.

164. Goodwin, "Hosea," 273-74.

165. On the former, cf. Pitre, *Jesus*, throughout.

to restore Israel."[166] Moreover, as Matthew adds "son of God" to the derision hurled upon Jesus on the cross, the overall thrust of his narrative will include the notion that his peculiar relationship with God is denied (cf. "In the place where it was said to them, 'You are not my people,'" Hos 2:1), only to have God vindicate and restore both the person of Jesus and the relationship. "Son of the living God" is a peculiarly Matthean riff on the son of God title that further underscores the tones of Jesus as an idealized human figure who embodies himself the destiny of the people of God.

5. WATER-WALKING, STORM-STILLING SON OF GOD

The scene of Jesus's water walking in Matthew 14:22-33 contains a number of details that can be taken as pointing in the direction of Jesus as a divine being: he walks on the sea, uses the phrase ἐγώ εἰμι, stills the wind, and in the end receives obeisance from the disciples who proclaim him "son of God." The comments of W. D. Davies and Dale Allison are worth citing in full:

> In the First Gospel Jesus exercises powers and displays attributes traditionally connected with God alone. In the present pericope, Jesus both walks on the sea and subdues its rage, and these are acts which the OT assigns to Yahweh himself. In other words, Jesus here exhibits an authority which the Jewish Scriptures associate exclusively with the deity. The fact speaks volumes. In addition, Jesus is bold enough to refer to himself with the loaded and numinous "I am." In view of all this, it does not quite suffice to say that, for our author, God has acted through Jesus the Messiah. It seems more accurate to assert that, in Matthew's gospel, God actively shares attributes characteristic of himself with another, his Son. The step towards the later ecumenical creeds, which affirm Christ's deity, appears undeniable.[167]

In addition to assessing whether the ways in which Jesus is described are "exclusively" the purview of God in the Old Testament (and the previous chapter has already laid out an extensive set of qualifications of such a claim), the logic of the argument Davies and Allison lay out needs to be explored.

---

166. Goodwin, "Hosea," 274.

167. W. D. Davies and Dale C. Allison Jr., *The Gospel according to Saint Matthew* (3 vols.; ICC; Edinburgh: T&T Clark, 1991), 2:512.

The distinction they draw is between God acting through Jesus as messiah and God actively sharing attributes characteristic of himself with another. The force of my studies in biblical and early Judaism was to demonstrate that such a distinction is unsustainable. To be God's representative on earth is, necessarily, to be one with whom God has shared God's unique characteristics: in the Priestly literature humans are created to be (like) theophanies. The creation story in Genesis 1 claims that this is so for all humanity, created as it is in the image of God. The subsequent biblical narratives and psalms demonstrate that the sharing of God's characteristics is precisely what differentiates Israel's king (and Israel itself) from the nations around it. Moreover, we should not underplay the significance of the claim that Davies and Allison rightly make, that God is sharing his characteristics with another. Such an assessment is exactly what the later creeds are written to deny. For the creeds, Jesus is not one other than God who shares in God-like properties or attributes; for the creeds, Jesus is the incarnation of none other than God himself. If we say that God is sharing with another, it is incumbent upon us to define who this other is, and to recognize that such a claim differentiates the Jesus of the Gospels from the theological system in which such attributes are exclusively true of God.

In order to assess Matthew 14:22-33 within the Jewish canon of possibility and expectation, I turn to Psalm 89 (MT, Eng.; Psalm 88, LXX).[168] The first point to make is that the psalm is messianic in most every sense of the term. It not only celebrates God's covenant with David to keep his seed on the throne (e.g., vv. 3-4, 35-36); it also stands at a point where the Davidic kings are, at very least, decimated in battle, and perhaps dethroned (e.g., vv. 43-44), thus leaving the psalmist crying out for a full restoration of what God has promised. Reading the psalm messianically is not a Christian peculiarity, either, as it is so employed in *Pesiqta Rabbati*, to which I return below.

Second, in addition to being a psalm about the king, and the king's relationship to God, it employs the father-son terminology that expresses royal theology in places such as Psalm 2 and 2 Samuel 7: "He will cry out to me, 'You are my father, my God, and the rock of my salvation! Indeed, I myself will make him firstborn, highest [MT, עֶלְיוֹן] of the kings of the earth" (Ps 89:26-27). Robert Rowe captures the force of Psalm 89 well when commenting on its use of the title "firstborn" of Israel's king: "This shows the special favour of his position — he is the one most entitled to represent the father's

168. Cf. J. R. Daniel Kirk and Stephen L. Young, "'I Will Set His Hand to the Sea': Psalm 88:26 LXX and Christology in Mark," *JBL* 133 (2014): 333-40.

kingship."[169] This underscores the importance of the royal category for carrying the connotations of "son of God" terminology in a text such as Matthew's that intentionally invokes the scriptures of Israel, and Davidic messiahship in particular, as co-texts for understanding the identity of Jesus.[170]

Third, as discussed in the previous chapter, Psalm 89 generally functions within the framework I have been arguing for throughout this book: the description of the Davidic king is derivative of the description of God, such that the actions of the king are shown to be, in fact, the actions of the God who is at work in him and thereby demonstrating his commitment to the human, earthly representative. God has a mighty arm and a strong hand (v. 13), and the Davidic king is powerful because God's hand establishes him and his arm strengthens him (v. 21). Tryggve Mettinger draws attention to the implication that the Davidic king rules as עליון (v. 27) and concludes, rightly, "the connection is unmistakable: the king does on earth what God does in heaven."[171] The fact that God is faithful and righteous (vv. 5, 8) is to manifest itself particularly in faithfulness to David (e.g., v. 24). While no one in the heavens can be compared to YHWH (v. 6), David's throne is to be a witness in the heavens like the sun or moon (vv. 35-36). God who demolishes Rahab and his other enemies (v. 10) will crush the enemies of David also (v. 23). Without directly alluding to this particular psalm, 4QAramaic Apocalypse (4Q246) picks up some of these very conjunctions. There, the king is called son of God and son of the most high (4Q246 II 1), and we read, "The great God is his strength, he will wage war for him; he will place the peoples in his hand and cast them all away before him. His rule will be an eternal rule" (4Q246 II 7-9).[172] The conjunction of sonship and God's own power being the power that enables victory are sufficiently well-established in both the biblical and post-biblical tradition that this provides a likely frame of reference for a first-century Jewish author invoking sonship in reference to Christology.[173] This lends credibility

---

169. Rowe, *God's Kingdom*, 52.

170. John Paul Heil, *Jesus Walking on the Sea: Meaning and Gospel Functions of Matt 14:22-33, Mark 6:45-52 and John 6:15b-21* (Rome: Biblical Institute, 1981), appears to agree with such a messianic reading of the son of God language in Matthew, as he posits "exalted Lord type of divine sonship (royal messianic tradition)" as the sonship of divine power involved in the storm stilling.

171. Tryggve N. G. Mettinger, *King and Messiah: The Civil and Sacral Legitimation of the Israelite Kings* (Lund: Gleerup, 1976), 263.

172. Martínez and Tigchelaar, *DSSSE*, 1:495.

173. Mark S. Smith, *The Priestly Vision of Genesis 1* (Minneapolis: Fortress, 2010), e.g., 12-13, 19, 101, 134-35.

to the conclusion of John Paul Heil that Matthew's water-walking story shows that "Jesus is the Son of God in the sense of the one equipped by God with absolute divine power for the salvation of his people."[174] The power is not innate, but comes from God.

Fourth, one specific way that the royal king manifests himself as a divine agent on the earth is through his control over the waters. Emblematic of God's own authority over the sea, we read in 89:9 that God rules (מוֹשֵׁל, MT; δεσπόζεις, LXX) the rising seas and stills its waves.[175] In parallel to this, we find that God bestows even this authority upon the Davidic king: "I will set his hand upon the sea, and his right hand upon the rivers" (89:25). The waters, symbolic of chaos, opposition, and death, stand under the king's hand because God has shared the authority over the created order with God's anointed son. Such authority is not unheard of elsewhere in the biblical tradition: Moses and God are both credited with splitting the waters of the Red Sea (Exod 14:16, 21, respectively).[176] The splitting of the Jordan's waters exalts Joshua such that he might take up Moses's mantle in leading the people (Josh 3:7).[177] As an important point of historical connection with the first century, Josephus tells us that the would-be revolutionary Theudas mounted his rebellion by claiming that the waters of the Jordan would open before him and that he would thus march across, like Joshua, to conquer the land (*Ant.* 20.97). In each case, the notion that only God can exercise authority over the waters is affirmed, even as the humanity of the person who is credited with the miracle is maintained. Psalm 89 appears to be drawing on the tradition of an agent on the earth through whom God is so powerfully at work that the person can act on God's behalf even over the uncontrollable powers of the waters. Thus, we can agree that "in the OT water is the special domain of Yahweh," and "only God can save from distress on the waters of the sea,"[178] but at the same time must recognize that

---

174. Heil, *Jesus Walking on the Sea*, 171.

175. Helmer Ringgren, *Israelite Religion* (London: SPCK, 1966), 226, suggests a connection between YHWH and the Davidic king as co-conquerors of the chaotic waters. Cf. Smith, *Priestly Vision*, e.g., 17-23, 31.

176. William R. Stegner, "Jesus's Walking on the Water: Mark 6:45-52," in *The Gospels and the Scriptures of Israel* (JSNTSup 104/SSEJC 3; ed. C. A. Evans and W. R. Stegner; Sheffield: Sheffield Academic, 1994), 212-34, argues that Exodus 14 is the intertext with which Mark is in intentional conversation in the penning of the water-walking scene. If so, then the conjunctions in that story between the work of Moses and the work of God provide even more important evidence for the plausibility that Jesus controls the water as an idealized human figure rather than a divine being.

177. Cf. Kirk and Young, "'I Will Set His Hand to the Sea,'" 337.

178. Heil, *Jesus Walking on the Sea*, 34.

both the tradition of God's power over the waters of chaos and the tradition of God's driving back the waters at the exodus find expression, in the scriptures of Israel, through the hands of idealized human agents.

This, in fact, is how the psalm is referenced in *Pesiqta Rabbati*. I mention this later rabbinic text, aware that it is too late to serve as "background." Sometimes, however, the existence of a messianic idea in later Judaism is particularly striking precisely because it reflects the Jesus tradition in ways that later Jews may have generally been keen to avoid. In this case, the rabbi did not shrink from imputing control over the waters to the coming messiah: "The Holy One, blessed be he, will reply, 'He is the messiah, and his name is Ephraim, my true messiah. . . . And even the seas and rivers will stop flowing,' as it is said (Psalm 89:25 [MT]), 'I will set his hand also on the sea, and his right hand on the rivers'" (*Pesiq. Rab.* 36:1). Scholarship has largely overlooked the extension of such divine prerogatives to human agents, an inattention that has led to conclusions about divine claims for Jesus on the basis of biblical allusions to divine saving action at sea.[179] The data discussed here open up another important and plausible line of interpretation that by and large coheres better with the overall Christological thrust of the Synoptic writers and that fits snugly within the idealized human framework developed in the previous chapter.

Summing up the evidence afforded by Psalm 89 and the broader biblical tradition, a son of God who has extraordinary powers over the waters might well be seen as the fulfillment of God's covenant promise to put a king on David's throne. Given Matthew's overt appeal not only to the Davidic throne itself but also to the Davidic line of kings in chapter 1 (contrast Luke 3), such a reading meshes well with both the specific Christology Matthew has been developing and the scriptural matrix to which Matthew has repeatedly pointed as providing the framework for making sense of his Jesus.[180]

Returning to Matthew 14 itself, Matthew provides a striking, unique moment in his story when he has Peter join Jesus on the water. Thus, despite Peter's ultimate failure, if water walking is indicative of divinity, then Peter is divine, at least for a few moments. Within the pericope itself, Peter's failure is not due to his possessing the wrong ontology, but being gripped by fear that overcomes his faith (vv. 30-31). Participating in Jesus's control of the waters, which is in turn a participation in God's own such control, is something

---

179. E.g., Peter Head, *Christology and the Synoptic Problem: An Argument for Markan Priority* (SNTSMS 94; New York: Cambridge University Press, 1997), 87-91.

180. Heil, *Jesus Walking on the Sea*, argues that the Old Testament and Jewish backgrounds make this a "sea-walking epiphany." However, a commonality among all the parallel literature he cites from the Jewish tradition is that none of it is epiphanic in the strict sense.

possible for a human with sufficient confidence in God. Peter's participation, however brief, curtails sharply the possibility that Jesus is being depicted as ontologically distinct rather than vocationally or dispositionally superior.

What, then, of Jesus's greeting, ἐγώ εἰμι (v. 27)? The first thing to be said is that this is not a magical phrase, the uttering of which entails a claim to being Israel's God as such. In Matthew's Gospel, we find the phrase on the lips of the disciples as they each ask apprehensively whether they are the one who will betray Jesus (μήτι ἐγώ εἰμι; 26:22, 25). We have no moment in Matthew's story where the mere utterance of the phrase causes those who hear it to bow as if in the presence of divinity as we find in John 18:5-6. This brings us to an additional important point of consideration, the narrative effect of Jesus's utterance in this particular pericope. The response is not one of shock that Jesus is making an exalted claim for himself, nor is the response to bow in silence as though some great revelation of God had been made. Instead, Peter addresses Jesus in the term by which numerous persons have addressed him throughout the story: κύριε (14:28). Further, as Matthew depicts Peter's response to Jesus's self-disclosure it is not one that signals a new revelation of Jesus's identity but, instead, that the one whom they thought was a phantasm is, instead, the Lord Jesus who was known to them: κύριε, εἰ σὺ εἶ, κέλευσόν με ἐλθεῖν ("Lord, if it is you, summon me to come!" v. 28). Jesus has disclosed himself as one who is known, and Peter responds in a way that shows he understands the signal and now wants proof or affirmation.[181] It is also worth noting that Peter's response to Jesus employs both the second-person singular pronoun and the second person singular form of the verb to be — precisely mirroring the self-disclosure that Jesus made in the first person. The English translation, "It is I" (RSV, NSV, NIV, ESV, NASB), or, perhaps better for our colloquial age, "It's me" (CEB), captures exactly the nuance of Jesus's words (v. 27). He is telling the disciples that no, he is not a ghost (v. 26), but instead the Jesus whom they know.

Thus, Peter's response in both word and deed helps steer us away from reading the passage as one of divine disclosure in the sense of making known Jesus's own divine identity. As in the confession of Peter, so here we see Peter as uniquely willing to act on his knowledge of Jesus as the Christ, the son of

181. In a different context, Norman Perrin, "The High Priest's Question and Jesus's Answer," in *The Passion in Mark* (ed. Werner H. Kelber; Philadelphia: Fortress, 1976), 80-91, here 81-82, argues that Mark uses ἐγώ εἰμι as a messianic claim formula, a phrase that indicates he does, in fact, claim to be the Christ, the son of God. He claims, further, that Matthew follows suit in Matthew 24:5. The possibility that the phrase might indicate a Christological rather than divine claim is another important qualifier to keep us from overreading divine identity into the words.

the living God, we see Peter's stumbling toward a sharing in Jesus's special actions, and finally we see Peter's failure to fully embody what is necessary to be the faith-full disciple prior to Jesus's resurrection.

I have indicated above that the disciples do not bow at the statement, ἐγώ εἰμι, but Matthew indicates that they do, in fact, bow before Jesus as they proclaim him son of God (14:33). Such obeisance (προσκυνέω) has been rendered to Jesus at several prior junctures in the story (2:2, 8, 11; 8:2; 9:18). The ones that demand our attention now constitute the first set: those pertaining to the magi from the east and their conversation with King Herod. When they make their mission known, they inquire of the king, "Where is the one who was born king of the Jews? For we have seen his star in the east and have come to worship [προσκυνῆσαι] him" (2:2). The narrator tells us that this is, in fact, what they do (προσεκύνησαν, 2:11). The narrative signal here is that Jesus is deemed an object of such worship/obeisance precisely because he is king of the Jews, not because a unique ontological status has been disclosed. As Margaret Barker comments: "Matthew is said to be the most Jewish of the gospel writers and yet he could write [this]. . . . The king was believed to be divine . . . he had a star . . . and the wise men brought offerings and worship. Whatever the pedigree of this story, this is how it was told by a Jewish writer. The King of the Jews was worshipped."[182] Barker suggests that there is an inherent notion of divinity in Israel's royal theology; here, of course, we disagree. However, the value of her observation is that it recognizes that to be king of the Jews is to be worthy of worship, as was Solomon before Jesus (1 Chron 29:20, 23).[183] Thus, the royal connotations are sufficient for explaining both obeisance and the son of God title, and Matthew himself demonstrates their sufficiency in the very first act of "worship" Jesus receives in the story.[184] Such a context points us toward royal Christology as the framework for understanding Jesus as son of God in the final scene of the water-walking episode.[185]

---

182. Margaret Barker, "The High Priest and the Worship of Jesus," in *The Jewish Roots of Christological Monotheism: Papers from the St. Andrews Conference on the Historical Origins of the Worship of Jesus* (JSJSup 63; ed. Carey C. Newman et al.; Leiden: Brill, 1999), 93-111, here 94-95.

183. Barker, "High Priest," 95.

184. More cautiously, Head, *Christology*, 130, concludes that "although Matthew's usage [of προσκυνέω] can be plausibly accounted for on the basis of his redactional preferences, there is insufficient evidence to establish that the term was a christologically loaded expression connoting the worship of Jesus as divine."

185. The disciples' bowing before the resurrected Jesus (Matt 28:17) is to the same effect:

With Psalm 89 as a model text for telling the story of an idealized human king, and other narrative cues from Matthew's Gospel, we can read
the final exclamation of the disciples neither as a profession of ontological
divinity, nor as a newly forming notion that "son of God" means divine in
some sense the meaning of which the early church was stumbling about
attempting to articulate, but as a declaration that Jesus is, in fact, the great,
idealized, uniquely authoritative king that they had been waiting for. Such
a conclusion fits well within the assessment of Heil, who despite amassing
data that would suggest his own view might be one of ontological disclosure
nonetheless concludes, "By walking on the sea and uttering the identifying
ἐγώ εἰμι Jesus has revealed and performed the will of God to save his people
in the concrete situation of the disciples' distress. As the agent of this divine
revelation Jesus has shown himself to be in the Son-Father relationship to
God."[186] Significant in this quote are the indications that Jesus performs the
will of God, and that Jesus is an *agent* of divine revelation. My reading fits
not only the stated, Davidic Christology of Matthew's story; it also fits within
both a particular scriptural context and a larger biblical theme in which
God's specially empowered agent is glorified in the sight of the people due
to his power over the waters.

Returning briefly to the quote from Davies and Allison with which this
section of my study began, we can see the importance of presupposed paradigms in shaping our reading of a text. If we read the story in Matthew and
the impressive catalog of ways in which it overlaps with Yʜwʜ texts in the
scriptures of Israel, and we do not have a working understanding of idealized
human figures, then the conclusion that Matthew is en route to Nicea and
Chalcedon seems to be foregone. However, once we approach the text with an
alternative paradigm that shows how such identifications were widespread in
early Judaism's depictions of idealized human figures the previous explanation
is shown to be in need of further development if it is to be sustained. Idealized
human Christology provides a rubric capable of assimilating this narrative
depiction of Jesus's identity, shedding different light on the question of who
this son of God is that even the wind and waves obey him.

---

all authority in heaven and on the earth has been, now, given to Jesus; Jesus is claiming to be
the raised and exalted king. I discuss this in more detail when I take up the resurrection narratives (chap. 4 below). The line of argument of Richard B. Hays, *Reading Backwards: Figural
Christology and the Fourfold Gospel Witness* (Waco, TX: Baylor University Press, 2014), 43-45,
also finds its rejoinder in what I have laid out here. It makes too many assumptions about who
can be worshiped and what that worship connotes in Matthew's particular story.

186. Heil, *Jesus Walking on the Sea*, 67.

6. FATHER AND SON(S) OUTSIDE THE SERMON

The passages from Matthew already covered have the strongest claims to pushing the son of God language beyond the realm of having a particular relationship to God as an idealized, human member of God's family and into the
realm of divinity as such. I thus run through a handful of remaining, uniquely
Matthean cases more briefly in order to round out the picture of Matthew's
son of God theology.

First, in Matthew 15:12-14 Jesus debriefs the disciples on his rebuke of the
Pharisees (15:3-9). Jesus shows no surprise at the Pharisees' taking offense,
saying, πᾶσα φυτεία ἣν οὐκ ἐφύτευσεν ὁ πατήρ μου ὁ οὐράνιος ἐκριζωθήσεται
("Every plant that my heavenly father did not plant will be uprooted," 15:13).
The father title in a saying that uses language of planting and uprooting draws
the reader's attention back to Matthew 13, in which the sower in the parable of
the soils and the son of man in the parable of the wheat and tares are clearly
representative of Jesus. The idea of being "uprooted" may be part of the eschatological harvest imagery in the latter parable especially. But the strongest
connection this allows is one in which God is at work in Jesus, not one in
which Jesus in any sense is divine. As we saw in the Sermon on the Mount,
Jesus's father language for God in Matthew regularly indicates the relationship
of the people who are rightly related to God because of Jesus. The Pharisees'
being scandalized at Jesus's saying (15:12) is an indication that they are not part
of the blessed family of God (cf. 11:6).

The notion of a larger family of God, in which being a son of God is applicable to many more people than Jesus, recurs in Matthew 18. There, at the
end of a parable about forgiveness, Jesus concludes, "Thus will my heavenly
father do to you if each of you does not forgive his brother from your hearts"
(οὕτως καὶ ὁ πατήρ μου ὁ οὐράνιος ποιήσει ὑμῖν, ἐὰν μὴ ἀφῆτε ἕκαστος τῷ
ἀδελφῷ αὐτοῦ ἀπὸ τῶν καρδιῶν ὑμῶν, v. 35). This saying is substantively the
same as the warning Jesus issues in the sermon that forgiving other people is
requisite for receipt of divine forgiveness (6:14-15). In issuing the warning in
chapter 6, however, Jesus refers to God not as his own father but as the father
of the hearers (ὁ πατὴρ ὑμῶν, v. 14). Such a conjunction of passages, each
issuing the same warning, both referring to God as father, but one referring
to God as the disciples' father and another referring to God as Jesus's father,
helps clarify that Jesus's sonship is something that in many respects makes
him like other representative or ideal humans rather than marking him out
as being ontologically distinct.

A similar point can be made from Jesus's warnings about embracing the pretensions of worldly authority. In Matthew 23:8-12 Jesus issues a series of warnings against adopting honorifics. The passage reminds Jesus's followers that they are all brothers before urging them not to call anyone on earth "father," "for your father in heaven is one" (v. 9). Interestingly, though Jesus warns them against calling others rabbi or teacher because the messiah alone is their teacher and instructor (vv. 8, 10), the notion that Jesus has a unique familial title does not come into the picture. The brothers share a father with each other and with Jesus as well.

Before proceeding to the passion narrative, I note in passing that in Matthew, following Mark, the idea that no one knows the eschatological hour is a limitation imputed to the son as well as to the angels (24:36). Sonship here is a way to speak of someone who stands in a peculiar relationship to God, but who at the same time is not God as such and bears the limitations of that distinction.

In Matthew's version of the trial, the high priest eschews the circumlocution of Mark and asks, "Are you the Christ, the son of God?" (εἰ σὺ εἶ ὁ χριστὸς ὁ υἱὸς τοῦ θεοῦ, 26:63). Matthew's Jesus answers more enigmatically than Mark's, replying, "You say this [σὺ εἶπας], but I say to you . . . ," followed by his prediction of the enthroned son of man. The following chapter will tackle the thorny son of man question; for now, I note that the character of the high priest makes the same equation that Peter had made in his confession in chapter 16 of "messiah" and "son of God." The reader knows that this is true, but also knows from the same preceding chapter that "Christ" as "son of God" needs to be modulated in light of Jesus's particular mission as suffering and then glorified son of man.

In the crucifixion scene the collation of "son of God" terminology with the royal pretensions for which Jesus is executed come more to the fore than they do in Mark. Twice Matthew records taunts leveled at Jesus for his claim to be son of God. The derision hurled at Jesus that he should save himself, coming down from the cross, recorded also in Mark, is punctuated in Matthew with, εἰ υἱὸς εἶ τοῦ θεοῦ ("If you are son of God," 27:40). Even more pointedly, the scribes and elders mock Jesus for not being able to save himself, using language both of kingship and of divine sonship: βασιλεὺς Ἰσραήλ ἐστιν, καταβάτω νῦν ἀπὸ τοῦ σταυροῦ καὶ πιστεύσομεν ἐπ᾽ αὐτόν. πέποιθεν ἐπὶ τὸν θεὸν, ῥυσάσθω νῦν εἰ θέλει αὐτόν· εἶπεν γὰρ ὅτι θεοῦ εἰμι υἱός ("He is the king of Israel! Let him come down now from the cross and we will believe in him! He has placed his trust in God; let him deliver him if he wants him! He said, 'I am God's son,' after all," 27:42-43). Here, the conjunction of Jesus as king of Israel and his claim to be God's son are joined by means of the allusion to Psalm 22, a song of the suffering (and rescued) Davidic king. In the mouths of Jesus's tormenters, the language appears to be royal language, evocative of a tradition of a rescued king. This tightens the connection between divine sonship and death that structured Mark's work.[187] For Matthew's readers, the plotline has already been established that Jesus's kingship will come, in fact, when Jesus is rescued from death and enthroned by the power of God. The claim to be son of God will be vindicated when Jesus returns as enthroned son of man. This is all a royal, Christological framework rather than a divine one, as we have seen throughout Matthew's story.

Finally, Matthew's centurion, like Mark's, professes the veracity of Jesus's divine sonship (27:54). Matthew's is responding to the earthquake and other things that happened (τὸν σεισμὸν καὶ τὰ γενόμενα, 27:54, though one wonders whether he could have seen the temple curtain ripped or the raised dead that Matthew reports). For a centurion, saying such a thing might be an indication that an emperor was about to become a god himself — but even this would be indicative of a royal (in this case imperial) status for the human being who died, or even deification after death, rather than a recognition of an ontological divinity during one's life on earth or of preexistence.[188] For the readers of Matthew, however, the point is much the same as for the readers of Mark: Jesus who is put on display as son of God at the baptism is the Davidic king whose kingship is consummated through being obedient to God to the point of death.

7. SON OF GOD IN ROMAN EARS?

Because the claims about early high Christology with which I am primarily engaging have been constructed, in large part, by theorizing Jewish limitations on the extent to which one could be identified with Israel's God before transgressing the bounds of Jewish monotheism, the focus of my research has been ways in which Jewish frameworks provide lenses for reading Jesus as an idealized human figure. Moreover, each of the Gospels invokes the scriptures of Israel at crucial junctures as a signal to the reader that Jesus's life and ministry finds its fullest significance when interpreted alongside such co-texts. However, the readers of the Gospels were also products of the Roman world

---

187. Dunn, *Christology in the Making*, 49.

188. See also the discussion of Roman parallels above, especially as delineated by Peppard, in the discussion of Jesus's sonship in Mark.

in which they lived, and thus the project of interpreting the Gospels with such singular focus on the Jewish tradition can have the effect of artificially limiting the interpretive possibilities. As I did above with an overview of the work of Peppard on Mark, so here also I will turn to the work of a scholar who has explored the connotations of "son of God" in the imperial context. This ground was well plowed by the giants of an earlier generation of New Testament scholarship who looked precisely to Greco-Roman traditions to explain the "son of God" phraseology in the New Testament.[189] More recently, Robert L. Mowery approaches the question with specific attention to Matthew's editorial hand.[190]

Mowery argues that Matthew has used "son of God" terminology in such a way as to more closely parallel claims that the emperors made for themselves in the first century than one finds in, for example, Mark's "son of God" terminology. Matthew is the only New Testament writer to use the precise phrase θεοῦ υἱός (anarthrous use of both nouns, genitive preceding the nominative head noun).[191] Moreover, he uses this particular phrase three times: once in the sea-stilling episode where he has introduced a son of God title where none existed in Mark (14:33); once in the taunts leveled at Jesus on the cross where, once again, Matthew has introduced a "son of God" reference where none existed in Mark (27:43); and finally in the centurion's confession where Matthew so renders Mark's υἱὸς θεοῦ (27:54; par. Mark 15:39).

Mowery situates these observations within another set of data: this very phrase was used to describe Roman emperors not merely in literary texts such as would have been available only to a small circle of elite, literate Romans, but also in coinage and statuary that pervaded the eastern empire. Due to the extensive and public use of the phrase, Mowery argues that at least some auditors of Matthew's Gospel would have heard ascribed to Jesus claims made elsewhere on behalf of the Roman rulers; and, given the uniqueness of Matthew's usage, and perhaps especially his changing of Mark's "son of God" phrase (in the mouth of a centurion), Matthew may have intentionally chosen the phrase in order to create such an allusion.

This, then, raises the question of how such an imperial allusion might influence the question of Matthew's Christology. The five emperors to whom this title is ascribed are Augustus, Tiberius, Nero, Titus, and Domitian. The first three were sons adopted by the "divine" progenitor.[192] Mowery generalizes

---

189. Once again, the shadow of Bultmann looms large; see *Theology,* 1:130-33.

190. Robert L. Mowery, "Son of God in Roman Imperial Titles and Matthew," *Biblica* 83 (2002): 100-110.

191. Mowery, "Son of God," 100-101.

192. Mowery, "Son of God," 104.

about the inscriptions within which son of God language is used of the Roman rulers, noting that such sources "proclaimed the 'good news' that imperial power was being transferred in an orderly manner from deified fathers to their sons."[193] Although such a generalization is open to nuance, it fits perfectly with the son of God Christology that I have argued for throughout this chapter on Jewish grounds. Pronouncing someone son of God is an indication that a heavenly being who has some say-so over which human being is entrusted to rule the world in its absence has chosen the person so designated. Notably, throughout the Julio-Claudian line, all the sons of the various gods were adopted, not natural-born sons, thereby curtailing any sense that "son of God" entails some sort of shared divine essence.

8. CONCLUSIONS: MATTHEW'S SON OF GOD

"Son of God" is a rich Christological category for Matthew; and, at the same time, it is a rich category of identity for Jesus's disciples. Matthew joins Mark in depicting "son of God" as, primarily, a messianic category when referring to Jesus; and this framework sustains even those passages where the height of Matthew's Christology might appear to have broken through the bounds of humanness. When such appearances occur, however, the capaciousness of the category of idealized humanity returns us, once again, to a Christology in which Jesus is readily interpreted as an idealized human given authority over every aspect of life on the earth. Even where we might see Matthew's Jesus pushing us to recognize aspects of idealized human Christology not fully enunciated or depicted in Mark, we nevertheless find ourselves dealing with a human Jesus and not, yet, incarnate God (and here again the absence of a son of God Christology in the birth narrative might be significant). This, in turn, shapes our expectations about how the other sons of God are going to define themselves on the earth and in the age to come.

D. CONCLUSION: SON OF GOD AS IDEALIZED HUMAN KING

"Son of God" is a royal category. From a Jewish perspective it draws on the reservoir of biblical precedent in which first Adam and then David were sons of God set apart for the purpose of ruling the world on God's behalf. The various

193. Mowery, "Son of God," 105.

pericopes that employ son of God language to speak of Jesus, and the overall Christologies of the Gospels themselves as they narrate the identity of Jesus using this category, are readily interpreted within the rich biblical framework of Israel's royal theology and its various heirs in post-biblical Judaism.

Once again, the work of Robert Rowe provides a helpful corrective to more recent arguments and assumptions about the nature of divine attributes and acts in ancient Israelite religion. Whereas the scholarly works discussed in the introduction to the current study regularly trade on a notion of the inviolable singularity of various divine prerogatives, the research presented in the previous chapter, along with the work of Rowe discussed here, bring to the fore the various ways that Israel's kings share in, extend, and represent those very divine prerogatives on the earth. The only reason the king has universal dominion is because he is a vassal of YHWH whose universal rule is both cosmic and singular.[194] And, importantly, "characteristics of Yahweh (e.g., 'glory,' 'splendor,' 'majesty,' and 'might,' Psalms 21:5; 45:3) are attributed to the king."[195] This biblical framework (Rowe is here focused on the Psalter) is the one in which it makes sense for Jewish writers, drawing on biblical tradition, to assign to Jesus powers over human bodies, chaotic waters, demonic forces, and the people of God.[196] Israel's king was an idealized human, which means he is depicted as ruling the world on God's behalf. Tryggve Mettinger sums up the evidence, complete with its Adamic force, when he says, "The king does on earth what God does in heaven. One is almost tempted to speak of the king as 'the image and likeness of God' on earth."[197] I might only suggest that we give ourselves over to such a temptation entirely — not only for Israel's king in general, but also for Jesus as the fulfillment of that royal, divine sonship in particular. We have also seen that approaching the question from a Greco-Roman background offers a complementary line of argument. As son of God, Jesus is the idealized human who has been empowered by God to rule the world on God's behalf, and these stories show that he only comes into his messianic throne by the way of the cross.

I have attempted to demonstrate in this chapter that for each of the Gospel writers "son of God" is not important simply because it is a Christological term. It is important also because of the way that it is used in the narrative to shape the readers' expectations of who Jesus is in the story that unfolds.

---

194. Rowe, *God's Kingdom*, 60.
195. Rowe, *God's Kingdom*, 60.
196. Cf. Collins and Collins, *King and Messiah*, 31.
197. Mettinger, *Civil and Sacral Legitimation*, 263.

Moreover, by studying the phrase we have seen that it guides us through the peculiarities of each Synoptic Evangelist's theological concerns, be those focused on a reorientation around the cross, an affirmation of Davidic promise, or a highlighting of the identity of the people of God. Thus, "son of God" is a faithful barometer for anticipating the larger Christological pattern that each Gospel will develop.

"Son of God," however does not stand alone in occupying such a position, because for each of our Gospel writers the phrase "son of man" modulates what might otherwise have been a triumphalistic vision of the coming Davidic king. I turn to this phrase next, a move that will, admittedly, once again privilege Mark, before turning to the birth and resurrection narratives where Matthew's and Luke's own storytelling will be drawn more to the fore.

3 *Son of Man as the Human One*

Turning to the son of man sayings, it is perhaps more necessary than in any other section of the book to bear in mind that this study's focus is on the Synoptic Gospels themselves. While important work continues to be done regarding the use of the phrase by the historical Jesus, including investigations into possible Aramaic forms, whether the phrase is titular in some sense, and the significance of predecessors in Daniel and *1 Enoch,* such historical questions are not the concern of the current project. Instead, I am investigating the related yet separate question of how this appellation is received and interpreted in the earliest surviving narratives about Jesus.

The importance of this chapter for my thesis is highlighted by the recent work of Daniel Boyarin. In *The Jewish Gospels: The Story of the Jewish Christ,* Boyarin maintains that it is precisely through the son of man title that the early Jewish Christians expressed their belief in Jesus's divinity.[1] This claim builds on Boyarin's reading of Daniel 7, which sees in Daniel's "one like a son of man" echoes, or perhaps the rewriting, of Canaanite myths in which the ancient god El presides over the investiture of a younger god, Baal.[2] Boyarin argues that this notion of two gods proved unacceptable to early readers of Daniel, such that it was reinterpreted as a depiction of the exaltation of Israel, reflected in the current canonical form.[3] Boyarin thus maintains, "The theology of the Gospels, far from being a radical innovation within the Israelite religious tradition, is a highly conservative return to the very most ancient moments within that tradition, moments that had been largely suppressed in the meantime — but not entirely."[4]

---

1. Daniel Boyarin, *The Jewish Gospels: The Story of the Jewish Christ* (New York: New Press, 2012), esp. 25-70.

2. Daniel Boyarin, "Daniel 7, Intertextuality, and the History of Israel's Cult," *HTR* 105 (2012): 139-62.

3. Boyarin, "Daniel 7."

4. Boyarin, *Jewish Gospels,* 47.

Of course, "the theology of the Gospels" to which Boyarin here refers is not the theology of the Gospels as the current study understands it. At least, it does not seem so on first blush. In a peculiar footnote that appears at the heart of his discussion of son of man as a divine title for Jesus, Boyarin quotes Adela Yarbro Collins's description of functional divinity as something distinct from ontological divinity. The former refers to exercising "divine activities" such as "ruling over a universal kingdom, sitting on a heavenly throne, judging human beings in the end-time or traveling on the clouds."[5] Boyarin says that it is this functional sense of divinity that he has in mind throughout his work.[6] It seems to me, however, that such a claim undermines the force of his larger argument. The claim that there are two divinities in heaven, and that Jesus is one of those deities, stakes out ground in notions of preexistence and some sort of heavenly ontology. It is difficult to imagine how one is supposed to hear that the son of man in the Gospels is a recovery of an ancient myth of two divinities in a heavenly court and not imagine that a divine ontology is entailed in some way that extends beyond "functional" divinity. Though I disagree with Boyarin that the Gospels recover a divine son of man in their renderings of Jesus, I agree with his mysterious footnote, to the effect that Jesus exercises divine functions, including those of Jesus as son of man. The argument of the current book is that "functional divinity" regularly typifies idealized human figures across various Jewish traditions, and that such functions are assigned to the human Jesus in the Synoptic Tradition.

We can address the argument from another angle by looking to the list of "functional" qualities Collins describes. She maintains that acting as eschatological judge, especially over humans, is an indication of functional divinity. I agree with this assessment. Thus, in the Synoptic Gospels not only Jesus but also the twelve disciples are capable of exercising a functional divinity, as seen in their destiny to sit on twelve thrones judging the twelve tribes of Israel (Matt 19:28). Early Jewish writers, both Christian and non-Christian, spoke regularly of people exercising divine functions without thereby indicating that the people are uniquely divine, or preexistent deities, in the sense that later Christians (including, in an incipient way, the Gospel of John) would speak about Jesus's divinity.

Because I agree with Boyarin's footnote to the effect that "functional divin-

5. Adela Yarbro Collins, "'How on Earth Did Jesus Become God?' A Reply," in *Israel's God and Rebecca's Children: Christology and Community in Early Judaism and Christianity: Essays in Honor of Larry Hurtado and Alan F. Segal* (ed. David B. Capes et al.; Waco, TX: Baylor University Press, 2007), 57.
6. Boyarin, *Jewish Gospels*, 55n.

ity" rather than "ontological divinity" best describes Jesus as we meet him in the Gospels, I find it important to distinguish the son of man of the Synoptic Tradition from Boyarin's larger argument (namely, that these books recover the ancient mythology of two divine powers ruling in the heavens as depicted in the vision of Dan 7:13-14). Boyarin sees an original hand behind Daniel 7, depicting two divine powers, providing the theological matrix for a divine Jesus in the Gospels. However, I show that what Boyarin sees as a second editorial hand, reinterpreting that ancient myth in Daniel 7 (vv. 17-18, 23-27), comes closer to what the Gospels depict. That thread of the story, in which the vision is interpreted, depicts the wielding of heavenly power such that it is borne by the idealized, vindicated people of God — Israel or its martyrs (vv. 18, 27).[7]

In this chapter we will see that the narrative arc of the son of man sayings in Mark draws us to recognize in the character of Jesus a specially designated human person embodying the divine prerogatives rather than a human embodiment of Israel's God as such. When I say that the son of man sayings have a "narrative arc," I am claiming that the significance of the title develops hand in hand with the larger developments in the plot of Mark. I demonstrate this below. As I address Mark's Gospel and follow his story line, I also turn to the Synoptic parallels. First, however, I demonstrate that there is a narratological unity to the son of man sayings in Mark's Gospel before tracing the narrative arc of Jesus as son of man across that story. Once these steps have been taken, I revisit the question of how Daniel's son of man might provide a framework for interpreting Mark's son of man. Then I turn to the son of man sayings that appear only in Matthew and/or Luke. Finally, I look at the important claim of Joel Marcus that the son of man should be understood as son of Adam. I give qualified assent to that claim, within the framework of a broadly defined "Adam theology" that we saw at work in a number of early Jewish texts, and incorporate Daniel's son of man into that important rubric.

A. NARRATIVE UNITY OF
THE SON OF MAN SAYINGS IN MARK

As is often noted, the phrase "son of man" appears in the Synoptic Tradition only in the mouth of Jesus. In the Gospel of Mark, these occurrences are sometimes grouped into those claiming authority for a person on earth, those predictive of suffering (and resurrection), and those indicating a future glorious

---

7. Boyarin, "Daniel 7," 140-41. See above, chapter 1, on the son of man in Daniel.

return.[8] A class of "proverbial" usages is also visible, though these are mainly in Matthew and Luke. As particular passages are dissected, and especially as historical Jesus studies exercise their influence, questions arise as to the provenance of various sayings, and whether they intend to refer to humanity in general, to the Jesus of the narrative world, or to a future, coming redeemer.

As important as such questions may be, the interpretation of Gospel stories demands a different approach. The Gospels are stories that create their own narrative worlds, and invite interpretations that do justice to the characters, events, sayings, and, perhaps most importantly, overall plots. Thus, in this first foray into Jesus's son of man sayings in Mark I demonstrate that the various sayings are not isolated from each other but form a coherent literary theme.[9] In the following section I build on this insight by providing a reading of the son of man theme within the larger narrative of Mark's story.

In his *New Testament Theology*, Rudolf Bultmann briefly addresses the son of man sayings in order to distinguish between the sayings of the historical Jesus and the theology of the early church.[10] For his purposes, a tripartite division of the sayings is crucial. First, Bultmann maintains that the predictions of the *parousia* do, in fact, go back to Jesus.[11] However, these predictions are of the arrival of the son of man (not his return); and Jesus did not understand this figure to be himself but some future coming messiah.[12] Second, Bultmann argues, the passion predictions were added to the Jesus tradition as *vaticinia ex eventu*, providing an indication that a violent death and resurrection must be undergone before the coming of the son of man (and in the Gospels the coming has been transformed into Jesus's return).[13] Moreover, Bultmann observed that the passages that speak of the *parousia* do not speak of passion and resurrection, while those that speak of passion and resurrection do not speak of *parousia*. Third, Bultmann asserts that the sayings indicating the presence of the son of man now already at work result from a misunderstanding of the Aramaic as the sayings were translated into Greek.[14] In Greek, and in these indications of the son of man presently at work, it is treated like a title rather

---

8. Rudolf Bultmann, *Theology of the New Testament* (trans. K. Grobel; Waco, TX: Baylor University Press, 2007), 1:30.

9. Cf. Edwin K. Broadhead, *Naming Jesus, Titular Christology in the Gospel of Mark* (JSNT-Sup 175; Sheffield: Sheffield Academic 1999), e.g., 132.

10. Bultmann, *Theology*, 1:29-32.

11. Bultmann, *Theology*, 1:30.

12. Bultmann, *Theology*, 1:29-31.

13. Bultmann, *Theology*, 1:29-30.

14. Bultmann, *Theology*, 1:30.

than as a circumlocution for "man" (as in the *parousia* sayings) or "I" (as in the passion predictions).

As is so often the case, Bultmann's keen eye has dissected the text in ways that subsequent scholarship is bound to address, even if in disagreement. In extracting the sayings from the narrative, Bultmann has not only drawn conclusions about the historical development of this slice of the church's Christology, he has also highlighted significant dynamics in the interpretation of the Synoptic Tradition: the son of man is depicted as presently at work, his death and subsequent resurrection are spoken of as divinely ordained and thus necessary, and he is an integral figure in the yet-to-come eschatological expectations of God's people. Bultmann provides one further piece of help for the current volume, which is not concerned about the historical Jesus per se, but rather the Jesus of the Synoptic Gospels, and of the Gospel of Mark specifically at this juncture: he acknowledges that the Evangelists make the equation that he sees lacking, historically, between Jesus and the coming eschatological deliverer. We must look more specifically at how that equation is established because this will be of utmost importance for discerning the story Mark tells that allows us to understand the identity of Jesus as expressed in the phrase "son of man," and this in turn will provide ground for recognizing that Mark's Jesus plays the role of son of man as an idealized human representative of God on the earth.[15] This will be my starting point, and I explore along the way how Matthew and Luke adopt and adapt Mark's presentation.

Within the narrative world of Mark, it is clear that their reference to Jesus unifies the son of man sayings.[16] The first time that the phrase appears in the Gospel (2:10), within the story of the healing of the paralytic (2:1-12), it clearly refers to Jesus as the one who has authority both to heal the paralyzed man and to forgive his sins.[17] That Jesus heals the man is proof that "the son of man on earth has authority on earth to forgive sins" (2:10). Similarly, in the juxtaposi-

---

15. Thus, the claims of Geza Vermes, "The Use of בר נש / בר נשא in Jewish Aramaic," in Matthew Black, *An Aramaic Approach to the Gospels and Acts* (3rd ed.; Oxford: Clarendon, 1967), 310-30, and Maurice Casey, *Son of Man: The Interpretation and Influence of Daniel 7* (London: SPCK, 1979), that "son of man" simply means "human," and that its origin is in generalized statements or simply as a circumlocution for "I" are set aside for my purposes inasmuch as the contexts of the three Synoptic Gospels have given the phrase much greater specificity.

16. Cf. Maurice Casey, *From Jewish Prophet to Gentile God: The Origins and Development of New Testament Christology* (Cambridge: James Clarke, 1991), 47: "In the Gospels, however, the term 'son of man' . . . functions as a title, and it generally refers to Jesus alone."

17. Werner G. Kümmel, "Jesus der Menschensohn?" *SbWGF* 20 (1984): 147-88, rightly comments that interpreting this verse as a reference to humanity in general leads to "exegetischer Gewaltsamkeit" (168).

tion of Peter's confession with Jesus's prediction of the son of man's looming death and resurrection, Jesus's self-references ("Who do people say that I am?" 8:27, and, "If anyone desires to follow after me, let that person deny himself, take up his cross, and follow me," 8:34) make it clear that he is the son of man so referenced. In the narrative of Mark's Gospel, the readers thus encounter Jesus and only Jesus as the son of man. To underscore the point: only Jesus uses the phrase, and within the Gospel it is self-referential even when referring to the *parousia*.[18] This latter point becomes evident when the warning against being ashamed of Jesus is tied to the son of man being ashamed of such a person upon his coming in glory (8:28). It is underscored at the trial when Jesus is asked if he is the messiah and provides an affirmative answer that entails the future return of the son of man (14:61-62). The character of Jesus provides unity to the son of man sayings as they all refer to him in some fashion.

Moreover, from both literary and historical perspectives, implied readers of the text hold together these sayings as collectively indicating significant dimensions of the identity of Jesus. First, whether or not the audience knew perfectly well what Jesus meant, as Joel Marcus concludes, the Gospels are consistent in always applying the term to the Jesus of the narrative.[19] Pre-critical and, in all likelihood, actual first auditors, do not (or did not) parse the sayings into separate layers based on prehistories or diversity of roles. Second, there is a surprising consistency in the handling of this phrase across the New Testament, inasmuch as it appears outside the Gospels only once (Acts 7:56), and other than in Jesus's own mouth only twice (John 12:34 and Acts 7:56). For the early church, "son of man" was consistently a way that Jesus referred to himself. Thus, despite the acute observations of Bultmann as to the distinctions in the three types of son of man sayings, his further observation that the Evangelists themselves conflated their referents points the way to asking what the significance of the phrase might be as it is interpreted within the narratives of the Gospels.

There is more to be said about the unity of the son of man sayings as they have been inscribed in our earliest Gospel narrative. First, and perhaps most evidently, Mark 8 so juxtaposes the first son of man passion-resurrection prediction (v. 31) with the first son of man *parousia* saying (v. 38) that the former's suffering and resurrection paradigm becomes inextricably linked to

---

18. Simon Gathercole, "The Son of Man in Mark's Gospel," *ExpT* 115 (2004): 366-72, also argues for this unity and for a common reference to Daniel 7 across the book (something I address in greater detail below).

19. Joel Marcus, *Mark 1–8: A New Translation with Introduction and Commentary* (AB 27; New York: Doubleday, 2000), 528.

the latter's depiction of glory and its locating of the cross at the center of the eschatological judgment. This connection happens by way of the middle term of discipleship (vv. 34-37). We revisit this scene with more exegetical detail below. For now, the important point is to notice how Mark has made two distinguishable ways of speaking about the son of man inseparable from each other. Followers of Jesus fulfill Jesus's call to discipleship when they embrace the same way of suffering, the cross, that Jesus takes to himself ("Let him deny himself and take up his cross and follow me," ἀπαρνησάσθω ἑαυτὸν καὶ ἀράτω τὸν σταυρὸν αὐτοῦ καὶ ἀκολουθείτω μοι, v. 34). Jesus promises that such loss of life will meet with the eschatological reversal that Jesus's own prior passion prediction entailed: "whoever loses his life for my sake and for the gospel will save it" (v. 35; cf. v. 31). It thus happens that when the passage ends with a saying about the son of man coming with the father's glory, that the basis for the final judgment he executes has been articulated as fidelity to Jesus as the suffering and resurrected son of man. In the story of Mark, the identity of Jesus as suffering and vindicated son of man and the identity of the son of man who comes in the eschaton as an active agent within the final judgment scene are inseparable, and thus are to be interpreted jointly as facets of the same reality.[20] The exegetical significance of this conclusion will become evident below as I trace the development of the son of man theme across the Gospel, and as we address the significance of Daniel for understanding Mark's usage of the title. For now, it is sufficient to note that Mark has provided a coherent picture of Jesus as son of man by joining the passion prediction with the coming judgment by way of a call to cross-bearing discipleship. This leaves us with the question of whether he has similarly joined these to the sayings indicating that the son of man is present and authoritatively at work in Jesus.

At first blush, the idea that Mark has similarly joined the sayings about the son of man present on earth with those about the coming eschatological judge seems unlikely. The two former sayings appear in chapter 2 of Mark (vv. 10, 28), some six chapters before the passion prediction and coming judge sayings of chapter 8 (vv. 31, 38). And yet, textual proximity is not the only way to link passages in a narrative. As it happens, Mark links the first and the final uses of the phrase son of man (2:10 and 14:62) such that they bookend Jesus's conflict with the Jewish religious leaders. The first usage occurs in the story of the heal-

---

20. This linkage has been suggested before, especially based on a reading of Daniel 7 that is quite similar to what this chapter suggests. See Morna Hooker, *Son of Man in Mark: A Study of the Background of the Term "Son of Man" and Its Use in St. Mark's Gospel* (Montreal: McGill University Press, 1967), and Christopher Tuckett, "The Present Son of Man," *JSNT* 14 (1982): 58-81.

ing of the paralytic, which is also the first conflict story in Mark's Gospel.[21] The final usage occurs in the story of Jesus's Jewish trial. In the previous chapter, I addressed the widely recognized structuring function that Mark's placement of the son of God title plays in his book. It may well be that a similar dynamic is at work with his deployment of the "son of man" phrase.

Besides being the first and the final occurrences of the phrase "son of man," these appearances of "son of man" share another key characteristic: they are the only two scenes in the book in which Jesus is charged with blasphemy. Jesus's first conflict in the Gospel entails his being accused of blasphemy, and this then becomes the charge on which he is condemned to death in his final confrontation with Jewish authorities before being crucified. Moreover, in both instances it is the authority that Jesus claims for himself as ὁ υἱὸς τοῦ ἀνθρώπου that generates the accusation. It is not simply that the phrase appears in both of the stories that happen to see Jesus charged with blasphemy; in both it is Jesus's assuming the prerogatives under that self-designation that leads to the charge. First, in Mark 2 Jesus tells the paralytic that his sins are forgiven, a pronouncement that elicits the response from the scribes, βλασφημεῖ· τίς δύναται ἀφιέναι ἁμαρτίας εἰ μὴ εἷς ὁ θεός; ("He blasphemes! Who is able to forgive sins except God alone?" v. 7). Jesus's reply is to demonstrate that the son of man has authority on earth to forgive sins, thus claiming for himself as son of man the prerogative for which he is accused of blasphemy.[22] Similarly, in the trial scene it is Jesus's close association with divine prerogatives, which he claims for himself using the phrase "son of man," that begets the accusation of blasphemy. In response to the question of whether he is the Christ, the son of the Blessed (14:61), Jesus replies affirmatively, ἐγώ εἰμι, καὶ ὄψεσθε τὸν υἱὸν τοῦ ἀνθρώπου ἐκ δεξιῶν καθήμενον τῆς δυνάμεως καὶ ἐρχόμενον μετὰ τῶν νεφελῶν τοῦ οὐρανοῦ ("I am, and you will see the son of man seated at the right hand of power and coming with the clouds of heaven," 14:62). As in chapter 2, Jesus uses the phrase "son of man" as he claims to be God's agent (the Christ), one who occupies a unique place in his exercising of authority on God's behalf (seated at the right hand of power).[23] Reflecting on this connection between the first and the final usages of the son of man language in Mark, Elizabeth Struthers Malbon observes, "Thus controversies over blasphemy, over deter-

21. This connection with Jesus's conflict with the Jewish leaders is well made by Tuckett, "Present Son of Man," 64-65, as another indication that Mark's son of man sayings form a unified whole: in each of them, Jesus's death looms ahead of any glory that might await.
22. Hooker, *Son of Man*, 84: "he claims this authority for himself as the Son of man, and not for himself *per se*."
23. Broadhead, *Naming Jesus*, 132.

mining the boundaries of God's authority and Jesus's authority, frame the 'Son of Humanity' statements in Mark's narrative."[24]

Mark has, in fact, managed to link within his narrative what Bultmann saw as the three layers of development in the son of man tradition. What he saw as the earliest layer, dating back to the historical Jesus, namely, the son of man as coming eschatological figure, has been linked with both the authoritative son of man on earth of Mark 2 and the dying and rising son of man of the latter half of the Gospel. Therefore, to best interpret the phrase within Mark's Gospel, the sayings must be interpreted together. This will entail both reading them all within the unfolding story of the Gospel and in light of literary clues to their meaning, such as the allusions sometimes found to Daniel's apocalyptic figure.[25]

B. THE SON OF MAN IN MARK'S NARRATIVE ARC

Having established the literary coherence of the "son of man" phrase in Mark, we are now poised to examine its function and meaning in the narrative. As Malbon notes, "the son of man" was not a technical term in the sense that it could simply be inserted into the story in order to provide a clear depiction of who Jesus is.[26] The phrase finds its meaning not only in the particular contexts of its various pericopes, but also in the larger narrative in which it is embedded. Due to its breadth of usage, it takes the entire Gospel of Mark to demonstrate what it means to call Jesus "son of man." As we will see in this

24. Elizabeth Struthers Malbon, *Mark's Jesus: Characterization as Narrative Christology* (Waco, TX: Baylor University Press, 2009), 203. An additional argument regarding the narrative unity of these texts is admittedly more speculative, thus I relegate it to a footnote. The observation is this: after both accusations of blasphemy we find a subsequent story in which the charge of blasphemy is turned back on the heads of Jesus's accusers by the narrator. First, it is the scribes who accuse Jesus of blasphemy in 2:6-7, only to then have the narrator tell us that Jesus's warning against blaspheming the spirit of God was given because the scribes had accused Jesus of having an unclean spirit (3:28-30). Second, in a deliberate echo of the trial scene, those who pass by Jesus on the cross are said to blaspheme him, taunting him in regard to his claim about the temple (15:29-30).

25. Daniel Boyarin, "How Enoch Can Teach Us about Jesus," *EC* 2 (2011): 51-76, follows Leo Baeck, *Judaism and Christianity: Essays* (Philadelphia: Jewish Publication Society, 1958), 28-29, in arguing that the "inexplicable" and "unintelligible" term "the son of man" in the Gospels can only be understood as an allusion to Daniel 7 in all of its appearances (52).

26. Malbon, *Mark's Jesus*, 202, in opposition to the claim of Jack Dean Kingsbury in *Conflict in Mark: Jesus, Authorities, Disciples* (Minneapolis: Fortress, 1989), 60-61.

section, such a claim is much more than a hackneyed appeal to "context" for determining meaning. The "son of man" phrase not only occurs within the major sections of the book; its uses also reflect the narrative developments in the story. Here we will see how the "son of man" phrase falls within the narrative structure supplied by the son of God title, and plays a key role in developing and redefining what it means to be "the messiah, the son of the Blessed" (14:61).[27] In fact, we will see that the titles are mutually interpreting. To be the son of God is to be the Christ who dies on the cross to come into the kingship that was first made manifest in deeds of power on the earth.[28] To be the son of man is to be the one authorized by God to act on the earth, as was King David, but who must come into his true glory by way of the cross.

1. TITLE AND MEANING

Thus far, I have put off discussing two important technical questions. First, what does the phrase ὁ υἱὸς τοῦ ἀνθρώπου mean? And, second, is it a title? That Mark seems to use the phrase as a title has sometimes tilted the interpretation of the word's meaning in favor of a fixed technical term, often thought to refer to "the one like a son of man" in Daniel. However, that the phrase likely means, simply, "human being," and has such a meaning in Daniel (where the one who appears is "like" a human) has sometimes unduly weighted the discussion against the phrase being interpreted as a title. In this case, it seems that the best way forward is a both/and: "son of man" means "human," but the Synoptic Jesus uses the phrase with titular self-referentiality.[29] I begin with the latter point. In response to the high priest's

27. Adela Yarbro Collins and John J. Collins, *King and Messiah as Son of God: Divine, Human, and Angelic Messianic Figures in Biblical and Related Material* (Grand Rapids, MI: Eerdmans, 2008), 130, 150.

28. Adela Yarbro Collins, *Mark* (Hermeneia; Minneapolis: Fortress, 2007), 70; Norman Perrin, *A Modern Pilgrimage in New Testament Christology* (Philadelphia: Fortress, 1974), 78.

29. So also James D. G. Dunn, *Christology in the Making: A New Testament Inquiry into the Origins of the Doctrine of the Incarnation* (2nd ed.; Grand Rapids, MI: Eerdmans, 1996), 66. Cf. Ulrich B. Müller, "Jesus als der 'Menschensohn,'" in *Gottessohn und Menschensohn: Exegetische Studien zu zwei Paradigmen biblischer Intertextualität* (BTS 67; ed. Dieter Sägner; Neukirchen-Vluyn: Neukirchener, 2004), 91-129, here 91-92. He affirms a titular use going back to Jesus while recognizing that the fixed, definite usage was not a preexisting messianic title Jesus was assuming. The hesitations of Donald H. Juel on this score are unwarranted, "The Origin of Mark's Christology," in *The Messiah: Developments in Earliest Judaism and Christianity* (ed. J. H. Charlesworth; Minneapolis: Fortress, 1992), 449-60, here 451, where Juel appears to demur

question of whether Jesus claims the title "Christ, son of the Blessed," Jesus replies affirmatively with an allusion to Daniel 7:13 (Mark 14:61-62). But his allusion also introduces an important change. In Daniel 7:13 the figure who comes riding on the clouds is one like a son of a human, that is, a human being (ὡς υἱὸς ἀνθρώπου). Jesus's words, however, are that the high priest and his court will see *the* son of man (τὸν υἱὸν τοῦ ἀνθρώπου). To the same effect is Jesus's prediction at the climax of the Olivet Discourse (Mark 13:26). The apocalyptic imagery of Daniel 7 has been transformed into a Christological title, referring to Jesus, by the way Jesus employs the phrase within the narrative of Mark.[30] In making the claim that Jesus uses the term as a title, I disagree with others such as Jack Dean Kingsbury.[31] Kingsbury maintains that since Matthew's Jesus does not use the phrase "to explain who he is," it is therefore not a title. This criterion, however, is not sound. For if Matthew or another writer intends to use the developing narrative to explain what a given title means, then the fact that the title is not self-explanatory to the characters within the story does not diminish its titular force for the reader. The phrase is not a preexistent technical term that can be simply inserted into the story to show the reader who Jesus is. However, it is a title inasmuch as Jesus uses it in a definite sense to refer to himself, and inasmuch as the stories in which it occurs demonstrate for the reader what the ramifications of the title are. A title need not explain per se; it might instead offer a pointer toward content that only gradually comes into focus.

What, then, does the phrase actually mean? As a phrase, "the son of the human being" or "son of humanity" simply means a "human being." This is how it is used repeatedly, for example, in the divine address to Ezekiel throughout his eponymous work. In Daniel 7 as well the point of the anarthrous phrase is that now one like a human being has arrived whose rule will displace the rule of the beasts. Combining the meaning of the phrase together with its titular use in the Synoptic Gospels lends prima facie validation to the decisions of the editors of both the Common English Bible and *The New Testament and Psalms: An Inclusive Version* to render the phrase in the Gospels as "the Human One."[32] In keeping with the thesis of this book, the current study will conclude

---

from the notion of a son of man Christology and son of man as a title because the phrase "son of man" does not convey some preexisting understanding of the phrase's connotations and is only used by Jesus himself.

30. As Tuckett notes, in Mark's Gospel the title always refers to Jesus, whatever the pre-Markan tradition might have meant ("Present Son of Man," 59).

31. Jack Dean Kingsbury, *Matthew as Story* (2nd ed.; Philadelphia: Fortress, 1988), 96.

32. Common English Bible (Nashville: Common English Bible, 2011); *The New Testa-*

that such a rendering captures the narrative perfectly: Mark's Jesus uses the title "the son of man" in order to claim that he is God's representative human being during his time on the earth, is so as he sits enthroned at God's right hand, and will continue to be such an idealized human figure in his future return. However, to adopt such a usage at this point in the study might be seen as premature. One could argue, as Boyarin does in his work discussed above, that the allusions to Daniel 7 entail depicting a being who is in some sense divine rather than quintessentially human. In such an instance, the use of the phrase "son of man" is allusive to the extent that it loses its literal meaning of "human being" altogether. It is the burden of this chapter to demonstrate that "the Human One" is, in fact, the better reading of Mark's story. Thus, I continue to use the phrase "the son of man" in order to maintain the titular force while the chapter explores the nuance that Mark provides for this title in his story of Jesus.

2. AUTHORITY AND KINGSHIP: THE SON OF MAN IN MARK 1–8

It is widely noted that Mark's story takes its fateful turn toward the cross with Peter's confession in Caesarea Philippi approximately halfway through the Gospel (8:27-30). Prior to this, Jesus's ministry is marked by miraculous feedings, numerous exorcisms, healing stories of various kinds, authoritative teaching, stilling storms, and walking on the sea. After this transition, the quality of Jesus's ministry changes markedly as his forthcoming death in Jerusalem becomes the driving theme and the miracles drop off precipitously. In the latter half there is but one exorcism and one healing. The disciples' failure to understand Jesus's mission becomes the focus of his teaching and correction en route to Jerusalem, and the final week of Jesus's life takes up the final six chapters of the Gospel. The importance of this skeletal outline is to enable us to see that the son of man sayings about authority (2:10, 28) fit within the portion of the narrative that delineates Jesus's authority on earth as the one in whom the reign of God has come near (1:1–8:30). Similarly, the son of man sayings about future suffering (8:31; 9:31; 10:33, 45) come into play when the narrative as a whole turns in chapter 8 toward Jesus's forthcoming death. The son of man sayings are integrated into the overall narrative development of Mark's Gospel and thus need to be interpreted within it.

---

ment and Psalms: An Inclusive Version (ed. V. R. Gold et al.; New York: Oxford University Press, 1995).

a. Authority on Earth to Forgive (Mark 2:1-12)

i. Forgiveness or Blasphemy in Mark

Jesus's first use of the "son of man" phrase comes in the first conflict story, the healing of the paralytic (2:1-12). When a man is let down through the roof by his friends, Jesus responds to the faith of these four people with the surprising declaration that the man's sins are removed (τέκνον, ἀφίενταί σου αἱ ἁμαρτίαι, 2:5). This is unusual in that typically Jesus addresses the presenting physical or spiritual ailment directly. In the historical context of first-century Judaism, moreover, the statement might surprise those who hear it for two reasons. First, as the scribes who hear this wonder among themselves, is it not the sole prerogative of God to remove sins (τίς δύναται ἀφιέναι ἁμαρτίας εἰ μὴ εἷς ὁ θεός; 2:7)? Second, has God not provided a means for attaining to such removal in the temple — the very place to which Jesus sent the cleansed leper in the previous story (1:39-44)?[33] This brings us to the crux of why this story is so important for the thesis of the current project. The debate about whether Mark's Jesus is a divine figure or an idealized human being runs right through the middle of this passage, as the scribes accuse Jesus of usurping the divine prerogative.[34]

For those who maintain that Mark reflects a divine Christology, the scribes are wrong in their accusation of blasphemy because they do not recognize that Jesus is right in exercising a claim that demonstrates himself to be God.[35] Chrys Caragounis argues that the very use of the "son of man" phrase conjures up Daniel 7 wholesale — such that Jesus is here claiming to be the "preexistent, heavenly Being, who appears as the leader of the saints."[36] My claim,

33. Cf. N. T. Wright, *Jesus and the Victory of God* (Minneapolis: Fortress, 1996), e.g., 647.

34. Dan McCartney, "*Ecce Homo*: The Coming of the Kingdom as the Restoration of Human Vicegerency," *WTJ* 56 (1994): 1-21, opts for a both/and, calling attention to Jesus as exercising human authority on earth (see esp. Matt 9:8) and claiming a prerogative of divinity (12). The idealized human category allows us to affirm the latter without concluding that Jesus is thereby claiming divinity itself.

35. This is the position of E. Earle Ellis, "Deity-Christology in Mark 14:58," in *Jesus of Nazareth: Lord and Christ: Essays on the Historical Jesus and New Testament Christology* (ed. J. B. Green and Max Turner; Grand Rapids, MI: Eerdmans, 1994), 192-203. As the title indicates, Ellis rightly links this opening salvo of the scribes with Jesus's final use of the title at the Jewish hearing and the accusation of blasphemy that follows.

36. Chrys C. Caragounis, *The Son of Man: Vision and Interpretation* (Tübingen: Mohr Siebeck, 1986), 188-89. His conclusion rests on two unlikely premises: (1) that this is how the son of man should be read in Daniel 7; and (2) that the son of man is a "figure with well-defined powers and rights" (188), something that the arguments against son of man as a fixed title in

however, is that in Mark's story the scribes are wrong because they do not recognize Jesus as someone whom God has uniquely appointed to exercise God's rule on the earth — even the prerogative of removing sins.[37] As Adela Yarbro Collins puts it, "the force of this saying, in the context of the healing of the paralytic and in the context of the collection as a whole, was that Jesus has the power to forgive sins because he is the chief agent of God."[38]

In determining what might be the best reading of Mark's story, we should note first of all that readers of Mark have already encountered "forgiveness of sins" in the opening scene of the Gospel. John's ministry in the desert is described as one of baptism and preaching. Baptism leading to the removal of sins is the content of his message: κηρύσσων βάπτισμα μετανοίας εἰς ἄφεσιν ἁμαρτιῶν (1:4). Thus, readers of Mark's Gospel already know that in this story human agents are capable of acting on God's behalf to perform the work necessary for sins to be forgiven. The pericope introducing John the Baptist and the pericope of the healing of the paralytic are joined not only by the conceptual and verbal repetition of "forgiveness" but also by their employment of the noun ἁμαρτία, a word that appears nowhere else in Mark's Gospel.[39]

So, while John signals that the one coming after him is much greater, dwarfing the disparity even between master and servant (1:7), the Baptizer also

---

early Judaism have adequately called into question. On point 1, Caragounis himself argues that the son of man being given over "into the hands" of people reflects the fate of the saints under Antiochus IV in Daniel 7:25, a reading that identifies the son of man both in the Gospels and in Daniel with the suffering humans, not a preexistent figure that only subsequently appears (199; cf. his attempt to answer this problem on 200-201).

37. Cf. Joel Marcus, "Son of Man as Son of Adam: Part II: Exegesis," *RB* 110 (2003): 370-86, here 371-72. Although Tuckett, "Present Son of Man," raises the important point that this being a conflict story ultimately makes it part of the time in which the son of man will suffer, I remain unpersuaded that Jesus's claim to authority is a secondary or incidental component to the story. It is not "tautologous" (Tuckett, "Present Son of Man," 62) to say that the son of man has authority as an indication of authority as such precisely because son of man is not a title with a given content that means "authority," and the story itself is written to demonstrate the precise nature of the authority that Jesus has as this son of man he claims to be.

38. Collins, *Mark*, 189. Collins proceeds to link this agency with the son of man figure from Daniel 7, a position with which I agree, but that I take up separately. See also the argument of Joel Marcus, "Authority to Forgive Sins upon the Earth: The *SHEMA* in the Gospel of Mark," in *The Gospels and the Scriptures of Israel* (JSNTSup 104/SSEJC 3; ed. C. A. Evans and W. R. Stegner; Sheffield: Sheffield Academic, 1994), 196-211.

39. Interestingly, Matthew changes the nature of John's preaching, so that his message is not a baptism of forgiveness of sins (Mark 1:4; Luke 3:3) but is, instead, Jesus's own message that the reign of God has drawn near (Matt 3:2). Matthew places the phrase εἰς ἄφεσιν ἁμαρτιῶν in the mouth of Jesus at the Last Supper, in reference to the cup of the covenant (26:28).

becomes a vehicle in which the narrator of Mark signals that being an agent of removal of sins on the earth is not an agency reserved for God alone (or a god incarnate). Thus, we should be cautious in following the scribes' conclusion regarding Jesus's claim.[40] Indeed, because the scribes are billed as opponents of Jesus in this story, through their accusation of blasphemy, the reader recognizes that they are untrustworthy interpreters of Jesus's claims. At best, we might expect a dramatic irony in which they impute a claim to Jesus as false that the reader knows to be true; however, at this point in the narrative (and indeed, by the time we reach the end in chap. 16), the audience is never told that God or God alone is an apt title for Jesus (in contrast with son of God, as the prior chapter demonstrates).

The narrator's description of Jesus's apprehension of the scribes' wondering "in his spirit" (τῷ πνεύματι αὐτοῦ, 2:8) maintains the link with the John the Baptist story. The differentiation between John and the one coming after him was described in terms of the Holy Spirit (1:8). In the baptism story, we see that the spirit is not a native possession of Jesus, but in Mark it is a gift of God, and, as we saw in the previous chapter, a demonstration of Jesus's kingship. In the story of the paralytic, though the scribes muse against Jesus in their hearts (ἐν ταῖς καρδίαις αὐτῶν, vv. 6, 8), Jesus perceives their disputatious questioning by his spirit (τῷ πνεύματι αὐτοῦ, v. 8). If, as we are arguing throughout this chapter, Mark's son of man sayings intend to demonstrate the nature of Jesus's messiahship, it may be that the expectations of the *Psalms of Solomon* are coming to the surface here: "He will condemn sinners by the thoughts of their hearts" (17:25).[41]

---

40. The detailed work of Daniel Johannson, "'Who Can Forgive Sins but God Alone?' Human and Angelic Agents, and Divine Forgiveness in Early Judaism," *JSNT* 33 (2011): 351-74, is of limited usefulness for interpreting Mark. The narratival considerations create ambiguity around the question, at the very least. Perhaps more importantly, Johannson does not consider that in the early Christian tradition, human agents were entrusted with the prerogative to forgive sins. We see this not only in John's Gospel (20:23), but also in the crowd's reaction to Jesus's work in the Matthean parallel of this account: οἱ ὄχλοι ἐφοβήθησαν καὶ ἐδόξασαν τὸν θεὸν τὸν δόντα ἐξουσίαν τοιαύτην τοῖς ἀνθρώποις (9:8). I address this latter statement in full below. Whatever the Jewish precedent might have been, and I tend to think Johansson has framed the issue in such a way that open questions are too neatly resolved in favor of an unmediated divine prerogative, early Christian literature clearly demonstrates a participation of people in this divine work. This movement makes most sense, in my estimation, as deriving from the conviction that Jesus was the first human so authorized and that others stake the claim derivatively (cf. Matt 16:18-19).

41. Translation is that of R. B. Wright, *Psalms of Solomon*, in *The Old Testament Pseudepigrapha*, vol. 2, *Expansions of the "Old Testament" and Legends, Wisdom, and Philosophical Literature, Prayers, Psalms, and Odes, Fragments of Lost Judeo-Hellenistic Works* (ed. James H. Charlesworth; New York: Doubleday, 1985), 639-70.

This psalm is reason enough to conclude that Jesus's ability to know what is in the heart of another person is not inherently a divine quality — it can equally well be understood as a messianic prerogative.[42] There may be more at work in this narrated contrast between Jesus and the scribes as well. If John's ministry by means of water is authorized by God for the forgiveness of sins, the reader is reminded that Jesus's ministry of the spirit is even greater than John's. Indeed, the next time that charges of blasphemy are leveled in the story it is precisely because work that Jesus is doing by the spirit's power is assessed by the scribes as being done by the power of Beelzebul (3:22-30). The supernatural ability Jesus has is a function of the spirit that God has given to Jesus upon his baptism.

In his verbal response to the scribes, Jesus draws together the forgiveness of sins with the action of healing in which he is about to engage.[43] The seemingly insoluble question of which might be easier to say to the paralytic, "Your sins are removed," or "Arise, take up your mat," recedes in importance as we recognize that Jesus sees the two as constituent parts demonstrating one coherent whole, namely, that "the son of man has authority to remove sins on the earth" (ἐξουσίαν ἔχει ὁ υἱὸς τοῦ ἀνθρώπου ἀφιέναι ἁμαρτίας ἐπὶ τῆς γῆς, 2:10).[44] The healing of the paralytic is to be the proof that Jesus did, in fact, remove the man's sins according to the authority he has as son of man.[45] As Simon Gathercole notes, the emphasis on authority on the earth (cf. Dan 7:14) may also be a first hint that Mark's son of man is the fulfillment of the son of man figure from Daniel 7, an important claim to which we will return.[46] Claiming authority on the earth maintains the distinction between "God above" and Jesus's own character as one who brings near God's reign.[47] Another possible facet of the phrase ἐπὶ τῆς γῆς is highlighted by Morna

42. Marcus, *Mark 1-8*, 222 seems to suggest that this is, in fact, an indication of some sort of divinity, though he goes on to describe the son of man in this pericope as one to whom God has delegated authority (223).

43. Cf. Peter Müller, "Zwischen dem Gekommenen und dem Kommenden: Intertextuelle Aspekte der Menschensohnaussagen im Markusevangelium," in *Gottessohn und Menschensohn: Exegetische Studien zu zwei Paradigmen biblischer Intertextualität* (BTS 67; ed. Dieter Sägner; Neukirchen-Vluyn: Neukirchener, 2004), 130-57, here 137.

44. Hooker, *Son of Man in Mark*, 88-89. Frederick Houk Borsch, *The Son of Man in Myth and History* (Philadelphia: Westminster, 1967), 321-22, notes the connection between authority and power that is significant here; I add that it was so previously in Mark 1, and also in the reign of the son of man in Daniel 7.

45. On the importance of the title at this point, see Perrin, *Modern Pilgrimage*, 88-89.

46. Gathercole, "Son of Man," 369. See also Marcus, "Authority to Forgive Sins," 201-5.

47. So also Marcus, "Son of Man: Part II," 372, though Jesus's own position will change with his resurrection, as he receives authority in heaven as well (e.g., Matt 28:18).

Hooker.[48] She points out that in the LXX of Genesis 1:26-30, a passage detailing the creation of humanity and its delegation to rule over the earth for God, the phrase is used three times. Thus, the claim to authority is one that marks out the son of man as one who "acts now as Adam was intended to act, as the representative of God on earth," a claim that she links also with the son of man figure in Daniel and *1 Enoch*.[49]

To this point we have seen four indications that the Christology disclosed in the first pericope where Jesus takes the son of man title is an idealized human Christology: his forgiving action builds on the prior work done by John; his ability to know people's thoughts may be attributed to the spirit, which marks him out as king; the ability to judge people's hearts is a description of an idealized messianic figure in *Psalms of Solomon*; and the use of the "son of man" phrase and the realm of his authority "on the earth" call attention to two scriptural precedents: Daniel's son of man who is emblematic of a glorified and reigning Israel, and Adam who is emblematic of a reigning humanity.

The theme of authority also builds on a prior moment in the story.[50] The first story Mark tells of Jesus's public preaching and healing is bookended by the response of the crowds, who are amazed at Jesus's authority (1:22, 27 — the only prior uses of ἐξουσία in the narrative). When Jesus teaches, the people respond with astonishment at his authority because his teaching is not like that of the scribes (1:22). The presence of the scribes in each story, as well as their use of ἐξουσία, both forge links between Jesus's first exorcism and his removal of the paralytic's sins, and suggest that the stories should be interpreted in concert with one another. In the former narrative, an unclean spirit discloses Jesus's identity as God's holy one, and as one who has the power to destroy this unclean specter and its ilk (1:24). In the Greek translations of the Old Testament, the substantive ὁ ἅγιος (the holy one) most often refers to God (e.g., Hab 3:3; Isa 40:25; Sir 23:9), and when modified by "of Israel" is a recurring title for God that spans all three sections of Isaiah (e.g., 1:4; 5:19; 17:7; 30:11; 37:23; 41:20; 43:14; 49:7; 55:5; 60:9; 63:15). However, when modified by a genitive that refers to God, this substantive refers to a person or people whose holiness derives from God's special presence with them (thus, Ααρων τὸν ἅγιον κυρίου, "Aaron the Lord's holy one," in Ps 105:16, and Ισραηλ τὸν ἅγιόν σου, "Israel your holy

48. Hooker, *Son of Man*, 91.

49. Hooker, *Son of Man*, 91, 93.

50. Perrin, *Modern Pilgrimage*, 80-81, 86-88, delineates Mark 1:16–3:6 as a section within which authority is a particular concern, a sequence crafted by Mark and in which the authority sayings find their appropriate context.

one," in Dan 3:35).[51] The authority that the unclean spirit recognizes in Jesus is the authority of God, but it is the authority of God that has been bestowed upon a sanctified human agent — an agent sanctified by the Holy Spirit of God at his baptism, the reader of this story might well surmise.

As with the story of the paralytic's healing, the story of Jesus's first exorcism combines two potentially discrete actions as demonstrations of the same singular authority.[52] The introduction to the earlier story stands well on its own, as Mark tells of Jesus teaching and the people's response of wonder at his teaching authority (1:22). And yet, what is not objectively verifiable in Jesus's teaching itself is whether he actually has the authority that his teaching implicitly claims — the same dilemma he faces in forgiving the sins of the paralytic. Thus, Mark joins the crowd's assessment of Jesus's teaching with the story of the exorcism. After Jesus bests his opponent, ridding the possessed man of the unclean spirit, Mark has the people express astonishment in such a way as to make clear that the story displays two indications of the same reality of Jesus's authority: τί ἐστιν τοῦτο; διδαχὴ καινὴ κατ᾽ ἐξουσίαν· καὶ τοῖς πνεύμασι τοῖς ἀκαθάρτοις ἐπιτάσσει, καὶ ὑπακούουσιν αὐτῷ ("What is this?! A new teaching with authority. He commands even the unclean spirits and they obey him!" 1:27). Jesus casts out unclean spirits precisely through the authority he has to speak directly for God — an authority that is his because he is the holy one of God, the person who has been sanctified by God to represent God (especially God's reign) on the earth. The first miracle story, in which we find the only prior mention of ἐξουσία and in which we find a first disjunction between Jesus and the scribes, depicts Jesus through deployment of an idealized human Christology.

As a further indication that in this first story about Jesus's authority Mark does not mean to tell us that Jesus is, in fact, divine in some proto-Chalcedonian sense, it is worth observing that Mark describes the mission of the twelve in precisely the same terms as he describes Jesus's work in 1:22-28.[53] He calls the twelve, in chapter 3, in order to be with him but then also to be sent out to preach and to have authority (ἐξουσίαν) to cast out demons. When he actually sends them out on their own in chapter 6, he bestows that very authority upon them (ἐδίδου αὐτοῖς ἐξουσίαν τῶν πνευμάτων τῶν ἀκαθάρτων, v. 7), and the narrator reports that they did, in fact, preach repentance, cast out

51. If one expands the parameters to include the word ὅσιος, the examples multiply and include references to the Davidic king (Ps 15:10, LXX).

52. Borsch, Son of Man, 321-22.

53. Hooker, Son of Man, 90, highlights the probability that "the authority of Jesus as Son of man is extended to his followers." For more discussion of the Christology entailed in Jesus's wonder working, see below, chapter 7, "Lord of Heaven and Earth."

demons, and heal the infirm (v. 13).[54] Because Mark depicts Jesus bestowing this authority upon other people, the narrative leaves little room for concluding that having such authority is an indication that a person is divine. Instead, this is an indication of being a human specially empowered and entrusted by God to exercise God's authority on the earth. In fact, such is arguably the significance of ἐξουσία in each of its ten usages in Mark (1:22, 27; 2:10; 3:15; 6:7; 11:28 [2x], 29, 33; 13:34).

Within the story of Mark's Gospel the interpretive grid provided by the scribes, that anyone professing to offer forgiveness of sins is transgressing an impassable divine boundary, is mistaken. Jesus is not the only human in Mark who removes sins. I have already mentioned the baptismal ministry of John. In addition, after the sign-act in which Jesus prophesies the temple's destruction, he locates the temple's function of forgiveness within the community of his disciples, whom he now describes as the house of prayer that the temple had failed to become (11:23-25).[55] Forgiveness of sins is, in fact, a divine prerogative, but it is one whose mechanisms are, at times, mediated by human activities on earth. In Mark, the refocusing of forgiveness around the eschatological acts of John and the ministry of Jesus continues in the followers whom Jesus leaves behind. Although the authority to forgive sins marks Jesus as one who is enacting a unique ministry, especially inasmuch as the parallel of John looks forward to Jesus while the parallel of the community looks back to him, it does not indicate an ontological status of divinity for which the readers have otherwise not been prepared. The connection with John is far from fortuitous. In the pericope immediately following the temple clearing and sayings on prayer, Jesus is questioned by the religious leaders about the authority he has to do the things he does (particularly in the temple, 11:28). To this, Jesus replies by asking about John's authority (11:29-30). The implication is clear: each has been authorized by God for his unique ministry.[56] Authority to act for God, even in the divine prerogative of establishing forgiveness of sins, does not indicate ontological divinity or preexistence.[57]

---

54. On the tight connection between Jesus and his disciples, see especially Suzanne Watts Henderson, *Christology and Discipleship in the Gospel of Mark* (SNTSMS 135; Cambridge: Cambridge University Press, 2006), e.g., 136-38.

55. For an extensive defensive of this reading of the temple and prayer pericopes in Mark 11:12-25, see J. R. Daniel Kirk, "Time for Figs, Temple Destruction, and Houses of Prayer in Mark 11:12-25," *CBQ* 74 (2012): 510-28.

56. So also Boyarin, *Jewish Gospels*, 57.

57. The contrary position asserted by Simon Gathercole, *The Preexistent Son: Recovering the Christologies of Matthew, Mark, and Luke* (Grand Rapids, MI: Eerdmans, 2006), 259, leans

Instead, the claim of Mark's Jesus with this son of man saying is to the effect that the future judgment and glory of the coming son of man is already present in the person of Jesus. So also Marcus concludes that "for Mark, the heavenly God remains the ultimate forgiver, but at the climax of history he has delegated his power of absolution to a 'Son of Man' who carries out his gracious will in the earthly sphere."[58] To this extent, Bultmann's assessment of the son of man stories is on target. The surprise of Mark's Gospel is twofold: first, that the expected eschatological redeemer is already present with divine authority in the ministry of Jesus on earth; second, that he must suffer and die before he comes again in the glory of God to judge and to reign. The first of these surprises is the subject matter of the son of man sayings in Mark 2.

Other early Christian interpreters of Jesus's ministry understood that the prerogative to take away sins was not the exclusive realm of divinity. In the Matthean parallel to this passage, the concluding statement is the crowd's interpretation of the event as God giving authority to humans: οἱ ὄχλοι ἐφοβήθησαν καὶ ἐδόξασαν τὸν θεὸν τὸν δόντα ἐξουσίαν τοιαύτην τοῖς ἀνθρώποις ("the crowds were afraid and glorified God who had given such authority to people," 9:8). In John's Gospel, the resurrected Jesus bestows this right upon his followers: ἄν τινων ἀφῆτε τὰς ἁμαρτίας ἀφέωνται αὐτοῖς, ἄν τινων κρατῆτε κεκράτηνται ("Whoever's sins you forgive, they will be forgiven them; whoever's you bind, they will be bound," 20:23). Thus, even in John's Gospel, where Jesus is most clearly depicted as preexistent and in some sense divine, the divine prerogative of taking away sins, expressed in the verb ἀφίημι, is extended to human agents acting in the world on God's behalf. With respect to Mark's passage itself, form critics claimed that the story's peculiar combination of healing and forgiveness indicates that it had been reworked in order to account for the fact that the early church itself was making such pronouncements. John's Gospel is ample evidence that the church was, in fact, making such claims for itself. In John, the immediately preceding words and actions of Jesus indicate (1) that the ministry of these sin-remitting followers is analogous to Jesus's being sent by God into

---

heavily on his understanding of the "I have come" sayings indicating preexistence. Thus, he reads the overall narrative context following clues down a different path that allows the son of man sayings to participate in a larger preexistence theology. As noted in the introduction, "I have come from heaven" is not the most likely reading. The flaws in Gathercole's argument are ably pointed out in Collins and Collins, *King and Messiah*, 123-26, including that the phrase "I have come" is an idiom, that a parallel expression is used of John the Baptist alongside Jesus (Matt 11:18-19; par. Luke 7:33-34), and that other Jewish people use the expression of one having come from God to designate eschatological agency without a notion of preexistence.

58. Marcus, *Mark 1–8*, 223.

the world to speak and act for God (20:21), and (2) that the presence of the spirit of God is an important qualification for exercising such authority. However one parses the particulars of Jesus's commissioning of the disciples in John, their task focuses on this one act, forgiving sins, that is certainly a divine task but now clearly one that humans can mediate on God's behalf.[59]

This book is continually putting forward the question, Is an idealized human paradigm sufficient for explaining the Christological data contained in the Gospel narratives? I have laid out various reasons why the blasphemy charge and Jesus's prerogative to forgive sins fit comfortably within that framework. The very title itself, meaning the "Human One," coupled with a realm of authority expressed as "on the earth" leads to a prima facie conclusion that Jesus is claiming an authority delegated by God. This may reflect primal human authority as well as the authority of the glorified people of God from Daniel 7.[60] The sphere of authority as forgiveness of sins is one that the narrative has already depicted as being mediated by another human agent whose source of authority is parallel to that of Jesus, and that it later locates in the community of Jesus's followers. The authority Jesus has is of a piece with his teaching and exorcising authority — gifts he can share with and bestow upon other humans. The way Jesus responds to the "heart" thoughts of his antagonists reflects God's gift to him of the spirit and his occupying the place of the expected eschatological messiah. Of course, someone reading the passage with a divine Christology or two natures Christology can also integrate all such facts within such a paradigm. But the sufficiency of the preexisting Jewish idealized human paradigm for containing the data makes it less likely that such Christian innovations in understanding the identities of both Jesus and God is at play in this text.

ii. Forgiving and Blasphemy in Matthew and Luke

a. The Paralytic. Matthew and Luke each include the story of the healing of the paralytic as well. For Matthew, this is not the first time Jesus has used the phrase "son of man." Previously, he had told a scribe who was a would-be follower, "The son of man has nowhere to lay his head" (8:20). I discuss this passage in more detail below, but for now it is sufficient to point out that Matthew's readers have encountered the son of man only as one who neither owns nor, apparently, is received into houses. Turning to the "son of man" phrase

---

59. To similar effect in the Synoptic Tradition may be the "keys of the kingdom" saying in Matthew 16:19.

60. On the likelihood of an allusion to Daniel 7, cf. Müller, "Zwischen," 138.

in the paralytic story, Matthew's version seems specially couched to curtail possible "divine Christology" interpretations. First, when the scribes accuse Jesus of blasphemy the charge is not elaborated. Matthew 9:4 reads simply, εἶπαν ἐν ἑαυτοῖς· οὗτος βλασφημεῖ ("they said among themselves, 'This one is blaspheming'"), eliminating Mark's, τίς δύναται ἀφιέναι ἁμαρτίας εἰ μὴ εἷς ὁ θεός ("Who is able to forgive sins except God alone?"). In another substantive change, Matthew allows the crowds' reaction to provide an interpretive cue for the story. The crowds were afraid, and ἐδόξασαν τὸν θεὸν τὸν δόντα ἐξουσίαν τοιαύτην τοῖς ἀνθρώποις ("they glorified God who gave such authority to people," 9:8). This response provides an interpretation of Jesus's prior claim that the son of man has authority on earth (9:6); τοῖς ἀνθρώποις might mean "among people." Frequently, another interpretive option is entertained, namely, that the phrase means "to humans."[61] But what is certain here is that Matthew intends to depict the authority as delegated: God has given this authority such that it can be exercised in the fashion that the crowds have beheld. Matthew's interpretation of Mark's story provides perhaps our earliest example of the story being read as signaling that Jesus is God's special agent on the earth, that he forgives on the basis of his empowerment as an idealized human figure rather than possessing his own authority as God.

In Luke's rendering of the story, we receive the narrator's first cue about how to interpret the scene in 5:17 where we read, καὶ δύναμις κυρίου ἦν εἰς τὸ ἰᾶσθαι αὐτόν ("and the power of the Lord was upon him so that he could heal"). These words contain some possible ambiguity. As Kavin Rowe notes extensively, the word κύριος in Luke's Gospel can refer to either Jesus or God.[62] This phrase might possibly be translated, "the Lord's [i.e., Jesus's] power was present for the purpose of healing him." The problem with this interpretation is that it lacks a masculine singular antecedent for the object of healing ("him"). Moreover, the textual variant that replaces αὐτόν with αὐτούς ends up referring back not to those who are sick but to the Pharisees and teachers of the law who have come to hear Jesus (5:17). Thus, as Rowe concedes, κυρίου in 5:17 refers to God, and αὐτόν is the subject of the infinitive ἰᾶσθαι rather than its object. Therefore, when the story comes to the moment in which Jesus claims that the son of man has authority on earth to forgive, the hermeneutical key has already been supplied: God's power is at work in this Jesus — the same authority by which God heals through Jesus is the power by which Jesus forgives

61. Douglas R. A. Hare, *The Son of Man Tradition* (Minneapolis: Fortress, 1990), 140.
62. C. Kavin Rowe, *Early Narrative Christology: The Lord in the Gospel of Luke* (Grand Rapids, MI: Baker Academic, 2009), 92-98.

sins. This close connection between God's power and Jesus's work is reiterated at the pericope's end. The man goes home praising God (δοξάζων τὸν θεόν), and the crowd, in turn, gripped with wonder, praises God (ἔκστασις ἔλαβεν ἅπαντες καὶ ἐδόξαζον τὸν θεόν). As in Matthew, there is an account of fear as well. Luke's pericope concludes: καὶ ἐπλήσθησαν φόβου λέγοντες ὅτι εἴδομεν παράδοξα σήμερον ("and they were filled with fear, saying, 'We have seen a great wonder today,'" 5:26). These comments indicate that both the paralytic and the people who witnessed the healing were able to perceive that it was God who was at work in Jesus to perform this miracle.

At both the beginning and the end of the pericope Luke has signaled to the reader that the point of this son of man story is that God is at work in Jesus, not that Jesus is somehow the God who can forgive sins.[63] Thus, the story functions as a perfect illustration of the claim of Peter at Pentecost: Ἰησοῦν τὸν Ναζωραῖον, ἄνδρα ἀποδεδειγμένον ἀπὸ τοῦ θεοῦ εἰς ὑμᾶς δυνάμεσι καὶ τέρασι καὶ σημείοις οἷς ἐποίησεν δι' αὐτοῦ ὁ θεὸς ἐν μέσῳ ὑμῶν καθὼς αὐτοὶ οἴδατε ("Jesus was a man attested by God to you by powers and wonders and signs that God did through him in your midst, just as you know," Acts 2:22). God is at work through the man Jesus in the signs and wonders Jesus performs. The praises with which the story ends are indications that the Lord God who was said to be with Jesus for healing at the beginning of the pericope has been rightly recognized by those gathered to see. Thus, when Peter says, "as you yourselves know" at Pentecost, the reader of Acts may well remember this particular passage as a point at which the people came to know that God was at work in the human Jesus to perform such wonders. A final point, raised by Douglas Hare, is important for grasping the Christological intentions of Luke in this passage. Luke intentionally follows Mark in coupling the authority to heal with the authority to forgive. The former is put on ample display by Jesus's followers in the book of Acts. Such authority is, therefore, readily understood as a heavenly delegation to earthly representatives rather than an indication of divinity.[64]

b. Unforgivable Blasphemy. In the discussion of Mark, I connected the healing of the paralytic with the blasphemy of the Holy Spirit passage in order to help get a handle on how the idea of blasphemy is conceived in the Gospel. The pericope is important for a more direct reason as well: in both Matthew and Luke the Beelzebub controversy, in which the notion of "blasphemy against the Holy Spirit" is found, also contains a son of man saying (Matt 12:32; Luke 12:10).

63. This is the conclusion also of Hare, *Son of Man Tradition*, 50.
64. Hare, *Son of Man Tradition*, 51-52.

In a peculiar twist, this saying appears to subordinate the son of man to the spirit who empowers him to act. In Matthew, the saying follows the Beelzebul controversy and constitutes its resolution.[65] In this passage, Matthew differs from Mark in four significant ways. First, in describing who can be forgiven their blasphemies, Mark describes people as τοῖς υἱοῖς τῶν ἀνθρώπων (3:28), a phrase Matthew renders as τοῖς ἀνθρώποις (12:31). The plural form of the "son of man" phrase, referring to humanity in general, occurs in one text, while the singular, referring to Jesus, occurs in the other. Second, Matthew states twice that those who blaspheme the spirit will not be forgiven — the second of which saying more closely resembles Mark's form.[66] Third, in between these twin assurances of the eternal consequence of such blasphemy, we find that there is forgiveness to be had for speaking against the son of man. Fourth, Mark connects the dots for the readers, telling them that Jesus said such a thing due to the mischaracterization of the Holy Spirit as an impure spirit (3:29).

The third point is our particular concern. The clause in question reads καὶ ὃς ἐὰν εἴπῃ λόγον κατὰ τοῦ υἱοῦ τοῦ ἀνθρώπου, ἀφεθήσεται αὐτῷ ("and whoever should say a word against the son of man, it will be forgiven him," Matt 12:32a). The most important dynamic for our consideration is the distinction Jesus draws between blaspheming the son of man versus blaspheming the spirit. The greater guilt would seem to imply that a greater figure had been spoken against: blaspheming the agent is forgivable, but blaspheming the presence of God through which the agent is empowered and is thus authorized to act is not.[67] Here we find the suggestion that the son of man finds his sanctity not in his own divine being as such, but in his being anointed by the spirit of God.

Luke deploys his version of this son of man saying in a different context (12:10), using it to link the son of man's eschatological confession or denial of a person (12:8-9; par. Matt 10:32-33) with the spirit's giving a person on trial the needful words when testifying (12:11-12; par. Matt 10:19-20; Mark 13:11). Luke's preceding verses contain a son of man reference, though Matthew's version simply contains "I." The result is that Luke creates a somewhat paradoxical juxtaposition in which denial of the son of man leads to being denied by the son of man, but speaking a word against the son of man (Luke does not use βλασφημέω with regard to the son of man) can, apparently, be followed by eschatological forgiveness:

65. Cf. W. D. Davies and Dale C. Allison Jr., *Matthew* (3 vols.; ICC; Edinburgh: T&T Clark, 1991), 2:345.

66. Cf. Davies and Allison, *Matthew*, 2:345.

67. Hare, *Son of Man Tradition*, 62-63, also reads the Lukan version as pointing to the humanity of Jesus on earth, even in contrast to the exalted son of man whom those in Acts are no longer free to disregard (e.g., 3:17-26; 13:27-31).

Λέγω δὲ ὑμῖν, πᾶς ὅς ἄν ὁμολογήσῃ ἐν ἐμοὶ ἔμπροσθεν τῶν ἀνθρώπων,
καὶ ὁ υἱὸς τοῦ ἀνθρώπου ὁμολογήσει ἐν αὐτῷ ἔμπροσθεν τῶν ἀγγέλων
τοῦ θεοῦ· ὁ δὲ ἀρνησάμενός με ἐνώπιον τῶν ἀνθρώπων ἀπαρνηθήσεται
ἐνώπιον τῶν ἀγγέλων τοῦ θεοῦ. καὶ πᾶς ὅς ἐρεῖ λόγον εἰς τὸν υἱὸν τοῦ
ἀνθρώπου, ἀφεθήσεται αὐτῷ· τῷ δὲ εἰς τὸ ἅγιον πνεῦμα βλασφημήσαντι
οὐκ ἀφεθήσεται.

But I say to you, whoever confesses me before people, so also the son of
man will confess that one before the angels of God. But whoever denies
me before people will be denied before the angels of God. And everyone
who speaks a word about the son of man, it will be forgiven him, but it will
not be forgiven for the one who blasphemes the holy spirit. (Luke 12:8-10)

Within the narrative of Luke, the paradox is soluble. Recognizing and confessing Jesus to be the Christ through whom God is at work and through
whom God will judge the world is crucial for eschatological salvation (cf.
Acts 2:22-24, 35-36; 3:13, 26). However, the message to the Jewish people, in
particular, is that turning from denial to faith is the route to forgiveness and
eschatological blessing (e.g., Acts 2:38-41; 3:14-20). Thus, denial of Jesus is a
criterion in the final judgment, but it is also one that can be reversed, from
denial to confession. Moreover, speaking against Jesus is the very thing that the
rulers (ἐξεμυκτήριζον, "sneered," Luke 23:25), soldiers (ἐνέπαιξαν, "mocked,"
23:36), and the crucified criminal (ἐβλασφήμει, "blasphemed," 23:39) do to
Jesus while he hangs on the cross — actions that stand under Jesus's invocation
of divine forgiveness (23:34).[68] These uses of the "son of man" phrase fit within
Luke's broader conceptual schema in which Jesus is "a man attested by God"
(Acts 2:22), one whom God makes Lord and Christ (2:36), "a man whom God
has appointed" to judge the world (17:31), and also within the soteriological
scheme in which acknowledgment of Jesus as God's agent is fundamental to
vindication in the final judgment. Words spoken against Jesus might, in fact,
be the very means by which a person later confronted with his resurrection,

---

68. I recognize the text-critical problem with this verse, but find its originality probable.
Luke's atonement theology largely rests on the notion that Jesus's death makes the Jewish
people realize that they, too, need forgiveness from God. As Bart D. Ehrman puts it, in *The
Orthodox Corruption of Scripture: The Effect of Early Christological Controversies on the Text of
the New Testament* (Oxford: Oxford University Press, 1993), 202, "the blood of Jesus produces
the church because it brings the cognizance of guilt that leads to repentance." Thus, the textual
variant seems to owe more to a later generation's discomfort with forgiving the Jewish people,
in particular, than to a harmonizing tendency with, e.g., Stephen's speech in Acts 7.

and the evidence of that resurrection by the outpoured spirit, recognizes her own need to be forgiven by God.

iii. Conclusions: The Agent of Forgiveness

The difficulty in holding the line between Jesus and God is understandable. The claim to be God's representative on earth is a claim to be God's stand-in to such a degree that the acts of such an idealized human figure are seen to be the very works of God.[69] Thus, at the end of this pericope the people do not praise Jesus, but instead glorify God (Mark 2:12; par. Matt 9:8; Luke 5:26). Such proximity between God and God's appointed representatives generally, and idealized human figures more specifically, filled the pages of our study of the Old Testament and early Judaism. Even as Matthew's Jesus calls his followers to be so engaged in good works that God their father would be glorified, so Mark depicts God as Jesus's father who is glorified by the works the child has done.

It will take the duration of this chapter to establish that Mark's son of man is, consistently, an idealized, representative human being (the conclusion drawn also by Morna Hooker).[70] But for now, we have shown that between the scribes' assertion that only God can forgive sins, on the one hand, and the possibility that someone who claims so to do is claiming to be God, on the other, lies the possibility that someone might be authorized by God to enact what otherwise would be an exclusively divine prerogative. By associating other people in the narrative with the authority to do the kinds of things that Jesus does, including forgiving sins as well as healing and teaching, Mark draws us toward this middle space, inviting the reader to recognize Jesus as a supremely empowered and authorized human, representing God and God's reign on the earth. Matthew and Luke each seem to follow.

b. Son of Man as Davidic Lord of the Sabbath

i. Mark's Jesus and Sabbath Authority

In Mark's Gospel, the Lord of the Sabbath claim (2:23-28) is the second deployment of the "son of man" phrase and also comes as part of a series of conflict stories that culminate in the first plot to take Jesus's life (2:1–3:6). Occurring as it does in the first half of Mark's Gospel, it is situated within the portion of

---

69. Cf. Hooker, *Son of Man*, 89.
70. Hooker, *Son of Man*, 90.

the narrative that illustrates the present power and authority of Jesus on the earth. This pericope adds substantial weight to the claim that Jesus employs the son of man title not as a hint toward divinity or preexistence but, instead, as a claim to be messiah — God's idealized human agent.[71] With its allusions to David, this passage stands together with the confession of Peter (8:31) and with Jesus's response to the high priest at his trial (14:62) as an indicator that Mark's son of man sayings provide new content for the title of Christ with which the Gospel begins.[72] In so doing, it also lends further definition and clarity to the title son of God that I addressed in the previous chapter. With its allusion to the original intent of the Sabbath, the pericope underscores that Jesus bears his authority precisely as he is a representative human figure.

The pericope of the grain plucking begins with an indication that Jesus's disciples are "making a way" by plucking heads of grain (2:23), an action that draws censure from the Pharisees who ask why they do what is not lawful (ὃ οὐκ ἔξεστιν) on the Sabbath (2:24). Rather than disputing the claim that the disciples are doing something unlawful, Jesus replies by telling a story about something unlawful (οὓς οὐκ ἔξεστιν) that David ate and gave to his companions (2:26).[73] Jesus also draws a comparison at the point of hunger (2:25). Jesus thus compares his situation to that of a royal figure from the past who is not yet enthroned, who sees to it that his companions are fed in a manner that is not lawful. Up through Jesus's summarizing of the David story itself one might conclude that the point of the story is to illustrate a principle that could be broadly applied, something to the effect that situations of need such as extreme hunger warrant a setting aside of the particulars of the law, or, perhaps, that mercy is the true fulfillment of the law.[74]

However, Mark's pericope does not end there, and the son of man saying

---

71. A point made from a different perspective as well in Marcus, "Son of Man: Part II," 374-76. See also the brief but important comments in Philip G. Davis, "Mark's Christological Paradox," *JSNT* 35 (1989): 3-15, esp. 9-11.

72. Walter Wink, *The Human Being: Jesus and the Enigma of the Son of Man* (Minneapolis: Fortress, 2002), 69, asserts that this saying refers instead to the authority that the disciples themselves have. Although the idea that Jesus's followers participate in Jesus's authority is an important part of Mark's Gospel, and a tremendously important factor in understanding the Gospels as depicting a high human Christology as opposed to a divine Christology, in this case the interpretation is not apt. Throughout the controversy stories the question is Jesus's authority, and if the disciples do have this authority it is not because it was always latent in them, but because it has been given to them as a share in what is originally and rightfully Jesus's.

73. Cf. Collins, *Mark*, 202-3; Müller, "Zwischen," 139.

74. Collins, *Mark*, 203, indicates that such a general principle is, in fact, established here. But this does not take account of either the unique role of David or verses 27-28.

demands a different reading of the David parallel. Jesus interprets the Sabbath such that it is subject to his authority because he is son of man: τὸ σάββατον διὰ τὸν ἄνθρωπον ἐγένετο καὶ οὐχ ὁ ἄνθρωπος διὰ τὸν σάββατον. ὥστε κύριός ἐστιν ὁ υἱὸς τοῦ ἀνθρώπου καὶ τοῦ σαββάτου (2:27-28).[75] In order to maintain the son of man title and the references to humanity in general, we might translate Jesus's saying like this: "The Sabbath came into being for the sake of humanity and not humanity for the sake of the Sabbath. So then, the son of humanity is Lord even of the Sabbath." The final sentence of the pericope, in which the son of man claim occurs, interprets the story as one that depicts Jesus's unique authority (I return to this below).[76] The two major interpretive decisions to be made pertain to the nature of Jesus's parallel with David and the claim he makes for himself as son of man.

First, I must establish that the significance of David in the Old Testament parallel lies in the analogous role Jesus occupies as the royal presence of God's anointed and spirit-bearing (cf. 1 Sam 16:13), if not yet enthroned, king who exercises the authority on earth to guiltlessly do what is not allowed by the law.[77] This is a significant moment in Mark's narrative Christology. Though he introduces Jesus as Christ in the introductory sentence, we find that both χριστός and Δαυίδ are ambiguous titles. Peter's confession of Jesus as χριστός in 8:29 meets with no approval, but rather redirection to a suffering son of man.[78] Analogously, when the high priest asks Jesus if he is the Christ, the son of the Blessed, Jesus answers affirmatively, but then proceeds to describe this vocation in terms of the glorified son of man. "Son of man" is the phraseology Jesus uses in Mark's Gospel to indicate for the readers what χριστός entails. Mark 2 is the first mention of David in the story, and the name next recurs on the lips of a blind man begging Jesus for mercy (10:47-48) before the crowds take up the chant of David's coming kingdom during Jesus's entry into Jerusalem (11:10). The blind man is healed — has he seen Jesus clearly through the mist of his blindness? Jesus's teaching on the Christ as son of David in Mark 12:35-37 muddies the waters considerably.

---

75. Cf. Müller, "Zwischen," 139.

76. Cf. Hooker, Son of Man, 102.

77. The conclusion, also, of John R. Donahue, "Temple, Trial, and Royal Christology (Mark 14:53-65)," in The Passion in Mark: Studies in Mark 14–16 (ed. Werner H. Kelber; Philadelphia: Fortress, 1976), 61-79, here 75; cf. Wright, Jesus and the Victory of God, 393-94. Collins suggests that the royal parallel goes back to Adam — the specific human for whom the Sabbath was created. This idealized human being is supposed to be repristinated in the king (Collins, Mark, 204). This seems to capture the point exactly.

78. Cf. Malbon, Mark's Jesus, 105-7.

There, Jesus asks how the messiah can be David's son when David refers to the messiah as his Lord (12:37).

The Gospel's ambivalence toward the association of Jesus with David parallels its ambivalence toward the term χριστός. In a section of the Gospel marked by the healings of two blind men (8:22–10:52), the narrative turns decisively toward Jerusalem as the fate of the son of man — whom Peter has called Christ (a title that the ideal reader knows to be valid due to the narrator's use of it in 1:1).[79] The first blind man's two-stage healing is emblematic of the disciples' own need for double sight: not only to see that Jesus is Christ, but also to see that as Christ he must suffer and those who would be his disciples must follow along the way of the cross. The second blind man "sees" Jesus as son of David, refuses to be silenced at the rebuke of the crowds, and follows along the way to which Jesus has summoned his followers. The reader knows the deeper significance of this connection, even if the blind man himself does not (parallel to the woman whose anointing with oil is a "preparation for burial" whether she knows it or not, and is to her credit, 14:8-9). Jesus can be seen as Davidic king, as he can be seen as Christ, but only if Davidic kingship is recognized within the parameters of the story of the suffering son of man, just as the title Christ is given similar refraction by Jesus's self-designation.

This paves the way for understanding the ambivalence about the Christ as David's son in Mark 12. Although Jesus as Christ might bear the title son of David, from the perspective of Mark's Gospel there might be two problems with this. First, as we have just argued, Davidic kingship carries connotations that do not fit the kind of Christ Mark's narrative depicts: one who comes into his heavenly glory by way of the cross. The well-worn notion that the expected Davidic messiah would likely be a military leader or one who would otherwise purge Jerusalem from its Gentile overlords is no less true for being so frequently iterated. Thus, for example, we find in the *Psalms of Solomon:*

> See, Lord, and raise up unto them their king, the son of David, to rule over your servant Israel in the time known to you, O God. Undergird him with the strength to destroy the unrighteous rulers, to purge Jerusalem from gentiles who trample her to destruction; in wisdom and righteousness to drive out the sinners from the inheritance; to smash the arrogance of sinners like a potter's jar; To shatter their substance with an iron rod; to destroy the unlawful nations with the word of his mouth; At his warning the nations will flee from his presence; and he will condemn sinners by

79. Malbon, *Mark's Jesus,* 105-6.

the thoughts of their heart. He will gather a holy people whom he will lead in righteousness; and he shall judge the tribes of the people that have been made holy by the Lord their God. And he shall not suffer unrighteousness to lodge any more in their midst, nor shall there dwell with them any man who knows wickedness, for he shall know them, that they are all sons of their God. (17:21-26)[80]

Mark's Jesus is an unpredictable combination of affirmation, denial, and transformation of such early Jewish messianic expectations. He is a Christ who is empowered by the Holy Spirit and wise in his teaching (*Pss. Sol.* 17:37). However, any purging of Jerusalem that Mark's Jesus anticipates will leave the temple and the city as a whole razed rather than purified (chap. 13; cf. 11:12-25). Rather than "driving out sinners" and "destroying unrighteous nations" (*Pss. Sol.* 17:22-24), Jesus calls them to himself (cf. Mark 2:17), and embraces the fate of a vanquished royal pretender as the very means by which his messianic claims are sustained. Thus, to embrace the title son of David runs the same risks as embracing the title Christ, inasmuch as both carry expectations that Mark's Jesus will not fulfill. The titles are appropriate only when given their specific outworking by the particulars of Mark's Gospel.

Returning to the pericope of the grain plucking, and the son of man saying that concludes it, we have surveyed Mark with sufficient depth to maintain that the connection Jesus draws between himself and King David is significant: there is a parallel between them in the authority they have to act; however, the precise nature of their authority and the means by which it is attained and wielded demand attention to Jesus's own story. In this case, the similarities are sufficient that the idealized Davidic predecessor can be seen as playing a role that Jesus later takes to himself: Jesus can superintend his disciples doing what is not lawful, and make such an act guiltless, because he, too, is the spirit-anointed king in waiting en route to his coronation.

I turn now to the son of man saying itself, expecting that the nature of this latter claim will be congruous with the claims implicit in Jesus's drawing a parallel between David and himself. The authority Jesus claims over the Sabbath is predicated in part in the statement, "the Sabbath was made for humanity, not humanity for the Sabbath" (Mark 2:27).[81] This statement allows us to sharpen somewhat our understanding of Jesus's use of the phrase ὁ υἱὸς τοῦ ἀνθρώπου. The first thing to say is that Jesus here situates his own being ὁ

80. Wright, *Psalms of Solomon,* 667.
81. Cf. Müller, "Zwischen," 139-40.

υἱὸς τοῦ ἀνθρώπου and the authority this entails with the place of ἄνθρωπος in the created order. As son of humanity, Jesus is claiming authority over things that were made for the sake of humanity. In the question that looms over this entire study, of whether the Synoptic Gospel writers intend to depict Jesus as an idealized human figure or whether their depictions transcend the realm of the human and demonstrate that Jesus is divine, the logic of Jesus's claim places strong weight on the former. The reason why Jesus, as son of man, has authority over the Sabbath is because the Sabbath represents a construct that was made for the benefit of humans. If son of man here carries connotations of divinity, then the connection between God's gift to humanity and Jesus's authority over that gift is broken. He does not claim that the title son of man makes him the kind of heavenly being whose own actions determine what Sabbath rest looks like — a reimagining the divine act of rest from Genesis 2:2-3 (cf. Exod 20:8-11) that should shape humanity's Sabbath keeping. Instead, he places himself solidly on the human side of the divine-human divide, claiming that his authority is based on his participation in the human. Moreover, we find here another hint that son of man might contain allusions to the biblical story of primeval humanity, thus identifying Jesus, as son of man, in some way as an Adam figure. The deduction (ὥστε, Mark 2:28) can only be posited if in the conclusion Jesus draws about the authority of ὁ υἱὸς τοῦ ἀνθρώπου the word ἄνθρωπος carries essentially the same meaning as it does in the premise that states that the Sabbath comes into being διὰ τὸν ἄνθρωπον.

Having established that the title refers to Jesus's humanity, it is now crucial to recognize that in Mark's Gospel, when Jesus employs the son of man saying at the end of the pericope, this is a titular use, not a general aphorism. Here, my conclusions diverge from those of Maurice Casey because he has taken the general statement about Sabbath being made for humanity as an indication that the subsequent statement about the son of man is, also, general.[82] The notion that "anyone who is obedient to God has the mastery over the Sabbath which God made for him at the creation" is slightly too indefinite.[83] Casey's work leans heavily on the prehistory of the saying, suggesting that the Aramaic original establishes, broadly, the place of humanity as lords of the Sabbath. However, we have already shown that it is reference to Jesus that unites the son of man sayings in the Gospel. In particular, readers have already met with the phrase once before in clear reference to Jesus (2:10). Moreover, both of

---

82. Maurice Casey, *The Solution to the "Son of Man" Problem* (LNTS 343; New York: T&T Clark, 2007), 124-25.

83. Casey, *Solution*, 124.

these authority sayings fall within a series of conflict narratives in which the special role that Jesus assigns to himself creates tension between him and the religious establishment. If Jesus's followers have a right to break Sabbath in this pericope, it is only because they are in service of the Lord of the Sabbath, whose authority opens up the possibility that they might do what is not lawful.

Thus, while the generalized notion of Sabbath as a gift to humanity is present in the first half of the saying (v. 27), within the eschatological narrative of the Gospel, in which he plays the leading role, Jesus as God's agent is the one uniquely empowered and authorized to take up the vocation of primal, idealized humanity and function as Lord of the Sabbath. Casey's claim provides a way of understanding the son of man phraseology in this passage that is even further removed from the idea that son of man connotes divinity than the reading I advocate, and it would seem that all Christological freight is thereby removed. Given the specific application to Jesus, the notion that son of man here is a Christological title is one that is sustainable not because Jesus inherited it as a title from his Jewish context, but because Mark's Gospel demonstrates its titular force and its messianic connotations through the uses to which he puts it. It is the framework within which Jesus claims authority to act for God as embodied in Davidic kingship.

The parallel Jesus draws between himself and David as he claims authority to determine the actions of his followers, together with the claim that it is as "son of humanity" that Jesus exercises authority over the Sabbath, weighs heavily in favor of the thesis of this book, that Jesus is being depicted as an idealized representative human being. In contrast to the assertions of Boyarin, for example, the claim Jesus makes is wholly one of human agency. "Lord of the Sabbath" is not a claim to the divine name of Yhwh from the Old Testament, as the story of David intimates and as the statement about humanity's relationship to Sabbath makes clear. It is, instead, a claim to be a particular kind of human being.

This pericope provides us with a crucial piece of evidence that the actual meaning of the phrase "son of man" as "human being" was not lost on Mark when he penned his Gospel. Though he uses it as a title, this interaction demonstrates that it was not an inherited title that had lost all of its original connotations of indicating a human person. Though later uses of the phrase in Mark will draw in the figure from Daniel 7, the phrase is not used in this instance as a title whose content referred to a known heavenly figure, as one would expect if Boyarin's thesis held true. Quite the opposite. Jesus's claim to authority over the Sabbath is made on the basis of the Sabbath's being made for human beings and his own position as *the* son of humanity. This is a clear claim that exercising authority as son of man is wielding authority as the Human One, the human who has been specially chosen and authorized by God to rule the world on God's behalf. Because we have already established that the son of man sayings must be interpreted as a group and across the entirety of the Gospel, this particular focus on what is given to humanity as the reason for Jesus's authority proves that the notion of an idealized human is at least a necessary component to explaining Jesus as son of man in Mark. It is, in fact, a significant exegetical argument in favor of Joel Marcus's claim that the son of man is son of Adam in the Gospel, a claim to which we will return at the end of this chapter.[84] In this pericope, the decision of certain Bible translations to translate son of man as the "Human One" finds preliminary validation. Jesus acts with authority over this world because as the son of man he has authority over the things that are made for humanity's sake.

The first two uses of the son of man title in Mark's Gospel are a rich proving ground for Mark's Christology. Although the forgiveness of sins and the overall reluctance of Mark to affirm a Davidic Christology might be seen as indications that Jesus is more than human, larger contextual and exegetical considerations begin to fill in a different picture. As authoritative son of man, Jesus is enacting the royal rule of God in power throughout chapters 1–8.[85] This constitutes a narratively constructed claim to Christological authority, which is often a claim to exercise divine authority on God's behalf, but it does not constitute a claim to divinity or preexistence. As mentioned above, this authoritative advent of the son of man is depicted in chapters 1–8 as a ministry whose opponent is Satan. The power that Jesus claims for opposing his enemy is that of the holy spirit (3:28-30). The power and authority of the son of man is not a demonstration of his divinity, but of his baptismal anointing.

ii. The Sabbath Lord in Matthew and Luke

Both Matthew and Luke follow Mark in telling the story of the grain plucking and Jesus's statement there that the son of man is Lord of the Sabbath. Once again, Matthew's readers have heard an additional saying about the son of man. Those who first heard that the son of man has nowhere to lay his head later hear of the son of man being derided as drunkard and glutton for eating

---

84. Cf. also Borsch, *Son of Man*, 322-23.

85. That the messiah can be king only because of God's exclusive kingship is a notion that not only upholds various Old Testament claims about Davidic kings but pervades the *Psalms of Solomon* as well; e.g., 17:1, 3-4, 21, 34, 46.

and drinking (11:19). In striking parallel with the first son of man saying in this Gospel, the glutton accusation indicates that Jesus as son of man is one who is rejected by his generation. I take up these two sayings in more detail below. In the grain-plucking story, Matthew fills in details that Mark skips over. Whereas Mark says that the disciples were making a way (ἤρξαντο ὁδὸν ποιεῖν), plucking heads of wheat, Matthew adds that the disciples were hungry and eating what they plucked (ἐπείνασαν καὶ ἤρξαντο τίλλειν στάχυας καὶ ἐσθίειν, 12:1). This opens the possibility that Matthew sees the pericope teaching a principle of need trumping Sabbath, but it does not play out that way. The mention of hunger does, however, tighten the connection between Jesus and his disciples on the one hand and David and his band on the other, as Matthew relates the latter simply as ἐπείνασεν ("he was hungry," 12:3) in contrast to Mark's χρείαν ἔσχεν καὶ ἐπείνασεν ("he had need and was hungry," 2:25). Matthew also clarifies that the bread of the presence was not lawful for David or his followers (not just David) to eat (12:4).[86]

The concluding statements are where Matthew's hand comes most visibly to the fore. Matthew both eliminates the saying about Sabbath being made for humanity, while retaining the statement about the son of man's authority over the Sabbath itself, and includes additional lines of defense. First, Matthew adds a saying that affirms even more clearly than the David story itself that what Jesus and his disciples do should be construed as guiltless law breaking. He draws an analogy with the priests in the temple: ἢ οὐκ ἀνέγνωτε ἐν τῷ νόμῳ ὅτι τοῖς σάββασιν οἱ ἱερεῖς ἐν τῷ ἱερῷ τὸ σάββατον βεβηλοῦσιν καὶ ἀναίτιοί εἰσιν; λέγω δὲ ὑμῖν ὅτι τοῦ ἱεροῦ μεῖζόν ἐστιν ὧδε ("Or have you not read in the law that on the Sabbath the priests in the temple profane the Sabbath and are guiltless? I say to you that something greater than the temple is here," 12:5-6). Thus, the law as such does not determine guilt or innocence. Jesus's introductory formula, λέγω δὲ ὑμῖν, displays a claim to personal, "Christological authority,"[87] evocative of a similar move Matthew's Jesus makes in the antitheses in the Sermon on the Mount.

The next statement Jesus makes cites Hosea 6:6 — a text that indicates, in concert with Jesus's illustration about the priests, that the law (regarding the temple) is not the ultimate arbiter of guilt or innocence ("I desire mercy, not sacrifice," Matt 12:7). The statement regarding Jesus's superiority to the temple

---

86. Davies and Allison, *Matthew*, 2:311, underscore that here, as argued above with reference to Mark, the comparison between David and Jesus is at the point of the authority held by each.

87. Davies and Allison, *Matthew*, 2:314.

might be taken as an indicator that Jesus is, in fact, claiming divinity for himself. Later, as Jesus excoriates the scribes and Pharisees for their casuistry in oath taking, he offers a series of contrasts in which the former and lesser thing is made holy by the greater thing associated with it: gold and temple (23:17), gift and altar (23:19), temple and God who dwells in it (23:21), heaven/God's throne and God (23:22). Thus, a good case can be made for Jesus claiming the status of the divine who makes the temple holy through his presence.

In order to assess these verses, we first need to recall the prior instance in which Matthew's Jesus quotes Hosea 6:6 to his opponents. In the pericope immediately after the healing of the paralytic, Jesus calls Matthew to become a disciple ("follow me," 9:9) and eats dinner at his house. In reaction to the sordid crowd gathered for the meal, the Pharisees question why Jesus eats with tax collectors and sinners (9:11). Jesus's first reply is identical in Matthew and Mark: "Those who are strong do not need a doctor, but those who have maladies." To this Matthew's Jesus adds the command, "Go and learn what this means, 'I desire mercy and not sacrifice,'" before concluding in concert with Mark, "I did not come to call righteous people but sinners" (Matt 9:13; Mark 2:17). A couple of points bear pointing out. First, the repetition of Hosea 6:6 three chapters later indicates that Jesus's opponents had not, in fact, learned the lesson of Hosea that Jesus told them to go and learn. Second, both stories work within the assumed framework of early Judaism with regard to "sinners," and yet in both Jesus claims that his own work or presence redefines innocence and guilt. In neither story does Jesus say that his interlocutors have misread the law itself. In the first, he maintains that his own role is to transform those whom the law or social custom would condemn. Similarly, in the latter story, Jesus maintains that with him something greater has arrived that keeps the law's judgment from having the last word. Thus, it is not merely a principle of "mercy" that the Jewish leaders are to go and learn, but that this mercy is present and embodied in the person of Jesus. As Davies and Allison put it, "Jesus adds that the command to keep the Sabbath, although it is worthy of observance, is subordinate to a greater law, which is his own person."[88]

Does Jesus's ministry as the embodiment of mercy, thus marking it (or him) as something who is greater than the temple, then, push the reader's understanding of Jesus's identity beyond the realm of a uniquely authorized human agent and into the realm of divinity? Few commentators follow such a path. Wrestling with the significance of the neuter form (something greater than the Sabbath is here), R. T. France comments, "it is the authority of Jesus

88. Davies and Allison, *Matthew*, 2:315.

himself which is immediately at issue, but not so much Jesus in his own person as in his *role*, as now (in comparison with priest, prophet, and king in the OT) the true mediator between God and his people; such a role is some*thing* new."[89] Even the strong statement by Adolf Schlatter, followed by Graham Stanton, falls short of an assertion of divinity: "God is present in Jesus to a greater extent than in the temple."[90] Jesus is the one in whom God is present, and in himself he becomes the one in whom God's presence with the people is mediated. A final answer to the sense in which Matthew's understanding of Jesus as "God with us" (1:23) and the one who "is with you even to the end of the age" (28:20) will have to wait for the chapter on birth and resurrection narratives. Matthew clearly sees Jesus as one in whom God is uniquely present with God's people. The idea that Jesus is greater than the temple might be a clue toward a divine identity or it may be an indication that here is a messiah who uniquely mediates the presence of God as God's anointed agent. In and of itself, it fits within the idealized human paradigm constructed above.

In the end, Matthew (like Luke) removes the saying about Sabbath being made for humanity rather than humanity for the Sabbath, concluding the pericope with, κύριος γάρ ἐστιν τοῦ σαββάτου ὁ υἱὸς τοῦ ἀνθρώπου (12:8). The innocence of the disciples, and of Jesus, is due to Jesus's own authority. Both of the son of man "authority" sayings that Matthew shares with Mark focus the reader of the First Evangelist on the unique authority with which Jesus functions on the earth. The first clearly indicates that Jesus is acting with an authority given by God to another in the human sphere. The second draws on analogies with an anointed king and an anointed priest, making a claim to divinity unlikely.

Luke's telling of the grain-plucking episode is the shortest of the three. In the introductory remarks, he indicates that the disciples were not only plucking and eating, but also ψώχοντες ταῖς χερσίν ("rubbing in their hands," 6:1). As Joel Green has commented, this passage in Luke's narrative introduces a new stage in Jesus's Sabbath actions — he had performed a Sabbath miracle previously (4:31-37; cf. the discussion of Mark above).[91] But here for the first time Jesus encounters opposition specifically for his work. Also, as in Mark, this is the second time Jesus has used the "son of man" phrase, the first being

---

89. R. T. France, *The Gospel of Matthew* (NICNT; Grand Rapids, MI: Eerdmans, 2007), 461 (italics original).

90. Graham Stanton, *A Gospel for a New People: Studies in the Gospel of Matthew* (Louisville, KY: Westminster John Knox, 1993), 130; citing Adolf Schlatter, *Der Evangelist Matthäus: Seine Sprache, seine Ziel, seine Selbstständigkeit: Ein Kommentar zur ersten Evanglium* (Stuttgart: Calwer, 1948), 396.

91. Joel B. Green, *The Gospel of Luke* (NICNT; Grand Rapids, MI: Eerdmans, 1997), 251.

in the healing of the paralytic. In light of the previous use of "son of man" in a context where Luke introduces κύριος language to refer to God, the final saying, κύριός ἐστιν τοῦ σαββάτου ὁ υἱὸς τοῦ ἀνθρώπου (6:5), takes on additional texture in its meaning. This added texture, however, as discussed in the discussion of Rowe's work in my introduction, is not one in which Jesus "is" the ΥΗΨΗ/κύριος of the LXX. It is, instead, one in which God is so at work in Jesus that Jesus exercises on the earth the lordship that is rightly God's in heaven. This is the point of dispute about Jesus's identity that runs through Luke's Gospel and into the book of Acts.

iii. Conclusions: Sabbath Authority

The exegesis offered stands over against the assertion of Oscar Cullmann that Jesus's claim of authority on earth, specifically as son of man, is an incarnational claim.[92] In the assertions that the son of man is present with authority, there is a claim to playing an authoritative role, but the source of this authority is not, as in John, Jesus's preexistent divinity or sonship (though even in John the authority is derivative and subordinate). As Philip Davis has argued, "Mark seems to have understood the phrase in a fairly literal way, as designating someone on the human side of the divine-human dichotomy."[93] When the son of man comes to earth from heaven, as we will see below, it is not to be born the first time but to revisit the world that rejected and crucified him. In terms of the structure of Mark's narrative in particular, the first two son of man sayings encapsulate the first half of Mark's Gospel with their indications of Jesus's authority to heal and forgive, and his ability to authorize his disciples to guiltlessly act out of accordance with the law. This coordinates with the larger texture of Mark 1–8, in which Jesus is present as authoritative inaugurator of the kingdom of God.[94] Again, Davis is apt: "Here we see more deeply Mark's paradox: the son of man is the man who does what only God can do."[95] Together, these two son of man sayings lay the groundwork for a rich, idealized human Christology in which Jesus is specially authorized to act on the authority given to him from God, and in such actions plays in himself the

92. Oscar Cullmann, *The Christology of the New Testament* (rev. ed.; Philadelphia: Westminster, 1963), 159.

93. Davis, "Mark's Christological Paradox," 9.

94. For a brief overview of how talk of a coming kingdom of God in Daniel might be part of the historical preparation for Jesus to proclaim such an advent, see Casey, *From Jewish Prophet*, 58-59.

95. Davis, "Mark's Christological Paradox," 9.

role of God's unique agent that Israel's scriptures originally assigned to Adam, Davidic kings, prophets, and Israel.

3. SUFFERING AND RISING CHRIST

In chapter 8 Mark's Gospel takes a definitive turn toward Jerusalem and the cross. The three passion predictions take the reader on a geographical march from Caesarea Philippi (chap. 8) to Galilee (chap. 9), and then on the road to Jerusalem, before Jesus's arrival at Jericho (chap. 10). The son of man sayings take on a different content with this turn toward Jerusalem as well. It is in Caesarea Philippi that Peter makes his pivotal confession of Jesus as Christ, but it is also here that Jesus explicitly and plainly (παρρησίᾳ, 8:32) begins to reframe his identity around a forthcoming suffering, rejection, death, and resurrection (8:31). In addition, the move from depicting the son of man as one possessing unique authority (chap. 2) to depicting the son of man as one who must suffer before entering resurrection glory comes with a precipitous falling off of Jesus's miraculous deeds: in chapter 9 Jesus completes an exorcism his disciples could not handle (vv. 14-29), and in chapter 10 he heals a blind man (vv. 46-52). Then in chapter 11 there is the cursing of the fig tree (vv. 12-14, 20-24). The mass healings, exorcisms, and feedings fall away. This is an important reminder that the significance of the son of man sayings is not simply in their function as a self-referential Christological title, but also in their integration with the narrative as a whole. When the story is depicting Jesus's authority on earth, so too do the son of man sayings stake this claim. When the story moves toward the cross, so too does the content of the son of man sayings.

The second half of the Gospel, however, does not simply look forward to the coming cross. It also looks forward to the son of man's return in glory to gather the elect. This thread of the son of man story weaves its way through the latter half of the Gospel, and its first appearance at the end of Mark 8 is insepa-rable from the first suffering son of man saying. I thus turn to the sayings about the coming son of man immediately after the discussion of Jesus as suffering and resurrected. However, the prior appearance of the passion predictions is significant: the son of man who comes is the one whose prior existence was on earth. The mutual interdependence of the sayings is important in this regard as well: Jesus's statements about a suffering son of man indicate that scripture predicts a suffering son of man who is then glorified, and the statements about the returning son of man will show us where in the scriptures of Israel such a son of man is anticipated.

a. Reframing Both Christ and Follower

Mark's Peter makes the simple confession, σὺ εἶ ὁ χριστός ("you are the Christ," 8:29). Unlike in the story in Matthew, Jesus's response to Peter is not a glowing celebration but the mandate of silence Mark's readers have come to expect for those who know something about Jesus's identity (e.g., 1:24; 3:12; 5:39; 7:36). The reader knows that Peter's chosen title is one of which the narrator approves (cf. 1:1), thus making the command to silence somewhat puzzling. The riddle does not last long, however, as Jesus adopts another rubric for explaining his mission. Here we have a situation parallel to Jesus's trial before the high priest: confronted with the title χριστός, Jesus refracts how he might play such a role by using a son of man saying.[96] In chapter 8 the narrative subtly leaves the χριστός title neither confirmed nor denied by Jesus, as he redirects the disciples' thinking; in the trial scene, however, Jesus directly says yes (ἐγώ εἰμι) to the question of whether he is χριστός (14:62).[97] Thus, Christ is a correct title in Mark's Gospel, but one whose content must be determined by who Jesus is as son of man.[98]

The first passion prediction is Jesus's initial move to so reframe the significance of Jesus as Christ.[99] It focuses on the son of man's rejection by the Jewish establishment (τῶν πρεσβυτέρων καὶ τῶν ἀρχιερέων καὶ τῶν γραμματέων — the very persons who Mark says are gathered for Jesus's trial in 14:53). These Jewish leaders are implicated in the son of man's fate, as he will suffer, be rejected, be killed, and later rise (8:31). In light of this book's thesis that the Synoptic Jesus is an idealized human rather than ontologically divine or preexistent, it bears stressing that the son of man about whom Jesus speaks is hereby delineated as participating in that most limiting and in some ways most defining of all human experiences: death. Moreover, resurrection is typically an indication that a dead human being has been or will be judged before God. Although, for example, John's Gospel can reframe resurrection glory as a return to what was previously had, without such a qualification resurrection is not an indication of divinity but, instead, of a person's having previously succumbed to the dreaded fate of death that lies ahead of all humanity. Here, son of man is not code for "one who plays the role that only God can play in

---

96. Cf. Malbon, *Mark's Jesus*, 105-7.

97. On the connection between the confession and the Jewish trial, including the common refraction of messianic titles with son of man terminology in each, see Perrin, *Modern Pilgrimage*, 109.

98. Cf. Malbon, *Mark's Jesus*, 204.

99. Cf. Hooker, *Son of Man*, 113.

Israel's drama"; it is an indication of a Christology in which the human king must endure what only creatures can: death. However, the prediction contains an expectation, also, of an almost immediate resurrection, an indication that Jesus is not "merely" human, but is enduring death as part of completing a particular task, and entering a new manner of life, as son of man.

The next moment in the story, Peter's rebuke of Jesus and Jesus's response (8:32-33), forms an important bridge to the subsequent call Jesus issues, which draws together Jesus's vocation as son of man and the nature of discipleship. The mutual rebuking forms an anti-discipleship story. After the passion prediction proper, Peter takes Jesus aside (προσλαβόμενος αὐτόν, 8:32). This is the first indication that things have gone wrong: rather than remaining in the place of follower to which he was called (δεῦτε ὀπίσω μου, 1:17), Peter assumes the role of leader. Mark's description of the physical movements symbolizes Peter's (no doubt well-intentioned) attempt to lead Jesus astray. Peter not only takes Jesus aside; he also rebukes him. The need for Jesus to regain his proper role as Peter's leader continues as Mark tells us that Jesus rebukes Peter after Jesus has turned and seen (ἐπιστραφεὶς καὶ ἰδών) his disciples (8:33). They are still behind Jesus, positioned as "followers," while Peter leads Jesus aside. Jesus's rebuke calls for Peter to resume his rightful place, among the other disciples, as a follower: ὕπαγε ὀπίσω μου (8:33; cf. 1:17). The language of Jesus's first invitation to Peter is now reissued as a command in the face of Peter's satanic temptation.

This is the second direct confrontation between Jesus and Satan in the Gospel (the first is in 1:13), with indications elsewhere that Jesus confronts Satan with each exorcism (3:23-26) and with each word preached (4:15). It is also the last mention of Satan in Mark. In light of the previous chapter's discussion of Jesus's baptism as a symbol of his forthcoming death, at which time Jesus is anointed with the spirit as king, the connections between the first and last appearances of Satan are striking. Each comes immediately after Jesus has been identified with what are essentially equivalent messianic titles (son of God and Christ), each appearance comes after an indication that to be the Christ entails a destiny of death, and each appearance is depicted as a satanic temptation Jesus must withstand.

The end of Jesus's rebuke broaches the divine-human tension in a somewhat paradoxical way: οὐ φρονεῖς τὰ τοῦ θεοῦ ἀλλὰ τὰ τῶν ἀνθρώπων ("You are not thinking the things of God, but the things of people," 8:33). The paradox is this: Jesus as ὁ υἱὸς τοῦ ἀνθρώπου knows and sets his mind on the things of God, but Peter as Satan sets his mind on τὰ τῶν ἀνθρώπων instead. This underscores the significance of recognizing the self-referential nature of ὁ υἱὸς τοῦ ἀνθρώπου as Jesus employs the title. While the meaning of "human being" has not been lost, as we saw in the grain-plucking episode, and while humanness is a crucial component of the one who bears this identity, as we see in his fate of suffering, dying, and rising, Jesus is "Human One" in the idealized sense of one who specially knows and is empowered to enact the will of God. As with the representatives from Israel's story such as Israel itself and the Davidic king, the role of idealized human being is assigned for the very reason that humanity in general is not fulfilling the role of faithful ruler under God. Refusal to acknowledge the way of the messiah as the way of suffering and death is a demonstration of humanity's being ruled by Satan — the strong man Jesus has come to bind.

Having said that humanity in general is not up to the calling of the son of man in particular, we must turn now to the inseparable conjunction between the way of Jesus and the way of his followers. Although humanity as such has its mind set on a kind of leader that is not God's way, the followers of Jesus are summoned to not only recognize the divine mandate that superintends a suffering messiah but also to recognize that to follow such a Christ means to follow him on the way to the cross.

This is the summons Jesus issues in 8:34. He calls the crowd back together and, in parallel to the call to follow he voiced after his first satanic temptation (δεῦτε ὀπίσω μου, "Come after me!" 1:17), he extends a call to any who would come after him (εἴ τις θέλει ὀπίσω μου ἀκολουθεῖν, "If anyone wants to follow after me"). However, whereas the first summons was succeeded by a demonstration of Jesus's authority in his first synagogue preaching and exorcism, in keeping with the pervasive theme of Mark 1–8, this newly issued call proceeds immediately into the suffering nature of both Jesus's own mission and the life of following after him to which he is inviting his audience, in keeping with the crossward theme of Mark 8–16. When the son of man was establishing his authority on the earth (Mark 1–8), his disciples were shown this authority and given a share in it. When the son of man is enacting his mission to die on the cross (Mark 8–16), his disciples are told of this mission and invited in to a cruciform participation.

Here we see a point at which failure to recognize the way Jesus's humanity is entailed in Synoptic Christology can skew our reading. Simon Gathercole suggests that the saints are "spared tribulation" because of the death of the son of man.[100] This only can be maintained by introducing a rift between the son of man and the saints in Daniel 7, and between Jesus and his disciples that neither text sustains. Both the suffering of the son of man itself and the

---

100. Gathercole, "Son of Man," 371.

subsequent suffering of the saints are indicators of the coming, or inaugurated, eschatological upheaval.[101] The conjunction between the death Jesus has just predicted and the nature of true discipleship is underscored in the particulars that "following after me" entails: ἀπαρνησάσθω ἑαυτὸν καὶ ἀράτω τὸν σταυρὸν αὐτοῦ καὶ ἀκολουθείτω μοι ("Let him deny himself and take up his cross and follow me," 8:34). The way of the son of man becomes the way in which other human ones see to it that they attain to the salvation of their own lives. The paradox of Jesus's call to salvation through self-giving is epitomized in the statement ὃς δ᾽ ἂν ἀπολέσει τὴν ψυχὴν αὐτοῦ ἕνεκεν ἐμοῦ καὶ τοῦ εὐαγγελίου σώσει αὐτήν ("Whoever then loses his life for my sake and for the gospel's will save it," 8:34). The significance of this saying is found in its embedding its paradoxical claim within the narrative of Jesus as told by Mark. The saying is not a generalized aphorism about life coming out of death; instead, it is an indication that Jesus's own movement from death to eschatological salvation (in the form of resurrection, 8:31) is determinative for those who are willing to give up everything to follow him on the road of his self-giving. The good news and the identity of Jesus are inseparable, perhaps even hendiadys in this case. The reward that Jesus promises for acting like the son of man is not a transforming deification but, instead, a gaining of one's own life (ψυχή, 8:35, 36, 37).

The connection between Jesus's death and the kind of discipleship Jesus demands provides us with a hint in chapter 8 itself as to why Peter did not want to follow such a crucified Christ. The reason for this is not simply because he had a certain set of hopes for Jesus but also because he was making a related set of deductions about himself. If Mark 8 shows us that a crucified messiah entails cruciform discipleship, Mark 9 and 10 show us that failure to comprehend a crucified messiah comes hand in hand with self-aggrandizing visions of discipleship. In chapter 10 the third prediction of the son of man's suffering, death, and resurrection is followed immediately by the request of James and John to sit at Jesus's right and left hands in his glory (ἐν τῇ δόξῃ σου, v. 37). This typifies the failure of the disciples throughout chapters 8–16: they were able to participate in the authoritative ministry in chapters 1–8, but they desire the future reign of glory without the intermediate step of the cross.[102] The question they pose finds a dramatic echo the next time we read of Jesus's right hand and left hand. Those so positioned are the two bandits

---

101. Cf. Dale Allison, *The End of the Ages Has Come: An Early Interpretation of the Passion and Resurrection of Jesus* (Philadelphia: Fortress, 1985), 38.

102. *Pace* Casey, *Solution*, 131, who claims they "must also have understood" that their request would mean suffering and death for them. The failure to understand lies at the heart of Mark's narrative.

who are crucified alongside him (15:27). But we do not have to wait until the crucifixion scene to recognize that the answer to the disciples' request for glory is to reimagine discipleship in light of Jesus's own messianic work.[103] His rhetorical questions of whether the sons of Zebedee can drink the cup that he will drink or be baptized with the baptism he is to undergo are, themselves, indications that the glory these disciples are seeking is only to be had by the way of the cross. The previous chapter demonstrated the connections between baptism and the cross in Mark's narrative; the imagery of Jesus's cup is similarly tied to his crucifixion. The latter is most clearly in evidence in Jesus's prayer in Gethsemane that the cup be taken from him — a prayer addressed to God as father, underscoring that the cup represents Jesus's peculiar task as son of God to die as freedom-bringing messiah (14:36). The other metaphorical association of Jesus's cup with his death is in the Last Supper scene, when the blessed cup is called "my blood of the covenant — poured out for many" (τὸ αἷμά μου τῆς διαθήκης τὸ ἐκχυννόμενον ὑπὲρ πολλῶν, 14:23).

The question-and-answer session between Jesus and the sons of Zebedee then expands to embrace the rest of the disciples, who are indignant with James and John (10:41). Jesus's response indicates that the cause of the indignity of the ten was the same as the cause of the request made by the two: all are operating with a vision of leadership and greatness that has been insufficiently transformed by an understanding of Jesus's mission. Those who would be great must play the role of servant (διάκονος, 10:43), and the one who would be first must be servant of all (πάντων δοῦλος, 10:44). Mark's Jesus grounds this claim in his own special task as son of man — the final son of man saying in this section of Mark devoted to Jesus's journey to Jerusalem: καὶ γὰρ ὁ υἱὸς τοῦ ἀνθρώπου οὐκ ἦλθεν διακονηθῆναι ἀλλὰ διακονῆσαι καὶ δοῦναι τὴν ψυχὴν αὐτοῦ λύτρον ἀντὶ πολλῶν ("For even the son of man did not come to be served but to serve, and to give his life — a ransom for many," 10:45).

The "ransom saying" rounds off this portion of the story in several ways. First, it provides an interpretation of why the son of man must die. The predictions themselves indicate the events, but do not clearly explain their necessity. Jesus's death is seen as a ransom — an act that frees many from the possession of Satan (cf. 3:23-37). Second, in so doing, it draws together even

---

103. Thus, in my reading the passage works in precisely the opposite direction as that argued by Casey, *Solution,* e.g., 132. He argues that general beliefs about humanity within Judaism are being affirmed and thereby claimed by Jesus as true of himself, whereas I am claiming that these things are true first of Jesus because he is a representative figure and only thereby generalizable to his followers precisely because they are participating in the reign of God he brings about.

more closely the authority sayings of the first section of the Gospel with the passion predictions of the second. The death of Jesus is, itself, the means by which the enslaving authority of one master will be conquered so that a new reign can begin. Third, it deploys a titular use of the "son of man" phrase in a saying that clearly ties Jesus's actions with what is expected of his followers. As the glorified son of man saying at the end of chapter 8 already indicated for Mark's readers, Jesus who gives his own life as servant of all will return as the most glorified and judge of all — the last will be shown to be first. Jesus is διάκονος, and calls his followers to play the same part. The titular use of the phrase and the redemptive significance of Jesus's own death keep Jesus set apart as a unique character who enacts a change in the story that the other characters cannot. However, the imitation to which Jesus calls the disciples indicates that all he does for them in his unique role are things that they are called to do for one another, and the world, as those who understand that the reign of God has come through this particular person. The mutual dependence between Jesus's messianic task, delineated under the son of man rubric, and the call to a discipleship that reflects this task, suggests strongly that what Jesus does as son of man he does not do as a divine figure, but as a human figure who holds a position as king, "leader," or "first" among a people who are to follow his lead into the life that demarcates a humanity in faithful relationship to the God whose reign is coming. If the son of man passion predictions trade on a notion of Jesus's divinity, this connection is lost.

The final passion prediction and concomitant ransom saying fill out what is left unsaid in the intermediate prediction found in chapter 9. There, as in chapter 10, Jesus's prediction of his death leaves the disciples sufficiently perplexed that their next immediate thought is about their own greatness (9:30-37). In the earlier chapter, Jesus also indicates that the way to greatness is to be last and servant (ἔσται πάντων ἔσχατος καὶ πάντων διάκονος, 9:35). It may well be that this call to be last is illustrated in the immediately subsequent action, when Jesus draws in a child and says that to receive such a one in his name is to receive him, and to receive him is to receive the father (9:36-37). The upside-down nature of greatness in the kingdom Jesus proclaims is illustrated in the identification of the son of man with the child, who occupies perhaps the lowest rung within each stratum of the ancient pecking order. The call to a service-seeking discipleship not only follows after the passion prediction in the narrative; it is also given its very grounds in the passion prediction itself as that prediction demonstrates the unique nature of Jesus's mission.

Here we arrive at one the most significant reasons for recognizing the depiction of Jesus as idealized human rather than divine. Despite the fact that in the Christian tradition the most significant one-off, unrepeatable, and final event in history is Jesus's saving death, and despite the unique saving significance it is allotted in the story of Mark itself, locating the son of man sayings in a claim to divine identity undermines the connection that Mark draws between Jesus's messianic role and the roles Jesus assigns to his disciples. In all three passion predictions, the way of Jesus as the way of the cross is, at the same time, the way of faithful discipleship. As with the first set of son of man sayings, those referring to Jesus's authority, so too with this second set, one of the key dynamics unfolding in Mark's Gospel is that what Jesus does as son of man is paradigmatic for those who would follow him. Both sharing in Jesus's authority and sharing in Jesus's suffering are definitive of discipleship in Mark's story.[104] Jesus as the Human One dramatizes in himself what it is to be faithful humanity, and calls his human followers to participate in that way of being.

As a representative and idealized figure Jesus is demonstrating what life is to be for his followers. Martin Hengel's conclusions regarding Jesus as earthly son of man demonstrate the appropriate amount of restraint: "The earthly and suffering Son of Man are a cipher with which Jesus, in certain situations, expresses both his authority as 'eschatological proclaimer of salvation' . . . and his humility and tribulation, which ultimately lead him to suffering and death."[105] Throughout the Gospel, Jesus is re-creating the people of God around himself, setting apart a people marked by adherence to himself as an embodiment of the reign of God (e.g., 3:34-35). As the idealized Human One, Jesus demonstrates what it means to be the new humanity that is faithfully loving God and loving neighbor (cf. 10:31).[106] The extensive connections between Jesus as suffering son of man and his disciples as those called to imitate his life bring into sharper focus that Mark's son of man rescues the world as a human, anointed by God to be sure, but nonetheless enacting salvation from within the narrative, rather than coming into the narrative from without as is the case with John's preexistent son.

b. Matthew's Passion Predictions

Matthew and Luke each use son of man language in the scene of Peter's confession and the first passion prediction. For our purposes, Luke follows

104. Cf. Perrin, *Modern Pilgrimage*, 92-93.

105. Martin Hengel, *Studies in Early Christology* (Edinburgh: T&T Clark, 1995), 61.

106. The claims of Hooker, *Son of Man*, e.g., 140, that "son of man" is a corporate term are to similar effect.

Mark closely enough in all three passion predictions to not merit a separate discussion except to highlight his removal of the ransom saying in keeping with his broader soteriology (22:27; par. Mark 10:45).[107] Matthew's rendering of the first prediction, however, introduces a change and an expansion that are helpful for the overall framework for understanding how representation can function in the First Evangelist. Whereas Mark and Luke frame Jesus's question as, "Who do people (or, for Luke, "the crowds") say that I am?" Matthew uses "son of man," instead: τίνα λέγουσιν οἱ ἄνθρωποι εἶναι τὸν υἱὸν τοῦ ἀνθρώπου ("Who do humans say that the son of humanity is?"). Conversely, when Matthew's Jesus moves into the passion prediction proper he uses the pronoun rather than the "son of man" phrase (αὐτόν, 16:21). For the reader of Matthew's Gospel, this creates slight differences in understanding. First, it situates Jesus as *the* son of humanity next to a designation of others as humans. Matthew has used the phrase a number of times to refer to Jesus, so it may be that he here simply expects his readers to hear it as self-referential. However, the close connection between Jesus as son of humanity and the responses of humans may also drive the reader to recognize that what Jesus does as son of man he does as the Human One. Second, by making Jesus's question pertain to his title as son of man, Peter's confession of Jesus as the messiah is more directly equated with the son of man idea in Matthew than in Mark. Here, the title is not so focused on rejection and suffering, but includes as well Peter's idea that Jesus is the Christ, the son of the living God (16:16).[108] Third, Matthew famously includes a lengthy blessing on Peter before mandating silence. Peter's being given the keys of the kingdom of the heavens and his power of binding and loosing on earth having heavenly force are telling indicators of how Matthew envisions earthly authority functioning. Earlier, the crowds responded to Matthew's son of man by celebrating the authority God had given among people (9:8; see above). Here we see that Jesus who has been given authority on the earth can also delegate authority with heavenly ramifications to his human followers.

Matthew's scene thus becomes a richer, more complex articulation of Jesus's identity and the ramification of it for discipleship. As the son of humanity, among other humans, Jesus is Christ with authority that reaches to heaven, and the Christ who must die. Peter is given a share in this authority

---

107. The removal of the ransom saying, together with the content of the sermons in Acts and a few other pieces of exegetical data, points toward Jesus's death bringing about cognizance of guilt among Jews rather than fundamentally changing the standing of humanity.

108. See John P. Meier, *The Vision of Matthew: Christ, Church, and Morality in the First Gospel* (New York: Paulist, 1979), 110-20.

before he, along with the others, is called to die. Peter's participation in Jesus's authority underscores that Jesus's own possession of it is no indication that he is God.

4. SUFFERING FOLLOWERS AND THE GLORIFIED SON OF MAN

a. Coming with the Father's Glory (Mark 8:38)

The break between my discussion of Jesus as suffering son of man and Jesus as son of man returning in glory is artificial from the perspective of Mark's narrative. Mark has made the future coming of the son of man in glory the resolution of the narrative that runs from Jesus as cross-bearing king to the final judgment. In between Jesus's own ministry and death and the coming of the son of man with heavenly glory come the lives of people who will either accept the summons to a self-giving life like Jesus's, or be ashamed of a crucified messiah and his call to a cruciform following.[109] Bultmann perpetuated the idea that the visions of a coming and glorious son of man were originally statements about a coming rather than a returning deliverer, even someone separate from Jesus.[110] The peculiar switch from first person to third person in Mark 8:38 may be an indication of this: ὃς γὰρ ἐὰν ἐπαισχυνθῇ με καὶ τοὺς ἐμοὺς λόγους ἐν τῇ γενεᾷ ταύτῃ τῇ μοιχαλίδι καὶ ἁμαρτωλῷ, καὶ ὁ υἱὸς τοῦ ἀνθρώπου ἐπαισχυνθήσεται αὐτόν, ὅταν ἔλθῃ ἐν τῇ δόξῃ τοῦ πατρὸς αὐτοῦ μετὰ τῶν ἀγγέλων τῶν ἁγίων ("For whoever is ashamed of *me* and *my* words in this adulterous and sinful generation, the *son of man* will be ashamed of him, when *he* comes in the glory of *his* father with the holy angels").

However, the question before us is not the self-understanding of the Jesus of history but, instead, the Jesus of the Synoptic Gospels. Thus, despite the clumsiness of the redaction in the eyes of Bultmann and others, the readers of Mark not only know that the identity of the son of man is none other than the Jesus who is here speaking, they have also come to know this in passages where Jesus speaks of the son of man in the third person while at the same time clearly referring to himself. This was the case in both the "authority" sayings in Mark 2 and in the passion prediction seven verses earlier (8:31). If there ever was a time when the coming son of man was distinct from Jesus, then at very

---

109. Cf. Hooker, *Son of Man*, 118-19.
110. Bultmann, *Theology*, 1:29-30.

least by the time that *coming* son of man found his way into Mark's narrative he has been inseparably united to Jesus and thus comes as the *returning* son of man. This is the crucial basis for recognizing, as well, that to the extent that Mark's coming son of man is preexistent, his preexistence is on earth as a human before being raised and then returning in glory.[111]

To grasp Mark's conjoining of the passion prediction with the statement about eschatological glory, we need first to note that "passion prediction" is somewhat of a misnomer. In addition to predicting his passion, Mark's Jesus also predicts his resurrection in each of the three suffering son of man sayings (8:31; 9:31; 10:34).[112] Once again, Bultmann is helpful, if in service of a point he was not interested in developing himself. Assessing the state of the tradition as it appears in the Gospels in contrast to what he deemed historically plausible, Bultmann notes that in order for the earthly Jesus to associate himself with the coming son of man, "He would have had to count upon being removed from the earth and raised to heaven before the final End, the irruption of God's Reign, in order to come from there on the clouds of heaven to perform his real office."[113] Setting aside possible quibbles one might raise with when it is that God's reign irrupts and what "his real office" entails, we can nonetheless recognize that not only is Bultmann correct that a removal from the earth to heaven would be needed before such a return, but also that this is exactly how Mark's Jesus views his own future, as Bultmann himself acknowledges. Similarly for Matthew, Leslie Walck demonstrates another way of articulating the unity between Jesus on earth and Jesus the coming eschatological judge. By introducing the question of Jesus's identity to the disciples under the rubric of the son of man (16:13), and then mentioning the title in connection with the passion-resurrection prediction (16:21), and finally denoting that the son of man will appear in eschatological glory (16:28), Matthew has linked what is known about Jesus as earthly son of man in connection with what is about to be revealed about his coming future.[114] This pattern shows, among other things, that Jesus is depicted as glorious judge only subsequent to his suffering and resurrection.

The one who returns in glory in Mark's Gospel is none other than the Jesus who suffers and is then raised to heaven. As Edwin Broadhead observes, "the

---

111. Dunn, *Christology in the Making*, 88.

112. On the notion that the resurrection enables the son of man to return, see also Müller, "Zwischen," 141.

113. Bultmann, *Theology*, 1:29.

114. Leslie W. Walck, *The Son of Man in the Parables of Enoch and in Matthew* (JCT 9; Edinburgh: T&T Clark, 2011), 179.

contrasting images of lowliness and power which circulate around the Son of Man title are merged within the narrative itself."[115] The significance of this observation for the thesis of the current project is not far to seek: in Mark's story the son of man who returns with heavenly glory was first of all the human Jesus who suffered and was raised from the dead. Coming from heaven with heavenly glory is not an indication of preexistent deity but of having been raised from the dead. Dunn states the matter with clarity:

> There is of course a conception of what Hamerton-Kelly calls "apocalyptic pre-existence" — the idea that the one who is to come from heaven existed in heaven *prior* to that coming — but in the passages in question the thought is obviously of Christ's coming *again* subsequent to his exaltation, not of his first coming, so that no thought of pre-existence prior to Jesus's earthly ministry and no precursor of a doctrine of incarnation is involved in any way.[116]

Moreover, as we have seen in the previous chapter, on Jesus as son of God, the death itself is the pathway to messianic enthronement even as it is Jesus's quintessential messianic act. Thus, the resurrection of Jesus entails his session on the throne that he was mockingly killed for claiming. In the overall narrative of the son of God as son of man that Mark is creating, the returning son of man can return in such glory because he is the messiah and faithfully filled that role during his time on earth.

The connection Jesus draws between his own fate and the fate of his followers further underscores the significance of Jesus's humanness for his identity as coming son of man. The passion prediction of 8:31 resolves with an expectation of resurrection after three days. Thus, when in the subsequent summons to follow Jesus not only demands that his followers take up the cross but also promises that those who lose their own self will save it, the salvation in view is the eschatological salvation of resurrection life. Jesus thus indicates that the disciples who follow him on the way of death will follow him also in being delivered from death. At the level of the disciples' hope, they can anticipate salvation because Jesus has also been raised — within the narrative (as in Paul's letters) their hope for a future resurrection is of the same order as Jesus's own

---

115. Broadhead, *Naming Jesus*, 133.

116. Dunn, *Christology in the Making*, 88; citing Robert G. Hamerton-Kelly, *Pre-existence, Wisdom and the Son of Man: A Study of the Idea of Pre-existence in the New Testament* (New York: Cambridge University Press, 1973), 45-47 (italics original).

resurrection because he was the first human raised. If the son of man is a title indicating divinity, and the resurrection an affirmation of that divine nature, then the son of man's own movement from death to life ceases to function in this manner as a source of hope for his human followers.[117]

Within the narrative of Mark, the son of man who comes in the glory of the father and his angels (8:38) is one who participates in that glory because he has been saved from death by God. God did not leave Jesus forsaken (15:34) but returned and delivered him in the end. The vision of the returning son of man is not a vision of the divine coming to the world from without, it is, within the framework of Mark's Gospel, the vision of the one who having become last, least, and servant of all on the cross subsequently being made first, greatest, and Lord of all thorough his resurrection.

In Mark 8:38 the precise role that the son of man plays when he comes with heavenly glory is not spelled out, but he appears to have a decisive role in the final fate of humanity.[118] It is worth noting that though this passage about the son of man's return appears to coincide with the final judgment, Mark never says so explicitly, reserving his sole use of words in the κρίνω, κρίσις, κρίμα family for a later comment of disapprobation directed at the scribes who will receive a greater condemnation (οὗτοι λήμψονται περισσότερον κρίμα, 12:40).[119] Nonetheless, this passage indicates a series of eternal ramifications for the son of man's assessment of a person at his return. Following the call to lay down one's life "for my sake and for the gospel" (8:35), if one would save one's very self, verse 38 threatens those who are ashamed of Jesus with having the son of man be ashamed of them when he comes in glory. Thus, a tight connection is forged between clinging to earthly life (rather than walking the way of the cross), being ashamed of Jesus, and finding oneself on the wrong side of the coming glory. The word

117. Mistaking Jesus's resurrection as a sign of his divinity is a trap into which, it seems to me, Simon Gathercole falls when he claims that the resurrection was merely Jesus's "returning to his pre-existent condition" ("What Did the First Christians Think about Jesus?" in *How God Became Jesus: The Real Origins of the Belief in Jesus' Divine Nature* [ed. Michael F. Bird; Grand Rapids, MI: Zondervan, 2014], 114). This perspective counters the narrative development of Mark, the Matthean Jesus's claim that all authority on heaven and earth has been given to him (28:18; cf. below on the resurrection narratives), and Luke's Jesus's insistence that he is not a ghost but has flesh and bones (24:39).

118. Cf. Collins and Collins, *King and Messiah*, 151.

119. The absence of "judgment" language is noted by Morna Hooker as well in "Is the Son of Man Problem Really Insoluble?" in *Text and Interpretation* (ed. E. Best and R. M. Wilson; New York: Cambridge University Press, 1979), 155-68, here 162. The language of condemnation, κατάκριμα, is reserved for Jesus's condemnation at his Jewish trial (Mark 10:33; 14:64).

that the son of man speaks about a person is decisive in this final judgment.[120] Whether the precise role he plays is that of judge or that of sole witness, his word is decisive.[121]

The question before us is whether a narrative in which Jesus is, in some sense, the decisive agent or even judge in the final judgment would amount to an indication that Jesus has so encroached on the divine prerogative of judgment that he is being depicted as God. The answer is no, as the early Christian tradition developed a both/and approach to the final judgment in which all answer to God, standing before God's judgment seat, and in which, also, God's human representatives are the agents who execute the final judgment. A possible suggestion of this is found in the parallel texts of Matthew 19:28 and Luke 22:30, where the twelve disciples are told that they will sit on thrones judging the twelve tribes of Israel. This may, however, have the sense of an ongoing rulership in the coming kingdom rather than the sense of final judgment. I address these passages in more detail below. First Corinthians 6:2-3, however, clearly claims that God's holy people will judge the world and even angels. While executing the final judgment may well be a divine function, it is a function that can be delegated and was so interpreted in the early Christian tradition.

If exercising such a defining role in the final judgment is no firm indication of divinity as such, what are we to make of the sharing in God's glory that qualifies this return? Jesus describes the coming of the son of man as ἐν τῇ δόξῃ τοῦ πατρὸς αὐτοῦ μετὰ τῶν ἀγγέλων τῶν ἁγίων ("in [or, "with"] the glory of his father and with the holy angels," 8:38). To claim a participation in God's glory could be seen as a claim to divinity itself. One might even muster Second Isaiah as a witness to the idea that the God of Israel does not give his glory to any other (42:8; 48:11). And yet, things are not so clear-cut. First, it must be noted that the glory is not Jesus's own glory, nor is it the native glory of the son of man himself. The glory is derivative; it is God's glory resting on or accompanying another. Second, as we saw in the previous chapter in the discussion of the transfiguration, idealized figures (including Moses) can and did become bearers of the divine glory. After Moses requested to see God's glory (Exod 33:18) Yʜwʜ passed in front of him (34:1-8) before giving Moses the words of the covenant. And it was upon descending from the mountain

---

120. Cullmann, *Christology*, comments briefly on the place of the son of man in the final judgment, including its Jewish roots and possible Christological modulations (158-59).

121. Perhaps this is one reason why the ultimate enemy of Jesus within Mark's story is Satan, one whose role in the mythology of ancient Israel is to accuse people before the throne of judgment. They play opposite roles in the final judgment.

after the fulfillment of his request to see God's glory that Moses's own face shone (34:29-35). In Psalm 8 we find that God's glory is set above the heavens (v. 1), which would indicate a uniquely exalted divine possession; however, we also see that when God makes humanity "a little lower than God" (v. 5, NRSV), he "crowns them with glory and honor" (v. 5). Idealized humanity has God's glory bestowed upon it. Third, we saw a development of this idea of bearing God's glory punctuating the Qumran writings as they anticipated a future in which the righteous would bear "all the glory of Adam." Indeed, idealized human figures were regularly so depicted. Fourth, in the Christian tradition the bearing of God's glory is not reserved for God alone. Paul uses the idea of glory as something that humans as God's children possess (Rom 5:2; 8:21, 29-30). Also, in the annunciation of Jesus's birth to the shepherds the Lord's glory shines as it is mediated by the angel and envelops the hearers, but without any notion that either the angel or the shepherds are divine (Luke 2:9).

Fifth, and most importantly, the narrative of Mark points us in a different direction than the idea that this son of man figure is coming in a divine glory that is actually his own divine glory now on display. The phrase τῇ δόξῃ τοῦ πατρὸς αὐτοῦ clearly references God as the father of the son of man. With this, we have a clear conjoining of the son of man and son of God titles. This anticipation of the son of man coming in glory, and thus being clearly marked out as God's son, finds immediate affirmation in the transfiguration narrative that follows in Mark's Gospel. The previous chapter dealt with this scene in detail, demonstrating how it affirms the way of the cross as the means by which Jesus plays his messianic role on earth.[122] The scene of shining glory is an anticipation of the future glory the son of man will have as one who has been raised from the dead. The connection with resurrection occurs in two directions. First, the passion prediction that Peter has rejected, and for which Peter is being rebuked by the divine voice, includes a prediction of resurrection. Second, on the way down the mountain Jesus tells the disciples not to make known what they had seen until the son of man rises from the dead (εἰ μὴ ὅταν ὁ υἱὸς τοῦ ἀνθρώπου ἐκ νεκρῶν ἀναστῇ, 9:9).[123] This is the third use of the "son of man" phrase since Peter's confession. It serves as a hermeneutical key for retrospectively interpreting the previous scenes: the transfiguration is an anticipation of Jesus's future resurrection glory; this future glory as resurrected son of God is the same glory in which he will come as glorious son of

---

122. Cf. Malbon, *Mark's Jesus,* 205.
123. Hooker, *Son of Man,* 124-25.

man; and this coming resurrection glory is what Jesus foretold for himself in the first son of man passion prediction.

The idea that resurrection entails glorification has roots as old as its appearance in the biblical tradition. Daniel 12 anticipates that the wise who are raised will shine (יַזְהִרוּ, MT; φανοῦσιν, LXX) like the brightness of the firmament, like stars (v. 3). This theme is picked up in other literature, including the *Psalms of Solomon*. There, God's righteous judgment includes raising the psalmist up to glory while, conversely, bringing eternal destruction to his enemy (2:31). In the third *Psalm* as well, the eternal life of the righteous includes the glory light of God: ἀναστήσονται εἰς ζωὴν αἰώνιον καὶ ἡ ζωὴ αὐτῶν ἐν φωτὶ κυρίου καὶ οὐκ ἐκλείψει ἔτι ("They will raise up to eternal life and their life will be in the light of the Lord and will no longer cease," v. 12). The point here is not a claim that Mark knew or was building on a particular Jewish tradition such as *Psalms of Solomon,* but instead to demonstrate that the way the narrative depicts Jesus has a possible and clear connotation of a glorified, which is to say resurrected, human being that the immediate context of Mark also suggests is the future being represented. Neither the coming of the son of man in glory nor the glory that besets him in the transfiguration need be indications of divinity; instead, they function well as indications that the son of man can come in glory because, having first died, he has been raised and thus glorified by God.

The glorified and coming son of man makes two more appearances in the speech of Mark's Jesus, one at the climactic moment of the Olivet Discourse and the other at his trial. In each of these it becomes clear that the coming son of man is an allusion to the "one like a son of man" in Daniel 7. These subsequent scenes pick up on many of the same themes that manifest themselves in Mark 8: the relationship between the glory of the coming son of man and the faithful suffering of Jesus's followers, his glory, and the presence of angels. Each theme is developed in chapter 13, especially as that passage is brought into conversation with the text from Daniel 7 to which it alludes. Keeping these connections with Mark 8 in view will enable us to see how the clear allusions to Daniel 7 in the latter son of man references are integrated into Mark's overall narrative. They do not provide a suddenly clear realization that the son of man is, in fact, a heavenly figure in the sense of the divine God coming in human form; instead, they provide an indication that the heavenly figure coming to earth is none other than the authorized, suffering, and risen son of man who is messiah based on his divine anointing.[124]

---

124. Cf. Collins and Collins, *King and Messiah*, 172-74.

b. Coming to End the Great Tribulation

In the first episode where Jesus mentions the coming son of man (Mark 8:38), willingness to endure suffering and death for the sake of the gospel is followed by a promised vindication at the son of man's coming. In chapter 13 a prophetic narrative of such suffering culminates with the son of man's arrival in glory. As such, this passage assigns typical roles in an anticipated eschatological drama to Jesus's followers and to Jesus. Jesus's followers play the role of the people of God who endure the great tribulation that anticipates the coming final deliverance. Jesus plays the part of the agent through whom God establishes an eternal kingdom.[125] In Mark 13 the eschatological assize is the interpretive lens through which Jerusalem's destruction is foretold (e.g., vv. 1-4, 14-20), a destruction that Jesus has prophesied through his temple protest (11:12-23) and that he has linked to his own rejection by the Jerusalem leadership (12:1-12, which should be read continuously with the preceding narrative of the temple clearing and the questioning of Jesus's authority).[126] This suggests that the salvation promised in chapter 8 is not only due to an imitation or patterning after Jesus's own movement from death to resurrection but also to the disciples' participation in the same eschatological tribulation that began with Jesus's suffering on the cross. Here, Allison is particularly helpful:

> For Mark, then, the denouement has commenced with the passion of Jesus, which is thus "the first act of the end of the world." Jesus has passed through the time of crisis, and the disciples must follow after their Lord, his way being their way (Mark 8:34-38). The sufferings of Jesus and of his church together constitute the labor pains after which the new world comes.[127]

The idea that the passion of Jesus is relived in the tribulation predicted in chapter 13 finds further corroboration in the redeployment of language and

---

125. This generalized scenario can be found across various descriptions of apocalyptic eschatology in early Judaism (e.g., Dan 7:21-22, 25-26; 1 En. 47; 90:6-27). In such scenarios, God does not always use a mediator figure. Importantly, Allison, *End of the Ages,* has demonstrated that early Christians consistently interpreted the death of Jesus itself as the inauguration of this eschatological tribulation, even as they looked to their own suffering as a continuation or fulfillment of it.

126. These themes are well strung together in Hooker, *Son of Man,* 150-56.

127. Allison, *End of the Ages,* 38, quoting Martin Dibelius, *From Tradition to Gospel* (New York: Scribner, 1965).

images from chapter 13 throughout the passion narrative.[128] Chapter 13 begins with a prophecy of the temple's destruction (13:2), which becomes a central charge at Jesus's trial (14:58) and which may be indicated in the splitting of the temple veil (15:38). Jesus warns of the false christs who will come saying, ἐγώ εἰμι (13:6), and then claims to be the Christ using that very phrase (14:62).[129] The climactic command to stay awake (γρηγορεῖτε, 13:37), issued not only to the disciples but also to those who are reading over their shoulders (ὃ δὲ ὑμῖν λέγω πᾶσιν λέγω, "What I say to you I say to all"), Jesus gives to the disciples in the garden (14:34), only for them to fail (14:37-38). Indeed, the very fate he warns of in chapter 13, that the master of the house might return and find the servants sleeping (13:36), is what unfolds in the garden when Jesus returns to his disciples from his angst-ridden prayer (14:37-38). The predicted trials of Jesus's followers before both Jewish and Roman authorities (13:9) find their anticipation in Jesus's two trials, before Jewish and Roman authorities, respectively. In parallel to Jesus's betrayal by Judas, a member of Jesus's reconfigured family according to Mark 3:34-35, his followers are told to anticipate familial betrayal unto death (παραδώσει . . . εἰς θάνατον, 13:12). The darkened sun of 13:24 (ὁ ἥλιος σκοτισθήσεται) finds its parallel in the darkening of the earth while Jesus hangs on a cross (σκότος ἐγένετο ἐφ᾽ ὅλην τὴν γῆν, 15:33). In Mark's Gospel, the son of man who comes as the agent of eschatological deliverance is the one who has himself successfully endured the same eschatological tribulations of which Jesus warns his followers.[130] The figure who arrives as rescuer is the Human One who has first been rescued himself.

The turning point of Jesus's eschatological discourse in Mark 13 draws on Old Testament imagery of cosmic catastrophe from Isaiah 13 and 34.[131] Although neither is decisive with respect to the identity of Mark's son of man, who appears immediately afterward, the passage from Isaiah 13 is instructive with respect to the possibilities of conjoining cosmic divine intervention with

---

128. This list is based on the work of Paul J. Achtemeier, Joel B. Green, and Marianne Meye Thompson, *Introducing the New Testament: Its Literature and Theology* (Grand Rapids, MI: Eerdmans, 2001), 139; cf. Allison, *End of the Ages*, 36-38.

129. Norman Perrin, "The High Priest's Question and Jesus's Answer (Mark 14:61-62)," in *The Passion in Mark: Studies in Mark 14–16* (ed. Werner H. Kelber; Philadelphia: Fortress, 1976), 80-95, here 81-82.

130. On the eschatological character of Jesus's suffering in Mark, cf. Werner H. Kelber, "The Hour of the Son of Man and the Temptation of the Disciples (Mark 14:32-42)," in *The Passion in Mark: Studies in Mark 14–16* (ed. Werner H. Kelber; Philadelphia: Fortress, 1976), 41-60.

131. The possible allusion to Isaiah 34 will be left aside here, as it does not contribute substantially to the issue at hand. It contains further apocalyptic imagery, but without the explicit indication of whether it is God or an agent at work in the coming day of judgment.

human mediatorial agency. Isaiah 13 is an oracle against Babylon in which the divine voice recurs in the first person. In verse 3 we read, "I myself have commanded my consecrated ones," followed in verse 4 by "YHWH is mustering an army." Isaiah labels the coming catastrophe "The Day of the Lord," a day that will come as destruction from the Almighty (v. 6). This day of wrath is then described using the imagery of cosmic upheaval, especially in verse 10, to which Mark appears to allude in Mark 13:24, though the LXX does not match exactly.[132] The first-person singular forms return in the following verse, as the divine voice promises, "I will punish" (פקדתי, MT; ἐντελοῦμαι, LXX, Isa 13:11) and "I will put an end" (השבתי, MT; ἀπολῶ, LXX, Isa 13:11), continuing through verses 11-13. Thus, it is somewhat surprising to come to verse 17 and discover that this great day of cosmic catastrophe and judgment is going to be executed on Babylon when God raises up the Medes against it. Not only is the cosmic upheaval itself an earthly occurrence of geopolitical change, but God's role as judge and captain of the avenging armies also finds its realization in an earthly agent. The cosmic imagery does indicate that God is at work, bringing about a great upheaval on the earth, but it need not indicate that the figure who appears to execute the apocalyptic transformation is God as such. That role may very well be played by a human agent. In the case of Isaiah, the agent is a foreign people. This, indeed, is the reality that has been too often overlooked in recent debates about early Christology: the claim that God is acting cannot predetermine whether said action is implemented by direct divine action or through a human or angelic mediator. And as we have seen clearly in our pass through early Jewish material, it is highly unlikely that one could determine in advance that certain prerogatives are so exclusively reserved for God that these could not be executed by a human agent.

Acting as a decisive figure in a great apocalyptic moment is not sufficient to indicate divinity as such. Moreover, in the narrative of Mark's Gospel, the narrative arc of the son of man has already provided a means by which the coming, glorious figure comes to be a preexistent, heavenly deliverer from the perspective of those who will see him return — not by eternal preexistence, but rather through rising from the dead. This is analogous to what we saw above in regard to 1 Enoch. In the final form of the document, the son of man is Enoch, thus making his preexistence in heaven prior to his eschatological activities a form of life that has as its starting point the time in which the human being

132. Compare Mark 13:24b, ὁ ἥλιος σκοτισθήσεται, καὶ ἡ σελήνη οὐ δώσει τὸ φέγγος αὐτῆς, with Isaiah 13:10 LXX, which is a literal rendering of the MT: σκοτισθήσεται τοῦ ἡλίου ἀνατέλλοντος καὶ ἡ σελήνη οὐ δώσει τὸ φῶς αὐτῆς.

is translated to heaven after an earthly life. So, too, with the expectations that Elijah would come before the day of the Lord: he comes from a state of heavenly preexistence that has as its starting point the time when the human was taken up into heaven. As I turn now to Daniel 7, alluded to by Mark at this crucial juncture, the discussion will demonstrate that nothing in Mark's use of the text indicates that this resurrection glory is actually a restoration of what was Jesus's prior to his death, but with more added. Instead, God has restored to him his life of authoritative divine representation, only now he is not solely authoritative on the earth, but at God's own right hand in heaven.

The most important intertextual link between Mark 13 and the scriptures of Israel is the one that employs the son of man language itself, when the apocalyptic signs are succeeded by the advent of the son of man as described by Daniel: καὶ τότε ὄψονται τὸν υἱὸν τοῦ ἀνθρώπου ἐρχόμενον ἐν νεφέλαις μετὰ δυνάμεως πολλῆς καὶ δόξης ("And then they will see the son of man coming in the clouds with great power and glory," v. 26). As with prior Old Testament allusions in this section, the imagery appears to indicate its scriptural antecedent clearly, but the verbiage is not exact. The LXX reads, ἰδοὺ ἐπὶ νεφελῶν τοῦ οὐρανοῦ ὡς υἱὸς ἀνθρώπου ἤρχετο . . . καὶ ἐδόθη αὐτῷ ἐξουσία καὶ πάντα τὰ ἔθνη τῆς γῆς κατὰ γένη καὶ πᾶσα δόξα αὐτῷ λατρεύουσα ("Behold! One like a son of a human came upon the clouds of heaven . . . and authority was given to him, and all the peoples of the earth according to their kind and every majesty will serve him," Dan 7:13-14). Although the LXX translates the Aramaic more literally than what we find in Mark, inasmuch as both Old Testament versions mention the clouds before the human figure, Mark provides a more literal rendering of the preposition indicating the human figure's relationship to the clouds. The MT reads עִם־עֲנָנֵי in comparison with the LXX's ἐπὶ νεφελῶν. Here Mark renders the phrase ἐν νεφέλαις, whereas in the parallel allusion to Daniel 7 in Mark 14:62 we read ἐρχόμενον μετὰ τῶν νεφελῶν. This raises the question of whether or not Mark viewed the clouds as a means of transport. That such a mode of locomotion is in view has been one argument deployed to claim that the son of man figure is divine, both in Daniel[133] and in Mark.[134] Evidence to the contrary of such a conclusion might be raised from within the New Testament itself, as the resurrected martyrs of Revelation 11 are summoned to heaven and travel there on a cloud (v. 12). Mark, however, does not say that the son of man comes riding on the clouds, only that he comes with them. In the first saying of the son of man's glorious return, he comes ἐν τῇ

---

133. John J. Collins, *Daniel* (Hermeneia; Minneapolis: Fortress, 1993), 290.
134. Marcus, *Mark 8–16*, 908.

δόξῃ τοῦ πατρὸς αὐτοῦ (8:34). It may very well be that the nebulose advent indicates the presence of the father's glory rather than the means of the son's transport. Such a conclusion with regard to the clouds finds some support in the pairing of 8:34 with the subsequent transfiguration scene. In the latter, the son's glorious radiance is accompanied by God's own presence in a cloud (9:7); on the other hand, the singular νεφέλης appears in the transfiguration scene whereas the plural form occurs with the coming son of man.

Perhaps the most significant change is that Mark's replacing the generic "one like a son of a human" (ὡς υἱὸς ἀνθρώπου; כבר אנש) with "the son of the human" (τὸν υἱὸν τοῦ ἀνθρώπου). It is worth repeating, in light of recent debates and scholarship, that in making such an observation, I do not claim that the son of man was a preexistent or fixed Christological title. Instead, I am arguing that there is a genuine difference between Mark's use of the phrase in question and the manner in which it is used in his biblical antecedent. The significance of this point must be underscored: we have already discussed the various possible interpretations of the son of man figure in Daniel 7, but the way that Daniel's character will be understood by Mark's readers, if the connection is made at all, will be given a peculiar shape by the ways in which prior son of man statements have already begun to indicate the particular identity of the figure. The reader knows that Jesus is the son of man. The reader knows, further, that as such Jesus has unique authority to act on God's behalf (which Jesus, at times, can extend to his followers). And the reader knows that as son of man not only must Jesus suffer and rise again, but so too must his followers, and this suffering is a shared endurance of the tribulation that precedes the great cosmic assize. The question as we turn to Daniel 7 is, generally, what it might add to our understanding of Mark's Jesus as son of man and, more specifically, whether there are indications that the allusion to Daniel 7 might push us to recognize that Mark intends to depict Jesus as a heavenly figure of inherent divine ontology.

As indicated in the previous investigation into Daniel 7, the figure who looks like a human being is most likely a symbolic representation of the people of God. Beginning with the interpretation of the vision itself, even Boyarin concedes that the interpretive frame claims that the one like a son of man is "a collective, earthly figure, Israel or the righteous of Israel."[135] The interpretation of the entire scene indicates that the heavenly vision represents an earthly set of events.[136] The fourth beast is a thinly veiled reference to the Greek empire,

135. Boyarin, *Jewish Gospels*, 43; cf. 51.
136. The failure to account for this is a significant weakness in the famous definition of

and its final, small horn a clear reference to Antiochus IV Epiphanes. This final horn wages war against God's people (v. 21), a conflict later described as blaspheming God, wearing out the saints, and attempting to change the laws of Sabbath keeping (v. 25). Throughout the passage, the Israelites who are so oppressed are referred to as the "holy ones" (קדישׁין, ἁγίους, vv. 21, 22, 25). Thus, when we read, also, that the kingdom (מלכותא, βασιλεία) and authority (שׁלטנא, ἐξουσία) are given to the holy ones (vv. 18, 27), the earthly ramification is clear: the faithful Israelites are given a kingdom on the earth in place of the one that had warred against them.[137] To the extent that the larger context of Daniel 7 may be influencing Mark's presentation of Jesus, we might note in particular connections between Mark's authoritative son of man from chapter 2 with this coming and glorious son of man in chapter 13. Like the Danielic predecessor, Jesus in 2:10 claims to have ἐξουσία of a kind bestowed by God. And as argued above, there are implicit claims to kingship in Jesus's appeal to Davidic warrant for his disciples' transgression, claims that mesh well with the bestowal of a reign (βασιλεία) upon the vindicated son of man in Daniel. The entirety of Jesus's ministry sits under the initial declaration that God's reign (βασιλεία) has drawn near (1:15) — after Jesus's own anointing at baptism. This, then, leaves us with essentially two options: either Mark is depicting the earthly ministry of Jesus as the first advent of the preexistent son of man, or Mark is depicting the earthly ministry of Jesus as the time when God's holy one is worn out by the enemy of God's people antecedent to his enthronement in glory.[138] While on earth, Mark's Jesus claims the prerogatives of Daniel's

apocalyptic literature coined by John Collins: "a genre of revelatory literature with a narrative framework, in which a revelation is mediated by an otherworldly being to a human recipient, disclosing a transcendent reality which is both temporal, insofar as it envisages eschatological salvation, and spatial insofar as it involves another, supernatural world." *The Apocalyptic Imagination: An Introduction to Jewish Apocalyptic Literature* (Grand Rapids, MI: Eerdmans, 1998), 5. In several pieces of apocalyptic literature the transcendent picture intends to disclose the mechanisms behind earthly realities. I note, for instance, the repeated indications that the beasts in Daniel 7 represent kings "from the earth" or "under [!] heaven" (vv. 17, 23, 27). In Daniel, the future reality being disclosed entails the removal of Antiochus IV Epiphanes, likely by the Maccabean revolutionaries.

137. Boyarin, *Jewish Gospels,* 43.

138. Tuckett, "Present Son of Man," argues that the movement in Mark, as in Daniel, is simply from suffering to vindication, without an explicit move from authority to suffering to vindication. This, it seems to me, does not do justice to the nature of Mark 1–8 more generally, though it does helpfully draw attention to the son of man sayings in Mark 2 coming in contexts of opposition to Jesus. Moreover, it does not seem necessary that Daniel itself indicate a prior authority antecedent to suffering in order for Mark's Jesus to be depicted as a Danielic son of man who embodies such a pattern.

vindicated son of man. Is this because the son has arrived to put on display his preexistent authority and glory? Or is it a preview of what will rightfully and fully be his only in the future?

Two factors point decisively toward the latter option, that Mark sees the future return of Jesus as the time when the son of man comes from heaven and gives no indication that the earthly ministry of Jesus is the first such advent. First, in the immediate context Mark depicts the tribulation that the vindicated son of man will bring to a halt as the suffering of the holy ones spoken of in the book of Daniel. Second, Mark's Jesus says clearly not only that he must suffer, and not only that the son of man as such must suffer, but also that it is written that the son of man must suffer, die, and be raised. I discuss this second point in the following section of this chapter, where we will see that Mark reads Daniel 7 as prophesying Jesus's death and vindication as son of man. Here, I want to examine the significance of Mark's allusion to another crucial text from Daniel: the reference to the desolating sacrilege.

Mark 13:14 alludes to Daniel 11–12, indicating that the time of the desolating sacrilege is the time in which the tribulations Jesus prophesies will come about: ὅταν δὲ ἴδητε τὸ βδέλυγμα τῆς ἐρημώσεως ἑστηκότα ὅπου οὐ δεῖ, ὁ ἀναγινώσκων νοείτω, τότε οἱ ἐν τῇ Ἰουδαίᾳ φευγέτωσαν εἰς τὰ ὄρη ("When you see the desolating sacrilege erected where it must not be — let the reader understand — then those in Judea must flee into the hills!"). In Daniel 11:31 and 12:11 this is a thinly veiled reference to the altar to Zeus set up in the temple complex in Jerusalem by Antiochus IV Epiphanes (Gr τὸ βδέλυγμα τῆς ἐρημώσεως; Ar שִׁקּוּץ שֹׁמֵם; cf. 1 Macc 1:54: ᾠκοδόμησεν βδέλθγμα ἐρησμώσεως ἐπὶ τὸ θυσιαστήριον). An identical phrase is used in Daniel 9:27 to refer to the same event. Besides this one allusion, Mark contains other parallels with its Danielic predecessor. The idea that this eschatologically fraught suffering is developing in the temple complex, and around Jerusalem more generally, is reflected in Mark 13:14 (cited above) as well as 13:1-4; Daniel's scenario entails desolation of the temple as well as a Judean war (Dan 11:45). Moreover, Mark's prophecy that the time of which Jesus speaks will be the greatest time of tribulation the world has ever seen (ἔσονται γὰρ αἱ ἡμέραι ἐκεῖναι θλῖψις οἵα οὐ γέγονεν τοιαύτη ἀπ᾽ ἀρχῆς κτίσεως ἣν ἔκτισεν ὁ θεός ἕως τοῦ νῦν καὶ οὐ μὴ γένηται, 13:19) clearly echoes the same notion from Daniel 12:1 (ἐκείνη ἡ ἡμέρα θλίψεως οἵα οὐκ ἐγενήθη ἀφ᾽ οὗ ἐγενήθησαν ἕως τῆς ἡμέρας ἐκείνης). One final factor is worth mentioning at this point, though it pertains to the prior discussions of the returning son of man more directly: this is the eschatological scenario that resolves in the only consistently acknowledged reference to resurrection in the canonical scriptures of Israel.

This heightens the plausibility that Daniel's vision of the end is influencing the prior son of man discussion in chapter 8, where the son of man comes as those who acknowledge Jesus are given the eschatological salvation that mirrors Jesus's own. Together, these points indicate that the narrative of Daniel's eschatological scenario is influencing the eschatological discourse of Mark 13 in more significant ways than simply providing a stock of words and images from which to draw. Mark employs the Danielic *Vorlage* as a prophecy that will be fulfilled when Jesus as "son of man" brings to an end the suffering of his followers. Moreover, in Daniel 7 the son of man who is exalted is also the saints who have been worn down by the enemy of God's people. The network of themes points in the direction of Jesus filling the role of God's persecuted people prior to divine exaltation and receipt of a kingdom.

The preceding paragraph provides sufficient points of contact with Daniel 11–12 for us to conclude that Mark has conflated the visions of Daniel 7 and 11–12, and possibly Daniel 9 as well. The son of man figure from Daniel 7 appears in Mark 13 as the resolution to the tribulation that finds its anticipation in Daniel 12. But to say that Mark 13 conflates the various visions is little more than that Mark has understood Daniel well. In chapters 7, 8, 9, and 10–12, respectively, Daniel's seer has visions of the future in which a final king of Greece will be defeated through divine intervention. Mark has transformed the corporate humanlike figure of chapter 7 into a person who arrives from heaven to bring to a close the period of tribulation that precedes the vindication of the age to come. The advent of the son of man in Daniel 7 brings to an end the war (v. 21) that exhausts God's saints (v. 25), the same war that is described in Daniel 12:1 as the world's gravest period of tribulation. The arriving son of man in Mark is supposed to bring to an end the time of tribulation surrounding the destruction of Jerusalem and the temple. Mark's son of man arrives as a glorious, heavenly figure precisely when he arrives to bring to an end the period of great tribulation that entails the desolating sacrilege and results in the people's glorification. And the echoes of Mark 13 in the passion narrative of Mark 14–15 show that Jesus has himself played the role of suffering faithful person whose tribulations bring about the age to come. Although Jesus claims to be the son of man while on the earth, in his first coming Jesus is not depicted in Mark as one who arrives in the fullness of preexistent glory in order to deliver God's people. In Mark's Gospel, the son of man attains to this heavenly glory not through creation or preincarnational existence, but only through his death and resurrection.

The question of whether the son of man's authority over the angels indicates divinity can be much more quickly dispatched. My preliminary study, above, on idealized human figures indicates that it is quite possible for an idealized human being to be depicted as exercising authority over the angels. As we saw, there are numerous ways of envisioning cosmology on offer in early Judaism, including those that see humanity's creation for the purpose of rule having the potential to extend even to the angels, who were created for the purpose of serving (cf. *Life of Adam and Eve*). Moreover, Paul tells the Corinthians that Christians will judge angels, indicating an early Christian understanding of the possible superiority of idealized humans with respect to angels.

Mark's Jesus speaks of the coming son of man as one who is imbued with heavenly glory and power. Although at first blush this may appear to lend prima facie evidence in favor of Jesus having some sort of divine preexistence, on closer inspection Mark has made things much more difficult for those who would take up such a line of argument. This is because Mark not only tells us that the son of man comes with heavenly glory, but also that the means by which Jesus attains to such heavenly glory is through his suffering and death on the cross followed by his resurrection. Thus, in Mark's story the mere fact that Jesus returns with heavenly glory is more analogous to Paul's claim that those who have been raised will return with Jesus (1 Thess 4:14) than it is to John's claim that Jesus's heavenly glory is simply returning to what was his before (e.g., John 17:5). This is truly a return of the Human One who was present before, not the coming of a preexistent heavenly being.

c. Coming as Christ Enthroned (Mark 14:62)

The scene of Jesus's trial before the Sanhedrin and high priests (Mark 14:55-61) is rife with complexities as it draws on earlier conflicts between Jesus and the Jewish authorities, entails the climactic ownership by Jesus of the Christological titles that he seems to so carefully avoid throughout the course of the narrative, and indicates a blasphemy conviction for reasons that are difficult to parse. And yet, this complexity also enables Mark to put the finishing touches on the particular subplot that is the identity of Jesus as son of man in his Gospel. Is this, as E. Earle Ellis has claimed, the "manifestation of deity" that has been brewing throughout the story?[139] Or is it a final indication that Jesus plays a surprising role as the exalted, idealized, and human Christ?

---

139. Ellis, "Deity-Christology," 196. Notably, Ellis also takes son of God to be a divine title, so his interpretation of the Gospel operates within a larger, holistic framework of divinity Christology that I am arguing does not best interpret the data of the Synoptic Tradition. It is somewhat perplexing that Ellis goes on to explain Jesus's reference to Daniel 7 as an allusion to Genesis 1:26-27 (197).

Mark establishes the farcical nature of the trial as he indicates that its purpose is, from the beginning, to find some witness who might provide some reason for putting Jesus to death (14:55). Twice Mark characterizes the witnesses as false (14:56, 57). The particular content of these false testimonies concerns the destruction of a humanly constructed temple and rebuilding of the temple without hands (14:58). For later Christian readers, the problematic nature of this report is heightened by the fact that John's Jesus says almost this very thing when he clears the temple (2:19-21).[140] But even within Mark itself the reader is invited to puzzle over where the facticity ends and where the falsity begins. After reporting this testimony, the narrator indicates that not even in this did their testimony align (14:59), a statement that seems to suggest that here, if anywhere, the witnesses are close enough to stating the truth that they should be able to have their testimonies converge on the truth.[141] In fact, Mark's Jesus has not only verbally prophesied the destruction of the temple complex in the presence of his disciples (13:1-2), but he has also prophesied its destruction through the temple-clearing incident (11:15-17).[142] The temple is the focus of Jesus's week in Jerusalem not only as the place where he teaches, but also as the symbol against which his prophetic words and actions are brought to bear. The connections between the temple and trial extend beyond Jesus's prophecies, however. They also include the hostility Jesus's actions generate among the religious leaders. After the temple-clearing incident, the narrator says, ἤκουσαν οἱ ἀρχιερεῖς καὶ οἱ γραμματεῖς καὶ ἐζήτουν πῶς αὐτὸν ἀπολέσωσιν ("The high priests and the scribes heard, and they began to seek how they might destroy him," 11:18). This bears striking verbal and conceptual similarity to the beginning of the trial scene where the reader is told, οἱ δὲ ἀρχιερεῖς καὶ ὅλον τὸ συνέδριον ἐζήτουν κατὰ Ἰησοῦ μαρτυρίαν εἰς τὸ θανατῶσαι αὐτόν ("The high priests and all the council were seeking a witness against Jesus in order to kill him," 14:55). Seeking Jesus's death and Jesus's prophetic action against the temple are linked. The scenes are tied together by one other feature as well: the question of what claim to authority emboldens Jesus to make such predictions.

In chapter 11, when Jesus returns to the temple after having cleared it the day before, he is immediately confronted by the high priests, scribes, and

---

140. See James D. G. Dunn, "'Are You the Messiah?' Is the Crux of Mark 14.61-62 Resolvable?" in *Christology, Controversy and Community: New Testament Essays in Honour of David R. Catchpole* (ed. D. M. Horrell and C. M. Tuckett; Boston: Brill, 2000), 1-22, here 4-6.

141. Dunn, "Are You the Messiah?" 7-8, argues that the royal sonship language of 2 Samuel 7:12-14, when reproduced in 4QFlor at Qumran, entails an expectation that the eschatological son of God will build a temple, even as Solomon does.

142. Cf. Kirk, "Time for Figs."

elders who ask, ἐν ποίᾳ ἐξουσίᾳ ταῦτα ποιεῖς; ἢ τίς σοι ἔδωκεν τὴν ἐξουσίαν ταύτην ἵνα ταῦτα ποιῇς; ("By what authority are you doing these things? Or who gave to you this authority so that you can do them?" 11:28).[143] Jesus provides an informative non-answer by affiliating himself with John, asking where John's baptism came from: heaven (i.e., God) or humanity? (11:30). The implication that both Jesus and John receive their authority from God is affirmed in the subsequent parable, when Jesus tells of the various servants and, finally, the son who are sent to the vineyard (12:1-12). That Jesus gets his authority from God makes him, on this question at least, an analogue of John. He is, of course, depicted as one greater than John, and as God's son, but both share in common that the authorization for their acts — be they forgiveness of sins through baptism, or through proclamation, or be they the pronouncement of judgment upon the temple and its leadership — are functions of an authority given from heaven. Unless I am mistaken in the previous chapter, and son of God is actually, for Mark, a title of preexistence, the authority Jesus claims as temple prophet is the authority of the human, messianic king, who has been authorized to speak and act for God on the earth.

This exposition of the question of authority surrounding the temple is crucial for making sense of the son of man claim at the trial because the high priest's direct question to Jesus about his identity constitutes a demand that Jesus respond to the particular charge of prophesying the temple's destruction and replacement. He summons Jesus to defend himself, not by answering directly whether he said such a thing but by owning up to the titles that imply the requisite authority to make such a pronouncement. The first statement the priest addresses to Jesus is an open-ended invitation to respond to the charges (14:60); when Jesus remains silent, he asks directly, σὺ εἶ ὁ χριστὸς ὁ υἱὸς τοῦ εὐλογητοῦ; ("Are you the Christ, the son of the Blessed?" 14:61). This more pointed question invites Jesus to claim a title under which he might simultaneously assert the authority that has been in dispute between him and the religious leaders since he first claimed to be authorized to act for God as son of man (2:10). Here we also receive an indication that the son of God title in Mark's Gospel is perceived to be a Christological rather than divine title. To be the son of God is to be the anointed one.[144] That "son of God" here means "king" finds tacit support in the following and final use of χριστός in Mark's

---

143. Hooker, *Son of Man,* also makes the connection between the son of man sayings and this dispute about authority, but does so with regard to the first son of man saying by highlighting that in both situations Jesus responds to a challenge about his authority by asking an unanswerable question.

144. On the interconnections between the various titles, see also Müller, "Zwischen," 150-51.

Gospel: the religious authorities taunt Jesus on the cross, saying, ὁ χριστός ὁ βασιλεὺς Ἰσραὴλ καταβάτω ("Let the Christ, the king of Israel, come down!" 15:32). The question at the trial is not asking Jesus whether he claims to be God, but whether he claims to be, as Israel's king, God's authorized temple replacer.[145]

In a surprising change from the coyness that has typified Jesus's posture toward various titles throughout Mark's narrative, Jesus begins by affirming that the high priest has correctly identified him (ἐγώ εἰμι, 14:62).[146] The secretive posture is overthrown by an explicit affirmation of what the reader has known since the opening verse.[147] But as he does with Peter, so here also Mark's Jesus refracts the connotation of the Christ title with his self-understanding as son of man: ἐγώ εἰμι, καὶ ὄψεσθε τὸν υἱὸν τοῦ ἀνθρώπου ἐκ δεξιῶν καθήμενον τῆς δυνάμεως καὶ ἐρχόμενον μετὰ τῶν νεφελῶν τοῦ οὐρανοῦ ("Yes, I am, and you will see the son of man seated at the right hand of Power and coming with the clouds of heaven," 14:62).[148] Three elements of Jesus's response merit further consideration: (1) Jesus here alludes, once again, to Daniel 7:13 and its vision of the son of man coming with the clouds, though with some difference in wording from Mark 13:26;[149] (2) Jesus uses the second-person plural, rather than the third-person plural as in Mark 13:26, to describe those who will see the son of man coming in glory; and (3) this citation includes a possible allusion to Psalm 110, a passage Jesus had quoted in his challenge about David being the Christ's father in Mark 12:36.

First, the redeployment of Daniel 7 provides another lens for understand-

---

145. Expectations of a new eschatological temple, living up to the prophecies of Isaiah and Ezekiel, were relatively common in the Second Temple period (e.g., *1 En.* 90:28-29; Tob 14:5); moreover, the tradition of David and Solomon as temple builders was ingrained in Israel's story (1 Chr 22:2-5 and 2 Sam 7:13, respectively), even if the notion of a temple-building messiah was not a frequent expectation in early Jewish eschatology.

146. Collins and Collins, *King and Messiah*, 151, comment, "In one way, this saying is a turning point in the theme of Jesus's identity in Mark. He reveals openly that he is the messiah and will be the heavenly, coming Son of Man." Cf. Juel, "Origin," 452; Collins, *Mark*, 71-72.

147. Edwin Broadhead, "Reconfiguring Jesus: The Son of Man in Markan Perspective," in *Biblical Interpretation in Early Christian Gospels*, vol. 1, *The Gospel of Mark* (ed. Thomas R. Hatina; LNTS 304; New York: T&T Clark, 2006), 18-30, says that Jesus's ἐγώ εἰμι invokes the name of Yнwн, and that thereby the Christology of the Gospel is made explicit. However, in the ensuing list of what is explicit, he enumerates nothing that indicates identity with Yнwн: messiah, son of God, son of man, prophet (26). The observation by Perrin, "High Priest's Question," 81-82, that this appears to be a Christological claim per se (cf. Mark 13:6) rather than a claim to divinity accounts better for Mark's Christology.

148. Malbon, *Mark's Jesus*, 208-9.

149. Hooker, *Son of Man*, 163, regards this as the closest parallel between any son of man saying in Mark and Daniel 7:13.

ing the eschatology of Mark's Jesus. As variously noted above, Mark 13 begins with a prophecy of the temple's destruction, continues through a reiteration of Daniel's "prophecy" about a desolating sacrilege, and then resolves when the son of man arrives to cut short the suffering of God's people. Thus, the destruction of the temple, presumably at the hands of Rome in AD 70, forms a crucial piece of the narrative that the advent of the son of man resolves. But unlike the prophecy of Daniel, the problem with the temple in Mark's narrative is not simply that of an arrogant foreign king. In Mark, the temple is marred by internal factors long before the external factor of Rome comes into view, however dimly, in chapter 13.

Jesus first enacts judgment against the temple by taking up the words of Jeremiah, who scolded the temple leadership for treating the temple like a talisman, thus indicating that the time of the temple's eschatological restoration (depicted in the "house of prayer for all nations" of Isaiah 56) must await yet another temple after the current one is torn down.[150] The Jerusalem leadership wants to kill Jesus after he makes such an indictment (Mark 11:18). As noted above, they subsequently challenge Jesus on the authority he has to do such things (11:28). After reframing the question of authority, Jesus immediately retells Israel's parable of the vineyard from Isaiah 5 in such a way as to locate himself as the decisive agent rejected by the vineyard workers, thereby bringing the wrath of the owner upon the farmers. The narrator provides us with a summary conclusion to the parable: καὶ ἐζήτουν αὐτὸν κρατῆσαι, καὶ ἐφοβήθησαν τὸν ὄχλον, ἔγνωσαν γὰρ ὅτι πρὸς αὐτοὺς τὴν παραβολὴν εἶπεν ("And they were seeking to seize him [and they were afraid of the crowd] because they knew he had spoken the parable about them," 12:12). Here we see even more clearly that the destruction of the temple that Jesus prophesies has the temple leadership, specifically the high priests, scribes, and elders, in view (cf. 11:27). In particular, the killing of the beloved son cements the fate of judgment that is to befall the Jerusalem leadership.

As in the destruction of the First Temple by the hands of Israel's non-Jewish neighbors, so here also the prophet indicates that the culpability for the temple's destruction lies with the Jerusalem leadership though the means seems to be the Roman armies. Mark draws together the two classes of rulers; in the eschatological narrative itself Jewish leadership and Gentile leadership exercise parallel functions in persecuting the faithful (13:9). Thus, Mark's deployment of Daniel 7's returning son of man functions not only to bring to an end the defilement of the temple by Gentile hands, but also to culminate in judgment

---

150. On the use of Isaiah and Jeremiah in Mark 11, see Kirk, "Time for Figs," 514-20.

on Israel's leadership that it represents. The son of man saying in the trial speaks to this same series of events, already tied to the Jerusalem leadership, and entails them in it directly.

We turn now to the use of the second-person plural at the trial. In the Olivet Discourse, Jesus switched from second person (addressing his disciples) to third person when describing the coming of the son of man (τότε ὄψονται, 13:26). In the trial scene, Jesus tells the court that they are the ones who will see the son of man coming (ὄψεσθε, 14:62).[151] Confirming the suggestion that the glorious return of the son of man is a return for the purpose of judgment, those who stand condemned by Jesus and under the sentence of destruction, both for their leadership in general and for their treatment of the beloved son, will see the coming son of man.

I previously mentioned that cloud travel is not restricted to divine figures in early Christian apocalyptic scenes. In Revelation 11 a surprisingly parallel set of events occurs: human prophets, prophesying in the context of the destruction of Jerusalem and the temple, are killed (in the same city, we are told, where the Lord was crucified, only to rise after three and a half days [cf. below on the connections between Daniel's three and a half days and Jesus's passion-resurrection predictions]), at which time they are summoned to heaven, to which they travel on a cloud in the sight of their enemies (vv. 1-12). Traveling on clouds is no indication of unique divine identity in early Christian apocalyptic literature, and being seen by one's enemies receiving heavenly exaltation after being raised from the dead can be predicated of humans as well. Here we receive tangential evidence of the viability of the reading being advanced: repetition of the coming son of man here underscores that the Jerusalem leadership, as much as the armies of Rome, will have to answer to the son of man for the war against his people, and the persecution of the faithful in particular.

Moreover, by recognizing that the coming son of man stands not only at the end of the Olivet Discourse but here, too, at the culmination of Jesus's trial, we can state a bit more fully the eschatology that is driving Mark's Jesus. I noted above several ways that Mark 13 anticipates the events of the passion narrative. Here Jesus draws together the judgment coming on the defiling temple leaders with the previous words about the son coming to deliver from the defiling Roman armies, such that the two events of the trials of Jesus's followers and the trial of Jesus are inseparably linked. The overlap between Jesus's own trials and suffering at the hands of Jewish and Roman leadership and that of his fol-

---

151. Cf. Rudolf Otto, *The Kingdom of God and the Son of Man: A Study of the History of Religion* (rev. ed.; Boston: Starr King, 1943), 227.

lowers and the need to stay awake and wait for the deliverance that comes after the sun has been darkened are connections between Jesus and the disciples signaling that Jesus's own narrative is an embodiment of the eschatological narrative that will subsequently befall his followers. The call to "take up your cross and follow me" is thus seen as a call to participate in the great tribulation that brings about the age to come. The climax of that narrative of suffering comes with the appearance of the risen, glorified Jesus in the fullness of his father's glory. Other factors being equal, this parity of experience between Jesus and his disciples would indicate that his own eschatological tribulations on the cross are of the same kind as theirs, if quantitatively and positionally greater: they are the sufferings of God's faithful human(s) that bring this current evil age to a close.

This brings me to the third point. The current age is brought to a close with the son of man's appearance, and here the idea that the "son of man" phraseology embodies Jesus's Christology gains still further support. Not only does the glorified son of man saying follow Jesus's affirmation that he is the Christ, but it also contains within it an allusion to a psalm that Jesus had previously cited as indicating that the Christ is greater than David. The allusion is found in the insertion, ἐκ δεξιῶν καθήμενον τῆς δυνάμεως ("seated at the right hand of Power," Mark 14:62), which alludes to Psalm 110:1, previously quoted by Jesus in 12:36, εἶπεν κύριος τῷ κυρίῳ μου· κάθου ἐκ δεξιῶν μου, ἕως ἄν θῶ τοὺς ἐχθρούς σου ὑποκάτω τῶν ποδῶν σου ("The Lord said to my Lord, 'Sit at my right hand until I place your enemies under your feet'"). Thus, the insertion of the phrase indicating that the coming son of man will be seen at God's right hand (δυνάμεως being a circumlocution for God) indicates that he is none other than this Christ whom Jesus says is so much greater than David as to be called David's "Lord." In addition, the Christology of the psalm text as Jesus cites it indicates that the messiah's role entails lordship over all things and subjugation of all enemies. Conflated with Daniel 7, the advent of the son of man in glory may be an indication of a final subjugation of these opponents — including those who sent the son to his death.[152]

As so often throughout these son of man sayings, we are confronted with a text that pushes Christology beyond its normal confines, as Jesus claims for himself interpretations of his messianic vocation that cannot be constrained by the common definitions and expectations. Indeed, Jesus's final articulation of his messianic role comes in a picture of a glorious messiah who is Lord over all things as he arrives from heaven. And yet, this "Lord" of whom David

152. Collins and Collins, *King and Messiah*, 151-52.

speaks, according to Mark's Jesus in 12:36, is one who is distinguishable from the "Lord" who is Israel's God. The son of man who comes is not the "Power of heaven," but one enthroned at the right hand of this Power. The coming son of man is, himself, rescued from eschatological tribulation by being raised from the dead and as such is the individual on whom the corporate hopes of Daniel 7 have devolved.[153]

The claim of Chrys Caragounis that the Christology on display is a preexistence Christology falters at the level of timing.[154] He reflects on the claim at the trial thusly: "This implies that in Jesus's view the Messiah is David's lord, not so much on account of his resurrection or exaltation, but because he was conceived from the outset in Danielic fashion as a heavenly, pre-existent Agent of God's Kingdom." In order for the claim to stand, Mark's Jesus would have to be making the point here that what they will see is what has always been, or what was previously, the case. In the narrative sequence, however, the son of man glorified at God's right hand appears only after life, death, and resurrection. Mere appeal to Daniel, and the possibility (and it is only a possibility, and not the most likely one at that) that there the son of man is a preexistent agent of God, is insufficient for establishing a preexistence Christology in Mark. Better in this regard, due to his attention to the development of the son of man's plot in Mark's Gospel, is John Donahue, who claims, "The future revelation of the Son of Man (8:38; 13:26; 14:62) will be a vindication of this suffering as well as a final revelation of Jesus."[155] Norman Perrin takes the futurist notion of the son of man's appearance at God's right hand a bit further, suggesting that for Mark the first time when Jesus will be revealed as risen and vindicated is at the *parousia* — and that this explains the absence of resurrection appearances.[156] This fits more smoothly with Mark's narrated son of man Christology than does a claim to preexistent deity.

If Jesus does not here claim to be God, why then is he accused of blasphemy? In Mark's Gospel, blasphemy accusations come from failing to recognize Jesus as the spirit-empowered agent of God. I discussed above how Mark's first and last son of man sayings both come in stories where Jesus is accused of blasphemy.

---

153. Hooker, *Son of Man*, 167-71, suggests that this coming on the clouds, as in its Danielic predecessor, is a reference to Jesus's exaltation rather than his return. If correct, this would lend yet another piece of evidence to my thesis that the Synoptic son of man, even in his most glorious, is an idealized human being rather than disclosed as God; however, my thesis does not require this interpretation.

154. Caragounis, *Son of Man*, 225.

155. Donahue, "Temple, Trial, and Royal Christology," 71.

156. Perrin, "High Priest's Question," 93.

Moreover, it is Jesus's identity as son of man that should insulate him from such a charge. Whether the claim is that a person is God's agent or Godself, the difference between whether or not one has blasphemed is to be found in the veracity of the claim. For Mark's Jesus, accusations of blasphemy are followed by actual blasphemy from his opponents. In chapter 3 Jesus speaks of the unforgivable nature of blaspheming the Holy Spirit, a comment the narrator glosses by telling the reader that Jesus said this because they were saying Jesus had an unclean spirit (3:28-29). In the mouths of Jesus's opponents, blasphemy is a charge leveled against Jesus for claiming to be God; but in the mouth of Jesus, blasphemy is a charge leveled against those who fail to recognize that the spirit of God is the one who is at work in Jesus's authoritative ministry. Analogously, the accusation of blasphemy at the trial is followed by Jesus himself being blasphemed while hanging on the cross in terms that echo the trial itself: οἱ παραπορευόμενοι ἐβλασφήμουν αὐτὸν κινοῦντες τὰς κεφαλὰς αὐτῶν καὶ λέγοντες· οὐὰ ὁ καταλύων τὸν ναὸν καὶ οἰκοδομῶν ἐν τρισὶν ἡμέραις, σῶσον σεαυτὸν καταβὰς ἀπὸ τοῦ σταυροῦ ("Those passing by blasphemed him, shaking their heads and saying, 'Aha! You who are going to destroy the temple and build it in three days — save yourself by coming down from the cross!'" 15:29-30). These bystanders echo the failure of perception that marred Jesus's trial, not only in that they repeat false testimony but also in the implied denial of Jesus's authority to be the Christ who is authorized to speak and enact God's judgment against the temple. The dramatic irony runs deep as well because the readers know that it is in going to the cross and losing his life that Jesus does, in essence, save himself (cf. 8:35). Blasphemy consists of a mocking denial of Jesus's Christological identity, put on display precisely by his going to death on the cross.

Following the narrative arc of Mark's son of man, we see a movement in this specific theme that parallels the broader career of Mark's Jesus: from authoritative ministry to one en route to suffering, death, and resurrection, to a subsequent return in glory.[157] Inasmuch as this title constitutes a claim to exercising divine authority on earth, it is a source of opposition from Jewish leaders who see this as a violation of divine prerogative and, perhaps, their own place as God's agents on earth. To the extent that the title entails Jesus's walking the way of the cross, it is a source of opposition from his own disciples who see this undoing their own pretentions to glory. As a vital component

---

157. A similar, simpler, elucidation with respect to Matthew's Jesus as son of man can be found in Kingsbury, *Matthew as Story,* 103: "Through Jesus's use of the public designation of the Son of man, therefore, Matthew calls the reader's attention to the twin elements of 'repudiation' and 'vindication.'"

of Mark's eschatology, the son of man sayings draw on a narrative where the Human One's suffering is, like that of his human followers, an instantiation of the great tribulation that is brought to an end by divine judgment made on the people's behalf (cf. 13:20), and that is, in the case of Jesus's followers, superintended by the glorified son of man himself. As Mark has carefully linked each of these sayings together, the son of man across Mark's Gospel has as its scriptural antecedent the one like a son of man in Daniel, the human figure who comes to rule an eternal kingdom in the place of the terrifying beasts that precede him. Such an endowment of power accounts for the authority sayings in chapter 2, and his coming in glory accounts for the returning son of man sayings in chapters 8, 13, and 14. But this brings us to the one dynamic of the son of man sayings we have not yet explored. Jesus sees a divine necessity in his coming death as son of man. Where does this facet of Jesus's understanding of his son of man role come from? I address this question below, but first we need to survey how Matthew and Luke depict the son of man's future glory.

d. Returning in Glory, according to Matthew and Luke

When Matthew recounts Mark's first statement about the son of man returning in glory (Matt 16:24-28; par. Mark 8:34-9:1), he shapes the statement in conformity with his own recurring Christological theme that Jesus is the eschatological judge.[158] Rather than a more open-ended statement about the son of man being ashamed of those who are ashamed of him, as found in both Mark and Luke, Matthew reads, μέλλει γὰρ ὁ υἱὸς τοῦ ἀνθρώπου ἔρχεσθαι ἐν τῇ δόξῃ τοῦ πατρὸς αὐτοῦ μετὰ τῶν ἀγγέλων αὐτοῦ, καὶ τότε ἀποδώσει ἑκάστῳ κατὰ τὴν πρᾶξιν ("For the son of man is about to come in the glory of his father with his angels, and then he will repay to each according to that person's deeds," 16:27). Although this assigns to the son of man a role that is often played by God in Jewish literature, such a role of judgment can also be assigned in later literature to humans such as Abel (*T. Ab.* 11-13),[159] Melchizedek (11Q 13 II, 13), the deliverer of the Animal Visions (*1 En.* 90:20), or Jesus's followers (Matt 19:28; 1 Cor 6:2-3).[160] For the story that Matthew tells, Jesus's role of judging by what people have done has more to do with Jesus as the one who gives a new law on the basis of which eschatological judgment will be determined than it does on Jesus's being

---

158. Cf. Walck, *Son of Man*, 181.

159. Cf. Marcus, "Son of Man," 56-57.

160. Marcus, "Son of Man," 58n79, also highlights Adam playing such a role in *Gen. Rab.* 34:14.

ontologically divine (see esp. 7:21-27, where knowing Jesus and doing the will of the father are both equivalents of hearing Jesus's words and doing them).[161]

Matthew also makes a potentially important change to Mark's description of the coming kingdom. Whereas both Mark and Luke say that some will not taste death before seeing "the kingdom of God" (τὴν βασιλείαν τοῦ θεοῦ; Mark 9:1; Luke 9:27), Matthew says that what will be seen is "the son of man coming with his kingdom" (τὸν υἱὸν τοῦ ἀνθρώπου ἐρχόμενον ἐν τῇ βασιλείᾳ αὐτοῦ, 16:28). In Matthew 16:28, as in the later glorious return passages, the son of man is the object of sight. But perhaps more importantly, Matthew has qualified this kingdom as belonging to the son of man. This move parallels others Matthew makes, one in the parable of the wheat and the tares and one in the request of the two disciples to sit at Jesus's right and left hands (13:41; 20:21). In all three instances the future advent of Jesus is described in terms of the son of man's or Jesus's kingdom. Clearly, this is the same as the "kingdom of God" or the "kingdom of the heavens" that we find elsewhere in Matthew's Gospel, a fact that presses the attentive reader to ask how a reference to Jesus can be so substituted for a reference to God. Gathercole suggests that such a possession of the eternal kingdom by the son might suggest that the son himself is preexistent as well.[162] But such a suggestion is easily set aside once we recognize that God's eternal kingdom was regularly thought to be administered by human agents (see above, chap. 1). The final answer to this puzzle within Matthew's Gospel does not come until Jesus speaks his final words in the Gospel: "All authority in heaven and on earth has been given to me" (ἐδόθη μοι πᾶσα ἐξουσία ἐν οὐρανῷ καὶ ἐπὶ τῆς γῆς, 28:18). Matthew's coming, glorious son of man, no less than Mark's, is such as a result of the transition that ensues upon his resurrection. An idealized human Christology is fully capable of explaining this shift: the kingdom is the son of man's not because he is ontologically divine and thus interchangeable with "God" as the defining possessor of the kingdom, but because the kingdom becomes the son's when Jesus is exalted and given all authority in heaven and on earth. Because he is, at his return, the king of God's kingdom, the kingdom is referred to as his own.

The Jewish trial in Matthew contains the Gospel's final son of man saying, as is the case with Mark, whereas it is the penultimate occurrence in Luke (in the latter, the two angelic messengers at the tomb remind the women about Jesus's words concerning the son of man who would suffer and rise again, 24:7). Matthew's changes are slight. His Jesus is more evasive in answering

---

161. Cf. Broadhead, "Reconfiguring Jesus," 27-28.
162. Gathercole, *Preexistent Son,* 264.

the high priest's question about being Christ, son of God. In a reversal of what we see in Mark, Matthew's Jesus roundly affirms Peter's saying that Jesus is the Christ, while deflecting the high priest's question with σὺ εἶπας. πλὴν λέγω ὑμῖν· ἀπ' ἄρτι ὄψεσθε τὸν υἱὸν τοῦ ἀνθρώπου καθήμενον ("You say so. But I say to you that from now on you will see the son of man seated," 26:64). Matthew's Jesus refracts the question by answering in terms of his son of man identity, which will soon be put on display through Jesus's exaltation. With his use of ἀπ' ἄρτι Matthew curtails the possibility left open by Mark's Gospel that this second-person plural referent was an indication of what the leaders would see in the immediate aftermath of the fall of Jerusalem, as I argued was a serious possibility for Mark. Instead, the reader of Matthew connects this with Matthew's prior indications that the future, coming kingdom is one that is defined by the reign of the son of man after Jesus's death and resurrection (esp. 16:13-28). This sitting is the enthronement (cf. 19:28 and discussion below) that he attains to with his resurrection (cf. 28:18).[163]

Luke goes his own way with Jesus's experience in the hands of the Jewish leadership (22:63-71). No mention is made of the temple, and the only blasphemy charge is made by the narrator, who describes the derision Jesus faces from his tormenters prior to the trial in this fashion (22:65). As noted above, this falls under the rubric of a sin that will be forgiven, according to Luke's rendering of the unforgivable sin passage (12:10). The questioning before the high priest is peculiar as well. Jesus is asked to say directly whether or not he is the Christ (22:67). He declines to answer directly, saying that such claims had not been believed before and would not be believed at this point (22:68). Eliminating the visual verb (ὄψεσθε) found in Mark and Matthew, Luke opts for the verb "to be": ἀπὸ τοῦ νῦν δὲ ἔσται ὁ υἱὸς τοῦ ἀνθρώπου καθήμενος ἐκ δεξιῶν τῆς δυνάμεως τοῦ θεοῦ ("From now on the son of man will be seated at the right hand of the power of God," 22:69). Like Matthew, Luke has brought Jesus's exaltation into the immediate future. The reader of Acts learns for certain that this interpretation of the son of man sitting at God's right hand is a reference to God's enthroning exaltation of the crucified Christ (e.g., 2:32-36; 5:31; 7:55-56). Within the narrative of Luke-Acts, such a heavenly appointment comes to Jesus as he is raised from the dead to be the fulfillment of the promise of a Davidic king. In Luke's telling, the correlation between Jesus as son of God and Jesus as son of man is not one that Jesus himself makes. Instead, this is the conclusion that the whole crowd draws (πάντες): εἶπαν δὲ πάντες· σὺ

---

163. On this connection between the son of man's near-enthronement and his saying in Matthew 28:18, cf. Allison, *End of the Ages*, 49.

οὖν εἶ ὁ υἱὸς τοῦ θεοῦ; ("All said, 'Therefore, you are the son of God?'" Luke 22:70). As I argued in the previous chapter, Luke's "son of God" terminology appears to interweave Davidic, Adamic, and Israelite connotations. Jesus being God's anointed son is declared to him at the baptism and immediately given an Adamic significance by the genealogy that runs back to Adam the son of God (3:22, 38) and is clung to by Jesus as he overcomes satanic temptations to relive the failures of Israel in the wilderness (4:3-13), a series of three temptations that begins and ends with temping Jesus to doubt or to prove his divine sonship (εἰ υἱὸς εἶ τοῦ θεοῦ, 4:3, 9). At the trial, the final use of "son of God" in Luke's Gospel appears as an accusation on the lips of Jesus's accusers, their interpretation of Jesus's son of man statement, confirming for them that Jesus claims to be the Christ. Jesus's reply to this is, once again, ambiguous: ὑμεῖς λέγετε ὅτι ἐγώ εἰμι ("You say that I am," 22:70), perhaps turning the ambiguity of their statement, which in Greek could be either interrogative or declarative, into a witness on his behalf.[164] The conclusion of the "trial" indicates no particular charge that Jesus is guilty of, simply the perhaps ironic conclusion that no more witnesses are needed because "we have heard it from his own mouth" (22:71). Indeed, in Luke's story, Jesus is not convicted of anything worthy of death; instead, the court having determined that Jesus confesses himself to be a king takes him to the only place where such a charge might carry the death penalty: the court of the Roman governor. Thus, when they hand Jesus over to Pilate accusing him of calling himself Christ, a king (λέγοντα ἑαυτὸν χριστὸν βασιλέα εἶναι, 23:2), they are presenting the conclusions of what turns out to be a sort of Jewish pretrial hearing. In keeping with Luke's larger concern to underscore the continuity between the law, Israel's story, and Jesus, the leaders of Israel finally discover nothing against Jesus, no charge that might render him anything other than δίκαιος (23:47). From the trial narrative, then, we learn that in Luke's view to be the exalted son of man is to attain to the already exalted position of being David's promised heir, the true fulfillment of Adam's vocation, enthroned at God's right hand in heaven. As enthroned son of man, Jesus is the human king exalted after suffering and death.

5. HOW IS IT WRITTEN?

There is one son of man saying in Mark that we have not yet examined. Though it anticipates the death of the son of man, it is not typically labeled as one of

164. Green, *Luke*, 796.

the three passion predictions, perhaps due to the form of the saying itself. While descending the mount of transfiguration in Mark 9, the disciples (who have just seen Elijah) ask Jesus why it is written that Elijah must come first. This is, apparently, an allusion to Malachi's אנכי שלח לכם את אליה הנביא לפני בוא יום יהוה ("I am sending to you Elijah the prophet, before the day of the Lord comes," Mal 3:23, MT; ἐγὼ ἀποστέλλω ὑμῖν Ηλιαν τὸν Θεσβίτην πρὶν ἐλθεῖν ἡμέραν κυρίου, Mal 3:22, LXX; Mal 4:5, Eng.). Mark's Gospel has mentioned John and Elijah in the same breath on two prior occasions, when the issue of Jesus's identity has arisen (6:15-16; 8:28). This is one of several signals of an important link between John's power and authority and that of Jesus, some of which this chapter has touched on already. In general, though, the connection between John and Elijah has been more subtle, demanding that the readers recognize an allusion to Malachi 3 in Mark 1:2 or to Elijah's dress in the description of John. In Mark, there is no comment parallel to that of Matthew's Jesus, who tells his disciples clearly that John is Elijah who was to come (11:14). But Jesus here states that Elijah in fact has already come first, meeting a fate that was itself scripted in the ancient writings (Mark 9:12, 13). This is a somewhat peculiar statement to make regarding the prophet whose fame entails being spirited to heaven without facing death, and yet perhaps John's death by sword in Herod's house at the demand of Herod's wife makes good on the threat of Jezebel, wife of King Ahab, in 1 Kings 19:1-2. But for Mark's story and our own purposes, the connection between Jesus and this Elijah figure are more important than the specifics of the scriptural antecedent for John's death. First, Jesus identifies the fate of the son of man and the fate of John. More importantly, he responds to the disciples' question about it being written that Elijah comes first by asking them, in turn, καὶ πῶς γέγραπται ἐπὶ τὸν υἱὸν τοῦ ἀνθρώπου ἵνα πολλὰ πάθῃ καὶ ἐξουδενηθῇ; ("And how is it written about the son of man that he must suffer many things and be despised?" 9:12). For Mark's Jesus, the necessity of the son of man suffering and being despised (the former of which is the first aspect of the first passion prediction in 8:31) are a matter of scriptural anticipation.[165] Another son of man saying we have not yet discussed asks the reader to wrestle with a similar question of a scriptural antecedent. In 14:21 Jesus says, "The son of man goes just as it is written of him." Where, then, does Jesus find such biblical warrant?

Having already established the unity of these sayings in Mark's Gospel, and

---

165. Interestingly, Matthew eliminates this portion of the Markan story, opting instead for a simple statement that the son of man is about to suffer because of them (μέλλει πάσχειν ὑπ᾽ αὐτῶν, 17:12).

having further seen that Daniel's son of man forms the biblical antecedent for this figure, the most likely explanation is that Daniel itself will provide the warrant for a suffering son of man.[166] What I have shown throughout this chapter is that son of man is not a casual self-reference, but one that has a narratological coherence in Mark. Thus, the use of son of man as a self-referent at this point, we can postulate, should indicate a specific scriptural reference to the son of man who suffers. This sends us to Daniel, especially but not exclusively Daniel 7, as a first possible reference point.[167]

Based on the interpretation of the vision in Daniel 7, a strong case can be made for seeing the glorified son of man as none other than those who suffered under the persecution of the fourth beast. In the first interpretation of the vision, the son of man figure is interpreted as "the holy ones of the most high" who receive the kingdom (v. 18). When the seer presses for greater clarity regarding the fourth beast, the kingdom that these holy ones displace, he is told that the final horn waged war against the holy ones and was victorious over them until God rendered judgment in their favor and they were given the kingdom (vv. 21-22). The holy ones are thus both those defeated in war and the enthroned victors. In an expansion of the vision's interpretation, the seer is told that this last king will wear down the holy ones (v. 25) until his rule is taken away and given to "the people, the holy ones of the Most High" (v. 27). Thus, again, the interpretation of the identity of the humanlike figure who comes in glory to receive the kingdom is (1) the holy ones of God, who were previously (2) those defeated in war by the beast.[168] The advent of the glorified son of man, in Daniel, is not only an arrival but also the exaltation of a previously beleaguered people.

As Jane Schaberg points out, there are additional reasons to posit Daniel 7 as the Old Testament background to Jesus's passion predictions — which are not only passion predictions but passion-resurrection predictions.[169] Schaberg points to verbal and conceptual similarities with the passion-resurrection pre-

---

166. Here I agree with Boyarin, *Jewish Christ*, 136-37. Alternatively, Müller, "Zwischen," 144, suggests that the psalms of the despised righteous form the scriptural backdrop. The use of the Greek ἐξουθενηθῇ is suggestive, but Daniel 7 appears more likely to me, for the reasons I go on to discuss.

167. Cf. Hooker, *Son of Man*, 108, 132-34.

168. This observation is also made by Francis Malone, "The End of the Son of Man?" *DR* 98 (1980): 280-90, here 284.

169. Jane Schaberg, "Daniel 7, 12 and the New Testament Passion-Resurrection Predictions," *NTS* 31 (1985): 208-22. It seems that Gathercole, "Son of Man," 370, has independently arrived at similar conclusions.

dictions. The final clause of Daniel 7:25 reads: וְיִתְיַהֲבוּן בִּידֵהּ עַד־עִדָּן וְעִדָּנִין וּפְלַג עִדָּן ("And they shall be given into his hands for a time, times, and half a time," MT), rendered essentially verbatim in the LXX as παραδοθήσεται πάντα εἰς τὰς χεῖρας αὐτοῦ ἕως καιροῦ καὶ καιρῶν καὶ ἕως ἡμίσους καιροῦ. Here she finds three elements that are repeated in Jesus's son of man sayings, in particular that of Mark 9:31: (1) the use of the passive of the verb to "hand over" (יתיהבון, MT; παραδοθήσεται, LXX; δοθήσεται, Theodotus; παραδίδοται, Mark 9:31; παραδοθήσεται, Mark 10:33); (2) the prepositional phrase "into the hands of" (בידה, MT; εἰς τὰς χεῖρας αὐτοῦ, LXX; εἰς χεῖρας ἀνθρώπων, Mark 9:31; cf. Mark 14:41); and (3) the notion of deliverance after the third day — as the Danielic prophecy indicates three and a half days, so too Mark's Jesus consistently prophesies resurrection *after* three days (μετὰ τρεῖς ἡμέρας, 8:31; 9:31; 10:34) not *on* the third day, as we find in Matthew's and Luke's renderings of the passion-resurrection predictions (τῇ τρίτῃ ἡμέρα, Matt 16:21; 17:23; 20:19; Luke 9:22; 18:33; 24:7; 24:46).[170]

Schaberg notes as well that Jesus's question why the son of man must suffer and be despised (ἐξουδενηθῇ, Mark 9:12) might find partial answer in the book of Daniel as well. In the LXX, Nebuchadnezzar is told that his kingdom will be taken away from him in order to be given to one who is despised (ἐξουθενημένῳ, Dan 4:31, LXX) in his house. The kingdom is one compared to the rising sun, possessing power and strength and authority that formerly belonged to the Babylonians (Dan 4:31, LXX).

In each of these observations, but especially the first three enumerated, we find further confirmation of what I argued above, that Mark's son of man sayings constitute a thematic and narratological unity in his telling of the Jesus story, a unity that entails not only Mark's own linkages among the sayings, but also a common anchor in a Danielic predecessor.

I have previously mentioned two aspects of Daniel and Mark's reading of it that are important for coming to terms with his son of man sayings: Mark conflates the various visions of Daniel, and Daniel is the place in the Old Testament where one finds the most unequivocal mention of resurrection. The passion predictions are, in fact, passion-resurrection predictions. This son of man of whom Jesus speaks is not only glorified after suffering, he is raised after dying. Schaberg observes that in Daniel 11–12 resurrection comes to those who are faithful and wise during the persecutions suffered under Antiochus.[171] The movement of the "holy ones" from defeat to enthronement, characterized by

170. Schaberg, "Daniel 7, 12," 210.
171. Schaberg, "Daniel 7, 12," 212.

the son of man's exaltation in Daniel 7, is depicted in terms of the resurrection and glorification of the faithful in Daniel 11–12.

Before Jesus asks his disciples "how it is written" that the son of man must suffer and be despised, he has told them not to make known the event of the transfiguration until the son of man has been raised from the dead. The scene from transfiguration through descent down the mountain works as a narratological reversal of the son of man's path to death. The disciples see a glimpse of Jesus's coming heavenly glory, after which they are told of his resurrection, and questioned about why it is written in scripture that the son of man must suffer and be despised. Thus, without being either a passion-resurrection prediction per se or a prediction of the son of man's return in eschatological glory, the passage holds together these two dynamics of the son of man sayings as they appear in the latter half of Mark, demonstrating to the reader that the suffering and resurrection dynamic, no less than the return in glory, is a facet of the son of man's biblically defined role.

The allusions to the son of man that, at the end, draw the reader's eye unmistakably to Daniel's figure as the grid for understanding Jesus's identity as the coming one (13:26; 14:62) are present earlier as well (8:31, 38; 9:12, 31; 10:33, 45), providing the framework for understanding the necessity of his suffering, death, and resurrection. This connection explains why for Mark's Jesus the title of Christ is only rightly understood under the rubric of son of man.[172] This reading of Mark does not profess to answer the "son of man problem" as such, with its various connections to the historical Jesus and its accounting for the changes introduced at various points in the tradition. It does, however, account for the use of the phrase by Mark's Jesus: here is one figure in the Old Testament who is both a future, coming eschatological deliverer and one who has been abused, died, and been raised before that coming glory. Moreover, we have argued above in the discussion of son of man as Lord of the Sabbath that Mark's use of the phrase maintains some of its connection with the literal meaning of human being. Jesus claims particular prerogatives in chapter 2 based not only on his being son of man, but what God has made for the sake of humans (2:27). And Jesus's vocation to suffer together with its promise of resurrection, along with their eschatological overtones in the Gospel, indicate that Jesus enacts this son of man role in a way that his disciples subsequently participate in. The original interpretations of Daniel's visions are, in this respect, not superfluous: they indicate the vindication of a persecuted people. Mark's Jesus, like Daniel's son of man, is an emblematic figure, experiencing

172. Cf. Boyarin, *Jewish Gospels*, 139-41.

in himself what will be true for the whole. There is a real difference, of course, in that in Daniel the one like a human being and the exalted holy ones are one and the same, whereas in Mark the son of man demonstrates and determines the destiny of God's people who must identify with him by following him and recapitulating his work in themselves. And yet, the sum of the evidence underscores the viability of reading Mark's Jesus as a representative, idealized human being. What he does as son of man anticipates what lies ahead for his followers; and even his return in glory is a depiction of what is his by virtue of faithfulness to the point of death. As the son of man, Mark's Jesus is playing the role of idealized humanity, as Israel (and the Davidic kings, as Psalm 110 is joined to Daniel 7) was supposed to do in the scriptural story that, according to Mark, Jesus fulfills. In this sense, also, Jesus is the son of man, not merely as the coming eschatological figure, but as the Human One who fulfills humanity's twin vocations of fidelity to God in the face of persecution and death and, perhaps even more importantly for Mark's narrative, ruling the world on God's behalf. This is a further deduction we can draw, both from Mark's Gospel itself and from Daniel's vision of the coming of one who looks like a human being.

C. THE SON OF MAN OUTSIDE MARK

I turn now to assess the son of man sayings found in Matthew and Luke. Most, but not all, of the following sayings are part of the double tradition. Here I meet with the challenge of attempting to honor the particular narratives of each Gospel writer, while covering a large quantity of material. Thus, I attempt to keep the discussion focused on how these sayings help inform the Christologies of the two books in question. Specifically, I ask whether the sayings point toward a divine or preexistence Christology, or whether they are best read as indicating the role played by an idealized human being.

1. SON OF MAN ON EARTH

Christopher Tuckett has argued that the location of the first two son of man sayings in Mark's Gospel within controversy stories has been too readily overlooked — by so placing the sayings Mark is showing even here that to be son of man is to be rejected.[173] Although I do not ultimately agree that these first

---

173. Tuckett, "Son of Man."

two stories are *not* about the son of man's particular authority, his point that they intimate the son of man's rejection is well made and enriches our understanding of those stories. The son of man stories form a unified whole and have to be read together — the authoritative son of man is the same one who will be rejected and, importantly, who will return in glory. At this particular juncture of my study, his observations are helpful in providing a link for several of the son of man sayings in Matthew and Luke. As Tuckett demonstrates, a considerable amount of the weight they bear indicates that Jesus as son of man is one whose life is marked by suffering and rejection.[174] The first son of man sayings in both Matthew and Luke confirm this.

Matthew's first son of man saying sets the tone that Tuckett suggests. Prior to Jesus's healing of the paralytic, Matthew tells the stories of two would-be disciples (8:18-22; par. Luke 9:57-60). The first is, in Matthew's telling, a scribe, who professes willingness to follow Jesus wherever he goes (8:19; par. Luke 9:57, where the man is simply called τις).[175] Jesus's response is that in contrast to foxes and birds, the son of man has no place to lay his head (ὁ δὲ υἱὸς τοῦ ἀνθρώπου οὐκ ἔχει ποῦ τὴν κεφαλὴν κλίνῃ, 8:20; par. Luke 9:58). Tuckett summarizes the meaning of the saying thus: "All that is said about the Son of Man is that he is homeless . . . it is a statement about Jesus's own life-style and the consequences which a commitment to Jesus' cause will bring . . . it is about the cost of discipleship, to be shared by Jesus and the would-be disciple. Thus again 'Son of Man' is used in a saying which refers to Jesus as one who arouses opposition and hostility."[176]

Although the references to opposition and hostility perhaps need to be read between the lines at this point in the story, the first time Matthew's readers hear of the son of man the context is one in which the figure could not be more earthly. Coming as it does in response to a would-be disciple, we see, also, that this saying (like the cross-bearing sayings later) indicates that the life of the son of man determines the quality of the lives of those who would follow him.[177] For the readers of Luke, this saying comes after the son of man has already been prophesied as having rejection and death ahead of him. This saying thus functions as another strong indicator that

---

174. Tuckett, "Son of Man," 67-70.

175. Dovetailing with the thesis of my work, Petr Pokorný, *Theologie der lukanischen Schriften* (Göttingen: Vandenhoeck & Ruprecht, 1996), 111, claims of the Lukan version, "Dieser Satz steht am Anfang der Entwicklung des Menschensohntitels als einer Bezeichnung für die menschliche Natur des Gottessohnes."

176. Tuckett, "Son of Man," 68.

177. Cf. Hare, *Son of Man Tradition*, 139-40.

the life of Jesus on earth is one of hardship and rejection — and will be so, as well, for his disciples.[178]

Luke's Jesus, like Mark's, first uses the son of man sayings in the two authority sayings (5:24; 6:5). The next usage is in Luke's version of the persecution beatitude (Luke 6:22; par. Matt 5:11, though Matthew uses the pronoun μου rather than "son of man"): "Blessed are you when people hate you and when they exclude you and when they insult you and cast out your name as evil for the sake of the son of man" (μακάριοί ἐστε ὅταν μισήσωσιν ὑμᾶς οἱ ἄνθρωποι καὶ ὅταν ἀφορίσωσιν ὑμᾶς καὶ ὀνειδίσωσιν καὶ ἐκβάλωσιν τὸ ὄνομα ὑμῶν ὡς πονηρὸν ἕνεκα τοῦ υἱοῦ τοῦ ἀνθρώπου). This beatitude, like the others, participates in a schema of eschatological reversal. Persecution here and now entails a promise of great reward "in heaven" (Luke 6:23). In this case, the particular cause of the suffering is fidelity to the son of man. Jesus intimates that this places his followers on the side of God over against those who oppose God's people when he compares such suffering to the afflictions of the prophets of old (6:23). To be a true prophet is to be met with opposition rather than praise (cf. 6:26). In Luke's narrative, this prophetic fate befalls Jesus before it befalls his followers. The comparison with prophets is one that underscores how the son of man is explicable by appeal to idealized human figures from Israel's past. This saying, too, indicates that as son of man Jesus is one who suffers rejection from his fellow people. Again, Tuckett is to the point: "the primary concern is with the consequences of following the Son of Man as involving suffering and persecution. Hence this saying too binds together the motif of suffering and the term 'Son of Man,' even though it is not explicitly stated here that the Son of Man himself is a suffering figure."[179]

The necessity of such rejection as a prophet is reflected in the "damned if you do, damned if you don't" son of man saying that appears in Matthew 11:18-19 and Luke 7:33-35. John and Jesus are each rejected, John accused of having a demon because he neither eats nor drinks, the son of man condemned as a glutton and a drunk and a friend of tax gatherers and sinners. In both Gospels, Jesus concludes with a saying about wisdom being vindicated. In Matthew, wisdom is vindicated by her works (11:19); in Luke, by all her children (7:35). The overall thrust of the son of man saying is that as son of man Jesus is rejected by his community, even as John the Baptist was. Thus, the verse fits

178. Caragounis, *Son of Man*, 175-79, argues that this is an allusion to Daniel 2, 4, where refuge for birds and animals is imagery indicative of the kingdoms God will uproot. The suggestion is intriguing, but its resolution does not influence the divine versus human Christology question on which this study is focused.

179. Tuckett, "Son of Man," 69.

neatly into the framework of Jesus as a kind of prophetic figure, rejected by the people, and thus in keeping with the rejection motif that recurs so frequently within the son of man sayings.[180] Such rejection links the son of man with God but does not unite them under a single identity. Rather, because the son of man is God's agent, rejection of the one sent is tantamount to rejection of the sender, even as rejection of the prophets of old was tantamount to reject-ing God. Moreover, the indication that the son of man has come (ἦλθεν, Matt 11:19; ἐλήλυθεν, Luke 7:34) is no indication of preexistence, since identical "has come" verb forms are used in each Gospel to refer to John the Baptist in the immediately antecedent sentences.[181] The reference to wisdom here does not force the pericope into any sort of preexistent wisdom Christology inasmuch as both Jesus and John are enacting the way of wisdom that is rejected by this generation but that will find ultimate vindication.

The idea that Jesus, as son of man, finds himself on the outs with his con-temporaries for feasting with the wrong people (tax gatherers and sinners) finds expression in the Zacchaeus story as well. In response to Jesus's self-invitation to the chief tax collector's (ἀρχιτελώνης) house, the people grumble at his going to stay with a sinful man (ἁμαρτωλῷ ἀνδρί, Luke 19:7). Thus, Zacchaeus embodies in himself the twin associations of which Jesus is ac-cused in the previously discussed son of man saying: friend of tax collectors and sinners. Upon Zacchaeus's declaration of repentance and restoration, Je-sus proclaims that salvation has come to the house of this son of Abraham, "For the son of man came to seek and to save the lost" (ἦλθεν γὰρ ὁ υἱὸς τοῦ ἀνθρώπου ζητῆσαι καὶ σῶσαι τὸ ἀπολωλός, 19:10). Here we have an indica-tion of the son of man's salvific mission, and a taste of how that very mission creates opposition, but no indication that being son of man entails any sort of preexistence or deity.

Jesus's uses of the "son of man" phrase continue to be self-referential and to indicate that the life of Jesus is one of suffering and rejection even as they highlight various aspects of his mission. None of this pushes toward a read-ing of the phrase that might call into question the sufficiency of an idealized human paradigm. Indeed, both the associations with suffering and death and

180. Cf. Dunn, *Christology in the Making*, 88-89. The notion that the son of man came eating and drinking is a generalizable statement, as Casey, *Solution*, claims, renders the passage incomprehensible. The point is that Jesus's normal way of life, or even his feasting, stands in contrast to John's asceticism. Casey maintains that there is a clear reference to Jesus himself (139), but this makes the earlier claim unnecessary if not forced.

181. Hare, *Son of Man Tradition*, 56, 145; Collins and Collins, *King and Messiah*, 123-26; *pace* Gathercole, *Preexistent Son*, 259.

those with earlier prophets circumscribe Jesus's son of man experiences as unfolding within the sphere of human experiences. Without directly arguing against a divine or preexistent messiah, they fill out the nature of the human life that Jesus lives during his time on earth.

2. IMAGES OF COMING DEATH AND RESURRECTION

From the well of son of man sayings we can draw additional sayings pertaining to Jesus's coming death and resurrection in Matthew and Luke. Most significant among these is the Jonah saying. In both Matthew and Luke, Jesus says that Jonah is to be the only sign his generation will be given (Matt 12:39; par. Luke 11:29). In Matthew, the specifications of the sign pertain to Jesus's death and resurrection. Jonah's time in the stomach of the sea monster is a metaphor of the son of man's time in the heart of the earth: "Thus will the son of man be in the heart of the earth three days and three nights" (οὕτως ἔσται ὁ υἱὸς τοῦ ἀνθρώπου ἐν τῇ καρδίᾳ τῆς γῆς τρεῖς ἡμέρας καὶ τρεῖς νύκτας, 12:40). As son of man Jesus is the one who dies and is raised after three days in accordance with the sign of Jonah, much in keeping with the passion predictions discussed previously. Also, this links Jesus yet again to a human person from Israel's prophetic tradition.

The sense in which Luke thinks Jonah to be a sign for the son of man's generation is a bit more complex. Luke here acts in accordance with his (and Matthew's) regular tendency and eliminates references to the resurrection of Jesus happening after three days (e.g., see the replacement of μετὰ τρεῖς in Mark 8:31 with τῇ τρίτῃ in Matt 16:21; Luke 9:22). Luke, then, continues the comparison with Jonah by having the biblical prophet function as a sign of the son of man in a different manner from Matthew due to the absence of the fish reference. Jonah is a sign by way of comparison with Jesus but of contrast with his audience. Like Jonah, Jesus is a prophet with a demand from God that the people repent. However, the Ninevites repented at Jonah's preaching, whereas Jesus's audience did not repent when something greater than Jonah arrived. So as son of man Jesus is greater than Jonah (or Solomon) and yet as one who, like them, possesses a prophetic and/or wise word from God that the people should be seeking out and responding to. This is enough to say that he is a prophet, or perhaps in this particular narrative that he is the promised Christ. More than this, Jesus claims to be greater than both Solomon and Jonah, thus staking a claim to higher ground than these idealized figures from the past. This is a high Christology, but it is far from a claim to divinity. In the case of Matthew in particular, it is a claim to be the Christ whose passion and resurrection looms — deeply human experiences of the earthly Christ.

Several other son of man sayings in Matthew and Luke point to the death of Jesus and to his betrayal in particular. As Matthew moves from Jesus's final teaching unit to the passion narrative in chapter 26, Jesus reminds the disciples that with the coming of Passover his death will come as well: "You know that after two days it will be the Passover, and the son of man will be handed over to be crucified" (οἴδατε ὅτι μετὰ δύο ἡμέρας τὸ πάσχα γίνεται, καὶ ὁ υἱὸς τοῦ ἀνθρώπου παραδίδοται εἰς τὸ σταυρωθῆναι, 26:2). This appears to be a reworking of the subsequent triple-tradition saying that the son of man will go as it is written (or destined, per Luke), but with attendant woe upon the one who makes it so (Matt 26:24; Mark 14:21; Luke 22:22). Matthew also shares a saying with Mark, altered, however, by inclusion of son of man language, in which Jesus, upon returning to his sleeping disciples, says, "Behold! The hour has come near, and the son of man is handed over into the hands of sinners" (ἰδοὺ ἤγγικεν ἡ ὥρα καὶ ὁ υἱὸς τοῦ ἀνθρώπου παραδίδοται εἰς χεῖρας ἁμαρτωλῶν, Matt 26:45; par. Mark 14:41). Once again the connection to Jesus's passion entails, specifically, being handed over. Luke takes up the same theme, but has Jesus direct it to Judas: "Judas, do you hand over the son of man with a kiss?" (Ἰούδα, φιλήματι τὸν υἱὸν τοῦ ἀνθρώπου παραδίδως; 22:48). These additional son of man sayings fill in the son of man as one who was betrayed unto death, thus underscoring the this-worldly character of the son of man identity in the Synoptic Gospels and perhaps picking up on the language of being handed over in Daniel 7. His identity is defined by a mission that entails betrayal, suffering, rejection, death, and resurrection.

Several threads of my study come together at this point. First, if Daniel's son of man figure stands behind the entire sweep of the Synoptic Gospels' son of man Christology, as I have argued, then these sayings from Matthew and Luke participate in a son of man Christology that has its beginnings here below rather than in heaven above. More specifically, the life of the son of man on earth below is one of rejection, suffering, and death. Tuckett's work thus comes back into view, demonstrating the consistency of the Christological vocation across the son of man on earth sayings. Matthew and Luke are following Mark, who in turn is following the interpreter of Daniel's vision, in depicting a career for the son of man in which his life prior to his appearance on the clouds of heaven is never spoken of in terms of an eternal preexistence but, instead, a time on earth of suffering antecedent to his heavenly vindication.

3. THE *PAROUSIA* OF THE SON OF MAN

Turning now to Matthew's and Luke's additional sayings about the son of man and the *parousia*, we are once again on the ground that most clearly draws on Daniel 7 and that some see as holding the best promise for a divine Christology. Both Matthew and Luke multiply son of man sayings in referring to the future coming of the messiah. As we discovered elsewhere, so here also we will find that the various dynamics of the son of man tradition form a coherent plot. In the words of Edwin Broadhead, "The present and the future destiny of the Son of Man cohere in the Sayings Tradition. . . . He has cast his lot with outcasts and wanderers as a homeless person, but his presence is decisive. His followers may be likewise rejected in this age, but they will be vindicated in his coming."[182]

Matthew places a returning son of man saying early in his narrative (10:23). It comes after the saying about the son of man having no place to lay his head (8:20) and after the healing of the paralytic (9:6). Thus, the current saying comes after the son of man has been said to wield authority in the face of official dissension and to be a homeless wanderer. The notion that he might be gone someplace from which he would return has not yet been introduced, but neither is there reason to think that here we have indication of a not-yet-arrived son of man who will come, for the first time, from heaven.[183] The passage in question consists of a mission discourse directed to the disciples whom Jesus is about to send out, but it also incorporates numerous elements from the Olivet Discourse of Mark 13. The instructions that appear to fit well within the ministry of Jesus give way, beginning around Matthew 10:17, to sayings that fit a time of eschatological crisis. There Matthew's readers hear of being flogged in synagogues and testifying before kings (10:17-18), of families splitting and members betraying one another (10:21), and of the need to flee from one city to the next in the face of persecution (10:22-23). It is here that we read, "Truly I tell you, you will not complete the cities of Israel before the son of man comes" (ἀμὴν λέγω ὑμῖν, οὐ μὴ τελέσητε τὰς πόλεις τοῦ Ἰσραὴλ ἕως ἂν ἔλθῃ ὁ υἱὸς τοῦ ἀνθρώπου, 10:23). Because this is the third time the "son of man" phrase is used, and the prior two clearly indicate Jesus, this statement also is most readily understood as referring to him and not to some coming heavenly figure whom the audience has not yet met. As Leslie Walck further observes, the subsequent mention of

---

182. Broadhead, "Reconfiguring Jesus," 27.

183. As I argued above, such a reading may very well be the prehistory of the sayings, as Bultmann contended, but it is not the story of the son of man in the Synoptic Gospels.

Beelzebul (10:25) demonstrates that the future advent indicated in verse 23 is a consummation of a cosmic battle in which the son of man aids the disciples.[184] This battle against Satan figures, as I have indicated at several points, is waged within the narrative of the Synoptic Jesus. Matthew's placement of so much of Mark 13's eschatological discourse into this juncture of the narrative, while Jesus is still very much an active part of the story on earth, is peculiar, but does not fundamentally transform our understanding of the son of man as one whose identity prior to his appearance is the one to whom God gave authority on the earth, but whom people did not receive.[185]

Another uniquely Matthean son of man saying comes in the interpretation of the parable of the wheat and the tares (13:36-43). This interpretation is rife with apocalyptic imagery, not only in its description of the coming eschatological judgment, but also in its account of the current activity of Jesus on earth as functioning in parallel with the current activity of the devil (vv. 37-38). The interpretation of the parable begins with this explanation: "The one who sows the good seed is the son of man" (ὁ σπείρων τὸ καλὸν σπέρμα ἐστὶν ὁ υἱὸς τοῦ ἀνθρώπου, v. 37). Following as it does on the heels of the parable of the sower, the identification of the one who sows the seed with Jesus as son of man is not a surprise for Matthew's readers. In a shift from that prior parable's interpretation, however, what is sown here is not the word of the kingdom (v. 19), but "the children of the kingdom" (οἱ υἱοὶ τῆς βασιλείας, v. 38) who are planted in the world. The description that follows, of the eschatological harvest, indicates that the son of man rules the angels who are commanded to gather out the tares and it also switches terminology, such that now the tares are weeded not from the κόσμος but from his kingdom (ἐκ τῆς βασιλεία αὐτοῦ, v. 41). These latter two points fit well within the claim made by the resurrected Jesus about the transformation that has taken place subsequent to his death and resurrection. Inasmuch as all authority has been given to him in heaven (28:18), he can exercise authority over the angels to send them on their eschatological mission. Inasmuch as all authority has been given to him on earth (28:18), the entire earth is his realm from which the tares are pulled. All of this is readily comprehensible within the paradigm of Jesus as an idealized human king, raised up to a heavenly throne.[186] The earlier statement about the son of man planting the wheat raises the question of whether Matthew views the earthly Jesus as the incarnation of a preexistent, heavenly son of man. The

184. Walck, *Son of Man*, 169.
185. Cf. Allison, *End of the Ages*, 49n11.
186. See the parallel observation by Walck, *Son of Man*, 172.

prior indications of the son of man's identity have not generated any such suggestion. Also, the reader has seen indications that the creation of faithful students (in contrast to the stumbling stones and lawless who are the "tares," 13:41) is a goal of Jesus's teaching (e.g., 5:1; 7:24). Matthew's readers have seen the mission discourse in which Jesus gives instructions for those who will take the message throughout the villages of Israel (chap. 10). And importantly, the audience knows that the earthly Jesus's mission is opposed by the devil (4:1-11; 6:13; 12:22-32; 13:19).

For the reader of Matthew, the son of man who sows sons of the kingdom is the earthly Jesus who will return with glory to purify and judge the world. Reading Matthew from the perspective of a community who knows Jesus to already be raised and enthroned might enrich the understanding of this parable. Such auditors might recognize that the enthroned Jesus continues to "plant" by sending his disciples into "all nations" (28:19). But all of this can function within an exalted human Christology. The penultimate statement of this parable is that the righteous ones "will shine like the sun in the kingdom of their father" (λάμψουσιν ὡς ὁ ἥλιος ἐν τῇ βασιλείᾳ τοῦ πατρὸς αὐτῶν, 13:43). Two observations are important for my study. First, the ability to shine in heavenly glory is not restricted to God or other celestial beings exclusive of humans. Shining with heavenly glory is a condition open to eschatological humanity. This reinforces the likelihood that Jesus's shining on the mount of transfiguration or coming as son of man with the father's glory are not indications of preexistent divine glory, but are more likely indications of his own glorified state as one exalted by God. Second, the kingdom that previously is referred to as belonging to the son of man (Matt 13:41) is here referred to as the kingdom of their father (clearly a reference to God). This comports well with the thread of Old Testament theology traced in the earlier chapter of this book, that God's kingdom consists, in part, in a human king who is enthroned to rule the world on God's behalf. The reign of God as depicted across the Synoptic Tradition is one in which Jesus is the king who mediates God's rule to the earth.

The idea that rule and enthronement, even at the eschatological turn of the ages, do not entail inherent divinity finds strong confirmation in the son of man saying of Matthew 19:28: "Truly I tell you that in the regeneration, when the son of man has been seated on his throne, you who follow me will also be seated upon twelve thrones judging the twelve tribes of Israel" (ἀμὴν λέγω ὑμῖν ὅτι ὑμεῖς οἱ ἀκολουθήσαντές μοι ἐν τῇ παλιγγενεσίᾳ, ὅταν καθίσῃ ὁ υἱὸς τοῦ ἀνθρώπου ἐπὶ θρονοῦ δόξης αὐτοῦ, καθήσεσθε καὶ ὑμεῖς ἐπὶ δώδεκα θρόνους κρίνοντες τὰς δώδεκα φυλὰς τοῦ Ἰσραήλ). Here, the son of man saying clearly contains the eschatological dynamic so prevalent in Matthew; moreover, the ideas of throne and glory draw on the imagery of Daniel that we saw undergirding Mark's son of man presentation. The imagery of a throne of glory has Jewish parallels in both the Similitudes (*1 En.* 69:27) and Sirach (47:11). While the former contains intimations of a possible link with preexistence or divinity (though, as I argued, it may well refer to a human whose heavenly existence comes via exaltation), the latter reference is to the throne of David.[187] The *Testament of Abraham,* moreover, contains two such scenes, one in which Adam is enthroned (8:5) and one in which Abel is so seated (12:4).[188] In the latter, Abel is depicted as like a son of God, and he judges all of humanity (12:5–13:6). Placing someone on a throne demonstrates that the person is royal, even in the context of exercising judgment on God's behalf (cf. Pss. 110:1-6; 132:11).[189] This calls into question Richard Bauckham's claim that only God can sit on God's throne, and that saying so of another agent is tantamount to a claim for divinity. Most importantly, however, Matthew's glorious son of man extends to his twelve human followers the markers of his coming position and function: being enthroned and exercising judgment.[190] As Joel Marcus argues, this is best understood as "their entry into a share of God's royal power."[191] The notion that the future coming enthronement of the son of man indicates divinity is undermined considerably by its applicability to the twelve disciples as well. Thus the conclusion of Hare is apt: "Throughout his Gospel [the "son of man" phrase] denotes the human Jesus, and in this saying more clearly than in any other of the Parousia sayings; there the man who calls himself the Son of man promises his Twelve that they will be associated with him in the coming judgment of Israel."[192] The parallel in Luke (22:28-30) does not contain the title

---

187. Hare, *Son of Man Tradition,* 164.

188. These latter two are noted by Walcke, *Son of Man,* 184. I should note that if the *Testament of Abraham* contains a significant amount of Christian redaction, or is of entirely Christian composition, then the placing of these human figures on the throne is demonstrative of how early Christians envisioned humanity being able to occupy the places that the heightened theological tradition of the church would increasingly restrict to Christ. If these are influenced by early Christian theology, then they demonstrate that early Christian theology envisioned Jesus's humanity enabling him to attain to enthronement in precisely the ways that I argue throughout the current study.

189. Walck, *Son of Man,* 185.

190. Cf. Joel Marcus, "Entering into the Kingly Power of God," *JBL* 107 (1988): 663-75, here 671. Interestingly, in the same context Marcus draws attention to such royal power being given over to the saints in Daniel 7:14, 27, as well. Herein lies another indication of the extensive manner in which Daniel's son of man forms the backdrop for the Synoptic Tradition.

191. Marcus, "Entering into the Kingly Power of God," 671.

192. Hare, *Son of Man Tradition,* 167.

son of man, but it is instructive in its parallel claim that Jesus shares his reign with other exalted humans: "You are those who have endured with me in my trials, and I will bestow upon you, just as my father has bestowed upon me, a kingdom, in order that you may eat and drink at my table in my kingdom, and that you may sit upon twelve thrones judging Israel." With both versions in front of us, numerous threads of my argument come together: exercising of sovereign authority is something that can be extended to humans within the Jewish tradition; it is, in fact, extended to exalted, representative humans within the early Christian literary tradition; such reign is encapsulated in the phraseology of "son of man" (Matt 19:28), and this in turn is a phrase whose function in the narrative is, in part, to delineate more clearly what it means to call Jesus "son of God" as a royal, representative figure (cf. Luke 22:28-30). The breadth of exalted, human Christology shows itself, time and again, as not only sufficient for explaining the Synoptic Christologies, but also as the best road to take given the numerous cues provided by the texts as to the identity of the Jesus they depict.

The bulk of Matthew's remaining son of man sayings come in chapter 24, in his version of the Olivet Discourse. Many of these, in turn, are paralleled by Luke 17 in the discourse that begins with Jesus's saying that days will come when his disciples will yearn to see one of the days of the son of man (v. 22). Luke's is a compressed eschatological discourse that runs from 17:22 through 17:35. Interestingly, Matthew introduces his additional son of man material at the point in Mark's discourse where Mark's Jesus alludes to Isaiah and then Daniel as markers of an eschatological culmination of the woes described. Effectively, then, Matthew is expanding on the coming of the son of man with this additional material. The question for the current study becomes whether any of these sayings about return push us to see that they are actually indications of a first coming or that the son of man as depicted in them is otherwise divine.

First, Matthew follows the warning of false christs, shared by both of the other Synoptic writers, with the saying comparing the coming (παρουσία) of the son of man with lightning visible from east to west (24:27). Matthew 24 is the only chapter in the four canonical Gospels where the word παρουσία appears. It is first spoken by the disciples, who ask Jesus what the signs of his παρουσία will be (v. 3), and then recurs in three of these final statements about the coming son of man (vv. 27, 37, 39). This all lends further weight to the claim that when Matthew speaks of the coming son of man, that son of man is coming as the return of the Jesus who lived on earth, not the arrival for the first time of the son of man who had previously dwelt only in heaven.

Luke modifies the statement about lightning, removing the word παρουσία and changing "from east to west" to something like "from one end of heaven to another" (ἐκ τῆς ὑπο τὸν οὐρανὸν εἰς τὴν ὑπ᾽οὐρανον, 17:24). But the effect of the verse is the same in both Gospels: it indicates that the arrival of the son of man will not be, as his first, a matter about which people must be told by word of mouth because everyone will be able to see and recognize his appearing.[193]

Matthew's version of the Olivet Discourse rejoins Mark, with his allusions to Isaiah 13 and 34 and Daniel 7. Between the signs in the heaven and the report that "they will see the son of man coming on the clouds," however, Matthew interjects: "And then the sign of the son of man will appear in heaven, and then all the tribes of the earth will mourn" (καὶ τότε φανήσεται τὸ σημεῖον τοῦ υἱοῦ τοῦ ἀνθρώπου ἐν οὐρανῷ, καὶ τότε κόψονται πᾶσαι αἱ φυλαὶ τῆς γῆς, 24:30). This is in keeping with the clarity of the son of man's coming that all three Synoptics underscore, with Matthew's own concern to demonstrate that the whole world will be accountable to Jesus's teaching,[194] and with Matthew's particular emphasis that Jesus superintends the final judgment.[195]

After rejoining Mark through the triple-tradition sayings about the fig tree (Matt 24:32-36; par. Mark 13:28-32; Luke 21:29-33), Matthew expands with further son of man sayings that have Lukan parallels, especially in Luke 17. The first of these is a comparison between the days of Noah and the παρουσία (Matt 24:37) or ταῖς ἡμέραις (Luke 17:26) of the son of man. In a warning directed particularly toward the unsuspecting wicked, Matthew's Jesus reminds his audience that all (ἅπαντες) who were eating and drinking were taken away (ἦρεν) by the flood (24:39), while in a similar vein Luke's Jesus reminds the audience that all (ἅπαντες) those who were so living were destroyed (ἀπώλεσεν) by it (17:27). Such sweeping away or destruction typifies what will occur, also, when the son of man appears (Matt 24:39; Luke 17:30).[196] Son of man sayings bookend this discourse unit, indicating similarity between the suddenness of past acts of judgment and the yet-to-come unexpected advent of the son of man. Matthew later employs the "son of man" phrase as an expansion on the Markan Jesus's word of admonition that people stay awake, not knowing when the Lord will return (Matt 24:42; par. Mark 13:35). Following an analogy about a householder being able to prevent a robbery if he had known the hour,

---

193. Cf. Ulrich Luz, *Matthew 21-28: A Commentary* (Hermeneia; Minneapolis: Fortress, 2005), 199.

194. Luz, *Matthew 21-28*, 200.

195. Hare, *Son of Man Tradition*, 173-74, is once again helpful in underscoring that the son of man who comes is none other than the crucified human who returns.

196. Luz, *Matthew 21-28*, 214.

Jesus admonishes people to be ready (ὑμεῖς γίνεσθε ἕτοιμοι) because they do not know the hour of the son of man's coming (ᾗ οὐ δοκεῖτε ὥρᾳ ὁ υἱὸς τοῦ ἀνθρώπου ἔρχεται, Matt 24:44). Luke 12:40 is nearly identical, though located in a different place. These points expand on the theme of the unpredictability of the future of the son of man, and they all fit well within the parameters of the story that have already established that this coming son of man is the returning Jesus, not a son of man who appears from the heaven for the first time or someone who appears in such a way as to be revealed as God in that advent.[197]

Luke's own rendition of Mark's mini-apocalypse culminates in a uniquely Lukan son of man saying. A pericope that warns against being caught on the last day as in a trap concludes, "But stay alert, praying at all times that you might be strengthened to flee all the things that are about to be and to stand before the son of man" (ἀγρυπνεῖτε δὲ ἐν παντὶ καιρῷ δεόμενοι ἵνα κατισχύσητε ἐκφυγεῖν ταῦτα πάντα τὰ μέλλοντα γίνεσθαι καὶ σταθῆναι ἔμπροσθεν τοῦ υἱοῦ τοῦ ἀνθρώπου, 21:36). Analogous to the instances discussed in the preceding paragraph, this son of man saying indicates that the day of final reckoning for which one must be prepared is the day when the son of man appears. Moreover, it suggests that the exalted Jesus will be the agent of this final judgment — something that we find confirmation for elsewhere from Luke's pen, for example, in Acts 17:31. Thus, the passage fits neatly within Luke's resurrection-exaltation Christology. The son of man's role as judge also accounts for a final Lukan passage, where Jesus muses, "But when the son of man comes, will he find faith on the earth?" (πλὴν ὁ υἱὸς τοῦ ἀνθρώπου ἐλθὼν ἆρα εὑρήσει τὴν πίστιν ἐπὶ τῆς γῆς; 18:8).[198]

Matthew provides one more son of man saying as he introduces the parable of the sheep and the goats, the final parable of the eschatological discourse that runs through chapters 24–25: "When the son of man comes in his glory and all his angels come with him, then he will sit on his throne of glory" (ὅταν δὲ ἔλθῃ ὁ υἱὸς τοῦ ἀνθρώπου ἐν τῇ δόξῃ αὐτοῦ καὶ πάντες οἱ ἄγγελοι μετ' αὐτοῦ, τότε καθίσει ἐπὶ θρόνου δόξης αὐτοῦ, 25:31). As the story unfolds, this son of man figure is the agent of the final judgment as he makes the separations (ἀφορίσει, 25:32) between those who enter the kingdom (25:34) and those who go

197. Hare, *Son of Man Tradition,* 64.

198. Gathercole, *Preexistent Son,* 268, concludes that Luke 19:10, the saying about the son of man coming to seek and save the lost, "is the only clear case of the Son of Man motif being brought into relation with preexistence." By this statement we may safely conclude that there is, in fact, no clear case in Luke of the son of man being brought into relation with preexistence. As Hare notes, the verbiage of a prophet "coming" is used of John the Baptist in Luke 7:33 (*Son of Man Tradition,* 69).

to eternal fire (25:41). But his involvement is more intimate still, as he himself becomes the standard by which this final judgment is executed: "I was hungry and you fed me, I was thirsty and you gave me drink" (25:35-36, 42-43). The narrator provides a first clue for interpreting the identity of the son of man as eschatological judge. The son of man figure is subsequently referred to as ὁ βασιλεύς (25:34, 40). Though it is sometimes argued that sitting on a throne in such an eschatologically charged scene indicates divinity, Matthew provides an alternate, and sufficient, explanation.[199] Jesus can sit on the throne because he is king. Here it is worth recalling that sitting on a throne and exercising judgment is also predicated of the twelve disciples in the eschatological future (19:28). Jewish texts outside the Christian tradition could reflect such things as well, as we see in a parallel scene from Ezekiel the Tragedian where Moses sits enthroned as king, a vision of the day when he will judge humanity (frags. 6-7), as well as the son of man in 1 Enoch. In all, the most significant clues as to Jesus's identity point toward an enthronement Christology rather than a divine Christology. Further, Walck notes, "The king is not identified with God, since the king calls God 'my Father.'"[200] Moreover, the basis of vindication is found in the familial solidarity between the son of man and those who have either been served or neglected: "Whenever you did it to any of the least of these siblings of mine [ἐποιήσατε ἑνὶ τούτων τῶν ἀδελφῶν μου τῶν ἐλαχίσων], you did it to me" (Matt 25:40).[201] Jesus is brother to these human siblings. There is a text-critical issue here, in that τῶν ἀδελφῶν μου is not in several manuscripts; moreover, the phrase does not appear in the parallel verse, where Jesus says that those condemned who "did not do it for the least of these [οὐκ ἐποιήσατε ἑνὶ τούτων τῶν ἐλαχίσων], . . . did not do it for me" (Matt 25:45). If the sibling reference is not original, and/or if we are to take its absence in the second clause as a significant omission, the same point I wish to make for my thesis stands in a somewhat different fashion.[202] In that case, the solidarity of the son of man with these is not simply found in familial solidarity, but in the experience of suffering and rejection that typified the life of the son of man on

---

199. Such a conclusion is the one to which Richard Bauckham would lead his readers in, "The Throne of God and the Worship of Jesus," 152-81, in *Jesus and the God of Israel: God Crucified and Other Studies on the New Testament's Christology of Divine Identity* (Grand Rapids, MI: Eerdmans, 2008).

200. Walck, *Son of Man*, 210. I would prefer to say that the king is not identified "as" God, but rather "with" God.

201. Cf. Luz, *Matthew 21–28*, 279-80.

202. Luz, *Matthew 21–28*, 282, argues that notion of siblings would have been read into the latter text as well.

earth (e.g., Matt 8:20; 11:19). With this parable, the final discourse unit ends as did the first — with an indication that the future eschatological judgment is going to be determined by how one responds to Jesus (Matt 7:21-27).[203] While this is an exalted Christology, to be sure, within this pericope the exaltation is that of an enthroned king. Such a king enacting a divine prerogative fits well within an idealized human paradigm.

D. THE HUMAN ONE: SON OF MAN AS SON OF ADAM

The overall thesis of my book is that the Jesus of the Synoptic Tradition is being depicted in a fashion that fits within an idealized human paradigm, and that the writers of these Gospels can thus be read as participating in the long tradition of telling the stories of humanity in general and those of particular peoples or persons as though the latter are the fulfillment or representative of the former. As I argued in my discussion of Daniel in chapter 1, such a back-and-forth between the creation narrative and the story of Israel is at work in Daniel 7. The story of Israel's enslavement to the nations is told as an anti-creation story, in which the beasts rule over the people. The first beast, terrible as it is in appearance, becomes truly frightening when it is allowed to stand on two feet like a human and when it receives a human mind (v. 4). The beast is acting like a human. The second beast is brutal inasmuch as it eats flesh, a striking contrast to the creation narrative in which people and animals are given the vegetation for their sustenance (v. 5; cf. Gen 1:29-30). The third beast is given authority (שָׁלְטָן, MT), itself an indication of possessing human pre-rogative (Dan 7:6; cf. Gen 1:26-27). Interestingly, the LXX renders this γλῶσσα, "speech," indicating that this beast, like the first, is being given characteristics that make it act in ways more appropriate to humankind than animal kind. Finally, I note that the last horn of the fourth beast had humanlike eyes (Dan 7:8). These features of the beasts, both explicit and implicit ways in which they are depicted as taking on human characteristics, underscore that the horror of the scene comes from the ways in which beasts are acting like humans. When, however, the judgment comes and the story is turned in favor of God's people, then things are rectified by a humanlike figure, rather than beasts, ruling the world on God's behalf. When Daniel 7 draws on creation imagery to portray

---

203. An observation that has a general parallel in Luz, *Matthew 21–28*, 282, but with a slightly different perspective as he focuses on deeds of love, judged by Jesus, as the point of commonality.

a world gone wrong, it depicts beasts wielding authority and dominion. When it illustrates a world restored, it employs the creation imagery of a humanlike figure being given rule over the earth by God. In doing so, Daniel 7 draws on what was, likely, the function of Genesis 1 in the first place: to indicate that Israel is the reembodiment of God's plan to have people rule the world on God's behalf. Thus, recognizing the explicit and implicit links between Mark's son of man and Daniel's one like a son of man is compatible with the idea that Mark's son of man is in some sense "son of Adam" (or, as I have been putting it, idealized human figure); Daniel's son of man is also a necessary step between the human primogenitor and Mark's Jesus.

Joel Marcus has argued extensively that the son of man should be understood as son of Adam. His argument begins with the contention that the construction ὁ υἱὸς τοῦ ἀνθρώπου should be read in full recognition of its dual definite articles: "the son of the man." This, then, raises the obvious question, "Which man?" to which the answer is, "Adam."[204] The designation of Adam as ὁ ἄνθρωπος throughout Genesis 1–2 strengthens the case, as does the fact that alternative explanations end up asserting that the phrase has been mistranslated consistently across diverse sources (e.g., Mark and Q) and, presumably, translators, as they all render the phrase with both definite articles despite its not being the expected form for "the son of (hu)man(ity)."[205] Marcus then demonstrates how the three types of son of man sayings (authority, suffering, and returning in glory) all draw on some facet of the Adam traditions of early Judaism: Adam was given primal authority, introduced suffering into the world, and was depicted as returning in restored glory.[206] Thus, Jesus as an Adam figure, one who represents a new humanity in his life, death, resurrection, and glorification, provides a unity to the son of man sayings that had previously proved elusive.

Marcus is leading readers down the right path, to interpretations of the son of man that are more theologically rich and exegetically compelling than those that have erred on the side of "generic sayings" and than those that have erred on the side of "divine identity." Jesus is not saying general things about people, nor is he simply saying "I" in a complicated way, nor is he claiming to be a preexistent divine figure. As I have demonstrated throughout this extensive chapter, Mark's Jesus is claiming to be a representative human figure. "Son of man" is a way of providing a portrait of what sort of idealized human figure

---

204. Joel Marcus, "Son of Man as Son of Adam," *RB* 110 (2003): 38-61.
205. Marcus, "Son of Man," 40-47.
206. Marcus, "Son of Man," 48-60.

this is. Moreover, in keeping with the Old Testament and Jewish literature surveyed at the beginning of my study, I find plausible Marcus's conclusion that Jesus is, as son of man, depicted as a new Adam.[207]

In terms of the argument itself, it seems to me that Marcus requires the intermediate step of Daniel's son of man to bridge the span between Jesus and Adam. The most important reason for this is that Mark clearly alludes to Daniel 7, especially in the glorified and coming son of man sayings of 13:26 and 14:62.[208] Moreover, the claim of Mark's Jesus that it is written of the son of man that he will suffer and be despised seems to demand a more explicit scriptural antecedent than the general notion of Adam's bringing suffering upon humanity — an antecedent that Hooker and Schaberg have helpfully pinned down in Daniel 7. Moreover, though Marcus rightly points out the associations between Adam's rebellion and the suffering and death of humanity, he provides no clear precedent for the redemptive value of this suffering, or that it is typological for the coming deliverer.[209] Ultimately, though, this is not a case of either/or, not merely because Adam and Daniel's son of man each are authoritative figures who suffer, but because, as we have noted, the son of man vision itself trades on the Adam theology that Marcus has helpfully highlighted.

The broader perspective of Marcus's article is akin to chapter 1 of this book, though with a tighter focus on Adam as such. Though there is no one pervasive "Adam myth," yet "the Adam story was profoundly influential in the OT period" and even comes to be merged with expectations of a coming Davidic messiah in passages such as Isaiah 11:1-9.[210] Both post-biblical Jewish writings and early Christian writings (e.g., 1 Corinthians 15 and Romans 5) contain reflections on the past and hoped-for eschatological future in terms of a glorious Adam figure. Daniel, standing as it does within the canon of Jewish scriptures but dating to the second century BC, indicates its eschatological hopes using anti-creation and restored-creation imagery. When the corporate image of the one who is like a human being is applied to Jesus in Mark's Gospel, it brings those connotations with it as well, albeit indirectly. Adam's appearance in the biblical story as a fully grown man, being given his life through the breath or spirit of God, and being imbued with royal authority to exercise dominion — each of these dynamics is in play in the story of Mark's Jesus. The expectation that Adam or his son will participate in the final judgment of humanity, even if

---

207. Cf. J. R. Daniel Kirk, "Mark's Son of Man and Paul's Second Adam," *HBT* 37 (2015): 170-95.

208. See also Christopher Tuckett, "The Present Son of Man," *JSNT* 14 (1982): 58-81, here 60.

209. Marcus, "Son of Man," 60.

210. Marcus, "Son of Man," 50.

a tradition developing later, demonstrates that it is perfectly feasible within the "monotheism" of early Judaism for a human figure to exercise eschatological prerogatives that are typically assigned to God.

In my argument, the phraseology "son of man" keeps its human connotations. The vast literature on the son of man problem as such reminds us that the Aramaic from which it is derived and parallel expressions that we find even in the Greek New Testament point to a shared identity between the person being spoken of and the person of whom they are said to be a son. The sons of Israel are Israelites. Sons of the devil are devil-like liars and murderers. Sons of humanity are humans. The idea that a pre-Danielic form of the son of man vision has broken through the linguistic constraints such that "human being" now means "God" demands more ingenuity from the reader than can be reasonably expected. "Son of man" means "human being"; in the case of Mark's Jesus, the phrase is applied as a title, indicating that Jesus is the Human One. The son of man is an idealized human figure who restores to humanity, in himself, what the first human one lost: rule over the cosmos as God's glorious vicegerent. Like that first human one, whose name simply means "the human," Jesus as the Human One acts in such a way as to determine the destiny of the humanity newly defined by him.

E. CONCLUSION: SON OF MAN AS THE HUMAN ONE

Whatever may be the prehistory of "the son of man," and whatever may be the alternative Jewish traditions of his preexistence, in the Synoptic Gospels the son of man's story begins with an authoritative agent of God on earth who is always rejected by the leadership, and is eventually killed by it, only to be exalted by God in the end. As such, the Gospels' Jesus follows the pattern of Daniel, in which the Israel who was chosen to exercise humanity's creational rule over the earth is persecuted and killed only to be exalted by God and given sovereignty over the world. Thus, the Gospels call Jesus "the Human One" with all its multifaceted resonances: he is the idealized human figure who, like primal humanity before him, rules on God's behalf; he is the figure from Daniel who comes into the Adamic role of rule by way of suffering; and as idealized human he is given a share in God's authority, participation in God's own rule, an embodiment of God's own glory. This is a narrative that moves from earth to cross to heaven without any indication of a heavenly prehistory to validate Jesus's role.[211]

---

211. Casey, *From Jewish Prophet*, 54, concludes his discussion of the Synoptic develop-

This study of the son of man in the Synoptic Jesus allows for some firm conclusions that lie at the heart of the claims of my work as a whole. First, the son of man sayings are amenable to interpretation within the larger rubric of idealized human figures. At times the human facet is at the fore, such as in the Lord of the Sabbath pericope and in the passion predictions. At other times, the human connotation suffices for containing the rendering of Jesus without explicitly demanding it. Throughout, this recognition of the son of man as the Human One allows for the title to retain its meaning: "the son of the human" is a way of saying "human being," and this meaning was not lost on the Gospel writers either through a tradition in which the phrase was transmitted as a title or through attention to an ancient myth about two deities that lies behind Daniel 7. Second, the son of man as an idealized human figure coheres with the narratives of the Synoptic Gospels as a whole, and with Mark's story in particular. Jesus is son of man as he is son of God: an authoritative agent who must suffer and die in order to come into his messianic glory. The glorified son of man is no less the Human One than the suffering son of man because the glorification and heavenly reign come after the human Jesus has died.

Third, the son of man sayings find their coherence in conversation with Daniel 7. Indeed, we can conclude that at the level of the Gospel narrative, especially of Mark, all son of man references allude to the Danielic predecessor. Bearing of authority, suffering and death, and subsequent resurrection and enthronement are all pieces of a narrative whole for the son of man in the Gospels, and each element is reflective of the one like a son of man in Daniel 7. Fourth, son of man finds its content, and thus narrates Jesus's relationship with God, in the function of rule, the vocation of suffering, and a subsequent heavenly glory. The functions of the son of man Christology do not indicate that Jesus has been included in God's unique identity as that is articulated by Richard Bauckham (participation in creation, sitting on God's own throne to rule, receiving worship, and bearing the divine name). Even if such criteria sufficed to demarcate a character as divine (and we have seen that they do not) the son of man sayings do not meet the threshold established for claiming a divine identity Christology. Even Jesus's heavenly enthronement is one in which he sits as king of God's kingdom, enacting God's final judgment in subordination to God.

---

ments in early Christology: "A Greek-speaking audience would understand ['son of man'] as indicating that Jesus was the outstanding member of mankind, and with 'son of God' in the tradition, the understanding of 'son of man' as a reference to Christ's human nature could not fail to occur eventually."

Beyond these firm conclusions about the son of man as an idealized human figure, the suggested connections between Adam and the son of man allow the reader to develop further the Adamic, and hence idealized human, connotations of Jesus's ministry in the Gospels. The Synoptic Gospels' son of man is the Human One, the idealized human who succeeds where Adam failed (in the face of satanic temptation) and thus has restored to him what Adam ceded (dominion over the earth). The ultimate act of resisting Satan, and of fidelity to God, was in going to the cross, an act that constitutes the onset of eschatological labor pains in which his disciples will share, but also marks the path to his enthronement, which will enable his followers to be set free. Here we tap into the necessity, from the perspective of the Jewish story of creation, of "the Human One" being, in fact, human: the dethroning of Satan is aimed not at instituting direct divine rule over the cosmos, but at reinstituting the rule of the world by a human acting on God's behalf.[212] In this sense, too, Mark's Jesus is the Human One. And it is with such a framework in view that Mark's son of man can and should be interpreted as an idealized human figure. The summary of Walter Wink captures the narratives well: "The so-called present Human Being is bound to suffer; the two cannot be separated. . . . Likewise, the 'present' Human Being is eschatological to the core; the inauguration of the new humanity is revealed in the ministry of Jesus, and that new humanity is the future of the species. Jesus's present *is* the human future. The 'coming' of the Human Being in the future will be the culmination of the Human Being revealed by Jesus."[213]

Daniel's son of man is a figure about whom the scriptures prophesy, one whose advent marks the arrival of the dominion of God, and one whose glorification is a divine reversal of death at the hands of Gentile enemies. Unlike the biblical Adam figure himself, the Adamic imagery of the human being in Daniel's vision provides all the pieces necessary to provide a scriptural backbone for the respective Gospels' narrative Christology of an authoritative, crucified, resurrected, and returning king. In the Adam-influenced messianic expectations of early Judaism, these roles are all assigned, not to an incarnate God but to an idealized and glorious man who takes up the mantle of ruling the world on God's behalf.

---

212. Such a notion of delegated rule is summed up well in Broadhead, *Naming Jesus,* 132: "Consequently, the Son of Man is not an isolated conqueror, but the sovereign designated to rule by Yahweh. He will come, not in his own name, but in the glory of the Father (8:38)."

213. Wink, *Human Being,* 64 (italics original).

4 *Messiah Born and Raised*

Each of the previous two chapters has privileged the Gospel of Mark. Both "son of God" and "son of man" serve as markers that guide Mark's readers through the narrative dynamics of the Second Evangelist's Jesus story. The current chapter shifts focus to Matthew and Luke as it examines the Christologies that arise from birth and resurrection narratives. In any story, the early chapters establish the expectations of the readers with respect to both plot and characterization (though, of course, it takes the entire story to either uphold, transform, or subvert those expectations). Final scenes play similar roles, concluding the given story, rounding off (or leaving open) the plots and characterizations that have unfolded. So as this chapter turns first to Matthew and then to Luke in order to examine their infancy and resurrection narratives, it affords these two Gospels the opportunity to reclaim their distinctive narrative voices in ways that have perhaps been sidelined in the prior two investigations. I turn now to plot the respective agendas of the First and Third Evangelists in terms that are more of their own making.

A. GOD WITH US: MATTHEW'S CHRIST IN BIRTH AND RESURRECTION

Matthew's birth narrative contains one of the most cherished ways of framing incarnation Christology — the notion that Jesus is "God with us" (1:23). This early introduction to the identity of Matthew's Jesus is recapitulated in Jesus's final words, the ultimate words of the Gospel, "Behold! I am with you always, to the completion of the age" (28:20). This pairing enables us to frame the question of the Matthew's Christology pointedly: in what sense is Matthew's Jesus "God with us"?

1. BORN IMMANUEL AND KING OF THE JEWS

Matthew's birth and infancy narratives are replete with Christological signifiers. From the opening declaration that Jesus is son of Abraham and son of David, through the virginal conception, the receipt of foreign worship, and the formula citations, Matthew 1–2 is teeming with indications that Jesus is specially located in the story of Israel at the spearhead of God's eschatological act of salvation.[1]

a. The Suffering Messiah and the End of Exile (Matthew 1:1-17)

Like Mark before him, Matthew introduces his entire narrative with a Christological heading. Echoing the genealogical markers from the book of Genesis, Matthew 1:1 reads, βίβλος γενέσεως Ἰησοῦ Χριστοῦ υἱοῦ Δαυὶδ υἱοῦ Ἀβραάμ ("The book of the genesis of Jesus Christ, son of David, son of Abraham"; cf. Gen 2:4; 5:1, LXX; etc.). The most obvious function of the genealogy is to situate Jesus in David's royal lineage, and the line of the kings in particular (contrast Luke 3:27-31).[2] Matthew signals that Davidic descent is tied with messiahship as he concludes the genealogy with "Jesus who is called Christ." Davidic messiahship is widely recognized to be a primary interest of Matthew's Gospel.[3]

A second, widely observed nod toward a royal, Davidic significance to the genealogy is in Matthew's summary statement, where he explains that there are fourteen generations in each of the three major periodizations of names he provides: from Abraham to David, from David to the exile, and from the exile to Jesus. The Hebrew letters of David's name, דוד, are worth the numerical value of fourteen (4 + 6 + 4), perhaps indicating that fulfillment of the Davidic line is the goal of Israel's history as Matthew tells the story.[4] Thus, the opening

---

1. Cf. Brian M. Nolan, *The Royal Son of God: The Christology of Matthew 1–2 in the Setting of the Gospel* (OBO 23; Göttingen: Vandenhoeck & Ruprecht, 1979), esp. 23-91.

2. On Matthew's particular emphasis on Jesus's Davidic descent, see W. D. Davies and Dale C. Allison Jr., *The Gospel according to Saint Matthew* (3 vols.; ICC; Edinburgh: T&T Clark, 1988), 1:156-57.

3. This claim is sufficiently well established that it can be assumed as scholars pursue other dynamics of Matthew's Gospel; e.g., Anthony LeDonne, *The Historiographical Jesus: Memory, Typology, and the Son of David* (Waco, TX: Baylor University Press, 2009); Lidija Novaković, *Messiah, the Healer of the Sick: A Study of Jesus as the Son of David in the Gospel of Matthew* (WUNT 170; Tübingen: Mohr Siebeck, 2003); Joel Willitts, *Matthew's Messianic Shepherd-King: In Search of "the Lost Sheep of the House of Israel"* (BZNW 147; New York: De Gruyter, 2007); Richard Van Egmond, "The Messianic 'Son of David' in Matthew," *JGRCJ* 3 (2006): 41-47.

4. Davies and Allison, *Matthew*, 1:162-65.

salvo of Matthew's Gospel performs a similar function to the "son of God" statements in Mark: an early indication that the most significant Christological reality is that Jesus is the human who is messiah. This is important, then, not simply for what it tells us (i.e., that Matthew thinks Jesus to be Davidic messiah), but for how it functions in Matthew's story. As Graham Stanton observes, "Narrative critics have reminded us of the crucial importance of the openings of writings. Matthew's gospel is no exception. 'Son of David' is the very first Christological title used by the evangelist in his opening line which functions as a heading (1:1)."[5]

There is more to these opening verses as well. In my discussion of the baptism narratives, I referred to Leroy Huizenga's work on allusions to Isaac in Matthew. He argues that "son of Abraham" is as Christologically significant as "son of David."[6] The heavy traffic that "son of David" has generated along the way of understanding Matthew's Christology suggests, by parity of reasoning, that "son of Abraham" is equally important.[7] In addition to this literary argument, that two titles presented side by side in the opening verse should be assumed to both carry definitive weight in identifying the main character, Huizenga also makes an important appeal to the literary encyclopedia of the ideal reader. Isaac's near-death is developed along several lines in early Judaism, including as an etiology of Passover (*Jub.* 18:18-19),[8] depicting Isaac as a willing sacrifice (e.g., 4Q225),[9] and being Isaac's own testing (Jdt 8:26).[10] Moreover, Philo depicts Isaac as being perfectly virtuous and "son of God."[11] Another first-century text, Pseudo-Philo's *Liber Antiquitatum Biblicarium,* participates in trends of depicting Isaac as a willing sacrifice and perhaps as a sacrifice of expiation as well.[12] The point of this is to suggest that with the binding of Isaac looming large in the imagination of early Jewish writers, and with that binding being reinterpreted so as to elevate both the character of Isaac himself and the significance of the (near-)sacrifice, Jesus as "son of Abraham," coming

---

5. Graham Stanton, *A Gospel for a New People: Studies in the Gospel of Matthew* (Edinburgh: T&T Clark, 1992), 181.

6. Leroy A. Huizenga, *The New Isaac: Tradition and Intertextuality in the Gospel of Matthew* (Leiden: Brill, 2009); Huizenga, "Matt 1:1: 'Son of Abraham' as Christological Category," *HBT* 30 (2008): 103-13.

7. Huizenga, *New Isaac,* 140-41.

8. Huizenga, *New Isaac,* 83-88.

9. Huizenga, *New Isaac,* 88-93.

10. Huizenga, *New Isaac,* 93-94.

11. Huizenga, *New Isaac,* 98-101.

12. Huizenga, *New Isaac,* 104-15.

as it does after "son of David," accounts for the great mystery of Jesus's messiahship. Not only must Jesus be king, but as king, Jesus must give himself over to death. As Huizenga concludes: "This second Christological category would solve the somewhat absurd and embarrassing conundrum of a dying messiah, as the messiah never undergoes martyrdom in any of the various portrayals in early Jewish traditions relevant for interpreting the Gospel of Matthew. In Matthew, the categories of Jesus as both Messiah and crucified savior are respectively undergirded by 'son of David' language and the Isaac typology, the latter providing the conceptual category of the atoning death of a martyr."[13]

Huizenga cites a piece of possible supporting evidence in the structure of the genealogy. In *Jubilees*, Isaac is sacrificed in the forty-second jubilee year. Thus, the forty-two generations between Abraham and Jesus (14 x 3) may be a pointer to the forty-two jubilees that are completed with the Akedah.[14] We need not choose between either the Davidic or the Isaac readings, as the structure of the genealogy itself may point to the same David-Isaac duality, that is, a sacrificed messiah, as the opening verse. With both pieces of Christological identification on the table, we have in Matthew's opening salvo an expectation for the reader that the story about to unfold will depict a Davidic messiah who will offer himself up in death. But to what end? The first hint of an answer is also found in the genealogy.

Matthew's threefold fourteen-generation genealogy depicts Jesus's birth bringing the era of exile to an end.[15] The extent to which the Judean situation in the first century was imagined to be an extension of exile is a much-mooted question.[16] However, there are a few points that cannot be set aside. First and foremost, the Gospel writers use prophecies and/or depictions of return from exile, such as Isaiah 40, to explain the events that unfold in the ministry of

---

13. Huizenga, *New Isaac*, 142.

14. Huizenga, *New Isaac*, 143-44, following Roy Rosenberg.

15. Davies and Allison, *Matthew*, 1:187.

16. N. T. Wright, *Jesus and the Victory of God* (Minneapolis: Fortress, 1996); Wright's thesis is appreciatively engaged by Craig A. Evans, "Jesus and the Continuing Exile of Israel," in *Jesus and the Restoration of Israel: A Critical Assessment of N. T. Wright's Jesus and the Victory of God* (ed. Carey C. Newman; Downers Grove, IL: InterVarsity, 1999), 77-100; Maurice Casey, "Where Wright Is Wrong: A Critical Review of N. T. Wright's Jesus and the Victory of God," *JSNT* 69 (1998): 95-103, vigorously objects to the idea that Israelites living in Jerusalem saw themselves as still in exile, see esp. 99-100; Wright is critically engaged by Brant Pitre, *Jesus, the Tribulation, and the End of the Exile* (WUNT 204; Tübingen: Mohr Siebeck, 2005), esp. 31-40, who redefines "exile" in a way more literalistic than Wright as the return of all twelve tribes to the land. The complexity of the issue is ably represented in James M. Scott, ed., *Exile: Old Testament, Jewish, and Christian Conceptions* (JSJSup 56; Leiden: Brill, 1997).

Jesus. Second, the later prophets such as Haggai and Malachi acknowledge that the full glory Israel had been promised as part of its return has not been attained. They thus look to a future act of God to bring it about — including the sending of Elijah that the Gospel writers affiliate with John the Baptist. Third, the heightened eschatological context, and the forward-looking expectation of a coming messiah (where it existed), are both sustained, at least in part, by reading as-yet-to-be-fulfilled, the future-oriented promises that were originally penned as depictions of the return from exile (Second Isaiah again comes to mind). Fourth, Brant Pitre has pointed out that one particular promise that had not yet been fulfilled was that all twelve tribes, not just the southern tribes of Judah, would be restored to the land — an expectation that still loomed large in the minds of many early Jewish writers.[17] Pitre sums up his project with the claim that Jesus "taught that he would die in this [the great eschatological] tribulation, and that his death would function as an act of atonement that would bring about the End of the Exile, the return of the scattered tribes from among the nations, and the coming of the kingdom of God."[18] Whether or not one ultimately agrees with Pitre's claims about the historical Jesus, such a conclusion fits the opening of Matthew's story like a glove. The kingdom of God, executed by a Davidic messiah through his Isaac-like death, brings to an end the "exile" that continues for the Jewish people.

b. Conceived by the Holy Spirit, Born of the Virgin Mary

A common reading of Matthew's narrative of the annunciation and birth of Jesus (1:18-25) suggests that it may well have been classified under the son of God rubric discussed previously.[19] However, that notion has been contested, especially by Donald Verseput, who suggests that Matthew eschews the opportunity and "avoids drawing any direct connection between the miraculous conception and the divine Sonship of Jesus."[20] In anticipation of the annunciation and birth stories, Matthew's genealogical account of Jesus's ancestry departs from the standard, active-voice "begot" formula ($x \, \dot{\epsilon}\gamma\dot{\epsilon}\nu\nu\eta\sigma\epsilon\nu \, y$) when

---

17. Pitre, *Jesus.*

18. Pitre, *Jesus,* 4.

19. So, e.g., Jack Dean Kingsbury, *Matthew: Structure, Christology, Kingdom* (Philadelphia: Fortress, 1975), 43. Kingsbury explains the lack of an explicit use of the son of God title as a literary choice by which Matthew uses the baptism scene to bring to fullest expression a notion that was growing from the Gospel's first narrative (15, 50-53).

20. Donald J. Verseput, "The Role and Meaning of the 'Son of God' Title in Matthew's Gospel," *NTS* 33 (1987): 532-56, here 532.

it arrives at Joseph and Mary. The former is husband to the latter, but is not spoken of as begetting Jesus. Instead, from Mary ἐγεννήθη Ἰησοῦς ("Jesus was begotten," 1:16). Although this may well be a divine passive to indicate that Jesus is begotten by divine rather than human means, the weight of the genealogy falls on Joseph as adoptive father legitimating Jesus's Davidic claim. The ambiguity of this situation is addressed in 1:18-25, as Matthew introduces the pericope, τοῦ δὲ Ἰησοῦ Χριστοῦ ἡ γένεσις οὕτως ἦν ("the origin of Jesus was thus").[21]

Specifically, the ensuing pericope specifies the Holy Spirit as the agent of Jesus's conception. Once in the voice of the narrator (1:18) and once in the voice of an angel of the Lord (1:20), we read that the baby is ἐκ πνεύματος ἁγίου. The use of the ἐκ preposition is somewhat surprising, given that previous genealogical uses in chapter 1 have all referred to the woman by whom a man begot a son (Tamar, 1:3; Rahab, 1:5; Ruth, 1:5; Uriah's wife, 1:6; Mary, 1:16).[22] Similarly, in 1:20 the Holy Spirit is named as the source of Mary's child: τὸ γὰρ ἐν αὐτῇ γεννηθὲν ἐκ πνεύματός ἐστιν ἁγίου ("That which is begotten in her is from the Holy Spirit"). This grammatical peculiarity points toward the conclusion that Raymond Brown reaches on other grounds; namely, "The Holy Spirit . . . is the agency of God's creative power, not a male partner in a marriage between a deity and a woman."[23] This differentiation is maintained not only through repeated insistence on Mary's virginity but also through the peculiar indication of the child being conceived ἐκ πνεύματός ἁγίου. Moreover, this language also coheres with the concern of the genealogy to maintain Jesus's (Abrahamic and) Davidic descent through the human father, Joseph.

It behooves us at this point to lay out the range of ontological possibilities for the child so begotten. On one end of the spectrum, this could be the special origination of one who is ideally human, a new creature of God in the sense that Luke suggests Jesus is when he ends his genealogy with "Adam, the son of God." At the other end of the spectrum, this could indicate that the God of Israel uses the divine spirit as a conduit to transport himself into human

21. Raymond E. Brown, *The Birth of the Messiah: A Commentary on the Infancy Narratives in the Gospels of Matthew and Luke* (ABRL; New York: Doubleday, 1993), 133-38, rightly contests Krister Stendahl's claim that this narrative is a mere footnote to the strangely ended genealogy, arguing instead that it is important as the beginning of the narrative proper as it cements the reader's understanding of Jesus's dual identity as son of David and son of God.

22. A point noted by John Nolland, "No Son-of-God Christology in Matthew 1.18-25," *JSNT* 62 (1996): 3-12, here 5-6. I will not follow Nolland, however, in drawing the conclusion that this strangeness points away from a son of God Christology entirely.

23. Brown, *Birth of the Messiah,* 137.

flesh. In between is a series of other options such as a superhuman whose divine parentage gives him peculiar endowments without making him divine as such or, closer to the divine end of the spectrum, a divine-human being who is quasi-divine to the point of endowing his human flesh with the level of divinity that might, for example, make death only the rarest of possibilities.

In negotiating among these options (or others like them) we have four pieces of data to adjudicate. First is the angelic announcement. Second is the narrator's gloss, citing Isaiah 7:14. Third is the Greco-Roman stories indicating supernatural conception of heroes. In summing up these possibilities, we will have to take account, fourth, of Matthew's larger son of God theology as discussed previously.

First, then, the announcement. The angelic declaration to Joseph indicates four things: (1) Mary's conception is of divine origin; (2) the child will be a son; (3) Joseph is to give the child the name Jesus; and (4) the reason for the name is that the child will save his people from their sins (1:20-21). The significance of such a breakdown will become more apparent as we see how it maps onto the citation of Isaiah 7:14. In asking the question of the ontology that Matthew intends for his readers to take away from the announcement, that is, how they are to interpret the importance of point 1, the interpretation of the name "Jesus" as one who will "save his people from their sins" is most relevant. In short, is this a claim that a Jewish person could make for any other than God alone? The answer is yes. Within the framework of human agency that I have demonstrated to be at work throughout biblical and post-biblical Judaism, the basic affirmation that God is the one who saves does not hinder the coordinate claim that a human being (or angel) is the one who saves as God's agent.

Josephus's telling of the Moses story provides a helpful point of comparison on this score, a point of comparison that is all the more significant given Matthew's use of Moses imagery in his depiction of Jesus.[24] In *Antiquities*, book 2, Josephus depicts the birth of Moses in ways that bear striking similarities to Matthew's birth narrative. First, in Josephus's story, Moses's father appeals to God on the basis of fidelity to the law (*Ant.* 2.211), an analogue to Joseph's standing before God as a righteous man (Matt 1:19). In response, God appears to Moses's father in a dream in order to disclose the future destiny of the child about to be born. The dream includes a reminder of Abraham and the miraculous birth that overcame Sarah's barrenness (*Ant.* 2.213). In this dream, Josephus reports a scenario much closer to Matthew than to Exodus

---

24. On the Moses typology, cf. Dale C. Allison Jr., *The New Moses: A Matthean Typology* (Minneapolis: Fortress, 1994).

itself, inasmuch as Moses is singled out as the one child on whose account Pharaoh is afraid and thus orders the boys to be slaughtered (*Ant.* 2.215; cf. 2.205; cf. the slaughter of the innocents in Matt 2:16-18; Exod 1:8-10). Moreover, the fame of Moses promises to extend beyond simply Israel to the nations as well (*Ant.* 2.216). These data together reinforce the connections between Jesus and Moses, even as Jesus is given the name of Moses's successor and the one who brought the exodus to its conclusion by leading the people into the land. More directly relevant to the significance of calling Jesus "savior," however, is the role Moses is assigned in *Antiquities.* God tells Amram that Moses will set the people free (ἀπολύσει) from the Egyptians (2.216). Such a pronouncement identifies Moses as the agent of the greatest and paradigmatic act of salvation in the Jewish scriptures, a shared agency that I showed above (chap. 1) to be at work in the original exodus story as well.

From a different angle, 11QMelchizedek is also instructive for numerous points of comparison with Matthew. First, both texts envision a saving figure arriving at the culmination of a periodized history. For Matthew, as we have seen, Jesus arrives at the end of the third fourteen-generation cycle, bringing to a close the period marked by Babylonian captivity. For 11QMelchizedek, the time of salvation comes at the beginning of the tenth jubilee (11QMelch II 6-8). Second, both Matthew and 11QMelchizedek couch this time of fulfillment in terms of return from exile. The Qumran text interprets the jubilee/sabbatical texts of Leviticus 25:13 and Deuteronomy 15:2 using language of liberty for the captives that is evocative of a return from exile: "[Its interpretation] for the last days refers to the captives, . . . whose teachers have been hidden and kept secret, and from the inheritance of Melchizedek. . . . All liberty will be proclaimed for them, to free them from [the debt of] all their iniquities" (11QMelch II 4-6).[25] This text contains a third important point of comparison: the state of captivity is due to iniquity, and its restoration is tied to remission of sins. Within this framework, the actions performed by Melchizedek are striking: he makes the captives return (11QMelch II 6, thus playing the role of deliverer); he is the subject of Psalm 82:1, which refers to God standing in the divine assembly and judging in the midst of gods (11QMelch II 10) as well as the statement from Psalm 7:9 that God will judge the peoples (11QMelch II 10-11); he not only judges the nations but also frees the people from Belial (11QMelch II 13). Given the connotations that the Synoptic Gospels make between Jesus's kingship and the reign of God, the further description of Melchizedek's work

---

25. Florentino García Martínez and Eibert J. C. Tigchelaar, *DSSSE* (2 vols.; Grand Rapids, MI: Eerdmans, 1998), 2:1207.

as bringing about the peace that is announced as the reign of God in Isaiah 52:7 is also pertinent. Thus, Melchizedek is the agent (whether human or angelic) through whom God saves God's people, fulfilling prophetic anticipations of jubilee, and bringing about the eschatological restoration anticipated as the fulfillment of the return from exile as described by the biblical prophets.

The Qumran text helps us get our bearings in at least a couple of ways. First, to be named as one who would save people from their sins can be a way to describe an agent who brings to an end the effects of the people's sin in their being subjected to some sort of continuing state of exile. Second, this salvation can include a salvation from sins that includes an eschatological judgment in which God's faithful people are vindicated and God's opponents not only condemned but also, in the case of spiritual forces, disempowered. To make such a claim is not to deny that God is the agent at work in saving the people, but to recognize that God who is at work can do so through an agent who is designated as the subject of the saving work. Thus, the angelic announcement, while clearly signaling that God is at work and will be at work to save, through Jesus, does not tell us precisely how to adjudicate the relationship between Jesus and God in the text.

Second, we turn to the narrator's gloss on the announcement, a gloss that to a great extent parallels the announcement itself. Here we find the first of Matthew's formula citations, indicating that what the angel proclaims all took place to fulfill the word of the Lord through the prophet: "Behold a virgin will have [a child] in her womb and will bear a son, and they will call his name, Immanuel." The verse indicates the following: (1) the woman having this child (as indicated by Matthew's context) conceives without having had sexual intercourse, corresponding to point 1 of the angel's announcement; (2) the child to be born will be a son, also corresponding to point 2 of the prior declaration; (3) the child is to be named "Immanuel," which correlates with the command to name from the prior story, but gives a different name. Point 4 is an explanation of the name. "Jesus" indicates that he will save. Isaiah itself does not provide an explanation of the name to be given, but the narrator provides it for the reader by translating "Immanuel" as "God is with us" (μεθ᾽ ἡμῶν ὁ θεός, Matt 1:23). The unit concludes with the narrator repeating points 1-3: Joseph took Mary but did not have sex with her, she bore a male child, and Joseph named him Jesus as he was instructed.[26]

---

26. This parallelism between the announcement, citation, and enactment is one reason why I do not find persuasive the argument that Andrew T. Lincoln lays out, *Born of a Virgin? Reconceiving Jesus in the Bible, Tradition, and Theology* (Grand Rapids, MI: Eerdmans, 2013),

Table 4-1 Announcement, Prophecy, Enactment

Announcement to Joseph in Matthew 1:20-21	Citation of Isaiah 7:14	Enactment
the child is begotten from the Holy Spirit	Behold! A virgin will have in her womb	He did not know her
She will bear a son	She will bear a son	until she bore a son
and you will call his name Jesus	and they will call his name Immanuel	and he called his name Jesus
for he will save his people from their sins	which is translated, "God [is] with us"	

The citation of Isaiah 7:14 poses a couple of challenges for interpreters seeking further enlightenment on the significance of the conception and birth of Jesus for Matthew's Christology.[27] Among the most significant of these challenges is that Matthew's ability to transform the meaning of scriptural texts, not least in the formula citations, is legendary. In this particular instance, the Isaianic context indicates that the παρθένος is simply a young woman. What is extraordinary in Isaiah is not the conception itself, but the abolition of Judah's enemies by the time of the child's early adolescence (7:15-16). In Matthew's deployment of the verse, however, Mary's virginity per se lies at the heart of the fulfillment. Turning to the name Immanuel, Isaiah is similarly earthly. "God with us" is not an indication of incarnation but of God's presence with Judah to deliver them from the Syro-Ephraimite coalition.[28] This consideration is important, but not definitive, for assessing the meaning of the word in Matthew. Its import lies in demonstrating that calling someone "God with us" need carry no intimations that such a person is divine, though we are probably correct to conclude that Jesus is "one in whom the community

---

69-86, that Matthew, no less than Isaiah, intends a "young girl" without reference to virginity per se. Lincoln himself does prefer the traditional reading of a virginal conception, despite his articulation of several strong arguments for a different reading (see 95-98).

27. Cf. Richard Beaton, *Isaiah's Christ in Matthew's Gospel* (SNTSMS 123; New York: Cambridge University Press, 2002), 89-97.

28. Richard B. Hays, *Reading Backwards: Figural Christology and the Fourfold Gospel Witness* (Waco, TX: Baylor University Press, 2014), 38-39, calls for an examination of the verse in context, but then ignores this important factor in its original articulation. The traditional incarnational understanding is allowed to stand without the sort of contextual investigation of Old Testament context that otherwise marks Hays's work.

experiences the presence of God."[29] It can simply be a name given to express the belief that God is with God's people, particularly to save or deliver.[30] As with the possibilities of assigning meaning to the term "virgin," however, the fluidity of possible connotation in naming the child so begotten "God with us" is something Matthew is free to exploit. Matthew's choice to translate Immanuel as "God with us" or "God is with us" (μεθ᾽ ἡμῶν ὁ θεός, 1:23) might be taken as an indication that a more literal interpretation of the name is in view as is a literal rereading of παρθένος.

In moving forward to adjudicate the significance of the name, I note again that it falls in parallel with the naming of Jesus and the explanation of his name. As "virgin bearing a son" corresponds to "she is with child by the spirit and will bear a son," so, too, the name Immanuel as "God is with us" corresponds to Jesus as one who will "save his people from their sins." John Nolland concludes that the transition from the name Jesus to the name Immanuel and then back again to Jesus works because Immanuel carries connotations of God's saving presence through a human person, not through God's own incarnation.[31] The paradigm of idealized human Christology suffices to contain the Immanuel identification, in the absence of other compelling evidence that a divine human is intimated.

In two ways, Isaiah sets the stage for using this prophecy to indicate the birth of a Davidic king who, in some way, indicates the presence of God with God's people.[32] As Raymond Brown points out, the addressee of the prophecy in Isaiah 7 is the "House of David."[33] Matthew has chosen a verse that not only indicates a miraculous birth, but also locates that prophecy within David's royal house.[34]

29. Beaton, *Isaiah's Christ*, 95.

30. Failure to consider the possibility that "God with us" might mean for Matthew something akin to what it meant for Isaiah causes Hans-Christian Kammler to conclude too quickly that Matthew claims a divine being ("gottliche Sein") for Jesus in addition to divine origin and work ("Sohn Gottes und Kreuz: Die Versuchungsgeschichte Mt 4,1-11 im Kontext des Matthausevangeliums," *ZTK* 100 [23]: 163-86, here 168).

31. Nolland, "No Son-of-God Christology," 9-10.

32. Larry W. Hurtado, *Lord Jesus Christ: Devotion to Jesus in Earliest Christianity* (Grand Rapids, MI: Eerdmans, 2003), 326-30, argues that a Davidic connection lies at the heart of birth narratives, and signals its continuity with biblical precedents even while demonstrating that it is "the most momentous of all" (329).

33. Brown, *Birth of the Messiah*, 153.

34. Nolland's overall thesis in "No Son-of-God Christology" is that this story is primarily directed toward detailing how Jesus is incorporated into the line of David, a conclusion with which I largely agree, even if I disagree that this comes at the expense of an idealized human, son of God Christology as well.

For Matthew, it may be that the address to David's house and his own concern for Jesus as son of David is significant. Second, Isaiah's subsequent paean of a coming Davidic king demonstrates just how close an Israelite king might be drawn into the divine identity without claiming ontological distinction for the royal figure. Isaiah 9 calls the newborn deliverer "wonderful counselor, mighty God, everlasting father, prince of peace" (v. 6). If Immanuel was the name given to a child of royal birth, then "God with us" is not only the promise of God's presence for deliverance, but also of God's presence in the person of the human, Davidic king. And so Dale Allison notes that the Immanuel title signals Jesus "as the unique one in whom God's active presence, favor, blessing, and aid manifest themselves. This fulfills the promise that God will be especially 'with' the saints in messianic times (Isa 43:5; Ezek 34:30; Jub. 1:17; Rev 21:3; etc.)."[35] Matthew has intensified the notion of a Davidic king as "God with us" by making God directly responsible for Jesus to be born son of David through the action of God's spirit.

The third question that needs asking as we attempt to sort out the narrated identity of Jesus in Matthew is how the audience might have heard this story if they were a mixed group of Jews and Gentiles. Specifically, do stories of supernatural conceptions in the ancient world create a cultural force toward understanding Jesus's identity in some particular way? Charles Talbert has helpfully cataloged various instances of divine-human lineage in Greek and Roman literature, indicating that various means of conception were imagined along with a range of results for the status of the children so conceived.[36] As for the mode of conception, Matthew's narrative, with its focus on Mary's virginity, differs from many of the ancient stories that are notable for the sexual contact between a divinity and a human.[37] But the idea of physical or, more specifically, sexual contact as the means for generation was by no means ubiquitous.[38] Thus, somewhat more closely akin to the birth narrative in Matthew we find claims such as that surrounding Plato's birth in Plutarch. In *Symposium* 8,

35. Dale C. Allison Jr., "The Embodiment of God's Will: Jesus in Matthew," in *Seeking the Identity of Jesus: A Pilgrimage* (ed. B. R. Gaventa and R. B. Hays; Grand Rapids, MI: Eerdmans, 2008), 117-32.

36. Charles H. Talbert, "Miraculous Conceptions and Births in Mediterranean Antiquity," in *The Historical Jesus in Context* (ed. A. J. Levine, D. C. Allison Jr., and J. D. Crossan; Princeton, NJ: Princeton University Press, 2006), 79-86.

37. E.g., birth narratives of Romulus and Remus that depict a divine figure raping a vestal virgin (Dionysius of Halicarnassus, *Rom. Ant.* 1.76-77) or a phantom phallus appearing to mate with a virgin member of a royal house (Plutarch, *Romulus* 2), and the birth narratives that depict Alexander's mother, Olympias, being impregnated by a god in serpentine form (Plutarch, *Alexander* 3).

38. See Talbert, "Miraculous Conceptions," 83-84.

question 1, the celebrants debate the nature of Plato's birth. Though one person at the table, Florus, thinks it no affront to Apollo to call Plato his son, another, Tyndares, is more cautious. He sees the bodily passions, and the separation of part of one's substance in ejaculation, as deficiencies belonging to mortals, and thus unbecoming of the gods. However, he allows for another manner in which a deity might be viewed as father: "But yet I take heart again, when I hear Plato call the eternal and unbegotten deity the father and maker of the world and all other begotten things; not as if he parted with any seed, but as if by his power he implanted a generative principle in matter, which acts upon, forms, and fashions it."[39]

In this case, it should be noted that while special conception of a particular human is not denied, allowance is made for such a specific case by appealing to a way in which an eternal god could be said to be father of all creation. Within such a rubric, no particular ontological distinction necessarily ensues to the creature due to divine paternity, even though such fatherhood is tied to the particular (in this case, intellectual) feats of which the human is capable. Talbert reads Plutarch's *Numa* (4.4) as indicating that Egyptians made a distinction between a woman being impregnated by a divinity's spirit and the possibility that a man would impregnate a god (or that a god would physically impregnate a woman).[40] Plutarch himself seems to reject this possibility. What he affirms, however, is that the people of greatness are rightly thought to have had close companionship of the gods (*Numa* 4.4-8). Plutarch recognizes the extraordinary nature of a particular human life as the source for stories about divine conception, and as the reason for affirming that a person had an intimate (if not sexual) relationship with a deity.

With a wide range of opinions on the question of divine begetting of human children, there are a few things that are consistent. First, the offspring so produced is always a genuinely new creature, and not the simple embodiment of the god or even a portion of the god. Second, such miraculous conception stories are used to explain the extraordinary life of a person on earth, accounting for greatness of various kinds from the power to heal to philosophy to rule.[41] Third, for the most part the divinity conferred by the divine conception extended only to the great superiority of the person in this life, not to an eternal sharing in the divine life of the gods or to equality with those who

---

39. Plutarch, *The Complete Works*, vol. 3, *Essays and Miscellanies* (Middlesex: Echo Library, 2006), 223.

40. Talbert, "Miraculous Conceptions," 83-84.

41. Cf. Talbert, "Miraculous Conceptions," 85.

had sprung from two divine parents.[42] Here, the deification of the Caesars is apropos inasmuch as the divinization was typically a postmortem glorification. Thus, even if we grant the conclusion that conception by God's spirit implies divinity in the child so begotten, this is still a significant distance from the notion that Jesus is being depicted as the self-same God of Israel. However, the Greco-Roman context opens up a sufficiently broad range of possibilities that it provides only the shakiest of grounds for concluding that the offspring of a deity bears the divine identity as such.

As a fourth point, I refer the reader back to the lengthy discussion of Matthew's son of God Christology in chapter 2. There I argued that a functional son of God Christology sustained even the most exalted demonstrations of Jesus's identity. Matthew introduces the title son of God at key moments of revelation, as at the water-walking scene (14:33) and at Peter's confession (16:16). While such scenes are certainly amenable to a reading in line with divine Christology, they do not require them, and Matthew's narrative does not appear to shatter the ceiling of exalted human Christology. Thus, Raymond Brown's contention that Matthew is inscribing the tradition of Jesus's sonship, first recognized as part of his resurrection and then as part and parcel with his baptism, on the birth of Jesus as well, seems well founded at the level of conceptual coherence, even if Jesus is not being depicted as son of God as such in the birth narrative.[43] Working with a narratological methodology, Jack Dean Kingsbury suggests that the divine sonship of Jesus is narrated through an introduction to his ministry that only concludes at the baptism.[44] This, too, suggests that the son of God Christology discussed previously is maintained here as well. Once we recall that the beginning of this extended episode is the genealogy that indicates a suffering messiah and its conclusion is a baptism that indicates a suffering messiah, the idea that a messianic significance to even the conception and birth narratives gains in plausibility.

The hypothesis I am testing in my study is that Jesus in the Synoptic Tradition is not being depicted as divine in the sense of later Nicene-Chalcedonian

---

42. Adela Yarbro Collins and John J. Collins, *King and Messiah as Son of God: Divine, Human, and Angelic Messianic Figures in Biblical and Related Literature* (Grand Rapids, MI: Eerdmans, 2008), 138-39, argue on the basis of Greek parallels that Jesus is, in fact, depicted as divine in Matthew's birth narrative, yet on that same basis they argue that he is a lesser deity, subordinated to God. Where I agree is that the miraculous conception story differs in kind from incarnation stories, and the latter would be necessary were the birth story itself to sustain the sorts of Christological claims advanced by Bauckham, Gathercole, and perhaps Hurtado.

43. Brown, *Birth of the Messiah*, 160-61; cf. Verseput, "Role and Meaning."

44. Kingsbury, *Matthew*, 50-53.

Christology, but is fully explicable as an idealized human being. In formulating an argument against the current trend toward early, high Christology in the sense of Jesus being depicted as God, the data clearly fail to uphold the thesis being argued for by so many: a miraculous birth story will not in and of itself carry connotations of incarnation to either a Jewish or Gentile audience in the first century. Further indications of preexistence or clearer narrative cues in the birth story itself would be required to reach such a conclusion.[45] In the ancient context, neither preexistence nor identity with the god who is fathering the child would be understood from a story told as Matthew's was.[46] The data point toward other possibilities quite at home within both of those Jewish and Gentile worlds: a human whose miraculous birth indicates that God is present, as promised, to save God's people, and a human whose miraculous birth indicates that God's empowering presence is a key component to the life described in the following pages.[47] I thus find apt the conclusion reached by Talbert about the significance of the birth narratives in Matthew and Luke: "they were saying that this type of life can be produced only by God's prior gracious, creative act."[48]

But we can say more, as well. The transformations that Matthew enacts on the biblical text he brings into conversation with the miraculous birth he narrates underscore the uniqueness of Jesus as the eschatological figure in whom God is fulfilling God's promises to save Israel by the hand of a Davidic king. Brown highlights this: "Even if the intervention of God through the Holy Spirit had been required many times in the long genealogical record of the Messiah, His intervention through the Spirit in the conception and birth of Jesus is not just one more in a series. Jesus is the final and once-for-all manifestation of God's presence with us, which is so much the work of the Spirit that for the first time in the genealogical record of the Messiah no human begetter can be listed."[49]

The humanness of Jesus that this book is highlighting throughout the Synoptic Tradition is not a humanness that Jesus has simply by virtue of being a man on the earth, but a humanness of extraordinary endowment as Jesus is the one who has been entrusted to bear within himself the title son of God that highlights his role as representative of God on the earth.

45. Cf. James D. G. Dunn, *Christology in the Making: A New Testament Inquiry into the Origins of the Doctrine of Incarnation* (Grand Rapids, MI: Eerdmans, 1996), 49-50.

46. Brown, *Birth of the Messiah*, 140-42.

47. Cf. Allison, "Embodiment," 130.

48. Talbert, "Miraculous Conceptions," 86.

49. Brown, *Birth of the Messiah*, 153.

c. Worshiping the King of the Jews

Immediately after the conception and birth narrative, Matthew tells the story of the magi from the east. Throughout the short episodes in which they appear, the identity of Jesus is depicted in terms that are royal but not divine: the one born king of the Judeans (2:2); the Christ (2:4) as the one who will be born in Bethlehem and shepherd Israel (2:6).[50] This royal connotation is the explanation provided by the magi for why they intend to bow before (προσκυνῆσαι) the child (2:3). Given that climactic, revelatory moments in Matthew's Gospel will be met with the response of prostration (14:33; 28:17), this point cannot be stated strongly enough. The reason why the Gentiles in the know are going to worship the child is because the child is king of the Jews, not because he is God incarnate or a god of some other sort.[51] Of course, it might very well be Matthew's literary strategy to introduce obeisance to Jesus by way of underinformed Gentiles, and that he will fill out the reasons for it as the story unfolds. But it is equally possible that in his relating of the story he deliberately had his foreigners combine their intention to worship with the very Christology that the narration itself introduces beginning from the genealogy: being Davidic king, king of the Jews, is reason enough to receive such homage. Such a conclusion is strengthened by the way in which the title of king is used in the story. Brian Nolan points out that Herod is referred to as king in 2:1, 3, and 9, when the magi arrive to worship the newborn king of the Jews. After they find and worship Jesus, however, "Herod is never dubbed king."[52] This is a passage about kingship as such.

Because προσκυνέω can carry connotations of worship, the question arises as to whether Matthew's readers should so understand the veneration paid to Jesus. The question becomes perhaps more acute as subsequent venerations include that given by the disciples after the storm-stilling episode, in which they confess Jesus to be son of God (14:33) and by those who see Jesus after his resurrection (28:9, 17). Other examples include the bowing of those who come to petition Jesus (8:2; 9:18; 15:25; 20:20). Perhaps more importantly, Jesus refuses to bow to the devil in keeping with the injunctions of Deuteronomy against worshiping anyone other than God (4:10; cf. Deut 6:13; 10:20).

Matthew has already provided the reader with sufficient clues to indicate

---

50. Cf. Kingsbury, *Matthew,* 44-45.

51. Kannler, "Sohn Gottes," 168-69, runs too quickly to an undifferentiated "hohe Christologie" in this text, in part because he does not consider the relationship between the title the magi affix to Jesus and the action they perform.

52. Nolan, *Royal Son of God,* 39.

a messianic rather than divine interpretation of this passage; and connections between the story of the magi and the crucifixion scene will further underscore that Jesus is due worship precisely because he is king of the Jews. Matthew's readers have already learned that Jesus is son of David and son of Abraham. The roles Jesus plays in the narrative are thus laid out in terms of Israelite sovereignty over the world, as Jesus is a specially empowered agent of God who nonetheless must suffer and die. In the wake of the divine conception from the prior story, the idea of Jesus as a king specially worthy of adoration from foreigners does not raise the Christology to the level of divinity.[53] The story also foreshadows other dynamics in Matthew's Gospel. As W. D. Davies and Dale Allison point out, the arrival of these Gentiles from afar represents an inaugurated eschatology — the command from the Great Commission finding proleptic fulfillment as the nations come to Jerusalem looking to adore Israel's king.[54] The future that Matthew envisions, however, will finally come about when Jesus sends out his followers after "all authority in heaven and on earth has been given to [him]" (28:18). In other words, the visit of the magi anticipates the time when Jesus will be enthroned as king. Matthew's story, rather than presenting presumed restrictions on who can receive worship from a monotheist, determines the significance of these actions that, nonetheless, fit well within the range of acceptable homage paid to a king in Israelite religion.[55] In addition to the resurrection, the crucifixion also provides important points of contact with this story. Davies and Allison point out that in both the point at issue is Jesus as "king of the Jews," and that the Jewish leaders gather and make a decision to put Jesus to death.[56] From the perspective of both the beginning and the ending of the book, bowing down before Jesus as "king of the Jews" is bowing down before him as Davidic Christ who will be crucified as such and raised to heavenly enthronement.

Appealing to the temptation narrative to argue that Matthew intimates that Jesus is divine by his receipt of obeisance may have a ring of truth to it, but is not decisive. The correlation between God and God's appointed agent is precisely the question at issue in studies of early Christology. The exalted human Christology that I established in chapter 1 makes ample room for the

53. Cf. Davies and Allison, *Gospel According to St. Matthew,* 253.
54. Davies and Allison, *Gospel According to St. Matthew,* 253.
55. This has been established in chapter 1 above, and accounts for the difference between my assessment and that of Hurtado, *Lord Jesus Christ,* throughout, and also of Simon Gathercole, *The Preexistent Son: Recovering the Christologies of Matthew, Mark, and Luke* (Grand Rapids, MI: Eerdmans, 2006), 69.
56. Davies and Allison, *Gospel According to St. Matthew,* 254.

notion that an idealized human like Jesus would, at times, demonstrate such
superiority to his followers that an awe-filled obeisance would be appropriate.
Moreover, in the biblical stories of the years in which Israel had kings, the
narrative easily slides between προσκυνέω as a term signifying divine worship
(1 Sam 1:19; 15:25, 31; 2 Sam 12:20) and as a term signifying deference to the
king or other revered figure (1 Sam 24:9; 25:23; 2 Sam 1:2).

But προσκυνέω may very well signify worship in the strong sense of the
term without indicating that Jesus is receiving a divine ascription previously
acceptable only for the One God of Israel. As discussed in chapter 1, 1 Chronicles 29:20 is instructive here. In that astonishing scene, the Chronicler tells
of David and all Israel making provision for constructing the temple that Solomon will go on to build. After his prayer celebrating God's faithfulness and
praying for Solomon and Israel, David invites the assembly to worship God.
They do, bowing down and worshiping not only YHWH but also the king
(וישתחוו ליהוה ולמלך). As God's representative on the earth, it is not too
much to say that the king might even participate in the worship due to God
alone without infringing on God's deity (see also Psalm 45). Once again we
find that the discrete categories of actions or attributes allegedly "reserved for
God alone" can at times contain sufficient fluidity to embrace God's appointed
human agents. This case, in particular, raises significant questions for Hurtado's thesis that being included in worship is a clear indication that the hard
line between deity and humanity has been crossed.

d. The One Who Fulfills the Prophets

A final indication of Jesus's identity comes from the formula citations, other
biblical citations, and how these provide the backbone for Jesus's life in the
early chapters of Matthew and thereby help create the expectations for the
ensuing narrative. In Matthew 1 we see how Jesus is the son of David and
son of Abraham who brings to an end the era of the exile. While no explicit
"fulfillment" language is used, these themes indicate that a host of expectations generated by biblical promises are claiming to be answered by Matthew's
Jesus. The principal significance of the virgin birth narrative is to affirm this
trajectory by indicating the miraculous birth of a person who will save the
people from their sins.

In chapter 2 the interaction of Matthean narrative and scriptural co-text
continues to fill out the identity of Matthew's Jesus.[57] First, the citation of Mi-

57. This is so even if we recognize the place that geography plays in the citations, as pointed

cah 5:13 in Matthew 2:6 is given in answer to the question of where the Christ is to be born (ποῦ ὁ χριστὸς γεννᾶται, Matt 2:4). The broader context of Micah 5 (which may or may not be relevant to Matthew's usage) is of a Davidic king who will rule Israel upon its return from exile: "And he shall stand and feed his flock in the strength of the LORD, in the majesty [גְּאוֹן] of the name of the LORD his God. And they shall live secure, for now he shall be great to the ends of the earth; and he shall be the one of peace" (vv. 4-5, NRSV). The passage is striking for its depiction of the Davidic king sharing in the divine attributes of strength and majesty, and for its assertions of royal glory as a result. This is the rich Christology of the Jewish tradition, not yet an incarnational theology.

Herod's opposition provides a route to an additional stream of Christological significance in Matthew's Gospel. Jesus's sojourn in Egypt and subsequent departure are said to fulfill Hosea 11:1, "Out of Egypt I have called my son" (Matt 2:15). Here we find the first explicit mention of the son of God Christology of Matthew, and it comes from Jesus's embodying within himself the identity of Israel.[58] Hosea's reference is to the exodus from Egypt in the past, but Matthew reads it as a narrative that finds its fulfillment in Jesus's own action.[59] This not only plays into the larger Moses typology that helps color the reader's understanding of Matthew's Jesus, but also contributes to a broader Israel typology, found especially in the formula citations, in which Jesus embodies in himself key moments from Israel's past in addition to enacting the fidelity to which it was called and embodying the powerful representation of God on the earth that was to typify its kings.[60] The citation of Hosea 11:1 demonstrates that Matthew is drawing on a son of God typology that does not entail divinity, and

---

out by Krister Stendahl, "Quis et Unde: An Analysis of Mt 1-2," in *Judentum, Urchristentum, Kirche* (BZNW 26; ed. W. Eltester; Berlin: Töpelmann, 1960), 94-105. Thomas R. Hatina, "From History to Myth and Back Again: The Historicizing Function of Scripture in Matthew 2," in *Biblical Interpretation in Early Christian Gospels*, vol. 2, *The Gospel of Matthew* (LNTS 310; ed. T. R. Hatina; London: T&T Clark, 2008), 98-118, sees the citations of place names as contributing "to the legitimization of Jesus as the divine hero, particularly in relation to the existing monarchy" (107). It does so by demonstrating that Jesus's "journey was divinely predetermined and thus factual" (110).

58. Collins and Collins, *King and Messiah*, 139-40.

59. Hays, *Reading Backwards*, 39-41, notes that a broader consideration of Hosea's context, in concert with the "God with us" promise Matthew has already articulated, suggests that Jesus plays the role of God as well, the one who is in Israel's midst according to Hosea 11:9. However, the switch in roles, such that Jesus plays the role of Exodus's Israel and Israel's present God, is too confused to be likely.

60. Cf. Peter Head, *Christology and the Synoptic Problem: An Argument for Markan Priority* (SNTSMS 94; New York: Cambridge University Press, 1997), 202.

it coalesces with other roles played by Jesus that mark him out as an idealized human figure (be that Israel's ideal prophet, like Moses, or Israel's ideal king, like David, or the idealized people of the earth, like Israel itself).[61]

Matthew continues his story of Herod's opposition by casting Herod in the role of the pharaoh-like ruler who slaughters the Israelite children (2:16). This event is interpreted as the fulfillment of Jeremiah 31:15 which, like Hosea 11:1, is a reference to the past and not a Christological prophecy in its original context. In Jeremiah, the weeping is the sorrow of death and exile, but an exile that is overcome by a new and greater exodus (cf. 31:32). In keeping with what one might infer from the structure of the genealogy in chapter 1, Matthew here correlates Jesus's harrowing escape from Herod with a description of exile that God is on the brink of overturning. The narrative Christology on offer is one in which Jesus's life becomes the stage for Israel's cosmic drama to be replayed and, ultimately, find its divinely determined resolution. Matthew's intent to depict the life of Jesus as the great exile-ending moment of return and restoration is highlighted by the otherwise awkward indication that after Herod's death Joseph took the child and his mother "into the land of Israel" (εἰς γῆν Ἰσραήλ, 2:20) before telling the reader that Jesus's family then relocated to Nazareth. The move from Egypt "into the land of Israel" cements the notion that Jesus's life means a new exodus for Israel, a fulfillment of the promises associated with return from exile.

The upshot of these associations between Jesus and the historical contours of Israel's story is that Matthew's Jesus finds his identity in associations with the great persons of Israel's biblical story along with Israel itself. In Matthew, Israel's scriptures are related to Jesus not by Jesus's playing the role of Israel's God in those stories, but by playing the role of the idealized human figures who represent that God to the world.

e. Conclusions: Matthew's Introduction

Matthew's introduction provides the reader with important clues for understanding the identity of Jesus: son of Abraham, son of David, and son of God; savior who brings the exile to its full and final end; Moses figure who will lead the people in the new exodus; Israel who will be saved. Though the miraculous conception provides a possible avenue for exploring a unique ontological identity for Jesus, it is a mistake of both quality and quantity to regard Jesus's being in some sense "divine" as a key for Matthew's telling of

---

61. Collins and Collins, *King and Messiah*, 139-40.

the story of Jesus. It is a mistake in quality because the sort of "divine" figure Jesus might be would not be identical with God in the sense meant by later Christian *homoousion* theology. And it is a mistake in quantity because the far more pervasive depiction of Jesus in Matthew 1–2 is of an eschatological human figure whose identity is understood through the roles that persons or people play in Israel's scriptures.

2. MATTHEW'S RAISED JESUS: GIVEN ALL AUTHORITY AND POWER

Matthew's resurrection narratives, like those of Luke and John, include appearances of the resurrected Jesus. As we approach these final episodes of the Gospel, we do well to remember that resurrection is a human experience, an expectation of the early Jewish people that God would be faithful to overcome the curse of death that, once again, is a quintessentially human experience.[62] Thus, the angel's words to the women at the tomb indicate that Jesus who was crucified has been raised from among the dead (ἠγέρθη ἀπὸ τῶν νεκρῶν, 28:7). Barring some extraordinary alternative explanation, a Jewish writer with a demonstrated concern for Jewish eschatological expectations (including resurrection life in the age to come) tells a story of resurrection in order to indicate the future life of glorified humans. In other words, resurrection does not carry connotations that a being is divine, but that the eschatological vindication of the humans who are the people of God has occurred. Matthew's Gospel both affirms the continuity of Jesus's resurrection life with the lives of other humans and depicts Jesus as discontinuous in the two senses of already being raised to the state that they will enjoy in the future and of being fully endowed with messianic authority over all things. These indications are Matthew's summary clues about the Christology of the Gospel.

a. "Tell My Brothers"

In the first of Matthew's two appearance stories, Jesus greets the women who had come to the tomb (28:8-10). They know Jesus by sight, which is perhaps an indication of the continuity of his resurrected appearance with his appearance prior to death. Jesus then reiterates the charge to the women that they let the

---

62. For a concise overview of how resurrection functioned in early Judaism, see J. R. Daniel Kirk, *Unlocking Romans: Resurrection and the Justification of God* (Grand Rapids, MI: Eerdmans, 2008), 14-32.

disciples know he will appear to them in Galilee. But where the angel had said to tell "his disciples" (τοῖς μαθηταῖς αὐτοῦ, v. 7), Jesus says to the women to go proclaim "to my brothers" (τοῖς ἀδελφοῖς μου, v. 10). The resurrected Jesus insinuates himself within the community of his followers rather than distinguishing himself from it. This shared familial bond reflects the claim from earlier that whoever does God's will is Jesus's mother or brother (12:46-50), and it also draws on broader usage of the familial language to indicate the kinship enjoyed by all who form the community of Jesus's followers (e.g., 5:22-24; 7:3-5; 18:15-21). The references in chapter 18 are particularly striking in that there Jesus promises to be present at a gathering of two or more who are assembled in his name (v. 20). This suggests that when the risen Jesus later tells the disciples "I am with you always," this is the promise of one whom Matthew understands to be among them as a brother who is a fellow subject of God rather than as God himself.

b. The King on the Mountain[63]

i. All Authority in Heaven and on Earth

The disciples' encounter with the resurrected Jesus leads to obeisance and to Jesus's disclosure of what has happened to him as he has passed from death to new life as one raised from the dead: "All authority has been given to me in heaven and on the earth" (28:18). The significance of this verse is clear, and helpfully detailed by Larry Hurtado: "First, the risen Jesus who speaks here claims to have been given cosmic authority in 28:18. On the one hand, the universal dimension of his statement ('all authority in heaven and on earth') reflect an august, divinelike [sic] status. On the other hand, that Jesus is given this authority (by God, as hinted by the 'divine passive' verb here) means that his status derives from, and is linked with, God, and that Jesus is neither hubristic nor a rival to God."[64] The significance of such an exposition for the question of Jesus's identity is difficult to overstate. If God gives the resurrected Jesus authority, then (1) Jesus did not fully possess such all-encompassing authority

---

63. In the following, I agree with the analysis of Jack Dean Kingsbury, "The Composition and Christology of Matt 28:16-20," *JBL* 93 (1974): 573-84, to the effect that the final resurrection appearance bears numerous marks of Matthew's hand, and reflects both vocabulary and thematic elements that integrate it into the overarching theology of the Gospel. Thus, not only is attention to the final scene good practice from the perspective of how literature tends to work, it is also indicated by the particularly Matthean nature of the passage.

64. Hurtado, *Lord Jesus Christ*, 331.

prior to his resurrection, and (2) the God who bestows the authority is other than the human Jesus to whom it is given. "Divinelike" (sic) authority within the Jewish traditions explored in this book is authority that God gives to another so that this other can act in the world on God's behalf. Such notions went into the constructing of idealized human Christology from early Jewish texts.

The overall theology at work is analogous to the resurrection-enthronement theology we find in Romans 1:4 and 1 Corinthians 15:20-28. In each of those Pauline contexts, the resurrection of Jesus marks his enthronement as royal son of God. As I demonstrate below, this is the case for Acts as well. Perhaps more to the point for Matthew's Gospel, such a claim for Jesus's new exalted status pairs perfectly with the son of man Christology studied in the previous chapter. Matthew's son of man both exercises authority on earth as the quintessential human being representing God to the world (e.g., in forgiveness of sins or in exercising authority over the Sabbath) and has a future in which he will exercise that authority through final judgment and vindication of the people of the world. Matthew's Jesus is enthroned "at the right hand of Power" (26:64) at his resurrection, the Human One given all authority to rule heaven and earth on God's behalf.

Expansive authority over all things echoes not only the royal Psalm 2 ("Ask of me and I will give you the nations of the earth as your inheritance and the ends of the earth as your possession," v. 8), but also, perhaps, the satanic temptation for Jesus to ascend to worldwide dominion through worshiping his tempter (Matt 4:8).[65] This is royal language of enthronement, perhaps being modulated through a Mosaic key.[66]

ii. Mission of Recapitulation

Above I mentioned the resurrected Jesus's use of the term ἀδελφοί to describe his disciples (Matt 28:10). Ideas of continuity between Jesus and his followers are continued in the so-called Great Commission. Matthew's Jesus, as the new Moses giving a new law, has been depicted as the consummate master in the master-student relationship.[67] The charge for the disciples to go and make

65. Trent Rodgers, "The Great Commission as the Climax of Matthew's Mountain Scenes," *BBR* 22 (2012): 383-98, here 394-95.

66. On the importance of Moses, cf. Rodgers, "Great Commission," as well as Kingsbury, "Composition and Christology."

67. Rodgers, "Great Commission," esp. 384-86, highlights the expansiveness of early Moses typology, including his depictions as prophet, priest, king, and lawgiver, to provide an interpretive framework for Matthew's Jesus on this final mountain of the Gospel.

disciples of all nations is for them to continue the mission of Jesus. Jesus gave the commandments (esp. chaps. 5–7), and these commands of Jesus are to be the stuff of his disciples' mission.[68] A Mosaic framework draws us to recognize the parallels with Moses appointing a successor who very much stands in his place (e.g., Josh 4:14). Moreover, the disciples are to go into Galilee, even as Jesus himself did (Matt. 28:16; 4:12).[69] The disciples are to be during the time of Jesus's resurrection what Jesus was during his time on the earth. The hints that the blessings of Abraham would overflow from the lost sheep of the house of Israel to all the Gentile nations will be fulfilled as the disciples extend the story of Jesus's ministry, superintended by his continuing presence.

It is a standard argument for the divinity of Jesus in many theology classrooms that baptism into the name of father, son, and Holy Spirit provides clear proof of the equal and unified divinity of the three. Although this makes for good Christian theology and practice in the post-Chalcedonian era, fitting well within the subsequently developed Trinitarian paradigm, that it was the takeaway for Matthew's first readers is unlikely.[70] Within the narrative of Matthew's Gospel, baptism finds its primary interpretive frame in Jesus's own baptism by John. There, Jesus is declared son of God while the spirit of God descends upon him. Matthew alone specifies the descending spirit is the spirit "of God" ([τοῦ] θεοῦ, 3:16). In the context of a story that began with a divine conception of Jesus by the spirit, the baptism becomes a moment in which the narrative marks Jesus out as God's son, specifically, in this case drawing on the specific functional markers of such sonship.[71] As argued above, the language of the baptism scene draws on antecedents in the Abraham and Isaac story and the coronation of David. To be the beloved son of God in this scene is to be the Davidic king who will "not be spared" by his father but offered up in sacrifice in order to atone for the people.[72]

An important corollary to this line of argument comes from John the Baptist's warning to the Pharisees and Sadducees not to presume upon their Abrahamic descent because God can raise up children from Abraham out of stones (Matt 3:9). This word of warning serves notice that physical descent

68. So also Davies and Allison, *Gospel According to St. Matthew,* 3:686.
69. Kingsbury, "Composition and Christology," 581-82.
70. So also Davies and Allison, *Gospel According to St. Matthew,* 3:686.
71. Kingsbury, "Composition and Christology," 581, suggests that this connection is one reason why the scene should be interpreted in line with Matthew's son of God Christology. More recently, Rogers, "Great Commission," has built on the idea that Jesus as son of God is the operative Christological framework for the scene.
72. Huizenga, *New Isaac.*

is insufficient for being reckoned Abraham's child. And it falls in between the genealogical indication that Jesus is Abraham's son and the Abrahamic allusions entailed in Jesus's baptism. Davies and Allison argue that the references to Abraham introduce the idea that the story of Jesus will be the means by which the promise of Abraham blessing the nations will finally come to fulfillment.[73] As discussed above, Huizenga has shown us that for Matthew a specific son of Abraham, Isaac, is being raised up only to be handed over to death. Matthew is thus providing in Jesus a reframing of the parameters in which one might rightly consider oneself a child of Abraham: bringing forth fruit in keeping with repentance, and more specifically, being aligned with Jesus in his cruciform mission. Putting this together, if Matthew's opening scenes mark out Jesus as David's son and Abraham's son, the baptism is his initiation into the specific vocation affiliated with those titles (not all Davidic descendants are enthroned as kings) as his identity as God's son is applied. This specific vocation, in turn, gives new definition to each of those terms as they are realized in Jesus's own ministry in Matthew.

Trent Rodgers links Jesus's exalted sonship in Matthew 28:16-20 with not only the baptism, but also the temptation narrative. The rich imagery is not only royal but also Mosaic, as the narrative highlights "the Son's legitimate authority and his special meeting with God."[74] By demonstrating how such son of God themes are Mosaic, Rodgers provides another angle for making sense of Matthew's exalted Christology through the notion of an exalted, idealized human being. Kingsbury sums up Matthew's use of the son of God title from a slightly different angle, but in a fashion complementary to my own thesis. First, he says that Matthew emphasizes Jesus as son of God across various time periods of Jesus's life in order to highlight the continuity between the one who is born son of God, is baptized son of God, is tempted as son of God, knows God's will as son of God, is crucified for not denying the title son of God, and is raised son of God.[75] Second, in terms of his relationship with God, "Matthew employs the title, the Son of God, in order to set forth the uniqueness of the person, and therefore the divine authority 'then' and 'now,' of the man Jesus who was born of Mary, and, after death, raised by God to life."[76] The title son of God tells us who the *man* Jesus is — this is the point, exactly.

73. Davies and Allison, *Gospel According to St. Matthew*, 1:158; a promise they see signaled again in the appearance of the magi (1:253).

74. Rodgers, "Great Commission," 389.

75. Kingsbury, "Composition and Christology," 582-83.

76. Kingsbury, "Composition and Christology," 583.

Jesus's own baptism and Jesus's command to baptize serve as bookends to his earthly ministry, and the former provides us with the interpretive grid for making sense of the latter. The disciples are to go out and make disciples of the nations (Matt 28:19), thus bringing to fulfillment the promise of Abraham, and making good on John the Baptist's warning that God can raise up such sons from rocks, not being constrained by physical descent. Baptism into the name of father, son, and spirit in this larger narrative is inauguration into the family of God. To have God as father is to have Jesus as brother (e.g., 6:9; 25:40), thus being made child of God (υἱὸς θεοῦ) by doing the will of God as revealed by Jesus (cf. 7:24; 12:50; 28:20). The familial relationship is determined by Jesus as shared teacher and God as shared father (23:7-8). So, while the unique relationship of Jesus to God is a crucial part of the identity into which the followers are baptized, this unique relationship is not one of deity to deity but of messiah to Israel's God.

Similarly, the spirit functions as a definitive marker of participation in the people of God and of sonship in particular. John the Baptist indicates that Jesus's mission entails baptism with the spirit as an eschatological marker of the people of God (3:11). The presence of the spirit in the baptismal formula is important for demonstrating the distinction assumed among the three named. The spirit is the agent determining Jesus's special identity at birth, and anointing him to his messianic office at baptism, and in the latter in particular is distinct from Jesus in an important fashion even while providing the direction (4:1) and power (12:18-28) for Jesus's ministry. Similarly, those who follow Jesus will have the spirit's guidance (10:20; cf. esp. 12:18). This fits well with the position of Davies and Allison that baptism "into the name" could mean either "in order that they may belong to" someone else or else "enter into relationship with."[77] Thus, substantively, the command to baptize in the threefold name(s) is not far from the theology of baptism reflected in Paul's notion of baptism "into Christ," where he can assume baptism also into and/or by the spirit (1 Cor 12:13) and that baptism makes God one's father as one participates in Jesus's own sonship (e.g., Gal 3:26-27), something that qualifies people as Abraham's seed and heirs (Gal 3:29). The Pauline example is important, not as though Pauline Christianity frames the theology of all the Gospels, but as a demonstration that the significance of the threefold name as indicated in Matthew's Gospel correlates well with what we otherwise know of baptism in earliest Christianity. Baptism into Jesus's name is not an indication that Jesus is a manifestation of the God

---

77. Davies and Allison, *Gospel According to St. Matthew*, 3:685.

of Israel due to ontological unity, but an indication of the role he plays as eschatological son of God who therefore defines the identity of the people of God in his particular mission.

3. FROM "IMMANUEL" TO "I AM WITH YOU"

I have already discussed Jesus as "God with us" in the birth narrative. This designation, together with Jesus's promise at the end, "Behold, I am with you always, unto the consummation of the age," has proved fertile ground for growing divine Christology in Matthean soil. In what way does Jesus's ability to be present with his followers indicate a realization of divine presence as such, God dwelling among God's people?

First, Jesus has undergone a real and radical transformation in being raised from the dead. Matthew's son of man Christology enters its next phase as Jesus is given all authority, a consummation of the son of man authority he exercised on earth (9:6, 8; cf. Dan 7:14). This entails a heavenly enthronement as well as a future as coming judge. Second, this authority is over both heaven and earth, indicating that Jesus is sharing in God's reign over all things. The extending of God's reign, through Jesus, to all things might well entail as well the extending of God's ability to be present throughout the earth even while properly being seen as dwelling in heaven. Third, Jesus provides a way of thinking about his presence on the earth that is mediated in the persons of his siblings. In Matthew 25 the parable of the sheep and the goats trades on an association of Jesus with the persons of the hungry, poor, and naked: "I was hungry . . . I was thirsty, I was a stranger . . . I was naked. . . . As often as you did this to one of the least of these brothers of mine, you did it to me" (vv. 35, 36, 40). Notably, this scene is depicted as the future of Jesus as glorified son of man (v. 31) and as "the king" (v. 34) — the very aspects of his identity that, according to Matthew, have been realized in his resurrection. The presence of the resurrected Jesus is known, at least in part, in the persons who are regarded as blessed in the beatitudes. Fourth, the promise of Jesus that he is present wherever two or three are gathered in his name (18:20) also indicates that his presence is represented in the gathering of his followers, which coordinates with the notion that Jesus is present in the community and perhaps by means of the community that is baptized into his name. That promise itself comes at the conclusion of the instructions on confrontation of sinners, together with its assurance that binding on earth entails a heavenly binding as well. The correlation between heavenly realm and earthly realm is assured by Jesus's father hearing the request due to Jesus's presence with those who make it (18:18-20).

Another possibility presents itself, one coupled with Jesus's depiction as eschatological Torah in Matthew's Gospel (e.g., 11:28-30). If Jesus is depicting himself as a new Moses who has given a new law that determines what obedience and worship should entail, then the parallel with the presence of God through the study of Torah takes on additional weight.[78] Allison draws attention to the parallel notion from the Mishnah that the divine glory was said to be present any time two or three gathered to study Torah (*m. Avot* 3:3) — Jesus might be envisioned here as the expression of "God's immanence."[79] When coupled with the passage from chapter 25, and when we recognize the ways that the disciples and the later church were charged with continuing Jesus's ministry, the possibility grows that Matthew's Jesus was not simply thought to be present *in* the church communities, but *as* those communities. Whether or not this is the case, Jesus continues to be the manifestation of God's presence with God's people to save them, as Immanuel connotes as well in chapter 1. How then does this presence take place? The best explanation would seem to be on analogy with the conception story. The original Immanuel was signaled by the spirit's provision of a new child who would save God's people. "I am with you" is not a promise of physical presence, and so the most likely interpretation is that Jesus is present by sharing in that same spirit with his followers (baptized into the name of the father and son and spirit).

Here again a Pauline parallel might prove instructive. In 1 Corinthians 5:3, 4 Paul claims to be present in spirit with the Corinthian church when they are gathered together. The specific context in which he mentions this is judgment of an offending member of the congregation. So, too, in Matthew 18:20 Jesus says he is present when two or three are gathered in his name, and the specific context is judgment. More generally, Colossians 2:5 reads, "Though I am absent from you in body, I am with you in spirit." In the case of Paul, readers feel no compulsion to ascribe to him a share in God's unique identity due to his claims to be present in churches from which he is physically absent. Similarly, the prophet Elisha says that his heart went with Gehazi as the latter went to claim money from Naaman the Syrian (2 Kgs 5:26). Spiritual presence can be predicated of idealized human figures in both the scriptures of Israel and the early New Testament writings. The prima facie likelihood of Jesus staking a claim to divine nature at the end of Matthew, then, is best seen as the product

78. So Kingsbury, "Composition and Christology," and Rodgers, "Great Commission."
79. Allison, "Embodiment," 130.

of an assumed Trinitarian or otherwise divine-Christ paradigm rather than the authorial intention or likely resonances with the first audience.

4. CONCLUSIONS: MATTHEW'S JESUS

Matthew provides ample signals as to the Christology of his depiction of Jesus in the early chapters of his Gospel and at its conclusion. Many of these indications, when approached with the presuppositions of later Trinitarian theology, can be readily and even helpfully appropriated within the Christian framework. However, the narrative draws our attention, more obviously and with greater emphasis, to the various human dynamics of Jesus's identity. Jesus is the Davidic king who must suffer as the son of Abraham and thus fulfill his identity as God's son and human agent enacting salvation on the earth. Jesus is the one to whom the nations will pay homage to as king of the Jews. Jesus becomes the resurrected king and enthroned son of man whose ways will be replicated in communities formed by his disciples. In all, the idealized human paradigm both fits more squarely with the narrative's emphases and is capable of accounting even for the data that might appear, given different presuppositions, to signal divinity as such.

B. THE SON OF DAVID: JESUS IN LUKE'S BIRTH AND RESURRECTION NARRATIVES

Luke is often thought of as a quintessentially Gentile author, concerned with placing Jesus on the Roman map for Gentile readers. However, he frames his birth narrative in a manner that is as Jewish as Matthew's. Luke tells the reader that the story of Jesus is one about "the things that have been fulfilled among us" (τῶν πεπληροφορημένων ἐν ἡμῖν, 1:1). Thus, the invitation is to read the entirety of the Jesus story as a fulfillment of Israel's scriptures. The final words of Jesus to the disciples in chapter 24 reiterate this expectation. There Jesus says, "All things written about me in the law of Moses, and the prophets, and the psalms must be fulfilled" (δεῖ πληρωθῆναι πάντα τὰ γεγραμμένα, v. 44). In this latter portion, Jesus also provides the specific content that he has in mind: the messiah must suffer, die, and be raised from the dead, and then repentance for forgiveness of sins must be proclaimed (vv. 46-47). As I show repeatedly, both here and in chapter 6, on intertextuality, Luke's understanding of Jesus's relationship to scripture is not as the incarnation of the primary actor (i.e., the

God of Israel) but as the fulfillment of that actor's promise to send an agent of deliverance who will restore the people of God.

1. BORN LORD AND CHRIST

Luke tells the story of the conception and birth with echoes of the miraculous births of Israel's scriptural tradition.[80] Thus, while I once again address, in brief, the possibility of the story being read as the birth of a god, the allusive force of the text places us much more firmly on the ground of the God of Israel bringing to life a new, extraordinary creature.[81] The resurrection narrative, and also Peter's speech at Pentecost, underscore that the identity of Jesus itself, and the biblical allusions that provide an interpretive grid for making sense of it, are a matter of exalted human Christology rather than divinity.

a. John Preparing a People for the Lord

The annunciation of John's birth to Zechariah (1:13-17) opens a number of Christological possibilities for the ensuing story of Jesus. But before addressing those directly, it is well to put on the table some of the attributes assigned to other characters in the narrative. First, Luke has no qualms about affirming faithful, law-keeping Jewish people as righteous (e.g., Elizabeth and Zechariah, 1:6). This makes them "special," but does not signal a peculiar dispensation of the spirit, much less divine ontology. John himself will be great before the Lord (1:15), and will experience a special endowment of the spirit even from the time of being in his mother's womb (πνεύματος ἁγίου πλησθήσεται ἔτι ἐκ κοιλίας μητρὸς αὐτοῦ, 1:15). The endowment by the spirit that empowers Jesus's own mission is not something that makes him ontologically unique, though it does empower him for a mission that is distinct from the mission of John.

The announcement about John's birth also avails itself of the tantalizing suggestion of a divine Christology for Jesus. Throughout, John's mission is spoken of in terms of preparing people for, and going ahead of, the Lord or the Lord God (e.g., 1:15, 16, 17).[82] And yet, the informed reader already knows,

---

80. Brown, *Birth of the Messiah*, highlights especially the echoes of the birth of Samuel, e.g., 268-69. Lincoln, *Born of a Virgin?* 101-2, shows how the announcement contains all five elements of an angelic annunciation from the scriptural tradition.

81. Cf. Justo L. González, *Luke* (Belief; Louisville, KY: Westminster John Knox, 2010), 19.

82. A possibility explored by C. Kavin Rowe, *Early Narrative Christology: The Lord in the Gospel of Luke* (Grand Rapids, MI: Baker Academic, 2006).

and those who do not yet know will find out soon enough, that the particular person before whom John goes, and whose way John prepares, is the Lord Jesus.[83] Kavin Rowe points the way forward for understanding the significance of this tension, though I disagree with the meaning he intends in the statement: "Luke . . . shares with Paul and John a remarkably similar — if not the same — underlying judgment about the identity of Jesus, namely, that as κύριος he is the human presence of the heavenly κύριος of Israel."[84] As we have seen repeatedly by this point, to be the human lord whose presence represents Israel's heavenly Lord is to be Adam, to be David, to be a great priest, to be Israel itself. The ambivalence surrounding the word "Lord" is encapsulated well in Psalm 110: "The Lord [God] said to my lord [the king]" (εἶπεν ὁ κύριος τῷ κυρίῳ μου, LXX). At this point, however, Jesus is not yet mentioned, and the mission of John is delineated as a preparation for the Lord God. How God will relate to Jesus is a matter for the unfolding of the story.

The story of a childless old couple who are enabled to conceive (through, it would seem, the otherwise normal processes of sexual intercourse, 1:23)[85] contains considerable allusive force to biblical precedents, to Sarah and Abraham in particular. Thus, the tradition of miraculous births in which Luke is so far participating is the Jewish tradition and not the Greco-Roman. The appeal to read the story in conversation with Jewish dialogue partners continues as allusions are made to the Nazirite vows (Luke 1:15; Num 6:3), to Elijah, and to the Malachi texts that predict Elijah's return (Luke 1:17; Mal 3:1; 4:5-6).

b. Mary, David, and Son of God

For the purpose of framing Luke's Gospel, and the identity of Jesus as presented in that Gospel, the annunciation to Mary is perhaps the most important passage in the birth narratives.[86] Here for the first time we hear directly about Jesus, and the entirety of the Christological content pertaining to Jesus's identity falls within a rubric of fulfilling David's kingship:[87] "This one will be great

---

83. Brown, *Birth of the Messiah*, 282-83, conjectures that John's own ministry, understood by John as preparing for God, was reinterpreted by later Christians as preparing for Jesus. Such a reconstruction might help explain why a John tradition that seems to refer to God nonetheless, within the narrative of Luke's Gospel story, refers to the Lord Jesus.

84. Rowe, *Early Narrative Christology*, 29.

85. Cf. Rowe, *Early Narrative Christology*, 35.

86. Mark L. Strauss, *The Davidic Messiah in Luke-Acts: The Promise and Its Fulfillment in Lukan Christology* (JSNTSup 110; Sheffield: Sheffield Academic, 1995), 87-97.

87. Cf. Lincoln, *Born of a Virgin*, 102. On kingship as a category in Luke-Acts, cf. Beverly

and will be called son of the Most High. And the Lord God will give to him the throne of his father David. And he will reign [βασιλεύσει] over the house of Jacob forever, and there will be no end to his kingdom [βασιλείας]" (1:32-33).

Here, Jesus is cast in the role of the promised son of 2 Samuel 7, the son of David who will also be God's son, promises that come to the surface in Psalms 2 and 89 as well.[88] Such a description fits well within the idealized depictions of humans who represent God on the earth, as the Davidic parallels demonstrate. Moreover, as Collins and Collins point out, and I discussed above in my section on Judaism, such language for a messiah figure also appears in the Aramaic Apocalypse (4Q246 II, 1): "He will be called son of God, and they will call him son of the Most High."[89] Even the description of the kingdom in the Qumran text coheres with the angelic announcement: "His kingdom will be an eternal kingdom . . . His rule will be an eternal rule" (4Q246 II, 5, 9).[90]

Mary's follow-up question ("How can this be since I know no man?" Luke 1:34) evokes a response from the angel that locates Jesus's divine sonship in the unique circumstances surrounding his birth: "The Holy Spirit will come upon you, and the power of the Most High will overshadow you. For this reason also [διὸ καί] that holy thing which is begotten will be called son of God" (1:35). Jesus is son of God due to the special circumstances of his birth. As with Matthew we are confronted with the question of what kind of role the Holy Spirit is playing, though here it is overtly stated that the intervention enables the child to be called God's son. The notion of the spirit "overshadowing" Mary has regularly been linked to the brooding of the spirit over the waters of creation (Gen 1:2).[91] The latter reference has been connected to Jesus's baptism as well.[92] Importantly, in both the baptism and the birth narrative Jesus's sonship is linked to the spirit of God. In fact, the link to creation is significant because it opens up one way of conceptualizing what divine

---

Roberts Gaventa, "Learning and Relearning the Identity of Jesus from Luke-Acts," in *Seeking the Identity of Jesus: A Pilgrimage* (Grand Rapids, MI: Eerdmans, 2008), 148-65.

88. So also Brown, *Birth of the Messiah,* 310; Petr Pokorný, *Theologie der lukanischen Schriften* (Göttingen: Vandenhoeck & Ruprecht, 1996), 112; cf. Joel B. Green, *The Gospel of Luke* (NICNT; Grand Rapids, MI: Eerdmans, 1997), 88; Strauss, *Davidic Messiah,* 88-89.

89. Collins and Collins, *King and Messiah,* 143-44; text from Martínez and Tigchelaar, *DSSSE,* 1:495.

90. Martínez and Tigchelaar, *DSSSE,* 1:495.

91. So Strauss, *Davidic Messiah,* 90-91.

92. Cf. Dale C. Allison Jr., "The Baptism of Jesus and a New Dead Sea Scroll," *BAR* 18 (1992): 58-60.

fatherhood might entail.[93] Luke's genealogy of Jesus, located immediately after the baptism, traces his line back to Adam, the son of God (3:38).[94] This genealogical record appears to lean on Genesis 5, a text that uses the "image and likeness" language of Genesis 1 to speak not only of humanity's creation but also of Adam's begetting of Seth: "When God created humankind, he made them in the likeness [בדמות] of God. Male and female he created them, and he blessed them and named them 'Humankind' [אדם] when they were created. When Adam had lived one hundred thirty years, he became the father of a son in his likeness [בדמותו], according to his image [וכצלם, cf. Gen 1:26, 27], and named him Seth" (Gen 5:1-3, NRSV).

Luke is reading the genealogical record as indicating that Seth is to Adam as Adam is to God, namely, a son. This, then, provides us with the framework we need for understanding how the hovering of the spirit over Mary signals the particular ontological status of Jesus. The resulting child is "son of God" not because he is God incarnate (in which case, the phrase "son of" becomes problematic)[95] but because he is begotten by God's creative power — he is son of God like Adam was son of God.[96]

Petr Pokorný offers an alternative reading, suggesting instead that the termination of the genealogy in Adam sets up an antithetical relation, "daß Jesus demnach als der wahre (gezeugte) Sohn Gottes das Gegenüber zu Adam ist, der ungehorsame Sohn Gottes war."[97] Such an evaluation, however, appears to be unduly influenced by Paul's Adam-Christ dichotomy. No such denigration of Adam is found in the genealogy, nor is Adam mentioned by name elsewhere in Luke-Acts. Moreover, the placement of this genealogy, between the baptism that proclaims Jesus as God's son and the temptation narrative that tests this identity, invites the reader to see correlation, rather than contrast, in the culminating moment of Jesus's genealogy.

As I discussed above in connection with Matthew's birth narrative, such a reading of the divine involvement in Jesus's birth accounting for the existence of an extraordinary human is not likely to be restricted to Jewish readers. Talbert refers to a conversation in Plutarch's "Table Talk" in which Plato's view of divine parentage is discussed:

93. Brown, *Birth of the Messiah*, 314, offers the new creation explanation as well, but without reference to Luke's subsequent Adam reference.

94. Cf. González, *Luke*, 55-56.

95. Dunn, *Christology in the Making*, 50-51, rightly discounts the idea of preexistence here.

96. Green, *Gospel of Luke*, 91, also chooses language of creation to represent the son of God Christology that comes through at this point.

97. Pokorný, *Theologie der lukanischen Schriften*, 115.

The first speaker, Florus, refers to those who attribute Plato's parentage to Apollo and claim that Ariston, Plato's father, had a vision in his sleep, which forbade him to have intercourse with his wife for ten months. The second speaker, Tyndares, replies that it is fitting to celebrate Plato with the line: "He seemed the child not of a mortal man but of a god." When, however, Plato himself speaks of the uncreated and eternal god as father and maker of the cosmos, "it happened not through semen but by another power of God (*dunamei tou theou*) that God begot in matter the principle of generation, under whose influence it became receptive and was changed."[98]

The points of contact are thoroughgoing: (1) the creative act leads to the child being referred to as a child of god; (2) divine parentage is discussed on analogy with creation; (3) the intervention happens through the power (δύναμις) of God (cf. Luke 1:35) and not through traditional sexual contact; and (4) such intervention is announced by a heavenly agent.[99]

From the twin perspectives of the biblical context Luke seems to be constructing as author, and the possible non-Jewish Roman context from which some of his actual first readers might be coming to the text, Jesus's conception as "son of God" indicates an act of divine creation rather than incarnation.[100] The nature of the being created is amenable to several possible interpretations. It may be that a Roman auditor would imagine that Jesus is a demigod, divine by virtue of divine parentage but not preexistent, as apparently Plutarch thought of Plato.[101] David Litwa says, "a divine conception in the Greco-Roman culture hinted at the divinity of the child."[102] The use of the language of power in conception often points toward mighty deeds of a person's life that are being elaborated on in the birth narrative. Of course, it is also possible that a Christian with a preexistence Christology will read this story as signaling the means by which Jesus came to be born in human flesh. However, from both a Jewish-creational perspective (my reading) and a divine-being perspective (Litwa's suggestion), the notion of Jesus being the incarnation of the one true God himself is absent.

98. Talbert, "Miraculous Conceptions," 83. Such a parallel seems more apt than the descriptions of Zeus fathering children in which Zeus plays the part of the male sexual partner in a more literal fashion (cf. Collins and Collins, *King and Messiah*, 145).

99. See M. David Litwa, *Iesus Deus: The Early Christian Depiction of Jesus as a Mediterranean God* (Minneapolis: Fortress, 2014), 37-67.

100. Cf. Litwa, *Iesus Deus*, 60-61.

101. Cf. Litwa, *Iesus Deus*, 45-54, 65.

102. Litwa, *Iesus Deus*, 65.

The connection between narratives of divinely enabled birth and creation in both Luke and Plutarch puts on the table, once more, what ramifications Luke wishes his readers to draw, given the connection between creation and the birth of Jesus that likely helps uphold the means of conception. Inasmuch as he later invokes the notion of Adam as son of God, creation of a new, idealized humanity in the person of Jesus may well be in view. Such an understanding of Jesus's identity, in turn, might coalesce with notions of Adamic humanity as "divinized," as we saw that humans can be theophanies in the Priestly strand of the biblical narrative. Though Luke may well be engaging in a divine birth story that has parallels in the ancient Greco-Roman world, it can also be simultaneously true that the appeals to Israel's God as creator, and creator of the first human in particular, would be intended to evoke a different set of resonances, those pointing toward creation of a new, idealized humanity.

As a final note, it should not be overlooked that the angelic messenger ends his conversation with Mary by coordinating, not contrasting, the birth of Jesus with the birth of John: the pregnancy of Elizabeth, who was called barren, is proof that this thing about to happen to Mary is possible (Luke 1:36-37). Though Jesus is, by all accounts, going to be the greater of the two, the notion of miraculous birth presents a continuum of options in Luke's Gospel for the identity of the God-enabled child.

c. Songs of John's Parents

i. Elizabeth's Greeting to the Mother of the Κύριος

Elizabeth's response to Mary's greeting (Luke 1:41-45) opens afresh the possibilities latent in the announcement regarding John's birth. Its usage of the κύριος language for both God and Jesus draws the two figures into what might be called a shared identity. The first use of κύριος is clearly a reference to Jesus, as Mary is called "the mother of my Lord" (ἡ μήτηρ τοῦ κυρίου μου, 1:43).[103] Rowe points out three crucial dimensions of this cry: (1) it is inspired by the Holy Spirit; (2) it is preceded by ten references to God as κύριος; and (3) it is the first label given to Jesus after he comes to exist as a character in the story, albeit in Mary's womb.[104] Moreover, the next usage of κύριος refers to God, who spoke the promise through the angel: "blessed is she who believed

---

103. Cf. Brown, *Birth of the Messiah,* 344, who brings the dual usage of κύριος to bear and concludes that this is a statement recognizing that Jesus is the Lord messiah.

104. Rowe, *Early Narrative Christology,* 39-40.

that there would be a completion of the things spoken to her from the Lord"
(μακάρια ἡ πιστεύσασα ὅτι ἔσται τελείωσις τοῖς λελαλημένοις αὐτῇ παρὰ
κυρίου, 1:45).

There are several reasons why I remain unpersuaded by Rowe's conclusion
that the conjoining of Jesus and God under the title κύριος is a move in the
direction of a divine Christology, some of which reasons will become clearer
as I work my way through the remainder of the birth and resurrection material in Luke. One of the most important reasons, however, is that I do not
take the presence of Jesus in this scene to be his narrative introduction. Rowe
makes much of the distinction between what we learn of Jesus in prospect
from the angel and what we hear of the baby who is present in Mary's uterus
from the mouth of another human character.[105] While these differences are
significant in the unfolding of the plot, I take it that the first set of Christological indicators, provided by the angel, gives the reader the framework for
making sense of the latter, and thus performs the function that Rowe assigns,
instead, to Elizabeth's greeting. The "character's first introduction"[106] is, to
my reading of Luke, the introduction provided by the promise of a Davidic
son of God. Indeed, this offers the lens through which I agree with Rowe's
astute observation, "Thus is Jesus . . . κύριος in relation to others, κύριος,
that is, within the web of human relationships that helps to construct his
identity."[107] Jesus is Lord of other humans inasmuch as he is God's anointed
king; Davidic kingship provides the context within which the conjunction of
Jesus as Lord and God as Lord cohere in the high human Christology that I
see Luke offering his readers.

Indeed, as Rowe continues his exposition, it becomes difficult to see how
the argument that unfolds argues for anything other than the exalted human
Christology that my own work sees at play in the text. That "the narrative
bespeaks a kind of unity of identity between YHWH and the human Jesus"[108]
is a strong point, but the connotations of it can be worked out either in the
direction of a "divine identity Christology," à la Richard Bauckham, where
"identity" entails ontological divinity, or in the direction of exalted human
Christology, in terms such as those developed from the Jewish antecedents
in the current study, where "identity" entails unique representation of God
on the earth. When Rowe later goes on to say that the "overlap created by the

105. Rowe, *Early Narrative Christology*, 42-43.
106. Rowe, *Early Narrative Christology*, 42.
107. Rowe, *Early Narrative Christology*, 43.
108. Rowe, *Early Narrative Christology*, 45.

particular context and use of κύριος does not in any way imply that Jesus is the same character or person as God the father. God the father is alone θεός and πατήρ for Luke, and it is the heavenly purpose of the Father that animates the events of Jesus's life,"[109] he draws the reader down a path that, to my mind, leads away from Bauckham and toward an idealized human Christology.

ii. Zechariah's Song

While Mary's song focuses specifically on God as Israel's help, Zechariah's song moves more directly into the roles that Jesus will play in the drama of salvation. Thus it is an important piece in directly assessing the Christology of Luke's narrative, and the Christology it depicts is thoroughly Davidic.[110] While Mary's song celebrates God's faithfulness in remembering Israel and fulfilling the Abrahamic promises (1:54, 55), Zechariah's song delineates more specifically what this divine visitation entails. God redeems Israel by "raising a horn of salvation in the house of David his παιδός" (1:69).[111] Of course, παιδός can mean "servant," but it can also mean "child," a multivalence that inheres in Mary's own description of Israel (cf. Acts 3:13).[112] Whether or not familial overtones are intended, the significant point for Luke's narrative is that the means by which God will redeem is through a Davidic savior. Moreover, in keeping with the claim made above, Luke specifies that this rescue, enacted by the messiah, is the specific way in which the scriptural promises find their fulfillment: "Just as he spoke through the mouths of his holy prophets of old: salvation from our enemies" (1:70-71). According to the clues that Luke provides his readers, the connection between Jesus and the biblical antecedents is not by playing the role of God as such, but by playing the role of the promised savior through whom God will act in fulfillment of God's promises.[113] The promise is salvation or redemption from enemies (1:70, 71, 72), and it comes by way of the scion of the house of David (1:69). Zechariah's song of celebration

109. Rowe, *Early Narrative Christology*, 49.

110. Strauss, *Davidic Messiah*, 97-108.

111. Green, *Gospel of Luke*, 113, says, "It employs Exodus typology and describes the agent of salvation in Davidic terms." Such a description is apt.

112. Brief allusion to the possibility of double entendre in Acts is made by Gaventa, in "Learning and Relearning," 151-52. Hurtado, *Lord Jesus Christ*, 191-93, draws the connection to the biblical precedents of Israel and David as God's servant, one of a number of instances in which Hurtado makes a compelling case that the category of messiah is large enough to hold the Christological data he brings to the table.

113. Green, *Gospel of Luke*, 115.

thus contains two clear indications about Luke's Christology: (1) we are to understand that Jesus saves precisely as Davidic king; and (2) this particular promise is what Luke understands to be Jesus's role in fulfilling scripture.

But of equal importance is the way that Zechariah goes on to speak of the role of his own son, John the Baptist. The words directed at John are important for the very reason that they speak of his ministry as the forerunner of the coming Davidic messiah, but do so in terms that otherwise sound like he is preparing the way for God. In other words, just as the initial introduction of Jesus by the angel in Christological terms helps the reader interpret Elizabeth's blessing in messianic rather than divine categories, so also Zechariah's elaboration of Jesus's Davidic mission aids the reader in understanding that the divine work for which John the Baptist prepares the people is the work that God does through God's chosen Davidic messiah. This task is depicted as going before the Lord to prepare his paths (1:76), giving knowledge of salvation to his people (1:77), a salvation that comes by forgiveness of sins, which, in turn, comes through God's own tender mercies (1:78), with the divine glory rising to shine on the people (1:78-79). John is forerunner of the Lord in preparing the people for the visitation of God in the Davidic king who is Jesus. Without the larger framework of understanding in which people respond to God through their responses to God's agent, such a conjunction of Jesus and God might lead one to conclude that Jesus and God share in divine identity in the ontological or incarnational sense. However, with such a paradigm in place, and with Luke's clear employment of such a divine representation framework in this very song, the words lend weight to an idealized human, rather than divine, Christology.

d. Born This Day in David's City: The Christ-Lord

In the birth narrative proper, Luke once again makes clear that the heart of Jesus's Christological identity is his Davidic kingship. For Luke, the birth in Bethlehem is not directly tied to the prophecy from Micah 5 that the messiah will be born in Bethlehem (cf. Matt 2:6), instead, it finds its immediate significance in Jesus's Davidic descent.[114] Before even naming the city as Bethlehem, Luke tells the reader that Jesus's father has taken the family to the city of David: ἀνέβη . . . εἰς τὴν Ἰουδίαν εἰς πόλιν Δαυὶδ ἥτις καλεῖται Βηθλεέμ (2:4). This, then, is immediately followed by the explanation that this was because he was of the house and line of David (2:4). In an almost heavy-handed way, Luke

114. Strauss, *Davidic Messiah*, 108-13.

directs the reader to find the significance of the ensuing birth in the realm of Jesus as Davidic messiah.[115]

This rubric continues to govern the Christology as Jesus's birth is announced to the shepherds in the subsequent pericope.[116] The angel declares to the shepherds good news for all the people (παντὶ τῷ λαῷ, 2:10): "A savior, who is Christ-Lord, has been born to you today in David's city" (2:11). From Zechariah's song, Luke's readers already know that the coming Davidic messiah is going to be the one through whom God brings salvation (1:69).[117] They also know that this Christ comes to make redemption for God's people (τῷ λαῷ αὐτοῦ, 1:68). Thus, the description of this newborn savior, whom they call Christ with yet another Davidic reference, is wholly caught up in Luke's messiah Christology. Here, also, we see Jesus referred to by the title κύριος, and again we encounter this title as a specification of Jesus's Christological identity. The first time it occurred was in Elizabeth's calling the baby κύριος, after the angel had established his identity as Davidic messiah; the second time was Zechariah's indicating that the fulfillment of the Davidic promise is the Lord before whom John would go, and now the Christ born in David's city is also called Lord. Thus, when the shepherds decide to act on what ὁ κύριος has made known to them (2:15), the reader can easily slide back to a divine reference for the title, without conflating the identity of the heavenly God and the earthly messiah, even while recognizing that Jesus is κύριος on earth, even from birth, solely because ὁ κύριος in heaven is the one who has selected, created, and empowered him to exercise lordship and bring about salvation on God's behalf. Thus far, my conclusions match those of Rowe, which he reaches by a slightly different exegetical path.[118] Further, I agree with Rowe that the binding of Jesus and God comes from a shared identity as κύριος;[119] however, the significance of saying that Jesus and God share in a basic identity as κύριος is a claim that I wish to carefully circumscribe around notions of agency such as I have been arguing for throughout this work, as I see insufficient evidence in this identification to gesture toward a proto-divine ontology of some sort.[120]

115. Cf. Green, *Gospel of Luke*, 127.

116. See also Strauss, *Davidic Messiah*, 113-17.

117. Brown, *Birth of the Messiah*, 424-25, indicates several ways that this initial giving of titles bestows upon Jesus roles that he will fulfill later in his life and resurrection.

118. Rowe, *Early Narrative Christology*, 53-55.

119. Rowe, *Early Narrative Christology*, 53-55. Less careful is González, *Luke*, 39, who points to the use of κύριος in the LXX for the name Yʜᴡʜ and says that the angels are thus announcing the birth of "the Lord" in this divine sense.

120. I choose vague words such as "gesture toward" and "proto-divine" intentionally, inas-

e. Simeon and "the Lord's Christ"

The reader is introduced to Simeon with several indications that he is a trustworthy character in the narrative: he is righteous, awaiting Israel's consolation, and, most importantly, is a bearer of the Holy Spirit and led by this spirit into the temple on the day of dedication (2:25-27).[121] The narrator tells us that this spirit had also promised Simeon that he would not die before seeing the Lord's Christ (τὸν χριστὸν κυρίου, 2:26). In contrast to the Christ-Lord of the angelic announcement, Jesus is here depicted as God's messiah. These, in fact, are the first two uses of the word χριστός in Luke's narrative, but they each connect the story with the larger theme of Jesus's Davidic kingship.[122] As Christ, Jesus is the embodiment of God's salvation (εἶδον οἱ ὀφθαλμοί μου τὸ σωτήριόν σου, 2:30). Both the unity between God and Jesus and their distinction from one another come through. Jesus is the personification of the great divine act of salvation that is, in fact, God's own act (σου); it is just because God is at work in Jesus to save the people that Jesus himself has already been called savior (2:11) and Israel's horn of salvation (1:69). This functional Christology that identifies Jesus with God runs throughout the passage, Simeon describing Jesus as a shining light of glory (2:32),[123] a cause of stumbling that will be rejected and disclose the contents of people's hearts (2:34-35). Throughout, there is no suggestion of ontological identity, but there is the continued building of a rich interconnectedness in which Jesus, as God's unique agent on the earth, represents God not only as an agent at work but also as the stand-in whose rejection entails the rejection of God, and whose embrace entails the embrace of God that leads to salvation. Such a relation is underscored further in the

---

much as Rowe is quite careful not to overstate the nature of his evidence while yet guiding the reader, so it seems to me, gently toward a conclusion that Jesus and God share an identity in a way that is well on its way to the clearer statements of divinity we see elsewhere in the Christian tradition (including John's Gospel). To my mind, however, it is precisely the hesitancy of such claims that underscores the likelihood of an alternative Christology functioning within the narrative, a Christology in which the distinctions between Jesus and the Father are clearly maintained because Luke does not see Jesus as either preexistent in general or an incarnation of the God of Israel in particular. Jesus is κύριος precisely because he is the Davidic messiah and therefore God's representative ruler on the earth.

121. Cf. Pokorný, *Theologie der lukanischen Schriften*, 53-54.

122. Cf. Strauss, *Davidic Messiah*, 117-20.

123. A role that seems to be picked up by Paul himself in claiming to be a light to the nations in Acts 13:47; cf. Pokorný, *Theologie der lukanischen Schriften*, 56. Here is another clue that we are not dealing with an inherent divine property, but with a communicated divine property that representative human figures might embody.

summary statement that concludes that Jesus "grew and strengthened, being filled with wisdom and the grace of God was upon him" (2:40). This is not only a summary passage, but perhaps also a transitional passage, allowing the reader to see that God is Jesus's father not only in the sense of creating Jesus in Mary's womb but also in the sense of "raising" Jesus. This will become clearer in the following pericope. Jesus's development is superintended by the God whom he will represent to the world as Christ and as Lord.

f. About His Father's Business

The final story of Jesus's youth, unique to the story of Luke and thus indicative of the particular Christology with which Luke desires to frame Jesus's ministry, is Jesus's presence in the temple as a twelve-year-old boy (2:41-52). This colorful story illustrates the narrator's claim about Jesus's growth in wisdom and the presence of God's grace that immediately precedes (2:40), as the people who hear Jesus are astonished at his understanding and his answers (2:47). The Christological crux, however, comes as Jesus turns his mother's declaration back to her and redefines who his father is. She says, "Look! Your father [ὁ πατήρ σου] and I have been in distress while looking for you!" (2:48). But Jesus has been concerned about another father: "Why is it that you were seeking me? Did you not know that I had to be [δεῖ] about the things of my father [ἐν τοῖς τοῦ πατρός μου]?" (2:49).

This final story prior to the appearance of John the Baptist shows a Jesus who has grasped the Christology developed throughout the infancy narrative. Jesus is son of God, both by peculiar creation and by having a particular role that he must perform (δεῖ, 2:49).[124] Moreover, God as Jesus's creating father has also been involved in developing Jesus in wisdom and insight. Finally, in this passage we receive a glimpse of what the ultimate necessity will be in Jesus's Christological calling: to articulate and demonstrate true faithfulness to God in the presence of Israel's temple leadership. This is a passage that underscores the Christological particularity of Jesus, but that does not entail a son of God Christology that transcends what we have seen before.[125]

---

124. Cf. Brown, *Birth of the Messiah*, 490-91.

125. Once again, the theologically oriented commentary of González is more far-reaching in its claims (*Luke*, 44). Discussing Jesus's relationship to the temple, he declares that the question with respect to the temple put in 1 Kings 8:27, "Will God indeed dwell on earth?" is answered with a resounding "Yes" by the incarnation. However true this may be theologically, it is my feeling that by so importing the incarnation (and temple) theology of John, that Luke's voice has been silenced rather than expounded or explained.

The Jesus to whom the reader has thus far been introduced fits extraordinarily well within the messianic expectations of at least some early Jews.[126] The *Psalms of Solomon* speaks of a king who is righteous because taught by God himself (17:31). In these psalms, the word "king" functions much like "Lord" does in Luke. In one breath the *Psalms of Solomon* is celebrating the "Lord's messiah" as king (17:32; cf. Luke 2:26), while in the next declaring that "the Lord himself is his king" (17:34). As Luke's readers move easily back and forth between God as Lord and Jesus as Lord, so the *Psalms of Solomon*'s readers move between God as king and messiah as king. The psalms also indicate that the messiah is marked out by the powerful presence of the Holy Spirit, and is wise and strong (17:37; 18:7), attributes Luke also ascribes to Jesus as he introduces us to him in Luke 1–2. The glory of this king, shining for even the nations (*Pss. Sol.* 17:31), matches the shining light who is Jesus, unto the revelation of the Gentiles (Luke 2:32). In the *Psalms of Solomon,* the way that God demonstrates that the Lord is Israel's king forever (17:46) is finally through the appointment of a Davidic king, in fulfillment of the promises made in 2 Samuel 7 (17:21). The only piece that is missing is the idea of the king himself as God's son, a title that the *Psalms of Solomon* ascribes, instead, to Israel as a whole (17:27; 18:4). Thus, the reading I have offered of Luke is not only internally coherent, but fits well within early Jewish conceptions of how to speak of a coming messiah and this figure's relationship to God.

g. Conclusion: The Birth and Childhood of the Lord's Christ

The beginning of a narrative performs an important function. It both creates expectations and establishes initial realities that are transformed by the ensuing story. In terms of expectations, Luke has generated a number of pointers toward the Christology that will unfold throughout the story of Jesus's life. Jesus is going to perform the functions of savior and redeemer and of bringing forgiveness. And he is going to do these things as he plays the role of Davidic messiah who therefore exercises God's own lordship over the world on God's behalf. The special creation of Jesus indicates that a second Adam figure is on the scene, a new opportunity for a human vicegerent to represent God's reign to the world and to fulfill faithful humanness before God. The conjunction of divine and human in Jesus is the conjunction we expect from biblical and post-biblical Jewish precedent: an exalted human being has arrived who stands in for God due to his unique place in the story of Israel. In this case, Jesus is

---

126. This is well established by Strauss, *Davidic Messiah,* 120-23.

the one through whom the promises of God are going to be fulfilled. Thus, Luke provides a clean picture, in his introduction, of the very kind of idealized human messiah that I propose as the grid for interpreting the Synoptic Gospels throughout this book. As for the possibility that the narrative will transform these expectations, I turn now to the resurrection narratives, and Peter's speech at Pentecost, to show that Luke's exalted human Christology as told through the first two chapters is maintained even after Jesus's death and resurrection.

2. THE CHRIST MUST BE RAISED

The resurrection narratives in Luke play a twofold role. On the one hand, they conclude the narrative of Jesus depicted in the Gospel; on the other, they provide a bridge into the continuing acts of Jesus through the deeds and experiences of the early church as depicted in Acts.[127] This section on the resurrection narratives examines how the resurrection itself finalizes the necessity of Jesus's messianic task as delineated in the passion and resurrection predictions; it then combs the resurrection narratives themselves for indications of Luke's Christology; and finally it turns to Peter's sermon on Pentecost to see a more extensive interpretation of the significance of Jesus's resurrection.

a. The Resurrection — as Predicted

In both Matthew and Luke there is some effort on the part of characters in the know to remind the nonplussed followers of Jesus that Jesus had predicted not only his death but also his resurrection (Matt 28:6; Luke 24:6, 44). Matthew issues a further reminder in the voice of the Pharisees that Jesus had predicted his resurrection (27:63). The specific places where such claims were made in the preceding narratives were the son of man sayings that predicted rejection, suffering, death, and resurrection. Luke, in fact, makes the connection with the son of man sayings explicit. The angels at the tomb say to the women, "Remember how he spoke to you while you were still in Galilee, saying, 'It is necessary [δεῖ] for the son of man to be handed over into the hands of sinful people and to be crucified and to rise on the third day.' And they remembered his words" (24:7-8). This uniquely Lukan rendering of the words of the angelic messengers at the tomb is of vital importance for understanding the Christol-

---

127. Cf. Green, *Gospel of Luke*, 832-33.

ogy of the resurrection narratives. It is an invitation to the reader to interpret the ensuing stories under the rubric of the son of man Christology that had previously been developed. As it turns out, the decision of my own study to focus first on the son of God and son of man titles has not skewed the Lukan Christology in the least, but provides the groundwork for making sense of the climactic revelation of Jesus's identity to his followers after that identity is fully, one might say eternally, possessed by the risen Jesus.

The Jesus whom we saw in Luke's son of man sayings was very much like Mark's in remaining firmly within the sphere of exalted humanity. Jesus as son of man is one with authority now, who must suffer and die, but who will also be raised to glory. As the one raised to glory, Luke's son of man will return as judge as well. The son of man sayings present a paradox that is captured by Luke's Gospel-Acts story in other terms as well: something truly happens for Jesus at the resurrection. He is glorified and enters into a state of authority over the cosmos as one enthroned at God's right hand. However, the son of man on earth exercised analogous authority already. Such is the Christology that Luke invokes when reminding the reader not only about the passion and resurrection predictions in general, but of Jesus as son of man in particular. This will be of utmost importance for making sense of Peter's claim that the one whom the angels call "Christ-Lord" at birth is nonetheless made Lord and Christ through his resurrection and exaltation to God's right hand. If the son of man is, as I argued, the quintessential human being ruling the world on God's behalf, then the resurrection is Jesus's entering into a heavenly existence as that Human One.

Such a recognition that Jesus's resurrection should be read within the narrative of the son of man, a narrative in which the earthly Jesus exercises an authority that will only fully be his in resurrection glory, helps explain an anomaly in Luke's story. In an article on the Christology behind Acts 2, Kavin Rowe notes, "Luke withholds the word κύριος from the mocking, trial, execution, and burial of Jesus."[128] The final use of the word is at Peter's denial, when ὁ κύριος looks at Peter and Peter remembered the word τοῦ κυρίου that he would deny him before the rooster crowed.[129] "Thus it is just here, at the moment that Jesus is rejected by the last disciple and begins to be mocked and beaten, that the word disappears from the story."[130] In the reading of Jesus's

---

128. C. Kavin Rowe, "Acts 2.36 and the Continuity of Lukan Christology," *NTS* 53 (2007): 37-56, here 52.

129. Rowe, "Acts 2.36," 52.

130. Rowe, "Acts 2.36," 52.

identity that I provide throughout this book, the silence of Jesus as κύριος during this rejection of Jesus by the disciples and authority figures fits perfectly. To be κύριος is to be one who holds a position of authority from God. The crucifixion is humanity's judgment against Jesus's right to make such a claim to authority. The son of man who has authority on the earth is paradoxically delivered into the authority of men. And yet, the paradox continues as this very setting aside of authority and lordship is reversed by God's raising Jesus from the dead and thereby restoring and giving to an even greater degree what was Jesus's already on earth in inchoate form. This is a reading of that narrative silence that makes good sense within the son of man Christology that Luke invokes at the beginning of the resurrection narrative — a narrative that kicks off with the women looking for the body of the Lord Jesus (24:3). More than this, however, the making of the crucified Jesus into Christ and Lord once again at the resurrection is the explicit proclamation of Peter on the day of Pentecost, as I demonstrate below.

b. Revelation of the Scriptural Christ

In Luke, Jesus appears in two scenes after his crucifixion: the road to Emmaus story (24:13-35) and his appearance to a larger group of followers (24:36-49). In both, Jesus has to reframe the people's understanding of what it means for him to be Christ, in both we are told that Jesus appeals to scripture to do so, and in both the movement from death to resurrection is a core component of how Jesus wants them to understand his work (though in the second the messianic tasks are a bit more expansive than in the first). Luke's Jesus thus tells the reader how it is that he is related to the scriptures of Israel and renders the final Christological statements that shape the readers' understanding of the narrative that has just unfolded. If Luke is a story about Jesus, then the story ends by telling the readers who this Jesus is whom they should have met.

In the first story in which Jesus reframes his auditors' understanding of what it meant for him to be Christ, the lesson is summarized this way: "'O foolish ones and hard of heart to believe all the things that the prophets have spoken. Were these things not necessary, that the Christ would suffer and enter into his glory?' And beginning from Moses and from all the prophets he interpreted for them in all the scriptures the things about himself" (24:26-27). The ironies of the story run deep. When Jesus first confronts them about their sadness, the two people on the road to Emmaus provide a virtual recitation of one of the son of man passion-resurrection predictions: the high priests and rulers handed him over to death, and he was crucified and now it has been three days and some women said they were told he was raised (24:20, 23). Moreover, in light of Jesus's mighty words and deeds before God and the people, they had hoped that Jesus would redeem Israel (24:19, 21). These two people have correctly delineated not only the events that have transpired, but also the relationship between Jesus and God and Jesus's role as redeemer of Israel (cf. 1:68). Thus, the problem that Jesus seeks to resolve with his exposition of scripture is the conjoining of these two strands: the events that have transpired are not a denial and fatal undoing of Jesus's vocation to be redeemer-messiah; they are the very events that make it possible.[131] This is the Christological correction issued by Jesus on the road to Emmaus: scripture indicates that to be the one in whom God is at work to redeem Israel is to be one who enters into resurrection glory only along the way of the cross. This is the paradoxical reality of Jesus's calling to be the Christ (24:26), who is also the Lord and the son of man.

When Jesus appears to the larger group of disciples, his first item of business is to establish continuity between the person they are seeing and the human Jesus who was crucified. Jesus is at great pains to prove that he is not a spirit (24:37-43). The proofs in which Jesus engages are a visual inspection of his hands and feet as demonstrations that he is, in fact, flesh and bone. (As an aside, I note the use of the phrase ἐγώ εἰμι in the demonstration to his followers that he is not simply spirit, as God would be.) The second demonstration of his identity is made in asking for and eating a piece of bread. In order for Jesus to demonstrate that the one who stands before the disciples is, in fact, Jesus, the actions he takes are specifically directed at proving that he is an embodied human being who has been raised from the dead. Luke's belaboring the point underscores not simply some apologetic purpose with respect to resurrection, but also an important Christological purpose: to be truly Jesus who is Lord and Christ is to be truly human in every sense of that word. The resurrected Jesus is the exalted human through whom God had already been at work during his life on earth. The Human One has been raised from the dead.

Jesus then turns, once again, to instruct his followers in Christological hermeneutics. To read the scriptures of Israel as a witness to Christ is to read them as saying that the Christ must suffer and rise again from the dead on the third day, events followed by repentance for forgiveness of sins being proclaimed to all nations (24:46-47). The specifically Christological content is largely the same as in 24:25-27, although here Luke's Jesus speaks of the resurrection per se rather than entering into his glory (cf. v. 26). A crucial expansion is also made, however. Jesus here foreshadows the following chapter in the story in which

---

131. Cf. Green, *Gospel of Luke*, 846-47.

repentance is proclaimed to all nations, a chapter for which the disciples are prepared because they are "witnesses of these things" (24:48), but for which they will be more fully prepared once Jesus sends the spirit upon them (24:49).

For wrapping our minds around Luke's Christology, here is the crucial point: when Jesus tells his disciples what it is about him that they need to know in order to proclaim him from the scriptures, he does not tell them about an identity with God in some sort of proto-Chalcedonian sense such that they are to go out and proclaim Jesus's divinity. Instead, he points them to the crucial Christological events of the death and resurrection. To be sure, the apostles will interpret these events. But what we see as we turn to Acts is that the interpretation is this: (1) the crucifixion demonstrates that humans stood against God who was testifying to Jesus by the work of the spirit in him — and humans therefore need to repent and be forgiven (this is especially Luke's message for Israel); and (2) the resurrection demonstrates that God has overturned the human judgment, reaffirming his original testimony and enthroning Jesus as the promised Davidic king, at God's right hand, forever. Luke's Jesus is not proclaimed and celebrated for his divinity, but for being the Christ of God. In neither of the closing scenes of Luke do we find any hint that Jesus's identity is to be understood in terms of being a God-like being; he is, instead, the suffering and resurrected Christ in, and only in, the full humanness that death and resurrection entail.

In light of some recent scholarship, it is important to highlight from another angle what Jesus does not say. Because New Testament writers apply to Jesus certain biblical texts, such as those that use κύριος to refer to YHWH in the LXX but now refer to Jesus as Lord, it has been argued that the force of the intertextual connection serves to identify Jesus as, in some way, the God of Israel. But when Luke's Jesus tells the reader what the connection is between himself and those biblical antecedents, it is the work of the messiah and not the ontology of Jesus as God or the unity of Jesus with/as YHWH that is articulated. This will be explained in more detail in chapter 6 below. Not only does Luke's Jesus state twice that it is the Christ event as such that the scriptures predict, Luke's preachers in Acts demonstrate the very hermeneutics that Luke 24 anticipates. We turn now to one example.

c. Proclaiming the Risen One

I have had the regular experience of hearing someone discuss the story of the road to Emmaus and lament that we do not overhear what Jesus says to his two companions. Such a longing seems to me entirely unnecessary inasmuch as the same author who made the claim that Jesus gave lengthy exposition of scripture as referring to a crucified and glorified Christ also provides several examples of sermons in which just this point is made from just that body of texts. The sermons in Acts demonstrate that for Luke the key Christological question is whether the man Jesus, who lived and was crucified, has also been raised from the dead and enthroned as the empowering presence behind the church's work. In order not to further stretch the length of a book that is already of such a girth as to try the patience of the reader, I limit my discussion to Peter's sermon in Acts 2. This speech provides for us an exposition of the identity of Jesus both before and after the resurrection, providing further confirmation that for Luke Jesus is best understood as idealized human being.

After interpreting the outpouring of the spirit in terms of Joel 3, Peter turns to address the Jesus who stands behind it. Acts 2:22 captures Luke's theology perfectly: "Jesus of Nazareth, a man attested to you by God [ἄνδρα ἀποδεδειγμένον ἀπὸ τοῦ θεοῦ] in deeds of power, wonders, and signs which God did through him in your midst, just as you know, this one . . . you killed, crucifying him through the hands of lawless people" (2:22, 23). At Pentecost, with the benefits of both the newly acquired spirit and the Christological disclosure handed to him by Jesus after the resurrection, Peter describes Jesus as a human being in whom God is at work. The mighty acts that we see throughout the pages of Luke's Gospel here receive their definitive interpretation: these are indications that God is at work in the particular man, Jesus. This also will provide a hermeneutical lens for understanding Acts: God who was at work in Jesus continues to be at work in Jesus as Jesus sends the spirit to be at work in the early church. For Peter's sermon, however, focused as it is on Jesus, the point is that God was the one who was working in Jesus. Jesus did not perform those works because he had an innate power within himself, or even because he had been bestowed an independent endowment of the Holy Spirit. Insofar as the spirit was at work, that was an indication that God was doing things in Jesus. Summarizing the life of the earthly Jesus before crucifixion, Peter's Christology is of a human being empowered by God to act on the earth. Coming as it does as a retrospective of Jesus's ministry, it would be difficult to imagine a more important or decisive proof that Luke's Jesus falls within the idealized human Christology I am developing in this book.

The crucifixion itself Peter interprets as humans making a judgment contrary to God's own, handing over to death one in whom God was clearly at work.[132] Without citing a particular scripture to uphold the necessity of

---

132. Cf. Gaventa, "Learning and Relearning," 150-51.

crucifixion (cf. Luke 24:26, 46), Peter nonetheless indicates its necessity by ascribing it to the "predestined will and foreknowledge of God" (Acts 2:23). Thus, the sermon moves from interpreting the life of Jesus to affirming the necessity of his death, bringing Peter's summary up to the final words of Jesus himself in Luke 24.

The ongoing interpretation of the resurrection fills out Luke's Christology by coloring in the lines that were already sketched in the Gospel. Moving into his words on Jesus's escape from death, Peter cites Psalm 15 LXX as the words of David (Acts 2:25) about a coming king in David's line (2:30).[133] Here then is the detail of what Jesus sketched in Luke 24: according to scripture (in this case Psalm 15, LXX) the Davidic messiah must suffer and die before being raised up into glory. Peter reads the psalm prophetically, claiming that knowledge of God's promise of an heir to his throne caused David to speak in terms of a descendant who would not see the decay of death (Acts 2:30). Echoing Jesus's demonstration of himself as one having flesh and bones, Peter says that the psalm sees beforehand "the resurrection of the Christ because he neither was abandoned to Hades nor did his flesh see corruption" (2:31). Peter is not simply providing a biblical proof or exposition of the resurrection, he is also articulating a Christology of a resurrected Davidic king. In other words, what Luke 1–2 trained the reader to anticipate for Jesus in its recurring refrain of his being the fulfillment of the Davidic promise and messiah is now fully and finally true of Jesus through the resurrection. When Peter brings God into the picture, it is not to say how Jesus has demonstrated his divinity by rising from the dead (as the Gospel of John seems to imply), but to say that the same God who attested to Jesus by powerful signs during his time on earth has acted powerfully in Jesus once again to raise the dead man back to life: τοῦτον τὸν Ἰησοῦν ἀνέστην ὁ θεός (Acts 2:32).

Jesus's resurrection is a literalization of the enthronement experienced by Israel's kings, as depicted in Psalm 110:1, in which the kings are envisioned as enthroned at God's right hand. Heavenly exaltation makes literally possible what was previously a figure of speech. The idea of God saying to a king, "Sit at my right hand," provided rich fodder for the early Christians who read the psalm messianically and depicted such enthronement at God's right hand as the consequence of Jesus's resurrection (e.g., Mark 10:37; Heb 1:13). Here, also, Peter says, "Therefore, having been exalted to the right hand of God," and he goes on to cite Psalm 110:1 (MT; 109:1, LXX) as indicating Jesus's newly exalted

133. On the thoroughgoing Davidic nature of this portion of the speech, see also Strauss, *Davidic Messiah*, 135-40.

status. Jesus's resurrection, in short, is his enthronement. In the Christology of Luke-Acts, the Jesus who was born Christ and Lord, but whose lordship is silenced through crucifixion, is made Lord and Christ through this literal enthroning at God's right hand: "God has made him both Lord and Christ, this Jesus whom you crucified" (Acts 2:36).[134]

The specific language that Peter uses, of a man attested by God, and the specific way in which Peter affiliates the man Jesus with the God who has enthroned him, both speak a word of caution as we attempt to discern what sort of correlation between Jesus and God is being drawn. Larry Hurtado suggests that the implication is an "astonishing" association of Jesus with God in the sense of shared divinity.[135] Peter applies the κύριος title to Jesus as Luke has done throughout the work, in such a way as to unite Jesus and God as those who are ruling the world; however, as elsewhere so also here Peter provides a thoroughly Davidic, messianic rubric for making sense of this title. Jesus is the one whom God has made Lord and Christ (Acts 2:36). Such a direct statement about the divine God and the human Jesus cannot be laid aside due to the purported significance of applying to Jesus a biblical passage originally about God. Jesus's incorporation into the church's celebration of God, and calling on the name of the Lord Jesus for salvation, reframes the identity of God only insofar as it tells us who this Davidic king is through whom God's reign is made known in the world. Again, one can say Lord is a "divine" title, but such divinity is a sharing in the rule of God over the world, as Adam and David did, not inherently a claim to share in God's own ontological divinity.[136] To call Jesus Lord is "revolutionary" because it is a claim that God's eschatological messiah is enthroned in heaven, but not necessarily because anyone who so claimed thereby was attributing divinity to him.[137] Again, when Hurtado claims that honoring Jesus with cultic action is a "startling conviction," it is only startling to include a human being if one is unfamiliar with the psalms that do this very thing for Israel's king (Psalms 2, 110, 89), or because this human is enthroned in a resurrected body in heaven.[138] If we attribute the exaltation of Jesus and his adoration by the church to an underlying conviction about his divinity, a

---

134. See also Strauss, *Davidic Messiah*, 140-43.

135. Hurtado, *Lord Jesus Christ*, 179. The language of "astonishing" is vague, while encouraging the reader to see the highest possible Christology being employed. The adjective creates a slippery conjunction that might appear to imply that Jesus is God without saying what the text cannot uphold.

136. Hurtado, *Lord Jesus Christ*, 182.

137. Hurtado, *Lord Jesus Christ*, 184.

138. Hurtado, *Lord Jesus Christ*, 185.

move in which, no doubt, Hurtado is striving to bring Jesus into closest possible connection with the scriptures of Israel and their God, we run the risk of severing Jesus from the story that those scriptures tell. Those scriptures are the story of a God whose kingdom is executed by faithful human agents, and it is precisely in his humanity ("See that a spirit does not have flesh and bones as I have!") that Jesus fulfills the role of Lord and messiah who rules the world on God's behalf.

The words of Peter, in fact, confirm several of the hypotheses of my study: both Christ and Lord are titles for Jesus that represent not an inherent identity such as is tied to ontology, but a function he performs within the story of Israel; Jesus is nonetheless a peculiar person within the narrative, playing a role that is specially his and not generically everyone's; and these titles are bestowed upon the man Jesus by the God who is at work in Jesus in various ways. Put differently, Jesus is Lord and Christ precisely to the extent that he is the man who is representing and enacting the saving power of God in God's stead.

In contrast to this reading, Kavin Rowe has argued that Jesus does not in any significant sense become something at the resurrection that he was not already from the time of his conception and birth. He claims: "The 'making' of which Acts 2.36 speaks does not refer, therefore, to an ontological transformation in the identity of Jesus or his status (from not κύριος to κύριος) but to an epistemological shift in the perception of the human community."[139] While I fully agree that this is not an ontological shift, as the insistence on ontological continuity is much the point of both the appearance scene and Peter's contrasting of David with the resurrected Jesus, I do not think that the shift in status can be brushed aside so easily. The most clear, and to my mind insurmountable, problem with Rowe's way of putting things is that ποιέω does not mean γνωρίζω. Rowe is correct that Peter admonishes the people to "know" (γινωσκέτω, 2:36);[140] however, what they are to know is not simply that God has disclosed something, but that God has *done* something. Two other arguments compel me to take Peter's ἐποίησεν in all its literalness. First, the entire section of the sermon is Peter's explanation of the resurrection. The resurrection fulfills scriptural promise because a son of God has been enthroned at God's right hand. Second, later sermons will continue to underscore the transformative significance of the resurrection. Acts 13:33 is a perfect example, as Paul there cites Psalm 2 as finding its fulfillment in the resurrection: "God has fulfilled this [promise] for us, their children, having

139. Rowe, "Acts 2.36," 55.
140. Rowe, "Acts 2.36," 55.

raised up Jesus from the dead, as also it is written in the second Psalm, 'You are my son, today I have begotten you.'" As with Lord and Christ, so also with the title son of God, there is a way in which this title is true of the earthly Jesus and there is also a way in which it becomes true of the resurrected Jesus in a manner that it was not true of him before. He is installed as son, as Christ, and as Lord. As I mentioned above, Rowe himself has observed that during the stretch from mocking through crucifixion and burial Jesus is never called κύριος. At a time when Jesus's endowment by God is wholly rejected, where he is entirely under the authority of other humans, and submits to the earth's great power in its crucifixion of him, Jesus does not play the part of Lord and Christ. This, it seems to me, weighs against Rowe's claim that "in the Lukan narrative, there was not a time when Jesus was not κύριος."[141] Perhaps more than a rich narrative technique, this silence in regard to Jesus's lordship is a deft indication of the reality at work in the plot: at this time, Jesus is not the Lord he was born to be and set aside to be from his mother's womb. What Jesus was on earth prior to his suffering and death he becomes once again, but to a fuller and more real degree, in heaven. This is the son of man Christology that shapes Luke's interpretation of the resurrection. But in between lies the crucifixion — the rejection of the Christ by the people of the Christ that is finally overturned when God makes the crucified Jesus, once again, Lord and Christ, through his resurrection and exaltation, which is Jesus's enthronement.[142]

The thrust of the sermon is, in the end, elegant and simple: God has rejected the people's rejection of Jesus. God has reaffirmed Jesus as the man through whom God will be at work in the world in great deeds of power and in the Holy Spirit. In none of it are we drawn toward Jesus's being divine; instead, there is a constant theme of pushing the people to recognize that the works brought about by the human Jesus are clear indications that God is at work through him.

In the discussion of Matthew's birth narrative, I cited Raymond Brown's claim that the church's resurrection confession gradually worked its way backward, from Paul's citation of a hymn in which Jesus as raised by the power of the spirit becomes the adopted son of God (Rom 1:4), to Mark's baptism scene in which Jesus is anointed son of God by the spirit and voice from heaven, to the birth narratives in which Jesus is son of God by the creative power of the spirit in the womb.[143] Luke includes such a tripartite establishment of Jesus's

141. Rowe, "Acts 2.36," 55.
142. Strauss, *Davidic Messiah*, 142-44.
143. Brown, *Birth of the Messiah*, 160-61.

identity within his own two-part work.[144] With Davidic Christology more at the fore than a son of God Christology, Luke depicts several key moments in which one might well say that Jesus here "becomes" what he was not before, except for the countervailing indications that he was, in fact, these things already.[145] The challenge, as I see it, is both to acknowledge that the reality of Jesus's identity as Lord and Christ is something Luke recognizes from conception and birth, and to see it as something bestowed at the resurrection, and likely at the baptism as well.[146]

3. CONCLUSIONS: LUKE'S JESUS

For Luke, as for Matthew, the investigation into the birth and resurrection narratives has provided an opportunity to better honor the literary shape of the Gospel. And yet, in Luke's resurrection narrative, it is clear that Luke's Christology has been well represented by the son of man Christology explored in the previous chapter. For Luke, Jesus is the fulfillment of the Davidic promise, the messianic Lord who exercises God's saving rule on the earth.[147] Though Luke might use a title or biblical reference that causes the reader to make the transition between God as Lord and Jesus as Lord, this transition is readily made and does not cause the two characters to be brought any closer than this: Jesus is the human Lord through whom the divine Lord rules and saves.

C. CONCLUSION: MESSIAH BORN AND RAISED

The birth and resurrection narratives set pieces in place that enable the reader to navigate the Gospel stories as disclosures of Jesus's identity. Though sum-

---

144. Cf. Strauss, *Davidic Messiah*, 92.

145. Cf. Dunn, *Christology in the Making*, 51.

146. Interestingly, Brown sees a parallel series of inaugurations in Luke's depiction of John the Baptist (*Birth of the Messiah*, 274-75). John's being filled with the spirit from the womb, says Brown, is "exactly the same thing" as the claim that the word of God came to John — an event that occurs years later.

147. Such a parsing of Jesus's function provides an opportunity both to do justice to the exalted nature of Luke's Christology and to have an alternative, more exegetically viable, way of describing the relationship between Jesus and God than one who is "equal with God" in ways that imply a latent Chalcedonian Christology, the trap fallen into by Thomas R. Schreiner, *New Testament Theology: Magnifying God in Christ* (Grand Rapids, MI: Baker Academic, 2008), 293-94.

ming up all of them is challenging, Larry Hurtado does well in his focus on the Gospel openings: "in both birth narratives, and in the common tradition upon which they depend as well, Jesus's unique conception functions as a way of asserting his significance as the true royal heir of David and the fulfillment of royal-messianic hopes."[148] Royal Christology, rather than divine identity, is the key to unlocking the narratives, even if Matthew's, especially, appears to shade beyond the notion of an idealized human being. The resurrection narratives, likewise, are most keen to indicate that the Jesus who walked the earth is now enthroned messiah and Lord over all. He is the one to whom all authority in heaven and on earth has been given (Matthew), the one who has been made resurrected Lord and Christ (Luke). In both, God has acted to bestow upon the human Jesus what was ideal humanity's in the beginning, what was mediated through David in Israel's past, and what would be embodied in the messiah at the great, eschatological turn of the ages. The messiah born and raised is the messiah who from the womb is the idealized Human One, and now sits enthroned over all things, the Lord at God's right hand.

To recognize these aspects as the core of Jesus's identity, as well as the depictions of Jesus as son of God and son of man explored in the previous chapters, is not to impoverish the Christology of the New Testament, but to enrich it by disallowing the entirety to be flattened by one aspect of the Johannine narrative. I take it that the popular theology of the church reflects, if in unnuanced and at times in caricatured form, the theology of its teachers. In that popular theology, the humanity of Jesus in churches that continue to affirm Jesus's divinity is good for little else than giving him a way to die on the cross. The creedal tradition that skips from "incarnate of the virgin Mary" or "was made human" straight to the crucifixion communicates all too little about Jesus's humanity, and appears to ignore the narratological necessity, within Israel's scriptures, of a human ruling the world on God's behalf, of that human being an agent of worldwide blessing, of that human standing in as God's representative on the earth and defining the identity of God's people. As Peter puts it in his speech on Pentecost, Jesus was a man attested by God.

---

148. Hurtado, *Lord Jesus Christ*, 328. I note in passing that Hurtado does not argue for his divine Christology from the material in the birth narratives.

5 Lord of All Creation

When at the end of Matthew the resurrected Jesus claims, "All authority in heaven and on earth has been given to me," he is (as argued in the previous chapter) asserting God's exaltation of him as king over God's kingdom. Similar is Peter's speech at Pentecost, claiming that the outpouring of the spirit is a manifestation of God's enthronement of Jesus at God's right hand. In both instances, the exalted Jesus is the fulfillment of God's promise to enthrone an Israelite king as lord over the nations. The point of this chapter is to argue that what the Synoptic Gospels claim for the resurrected Christ is a final vindication and securing of what they narratively depict of the human Jesus while on earth. The miracles of Jesus raise the question of who Jesus is that he can perform such deeds.[1] These are questions that the narratives guide the reader to ask as characters within the story wonder aloud, "Who is this?" (e.g., Mark 4:41; 6:14-16) or as Jesus wages a war of information control with those who know the answer (e.g., Mark 3:11-12; 5:43). The stories of Jesus's miraculous works of power are told, at least in part, to press upon the reader the question of Jesus's identity. Inasmuch as the questions are raised in stories, it will take the whole story to answer the question of who this is whom wind and waves, spirits and bodies obey. And so we should use caution against overly weighing any one particular pericope or group of pericopes.

But by the same token, the functioning of the whole narrative to answer the question of Jesus's identity creates a strong presupposition in favor of the Christological indications already surveyed continuing throughout the stories of Jesus's life. In surveying the son of God title, I showed how it frames the entirety of Mark's Gospel, even as its specific messianic content is more

---

1. An observation made also by Barry L. Blackburn, "The Miracles of Jesus," in *The Cambridge Companion to Miracles* (ed. Graham H. Twelftree; New York: Cambridge University Press, 2011), 113-30, here 114.

overtly articulated by the later-surveyed son of man title. The connotations of a suffering royal figure, authoritative on earth and later exalted to a heavenly securing of kingly power, carry over to Matthew and Luke as well. And in the latter Gospels' birth and resurrection narratives we saw a concern to depict a Davidic messiah, specially created by God to represent and to rescue God's people through suffering, death, resurrection, and rule. Although all three Gospels, using the authoritative son of man motif, provide us with a grid for understanding Jesus's work as that of an idealized, uniquely authorized human figure, Luke is particularly clear in drawing these lines. While the events of the day of Pentecost are interpreted as Joel's signs and wonders (Acts 2:16-21, esp. τέρατα and σημεῖα in v. 19), Peter says the same of Jesus's time on earth: God was at work in him to perform signs and wonders (δυνάμεσιν καὶ τέρασιν καὶ σημείοις, 2:22). As the resurrected Jesus is a man exalted to heavenly authority and power, so also Jesus during his time on earth was "a man attested by God" (2:22, NRSV). This is Luke's hermeneutical key to the identity of Jesus as put on display during Jesus's earthly ministry. In surveying a cross section of these signs and wonders below, I aim to demonstrate that it applies equally well to the tellings of Mark and Matthew. The argument running throughout this chapter, as throughout this book, is that idealized human figures were sufficiently amenable to participation in divine ascriptions, actions, and attributes to account for Jesus's sharing in the same without recourse to notions of divinity as part of the Christological equation. The chapter as a whole, then, will stand against an earlier approach to the miracle traditions, which saw in them such clear indications of divinity that a Hellenistic setting was posited to account for Jesus's depiction as a *theios anēr*.[2] Against the notion that a Hellenistic environment was necessary due to the scruples of Jewish monotheism, and against the notion that Jewish scruples nonetheless led to shocking ascriptions of divine identity to Jewish figures from earliest Palestine, I demonstrate that the miracle and exorcism traditions fit neatly within Jewish categories of idealized human figures acting for and empowered by Israel's God. Jesus's performance of his role as idealized human figure is well captured in Barry Blackburn's assessment that "Jesus performed miracles because he believed himself to be gifted to do so through the Spirit of God."[3] In this assessment of the Christology behind exorcisms, nature miracles, and healings, we discover early Christian stories

2. Rudolf Bultmann, *History of the Synoptic Tradition* (trans. John Marsh; New York: Harper & Row, 1963), 241, does not use the phrase *theios anēr*, but does describe Mark's Jesus, in contrast to that of Q, as "a θεῖος ἄνθρωπος."
3. Blackburn, "Miracles of Jesus," 121.

describing the fulfillment of an expectation that was expressed at Qumran in these words: "Heaven and earth will listen to his messiah" (4Q521 frag. 2 1).

A. EXORCISMS

Stories of exorcisms function in the narrative to draw attention to the surprising power or authority (ἐξουσία, Mark 1:27; par. Luke 4:36) at work in or through Jesus. In this way, the exorcisms cohere with the early son of man sayings that highlight Jesus's authority on the earth (Mark 2:10, 28). The demonic forces Jesus faces in the exorcisms also provide a sort of breech in the great secret of Jesus's identity, indicating to the reader that not only God but also these malevolent spirits know who Jesus is and what Jesus's role is to be in the cosmic drama that is unfolding (e.g., Mark 5:7). Another aspect of Jesus's ministry is encapsulated in these particular mighty acts: they demonstrate that Jesus is engaged in a sort of battle with Satan through the power of the spirit he received at his baptism (Mark 3:23-30). In the narrative flow, Jesus's exorcisms parallel the healing miracles in general in tapering off after Peter's confession (Matthew and Mark only contain one exorcism after the confession; Matt 17:14-20; Mark 9:14-27). But to that point Jesus's exorcisms had been a quintessential part of his ministry, appearing not only in particular episodes but also in summary statements such as Mark 1:39: "And he was going around in all of Galilee, preaching in their synagogues and casting out demons."

Even such a brief summary paragraph highlights some important ways that the exorcism stories will function in tandem with the narrative arcs that have already been traced. This section shows that the exorcism narratives, highlighting as they do Jesus's ἐξουσία, will, like the son of man passages that do the same, demonstrate that Jesus is a specially empowered and authorized human agent of God.[4] Similarly, we can expect that the demonic knowledge of Jesus's divine sonship (Mark 3:11) will function in tandem with the other disclosures that Jesus is son of God and underscore that he is king. Moreover, the idea that Jesus is engaged in a battle with Satan draws the demonic contests into a battle for the throne of rule over the earth (e.g., Matt 4:8-10). Inasmuch as the work done in previous chapters has provided us with holistic, framing

---

4. Dan McCartney, "*Ecce Homo*: The Coming of the Kingdom as the Restoration of Human Vicegerency," *WTJ* 56 (1994): 1-21, cites exorcisms, especially as these are said to be harbingers of the kingdom's arrival in Matthew 12:28 and Luke 11:20, as indications that humanity has regained its place as God's vicegerent through Jesus's authority (9-10).

indications of Jesus's identity as that identity is gradually disclosed across the narratives, and inasmuch as the exorcism stories provide preliminary indication that they address similar themes in the identity of Jesus, I argue here that they further the picture of Jesus as idealized human being rather than adding a unique piece of divine ontology.

One further preliminary consideration, internal to the narrative dynamics of the Synoptic Gospels, is in order at this point. Jesus is not the only person who casts out demons. When Jesus calls his disciples, the very reason for their call as Mark relates it includes participation in Jesus's ministry of exorcism (3:15). Moreover, when he sends them out on their own mission, he gives them authority over these spiritual forces (Mark 6:7; Matt 10:1; Luke 9:1). Thus, in the narrative world of the Synoptic Gospels, the ability to cast out demons per se is not an indication of any peculiar ontological status, but is indicative of possessing an authority or power of such a sort as human beings can exercise. Put differently, if the Synoptic Gospels are willing to show the reader that exorcism is a part of Jesus's ministry that humans can share in, then exorcisms are not attempts to point the reader to a divine Christology. To the contrary, by locating the power of Jesus's ability to exorcise in his possession of the spirit (Mark 3:22-30; pars.), we receive clear indication that even Jesus has such authority inasmuch as he acts within this narrative world as God's specially authorized agent.[5]

1. EXORCISTS IN THE JEWISH TRADITION

As I mentioned already in the chapter on Jesus as son of God, power over demons fits easily within a royal framework in early Judaism.[6] After his anointing, David not only was endowed by the spirit but also served as an exorcist (1 Sam 16:23), a tradition that appears to be preserved in 11QPs[a] XXVII, 9-10 as it lists among David's compositions four songs to sing over the possessed.[7]

---

5. Mary E. Mills, *Human Agents of Cosmic Power in Hellenistic Judaism and the Synoptic Tradition* (JSNTSup 41; Sheffield: JSOT, 1990), 98, puts it thus: "The narrator's attitude tends toward the view that Jesus is divine in the sense of being 'son of God,' i.e. one chosen by the deity as his human agent and given the ongoing presence of divine energy in his own self."

6. The traditions of Solomon and David being regarded as exorcists are widely noted. In addition to the sources noted below, see also Graham H. Twelftree, *Jesus the Exorcist: A Contribution to the Study of the Historical Jesus* (WUNT2 54; Tübingen: Mohr Siebeck, 1993), 35-39.

7. A conjunction widely noted; e.g., in Eric Sorensen, *Possession and Exorcism in the New Testament and Early Christianity* (WUNT2 157; Tübingen: Mohr Siebeck, 2002), 53; Eric Eve, *The Jewish Context of Jesus's Miracles* (JSNTSup 231; New York: Sheffield Academic, 2002), 212.

As Amanda Witmer points out, in Josephus's telling of the David story, the explicit language of exorcism (ἐκβάλλω) is deployed (*Ant.* 6.11).[8] Josephus, writing in the late first century, also reflects a tradition in which God enabled Solomon to learn the arts of exorcism (*Ant.* 8.45).[9] Josephus claims more for Solomon as well: he not only learned incantations for exorcising demons but also compiled these in writing (*Ant.* 8.45). Here, Josephus appears to be comparing Solomon's work as an exorcist with the tradition of Solomon as sage who left behind books such as the biblical Proverbs. Two additional points Josephus makes are worth highlighting. One is that the spells recorded by Solomon ensure that the departing demon is unable to return to its host once cast out (*Ant.* 8.45), a concern echoed in Jesus's teaching in Matthew 12:43-45 (par. Luke 11:24-26). The First Evangelist cultivates the connection between Jesus and Solomon. In Matthew, the saying about a cast-out spirit returning follows immediately after Jesus's claim that one greater than Solomon is present in himself (12:42): his generation will be worse off (like the demoniac whose possessor returns with seven others) because it did not have the eyes to see the great son of David who was in its midst — unlike the queen of the South. The second aspect of Josephus's tale about Solomon significant for our purposes is that Solomon's powers as exorcist, recorded in books, enabled others to cast out demons as well (*Ant.* 8.46-49). Josephus tells of his own contemporary, Eleazar, who not only mimics the spells, but also invokes the name of Solomon (Σολόμωνος μεμνημένος) as he commands the demons to leave (*Ant.* 8.47).[10] Josephus's Solomon tradition thus provides apt parallels to the Synoptic Gospels and Acts not only in its exorcising king, but also in that king's followers' ability to cast out demons in his name. Inasmuch as my primary conversation partners on the question of Gospels Christology draw our attention sharply to the Jewish religious context as the one in which the depictions of Jesus's actions signal a parity with Israel's God, such biblical and post-biblical reflections on exorcising royalty are significant: power to exorcise fits within a royal framework. In the case of David, it is a signal of his empowerment by the spirit; in the case of Solomon, it is an extension of his wisdom. The development of these traditions in post-biblical Judaism comes hand in hand with the development of demonology and angelology

---

8. Amanda Witmer, *Jesus, the Galilean Exorcist: His Exorcisms in Social and Political Context* (LNTS 459/LHJS 10; Edinburgh: T&T Clark, 2012), 43.

9. See the full discussion in Dieter Trunk, *Der Messianische Heiler: Eine redaktions- und religionsgeschichtliche Studie zu den Exorzismen im Matthäusevanglium* (HBS 3; Freiburg: Herder, 1994), 299-312.

10. Cf. Witmer, *Jesus, the Galilean Exorcist,* 45-46.

that occurred in the same period.[11] Moreover, both of these connotations re-verberate through the Synoptic Tradition, with Jesus's spiritual power and au-thoritative teaching being coupled with the traditions of exorcising demons.[12]

2. AUTHORITY, SPIRIT, ROYALTY

a. Matthew: Exorcism and Davidic Kingship

Matthew 12:15-32 provides us with a uniquely Matthean depiction of Jesus as God's beloved, spirit-bearing child who is also an exorcising son of David. In chapter 2 I discussed Jesus's spirit-bearing sonship as an indication of royal power, demonstrating how Jesus's baptismal anointing is an indication of his kingship. Matthew draws those very themes together by juxtaposing his ci-tation of Isaiah 42:1-4 with the Beelzebul controversy, the latter of which he frames as a debate that arises when the crowds muse on whether Jesus might in fact be the son of David (12:21).

The lengthy formula citation in Matthew 12:18-20 quotes a passage from Isaiah (42:1-4) that is often cited as a possible intertext for the baptism scene. It reads in part, "Behold my child (or "servant," Gr παῖς) whom I have chosen, my beloved in whom my soul delights, I will place my spirit upon him and he will proclaim judgment to the nations . . . and in his name the nations will hope." The formula citation itself is said to be the fulfillment of Jesus as a healer who will not allow his deeds to be made known. Ideal readers of Matthew have been given several early indications of what the Christological connotations might be. A spirit-bearing, elect child (or servant) of God, as I already men-tioned, coheres with the baptismal anointing of Jesus as royal son.[13] Also, in the birth narrative we saw how the gathering of the nations to the newborn child Jesus occurs under the rubric of Jesus as king of the Jews. Moreover, the final sending of the disciples into all the nations happens within a scene superintended by Jesus's resurrection-enthronement, as we saw in the previous chapter as well. These hints nudge the reader toward assimilating the servant text of Isaiah within Matthew's larger son of David, messianic Christology.[14]

11. Sorensen, *Possession and Exorcism*, 59-74.

12. See Sorensen, *Possession and Exorcism*, 139-42.

13. On the connection with the baptism, see also Richard Beaton, *Isaiah's Christ in Mat-thew's Gospel* (SNTSMS 123; New York: Cambridge University Press, 2002), 142-43.

14. Cf. Beaton, *Isaiah's Christ in Matthew's Gospel*, 151-73, who concludes that this citation of Isaiah 42:1-4 builds on Matthew's notion of Jesus as an ideal Davidide messiah. See also

Matthew's redactional introduction of the Beelzebul controversy makes the connection even stronger.

For all three Synoptic Evangelists, the controversy begins with an exorcism of a demon that was making a man mute. Matthew ups the ante somewhat by making the man not only mute but also blind (12:22). More importantly, Matthew describes this man's restoration using not the language of exorcism (e.g., Mark's ἐκβληθέντος or Luke's ἐξελθόντος) but the language of healing (ἐθεράπευσεν, 12:22). Matthew's peculiar word choice links the exorcism with the previous pericope in which Jesus healed (ἐθεράπευσεν, 12:15) all of the people who were following him.[15] The conjoining of healing and exorcism is common in the Synoptic Tradition, particularly in summary statements (Mark 10:1; Luke 6:18-19), and one might argue that the line between "spiritual" and "physical" restoration was much blurrier in the ancient world, particularly in the East, than it typically is in modern Western societies.[16] Matthew is elaborating on the summary statement that Jesus healed (12:15) by providing a particular instance of healing, one that brings speech and sight through the overcoming of a possessing demon.

The hints that Jesus is being depicted as a messianic healer, put in place by Matthew's citation of Isaiah 42, find still more explicit confirmation in the response of the crowds to Jesus's healing of the demoniac. In Matthew, the astonished crowds ask, "Might this one possibly be the son of David?" (μήτι οὗτός ἐστιν ὁ υἱὸς Δαυίδ, 12:23). This response is Christologically significant. First, it demonstrates the plausibility that Jesus as exorcist (and healer more generally) might be interpreted in terms of Davidic messiahship.[17] Second, the ideal reader knows from Matthew 1:1 that Jesus is, in fact, "son of David," and so knows that at this point the crowd's inference can be trusted. Third,

---

Alicia D. Meyers, "Isaiah 42 and the Characterization of Jesus in Matthew 12:17-21," in *"What Does the Scripture Say?" Studies in the Function of Scripture in Early Judaism and Christianity,* vol. 1, *The Synoptic Gospels* (LNTS 469/SSEJ 17; ed. C. A. Evans and H. D. Zacharias; London: T&T Clark, 2012), 70-89. Meyers argues that allusions to Herod Antipas as "a useless 'bruised reed' and 'smoldering wick'" are at work, creating a counterpoint in which "the royal overtones" of the servant language as deployed here in Matthew become even more clear (84).

15. Matthew uses θεραπεύω as the blanket word for healing and exorcism in the summary statement of 4:24 as well.

16. Sorensen, *Possession and Exorcism,* 6, points out that exorcism is largely absent from the Greek healing traditions prior to the turn of the era, though the conjunction is fairly ubiquitous in early Christianity. He then turns to demonstrate the precedent for exorcism, and its conjunction with healing, in Mesopotamia (18-32).

17. Cf. Peter Head, *Christology and the Synoptic Problem: An Argument for Markan Priority* (SNTSMS 94; New York: Cambridge University Press, 1997), 180-86.

this claim of the crowd is what the Pharisees immediately attempt to deflect when they offer an alternative explanation: "This one does not cast out demons except by Beelzebul, the prince of demons" (12:24). Thus, the controversy that unfolds in the pericope is set by the differing judgment of the crowds and the Pharisees, a difference that Matthew alone frames, in keeping with his amplification of Davidic messiahship, as Jesus being son of David or Jesus being an agent of Beelzebul. The latter conflict itself turns on the question of authority to rule, as Beelzebul is named the "prince" of demons.

Within the specific context of exorcism, Matthew affirms the more general argument made especially in the son of God chapter above: Jesus's supernatural acts on the earth are indications that he possesses the spirit of God and is therefore God's specially appointed agent; specifically, that he is the promised messianic king.[18] At the heart of the controversy we find a Mark-Q overlap, where Matthew and Luke have versions of a saying that reads, in the former, "If by the spirit of God I am casting out the demons, then the kingdom of God has come upon you" (Matt 12:28).[19] Jesus's possession of the spirit makes itself known in the deeds of power that show him to be standing against the kingdom of Satan. Within a narrative that unfolds under the rubric of whether or not Jesus is son of David, the possession of the spirit and advent of God's kingdom are indications that Jesus himself is the Davidic king in whose rule God's own reign is made known.[20] This is a strong, preliminary indication that for Matthew the Christological significance of exorcisms is Davidic: an idealized human king, manifest in Jesus, is God's agent to restore God's rule to the world. Moreover, this provides further evidence that the arrival of the βασιλεία τοῦ θεοῦ is conceived in terms of Jesus as anointed king rather than Jesus as the God-king. As such, the association of Jesus's role as idealized human being with the pervasive theme of the kingdom of God carries high human Christology across wide swaths of the Synoptic Gospels, further diminishing the possibility that they intend to disclose Jesus as divine in some proto-Chalcedonian sense.

The preliminary indication Matthew provides here that exorcisms are demonstrations that Jesus is, in fact, the long-awaited "son of David," finds

---

18. On Jesus acting as one empowered by the spirit, see Sorensen, *Possession and Exorcism*, 141-42.

19. Without specifying the Christology in view, E. P. Sanders, *The Historical Figure of Jesus* (London: Penguin, 1993), 168, takes this as an indication that the historical figure of Jesus, as well as the Evangelists, "probably saw his miracles as indications that the new age was at hand. *He shared the evangelists' view that he fulfilled the hopes of the prophets*" (italics original).

20. Cf. Beaton, *Isaiah's Christ*, 181-83.

further confirmation in the plea of the Canaanite woman (15:22). She includes this title in her address, "Have mercy on me, Lord, son of David! My daughter is badly demon possessed" (ἐλέησόν με, κύριε υἱὸς Δαυίδ· ἡ θυγάτηρ μου κακῶς δαιμονίζεται).

Other exorcisms are occasions for the Christologies of Jesus as son of God and of coming eschatological judge to surface. In Matthew's telling of the Gadarene demoniac story (8:28-34), the demons address Jesus with the royal title son of God (υἱὲ τοῦ θεοῦ, 8:29) and ask whether he is going to administer in an untimely fashion the presumably eschatological torment that is the son of God's to bring about (ἦλθες ὧδε πρὸ καιροῦ βασανίσαι ἡμᾶς, 8:29). I argued in the son of man chapter that such a role in the final judgment is regularly assigned to glorified human beings in Jewish traditions, and that the early Christian tradition itself could envision humans playing the role of cosmic judge over the angelic realm (1 Cor 6:3). In Matthew, Jesus clearly plays that role, specifically as son of man. Here, too, the connotations of exorcism fall within the framework of idealized humanity executing God's rule on God's behalf.

b. Mark: Exorcism and Authority to Teach

Mark's Gospel provides another angle for gaining perspective on the Christological implications of exorcisms. The authority to exorcise is one facet of the overall authority of Jesus that fits within the rubrics created by the son of God and son of man titles.[21] Mark signals the significance of Jesus's encounters with malevolent spirits by placing an exorcism narrative (1:21-23) at the head of a string of miracle stories (1:21–2:12) that constitute the first depiction of Jesus's ministry after he calls his first followers. Like the stories in Mark 2 in which son of man sayings signal a focus of Jesus's authority, so too in this first exorcism story facets of Jesus's authority are put on display. The question, then, is what sort of authority this might be.

The pericope relating Jesus's first encounter with an "unclean spirit" (πνεῦμα ἀκάθαρτον), Mark 1:21-28, bears clear marks of redaction, as verses 21-22 provide a succinct summary statement of Jesus's teaching, including the astonished response of the crowd that typically comes at the end of a

21. Mills, *Human Agents*, 93-108, nicely situates Jesus's wonder-working, including exorcisms, healings, and nature miracles, within the overall narrative in which Jesus functions as God's chosen human agent, empowered by God from the point of his baptism and exercising that power through the eschatological future of the son of man.

pericope, an element of the story that is repeated in verse 27.[22] My interest in highlighting the likely redactional history is twofold. First, this indicates that Mark's hand is at work to interweave a story of Jesus as authoritative teacher with Jesus as authoritative exorcist, combining the two such that the teaching authority has power even over the spirits.[23] Second, this is a closely analogous redaction to what we find in Mark 2:1-12, where a self-contained healing narrative (2:1-5a, 10c-12) appears to be edited such that the story also carries the weight of the forgiveness of sins conflict narrative. In this latter story, the result of the redaction is to make the story a demonstration of Jesus's authority, a commanding power that encompasses both the "spiritual" sphere of people's sins and standing before God as well as the physical sphere of broken bodies.[24] In both instances, shorter stories about Jesus have been expanded to demonstrate that the ἐξουσία of Jesus's ministry extends beyond words and deeds on the physical plane to the "spiritual" world that stands behind it, or above it, and in some ways empowers it. We might ruminate further on the parallels between the passages by remembering also that each stands at the head of a series of like stories: the exorcism is the first in a string of healing narratives, and the healing of the paralytic bridges the story from that series of healing stories into a series of controversy stories (2:1–3:6). The significance of the first exorcism story is heightened as we recognize that its demonstration of the kind of authority Jesus possesses is reiterated in the subsequent healing pericopes, even as Jesus's authority as son of man on earth reverberates throughout the controversy stories.[25] The question before us is whether the kind of authority Jesus possesses as "son of man," namely, as God's representative agent on the earth and thus an idealized, empowered human figure, is the proper rubric for deciphering the Christology in play in Mark 1, and the exorcism in particular.

The crowd's declarations that Jesus teaches with authority bookend the exorcism of Mark 1. In 1:22 they marvel at his teaching because he teaches like one who has authority (ὡς ἐξουσίαν ἔχων) and not like one of the scribes.[26]

22. On the composition of the story, see Christian Strecker, "Mächtig in Wort und Tat (Exorzismus in Kafarnaum): Mk 1,21-28," in Kompendium der frühchristlichen Wundererzählungen, Band 1, Die Wunder Jesu (ed. Susanne Luther and Jörg Röder; Gütersloh: Gütersloher Verlaghaus, 2013), 205-13.

23. See Herman Hendrickx, The Miracle Stories of the Synoptic Gospels (San Francisco: Harper & Row, 1987), 52-55.

24. Cf. Hendrix, Miracle Stories, 53-54.

25. Similar narratological weight to this story and its Christology is noted by Strecker, "Mächtig in Wort und Tat," 206-7.

26. Mills, Human Agents, 106, sees this combination as tying together the notions of wis-

When the same rubric of teaching authority occurs at the end of the pericope, it includes the ability to issue orders to demons: "What is this? A new, authoritative teaching [διδαχὴ καινὴ κατ᾽ ἐξουσίαν]! He commands even the unclean spirits and they obey him" (1:27). To the extent that the crowds articulate the Christological implications of the narrative, they undergird Jesus's identity as an authoritative teacher. Ἐξουσία entails a significant element of effective power, as it does also in the healing of the paralytic/forgiveness of sins story.

Christological implications also arise from the voice of the demon, who confronts Jesus by saying, "What is it between us, Jesus the Nazarene? Have you come to destroy us? I know who you are — God's holy one!" (1:24). The first thing that the demon demonstrates knowledge of is Jesus's name, who he is in terms of his basic human identity. Then, in a fashion analogous to Matthew's Gadarene demoniac discussed above (8:29), this demon views Jesus as a potential judge/executioner. Third, there is the title God's holy one (ὁ ἅγιος τοῦ θεοῦ).[27] As I noted in the discussion of Jesus as son of God, this title is somewhat vague. The closest biblical precedent seems to be found in Psalm 16:10 (15:10, LXX), a verse picked up in Acts, in which the Davidic speaker expresses confidence that God will not allow "your holy one" to see the pit (חתשׁ, MT) or decay (διαφοράν, LXX). The match is not exact, however, as the LXX reads ὅσιον whereas Mark uses the word ἅγιος. As I also pointed out in that previous chapter, Mark's own Beelzebul controversy story provides a key to understanding who Jesus is in the exorcism stories. There, he attributes his ability to cast out demons to the power he possesses through the Holy Spirit (3:29-30). Thus, Jesus may very well be marked as "God's holy one" because he has received God's Holy Spirit at his baptism.[28] Such a correlation finds some confirmation in the sociological work of Witmer, who argues that Jesus's own reception of the spirit at baptism locates him within the tradition of ancient exorcists who received a visionary induction into the spiritual realm, including the visionary prophets of Israel's biblical tradition.[29]

---

dom and kingship, the former including knowledge of how the cosmos functions, which, in Jesus's case, is knowledge about the kingdom of God.

27. Strecker, "Mächtig in Wort und Tat," 207, 210, sees the scene as an indication of Jesus's "göttliche Identität," but does not clarify what divinity might mean in this instance. He sees here also an indication of Mark's "sending" theology, a motif that he appears to align with preexistence (citing Simon Gathercole). For both claims, greater specificity is required to enable us to adjudicate whether they are attempting to uphold a divine Christology as such, or the exalted sort of human Christology that I am arguing for here.

28. This is the position of Hendrickx, *Miracle Stories*, 44.

29. Witmer, *Jesus, the Galilean Exorcist*, 97-103. I should note that although I find Witmer

Without attempting to pin down further what the connotations of the title holy one of God might be, this first exorcism sets some markers for the story's Christology that coalesce smoothly with Mark's son of man Christology: Jesus is a human being to whom has been given sweeping authority to act and to speak for God, an authority that will be finally put on display through his participation in the coming eschatological assize and its attendant judgment.[30] Drawing a similar conclusion, Herman Hendrickx claims, "The Holy One of God performs the function of God; in his activity God's rule — and thereby the destruction of the rule of Satan — dawns."[31]

Mark builds on this first demonic encounter two chapters later, with a summary statement about demons falling before Jesus and declaring his identity. As a summary statement, it may be intended to shed light on the connotations of the particular statement made by the first demon in chapter 1, though this is not a necessary conclusion. As discussed in the son of God chapter above, Mark says, "The unclean spirits, when they saw him, were falling before [προσέπιπτον] him and crying out, saying, 'You are the son of God!'" (σὺ εἶ ὁ υἱὸς τοῦ θεοῦ, 3:11). What I think is hinted at in the first exorcism story is stated clearly here: the demons know who Jesus is, as that identity was established at the baptism. The coalescence between the divine voice's identification of Jesus and the demonic identification assures Mark's readers that the demons are rightly naming Jesus. As I demonstrated above, the "son of God" phrase itself shows that the Christological implications of exorcism are, for Mark, messianic rather than divine. Jesus can exorcise demons because he is God's king, anointed by the spirit, exercising God's reign with full divine authority on the earth. The same concern unfolds in Luke, as I also discussed in the son of God chapter, as Jesus silences the demonic cry, "You are the son of God" because those spirits know that Jesus is messiah (4:41).

It might be argued that this knowledge of Jesus is, itself, a sign that Jesus bears some sort of transcendent identity. However, for the author of Luke this is manifestly not the case. In his sequel, demonic knowledge of human

---

helpful for shedding light on some of the social contextual cues for how to read the text, I have reservations about her conclusions at the level of the historical Jesus. For the purposes of my study, the immense value of Witmer's work is in underscoring how the patterns of Jesus's ministry from visionary experience to testing to exorcism fit within a larger pattern of exorcist traditions across cultures in the ancient world.

30. Strecker, "Mächtig in Wort und Tat," 211, makes a similar connection with the authority of Jesus throughout the book. On the combination between Jesus as God's human agent and the larger story of the cosmos, cf. Mills, *Human Agents*, esp. 108.

31. Hendrickx, *Miracle Stories*, 45.

exorcists extends to Paul as well (Acts 19:13-15).[32] This scene embodies well the both/and approach of my own study, in which we are returning repeatedly to the notion that Jesus is a unique figure with a unique role to play, but that his followers can also share in his role and actions. The demons know Jesus as well as Paul; however, they do not know the seven sons of Sceva. This differentiates the Jesus movement from "magic," in which incantations might simply be learned and recited.[33] Jesus himself is known to the demons, and those who are known and sent by Jesus will be known as well.

3. THE KING AND HIS MEN

The Synoptic Gospels use Jesus's exorcising power to highlight his particular authority as one who has been empowered by the spirit of God in order to enact God's rule even over the demonic realm.[34] In addition to the Christological indications given in the various pericopes above, which build a positive case for Jesus acting as an idealized representative human figure, the texts also provide another body of evidence that weighs heavily against the possibility that authority over demons carries divine connotations. This other body of evidence is the mirroring of Jesus's exorcism ministry in the ministry of his disciples.[35] Any action performed by other people can hardly be taken, when applied to Jesus, as an indication of Jesus's ontological distinctness. Various indications in each of the three Gospels make it clear that exorcism is a sign of the eschatological advent of the reign of God, a sign embodied by the disciples as they continue and extend the ministry of Jesus.

Mark summarizes the purpose of Jesus calling the twelve to include the exorcism ministry Jesus himself has been carrying out: "And he made twelve, in order that they might be with him and in order that he might send them to preach and to have authority [ἔχειν ἐξουσίαν] to cast out demons" (3:15). The authority by which Jesus casts out demons can be bestowed upon other persons, and is thus not inherent in any sort of distinct divine identity that other representative humans cannot share.

This same authority, Mark again tells the reader, is conveyed by Jesus to the

32. Graham H. Twelftree, "Jesus and Magic in Luke-Acts," in *Jesus and Paul: Global Perspectives in Honor of James D. G. Dunn* (LNTS 414; ed. B. J. Oropeza et al.; New York: T&T Clark, 2009), 46-58, here 52-53.

33. Twelftree, "Jesus and Magic."

34. Sorensen, *Possession and Exorcism*, 138.

35. Cf. Sorensen, *Possession and Exorcism*, 131.

disciples when he sends them out two by two in 6:7. Mark issues a summary statement of their missionary labors, saying that they preached repentance, cast out many demons, and healed people by anointing them with oil (6:12-13), a summary statement that expands on the purpose of the disciples as stated in 3:15 by the inclusion of healing.[36] For the question of what sort of Christology is in play in this Gospel, Mark's narrative turns to Herod's speculations about Jesus based on what the disciples have done (ἤκουσεν ὁ βασιλεὺς Ἡρῴδης, φανερὸν γὰρ ἐγένετο τὸ ὄνομα αὐτοῦ, 6:14). First, this indicates (as will be stated more explicitly elsewhere in the Synoptic Gospels) that Jesus mediates to the disciples the authority to exorcise. They do not have the authority simply because they are humans, but because they are acting in the name and with the authority of the idealized authoritative human. Second, the report of their actions leads to a report of speculations about who Jesus might be. Herod thinks that this power is at work because John the Baptist has been raised from the dead (6:14); other people speculate that it might be Elijah or a great prophet who has arisen (6:15). Each of these conclusions, while wrong, signals that the speculation that such wonder-working might generate among Jesus's contemporaries all revolves around specially empowered human agents. No one speculates, for example, that an angel or God has come down and that this is the reason for the power. Here we have a tacit indication that the identity put on display in exorcism would have been understood as a sort of exalted human, perhaps the work of a peculiarly endowed prophet. This list of speculations might appear to be of limited value, inasmuch as the ideal reader knows each answer to be wrong, thus leaving open the question of what the right answer is. However, the question is not left open forever, as the same list of possible identities for Jesus is rehearsed in chapter 8. There, Jesus asks his followers, "Who do people say that I am?" to which they respond with the same three options: John the Baptist, Elijah, or one of the prophets (v. 28). This time, of course, we are given the right answer in the voice of Peter: "You are the Christ" (v. 29). The great works that Jesus does, even when those works are administered through the persons of his followers, point to his identity as the messiah, and not to divinity as such.

Matthew's mission discourse underscores the notion that the disciples em-

---

36. An inclusion that might, importantly, link healing with exorcism as an expression of power of oppressive spirits. Cf. Pierre Grelot, "Les Miracles de Jésus et la Démonologie Juive," in *Les Miracles de Jésus selon le Nouveau Testament* (ed. J. N. Aletti et al.; Paris: Éditions du Seuil, 1977), 59-72, here 67: "Les Douze chassent beaucoup de démons et guérissent les malades en leur faisant des onctions d'huile: cela suppose un mélange inextricable d'exorcismes et de pharmacopée popularie."

body and extend the ministry of Jesus, and in so doing highlights how the various aspects of Jesus's work, including exorcisms and healings, are signals of an idealized humanity rather than tokens of a hidden divinity. Like Jesus, the disciples are to go only to the lost sheep of the house of Israel (10:6; cf. 15:24). Like Jesus, they are to go out preaching that the reign of God has drawn near (10:7; cf. 4:17). Like Jesus, they are to heal the sick, raise the dead, purify lepers, and, finally, cast out demons (10:8). The ability to exorcise is thus one component of a holistic reembodiment of the ministry of Jesus as they go about their own mission. Throughout the mission discourse, this connection is reinforced in various ways. The disciples will be hated because of Jesus's name (10:22) and thus will experience betrayal unto death, even as Jesus does at the end of the story (10:21). As Jesus was accused of collusion with Beelzebul for his authority over demons, so too will his followers be (10:25). Indeed, the disciples embody the authority and presence of Jesus to such an extent that whoever receives them receives Jesus and the God who sent him (10:40-41). Such a lengthy accounting of the similarity between what Jesus does and what his disciples are to do provides another key piece of evidence that the depictions of Jesus in the Gospel, including his power over demonic spirits, intend to show Jesus not as ontologically other, but as one who embodies the idealized potential that other humans can attain to as they follow him and are empowered by the same spirit who empowers Jesus's own ministry.

Luke's sending of seventy disciples provides another window into the place of people within the cosmic battle that is entailed in the various exorcism stories. In sending this group, Luke's Jesus seems primarily concerned with how missionaries are received in various towns. He gives them simpler instructions than we find in other sending narratives, telling the seventy to heal the sick and declare, "The reign of God has come near to you" (10:9). Like Matthew, Luke also includes an indication that the way one responds to Jesus's followers is how one responds to Jesus himself and to the God who sent him (10:16). The report of the seventy upon their return is a celebration that even the demons are subject to them because of Jesus's name (κύριε, καὶ τὰ δαιμόνια ὑποτάσσεται ἡμῖν ἐν τῷ ὀνόματί σου, 10:17), a report that is particularly striking since exorcism as such was not part of Jesus's original commission. Jesus responds by telling the disciples that he has seen even greater cosmic effects as a result of their work than even they have seen: "I saw Satan falling like lightning from heaven" (10:19). Such a depiction of the power that the disciples have mediated to them from Jesus, as a power that can affect the cosmic order including, perhaps, the dethronement of the wrongly enthroned Satan, demonstrates the virtually unlimited capacity of an idealized human figure to rule over the created order.[37] The explanation for this ability is that they have been given authority: "Look! I have given you the power to tread upon serpents and scorpions, and upon all the powers of the enemy, and nothing will harm you" (10:19). Authority to exercise power over the satanic enemy is borne by humans who have been so appointed. In the Gospel narratives, this appointment belongs to Jesus, first of all, as the one whom God has sent, and then to those whom Jesus sends in turn, who act with his name, authority, and power.

The picture being formed across the Synoptic Gospels is one in which Jesus possesses authority over demonic spirits due to his peculiar role in the narrative as God's agent on the earth, and in which this authority can be further transferred to other people. There are no indications that such authority in Jesus's case depends on a unique ontology or preexistence; there are several indications that it depends on his being uniquely empowered by the spirit of God; and the fact that other human beings can extend this role is a sure indication that divinity is not prerequisite to exercising such power and authority.

I wish to further this last point by giving attention to two other passages in Mark and by making a few observations about Luke's narrative world(s). With respect to Mark, there are two episodes after Peter's confession where exorcism comes to the fore, in particular, the place of the twelve disciples in extending this aspect of Jesus's work. First, there is the failed exorcism of the boy whom we would probably recognize today as having epilepsy (9:14-29). When Jesus receives the report of the disciples' failure, he expresses his exasperation by chiding the "faithless generation" (γενεὰ ἄπιστος, 9:19). The theme of faith introduced in Jesus's response continues throughout the pericope, as the father expresses some hesitation about Jesus's ability to cast out the demon (εἴ τι δύνῃ, 9:22), to which Jesus replies, "'If it is possible for you'?! All things are possible to the one who believes" (9:23). This passage suggests a sort of synergy between the power of the wonder-worker and the faith of the recipient. While it initially might seem that Jesus's concern about the "faithless generation" lands squarely on the shoulders of his disciples, the unfolding interaction with the father indicates that he, too, shoulders some of the blame. In a previous episode, Jesus responds to the faithlessness of his hometown crowd by sending out his twelve on a mission of preaching and exorcising; here, the disciples show themselves to be unlikely surrogates. When the twelve debrief the episode with Jesus later, the reason he articulates for their failure is not that the father lacked faith,

---

37. Twelftree, *Jesus the Exorcist*, 126-27, also recognizes here that the disciples participate in Jesus's mission, including the eschatological overthrow that is signaled in the exorcisms.

but that such a type of demon only comes out by prayer and fasting (9:29).[38] Thus, the disciples have truly failed in properly disposing themselves toward the God from whom the power over demons comes. Moreover, Jesus walks precisely the line we would expect from his playing the role of an idealized human figure: he does not claim any sort of ontological distinction for himself in the ability to command the spirit, but he speaks and acts as one whose ability is not subject to the same wavering as that of his followers. In giving the final instruction, he is telling the disciples the manner in which they do, as his followers, have access to the needful power and authority.

Second, John proudly reports to Jesus that the disciples had forbidden a man to cast out demons in Jesus's name because "he did not follow us" (οὐκ ἠκολούθει ἡμῖν, 9:38). Jesus's rebuke signals that his circle of followers is not so easily circumscribed. "Do not forbid him. For there is no one who might do a work of power in my name and be able soon after to speak ill of me. For the one who is not against us is for us" (9:39-40). The power that Jesus bears as representative of God on the earth is extended through a web of followers who are able to share in it by acting in his name. Moreover, this last mention of demonic spirits in Mark's Gospel correlates with the first (1:21-27) in that the power to exorcise and the power to speak the good news are joined in the person of the exorcist. Exorcism is one component of Jesus's ministry as an idealized human figure who is restoring the reign of God on the earth, and the extension of this and other such functions to his followers demonstrates that they are being offered the opportunity to share in that idealized humanity in a derivative fashion.

This notion that the power over demonic spirits comes to people as they represent the reign of God on the earth finds extended confirmation in book 2 of Luke's work. While the disciples are ministering in Jerusalem, deliverance of those harassed by unclean spirits is one hallmark of their work (Acts 5:16). When Philip takes the ministry beyond Jerusalem, his ministry as well is marked by the expulsion of spirits (8:7). When the focus shifts to Paul, the stories of exorcism become somewhat more entailed. The casting out of a spirit of divination (πνεῦμα πύθωνα, 16:16) from a slave girl is particularly significant in that it includes a disclosure, in the voice of the possessed girl, as to the identity of Paul and his companions: "These people are servants of the Most High God, who proclaim to you the way of salvation" (16:17). When Paul's annoyance gets the best of him, he commands the demon to exit in the name of Jesus the messiah (16:17). Such a brief snapshot into Paul's authority to

---

38. I read νηστεία in verse 29 as original, but it is not of immediate consequence for my purposes here.

exorcise confirms that on the plane of Luke's narrative this power exists within people (ἄνθρωποι, 16:17) who are God's servants, and that this power comes to other people as it is mediated through the person of the now-exalted Jesus. Jesus is the representative bearer of God's reign, and he extends the power and authority of his rule to and through his fellow human followers.

The framework of Jesus as idealized human who shares his authority with his followers explains both dynamics of the peculiar story told in Acts 19:11-17. On the one hand, there is a description of the unusually strong miracles God worked through Paul's hands (v. 11), such that the power coming off Paul could be carried by a piece of cloth that had touched him and prove an effective salve for sickness or evil spirits (v. 12). The idea that Paul, like Jesus, is a "man attested by God" would be, at one level, correct. However, when people attempt to derive authority to exorcise in the name of the Jesus whom Paul preaches, they are rebuffed by the demon and run off, beaten and naked (vv. 13-16). The result, Luke claims, is that "the name of the Lord Jesus was exalted" (v. 17). Paul can extend the ministry of Jesus on the earth; however, he cannot stand in the place of Jesus as the one whose name is invoked in order to become a conduit of heavenly power. That role belongs to the "Lord Jesus" alone. In this pericope, both the peculiar place Jesus occupies as risen Lord and thus God's appointed king over the earth and the possibility of shared authority, extending God's work through Jesus's reign by the hands of other humans, are held together. And so, with the extension of our gaze to the book of Acts, the notion of Jesus as an idealized human figure continues to wield fruitful explanatory power. This is a positive indication that we are working within the correct paradigm.

4. ESCHATOLOGICAL JUDGMENT

In Jesus's confrontation of the demon-possessed man at Gerasa (Gadara in Matthew), all three Synoptic Gospels depict the demons responding in fear that Jesus might torture them. In Mark's and Luke's version, this is simply a call that Jesus not torment them/it (μή με βασανίσῃς, Mark 5:7; Luke 8:28). In Matthew's Gospel, however, the plea implies that Jesus will in fact afflict them, at a time, however, that has not yet come: "Have you come here before the time to torment us?" (ἦλθες ὧδε πρὸ καιροῦ βασανίσαι ἡμᾶς, 8:29). Matthew's Legion not only recognizes Jesus as "son of God" (8:29), it seems that they recognize him as one who will be executing their own eschatological judgment.[39] This

39. Cf. Blackburn, "Miracles of Jesus," 122.

expectation comports with an observation I made in comparing Matthew's son of man with Mark's. In depicting the eschatological return of the son of man immediately after the call to cross-bearing discipleship (Mark 8:38; Matt 16:27; Luke 9:26), Luke and Mark speak of the son of man being ashamed of those who are ashamed of him, whereas Matthew says that the son of man will repay to each according to his works (ἀποδώσει ἑκάστῳ κατὰ τὴν πρᾶξιν αὐτοῦ). Similarly, in the parable of the weeds in the field the son of man superintends the final judgment by sending forth his angels into the world to gather all the causes of stumbling and all those who practice lawlessness (Matt 13:41). It seems, then, that Matthew's focus on Jesus as agent of the final judgment leads him, in the story of the Gadarene demoniac, to extend this purview to the judgment of demons as well.[40]

As noted before, such authority to enact divine judgment even over celestial beings was not thought to transcend the human in early Christianity. First, this authority to judge in the end is of a piece of the larger whole of Jesus's exorcism ministry, one that we have seen developed under the rubric of Jesus as authoritative son of God and, in the Beelzebul controversy in Matthew and Luke, one whose power signals that the kingdom of God has begun to arrive (Matt 12:28; Luke 11:20). In Matthew, moreover, this has been tied to Jesus as son of David. In the ministry of Jesus itself as a ministry of exorcism the eschatological judgment is coming to bear on the spiritual forces hostile to humanity.[41]

Second, throughout Matthew Jesus's role as judge is pronounced and yet simultaneously subordinate to and in service of God the father. In Matthew 7:21-23, for instance, Jesus is addressed as the Lord who determines entrance into the kingdom of the heavens; however, the standard of judgment is whether someone has done the will of the father in heaven (v. 21). The standard thus comes back around to Jesus, as his saying "I never knew you" becomes the measure for final exclusion. This is reiterated as Jesus then proceeds to claim that his own words are the standard for eschatological endurance versus eschatological destruction (7:24-27). Similarly, when Jesus as son of man and king plays the role of eschatological judge in Matthew 25:31-46, he not only judges on the basis of how those judged treated him, but also says that those who are vindicated receive "the blessing of my father" (25:34) in the form of a

---

40. It may be that Luke's version, which later has the demons pleading not to be sent into the abyss, is similarly evocative of Jesus as one who plays a role in eschatological judgment (Luke 8:31).

41. Cf. Grelot, "Les Miracles de Jésus," 69.

kingdom made ready for them. Another important component of this scene is that those who are condemned are sent to "the eternal fire prepared for the devil and his angels" (25:41), thus indicating that this judgment over which Jesus presides as king is not qualitatively different from that to which the spiritual beings will be subject.

Third, elsewhere in the New Testament early Christians speak of humans judging spiritual beings. Paul in 1 Corinthians 6:2-3 claims that the saints will judge the world, and specifies thereafter that "we shall judge angels." This not only indicates that the judgment of the world more generally and the judgment of angels more particularly were seen as part and parcel of the same eschatological judgment, it also demonstrates that those who are envisioned as coming to rule the age to come (cf. Rom 5:17) are also envisioned as reigning over the entirety of the created order, including its angelic, and by extension demonic, components. Thus, the arguments made above in discussion of Matthew's son of man, to the effect that he judges the world as an idealized human figure rather than as one who is inherently divine, carries over to this judgment of the demons as well.

Finally, in Matthew's Gospel the demons who anticipate eschatological judgment from Jesus do so as they recognize him to be "son of God" (8:29). This suggests that the royal, Davidic connotations of son of God, discussed at length in a prior chapter, provide the Christological grounds for their expectation.

The eschatological dimensions of Jesus's ministry are widely recognized. Preceded by John the Baptist who comes with a warning that the eschatological separation of humanity is immanent (Mark 1:7-8; Matt 3:11-12; Luke 3:15-18), Jesus himself appears proclaiming that the time has been fulfilled and that the kingdom of God has drawn near (Matt 4:17; Mark 1:14-15). The holistic picture of a world set to rights with the advent of God's anointed messenger includes exorcisms, which are not only momentary acts providing freedom for particular persons, but also signs of a wholesale defeat and conquest of these enemies of humanity.[42] This is clear not only in Jesus's claim to be "binding the strong man," but also in his first encounter with demonic forces in Mark and Luke, when he is asked, "Have you come to destroy us?" (Mark 1:24; par. Luke 4:34).[43] Luke elaborates on this when, in response to the disciples' happy report about being able to exorcise demons during their missionary journey, Jesus says, "I saw Satan fall like lightning from heaven" (10:18). The exorcisms

42. Blackburn, "Miracles of Jesus," 122-23.
43. See Howard Clark Kee, *Miracle in the Early Christian World: A Study in the Socio-historical Method* (New Haven, CT: Yale University Press, 1989), 161-63.

on earth are part of a larger cosmic reality that includes the time of Satan's downfall, a reality that is turning with the arrival on the scene of Jesus, and with the extension of his God-given authority at the hands of his followers.[44]

In the larger picture I have been drawing of a world set to rights by God's idealized human agent, such human control over spiritual forces fits like a glove. The world was created to be ruled by humans. When God's chosen human king arrives on the scene, however, he finds a world under the power of satanic forces including not only possessing demons but also the forces of sin and death, exile and exclusion, destructive forces of nature, and lack of daily provision. The Human One entrusted to rule over the kingdom of God therefore sets about confronting these forces, and overcoming them, in demonstration of the full and final restoration that has begun. That the king of this royal realm should judge those responsible for holding his people captive is entirely expected.

B. NATURE MIRACLES

I shift attention now to what are commonly called nature miracles, looking at Jesus's authority over the waters and miraculous feedings. In the scenes where Jesus exercises authority over waters, in particular (Mark 4:35-41; 6:45-52, and pars.), scholars regularly see echoes of Old Testament theophany stories and of divine control over the waters of chaos.[45] And yet, both the idea of power over waters and the hopes for abundant provision of food are aspects of the Jewish cultural canon that are taken up in the descriptions of idealized figures such as coming messiahs or Davidic kings.

1. POWER OVER THE WATERS

a. Messiah and Power over Waters

Two stories depict Jesus's power over the waters as such. One is the stilling of the sea in Mark 4:35-41; par. Matthew 8:23-27; Luke 8:22-25; the other is the

---

44. Cf. Blackburn, "Miracles of Jesus," 122; Sanders, *Historical Figure of Jesus*, 168; Grelot, "Les Miracles de Jésus," 70.

45. E.g., Pamela Lee Thimmes, *Studies in the Biblical Sea-Storm Type-Scene: Convention and Invention* (San Francisco: Mellen Research University Press, 1992).

water-walking episode in Mark 6:45-52; par. Matthew 14:22-33. The last passage, Matthew 14:22-33, became a focus of this study in my discussion of Jesus as son of God. Once again, I begin the discussion by citing W. D. Davies and Dale Allison's Matthew commentary, as it clearly sets before us the claims for deity that arise from Jesus's authority over the waters:

> In the First Gospel Jesus exercises powers and displays attributes traditionally connected with God alone. In the present pericope, Jesus both walks on the sea and subdues its rage, and these are acts that the OT assigns to Yahweh himself. In other words, Jesus here exhibits an authority which the Jewish Scriptures associate exclusively with the deity. The fact speaks volumes. In addition, Jesus is bold enough to refer to himself with the loaded and numinous "I am." In view of all this, it does not quite suffice to say that, for our author, God has acted through Jesus the Messiah. It seems more accurate to assert that, in Matthew's gospel, God actively shares attributes characteristic of himself with another, his Son. The step towards the later ecumenical creeds, which affirm Christ's deity, appears undeniable.[46]

The conclusion being drawn depends on at least three presuppositions that my study has gone a long way toward undermining. First, in positing a broader category of idealized human beings, and recognizing the ways that such figures transcend what modern people might see as boundaries between the deity and humanity, I have demonstrated numerous ways in which people can be spoken of as sharing in actions and attributes that are otherwise spoken of as God's exclusive purview.

Second, Davies and Allison make a distinction between God acting through Jesus and God actively sharing attributes characteristic of himself with another. The force of my studies in biblical and early Judaism was to demonstrate that such a distinction is unsustainable. To be God's representative on earth is, necessarily, to share in one or more characteristics of God. In his work *The Jewish Context of Jesus's Miracles,* Eric Eve offers a definition of miracles as Josephus describes them.[47] The first-century Jewish historian describes as miracles events that are taken by believers to be acts of God.[48] And yet, the

---

46. W. D. Davies and Dale C. Allison Jr., *The Gospel according to Saint Matthew* (3 vols.; ICC; Edinburgh: T&T Clark, 1991), 2:512.

47. Eve, *Jewish Context of Jesus's Miracles,* 25.

48. Eve, *Jewish Context of Jesus's Miracles,* 25.

fact that God is at work does not diminish the notion that the miracles are often described as being worked by prophets (e.g., Moses in *Ant.* 2.284-87). Miracle-workers are conduits for God's own work and power.

Finally, the conclusion of Davies and Allison may well be historically true; namely, that Jesus is being attributed with such God-like characteristics that the later creeds would say that Jesus is none other than God. However, this is a far cry from the notion that Matthew's Christology is a narrated version of what we later discover in the creeds. The idea that "God actively shares attributes characteristic of himself with another, his Son," is one that I can only imagine would lead to one's excommunication, if not execution, in the era when the *homoousion* was being articulated. If God is sharing God's attributes with another, then there is some way in which that other is not, or at least was not, God. The idealized human Christology that I have been developing is a container in which such a description of Jesus fits exceptionally well, but it is not a description of the divine Christ of the creeds.

In my study of Matthew 14:22-33 in the son of God chapter above, I detailed a series of considerations that I only outline here in brief. The upshot of these data points is to demonstrate that there is an early Jewish lens for interpreting Jesus's authority over the seas, and it the lens of a messiah, or other such divinely approved human agent.[49] First, Psalm 89 articulates a longing for the restoration of an idealized Davidic kingship that was later read as anticipating a coming messiah. Second, it depicts the king calling out to God as "My father, my God" (v. 26), an anticipation that not only coheres with Jesus's portrayal as son of God, but that also matches Jesus's "*abba*, father" prayer (Mark 14:36) and its parallels (Matt 26:39; Luke 22:42). Third, the psalm delineates various attributes of God, only to then apply these as its description of the greatness of David's kingdom. Fourth, one particular way that the coming king manifests his sharing in divine power (cf. Ps 89:9) is through control over the waters: "I will set his hand upon the sea, and his right hand upon the rivers" (v. 25). The psalm itself thus provides an analogue to the Gospel narratives in depicting a royal son of God who addresses God as father and who then extends God's rule over the earth — even to the waters of chaos.

Given the idealized nature of the Davidic king in the psalm, it is important to highlight that its expectations both reflect other biblical narratives and find expression in post-biblical expectations. Looking backward, both Moses (Exod 14:16) and Joshua (Josh 3:7) are depicted as agents of God who had power over

49. Cf. J. R. Daniel Kirk and Stephen L. Young, "'I Will Set His Hand to the Sea': Psalm 88:26 and Christology in Mark," *JBL* 133 (2014): 333-40.

the waters.[50] In the former case, especially, the power over the waters enables salvation, even turning the waters into weapons of salvation.[51] The early moments of Elisha's ministry are speckled with instances of authority over water as well. He parts the waters of the Jordan using the mantle of Elijah (2 Kgs 2:13-14); purifies the water of Jericho so that it becomes drinkable (2:19-22); mediates God's provision of water for the armies of Judah, Israel, and Edom (3:13-20); and causes an ax-head to float (6:1-7).[52] In this vein the first-century revolutionary Theudas is also important, inasmuch as he claimed that God would part the waters of the Jordan so that he and his army could conquer the land (Josephus, *Ant.* 20.97). Finally, the later rabbinic text, *Pesiqta Rabbati*, includes an interpretation of Psalm 89:25 to the effect that the messiah will exercise Joshua-like power, and stop rivers from flowing (*Pesiq. Rab.* 36:1). In both the psalm itself and the traditions that it may reflect or help generate in later generations, the notion that only God has authority over the waters is affirmed, thus making it clear that only the human agent authorized and empowered by God can extend such control over the cosmos.

b. Storm Stilling

The storm-stilling episode appears in all three Synoptic Gospels (Mark 4:35-41; Matt 8:23-27; Luke 8:22-25), and in each the final note sounded is the disciples' wondering who (τίς; Mark 4:41; Luke 8:25) or what sort of person (ποταπός, Matt 8:27) Jesus is, that the wind and sea obey him. The story thereby invites

50. Philo attributes such power to Moses quite baldly in *De vita Mosis* 1.155-56, stating that Moses's standing before God as friend led to his being given authority over the elements as their master. See the discussion in Eve, *Jewish Context of Jesus's Miracles,* 69-74.

51. William R. Stegner, "Jesus's Walking on the Water: Mark 6.45-52," in *The Gospels and the Scriptures of Israel* (JSNTSup 104/SSEJC 3; ed. C. A. Evans and W. R. Stegner; Sheffield: Sheffield Academic, 1994), 212-34, argues that Exodus 14 is the primary intertext for Mark 6. If so, the conjunction of Moses's actions and divine action in the story provide another avenue for recognizing that idealized human figures are depicted as participating in God's control of the seas.

52. Maurice Carrez, "L'héritage de l'Ancien Testament," in Aletti et al., *Les Miracles de Jésus selon le Nouveau Testament,* 45-58, demonstrates a number of correspondences between Jesus's miracles and those of Elisha, including a cycle of exercising authority over water (Mark 4 and 2 Kgs 2:13-14), raising a child (Mark 5 and 2 Kgs 4:18-37), multiplying bread (Mark 6 and 2 Kgs 4:42-44), and a second feeding (Mark 8) paralleling the end of the famine (2 Kgs 6:25–7:20). These and other parallels suggest that the connection between Jesus and Elisha is likely to be more than fortuitous, underscoring that Jesus's miraculous activity falls well within the prophetic traditions of Israel.

the reader to reflect on the significance of the episode for disclosing the identity of Jesus. This is a helpful reminder that to pursue the question of Jesus's identity is to read with the grain of these texts, not to bring an alien agenda to them.[53]

In Mark's rendition, this episode occurs directly after the first extensive teaching unit, Jesus's teaching in parables (4:1-34). Mark uses the transitional statement, "And he said to them on that day, when evening came, 'Let's cross to the other side'" (καὶ λέγει αὐτοῖς ἐν ἐκείνῃ τῇ ἡμέρᾳ ὀψίας γενομένης· διέλθωμεν εἰς τὸ πέραν, 4:35), and proceeds to tell the reader that Jesus dismisses the crowd from the boat where he had been teaching (v. 36; cf. 4:1). Mark thus provides two links backward to the teaching unit as the story moves into the storm-stilling episode, indicating that the reader should not merely see this as the next in a series of stories, but somehow connected to the one that came before. As we will see below, he makes a similar move in the water-walking episode in chapter 6, concluding that the disciples' understanding of their maritime adventure was marred by their failure to comprehend the "loaves" of the feeding narrative that had come immediately before (v. 52). Neither Matthew nor Luke follows this part of Mark's strategy, Matthew placing the episode immediately after Jesus expresses the cost of discipleship to two would-be volunteers (8:18-22). Luke is more true to Mark in situating the episode just after his parallel to Mark 4's parables, but he also inserts the redefinition of family pericope (8:19-21) in between the two, and introduces the storm stilling with the nondescript, "It happened on one of those days" (8:22).

There are a couple of ways that Mark's pairing of the teaching unit with the storm stilling might shed light on the latter when read in tandem. One shared thread is that the disciples have privileged access to Jesus, but this proximity fails to produce the understanding that Jesus seems to expect (cf. 4:10-13, 40-41).[54] The conjunction of the stories might, however, help the reader perceive the particular understanding Mark's Jesus seems to be after. At several key junctures in the text, Mark has coupled Jesus's teaching with a miracle in order to demonstrate by way of the latter that Jesus's teaching itself is truly an authoritative word, authorized by God.[55] As discussed above, the first mighty

---

53. Cf. John Paul Heil, *Jesus Walking on the Sea: Meaning and Gospel Functions of Matt 14:22-33, Mark 6:45-52 and John 6:15b-21* (Rome: Biblical Institute, 1981), e.g., 84-94.

54. Heil, *Jesus Walking on the Sea*, 121-25, makes much of the privileged position of the disciples in each unit, suggesting that the storm stilling is a crucial moment of insider knowledge given to the twelve.

55. Adela Yarbro Collins, *Mark: A Commentary* (Hermeneia; Minneapolis: Fortress, 2007), 259.

act of the story is the exorcism in the synagogue at Capernaum (1:21-28). The people had marveled at Jesus's teaching authority already in verse 22, but after the ensuing exorcism their praise is expanded: "What is this? A new teaching with authority. He commands even the unclean spirits, and they obey him!" (v. 27). In Mark's Gospel, there is an authority inherent in Jesus's teaching that shows itself through his ability to command the world of demonic forces and heal the bodies of the sick. The latter point is illustrated in the healing of the paralytic, where the healing becomes the means by which the authority to forgive sins is confirmed (2:1-12, esp. v. 10). These two stories are significant in the flow of the Gospel as well: the exorcism was Jesus's first in a series of miracles that run through chapter 1; the healing of the paralytic is the first in a series of conflict stories that run through the beginning of chapter 3. The parable chapter, in turn, is the first teaching unit of the Gospel. Thus, the conjoining of a teaching unit with a miraculous stilling of a storm falls into a narrative pattern in which a miracle affirms the authority and validity of Jesus's spoken word.

The first parallel, the exorcism at Capernaum, invites further comparisons, and since Luke also contains the story of this particular exorcism I include it in this discussion. First, the same verb is employed to express the fear of destruction experienced by the demons (ἀπλέγει, Mark 1:34; Luke 4:34) and by the disciples (ἀπολύμεθα, Mark 4:38; Luke 8:24).[56] Mark employs the same two verbs to describe Jesus's response to each situation, and Luke follows suit. In the exorcism story, we read of Jesus's response to the spirit, "And Jesus rebuked [ἐπιτίμησεν] him" (Mark 1:25; Luke 4:35). In the storm-stilling episode, Jesus's response to the disciples begins, "And getting up he rebuked [ἐπιτίμησεν] the wind" (Mark 4:39; Luke 8:24).[57] The second verbal repetition is found only in Mark, in Jesus's words to the opposing force, "Be silent [φιμώθητι] and come out of him!" (Mark 1:25; Luke 4:35) in the first instance, and "Shut up! Be silenced [πεφίμωσο]!" (Mark 4:39) in the second.[58] Moreover, the reaction of those who witness the two miracles bears striking resemblance. After the exorcism, the crowd responds, "What is [τί ἐστιν] this? A new teaching with authority! He commands even the unclean spirits [καὶ τοῖς πνεύμασι τοῖς ἀκαθάρτοις] and they obey him [ὑπακούουσιν αὐτῷ]!" (Mark 1:27). The storm stilling is followed by, "Who then is this [τίς ἄρα οὗτός ἐστιν] that even

---

56. On the possible widespread depiction of not only the sea stilling but also Jesus's healing miracles as overcoming the demonic, see Grelot, "Les Miracles de Jésus," esp. 65-66.

57. Thimmes, *Studies in the Biblical Sea-Storm Type-Scene*, e.g., 138-41, sees the very use of the verb ἐπιτιμάω as sufficient indication that the scene is an exorcism of some sort. See also Strecker, "Mächtig in Wort und Tat," 209-10.

58. Cf. Sorensen, *Possession and Exorcism*, 134.

the wind and the waves [καὶ ὁ ἄνεμος καὶ ἡ θάλασσα] obey him [ὑπακούει αὐτῷ]?" (Mark 4:41).[59] These are the only two uses of the verb ὑπακούω in Mark's Gospel. In Luke's telling, the common verbal tie between the texts is in the verb ἐπιτάσσει (4:36; 8:25).[60]

Jens Dechow recognizes these links and suggests, "So wird die Stillung des Seesturm von Jesus Mk 4,35ff. in deutlicher Anlehnung an Berichte exorzistischer Praxis geschildert."[61] The common language Jesus employs in his rebuke and silencing of both unclean spirit and sea suggests that the sea is not simply functioning as a force of "nature" in the modern sense, but has taken on the character of hostile, primordial chaos, a symbol of opposition to order, humanity, and God's people in particular (e.g., Pss 18:15-16; 29:3; 65:7; 74:13; 77:16; 89:9-10, 25).[62] As a theologized symbol, the sea occupies much the same cosmic space as the unclean spirits: it is emblematic of what we might call "spiritual" forces that array themselves against the flourishing of people and the reign of God.[63] Joel Marcus summarizes the effect of Mark's depiction of Jesus in this and the subsequent water-walking narrative: "He is speaking in and acting out the language of the Old Testament divine warrior theophanies, narratives in which Yahweh himself subdues the demonic forces of chaos in a saving, cosmos-creating act of holy war."[64] In speaking of these forces of chaos as "demonic," Marcus is intentionally linking them to the power Jesus exercises over demons.[65]

Adela Yarbro Collins concludes that the Jewish tradition of God's power over the seas colors this story as a revelation of Jesus's divinity: "they have God manifest in the boat with them!"[66] We have seen enough of the tight correla-

59. See also Hendrickx, *Miracle Stories*, 171-72, 177-78.

60. Such an assessment of parallels runs counter to the claim of Heil, *Jesus Walking on the Sea*, 87, that "the very nature of the power to still a storm is different than that of healing and exorcizing."

61. Jens Dechow, *Gottessohn und Herrschaft Gottes: Der Theozentrismus des Markusevangeliums* (WMANT 86; Neukirchen-Vluyn: Neukirchener Verlag, 2000), 87; see also Kee, *Miracle in the Early Christian World*, 163.

62. Cf. Dechow, *Gottessohn*, 87-88; Collins, *Mark*, 260-62.

63. See also John Meier, *A Marginal Jew: Rethinking the Historical Jesus*, vol. 2, *Mentor, Message, and Miracles* (ABRL; New York: Doubleday, 1994), 926-27.

64. Joel Marcus, *The Way of the Lord: Christological Exegesis of the Old Testament in the Gospel of Mark* (Louisville, KY: Westminster John Knox, 1992), 144-45.

65. Marcus, *Way of the Lord*, 144.

66. Collins, *Mark*, 260. Richard Hays, *Reading Backwards: Figural Christology and the Fourfold Gospel Witness* (Waco, TX: Baylor University Press, 2014), 22-23, makes the same claim but from Psalm 107 specifically.

tion between God and idealized humanity in the Jewish, especially Priestly, tradition to say that even such theophanic language might be indicative of a particular kind of idealized humanity. However, Collins also offers evidence that may point in another direction. She cites a story from Herodotus in which Xerxes has the Hellespont scourged and castigated for destroying a bridge his men had attempted to build.[67] Whether true or not, the tale depicts a king who thought that he might bring under control the powers of the sea that opposed him. She also cites a magic spell for calming winds, and finally cites the *Testament of Solomon,* in which a demonic figure claims the role of rising up against ships like a wave and crashing down on them.[68] Together, these data have the potential to open another possible interpretation of a person who has power over the wind and the waves: such a one might not be divine but a specially empowered human agent with the knowledge and/or power to command the hostile spirits manifesting themselves in the oppositional seas.[69] The connections between the exorcism story and the storm stilling point in such a direction;[70] and such a divinely empowered human agent exercising control over demons, and even the waters, is not foreign to the Hebrew scriptures.

Marcus uses the supernatural dynamics of Jesus's "filial plenipotentiary" power over the world to argue that the category "son of David" is insufficient to contain the scope of Jesus's embodiment of the power and reign of God.[71] I fully agree with Marcus that the power Jesus exercises is demonstrative of the power Jesus has as son of God. Thus, the storm stilling no less than the exorcisms proper are displays of Jesus's kingship. I would differ slightly from his ultimate conclusion, however, arguing instead that Mark's Jesus redefines the nature of Davidic kingship as he redefines what it means to be "Christ," more generally. Or, better put, Mark's Jesus embodies and performs the func-

67. Collins, *Mark,* 261; citing Alfred D. Godley, *Herodotus* (4 vols.; LCL; Cambridge, MA: Harvard University Press, 1922), 3:334-71.

68. Collins, *Mark,* 261-62.

69. Wendy J. Cotter, *The Christ of the Miracle Stories: Portrait through Encounter* (Grand Rapids, MI: Baker Academic, 2010), 212, draws such a conclusion: "All of these demonstrate the idea that special, divinely empowered heroes have power over the sea; it cannot overpower them or their plans."

70. Collins, *Mark,* 262-63, makes such a signal as well, drawing attention to the echo of the concluding questions of this episode ("Who is this that both wind and sea obey him?" 4:41) with that which concludes the first exorcism ("What is this? . . . He commands even the unclean spirits and they obey him!" 1:27), and saying, "From the point of view of the audience, these mighty deeds are part of the unfolding of the significance of Jesus's portrayal as 'messiah' or 'Christ' (1:1) and as God's son (1:11 and 3:11)."

71. Marcus, *Way of the Lord,* 144-45.

tions of an idealized human figure that cannot be contained in a normal human king; however, these very functions of ruling the world on God's behalf, including the world of demonic spirits and raging waters, is part and parcel with the idealized portraits of Davidic kingship that we see in both the narrative of 1 Samuel 16:13-23 and the lyrical anticipations of Psalm 89. I have discussed Psalm 89 at length above, so here I only sharpen the focus slightly: in Psalm 89:9-10 we see echoes of the *Chaoskampf* motif, where God conquers the seas as a warring enemy. Far from demonstrating that such a power, demonstrated by Jesus, signals his divinity, this same psalm points in a very different direction by later returning to the theme and having God declare of the Davidic king:

> I will crush his foes before him
>> and strike down those who hate him.
> My faithfulness and steadfast love shall be with him;
>> and in my name his horn shall be exalted.
> I will set his hand on the sea
>> and his right hand on the rivers.
> He shall cry to me, "You are my Father,
>> my God, and the Rock of my salvation!"
> I will make him the firstborn,
>> the highest of the kings of the earth. (89:23-27, NRSV)

In this psalm, God's victory over enemies and watery chaos is extended through the Davidic king.[72] Verse 25 carries such connotations, as is clear from its positioning in the midst of a series of promises about deliverance from enemies. I thus find Richard Hays's conclusion about this passage to be too hasty. Speaking of the disciples' question, "Who is this that the wind and the sea obey him?" Hays asserts, "For any reader versed in Israel's Scripture, there can be only one possible answer: it is the Lord God of Israel who has

---

72. This possibility is too little considered in much literature surrounding the text, in which the divine power at work in Jesus is seen to be an indication of Jesus as the embodiment of God himself. So, e.g., Hans-Georg Gradl, "Glaube in Seenot (Die Stillung des Sturms): Mk 4,35-41 (Lk 8,22-25)," in Luther and Röder, *Die Wunder Jesu*, 257-65: "[Jesus] wirkt das Wunder. Er ist nicht nur das Medium der Wirkmächtigkeit Gottes. Er steht im Zentrum der Erzählung, weil ihm der Wind und die See gehorchen. Damit wird eine soteriologische Grundaussage der alttestamentlichen Enzyklopädie Gottes auf Jesus übertragen, um die zentrale Frage nach seiner Identität zu beantworten" (261). The power of Jesus's word, and the obedience rendered to it by wind and sea, are perfectly capable of demonstrating an idealized human mediary.

the power to command wind and sea and to subdue the chaotic forces of nature."[73] Certainly this is divine power, but Psalm 89 shows us that even in this particular God is capable of extending this power such that it is embodied in a human agent.

For Jesus to embody such characteristics (as son of God and Davidic messiah) is not to discount Davidic messiahship, but to idealize it on a cosmic scale. Through the echoes of the exorcism story in the storm-stilling episode, Mark is signaling that the answer is the same to the Christological question each engenders: Jesus is the son of God, the vicegerent who rules the entirety of the world on God's behalf, who is therefore also authorized to speak for God, demonstrating in both word and deed the nature of God's dominion.[74] This is also not to argue against the notion that Jesus is here playing the role that the biblical antecedents typically reserve for God.[75] However, as throughout this study I am arguing here that playing the role of Israel's God is precisely what idealized human figures do. Sanders argues for a similar interpretation: because storm stilling is characteristic of God, particularly in God's defeat of the hostile forces of the deep, Jesus's wielding of such power indicates "that he could call on the power of God, rather than that he himself was a supernatural being."[76] This layer of resonance carries over into the other Synoptic Gospels as well.

Matthew's telling carries many of the same connotations as Mark's and Luke's, but he also reframes and otherwise alters the story in significant ways. First, Matthew frames his version as a story of discipleship that stands in contrast to the would-be followers whom Jesus rebuffs immediately before. The order to depart in the boat is given in Matthew 8:18 prior to the coming of these two would-be disciples. A scribe asks to follow, only to have Jesus explain that the son of man has no home (vv. 19-20); another man asks for permission to bury his father first, only to have Jesus summon him to follow and leave the dead to bury their own (v. 21). Second, when the order itself is executed, Matthew tells us that the faithful disciples not only went along with Jesus, but also followed him, specifically: ἠκολούθησαν αὐτῷ οἱ μαθηταὶ αὐτοῦ (v. 23). The story thus begins by underscoring the great cost at which

---

73. Hays, *Reading Backwards*, 22.

74. See also the similar conclusion of Hendrickx, *Miracle Stories*, 185, after highlighting the extensive biblical parallels between God as one who masters the sea and the storm-stilling episode: "Jesus is the Lord. However, he does not compete with God, but *acts on his behalf*, as his 'Son' who is equipped with his divine power" (italics added).

75. Cf. Meier, *Mentor, Message, and Miracles*, 931-33.

76. Sanders, *Historical Figure of Jesus*, 166.

the disciples accompany Jesus in the boat across the lake. Picking up on such threads, Davies and Allison concur with Günther Bornkamm that Matthew's version of the pericope is "a kerygmatic paradigm of the danger and glory of discipleship."[77] They proceed to describe other dynamics of the story that make it indicative of a life of discipleship, including biblical precedents for wild seas as emblematic of the trials of God's people (e.g., Pss 29:3, 65:7),[78] and Matthew's unusual choice to describe the storm as a σεισμός (8:24; cf. λαῖλαψ in Mark 4:37), a word that typically means "earthquake," and that is regularly associated with the eschatological tribulations of the faithful.[79] Matthew thus narrates his story in such a way that the Christological question that is the passage's culmination impinges directly on who it is that can so rescue his faithful followers, even from the chaos of the storm-tossed sea.[80] Interestingly, Matthew describes those who ask after Jesus's identity in the end as "the humans" (οἱ ἄνθρωποι, 8:27). This might differentiate Jesus as, in some way, more than human when the question immediately follows, "What sort is this one?" (ποταπός ἐστιν οὗτος, 8:27).[81] Alternatively, ἄνθρωπος might supply the missing qualifier for ποταπός: "What sort of human is this?"[82] In light of the son of man sayings with which the story is linked, this latter appears to be on track. By tying this passage to the son of man sayings on discipleship as he has done, Matthew provides a preliminary indication that the son of man title might provide an important clue to the disciples' question — a suffering and rejected human figure who nonetheless rules the world on God's behalf.[83] And yet, it might well be argued that the reader has to wait for a

77. Davies and Allison, *Matthew*, 2:68; citing Günther Bornkamm, "The Stilling of the Storm in Matthew," in *Tradition and Interpretation in Matthew* (ed. G. Bornkamm et al.; Philadelphia: Westminster, 1963), 52-57.

78. Davies and Allison, *Matthew*, 2:68.

79. Davies and Allison, *Matthew*, 2:69.

80. Davies and Allison, *Matthew*, 2:67, observe that the Christology of Matthew's passage is "more circumspect" than that of Mark, inasmuch as the disciples follow Jesus (Matt 8:23) rather than the disciples taking Jesus along with them (Mark 4:36); the disciples address Jesus as "Lord" (Matt 8:25) rather than "teacher" (Mark 4:38); and the disciples cry out to him, "Save!" (Matt 8:25) rather than the potentially reproachful, "Don't you care that we are being destroyed?" (Mark 4:38). None of these Christological refinements, however, invites a substantial reframing of the Christology from an exalted human Christology to one in which Jesus is conceived of as divine in a traditional sense.

81. Davies and Allison, *Matthew*, 2:75-76.

82. So McCartney, "*Ecce Homo*," 10.

83. This story may also contain allusions to Jonah; if so, it is not a far leap to recognize, as Davies and Allison have done (*Matthew*, 2:72), that here the reader sees Jesus as one who is greater than Jonah — a claim Jesus makes for himself explicitly in Matthew 12:41. In that

fuller answer until the second scene on a lake, when the disciples recognize Jesus as God's son (14:33).[84]

c. Storm Stilling in Roman Ears

In her *Miracles in Greco-Roman Antiquity,* Wendy Cotter demonstrates that some heroes of the hoary past were remembered as having power over the elements as well as the power to heal bodies.[85] She theorizes that the ability to drive off pestilence and control rivers and seas was due to the philosophers' probing of nature's secrets.[86] In a cosmology where "the elements of creation are both living and rational entities," those who probe nature come to be on intimate terms with the elements studied.[87] The legends surrounding Pythagoras, as relayed by Porphyry in the third century, demonstrate the possibility that a Roman auditor would have understood Jesus as such a quintessential philosopher. Porphyry writes,

> Verified predictions of earthquakes are handed down, also that he immediately chased a pestilence, suppressed violent winds and hail, calmed storms both on rivers and on seas, for the comfort and safe passage of his friends. As their poems attest, the like was often performed by Empedocles, Epimenides and Abaris, who had learned the art of doing these things from him. Empedocles, indeed, was surnamed Alexanemos, as the chaser of winds; Epimenides, Cathartes, the lustrator. Abaris was called Aethrobates, the walker in air; for he was carried in the air on an arrow of the Hyperborean Apollo, over rivers, seas and inaccessible places. It is believed that this was the method employed by Pythagoras when on the same day he discoursed with his friends at Metapontum and Tauromenium. (*Life of Pythagoras* 29)[88]

---

instance as well, Jesus compares himself to Jonah under the rubric of "son of man," lending further weight to the possibility that Jesus as son of man is at least a partial answer to the disciples' query.

84. Davies and Allison, *Matthew,* 2:69.

85. Wendy Cotter, *Miracles in Greco-Roman Antiquity: A Sourcebook* (New York: Routledge, 1999), 35-38.

86. Cotter, *Miracles,* 35.

87. Cotter, *Miracles,* 35.

88. Porphyry, *Life of Pythagoras,* in *The Pythagorean Sourcebook and Library: An Anthology of Ancient Writings Which Relate to Pythagoras and Pythagorean Philosophy* (comp. and trans. Kenneth S. Guthrie; Grand Rapids, MI: Phanes, 1987), 123-36, here 128-29.

This paragraph demonstrates a wide-ranging control over the natural world, including both healing miracles and the calming of seas for the safe passage of friends. Importantly, these capacities are ones that Pythagoras hands on to his disciples, which is a clear indication that they are "arts" that can be performed by the initiated, not powers that inhere in a thinly veiled divinity. Thus, although the numerous strands of the Pythagoras tradition in which he is the son of Apollo, or even the Hyperborean Apollo himself, might provide a route toward understanding how the miracle tradition of Jesus would signal the latter's divinity, the feats attributed to him are not themselves sufficient for such an ascription.[89]

Peter Kingsley has delved into the work of Empedocles, one of the Pythagorean pupils mentioned above, and argued that lines regarding healing, ability to control wind and rain, and the knowledge requisite to raise the dead are central dynamics of his teaching, stretching the self-depiction of this idealized philosopher well into the realm of "magic."[90] Importantly, the fragment that boasts of these abilities is one in which Empedocles is promising to entrust his abilities to his pupil, once again demonstrating that such possession is a matter of learning and study rather than divine ontology.

The fragment from Empedocles is significant not only due to its correlation with the tradition about Pythagoras, but also because it demonstrates that the third-century AD tradition about the Pythagoreans contains the same major elements as the fifth-century BC fragments from a Pythagorean's own hand. It is also noteworthy that for both these figures the traditions about them casually link power over the human body with power over the natural elements.[91] This lends additional weight to the notion that the various powers of Jesus that the current chapter explores would have functioned together in the mind of a Roman reader as indicative of a certain kind of being.

A third philosopher associated with the Pythagoreans, Apollonius of Tyana, lived at the time in which the Gospels were written, and his legend was inscribed about a century later by Philostratus.[92] Although he was more widely

89. On the divine nature of Pythagoras, see Barry Blackburn, Theios Anēr *and the Markan Miracle Traditions: A Critique of the* Theios Anēr *Concept as an Interpretive Background of the Miracle Traditions Used by Mark* (WUNT2 40; Tübingen: Mohr Siebeck, 1991), 37-51.

90. Peter Kingsley, *Ancient Philosophy, Mystery, and Magic: Empedocles and the Pythagorean Tradition* (Oxford: Clarendon, 1995), 217-370. Kingsley refers specifically to fragment 111, which he sees as authentic and as belonging at the head of the work to which critical editions have appended it at the end.

91. Cf. Kingsley, *Ancient Philosophy*, 223.

92. Cotter, *Miracles*, 145; Robert Garland, "Miracles in the Greek and Roman," in Twelftree, *Cambridge Companion to Miracles*, 86-87.

renowned for his healing, one passage in Philostratus's *Life of Apollonius of Tyana* describes him in a manner evocative of Pythagoras's gift of being able to still storms for the benefit of his friends. In describing Apollonius's travels, a comment is made in passing about people desiring to sail in the same ship as Apollonius because fall had arrived with its unpredictable weather: "They all then regarded Apollonius as one who was master of the tempest and of fire and of perils of all sorts, and so wished to go on board with him" (4.13).[93] Safe passage would be guaranteed by the presence of the philosopher-healer due to his mastery of the elements.

Finally, in her more recent work on miracles in their ancient context, Cotter demonstrates ways in which first-century literature depicts Roman emperors in authority over storms at sea.[94] In one passage from Lucan, Julius Caesar stirs a ship captain to courage with the notion that Fortune will see to it that he is delivered safely, and claims that he himself will be the salvation of the ship (*Bell. civ.* 5.577-93).[95] She also cites the metaphor of sea stilling invoked by Philo in his *Embassy to Gaius,* in which he credits Augustus for "calming the torrential storms on every side" (144-45). Cotter concludes that the notion of a man empowered to still the seas could either signify a god come to earth "or that God had empowered a special man to do his will on earth."[96]

Modern readers regularly take Jesus's control over the waters as a signal of divinity. But ancient auditors both Jewish and Roman had other options available to them. The latter might appeal to the demigods of their cultural encyclopedia for making sense of Jesus, but they might just as well appeal to the philosopher-magicians who not only taught but also healed and exercised power over the natural elements of the world. Jews, in turn, have not only stories of water-controlling heroes in Moses and Joshua, but also idealized depictions of a Davidic king who will exercise God's reign over the seas on God's behalf.

d. Water Walking

I addressed Matthew's water-walking incident (14:22-33) in the son of God chapter above. There I noted that Peter's own walking on water provides a

93. Philostratus, *The Life of Apollonius of Tyana* (trans. F. C. Conybeare; LCC; London: Heinemann, 1912), 371.

94. Cotter, *Christ of the Miracle Stories*, 228-30.

95. Cotter, *Christ of the Miracle Stories*, 228.

96. Cotter, *Christ of the Miracle Stories*, 230.

significant warning against associating the action itself with a divine ontology.[97] The obeisance that the disciples render to Jesus as they proclaim him son of God (προσεκύνησαν αὐτῷ λέγοντες· ἀληθῶς θεοῦ υἱὸς εἶ, Matt 14:33) echoes that rendered by the magi when they come to worship the one who had been born king of the Jews (Matt 2:2, 11). The adoration thus fits within Matthew's schema of what is appropriate for Jesus given that he is messiah.[98] Further proof of this comes from the confession of Peter in 16:16, where Peter's hendiadys, "Christ, son of the living God," meets with Jesus's enthusiastic approval (16:17). Together, these data point us in the direction of Jesus's water walking as executing the sort of idealized portrait of a coming messiah depicted in Psalm 89, or perhaps even a prophet like Moses who can execute authority over the seas — a messiah with the kind of power Theudas thought would be at his disposal when he gathered his followers at the Jordan River (*Ant.* 20.97).[99]

The urge to recognize divinity in the Gospels' depictions of Jesus runs the risk of separating or dividing Jesus's humanity from the actions he performs, or else of turning Jesus into an odd admixture of humanity and divinity. In an uncharacteristic foray into the Chalcedonian Definition, E. P. Sanders warns readers of such interpretations that are not only commonplace among contemporary Christians but also heretical according to the so-called ecumenical creeds: "Ever since the fifth century . . . orthodox Christians have believed that Jesus was 'true man of true man' and that his divinity (which they also affirm) neither combined with nor interfered with his humanity: he was not an odd mixture. It is heretical to say that his divinity buoyed up while his human feet lightly grazed the water. The definitive statement on

97. Thimmes, *Studies in the Biblical Sea-Storm Type-Scene,* 170, puts it well: "The Jesus of Matthew extends to Peter the authority/ability to do what the divinity can do." Such an ability for humans to share in divine authority and ability should provide a significant curb on the tendency to equate someone with God when that figure exercised divine prerogatives. Judith Hartenstein, "Jenseits der Komfortzone (Jesu Erscheinen auf dem See): Mt 14:22-33," in Luther and Röder, *Die Wunder Jesu,* 454-64, sees Peter's participation as one factor that puts any possible epiphanic aspect to the sidelines and keeps Jesus's relationships with the disciples as the focus of the pericope.

98. *Pace* Simon Légasse, "Les Miracles de Jésus selon Matthieu," in Aletti et al., *Les Miracles de Jésus selon le Nouveau Testament,* 227-47, here 232.

99. As a further option, Sanders, *Historical Figure of Jesus,* 161-62, suggests that Jesus is here referred to as "son of God" in the same sense that Honi the Circledrawer is referred to as God's son in *m. Ta'anit* 3.8. Honi would be guilty of something close to blasphemy ("I would have pronounced a ban against you") except that God responds to his solicitations "like a son who importunes his father and he performs his will."

this issue is that he is 'of one substance with us as regards his manhood; like us in all respects, apart from sin' — not, 'apart from the ability to walk on water.'"[100]

This statement comes as Sanders introduces his chapter on miracles, urging just the sort of caution that my own study is concerned with. Theologically within the creedal Christian tradition, as well as historically and literarily, every story about Jesus depicts something about a human being. I am arguing, in agreement with Sanders, that such anthropological implications are both necessary and sufficient for the interpretation of the Synoptic Gospels in their historical and literary contexts, even if the canonical or ecclesial contexts in which they are also read demand an additional layer of meaning.

One further set of considerations is in order at this point, to broaden the assessment of how a Roman reader of a water-walking episode might interpret the identity of such a protagonist. Cotter lays out several pieces of evidence that the notion of walking on the sea was considered something specially appropriate to the gods, a conviction that helped generate exalted descriptions of the humans who could accomplish such a feat.[101] Several such assessments swirl around Xerxes and his crossing of the Hellespont. Dio Chrysostom has one of Socrates's dialogue partners say that of all men under the sun Xerxes "is most powerful and in might not inferior to the gods themselves, who is able to accomplish the seemingly impossible — if it should be his will, to have men walk dryshod over the sea, to sail over mountains, to drain rivers by drinking" (3 Regn. 30). Xerxes's construction of a bridge of boats is recalled as "riding upon a chariot just like Poseidon in Homer's description" (3 Regn. 31). Although crossing the sea on a bridge of boats bears a significantly different quality than simply walking on the water on foot, it is described using the same imagery (walk dryshod over the sea) and as embodying the likeness of the gods' own water-riding capacities.

When Gaius Caesar (Caligula) mimicked such a deed to cross the Bay of Baiae, it, too, was interpreted as a completion of the impossible.[102] Suetonius records the story as one in which some thought Caligula was attempting to imitate Xerxes. But he also provides another interpretation, that the deed was done due to an astrologer's prophecy to Tiberius that "Gaius had no more chance of becoming emperor than of riding about over the gulf of

---

100. Sanders, *Historical Figure of Jesus*, 134.
101. Cotter, *Christ of the Miracle Stories*, 240-45.
102. Cotter, *Christ of the Miracle Stories*, 244-45.

Baiae on horseback" (*Cal.* 19).[103] In Dio Cassius the deed is recounted with this comment about the calmness of the sea: "This, too, caused the emperor some elation, and he declared that even Neptune was afraid of him" (*Hist.* 59.17.11).[104] Such a crossing signaled a human who rivaled the gods. Josephus pushes the interpretation a bit further, ascribing a presumption of divinity to Gaius, who considered himself "master of the sea," and rode across it as was befitting his "divinity" (*Ant.* 19.6). This shows that there is a range of possible connotations for passing over the water, from a human performing a great action that demonstrates subjugation of the gods, to a claim for divinity itself.

Alexander, too, was remembered as possessing lordship over the sea.[105] Though the writings of Callisthenes have been lost, and these appear to be the most ancient source of the legend, sources as early as Josephus recall that the Pamphylian Sea retreated before Alexander's army to allow passage. Josephus recalls the episode in his admonitions to his readers not to find the story of the Red Sea crossing incredible: "Let nobody be amazed at this strange thing, if a way of salvation was found, even through the sea, for people of old who were innocent of evil, whether by the will of God or by chance [κατὰ ταὐτόματον], since also the Pamphylian Sea withdrew for those who were with Alexander the king of Macedonia, people born just yesterday. And they not having another way, the sea provided them one through itself in order to destroy the Persian rule when God so desired" (*Ant.* 2.347-48). Since passing through the waters dryshod is largely the purview of God, such a feat accomplished by a human signals divine favor. In sum, the accounts of people miraculously crossing water from the Greek and Roman worlds signal their great power and often attest to the divine sanction of their royal power or task. Such actions might be considered tokens of some sort of divinity, but quite often attest to the person's possession of divine favor.

Returning to the Synoptic Gospels, Mark's portrait of this episode lacks Peter's zealous joining with Jesus, the disciples' exclamation of Jesus's divine sonship, and their act of obeisance. The reader or the "listener to the story would have already recognized that Jesus's walking on the sea is a claim to his divine empowerment, for the sea's submission to Jesus is a sign of its recogni-

103. Suetonius, *Gaius Caligula*, in *Lives of the Caesars* (trans. J. C. Rolfe; 2 vols.; LCL; Cambridge, MA: Harvard University Press, 1959), 1:433.

104. Dio Cassius, *Roman History* (trans. Earnest Carey; 9 vols.; LCL; Cambridge, MA; Harvard University Press, 1914-27), 7:313.

105. Cotter, *Christ of the Miracle Stories*, 241-42.

tion of his special status, his authorization over the earth."[106] For the disciples, however, the story leads to their astonishment due to their hardness of heart rather than a moment of revelation (6:52). Specifically, Mark signals that their failure to comprehend the loaves leads to their missing the opportunity to recognize Jesus in this moment of Christological disclosure (λίαν ἐν ἑαυτοῖς ἐξίσταντο. οὐ γὰρ συνῆκαν ἐπὶ τοῖς ἄρτοις, ἀλλ᾽ ἦν αὐτῶν ἡ καρδία πεπωρωμένη, 6:51-52). Thus, the interpretation of Jesus's water walking in Mark will be inseparable from the interpretation of the antecedent pericope. I turn now to the feeding story, where we will see not a divine Jesus but a royal, Mosaic shepherd.

2. MESSIANIC BANQUETS

Mark 6:1-52 contains an extensive unit of interrelated stories. Specifically, Mark intercalates the story of Herod's banquet between the sending and the return of the disciples, the latter of which bleeds into the feeding of the five thousand.[107] This sandwiching effect signals to the reader that the stories should be read in tandem.[108] Another narrative clue that Mark is linking the pericopes comes in the narrator's depiction of Jesus's desire to give his followers some rest — they had not even had time to eat (οὐδὲ φαγεῖν εὐκαίρουν, v. 31). This sets up the reader for the pervasive contrast that is beginning to unfold between Jesus's setting a feast in the desert and the "day of opportunity" (ἡμέρας εὐκαίρου, v. 21) that arises for Herodias at Herod's birthday banquet.

Significant for this contrast is the almost heavy-handed way that Mark depicts the first scene as a king's feast. Though Herod Antipas was a tetrarch, the pericope refers to him as king (βασιλεύς) no fewer than four times (vv. 22, 25, 26, 27), and includes his promise to give up to half his kingdom (βασιλείας) to his stepdaughter (v. 23). "King" Herod's feast is one at which the great people of the "kingdom" are present (v. 21). But in the end, the story subverts the would-be greatness of this purportedly royal figure that such a banquet might be thought to depict. Herod finds himself not imbued with royal sovereignty, but bound to act against his will by an oath, a woman's request, and his fear of losing face in front of his guests (v. 26). When the head of John the Baptist

106. Cotter, *Christ of the Miracle Stories,* 251.
107. Cf. Suzanne Watts Henderson, *Christology and Discipleship in the Gospel of Mark* (SNTSMS 135; New York: Cambridge University Press, 2006), 170-74.
108. See Paul J. Achtemeier, "*Omne Verbum Sonat:* The New Testament and the Oral Environment of Late Western Antiquity," *JBL* 109 (1990): 3-27.

is brought out on a serving platter (πίνακι, v. 28) as though it is the gruesome course of Herod's feast, the reader is given a final or ultimate picture of earthly kingship as a harbinger of death (cf. 10:42-45). Not only will Jesus, as the heir to John's prophetic program, fall into the same fate, the entirety of Mark is spent depicting his as a different kind of kingship over a different kind of kingdom. One such portrait is painted in the feeding narrative that Mark has signaled to his readers to interpret in tandem with Herod's royal feast.

The contrasts between the two scenes are pervasive. Whereas Herod's gathering is populated with the Galilean and Roman elite, Jesus's gathering is overflowing with οἱ πολλοί (vv. 31, 33), and the setting in the scarcity of the wilderness could not be farther from the lavish banqueting halls of the "king." And yet, the story invites comparison as well as contrast, providing two crucial cues that what is unfolding is the life-giving banquet of the true king of Israel, in contrast to the death-feast of Herod the pretender. First, when Jesus disembarks and sees the crowds that have run on foot ahead of him, he has compassion on them because they are like sheep without a shepherd, and he begins to teach them (v. 34). Second, when Jesus commands the people to recline for the meal, he has them do so in banqueting groups (συμπόσια συμπόσια, v. 39).

The narrator's comment that Jesus saw the people as "sheep without a shepherd" provides a rubric for understanding both the critique of Herod entailed in the prior pericope and the Christological disclosure that occurs in the feeding narrative. These words are likely an allusion to one of two scriptural texts. In Numbers 27:16-17 Moses is asking God to raise up someone to assume his mantle of leadership after he is gone so that God's people will not be like sheep who have no shepherd (ὡσεὶ πρόβατα οἷς οὐκ ἔστιν ποιμήν, v. 17). In 1 Kings 22:17 the prophet Micaiah prophesies to King Ahab of Israel that he will be defeated in battle, saying, "I saw all Israel scattered on the mountains like sheep that have no shepherd" (ὡς ποίμνιον, ᾧ οὐκ ἔστιν ποιμήν). These verses come closest, verbally, to Mark 6:34; however, it may also be that the conceptual idea of God's people not having a shepherd and the divine provision of such a shepherd through God's own shepherding and that of an idealized royal figure in Ezekiel 34 provide the conceptual grid for interpreting Jesus's work.[109] Choosing among these options is not entirely necessary for our purposes, inasmuch as they contain common threads to guide us through the labyrinth of Mark 6.

The shepherd image is used of Israel's various leaders. In Numbers 27:16-23 Joshua is the answer to Moses's petition: a leader of the people especially

---

109. See also Kee, *Miracle in the Early Christian World*, 169.

as they need to be guided out of the wilderness and into the Promised Land. Working in tandem with Eleazar the priest, Joshua is appointed to a role much like that of the later judges or kings, a political, judicial, and military role (v. 21). Importantly, Joshua fills this role as Moses bestows his own authority upon him (v. 20). Although scripturally Moses is remembered as the great prophet and David as the great king, the lines between prophet and king were blurred at times in the history of interpretation, Moses being depicted as king (cf. Philo, *Mos.* 1.155-58; Ezek. Trag. 68-89) and David being referred to as prophet (e.g., Acts 2:30). Both figures were also said to be taken from shepherding sheep in order to fill their roles as leaders of God's people (Exod 3:1; 1 Sam 16:11-12; 17:15).

In the context of Mark 6, the web of connotations points in the direction of Jesus being depicted as a royal Moses figure, one who shepherds shepherd-less Israel in the wilderness by teaching the people (v. 34) and ultimately by feeding the people by the hands of his disciples and the miraculous provision of bread (vv. 39-44).[110] The echoes of the exodus in the feeding of Israelites in the wilderness certainly foregrounds a Mosaic connection; however, the notion of superabundant provision of food with the restoration of David's line (Amos 9:11-15) provides another indication that the figures might be combined here. Between the juxtaposition with the Herod episode and the allusion to the Old Testament shepherd figures, Mark signals that this scene describes Jesus as a messianic, if simultaneously Mosaic, shepherd. Indeed, the exodus had proven paradigmatic within biblical and post-biblical Judaism, such that the wilderness itself became associated with God's eschatological deliverance, making such a conjunction of Mosaic and messianic imagery readily acces-sible to Mark's hearers.[111] With the "sheep without a shepherd" comment, Mark's feeding narrative is framed by an indication that the story contains a Christological disclosure.[112]

Jesus's first response to the people's shepherdless situation is to teach. This is now at least the fourth time in Mark's Gospel when a Christological claim is established through a conjunction of teaching and acting with unique au-

---

110. The occurrence of the miraculous feeding in the wilderness certainly echoes the ex-odus narrative, and thus Jesus playing the role of Moses is strongly indicated, though David's own ascendancy to the kingship is marked by extensive time in the wilderness as well (cf. 1 Sam 17:28; 23:13-29; 24:1; 25; 26:1-3).

111. Henderson, *Christology and Discipleship*, 184, highlights Second Isaiah (43:19), descrip-tions of would-be revolutionaries in Josephus's *War* (*J.W.* 2:258-63), and theologization of the wilderness setting of the Qumran community.

112. Cf. Henderson, *Christology and Discipleship*, 187.

thority (cf. 1:21-28; 2:1-12; 4:1-41). The conjunction is maintained when Jesus empowers his followers to act on his behalf as well (3:14-15; 6:7, 12-13). Suzanne Henderson, making a parallel observation, suggests that "for Mark, wonder-working and teaching represent two facets of the same overarching reality. . . . Indeed, this convergence fits well the gospels' Mosaic typology, since Moses' mediation of the Torah and his mighty deeds both attest God's power at work through him."[113] That Mark uses such conjunctions to demonstrate through Jesus's action the authority that he claims in the teaching underscores the likelihood that teaching the people does not exhaust the significance of Jesus as shepherd, and it also further strengthens the case that Mark is making yet another Christological point by such a conjunction of word and deed. It also increases the likelihood that Mark is not here introducing a new, divine Christology such that Jesus is playing the role of divine shepherd as such (e.g., Psalm 23; Ezek 34:11-16) but is instead building on the high human Christology where the faithful human king represents the divine shepherd through his tending of the flock (e.g., Ezek 34:23-24).[114]

Throughout this study I have regularly had recourse to one particular line of argument: if a human being does the things that Jesus does, then Jesus's performance of such actions is no indication of ontological distinction. In Mark's Gospel, the disciples participate in the feeding.[115] In fact, the command Jesus issues them upon their request that the people be sent away is that they provide the people with food to eat (Δότε αὐτοῖς ὑμεῖς, 6:37).[116] In the actual distribution of the bread and fish, Jesus gives to the disciples and they set the bread before the people (v. 41).[117] A similar inclusion of the disciples occurs in the feeding of the four thousand (8:1-10), where it seems that Jesus is trying to lead his disciples into offering to feed the people without stating this directly

113. Henderson, *Christology and Discipleship*, 186-87.

114. See also Roger David Aus, *Feeding the Five Thousand: Studies in the Judaic Background of Mark 6:30-44 Par. and John 6:1-15* (Lanham, MD: University Press of America, 2010), 155-59. Bernd Kollmann, "Brot und Fisch bis zum Abwinken (die Speisung Fünftausend): Mk 6,30-44 (ActJoh 93)," in Luther and Röder, *Die Wunder Jesu*, 294-303, refers to Psalm 23 as one possible intertext, suggesting the detail about green grass as a point of contact (298).

115. Henderson, *Christology and Discipleship*, 169-203.

116. Joel Marcus, *Mark 1–8* (AB 27; New York: Doubleday, 2000), 418, draws attention to the emphatic ὑμεῖς, perhaps a contrast to the disciples' suggestion that the people be sent to get food for themselves.

117. Henderson, *Christology and Discipleship*, 178-79, highlights the involvement of the disciples as a pervasive difference between Mark's and John's telling of this story. This sort of differentiation in functions parallels the different Christologies: John's disciples, following a truly divine figure, are further removed from Jesus's ministry.

(vv. 1-3). Jesus does not reserve this miracle for himself as one indicating his unique divine authority or ontology, but instead extends the authority to his disciples as those capable of doing the same.

The claim that Mark depicts Jesus here as a Moses-like messiah, and hence as an idealized human rather than divine, finds three additional supports. First, Mark has conjoined this feeding narrative with the subsequent water-walking episode by telling the reader that the disciples' astonishment is due to their failure to understand the loaves (6:52). Above I have argued that the authority Jesus exercises over the waters is a striking embodiment of the divine power over watery depths — an authority previously exercised by Moses at the Red Sea and Joshua at the Jordan River, an authority Psalm 89 anticipates devolving upon the coming Davidic king, and that Theudas expected to be at work in his own messianic charge across the Jordan into the Promised Land. Jesus's intention to pass the disciples by, in the context of Mark's Gospel, can only signal that he intends to resume the proper place of leader whom his disciples are following. As Mosaic-messiah shepherd, Jesus will lead his disciples on the sea to the place of safety (cf. Ps 23:2, ἐπὶ ὕδατος ἀναπαύσεως, LXX; Ps 89:25, θήσοαι ἐν θαλάσσῃ χεῖρα αὐτοῦ, LXX).

The second piece of evidence confirms that Jesus is depicted as messiah-shepherd in contrast to "King" Herod. After the second feeding narrative, upon the Pharisees' requesting a sign from Jesus, he tells the disciples to beware of the yeast of the Pharisees and of Herod (Mark 8:15). The disciples' misunderstanding leads Jesus to remind them about the abundance that came in the two feeding narratives, and he asks how they do not yet understand and, as in the narrator's assessment at the end of the water walking, whether their hearts are hardened (8:17; cf. 6:52). This strange juxtaposition of the Pharisees and Herod has a predecessor in the climactic conflict story of Mark 3:1-6, after which the Pharisees go out to plot with the Herodians how they might kill Jesus. Thus, the warning in 8:15 juxtaposes the feeding narratives with the murderous "shepherding" of Herod and his ilk, both through the overt mention of Herod himself and through the prior conspiracy of the Pharisees with Herod's partisans. The feeding narratives, then, are displaying a means of shepherding the people of God that stands in sharp contrast to the would-be "king" and Israel's religious guardians.

A third signal that the abundance of bread is provided by Jesus as messiah and not as divine comes from the troubling story of the Syrophoenician woman (7:24-30). The story is one of Jesus as exorcist, a role I have already established to be one Jesus plays as messianic son of God. In his rebuttal of the woman, Jesus says that it is wrong to give the children's bread to dogs before they are filled (χορτασθῆναι, v. 26), to which she replies that even the dogs eat the crumbs that fall from the table (v. 28). The reader knows that this kingship Jesus exercises has already filled the children with bread (ἐχορτάσθησαν, 6:42). The echo of the feeding story suggests that the more-than-abundant power Jesus exercises in the exorcism is of the same order as that which he employs in dispensing a more-than-abundant provision of bread for the children of Israel.

Henderson's insightful study of the feeding narrative not only highlights the entailment of Jesus's followers in this great miracle, it also demonstrates that such human participation in making bread abundant in desolate places is a component piece of Israel's eschatological expectation. Isaiah 58:9-12 invites Israel into practices of sharing its bread with the poor (δῷς πεινῶντι τὸν ἄρτον) so that the Lord will fulfill its need and rebuild the desolate ruins.[118] Thus, from multiple angles of biblical expectation, in addition to the unfolding Christology of Mark itself, the story presents a Christology of an idealized humanity — Jesus as idealized human, the Moses-like messiah, and his followers entering into this idealized humanity through their participation in the miracle.

Matthew and Luke make several adjustments to Mark's story, including the elimination of Mark 6:34b, "because they were like sheep without a shepherd, and he began to teach them many things." Both Matthew and Luke add an indication that Jesus healed the sick who had come to him, and Luke also says that Jesus spoke to them about the kingdom of God. Moreover, Luke has eliminated the antecedent Herod story altogether, while Matthew has kept it but deployed it somewhat differently. Matthew's Jesus retreats with the twelve specifically in response to hearing about John's murder (14:13). This connection in Matthew lends itself toward an indication of Jesus's compassion (14:14) overcoming any grief or fear he might feel at the news of John's death. Thus, both of the other Synoptic Gospels mute the signals that this banquet demonstrates Jesus as the messianic shepherd of Israel. However, neither reading offers an alternative Christology, either higher or lower. In the history of Israel there is precedent for a prophet to superintend a miraculous feeding — not only Moses in the wilderness, but Elisha hosting a filling feast for one hundred people through the twenty loaves he commanded his servant to distribute (2 Kgs 4:42-44).[119] Jesus in the Synoptic Gospels initiates the same type of miracle

118. Henderson, *Christology and Discipleship*, 190.
119. For an extensive comparison between Jesus and Elisha, including not only feeding miracles but also being noted for having disciples, see Aus, *Feeding the Five Thousand*, 18-44.

while amplifying its abundance to proportions befitting the eschatological advent of God's anointed.

3. CATCHING FISH

Both Luke and Matthew narrate stories in which Jesus superintends a miraculous fishing expedition at the hands of Peter. In Luke, the miracle is a catch of fish so great that the nets began to tear and two boats are filled to the point of nearly sinking (5:4-11). In Matthew, Jesus sends Peter to catch a fish that will have a coin in its mouth for the temple tax (17:24-27). Both actions are miraculous, and thus display within the world of the narratives access to divine power, but neither pericope signals that this divine power is native to Jesus rather than an endowment he possesses as God's authorized agent.[120] As the Elisha cycle provides recurring indications of the prophet's divine power through various miracles, and especially those having to do with water, so too the Synoptic Gospels include such fish tales as fit within a larger tapestry of Jesus's deeds that demarcate him as a human agent specially authorized by God.

a. Luke's Catch and Commissioning

Luke's story of the miraculous catch of fish (5:4-11) serves several purposes. Not only does it demonstrate Jesus overcoming the natural world in service of the men who would become his disciples, it also serves as a christophany of sorts as well as the call narrative for the first four disciples. Kavin Rowe has demonstrated how these dynamics are captured through the change in Peter's address to Jesus.[121] When first commanded to put out his nets, Peter addresses Jesus as ἐπισάτα, explaining that a hard night's work has proved fruitless, before acceding to Jesus's command (5:5). This title, which means "master," but sometimes with overtones of one who is a teacher (BDAG), is found in Luke on the lips of those who are addressing Jesus with insufficient

---

120. Cf. Susanne Luther, "Steuersünder mit Angellizenz (die Zahlung der Tempelsteuer): Mt 17:24-27 (EpAp 5,12f.),” in Luther and Röder, *Die Wunder Jesu*, 485-93, who associates the miracle with the power of Jesus's word and sees the fish as a symbol of the gift of God throughout Matthew (490-91).

121. C. Kavin Rowe, *Early Narrative Christology: The Lord in the Gospel of Luke* (Berlin: De Gruyter, 2006), 82-89.

awareness of who he is and what this should mean for them.[122] It is the address of the disciples when they fear for their lives on a storm-tossed boat (8:24), of Peter when he tells Jesus that with such a great crowd there is no point asking who touched him (8:45), of Peter when he wants to set up tabernacles on the mount of transfiguration because he does not know what he is saying (9:33), of John when he tells Jesus that they had silenced an exorcist (9:49), and of the lepers who with but one exception did not return to give thanks to Jesus after being healed (17:13). As the story begins, Peter does not address Jesus with a title that evidences fullness of faith and understanding.

After the catch of fish, however, Peter's address is different. Falling before Jesus he says, "Go away from me, for I am a sinful man, Lord" (5:8). Two points are worthy of note. First, Peter now addresses Jesus with the commendable title κύριε, a title the reader knows to be an accurate representation of Jesus from its use in the birth narrative (1:43, 76; 2:11).[123] Second, Peter's response of recognizing himself to be a sinner in need of repentance embodies the exact response that, in Luke-Acts, Jesus comes to engender within the people of Israel (e.g., 5:30-32; 7:36-50; 15:1-32; 18:9-14; 19:1-10 — nearly all these instances of sinners repenting are unique to Luke's Gospel or redacted by him in significant ways; cf. Acts 2:38; 3:19; 5:31).[124] The story, then, functions as an epiphany of sorts for Peter, who in response to the nature miracle understands Jesus's character in a way closer to what the reader knows to be true. The change in Peter "corresponds to the change in Christological title from ἐπιστάτης to κύριος, wherein, on the basis of the miracle, Peter sees who Jesus is and responds accordingly: Jesus is in fact the κύριος who deals with sinners."[125] This passage is freighted with Christological significance, and Rowe has rightly signaled that the title κύριος is not simply a polite address (e.g., "sir"). What, then, does Luke's κύριος Christology entail at this point?

Joel Green compares the story with Isaiah 6:1-10 as a parallel "commission story." In each there is an epiphany (Luke 5:4-7; Isa 6:1-4), a reaction (Luke 5:8; Isa 6:5), an assurance (Luke 5:10a; Isa 6:7), and a commission (Luke 5:10b; Isa 6:8-10).[126] Green walks the line of affirming that this scene is "theophanic for Luke," but simultaneously warning against the notion that such a depiction means that Jesus "*is God*" — such a conclusion would "employ alien catego-

---

122. Rowe, *Early Narrative Christology*, 84-85.

123. Rowe, *Early Narrative Christology*, 85-89.

124. Rowe, *Early Narrative Christology*, 87-88, makes a similar point.

125. Rowe, *Early Narrative Christology*, 86.

126. Joel B. Green, *The Gospel of Luke* (NICNT; Grand Rapids, MI: Eerdmans, 1997), 233.

ries."[127] To hold together the categories available to Luke and, presumably, his first readers, Green suggests instead that the commissioning scene "encourages the view that Peter recognizes in Jesus the agency of God."[128]

The idea that this initial commissioning of the disciples occurs due to Jesus's agency rather than his inherent divinity finds some validation in the commissioning story that concludes the Gospel (24:44-53). There, Jesus ties his death and resurrection to scripture, explaining that these are the things that must happen to him as "the Christ" (τὸν χριστόν, v. 46). Not only is this the narrative that the disciples are to take to all the nations in order to bring the forgiveness of sins, it is the very proclamation of this narrative in the book of Acts that has the potential to convince people that they are sinners who need God's forgiveness (e.g., 2:27-38; 3:26). We see in the later narrative that it is not confrontation with Jesus as God that causes people to recognize their sinfulness, but their confrontation with Jesus as God's promised, attested, and raised messiah who is also the coming judge. Importantly, in this final commissioning story Jesus makes it clear that, as messiah, he is the agent through whom God is at work: "I will send the promise of my father upon you" (Luke 24:49). The mediatorial nature of Jesus's pouring out the spirit is confirmed specifically in Peter's speech on Pentecost: "Therefore, having been lifted up to the right hand of God, and having received the promised Holy Spirit from the father, he has poured out this which you both see and hear" (Acts 2:33). In the unfolding story, the question about what sort of κύριος it might be who so enables a remarkable catch of fish that it inspires his followers to confess their sinfulness before they are commissioned to gather people is answered as the reader discovers that recognition of sinfulness comes from an encounter with Jesus as God's messiah, and that Jesus as the commissioning sender is playing this very messianic role. The further fact that both commissioning stories signal that the followers venerate Jesus through some act of obeisance (Luke 5:8; 24:52) underscores the connection between the first and the last commissionings of Jesus's disciples in Luke, and demonstrates the honor that is due Jesus as God's anointed.

b. Matthew's Tax-Paying Fish

Matthew's unique fish story unfolds around the question of whether or not Jesus pays the two-drachma tax (τὰ δίδραχμα, 17:24). Davies and Allison have

127. Green, *Gospel of Luke*, 233 (italics original).
128. Green, *Gospel of Luke*, 233.

persuasively argued for the majority view: the tax in view is the temple tax and not a Roman tax.[129] The discussion that ensues between Jesus and Peter uses state tax collection to make a Christological point about Jesus and his relationship to God. Kings of the earth, Jesus and Peter concur, collect taxes not from their own children but from others' (17:26). The implicit conclusion from this is that Jesus, as son of the God for whose sake the temple tax is being collected, is free from the tax. Nonetheless, "in order not to scandalize them [ἵνα μὴ σκανδαλίσωμεν αὐτούς]," Jesus has Peter go fishing for a fish whose mouth will contain the needful coin for both of their temple taxes (17:27). Unlike Luke's surprising fish story, the miracle itself is not a moment of disclosure in this pericope. Peter's catch does not, for example, draw forth a concluding exclamation about Jesus's identity. However, the pericope does hinge on the question of Jesus as son of God. For readers who have recently heard the exchange between these same two characters that equated the title of "messiah" with "son of the living God" (16:13-20), this pericope points to Jesus exercising miraculous powers as God's anointed son without signaling divinity as such.

4. CONCLUSION: NATURE MIRACLES

The ability to exercise power over nature demonstrates that God is at work.[130] In the scriptures of Israel, such power resides in extraordinary prophets (e.g., Moses, Elijah, and Elisha).[131] In the Gospels, such power resides in Jesus as God's son, the messiah. The point of these depictions, and of my argument about them, is not to deny divinity to Jesus, but to demonstrate the height to which humanity obtains in its idealized embodiment. In a religious framework within which humanity in its idealized, primordial state was created by God to reign over the earth, Jesus's actions demonstrate the breadth of what such rule might entail. Jesus rules the powers of primordial chaos, of which the sea is emblematic, because God has so empowered Jesus by the spirit and the inchoate kingship proclaimed at Jesus's baptism. Jesus is the messianic king

129. Davies and Allison, *Matthew*, 2:738-41.

130. This is a special emphasis in Philo, but even there God acts through mediators, such as in the case of Moses and Aaron in the exodus plagues. See Eve, *Jewish Context of Jesus's Miracles*, 65-68.

131. On the more general question of miracles, Eve, *Jewish Context of Jesus's Miracles*, e.g., 249, demonstrates that a majority of miracles in Josephus and in Second Temple literature more generally were ascribed to human agents. For the connection between Jesus's actions and Elijah and Elisha, cf. Strecker, "Mächtig in Wort und Tat," 209.

who presides over a banquet of abundance in the wilderness. Jesus is the Lord whose lordship extends the rule of the heavenly Lord God precisely because the latter has created humanity, and set aside Jesus, precisely for this purpose.

C. HEALING HANDS

Although modern readers will see the three categories of exorcisms, nature miracles, and healings as three essentially discrete types of actions, for the ancients they were more likely on a continuum.[132] In the storm-stilling episodes we saw extensive parallels with exorcism stories. In Jesus's practice of healing, as well, the conjunction between physical and what we might call "spiritual" power is sometimes seen.[133] In this vein, Luke's description of a hunched over woman as one having a spirit of sickness (πνεῦμα ἔχουσα ἀσθενείας, 13:11) and Jesus's claim that she had been bound by Satan for eighteen years (13:16) are windows into what was often a tightly connected world of spirits and bodies in the ancient way of viewing the world.[134] For Matthew's part, he tells of a blind and mute man who was demon possessed (δαιμονιζόμενος), whom Jesus healed (ἐθεράπευσεν, 12:22). Perhaps sounding a similar note, the healing of the paralytic (Mark 2:1-12; pars.) is significant inasmuch as the authority to heal and the authority to forgive are conjoined and demonstrative of each other.[135]

This third instance paves the way for considering what sort of authority it is that someone might have as one who heals. Mark's early signal is that this is the same authority Jesus possesses as "son of man," thus lending initial plausibility to the notion that Jesus heals as an idealized, representative human figure. This idea that healing demonstrates the authority that specially authorized humans possess is validated as well by the fact that this defining facet of Jesus's ministry (e.g., Matt 4:23-25; 9:35; 12:15; 14:14; 15:30; 19:22; 21:14; Mark 1:34; 3:7-12; 6:53-56; Luke 4:40; 5:15; 7:21; 8:2; 9:11) also defines the disciples' missionary endeavors (Matt 10:1, 8; Mark 6:12-13; Luke 9:1, 6; 10:9).

---

132. *Jubilees,* for instance, reflects a shared etiology. When Noah's prayer for an expulsion of demons who have been blinding and killing his descendants is only partially granted, God commands angels to disclose ways to heal using "the herbs of the earth" (*Jub.* 10:1-14). This seems to indicate a demonic source for physical ailments that are, in turn, cured with primitive medicines (cf. Eve, *Jewish Context of Jesus's Miracles,* 163-64).

133. Cf. Grelot, "Les Miracles de Jésus."

134. McCartney, "*Ecce Homo*," 10, highlights healing, and the healing of a royal figure, as a sign that the reign of God was being restored, with humanity ruling over the created world.

135. Sanders, *Historical Figure of Jesus,* 165.

1. JEWISH AND GRECO-ROMAN HEALERS

a. Jewish Healers

At various junctures in this study, I have drawn attention to the conjunction between Jesus's authority as one who speaks for God and his authority as one who acts with miraculous power. We have seen this, for instance, in his healing of the paralytic, where the speech signifying forgiveness is confirmed by the healing miracle, and a similar conjunction is in view in the first exorcism, where teaching with authority encompasses the authority to command demons. In Israel's biblical tradition, such power was regularly associated with prophets.[136]

The notion that someone's miraculous, healing actions prove his empowerment to speak for God finds precedent in the story of Elijah raising a widow's son (1 Kgs 17:17-24).[137] The boy's restoration comes by a combination of Elijah's actions, including both spreading himself on the boy three times and prayer to God, and divine response to the prophet's petition ("YHWH listened to the voice of Elijah," v. 22). The culmination of the miracle story, however, is the affirmation of Elijah's identity by the woman: "Now I know that you are a man of God, and that the word of YHWH in your mouth is truth" (17:24). The ultimate healing miracle of raising the dead signals that God is, in fact, at work in and through the prophet who is God's human agent. In Josephus's telling of this story, despite other alterations, he reiterates this point of the healing narrative confirming for the widow that God did, in fact, speak through Elijah (τότε σαφῶς ἔλεγε μεμαθηκέναι ὅτι τὸ θεῖον αὐτῷ διαλέγεται, *Ant.* 8.327).[138]

The healing of Naaman the Syrian in the Elisha cycle provides analogous evidence as to the interaction between divinity and an earthly wonder-worker (2 Kgs 5:1-19). When Naaman comes to the king of Israel with a letter from Aram asking for Naaman's cure, the king replies, "Am I God, to give death or life, that this man sends word to me to cure a man of his leprosy?" (5:7, NRSV). Thus, the initial requirement for performing such an action appears to be nothing less than divinity. However, Elisha sends for Naaman with these words: "Let him come to me, that he may know that there is a prophet

---

136. Kee, *Miracle in the Early Christian World,* 147-49.

137. See Cotter, *Miracles,* 48-49.

138. This fits the broader pattern within Josephus of interpreting the miraculous as acts of God (cf. Eve, *Jewish Context of Jesus's Miracles,* 24-52).

in Israel" (5:8). The person on earth who can perform a task that demands divine power is God's prophet.[139] The result of the miracle, in turn, includes Naaman's confession that "there is no God in all the earth except in Israel" (5:15).[140] Each of these stories provides a common framework for how a Jew might understand a miracle-worker who was, at the same time, claiming to speak for God: a uniquely empowered prophet. The unity between God and the agent in such a case would not be one of ontological identity, but of a representation in which God is at work in the human person. As Sanders puts it in his summary of Jewish healers, "The Jewish assumption in all these cases was that an individual could influence God, who could of course do anything he wished."[141]

As a final piece of peculiarly Jewish background, the Qumran text 4Q521 contains numerous points of contact with the Jesus narratives. The challenge in employing it for our understanding of early Christology, however, especially on the point of the divinity versus the agency of Jesus, is that the Qumran text itself is ambiguous as to what actions are performed by God and which are performed by God's messiah.[142] As discussed in chapter 1 above, the scroll clearly anticipates an eschatological age in which the messiah and then the holy ones will rule the world on God's behalf (frag. 2). Moreover, the text clearly anticipates that this eschatological age will entail healing, proclamation of good news, resurrection, and feeding of the poor. The debated question is whether God or the messiah is subject of these latter activities. Above I echoed the argument of John Collins that the action of proclaiming good news is more likely to have a human subject than divine, thus highlighting the possibility that a human agent is the means by which such divine activities will be manifest on earth.[143] Such an expectation can help underscore the eschatological character of Jesus's ministry as depicted in the Gospels, and may illustrate a messianic expectation wherein a human figure is God's agent in healing, resurrection, and feeding miracles.

139. Hendrickx, *Miracle Stories*, 84-91, repeatedly draws attention to parallels between Elisha's healing of Naaman and Jesus's healing of the leper (Mark 1:40-45), concluding that Mark depicts Jesus as an eschatological prophet, in the same tradition of, but greater than, the biblical precedents.

140. Cf. Kee, *Miracle in the Early Christian World*, 149.

141. Sanders, *Historical Figure of Jesus*, 140.

142. See the judicious discussion in Eve, *Jewish Context of Jesus' Miracles*, 189-97.

143. See Émile Puech, "Messianism, Resurrection, and Eschatology at Qumran and in the New Testament," in *Community of the Renewed Covenant* (ed. E. C. Ulrich and J. C. Vander-Kam; Notre Dame, IN; University of Notre Dame Press, 1994), 235-56, here 242.

b. Greco-Roman Healers

Roman hearers, and Jews with exposure to Greek and Roman legends, had a broader array of interpretive options available to them. In particular, the notion that healing is the provenance of the gods bore fruit in tales of gods who healed on earth. Hercules is one such figure. Born of a divine father and human mother, he was not only remembered for his eponymous labors but also venerated as a healer.[144] However, the preponderance of evidence for Hercules as a healer comes from after his life on earth when he had been deified. In Aelius Aristides's *Heracles,* Apollo is said to mandate the establishment of temples and sacrifices made to Heracles upon his death (40.11). Immediately thereafter, Aristedes lists both healing and escape from dangers at sea as the provenance of this god (40.12). This literary evidence of Hercules being honored for his healing powers finds confirmation in various pieces of material evidence, including inscriptions from cultic sites throughout the Roman world.[145] Thus, although the connection of a divine father and human mother might make Hercules an appealing parallel in the Gospels of Matthew and Luke, his powers as healer are associated not so much with his time on earth, which bears quite a different character (even if, ultimately, the two are related), but with his status as an enthroned God. This makes Hercules an unlikely parallel in terms of providing a category for interpreting Jesus's work as healer; however, it does raise the possibility that an ancient would associate healing powers with a person's divinity.

A more likely candidate for an ancient parallel deity might be Asclepius, the famous healer, who was said to be the offspring of the god Apollo and the human princess Coronis (e.g., Homer, *Hymns* 16.1-4).[146] Generally speaking, one might say that the divinity of Asclepius is an important explanation for his powers as a healer. However, there are some important differences as well. In Plato's *Republic,* the healer's work is described very much as the work of medicine, the working of a hero, rather than divine power, reflecting the Homeric tradition as well.[147] There a comment is made that for "localized

144. Cf. Christina Salowey, "The Peloponnesian Herakles: Cult and Labors" (PhD diss., Bryn Mawr College, 1995).

145. Christina Salowey, "Herakles and Healing Cult in the Peloponnesos," cited June 4, 2015, http://www1.hollins.edu/faculty/saloweyca/Saloweytext.htm.

146. Cf. Enno Edzard Popkes, "Antikes Medizinwesen und antike Therapieformen," in Luther and Röder, *Die Wunder Jesu,* 79-86, esp. 79-82.

147. See also the assessment in Emma J. Edelstein and Ludwig Edelstein, *Asclepius* (2 vols.; Baltimore: Johns Hopkins University Press, 1945), 2:1-64; Kee, *Miracle in the Early Christian World,* 89.

disease" Asclepius "revealed the art of medicine, driving out their disease by drugs and surgery, prescribed for them their customary regimen in order not to interfere with civic duties" (*Rep.* 407).[148] Plato goes on to reflect the Homeric tradition that Asclepius's sons learned such arts from their father, especially as pertains to blood letting and healing of wounds (cf. *Il.* 2.729-33). Of course, his legend grows as the deified Asclepius is remembered as a god who appears to worshipers as they sleep in his shrines and provides remedies for their illnesses. The widespread reputation of Asclepius as healer might invite comparisons with Jesus as healer, and his deification seems to have been his path to effecting miraculous healing thus, perhaps, signaling that to heal entails divinity. However, the differences between the life of Asclepius and his means of healing and those narrated of the Synoptic Jesus make for minimal points of comparison. The question left for us by both the Hercules and Asclepius legends, given that their healing powers are associated with their deification, is this: would a Roman reader assume that one with miraculous powers to heal is, in fact, divine? A survey of healing heroes leads me to say no.[149]

Wendy Cotter assembles evidence of healing by classical philosophers, rulers, the late first-century itinerant philosopher Apollonius, and Augustus's physician Asclepiades in addition to evidence from the Jewish scriptures.[150] The evidence Cotter cites for much of this material is later than the first century; for instance, Porphyry is offering remembrances of the late sixth-century BC philosopher Pythagoras in the third century AD. Nonetheless, the material is instructive for demonstrating possible ways in which a Greco-Roman audience would hear a hero story. Importantly, as mentioned above, the literary evidence of Pythagoreans as healers reaches back to the *Fragments* of Empedocles himself, thus indicating that such traditions predate their later inscription.[151] As already discussed above, the traditions surrounding the Pythagoreans link healing powers with the ability to control nature.[152] Thus, Pythagoras is described as one who "chased away a pestilence, suppressed violent winds and hail, calmed storms on both rivers and seas."[153] And Empedocles

---

148. Plato, *Plato in Twelve Volumes* (trans. Paul Shorey; LCL; Cambridge, MA: Harvard University Press, 1969).

149. Popkes, "Antikes Medizinwesen," 79-81, helpfully outlines the ambiguity in Asclepius's own status between empowered human and quasi-divine figure.

150. Cotter, *Miracles in Greco-Roman Antiquity*, 35-53.

151. Kingsley, *Ancient Philosophy*, 218.

152. See also Robert Garland, "Miracles in the Greek and Roman World," 82-83.

153. Porphyry, *Life of Pythagoras*, 128-29.

promises that his pupil will learn the remedies "that exist as defense against sufferings and old age," will "stop the forces of the tireless winds" and stir them back up again as desired, will cease or conjure up rains as needed, and will "fetch back from Hades the life-force of a man who has died" (frag. 111).[154] The Pythagoreans, in particular, are associated with a holistic control over nature that includes the healing and revivification of the human body.

Finally, there are two cases in which kings are said to have healing powers. In a largely derogatory account of King Pyrrhus, Plutarch describes the king's ability to heal ailing spleens: the combination of a sacrificed white cock and the king's right foot pressed against the prone patient's spleen were said to be curative.[155] A second case is much closer to the time of the Gospels, in legends surrounding Vespasian.[156] Tacitus tells of divine omens, including Vespasian's own healing acts, which worked to confirm Vespasian in his rule over Rome (*Histories* 4.81-82). The healing narrative relates to two men who come to Vespasian while he is in Alexandria. Tacitus sets the stage for the healing by saying that the god Serapis prompted the men, one blind and another with a lame hand, to come ask for the healing. Thus, divinity plays an important part in the story, though that role is not Vespasian's. As Vespasian mulls over whether or not to attempt the healing, Tacitus comments that such restoration "perhaps was the will of the gods." Then, strikingly, he claims that, if successful, "the glory would be Caesar's." Though the impetus for this healing is the divine intervention of Serapis, and though the power to heal appears to be a peculiar gift for this one moment as Vespasian is ascending his throne, the glory is not ascribed to the gods who empowered him, but to the new Caesar. The point of the healings is to demonstrate the "partiality of the gods" toward him — not to show that he is in some sense divine, but that the gods approve of his ascendancy.

There is no one category in ancient Rome that would have had exclusive claim to providing a framework for making sense of Jesus's identity. Divinity is a possibility, but the differences between the divinized healers and those who healed on earth are significant. The closest analogue appears to be the heroes of the Pythagorean tradition, whose knowledge of the world was such that they were not only renowned philosophers but also healers who had control even over the wind, seas, and rains. Ultimately, the readers will have to situate these

154. As cited in Kingsley, *Ancient Philosophy*, 218.

155. Plutarch, *The Parallel Lives: Pyrrhus* (trans. B. Perrin; LCL; London: Heinemann, 1920), 3.4; cited in Cotter, *Miracles in Greco-Roman Antiquity*, 39-40.

156. Cf. Garland, "Miracles in the Greek and Roman World," 84-85.

miracles in the larger context of the unfolding narratives in which they appear, an exercise, I am arguing throughout, that would repeatedly underscore that Jesus is functioning as some sort of idealized human figure, including ways that such figures are empowered and directed by divinity, rather than being divine figures as such.[157]

2. MESSIAH AS HEALER IN MATTHEW

In her study *Messiah, Healer of the Sick,* Lidija Novaković demonstrates how healing might be seen as a messianic activity in early Judaism, and that Matthew specifically ties Jesus's healing ministry to his Davidic messianism.[158] Already I have discussed Jesus as Davidic messiah and son of God in Matthew. Novaković's research homes in on the manner in which this title is deployed to govern Jesus's activity as a healer. The paradigmatic announcement of the angel that Jesus will save his people from their sins is interpreted as including his healing ministry.[159] The notion of Jesus as a healing Davidic messiah is sustained through close attention to the son of David passages in Matthew.

Matthew 9:27-31 contains a pericope unique to Matthew in which two blind men are healed. These men, like blind Bartimaeus in Mark 10:46-48, address Jesus as son of David: ἐλέησον ἡμᾶς, υἱὸς Δαυίδ (9:27). When Jesus asks if they believe he can perform this miracle, they reply, "Yes, Lord" (ναὶ κύριε, 9:28), an indication that if "Lord" means more than "sir," it means "Lord" with all the reverence due to Israel's rightful king. The men receive sight, according to their faith (9:29). In assessing the use of the son of David title, we do well to remember that readers of Matthew's Gospel encounter this as a title first bestowed upon Jesus in 1:1 by the narrator, and they recognize that this address is appropriate. Novaković further concludes that the Davidic address not only is appropriate for Jesus as healer, but is also summative of the identity of Jesus under which the entire healing cycle of chapters 8–9 takes place:

---

157. Légasse, "Les Miracles de Jésus," provides a thoroughgoing summary of the ways in which Matthew appears to elevate the Markan Christology, attributing greater majesty to Jesus. However, his assertions of divinity stand largely in the absence of alternatives: he offers no arguments as to why an exalted human Christology might not contain such a figure, nor methodological considerations for how we might know that a character is divine or what such divinity might mean for a pre-Chalcedonian Jewish author.

158. Lidija Novaković, *Messiah, Healer of the Sick: A Study of Jesus as the Son of David in the Gospel of Matthew* (WUNT2 170; Tübingen: Mohr Siebeck, 2003).

159. Novaković, *Messiah,* 73.

Yet the fact that a quite unanticipated identification of Jesus as the Son of David by two invalids in 9:27 is not accompanied by any explanatory note leaves the impression that the Davidic title somehow sums up the experience of Jesus as a healer in the preceding episodes. This strategic significance of the healing of the two blind men within the whole miracle cycle in chapters 8–9 has been generally recognized. By such arrangement, the entire cycle in chapters 8–9 has been placed into the Davidic framework.[160]

In this story, the capacity in which Jesus heals is his role as Davidic messiah. The final pericope of the Matthew 8–9 healing cycle is one in which Jesus's exorcism meets with the charge of casting out demons by the prince of demons (9:32-34). And so as Matthew turns to a summary statement about Jesus's mission of preaching the gospel of the kingdom and healing every illness and malady (9:35), the reader is left with the choice of recognizing Jesus as son of David, anointed, presumably, by God for his task, or else as agent of Satan. As this section of the Gospel draws to a close, Matthew underscores the high human Christology in which Jesus heals because of his messianic authority.

Matthew's intentionality in conjoining of the blind men's Davidic Christology and the accusation of collusion with Satan is affirmed when we turn to the Beelzebul controversy itself (12:24-31). Matthew introduces the latter controversy with heavily redacted material in which Jesus is depicted as a healer and exorcist, generating the question of the crowds as to whether he is, in fact, the son of David (12:15-23). In the verses leading up to the controversy Matthew conjoins healing and exorcism:

vv. 15-16 Jesus heals all who follow and orders silence
vv. 17-21 Formula citation of Isaiah 42:1-4
v. 22 Jesus heals (ἐθεράπευσεν) a man with a blind and mute-making spirit
v. 23 Crowd wonders if Jesus is son of David

The movement from a generalized statement about healing to a description of an exorcism as a healing corroborates the claim made above that power over malevolent spirits and power over broken bodies indicate points on a shared continuum in many ancient writings, including Matthew's Gospel.[161]

---

160. Novaković, *Messiah*, 81.

161. Though both Mark and Luke have similar short exorcism stories, only Matthew uses θεραπεύω rather than ἐκβάλλω to describe the incident (cf. Novaković, *Messiah*, 82).

The citation of Isaiah 42:1-4 raises any number of issues, but germane for my purposes are these observations. First, this is a "servant song" that depicts the beloved child as one on whom God bestows God's spirit (v. 18). The very point of contention in the ensuing controversy will be whether Jesus casts out spirits by Beelzebul or by the spirit of God (12:24, 26-28). Thus, the broader context signals that Jesus fulfills scripture as one who has a spirit of healing and exorcism that is given to him by God. Second, the notion of not crying out (v. 19) might well correspond to the command to silence (v. 17). Third, the final note sounded in Matthew's citation of Isaiah 42 is, "In his name the nations [ἔθνη] will hope" (12:21), a verse that echoes the promise of a Davidic messiah from First Isaiah (11:10). Although Isaiah 42:4 does not in itself carry such Davidic overtones (and, one might argue, it may reproduce the language to redirect the hope away from Davidic messianism), it may well be that Matthew imputes such overtones to the verse, as the subsequent conclusion of the crowds that Jesus might be "son of David" flows from Jesus's healing of the demoniac. Whether or not the final clause cited from Isaiah 42:4 is to be taken as textual basis for Jesus's Davidic role, the overall force of these verses is to situate Jesus's healings in general and his exorcisms in particular within the rubric of Davidic messianism — a textbook example of Jesus fitting the mold of an idealized human figure.

As in Matthew 9:27-34, the affirmation of Jesus as son of David is met with a counter-charge that Jesus is colluding with Satan (12:24). Jesus's rebuttal is that he is casting out demons by the spirit of God, and that this is a signal that the kingdom of God has come upon them (12:28). As I discussed above, such a conjunction of themes signals that Jesus's claim is to the role of Davidic messiah, anointed by the spirit of God, as the king of God's kingdom. In a later story, Matthew will have the Canaanite woman who asks for an exorcism on behalf of her daughter address Jesus, "Have mercy on me, Lord, son of David" (15:22). In this case, too, Matthew indicates that a healing has taken place (ἰάθη, 15:28), parting from Mark's language of the demon's departure (ἐξεληλυθός, 7:30).[162] A consistent pattern begins to emerge in which Matthew's Jesus heals precisely because he is Davidic messiah.

The story of Jesus healing two blind men who address him as son of David recurs in Matthew's redaction of the Bartimaeus story (20:29-34). Matthew so renders the story, turning the one blind man into two, that it serves as a book-end of sorts to Jesus's ministry of healing prior to his entry into Jerusalem. In all three Synoptic Gospels the blind men outside Jericho address Jesus as son

---

162. Novaković, *Messiah*, 83.

of David, but whereas for Mark's readers the appellation is first heard at this point in the story, for Matthew's it has been a recurring theme, and serves as a strong indication that, paradoxically, the blind can see who Jesus truly is.[163] Jesus is David's son precisely as one who has the power to heal.

Matthew provides one further scene that interprets Jesus's healing ministry within Davidic messianism. After the temple-clearing incident (21:12-13) Matthew alone tells of a healing ministry that takes place in the temple (προσῆλθον αὐτῷ τυφλοὶ καὶ χωλοὶ ἐν τῷ ἱερῷ, καὶ ἐθεράπευσεν αὐτούς, 21:14). The indignation of the high priests and scribes is stirred when they see (1) the wonders (θαυμάσια) Jesus is doing, and (2) the children who are crying out, "Hosanna to the son of David" (21:15). As was the case in the Beelzebul controversy (12:23-24) Jesus's healing action is seen by all, but it is the interpretation of the deed by the crowds, that such healing signals Jesus's identity as the son of David, that agitates the religious leadership.[164] Jesus, in turn, cites Psalm 8:3 LXX, "Out of the mouths of babies [νηπίων] and nursing infants you have ordained praise" (21:16). This response performs at least two functions. First, it affirms for the reader that in celebrating Jesus as son of David, the children are not merely echoing what they heard in the entry procession (12:9), they are rightly interpreting Jesus's acts of healing. Second, they are fulfilling the words of Jesus, spoken in 11:25, that God has hidden "these things" from the wise and understanding and revealed them to babies (νηπίοις).[165]

Matthew paints a consistent picture in which healing is a facet of Davidic messianism. As Novaković summarizes the results of her survey of this material, she draws attention to several dynamics: Jesus "is appealed to heal exactly in his capacity as Son of David," the various figures implore him to have mercy, and the assorted petitioners refer to him also as κύριος.[166] As Matthew tells the story, healing is not part of an inherent divine identity, but of Jesus's Davidic kingship. Moreover, we receive a hint through Jesus's citation of Psalm 8:3 in the final episode surveyed that praise and adoration of the Davidic king is an appropriate, God-given response (Matt 21:16-17), even as the magi come to do obeisance before Jesus as "king of the Judeans" (2:2, 11) and as the disciples do obeisance before Jesus as "son of God" (14:33).

The framework Matthew has established, in which Jesus as messiah is healer, provides an important clue for the interchange between Jesus and the

163. Cf. Novaković, *Messiah*, 85.
164. Novaković, *Messiah*, 87-88.
165. Novaković, *Messiah*, 94-95.
166. Novaković, *Messiah*, 89.

messengers sent to him by John the Baptist (11:2-6). In response to Jesus's works, John asks, "Are you the coming one, or do we expect another?" (11:2-3). The narrator tells the reader that John hears about the works of the messiah (τοῦ χριστοῦ, 11:2), so that the reader knows what "coming one" means in this case. Jesus responds, "Go and report to John what you hear and see: blind people see and the lame people walk, lepers are cleansed and deaf people hear, and dead people are raised and poor people have the gospel proclaimed to them. And blessed is the one who does not stumble on account of me" (11:4-6). For those with eyes to see and ears to hear, the healing miracles of Jesus should be sufficient indicators to demonstrate Jesus's identity as the one who comes after John, that is, the Christ (cf. 1:11; 11:10).[167] For John, this coming one was to be a figure of eschatological judgment (1:12). As Matthew 11 unfolds, we see that Jesus is himself the means by which the eschatological division of humanity begins to be made, as those cities that cannot rightly interpret Jesus's deeds of power (αἱ πλεῖσται δυνάμεις αὐτοῦ, 11:20) are warned about their fate on the day of judgment. Thus, the deeds should show John what they failed to show Chorazin, Bethsaida, and Capernaum (11:21, 23). What God has hidden from the wise (11:25) will be disclosed to the babes in 21:15-17 — the healer is the Christ, the son of David.

I argued above that the notion of Solomon as exorcist provides a fitting point of comparison for how first-century Jews might envision a person who both has such control over demons himself and has the ability to extend this power to his followers. Here two additional points should be made. First, Solomon is the quintessential, royal "son of David." Thus the title Matthew chooses to deploy in the healing episodes surveyed forges a connection with the Solomon-as-exorcist tradition. Second, in the tradition as related by Josephus Solomon's ability to exorcise is juxtaposed with his ability to heal: he learned the art of exorcism for the help and healing (ὠφέλειαν καὶ θεραπείαν) of people (*Ant.* 8.45); he also arranged spells by which illness were relieved (παρηγορεῖται τὰ νοσήματα, *Ant.* 8.45).[168] This evidence helps substantiate

---

167. Cf. Novaković, *Messiah*, 91, 95. Vernon K. Robbins, *Who Do People Say I Am? Rewriting Gospel in Emerging Christianity* (Grand Rapids, MI: Eerdmans, 2013), 19, cites this passage as an indication that Q shows little to no interest in Jesus as a messiah figure per se. My differing interpretation here is due to my focus on Matthew's deployment of the scene, in which signals that Jesus is "Christ" are important. However, Robbins's point that Jesus is depicted in terms that resonate with the biblical prophetic tradition (Isaiah, Elijah, Elisha) is likely an important dimension of Jesus's wonder-working in the Synoptic Tradition.

168. See also Lidija Novaković, "Miracles in the Second Temple and Early Rabbinic Judaism," in Twelftree, *Cambridge Companion to Miracles*, 95-112, here 100-101.

the notion that exorcism and healing were reckoned by some first-century Jews as coordinate activities, that Matthew's movement between the two ideas affirms that the same framework of identity and authority are in view in each, and that a Solomon-like son of David — indeed, one greater than Solomon (Matt 12:42) — would be exactly the person to embody such authority from God (cf. *Ant.* 8.45).[169] Jesus heals, as he exorcises, in his role as Davidic messiah.

Although Davidic messiahship is a primary category for Matthew's depiction of Jesus as healer, such an appellation does not exhaust the topic. Or, perhaps it is better to say in light of Matthew's citation of Isaiah 42:1-4, discussed above, that Matthew also interprets Isaiah's servant figure as finding its fulfillment in Jesus's healing actions. One final reference to Jesus as healer expands that category. The passage in question is Matthew 8:17, which entails a formula citation that quotes Isaiah 53:4: "He took our sicknesses and bore the diseases" (αὐτὸς τὰς ἀσθενείας ἡμῶν ἔλαβεν καὶ τὰς νόσους ἐβάστασεν). As Novaković rightly points out, this rendering maintains the reference to physical ailments, as in the MT, in distinction from the spiritualizing interpretation of the LXX, in which "infirmities" (חליינו) is rendered ἁμαρτίας.[170] Matthew interprets Jesus's healing ministry in terms of the servant who ministers to God's people by taking away their physical ailments. Whether this is part of a larger Davidic Christology,[171] or perhaps a parallel servant Christology, Jesus so acts as an idealized human figure, representing the people from within.

As with so many other categories of Jesus's unique agency as messiah, the sharing of this gift with his disciples provides clear indication that the action in view is not the product of a unique divine ontology. Jesus's words to John's disciples in Matthew 11:4-6 signal that the eschatological "coming one" is on the scene. And the very actions by which he signals this, including healing, raising the dead, and proclamation of the gospel to the poor, are constituent parts of his commissioning of the twelve disciples in the previous chapter (10:5-8).

Healing, both as an action and as a word designating the restoration Jesus brings to people in situations such as those involving demonic activity, is a peculiar focus of Matthew's Gospel. As Novaković has pointed out, Mat-

---

169. Cf. Novaković, *Messiah*, 96-98.

170. Lidjia Novaković, "Matthew's Atomistic Use of Scripture: Messianic Interpretation of Isaiah 53:4 in Matthew 8:17," in *Biblical Interpretation in Early Christian Gospels*, vol. 2, *The Gospel of Matthew* (LNTS 310; ed. Thomas R. Hatina; London: T&T Clark, 2008), 147-62, here 155.

171. This is the conclusion of Novaković, "Matthew's Atomistic Use of Scripture." See, e.g., 159.

thew's summary statement of Jesus's ministry in 4:23 redacts Mark's "casting out demons" (δαιμόνια ἐκβάλλων, 1:39), replacing it with "and healing every sickness and every disease among the people" (θεραπεύων πᾶσαν νόσον καὶ πᾶσαν μαλακίαν ἐν τῷ λαῷ).[172] Matthew 9:35 contains a nearly identical summary statement. Matthew thus makes healing the sick (including those whose sickness is induced by demonic presence) a hallmark of Jesus's ministry. This hallmark, in turn, signals for those with eyes to see that Jesus is the Davidic messiah. And this touchstone messianic activity is extended into the world through the faithful activity of Jesus's closest followers.

3. JESUS, HEALING, AND THE KINGDOM OF GOD IN MARK

Turning to the Second Evangelist, we are on ground where the notion of Jesus as Davidic messiah is muted, at best. And yet the healing miracles are no less indicative of Jesus's Christological identity in Mark than they were in Matthew. Importantly, Mark has conjoined Jesus's first healing miracles with his first exorcisms. Mark 1:23-34 contains a series of miracles that all happen on the same Sabbath day: astounding, authoritative teaching sandwiching the first exorcism (1:23-28), healing Peter's mother-in-law (1:29-31), and a report of Jesus healing various illnesses and sicknesses and casting out many demons who were ordered to silence (1:32-34).[173] The net effect of this series of scenes is to link Jesus's authority with a variety of activities, and further, to tie that authority to Jesus's identity as God's holy one. These conjunctions continue, especially in summary statements (e.g., 3:10-12). One further piece of evidence links the Christology of the exorcisms with that of the healing miracles: the messianic secret motif. When Jesus raises Jairus's daughter (5:21-24, 35-43), he orders that no one know about what transpired (5:43). The "secret" of Jesus's identity in the case of the demons is their knowledge that he is son of God, that is, messiah, and so the reader expects that the same secret is put on display when Jesus heals.[174] Thus, whether or not Mark envisions sickness as some-

172. Novaković, *Messiah*, 104.

173. We might even question whether the author recognized a sharp distinction between healing and exorcism; cf. Paul Lamarche, "Les Miracles de Jésus selon Marc," in Aletti et al., *Les Miracles de Jésus selon le Nouveau Testament*, 213-26, here 214.

174. Hendrickx, *Miracle Stories*, 65-66, reaches the same conclusion by other means, beginning with the notion that sickness (especially fever) might be seen as a punishment for sin, and conjoining such a notion with the expectation that the messiah would free people from the afflictions that arise due to their sins.

thing caused by spiritual powers, he nonetheless ties Jesus's authority to heal with Jesus's authority to speak and exorcise, so that the messianic overtones established above as the Christology upholding the latter is also the Christology that explains the former.[175] Similarly, in discussing Mark's son of man I argued extensively that this is an idealized human figure, so that when in the healing of the paralytic the authority to forgive sins is tied to the ability to heal (2:10) we have on display not an inherent divine authority, but a mediated, Christological authority.

The two healings in chapter 5 set the stage for a deflating homecoming for Jesus in chapter 6. In the former chapter, faith comes to the fore as a core component of Jesus's healing ministry.[176] First, the woman with the flow of blood is told, "Daughter, your faith has saved you" (ἡ πίστις σου σέσωκέν σε, 5:34). Immediately thereafter Jairus receives a report that his daughter has died, to which Jesus replies, "Do not fear, only believe!" (5:36). The faith of the petitioners lies at the heart of this intertwined literary unit.[177] The focus on faith not only links this scene to other healing miracles (2:5) and exorcisms (9:24), but also signals that Jesus's ability to heal is not simply an innate, supernatural power, but is to some degree contingent on the disposition of the petitioner. Such an inference is borne out when Jesus returns to his hometown (τὴν πάτρια αὐτοῦ, 6:1), where he cannot do many miracles because of the people's unbelief (ἀπιστία, 6:6).[178] Like the previous scene where Jesus's mother and siblings are mentioned (the Beelzebul controversy, 3:20-35), the point at issue is not what Jesus can do, but how to interpret the significance of what is on display. In this case, Jesus's teaching raises questions about where he gets his wisdom and deeds of power (6:2). The contrast with Jesus's first synagogue teaching (1:21-28) is palpable, especially as these later auditors are scandalized by Jesus (6:3).

Two points of Christological import arise from the scene of Jesus's rejection. First, Mark underscores that the people's unbelief is, in fact, a limiting factor in Jesus's ability to do miracles. Although he does heal a few small sicknesses, the overarching assessment is "He was not able to do any deeds of power there" (6:5), and the reason cited is the people's unbelief (τὴν ἀπιστίαν

---

175. Lamarche, "Les Miracles de Jésus," both highlights the conjunction between the miracles and the authority of Jesus's teaching and argues that the purpose of them is to put on display the thoroughgoing power of God as an inauguration and foretaste of eschatological salvation.

176. Cf. Sanders, *Historical Figure of Jesus*, 144-46.

177. Werner Kahl, "Glauben lässt Jesu Wunderkraft heilsam überfließen (die Tochter des Jaïrus und die blutflüssige Frau): Mk 5,21-43," in Luther and Röder, *Die Wunder Jesu*, 278-93.

178. Kahl, "Glauben lässt Jesu," 284.

αὐτῶν, v. 6). Matthew cleans up the potentially scandalous Christological implications, saying simply that Jesus did not do (οὐκ ἐποίησεν) many miracles because of the people's unbelief (Matt 13:58) rather than Jesus could not (οὐκ ἐδύνατο) do the miracles (Mark 6:5). This is a slight Christological correction, which, while not making Jesus divine, likely indicates a discomfort with the contingency Mark articulates. Jesus's power is not absolute, nor is it even entirely at his discretion. On the latter point, the healing of the woman with the flow of blood is once again apropos. As those closest to Jesus can stanch the flow of his power by their unbelief, so also the woman who comes for healing can open the flow of his power through her act of faith (5:30).[179]

A telling misidentification of sorts occurs in Mark 6:3. The people ask if this is not the craftsman, the son of Mary, whose brothers are known and named. In the redefinition of family that occurred the last time these characters appeared, the reader learned that Jesus's mother and brothers and sisters are his followers (3:33-35). More importantly, however, the reader knows that Jesus is most correctly identified not as "son of Mary," but as either son of man or son of God. This latter title is the truth of Jesus's messianic identity that is known to the demons but which he forbids them from disclosing (3:11-12). To rightly interpret Jesus's identity in conjunction with his authoritative teaching, miraculous deeds, and healing in particular is to recognize that he is son of God.

Once we have said that Jesus's power to heal is a function of his own divine sonship, the question immediately poses itself as to what this means for those whom Jesus calls sisters and brothers. It would seem that they, too, are children of God. On the basis of my argument that Jesus can heal because he is son of God in a Christological sense (as opposed to possessing ontological divine sonship) we might expect that they, too, could posses such authority. In fact, this is precisely what we find. Jesus gathers the twelve and bestows upon them authority to preach and to exorcise (6:7), and the narrator's report about their mission is that they not only preached and exorcised, but also healed (6:8). Here we have not only further confirmation that the same sort of authority is in view for the three tasks of speaking, exorcising, and healing, but also further indication that possession of such authority is not a matter of ontological divinity but of entrusted authority. If the human characters in the story can perform the same actions, then those actions are no indication that Jesus is God.

179. Cf. Candida R. Moss, "The Man with the Flow of Power: Porous Bodies in Mark 5:25-34," *JBL* 129 (2010): 507-19.

One final foray into Mark's healing narratives will underscore that the Christological indicators in these texts point toward an authoritative Christ without signaling divinity. The two-stage healing of the blind man at Bethsaida has created discomfort for readers at least as early as those first interpreters of Mark, namely, Matthew and Luke, who in a rare showing of solidarity against their forerunner both omit the story entirely. The story at first blush appears to be a failed healing that Jesus then has to rectify. After he spits on the man's eyes and lays hands on him, the man sees, but perceives wrongly — people look like trees walking about (8:23-24). A second time Jesus places his hands on the man, and then he sees rightly (8:25).

The likely solution to this conundrum is that the healing is metaphorical.[180] Immediately prior to this pericope, Jesus upbraids the disciples for their inability to perceive the ministry of Jesus in which they have been participating. Included in his rebuke is, "Having eyes, do you not see? Having ears, do you not hear? And do you not remember?" (8:18). These words, perhaps an allusion to Jeremiah 5:21, echo as well the reference to Isaiah 6:9-10 that Jesus makes in response to the disciples' query about why he speaks in parables (Mark 4:12). The disciples have been seeing, but apparently without perception. What they have seen and what they have failed to perceive come into sharp focus in the immediately following pericope, the confession of Peter at Caesarea Philippi (8:27-33). The first half of Mark's Gospel, leading up to the confession, is focused on Jesus's authority and power. This, it seems, has been sufficient for his followers to see that he is, in fact, the messiah (8:29) — a title that has appeared previously only for the benefit of the reader in 1:1, so that the ideal reader knows Peter's confession to be correct. However, when Jesus turns to describe his mission as one of rejection, suffering, death, and resurrection, Peter rebukes him, despite the fact that Jesus is speaking clearly (8:32). The second half of Mark's Gospel is the story of Jesus on the way of the cross as he heads south into Galilee in chapter 9 (v. 30) and is heading toward Jerusalem in chapter 10 (v. 32) before making his so-called triumphal entry in chapter 11 into Jerusalem, where he will be tried and killed. The disciples continually reject the passion as Jesus's vocation, a failure to see what kind of messiah he is that plays out after each of the subsequent passion predictions (9:33-37; 10:35-45). This dissonance from the mission of their master plays out in their failure to extend Jesus's power of word and over spirits in the case of the mute demoniac who was brought to them by his father (9:14-27), and in their rejection of children (10:13-16) after Jesus

180. See the pithy discussion in Cotter, *Christ of the Miracle Stories*, 44-46.

had explicitly told them that to receive a child is to receive Jesus himself and the God who sent him (9:37).

With such a narrative of the disciples unfolding, the two-stage healing of the blind man plays a symbolic role in the story. There is a first stage of the healing encounter with Jesus that results in sight but with a failure to perceive people (ἀνθρώπους, 8:24) correctly. At this juncture of the disciples' story, they have had an extended encounter with Jesus that results in being able to see that he is the Christ, but with a failure to perceive correctly what Jesus must do as the son of man (τοῦ ἀνθρώπου, 8:31; 9:31; 10:33). Thus, when we come to the question of what sort of Christology, if any, is in play in this healing narrative, we go far afield if we look to anything other than a Christ whose earthly vocation is to suffer and die. While not all healings have to have the particular kind of symbolic resonance that this story does, it is instructive for gripping the complementary nature of healings with the broader narrative dynamics of Mark's story. If the purpose of the healings is to lend their weight to a composite picture of Jesus as divine in a proto-Chalcedonian sense, this story is entirely out of place. If they are part of a narrative whose major thrust is to demonstrate that Jesus is a messiah who must, paradoxically, die to come into full share of God's authority, then the story (and the consensus interpretation of it) fits like a glove.

This reading finds support in the final healing miracle Mark narrates, a second healing of a blind man, this time as Jesus is coming to Jericho (10:46-52). In this pericope, Bartimaeus addresses Jesus, υἱὲ Δαυὶδ Ἰησοῦ, ἐλέησόν με (10:47, 48). Unlike Matthew, Mark demonstrates a marked reticence about Jesus as a Davidic messiah per se, as he is never called "son of David" by the narrator, nor does Jesus take this title for himself. He is only so addressed by a blind man, he is hailed as the bringer of David's kingdom by the crowd celebrating his arrival in Jerusalem, and he then distances himself from Davidic sonship in his interaction with the religious experts in the temple (12:35-37). And yet, Jesus neither accepts nor rejects the title that Bartimaeus takes up, a title that would seem to be roughly equivalent to "Christ." The blind man who can see that Jesus is a Christ figure asks Jesus, nonetheless, for sight. And he then follows Jesus on the way to Jerusalem (10:52), which the reader knows to be the way to Jesus's death on the cross. The strategic placement of this story, a second healing of a blind man at the transition point in the narrative prior to passion week, signals its narrative correspondence with the prior healing. This blind man, however, demonstrates that even those who can see that Jesus is Christ, the son of David, are still in need of sight. In other words, at the beginning of the pericope, by addressing Jesus in Christological terms, he occupies the very position occupied by the twelve, who know that Jesus is the Christ but do not yet see that the Christ must be rejected, suffer, and die — a failure to see that has them clamoring for positions of greatness while Jesus is leading them along the way of humility and death. Bartimaeus, after he is healed, follows Jesus as he goes toward suffering and death, thereby symbolizing the discipleship that the twelve have rejected.

Here we are at a critical juncture, where the value of recognizing Jesus as an idealized human figure contains an exegetical payoff that a "higher" Christology has the power to silence. The two-stage healing is, no doubt, a difficult text, as it so proved to be for both Matthew and Luke. But the very difficulty it provides the modern reader, no less than the ancient, is exacerbated to the extent that we allow a divine Christology to shape our expectations. A divine Christology that sees a "failed" healing as unbecoming of Jesus is edging dangerously close to assessing Jesus through the very lenses of the disciples that the two-stage healing story is written to illustrate as a failed perception: a Christology of glory that has no thoroughgoing place for the reign of God to come through a human's rejection, suffering, death, and resurrection.

4. THE HEALER AS GOD'S VISITATION IN LUKE

In ways both subtle and direct, Luke ties Jesus's ministry of healing to Jesus's power over the spiritual realm.[181] Such connections suggest that the idealized human Christology we saw at work in the exorcism scenes is the same Christology that explains Jesus's authority over sickness. As an example of a subtle connection between illness and the spiritual realm, Luke writes that when Jesus heals Peter's mother-in-law he rebukes (ἐπιτίμησεν) the fever (4:39).[182] The same verb is used four verses prior in Jesus's rebuke of a demon (4:35) as well as two verses later as Jesus is silencing his spiritual foes (4:41; cf. 9:42).[183] Such a personification of the malady treats fever as though it is itself some sort of personal agent of oppression, or else might suggest that some such agent lies

181. See also Kee, *Miracle in the Early Christian World,* 202; Augustin George, "Le Miracle dans l'Oeuvre de Luc," in Aletti et al., *Les Miracles de Jésus selon le Nouveau Testament,* 259-68, here 250-51.

182. Cf. Hendrickx, *Miracle Stories,* 71-72; George, "Le Miracle dans l'Oeuvre de Luc," 251.

183. Hendrickx, *Miracle Stories,* 71-72. Conversely, Luke describes exorcisms using terminology for healing (George, "Le Miracle dans l'Oeuvre de Luc," 251).

behind it.[184] Thus, Peter's speech in the house of Cornelius may well provide a wide-ranging interpretive grid for Jesus's miracles in Luke-Acts: "Jesus from Nazareth — how God anointed him with the Holy Spirit and power, who went around doing good and healing everyone who was oppressed by the devil, because God was with him" (Acts 10:38). Such a statement not only epitomizes Jesus's healing work as part and parcel with his "spiritual" war against Satan, it also provides a Christological indicator that these miracles are possible because God, by the Holy Spirit, is with the human, Jesus of Nazareth.

A more direct indication of the interwoven nature of physical malady and spiritual oppression comes in the story of the hunched over woman whom Jesus heals on a Sabbath (Luke 13:10-16). Describing the woman, Luke says that she had a spirit of sickness (πνεῦμα ἔχουσα ἀσθενείας, 13:11). The word of healing Jesus speaks is that the woman be released from her sickness (ἀπολέλυσαι, 13:12). And in defending his actions to the synagogue official, Jesus says that Satan had bound this woman for eighteen years (13:16). Pierre Grelot sees this reflecting a pervasive conjunction of Jesus's healing activity with his power over the spirit world: "Elle suppose uné representation très précise de Satan et des esprits, responsables des divers maux humains."[185] The conjunction between healing and exercising authority over spirits is strengthened at several points in Luke's Gospel. In 5:15, after Jesus cleanses the leper, people come to him to hear and to be healed (ἀκούειν καὶ θεραπεύεσθαι) from sicknesses. In the summary statement in 6:17-19, people are coming to hear and be healed, and Jesus is healing (ἐθεραπεύοντο, v. 18) those who are inhabited by unclean spirits.

Luke signals to his readers early on what Christological framework suffices for this authority over spirits and bodies. Immediately after the healing of Peter's mother-in-law, Luke follows Mark in describing a scene of mass healings after the sun had set on the Sabbath (4:40-41). However, he does not parrot Mark in saying that those who had maladies and the demon-possessed came; instead, he simply says that Jesus healed many kinds of illnesses by laying his hands on the sick (4:40). However, in further describing the healing he says that demons came out, crying that Jesus was son of God (σὺ εἶ ὁ υἱὸς τοῦ θεοῦ, 4:41). The narrator says that Jesus rebuked the demons into silence and also

---

184. A similar conjunction of spiritual oppression and physical ailment may be reflected in the Genesis Apocryphon (1QapGen 19-20), in which Abraham lays his hands on Pharaoh to heal him from the affliction that came with the abduction of Sarah — a healing that comes as the afflicting spirit is rebuked and thereby sent away (see the discussion in Eve, *Jewish Context of Jesus' Miracles*, 177-82).

185. Grelot, "Les Miracles de Jésus," 67.

provides the reason: "because they knew him to be the messiah" (ὅτι ᾔδεισαν τὸν χριστὸν αὐτὸν εἶναι, 4:41). Thus, not only does Luke link Jesus's ability to heal with that to exorcise demons, he also frames both together under his son of God Christology, a Christology that he further delineates in terms of being the messiah. As God's anointed messiah, Jesus has authority on earth over both ailing human bodies and the spiritual forces that might cause such infirmities.

The thesis that I am arguing, that Luke's Jesus is an idealized human figure, does not in any way minimize the place of God at work in Jesus; instead, it reframes our understanding of how it is that God is at work. In the sermon on Pentecost from which the title of this book is taken, Peter makes it clear that the way in which God witnesses to the veracity of Jesus's messianic identity is through Jesus's dramatic deeds. These, in fact, are God's own doing in the man Jesus (Ἰησοῦν Ναζωραῖον, ἄνδρα ἀποδεδειγμένον ἀπὸ τοῦ θεοῦ εἰς ὑμας δυνάμεσι καὶ τέρασι καὶ σημείοις οἷς ἐποίησεν δι᾽ αὐτοῦ ὁ θεὸς ἐν μέσῳ ὑμῶν, Acts 2:22). To be God's Christ is to be the one in whom God is working.[186] This, I suggest, is the rubric for interpreting one further emphasis of Luke's healing narratives: Jesus is a human attested by God.

In all three Synoptic Gospels, when Jesus heals the paralytic the people around Jesus glorify God (Matt 9:8; Mark 2:12; Luke 4:26). Luke adds to this by having the healed man himself go on his way glorifying God (4:25). In the healing of the woman who had been hunched over for eighteen years, Luke says that immediately she was straightened and glorified God (παραχρῆμα ἀνωρθώθη καὶ ἐδόξαζεν τὸν θεόν, 13:13). In the same story, we find a stark contrast in the figure of the synagogue official who upbraids the crowd for coming for healing on the Sabbath. In light of the depiction of Jesus's deeds in Acts 2, the significance of the contrasting responses are placed in sharp relief: the woman rightly interprets the healing as a signal that God is at work in Jesus through this deed of power, while the synagogue official fails to see that God is at work and strives instead to protect God's law from Jesus's violations of it.[187] Another brief example of the close conjunction between Jesus as God's agent and God's own action comes in the healing of the Gerasene demoniac (8:26-39). At the conclusion of the story, Jesus commands the man to return

186. In so connecting the miracles with God, Luke bears some resemblance to Philo, whose miracles are evidence of God's own presence, power, and trustworthiness; cf. Eve, *Jewish Context of Jesus' Miracles*, 74-76.

187. Paul J. Achtemeier, "The Lukan Perspective on the Miracles of Jesus: A Preliminary Sketch," in *Perspectives on Luke-Acts* (ed. C. H. Talbert; Edinburgh: T&T Clark, 1978), 153-67, similarly concludes that these are signals that "identify by what power Jesus performed such acts" (158).

to his home and make known what God has done for him (ὅσα σοι ἐποίησεν ὁ θεός, 8:39). What the man does, then, is to proclaim what Jesus has done for him (ὅσα ἐποίησεν αὐτῷ ὁ Ἰησοῦς, 8:39). This is neither, on the one hand, a mistake nor, on the other, an indication that Jesus is God after all.[188] In light of the idealized human paradigm indicated in the conjunction between God's actions and the ἄνθρωπος Jesus delineated in Acts 2:22, this is clear perception that God is at work in the deeds of the human Jesus. God's own authority and power are working in God's idealized human agent.[189]

Jesus's raising of the widow of Nain's only son sheds further light on the relationship between Jesus and God in the former's role as healer. The story of Elijah's raising of the son of the widow of Zarephath (1 Kgs 17:8-24) looms in the background of Luke's tale, not only in some general sense of a scriptural precedent, but also in the specific sense of having been mentioned previously in Jesus's sermon in Nazareth (Luke 4:26).[190] In both cases a widowed woman receives her only son back from death. As mentioned above, in the Elijah story the climactic moment comes with the widow's declaration that Elijah truly is a man of God and that YHWH's words in his mouth are true (1 Kgs 17:24). In other words, for the earlier story raising the dead signaled someone's playing the role of God's prophetic agent on the earth. In Luke 7:13 Jesus is called κύριος, indicating his authorization to enact lordship over the earth on God's behalf. The crowd's reaction to Jesus's miracle is multifaceted. In keeping with the theme of glorifying God, Luke says, "Fear took hold of them all and they glorified God" (ἔλαβεν δὲ φόβος πάντας καὶ ἐδόξαζεν τὸν θεὸν, 7:16). The key to the Christology of the passage is then found in their two ejaculations of praise: "A great prophet has arisen among us!" and "God has looked after his people!" (7:16).[191] The first of these exclamations is di-

---

188. It is worth pointing out that *theios anēr* Christology has been tried and found wanting as an explanation of Luke's Jesus. E.g., Marilyn McCord Adams, "The Role of Miracles in the Structure of Luke-Acts," in *Hermes and Athena: Biblical Exegesis and Philosophical Theology* (UNDSPR 7; ed. E. Strump and T. P. Flint; Notre Dame, IN: University of Notre Dame Press, 1993), 235-74, esp. 247-52; Thomas H. Tobin, "Miracles, Magic and Modernity: Comments on the Paper of Marilyn McCord Adams," in Strump and Flint, *Hermes and Athena*, 275-81.

189. Kee, *Miracle in the Early Christian Tradition*, 203-4.

190. Cf. Hendrickx, *Miracle Stories*, 205-6, who also points out that the healing of the centurion's servant bears some resemblance to Elijah's healing of an enemy military official (so also George, "Le Miracle dans l'Oeuvre de Luc," 252-53). Such a connection with Luke 4 also has Christological implications, inasmuch as Jesus's sermon is programmatic for the Gospel and in it he identifies himself as God's agent, anointed by the spirit before comparing himself to Elijah and Elisha. This, too, points in the direction of an idealized human Christology.

191. On the importance of the category of "prophet" for understanding Jesus as a miracle

rectly in keeping with the expectations created by the precedent we find in Elijah: when Israel's God is at work in a prophet, that prophet has the power even to raise the dead. Here, I am assuming that the crowd's assessment of Jesus's identity is on target, an assumption that finds some validation in Acts 3:22-26, where Peter applies Moses's prophecy of God raising up a prophet like himself to Jesus.[192]

The second exclamation has the potential to push the Christology of the passage beyond the sphere of human representation, but such potential is not realized in Luke's narrative. The people recognize divine visitation in the action of Jesus (ἐπεσκέψατο ὁ θεὸς τὸν λαὸν αὐτοῦ, 7:16). This is the third time Luke's readers have encountered the verb ἐπισκέπτομαι (ἐπισκοπτέω), the others occurring in 1:68, 78, and the second time in which ὁ θεός has been the subject of the verb, the first being 1:68. The prior uses are in Zechariah's song at the birth of John. This is significant in that it demonstrates that divine visitation or care does not immediately carry connotations of incarnation, but may very well carry connotations of agency. That is to say, nobody argues that John the Baptist is divine in light of the fact that, at his birth, Zechariah is filled with the spirit and proclaims that God has visited his people. More positively, as Zechariah expounds on what the divine visitation entails, he celebrates the Davidic messiah for whom John will prepare the way: a horn of salvation in the house of David (1:69) in fulfillment of God's promises (1:70-73). Such a context within Luke's Gospel shows the implied reader that the rich Christology of the narrative is coalescing with the story of the widow of Nain's son: Jesus is Lord and prophet and messiah, and in this richly variegated human agent those with eyes to see can recognize God's visitation of Israel.[193] Thus, the fear that grips the people, leading to their glorification of God, is not a recognition of God as such in their very midst, but a recognition that God is in their midst through the great and powerful deeds that God is working in the man Jesus.[194]

The query of John the Baptist as to whether or not Jesus is "the coming one" follows immediately after the raising of the widow's son (7:18-35). Throughout

---

worker in Luke, see also Ruben Zimmermann, "Hinführung," in Luther and Röder, *Die Wunder Jesu,* 513-25, esp. 523-24.

192. So also Hendrickx, *Miracle Stories,* 213.

193. On "Lord" in verse 13 as a messianic title, cf. Hendrickx, *Miracle Stories,* 219.

194. Achtemeier, "Lukan Perspective," notes throughout that one of the major Lukan emphases is the ability of Jesus's miracles to generate faith because they "validate Jesus as the one sent by God" (165). This language of a sent representative accurately reflects the idealized human Christology of Luke, in my view.

Jesus's response to John, there is no indication that his identity as "coming one" entails divinity. Instead, the series of responses signals the eschatological arrival of the reign of God. In listing the miracles that he has performed, and appending to it "blessed is the one who does not stumble because of me," Jesus both points to his works as signs of the dawning of the reign of God and places response to himself at the decisive center of inclusion in or exclusion from God's eschatological blessing (7:22-23).[195] Jesus next exalts John above all those born from women due to his role as forerunner and one who prepares the way. And yet, Jesus also declares as greater than John the great prophet anyone who is in the kingdom of God (7:27-28). Again, the point rests on the eschatological turning of the ages that Jesus brings; and greatness in this era is defined by the reign of God, a reign we see executed by Jesus the κύριος (7:19). The interconnection between John as one who prepares the way and Jesus as the coming one is strengthened as Luke includes a response of the crowds: the tax collectors, having been baptized by John, justified God, while the Pharisees and lawyers rejected God's purpose for them because they had not been so baptized (7:29-30). In Luke's salvation-historical schema, John is the forerunner of the decisive eschatological moment of divine visitation, whereas Jesus is the Christ figure in whom that divine visitation takes place. The final pericope in this string of sayings about John is Jesus's mournful comparison of his generation to children singing in the marketplace (7:31-35), a saying in which Jesus laments the unwillingness of that generation to respond to either the austerity of John or the messianic banquet of Jesus in the company of tax collectors and sinners.

By placing back to back the raising of the widow's son and the query of John the Baptist, Luke provides the reader with a specific Christological reflection on one miracle followed by a more generalized Christological reflection on Jesus as a miracle worker (which miracles include raising the dead, 7:22). Taken together, the passages provide a framework for interpreting Jesus's miraculous healings as work performed by the greatest of all prophets as the embodiment of God's eschatological visitation of God's people.

Jesus's healing of ten lepers brings us back to the tight interconnection between Jesus and God that permeates Luke's work (17:12-19). In this healing episode, the lepers are sent away to show themselves to the priests, and as they go they are cleansed (v. 14). One of the ten, a Samaritan, returns, "glorifying

---

195. Achtemeier, "Lukan Perspective," 158, demonstrates how Luke's redaction of the passage, including the information that "in that hour" Jesus performed a number of miracles, demonstrates Luke's emphasis on miracles validating Jesus's identity and claims about himself.

God with a loud voice," and falls before Jesus's feet, thanking him (vv. 15-16). Jesus, in turn, questions why only one of the ten returned to give glory to God, and why, in particular, it would be the foreigner (vv. 17-18). By highlighting the identity of the faithful man as a Samaritan, this pericope contributes to the larger theme of Israel's failure to recognize the time of God's visitation in the person of Jesus and also echoes Jesus's remembrance of Elisha's healing of Naaman the Syrian in Luke 4:27.[196] The immediately subsequent pericope has the Pharisees asking Jesus when the kingdom of God comes, which meets with a reply that it "is among you" (ἐντὸς ὑμῶν ἐστιν, v. 21). They do not recognize that the reign of God is present in the person and work of Jesus. Returning to the story of the cleansed lepers, we have a story that demonstrates that Jesus is not only the conduit "downward" to the earth of God's restorative power, but that he is also the appropriate conduit of glory and praise "upward" to God. As Herman Hendrickx puts it, "As God's representative, Jesus is the locus where God is to be praised."[197] The glorification of God is intimately tied to the thanksgiving rendered to Jesus because as God's agent Jesus is the earthly embodiment of God's presence and power. As with the idealizations of Abraham and David before Jesus, Luke's narrative indicates that how one responds to Jesus is how one responds to the God who is at work in him.[198] Once again Peter's sermon in Acts 2 is apropos, as Peter there says that God did signs and wonders and miracles in the midst of the Israelites through Jesus (v. 22). This is why glorifying God in the presence of Jesus is the appropriate response for the miracle: not because monotheism has been redefined to include Jesus in the divine binitarian identity, but because it is truly the power of God who is at work in the human Jesus.

One line of argument that I have returned to repeatedly has been that anything the Gospel writers depict Jesus's followers as doing cannot be a deed by which they intend to signal, in and of itself, that Jesus is divine. When it comes to the healing miracles, we not only have such parallels in Luke's version of the sending of the twelve (9:1-6) and the additional sending of the seventy (10:1-12, 17-20), but also in the entirety of the book of Acts.[199] In the first, we see that Luke, like Matthew, includes healing within the authority that Jesus extends to the twelve (9:1-2). We also see in the conjunction between healing and exorcism that there is a somewhat blurry line between physical

196. Cf. Hendrickx, *Miracle Stories*, 225-27.
197. Hendrickx, *Miracle Stories*, 238.
198. Achtemeier, "Lukan Perspective," 159-60.
199. Adams, "Role of Miracles."

and spiritual ailments. The summary report indicates that the disciples went around proclaiming the good news and healing (9:6). The instructions to the seventy in Luke 10 include healing those who are sick in any city (v. 8). Upon their return, the seventy report that even demons are subject to them in Jesus's name (v. 17), news that Jesus responds to with what appears to be an indication of eschatological heavenly warfare: by the extension of Jesus's reign, Satan has been thrown down and the powers of wickedness have lost their ability to harm his followers (vv. 18-19). These provide a few early glimpses of the notion that Jesus's followers are arrayed under Jesus to be the kind of people in and for the world that Jesus himself is: a people who exercise the reign of God over all the earth on God's behalf. This hint is carried through in the book of Acts.

The keynote sermon in Acts 2 to which I keep returning not only tells the readers about Jesus, but also sets the stage for the subsequent description of the apostles within the community that begins to form. In the sermon, Peter cites a lengthy portion of the prophet Joel. In the middle of this prophecy is the promise that God will give wonders (τέρατα) in the heavens above and signs (σημεῖα) on the earth below (v. 19). The word σημεῖα is poorly attested in the Greek manuscripts of Joel, and may represent Luke's own editing of the passage.[200] Immediately after the citation, Peter then turns to describe Jesus as a man attested by God through deeds of power and wonders and signs (δυνάμεσιν καὶ τέρασιν καὶ σημείοις, v. 22). The life of Jesus, then, becomes a primary way in which God has fulfilled the prophecy of Joel. This makes it all the more striking that in the summary statement in verses 42-47 the description of the community includes "many wonders and signs [τέρατα καὶ σημεῖα] were happening through the apostles" (v. 43; cf. 4:30; 5:12; 6:8; 8:13).[201] Whether those signs and wonders be healings (as 5:12-16 implies), exorcisms (cf. 8:6-7), or some other mighty works, Luke is demonstrating that the power and authority to perform them is simultaneously a divine power and authority and a power and authority that can be executed through representative humans.[202] This does not, however, diminish the unique role that Jesus plays in the story as Lord and Christ.[203] The first healing narrative

200. Cf. Theodore J. Weeden Jr., *Mark: Traditions in Conflict* (Philadelphia: Fortress, 1971), 75; followed by Adams, "Role of Miracles," 236.
201. Adams, "Role of Miracles," 236-38, draws attention to the parallels between Jesus in Luke and the disciples in Acts, arguing that the miracles perform similar functions in each story.
202. Adams, "Role of Miracles," 248.
203. See also Mills, *Human Agents*, 109.

in Acts makes this clear, as Peter extends healing to a crippled man "in the name of Jesus Christ the Nazarene" (3:6). Just as Peter interprets the miracles of Jesus's life on earth as God's bearing witness to Jesus, so too the miracles of the early church are witnesses to Jesus as Lord and Christ, as Peter goes on to explain: "The God of Abraham, Isaac, and Jacob . . . glorified his servant Jesus" (v. 13). Jesus now plays the role of idealized human figure at God's heavenly right hand, while the apostles on the earth mediate that power Jesus has received.[204] Echoes of Jesus's ministry continue as Peter heals a paralyzed man (9:32-35) and raises Dorcas from the dead (9:36-43). Each of these miracles draws people to Jesus the heavenly Lord, not the disciples themselves (9:35, 42).[205] Like Jesus's miracles on earth, these works of power are indicative of heavenly power at work in the person on earth, not the inherent divinity of the earthly agent. In this case, however, it is the human Jesus, enthroned as Lord and Christ by virtue of his resurrection (2:36), pouring out on his followers what he has received from God the father (2:33), who provides the power to heal. Throughout Acts, God is still attesting to Jesus through works of power, wonders, and signs; however, now that witness comes through the apostles and others enacting such deeds in the power that God has given the human, now raised and exalted, Jesus.[206]

The miracles of Jesus are significant for Luke's Christology. They demonstrate the closest possible connection between Jesus and God, such that the way one responds to the works of Jesus is nothing less than the way one responds to God. As Paul Achtemeier concludes, "Thus, in Luke, the reaction to miracles is to see God behind the activity of Jesus, thus acknowledging Jesus to be the one whom God has chosen to do his work."[207] Augustin George suggests that Luke's emphasis on God's activity is Christologically motivated: "Elle est probablement motivée aussi chez lui par une reaction contre la conception grecque de l' 'homme divin.'"[208] The nature of this relationship is not one of ontological identity but instead one of idealized, in this case eschatological, representation. The way one responds to Jesus is itself a response to God because it is God who is at work, empowering Jesus and thereby testifying on his behalf.[209] In the story Luke tells, Jesus can heal (and exorcise and exert

204. Cf. George, "Le Miracle dans l'Oeuvre de Luc," 255-56.
205. Cf. Achtemeier, "Lukan Perspective," 159.
206. A point well made in Mills, *Human Agents,* 108-23.
207. Achtemeier, "Lukan Perspective," 159.
208. Cf. Grelot, "Les Miracles de Jésus," 70: "le règne de Dieu ne s'instaure que parce que Dieu, agissant par son Envoyé, triomphe radicalement d'une Puissance obscure."
209. So also George, "Le Miracle dans l'Oeuvre de Luc," 257-58.

control over nature) not because he is ontologically divine, but because God has made him Lord and Christ.

D. CONCLUSIONS: HUMAN AGENT OF DIVINE POWER

The interrelated themes of exorcism, healing, and nature miracles are tied together well by Blackburn: "And what we have is a Jesus who believed himself to be God's agent — probably specifically the royal messiah — for inaugurating the kingdom of God and heralding its consummation. In executing this mission, Jesus exorcised demons, healed the sick and even raised a few people from the dead. Through such actions God was, in Jesus's eyes, compassionately implementing his long-awaited reign."[210] This summary helps underscore that the idealized human Christology I am advocating is not the "low Christology" of Jesus the Galilean peasant (for example). It is the high, human Christology of the agent specially entrusted by God to demonstrate the advent of God's own reign.[211]

As Eric Eve approaches his synthetic comments about the miraculous in Second Temple Judaism, he cautions that miracles were not a common theme in its literature, and that talk of exorcism, too, was rare; instead, the authors of such works "were more interested in keeping the law, in the history or prospects of the nation, or in wisdom and right living, or in the revelation of heavenly realities, or in promoting their own party."[212] The contrast in content between literature that engages such concerns without appeal to a miracle tradition and the Synoptic Gospels that engage many of the same themes within a story peppered by miracles and reports of the miraculous is, itself, telling. The difference seems to be captured by a combination of the eschatology of the Gospel writers and their understanding of the person of Jesus and the role he plays in inaugurating the end that they believe has arrived.

Throughout this chapter I have surveyed the miraculous elements of Jesus's ministry and striven to understand their possible significance through comparison with comparable Jewish traditions. Such traditions exist, and they demonstrate the viability of the thesis that Jesus in the Synoptic Gospels is

---

210. Blackburn, "Miracles of Jesus," 124. Sanders articulates a similar conclusion (*Historical Figure of Jesus*, 165-66). Blackburn is making a point about the historical Jesus; while I am not persuaded that we can know this much about such a one, this paragraph does reflect well the theology of the Synoptic Gospels as I have analyzed it in this chapter.

211. Sanders, *Historical Figure of Jesus*, 164-68.

212. Eve, *Jewish Context of Jesus' Miracles*, 244.

functioning as an idealized human figure through whom God is at work in the world. To say this, however, is in no way to minimize the centrality of Jesus as the decisive figure in the Gospel narratives or the ways that Jesus therein differs from other Jewish prophets or kings of the past. Eve concludes his rich study of Jewish miracle traditions by highlighting (1) that "there is relatively little interest in miracles of healing anywhere," (2) that there is much more interest in miracles of national deliverance, (3) the texts of *Enoch* and those from Qumran do have "an interest in healing and the ultimate defeat of demonic powers."[213] Thus, the Gospels offer a unique combination of various abilities in one person, as well as a unique focus on such powers. Moreover, they embed these miraculous deeds within stories rife with eschatological connotations, thereby drawing some future-oriented expectations of various Jewish communities into the present of Jesus's life on earth. Thus, while the concentration and diversity of miraculous powers attested of Jesus do not connote that he is something ontologically more than human, they do suggest that this particular human figure is of decisive significance for the history of Israel and the world more generally.

Eve's investigation contains one further conclusion of interest for the purposes of ascertaining the Gospels' Christology. Following the taxonomy of Werner Kahl, Eve notes that the Gospels tend to depict Jesus as a "bearer of numinous power" (BNP) rather than a "mediator of numinous power" (MNP) or a "petitioner of numinous power" (PNP).[214] In miracle stories in the Jewish tradition, God is typically the BNP, with prophets functioning as mediators of that power or petitioning God to enact that power on their behalf or on behalf of the people. Thus, one might argue that by casting Jesus in the role that other Israelites typically assigned to God, the Gospel writers intend to demonstrate Jesus's inherent divinity, an argument that would complement Bauckham's thesis nicely. However, Eve also recognizes that the power at work in Jesus as a BNP is, in the Gospels, God's and not Jesus's own: "If Jesus is a BNP, it is because he is a bearer of God's Spirit, which is the source of Jesus's power. Indeed, if God were not in some sense behind Jesus's acts of power, they would not count as miracles."[215] Thus, the larger narratival indications of Jesus's relationship with God, and possession of the spirit, curtail the conclusion that the Gospels depict Jesus as inherently divine. The evidence offered

---

213. Eve, *Jewish Context of Jesus' Miracles*, 270.

214. Eve, *Jewish Context of Jesus's Miracles*, 376-86; Werner Kahl, *New Testament Miracle Stories in their Religious-Historical Setting: A Religionsgeschichtliche Comparison from a Structural Perspective* (FRLANT 163; Göttingen: Vandenhoeck & Ruprecht, 1994).

215. Eve, *Jewish Context of Jesus' Miracles*, 378-79.

in this chapter points in the same direction. The exalted depictions of Jesus fit within the idealized human paradigm established earlier, even though they could also fit within the rubric of a divine man as such. I have shown that within the Jewish frame of reference with which I am primarily engaging that idealized human Christology is more likely, and that within the Roman context a similar paradigm often fits as well.

6 *Jesus and the Scriptures of Israel*

In our quest to understand the Christologies of the Synoptic Gospels, we have covered the titles son of God and son of man; the birth and resurrection narratives; and the stories of Jesus's power over spirits, bodies, and nature. In each, I have attempted to demonstrate that reading Jesus as an idealized human figure makes sense of the various presentations, indicates a strong grasp of the interpretive cues in each given pericope, and also best coheres with the overall story each Gospel tells. In this final set of studies, I turn to the issue of intertextuality, taking up the question, Do citations of or allusions to the scriptures of Israel so coordinate Jesus with God as to indicate, however subtly, that Jesus and Israel's God are one and the same?[1]

In the introduction I discussed the approach of this book as testing the explanatory power of the idealized human paradigm. Here, perhaps more than anywhere, the importance of paradigmatic assumptions comes to the fore. If Christological presuppositions can influence or even determine a reader's interpretation of any one passage, that possibility increases exponentially when one scriptural text is embedded within another. Many of the texts that this chapter explores can be interpreted as indicating Jesus's divinity if certain measures are assumed (e.g., that the application of a YHWH text to Jesus indicates that Jesus is, in some sense, the God of Israel). And yet, the capacious realm of possibility opened up by the idealized human paradigm enables an alternative set of conclusions. While at times this chapter points to an explicit indication that idealized human Christology is intended by the author in the

---

1. In this chapter I focus on specific, detectable allusions or references to particular verses rather than more generalized scriptural motifs such as "Exodus and Sinai Traditions" or "Kingship Traditions." For a discussion of several themes in the latter vein, see Willard M. Swartley, *Israel's Scripture Traditions and the Synoptic Gospels: Story Shaping Story* (Peabody, MA: Hendrickson, 1994).

scriptural citations (such as Luke's paradigmatic statements in the final chapter of his Gospel), the more common approach will be to demonstrate that early Jews deploying or hearing scripture in the manner we find in the Synoptic Gospels (and Acts) could well use such deployments to characterize an ideal, human messiah.

Before turning to the New Testament directly, it will be profitable to recall some data that turned up in the discussion of early Judaism. There are examples outside the New Testament of early Jewish interpretations of scripture in which passages that originally spoke about God have been applied to an idealized human figure. Three examples of this come from Qumran. First, in the Habakkuk Pesher, the Teacher of Righteousness replaces God as the object of faith in Habukkuk 2:4: "Its interpretation concerns all observing the Law in the House of Judah, whom God will free from the house of judgment on account of their toil and of their loyalty to the Teacher of Righteousness" (1QpHab VIII 1-2).[2] A second example comes from a likely citation of Hosea 5:14 in 4Q166-67[b]. There, God's words, "I will be like a lion to Ephraim and like a young lion to the house of Judah," are ascribed to the priest: "For I will be like a lio[n to E]ph[ra]im [and like a lion cub to the House of Judah. Its interpretation con]cerns the last priest who will stretch out his hand to strike Ephraim" (4Q167 2, 2-3).[3] Third, in 11QMelchizedek "the year of the Lord's favor" (Isa 61:1) is rendered "the Lord of Melchizedek's favor." This and other evidence leads Carl Davis to conclude, "Application of such texts occurred both to divine and non-divine figures. . . . The evidence does show that one cannot claim that application of such passages necessitates a view that Jesus was divine or that the early Christians worked with a Trinitarian view of God, nor can one claim such application necessarily depends on viewing Jesus as God's agent."[4] Applying to other figures verses that originally referred to God is a daring move, but not necessarily so fraught as to suggest a transformation of the divine identity. Only interpretation of the passages cited within their new contexts can determine the relationship between God and the other figure in each given instance.

---

2. Florentino García Martínez and Eibert J. C. Tigchelaar, *DSSSE* (2 vols.; Grand Rapids, MI: Eerdmans, 1998), 1:17. Maurice Casey, "Chronology and the Development of Pauline Christology," in *Paul and Paulinism: Essays in Honour of C. K. Barrett* (ed. M. D. Hooker and S. G. Wilson; London: SPCK, 1982), 128; Carl Judson Davis, *The Name and Way of the Lord: Old Testament Themes, New Testament Christology* (JSNTSup 129; Sheffield: Sheffield Academic, 1996), 47-48.

3. Martínez and Tigchelaar, *DSSSE*, 1:333. Davis, *Name and Way of the Lord*, 47.

4. Davis, *Name and Way of the Lord*, 60.

A. MARK

Appeal to scripture is a key way that Mark frames his narrative as unfolding within a Jewish, and specifically scriptural, milieu. Stephen Ahearne-Kroll summarizes the result this way: "Through the lens of Scripture, we see a Markan Jesus that is at once powerful and God-like, utterly human, and mediating between the divine and the human as a prophetic figure. All of these images constitute what it means for Jesus to be the Messiah for Mark."[5] And yet the scriptural citations that contribute to Mark's Christology typically reside in the background, signaled only through wording that calls to mind a possible biblical precedent. An exception to this rule is Mark's first and clearest scriptural citation.

1. THE LORD

a. Isaiah 40:3: The Way of the Lord

Within the Gospels' presentation of Jesus it is possible to argue that an implicit Christological claim is made when biblical texts that originally applied to God, especially those containing the divine name (יהוה, MT; ὁ κύριος, LXX), are quoted in such a manner that a title, noun, or pronoun that refers to divinity in its original Old Testament context refers to Jesus in the Gospel.[6] There are at least two plausible explanations for such phenomena that fit within the thesis of this book, and they might both be at work. First, C. H. Dodd has shown that several scriptural texts were foundational for the preaching of the first-century church such that they recur independently across our earliest witnesses.[7] Among these foundational texts is Psalm 110:1, which appears in the Synoptic Gospels, receives independent elaboration in Acts, is quoted in 1 Corinthians and alluded to in Romans and Ephesians, and finds a place in the argument of Hebrews. Since the

---

5. Stephen P. Ahearne-Kroll, "The Scripturally Complex Presentation of Jesus in the Gospel of Mark," in *Portraits of Jesus: Studies in Christology* (WUNT2 321; ed. Susan E. Meyers; Tübingen: Mohr Siebeck, 2012), 45-68, here 47-48.

6. Such is the assertion of Richard Bauckham, *Jesus and the God of Israel: God Crucified and Other Studies on the New Testament's Christology of Divine Identity* (Grand Rapids, MI: Eerdmans, 2008), 265. However, the very change in referent might be the most significant clue that the role of God is being played by a divine agent who is not God as such.

7. C. H. Dodd, *The Apostolic Preaching and Its Developments: Three Lectures with an Appendix on Eschatology and History* (New York: Harper & Row, 1964); Dodd, *According to the Scriptures: The Substructure of New Testament Theology* (New York: Scribner, 1953).

Tetragrammaton is rendered as ὁ κύριος in the LXX, this widely quoted psalm refers to two separate persons as κύριος in the same breath: "The Lord said to my Lord" (εἶπεν ὁ κύριος τῷ κυρίῳ μου). Such a conjunction opens up the possibility of applying to the royal Lord (in the New Testament universally interpreted as referring to the messiah, and usually a reference to Jesus is clear) passages that originally referred to the divine Lord. Because the Tetragrammaton fell out of use, and was replaced by a noun, κύριος, which the earliest Christians applied to Jesus, it became a simpler matter to apply to Jesus texts whose original referent was YHWH. Psalm 110 facilitates a change in person, not simply a change in referent, by holding the two κύριος figures in such tight connection. This, then, leads into a second possible explanation, in line with the conceptual framework of this book; namely, that the human agent of God so represents God to the world that texts originally referring to God are interpreted as finding their fulfillment in God's human agent. This latter possibility, perhaps under the influence of the first (it is impossible to say for sure), may well account for Mark's opening salvo, in which the narrator calls attention to a scriptural citation by means of a citation formula.

Mark introduces an amalgamated citation of three scriptural references with, "Just as it is written in the prophet Isaiah." The ensuing quote comes from Exodus 23:20, Malachi 3:1, and Isaiah 40:3. Table 6-1 on page 493 lays out the possible source texts alongside the text of Mark.

The Hebrew texts of Exodus 23:20 and Malachi 3:1 use the same verb for "send" (שׁלח), making them somewhat closer to one another than the extant Greek translations. This has led both Rikki Watts and Joel Marcus to suggest that the MT rather than the LXX is the source for Mark's citation.[8] For our purposes, the important point is that despite a somewhat vague connection between Mark's Greek text and that of the LXX translations we are aware of, an allusion to Malachi is nonetheless likely.[9] Malachi's messenger is later identified with Elijah (Mal 4:5, Eng.; 3:23, Heb, LXX), and Mark depicts John the Baptist as fulfilling the role of forerunning messenger here in chapter 1, and later indicates that he was Elijah (1:6; 9:11-13).[10]

---

8. Rikki E. Watts, *Isaiah's New Exodus in Mark* (Grand Rapids, MI: Baker Academic, 2000), 61-62; Joel Marcus, *The Way of the Lord: Christological Exegesis of the Old Testament in the Gospel of Mark* (Louisville, KY: Westminster John Knox, 1992), 13.

9. As Joel Marcus, *Mark 1–8: A New Translation with Introduction and Commentary* (AB 27; New York: Doubleday, 1999), 142, points out, Malachi 3:1 and Exodus 23:20 were joined in several Jewish traditions as well as in Q.

10. Adela Yarbro Collins, *Mark: A Commentary* (Hermeneia; Minneapolis: Fortress, 2007), 136; Marcus, *Mark,* 142.

Table 6-1 Citations in Mark 1:2-3

Mark 1:2-3	Old Testament Text
ἰδοὺ ἀποστέλλω τὸν ἄγγελόν μου πρὸ προσώπου σου,	ἰδοὺ ἐγὼ ἀποστέλλω τὸν ἄγγελόν μου πρὸ προσώπου σου (Exod 23:20, LXX) הנה אנכי שלח מלאך לפניך (Exod 23:30, MT)
ὃς κατασκευάσει τὴν ὁδόν σου	ἰδοὺ ἐγὼ ἐξαποστέλλω τὸν ἄγγελόν μου καὶ ἐπιβλέψεται ὁδὸν πρὸ προσώπου μου (Mal 3:1, LXX) הנני שלח מלאכי ופנה־דרך לפני (Mal 3:1, MT)
φωνὴ βοῶντος ἐν τῇ ἐρήμῳ· ἑτοιμάσατε τὴν ὁδὸν κυρίου, εὐθείας ποιεῖτε τὰς τρίβους αὐτοῦ	φωνὴ βοῶντος ἐν τῇ ἐρήμῳ ἑτοιμάσατε τὴν ὁδὸν κυρίου εὐθείας ποιεῖτε τὰς τρίβους τοῦ θεοῦ ἡμῶν (Isa 40:3, LXX) קול קורא במדבר פנו דרך יהוה ישרו בערבה מסלה לאלהינו (Isa 40:3, MT)

The Christological ramifications of the verse come into focus when we shift from Elijah the forerunner to the one for whom the way is prepared. Whereas in Exodus 23:30 the divine voice speaks of preparing the way for God's people, in both Malachi 3:1 and Isaiah 40:3 the way is prepared for God, indicated by the pronoun μου in the former and by the words κυρίου and τοῦ θεοῦ ἡμῶν in the latter. The question thus becomes, Does such an application of verses whose original referent was Yhwh, including Isaiah 40:3, whose κυρίου translates יהוה, signal an identification of Jesus with the God of Israel in a manner that exceeds representation by an idealized human figure?[11] The question is heightened by the use of the same pair of words, פנה דרך, as an indication of preparing Yhwh's way in both Malachi 3:1 and Isaiah 40:3 (cf. Isa 57:14; 62:10).[12]

Watts concludes that the deployment of these verses in Mark 1:2-3 carries

11. This is precisely the line of interpretation taken by Richard B. Hays, *Reading Backwards: Figural Christology and the Fourfold Gospel Witness* (Waco, TX: Baylor University Press, 2014), 20-21.

12. Watts, *Isaiah's New Exodus*, 73. Although, interestingly, the repetition of the phrase in the latter chapters of Isaiah is used in anticipation of the people's, not Yhwh's, return.

profound Christological implications. His claim is vague, but suggestive. Watts does not say that Mark depicts Jesus as Yhwh, but seems to want to lead readers down such a path: "he is to be identified in some way, not so much with 'the Messiah,' but with none other than the הָאָדוֹן and מַלְאָךְ הַבְּרִית of Malachi and, in terms of Isaiah 40:3, the presence of Yhwh himself."[13] Richard Hays suggests that this is the first in a string of clues that might point toward Jesus's "divine status" in the Gospel.[14] Joel Marcus also argues extensively that the way of Lord is not merely the way of those who want to be ethically faithful to God or even just the way of Jesus, but the way of Yhwh that is inseparable from the way of Jesus as depicted in the Gospel.[15] However, in assessing the Christological implications of such a claim, Marcus is keen to preserve the differentiation that Mark's Gospel maintains between the two characters of Jesus and God even as it draws them together as, in some ways, inseparable.

In interpreting the Christological significance of these citations, one of the most important pieces of evidence is that the referents have been changed such that verses that originally spoke directly about Yhwh no longer do so. In the voice of Yhwh, Malachi 3:1 uses the first-person singular pronoun μου to delineate the one for whom the way is prepared. In Mark 1:2, however, the pronoun shifts to the second-person singular, so that another figure is added: from the two figures of the messenger and Yhwh in Malachi 3:1, Mark produces a text of three figures in which Yhwh is still the speaker, but he speaks of not only a messenger but also an unnamed "you." In an analogous manner, Mark's citation of Isaiah 40:3 eliminates an opportunity to clearly state that the path being prepared is for God. Rather than "make straight the paths of our God [τοῦ θεοῦ ἡμῶν]," Mark reads, "make straight his [αὐτοῦ] paths." Confronted with the possibility of applying scriptural texts to Jesus that would directly identify Jesus with God, Mark instead changes those texts so that no such direct identification is made.[16]

In this composite biblical citation, both God and the messenger speak. This accounts for the shift in pronouns that refer to Jesus: σοῦ in verse 2, when God is addressing the one for whom the way is prepared, and αὐτοῦ in verse 3, when the messenger is proclaiming the preparation. In the latter, the one for whom the way is prepared is the "Lord" (κυρίου). This is a reference to Jesus, a title

---

13. Watts, *Isaiah's New Exodus*, 87.

14. Hays, *Reading Backwards*, 21.

15. Marcus, *Way of the Lord*, 12-47.

16. As Marcus points out, this argument has been made by both Krister Stendahl, *The School of St. Matthew and Its Use of the Old Testament* (2nd ed.; Philadelphia: Fortress, 1968), 48, and Rudolf Pesch, *Markusevangelium* (HTKNT 2; 2 vols.; Freiburg: Herder, 1976), 1:77.

that, throughout the Gospel, indicates Jesus's authority to exercise God's rule over the earth while still functioning as one who is distinct from God. Jesus is Lord of the Sabbath (Mark 2:28, a claim, as we saw above, of his being an idealized, representative human figure); he is either the Lord who showed mercy to the Gerasene demoniac or else the agent through whom it came (5:19-20); he is the Lord who can command use of a colt (11:3).[17]

In this Gospel, God is also κύριος: the one in whose name Jesus comes (11:9); the master of the vineyard (12:9) who exalts the rejected stone (12:10-11); the one who is to be loved with all that a person is (12:29-30). Throughout, there is a close identification of Jesus with God; however, Jesus is not identified as God. Such proximity fits well within a Jewish idealized human framework.

The Christological implications of these opening verses are significant, but do not in themselves indicate that Jesus is identified as the God of the biblical texts. The ramifications are, first of all, eschatological, in demonstrating that the story of Jesus is the moment toward which Isaiah and Malachi looked forward. The latter prophet's eschatological vision, and its association with John the Baptist, comes up again in Mark 9:11-13. The pairing of John with Jesus is a crucial component for imbuing Mark's story with its claim to be taking place at the time of fulfillment (cf. 1:15). Jesus is the one whose way is prepared by John the Baptist, the "stronger one" whom John anticipated (1:7-8). Jesus's Christological significance comes, first of all, from his being God's eschatological agent.

Additionally, playing the role of God on earth, as that role is prophesied by Isaiah and Malachi, does in fact establish Jesus as a unique agent of the dawning eschatological age. The idealized human paradigm allows us to say that God is visiting the people through Jesus, who is the agent identified with God's actions on the earth. The good news is about Jesus the messiah (1:1), and this is precisely how it is also the good news of God (1:14). Making straight the ways for God's anointed messiah is how the way is prepared for the kingdom of God to come through God's chosen human king.

In interpreting this passage, the paradigm that the reader brings to the text will likely determine the outcome. For those who assume a divine Christology, the replacement of divine referents with references to Jesus will clearly indicate that Jesus plays the role of God, in some mysterious way, as God. For those who approach with an idealized human Christology, the possibility demonstrated at Qumran that the divine name might be replaced with a divine agent looms large. The pervasive indications that human agents are identified with

17. Cf. Marcus, *Way of the Lord*, 38-39.

JESUS AND THE SCRIPTURES OF ISRAEL

God in the biblical and post-biblical Jewish traditions provide another lens for coming to terms with the text. An idealized human paradigm cannot prove that the text refers to a human agent of God, but it can show that the textual dynamics are well accounted for on such a reading and that, therefore, a divine Christology cannot be proved from Mark's hermeneutical move.

b. Psalm 110:1: The Lord Said to My Lord

It may well be that the widespread citation of Psalm 110:1 accounts for the sort of conjunction in differentiation that attends to the use of the word κύριος in the Gospel. Mark 12:35-37 contains one such citation of Psalm 110:1. The passage offers a number of challenges for the interpreter. Unprompted, Jesus challenges the people, "How do the scribes say that the Christ is son of David? For David himself says by the Holy Spirit, 'The Lord says to my Lord, "Sit at my right side, until I place your enemies as a footstool for your feet."' Therefore David himself calls him Lord; and so how is he is his son?" (12:35-37). This passage presents two puzzles simultaneously: (1) what is the relationship between the two Lords? and (2) what is Jesus's relationship to the Davidic king?

The latter question frames Jesus's challenge, and embodies the ambiguity of the Markan narrative with respect to the notion of a Davidic messiah. Jesus's only other invocation of David is in 2:25-26, where David's lawbreaking becomes precedent for that of Jesus's disciples. As discussed in chapter 3 above, this likely suggests a parallel between Jesus and David as figures anointed to be king by God's spirit who have yet to come fully into their thrones. Importantly, the former passage is in the first half of Mark's Gospel, the portion in which Jesus is putting on display his powerful authority prior to Peter's confession. Peter's confession itself might be thought of as an allusion to a Davidic Christology in its absolute use of "Christ." If so, it is telling that he and Jesus immediately thereafter part ways over the significance of this title. Like "Christ" itself, "son of David" in Mark's Gospel must be reframed around Jesus's peculiar mission if it is to be understood.

The second and third appearances of the name David in Mark are on the lips of the blind man outside Jericho (10:47-48): "Jesus, son of David [υἱὲ Δαυίδ], have mercy on me!" (v. 47).[18] This is the second blind man that the reader encounters in Mark, the prior coming in 8:22-26. The healings of these

18. Stephen P. Ahearne-Kroll, *The Psalms of Lament in Mark's Passion: Jesus's Davidic Suffering* (SNTSMS 142; New York: Cambridge University Press, 2007), 139, points out that this is the only pericope in Mark's Gospel to use the son of David title.

two men bookend the middle section of Mark, which otherwise runs from the scene of Peter's confession at Caesarea Philippi (8:27-30) through Jesus's third passion prediction and the conversation that ensues around it (10:32-45). The healing of the first blind man is widely recognized as a metaphor for the disciples' own need for sight, a recovery from "blindness" that takes place in the two stages of (1) knowing that Jesus is Christ, but then (2) having to subsequently learn that the mission of this particular Christ entails rejection, suffering, death, and resurrection. This twofold eye opening is critically important for interpreting the subsequent healing of Bartimaeus. The metaphor of blindness for lack of understanding renders his appellation "son of David" suspect. However, the request for mercy and for sight, together with his assuming the posture of faithful discipleship by following Jesus in the way (ἠκολούθει αὐτῷ ἐν τῇ ὁδῷ, 10:52),[19] which the reader knows to be the way not only to Jerusalem but also to the cross, signals that his blindness is not complete. Instead, his vision of Jesus as "son of David," like Peter's vision of Jesus as "Christ," needs to be transformed by Jesus's journey to the cross.

Together, the two stories of Jesus healing the blind, bracketing the section in which Jesus travels from Caesarea Philippi to Jerusalem and issues his passion predictions, metaphorically depict understanding Jesus and his ministry. Like the term "Christ" itself, Davidic messiahship is not a sufficient category for interpreting Jesus's ministry. It needs reframing and reinterpretation by Jesus's own ministry. The importance of this for my current purpose is to suggest that son of David is not a wholly inappropriate title for Jesus within Mark, but that it demands a radical reorientation around the fate of Jesus that includes not only authority, suffering, and death, but also resurrection and enthronement.

Returning, then, to the citation of Psalm 110 in Mark 12:36, we see that Jesus raises the question of how Christ can be equated with "son of David." The psalm is interpreted as referring to the coming messiah, and will later be alluded to in Jesus's response to the high priest when he affirms the latter's question, "Are you the Christ, the son of the Blessed?" (14:61-62). Thus, in Mark's narrative world, Jesus is the Lord Christ about whom David prophesied, who will be enthroned at the right hand of the Lord God. The question, then, is whether this association of Jesus as Lord with the Lord God, and unraveling

---

19. Ahearne-Kroll, *Psalms of Lament,* 140-44, argues that Bartimaeus is a reliable character based on his willingness to leave behind his cloak and follow Jesus, thus confirming the title he has spoken. Ahearne-Kroll also argues that Mark is reinterpreting the significance of this title, but does not explore the metaphor of blindness per se.

the notion of Davidic sonship, entails an identification of Jesus with God that signals a divine or preexistence Christology.

The mixed citation of Psalm 110:1 with Daniel 7:13 in Mark 14:62 suggests that within Mark's narrative the resolution of the question is to be found in Mark's son of man Christology; specifically, it is to be found in the exaltation dimension of that narrative arc. As I argued in chapter 3, Mark's exalted son of humanity is not a preexistent divine figure, but takes his seat at God's right side as the earthly, human Jesus is exalted to heavenly glory. As Peter's Christ Christology has to be refracted through the lens of the suffering son of humanity, so also any son of David Christology must be refracted through the lens of the exalted son of humanity. Although it is possible to conceive of this Christology as a divinization, there is no indication in Mark's Gospel that it suggests preexistence, such that Jesus would be identified as YHWH of the Hebrew Bible.

Interpreting Psalm 110:1 as a psalm about the coming Christ, and reading the enthronement as a literal, heavenly exaltation, renders Christ greater than David and hence David's Lord. The psalm indicates one clear element of this coming Lord's reign that differentiates him from David: the place of his enthronement. A "son of David" would be expected to take his seat on a royal throne in Jerusalem, the city of David. But with the literalization of the language of being positioned at "the right side" (ἐκ δεξιῶν) of God (Mark 12:36), a heavenly enthronement is now in view. Importantly, this has dramatic consequences for how the throne must be attained, as recovery of David's earthly throne would likely entail geopolitical, military methodologies — even as David's coming to and securing the throne in Jerusalem required the death of the reigning king Saul and numerous battles against other people.[20]

Psalm 110:1, as cited and queried in Mark 12:36-37, maintains the distinction between the two characters of God and the Christ that runs throughout Mark's Gospel. Though the title "Lord" is used of each, Jesus distinguishes which "Lord" is addressed by David as "my Lord." The Lord God speaks to and seats the Lord Christ. This session indicates a union of the reign of God with the reign of God's messiah, but it is a union of precisely the type that we expect given the closeness between God and idealized human figures that we have observed throughout this book.

As noted above, Psalm 110:1 is a widely cited verse that uses the same title for God and for God's Christological agent, whom the earliest Christians inter-

20. Ahearne-Kroll, *Psalms of Lament*, 161-66, offers a reading that concludes similarly: heavenly versus earthly enthronement and redefinition of Davidic kingship away from militant messianism are the key forces at work.

preted as Jesus (Mark 12:36; par. Matt 22:44 and Luke 20:42; Acts 2:34-36; 1 Cor 15:25; Heb 1:13, in addition to a number of other likely allusions). The verse maintains the two as distinct characters, and yet speaks of the enthronement of the Christ figure "at God's right side," thus indicating a close proximity, even to the point of the Christ mediating and enacting God's reign. Moreover, it speaks of God's own power continuing to be the means by which the rule of the messiah is established through the conquering of the messiah's enemies. As we would expect from our survey of early Judaism, the Lord God is known through the rule of the Lord Christ, and the Lord Christ's rule is put on display through the ruling and subduing power of the Lord God.

c. Psalm 118:22-23, 26: The Coming Kingdom Is the Lord's Doing

The association of the Lord God with Jesus as the son of David is iterated also in the cry of the crowds during Jesus's entry into Jerusalem (Mark 11:9, alluding to Ps 118:26). The citation itself mentions only God as the Lord. Importantly, this same psalm appears on the lips of Jesus a chapter later, in explanation of the parable of the vineyard: "The stone which the builders rejected, this one has become the chief cornerstone. This is from the Lord, and it is marvelous in our eyes" (Mark 12:10-11; citing Ps 118:22-23). Together, these passages provide the same sort of reorientation about Jesus's messianic identity that both Peter and Bartimaeus require: a move from identifying God's chosen agent in undifferentiated messianic terms ("the coming kingdom of our father David," Mark 11:10), to a Christology of divine vindication of the rejected and murdered son (Mark 12:1-12, esp. vv. 8-11).[21]

In both citations from Psalm 118, "Lord" clearly refers to God rather than Jesus. In the first, the coming one comes in the Lord's name, signaling precisely the sort of conjoining of God and messiah that I articulate above. Moreover, the language of coming in the Lord's "name" provides another perspective on the possibility that someone other than God, who comes as one authorized and empowered by this Lord, might also be referred to as Lord in a mediated, derivative fashion. In the citation of Psalm 118:22-23 that concludes the parable of the vineyard, the Lord corresponds to the vineyard owner who has sent his sole, beloved son, only for that son to be killed. This places the parable squarely within the son of God Christology discussed in the son of God chapter above.[22]

---

21. Cf. Ahearne-Kroll, *Psalms of Lament*, 156-61.

22. See also Klyne Snodgrass, *Stories with Intent: A Comprehensive Guide to the Parables of Jesus* (Grand Rapids, MI: Eerdmans, 2008), 292-95.

Moreover, this citation hints at something that the parable does not itself point to — that the murder of the son will not be the end of his story.[23] The character to whom responsibility for the continuation of the son's story falls, however, is not the son himself (cf. John 10:18), but the Lord God, who is the father of Jesus. Both Jesus and God can be referred to using the title Lord. In the Psalm 118 citations, God maintains the role of Lord that Yhwh has in their original setting. But in each, the Lord God is also represented by Jesus, who in the first bears Yhwh's name, and is known by what happens to and through him.

d. Deuteronomy 6:4-5: The Lord Is One

The singularity of Israel's God that forms the basis for many arguments in favor of early high Christology is captured in the *shema* of Deuteronomy 6:4-5. Jesus cites just this passage in his debate with a scribe in Mark 12:29-30. In response to the scribe's query as to which is the first commandment of all, Jesus replies, "Hear, Israel, the Lord our God, the Lord is one [ἄκουε, Ἰσραήλ, κύριος ὁ θεὸς ἡμῶν κύριος εἷς ἐστίν]. And you shall love the Lord your God from your whole heart and from your whole self and from your whole mind and from your whole strength," and he then proceeds to cite Leviticus 19:18 as the second great command. The response of the scribe and Jesus's final return are important for our purposes. First, the scribe commends Jesus's answer, and largely repeats it back to him, but slightly modifies the description of God: "Well done, teacher, you have said truly that he is one and that there is no other but him [εἷς ἐστιν καὶ οὐκ ἔστιν ἄλλος πλὴν αὐτοῦ]" (12:32). The scribe also elaborates on the citation of Leviticus 19:18, affirming that the mandate to love neighbor is greater than all sacrifices and burnt offerings (12:33). Finally, Jesus commends the scribe as not being far from God's kingdom (12:34).

In the narrative world of Mark's Gospel, the scribe's response to Jesus shows that Jesus's manner of configuring the singularity of God has not been so modified as to be a point of dispute between Jesus and the traditional Jewish religious elite. The significance of this point is amplified once we recall that the first controversy story in Mark also pits Jesus against the scribes and may also have echoed the *shema* (2:6-7). In the earlier episode, Jesus's forgiving of the sins of the paralytic is met with a charge of blasphemy due to Jesus's infringement on the divine prerogative: "Who can forgive sins but God alone [εἰ μὴ

---

23. See also J. Samuel Subramanian, *The Synoptic Gospels and the Psalms as Prophecy* (LNTS 351; London: T&T Clark, 2007), 53-57.

εἷς ὁ θεός]?" (v. 7). Mark tells the reader that the interchange with the scribe in chapter 12 is the final time any of the religious authorities dared ask him questions (v. 34), making this a bookend of the conflicts that ultimately lead to Jesus's arrest. Thus, Mark appears to be linking the two episodes intentionally: a first and a final debate with scribes and each concerning Jesus's ministry in relationship to the *shema*.

The importance of the connection is to underscore that in Mark 12 Jesus invokes the *shema* in a manner that is completely acceptable to the religious leader who likely does not follow him, and that the religious leader's reiteration and modification of what Jesus had said is, in turn, completely acceptable to Jesus. Thus, there is no thoroughgoing modification of the divine identity, or the monotheism of the *shema*, that transforms the meaning either of "God" or of "Lord" when it is referring to that God. It seems, instead, that Mark maintains a distinction between these two characters in the story, even as his conviction that Jesus is Christ and Lord allows him to speak of Jesus as the κύριος in whose life the way of the Lord God is made known.

e. Conclusions: Mark's Κύριος Christology

Mark's κύριος Christology, as it appears in biblical citations from Isaiah 40:3, Psalm 110:1, and Psalm 118:22-26, and ripples throughout the Gospel, does not present us with a Christology of Jesus's ontological identity with Yhwh, but fits well a Christology of representation and even embodiment of the reality of Yhwh's actions. When the Lord Jesus acts and speaks, it is a mediation of the action and authority of the Lord God. Maintaining this proximity in differentiation between Jesus and God is crucial for the integrity of Mark's narrative. The story requires a Jesus who prays to a father who is other, and who is ultimately in charge of the plan that Jesus go to the cross (Mark 14:36). Even more importantly, perhaps, the identities of Jesus and God, however closely joined in action and heavenly enthronement, are sufficiently distinct for the character Jesus to cry out to God from the cross, "My God, my God, why have you abandoned me?" (15:34). The mystery of Mark's Gospel is not so much that Jesus "seems to be at the same time . . . both the God of Israel and a human being not identical with the God of Israel,"[24] but that Jesus is somehow both the authoritative messiah who is king of God's kingdom and the one who must suffer and die on the cross. Such a messianic vocation is embodied in the κύριος Christology as it surfaces in Mark's biblical citations.

24. Hays, *Reading Backwards*, 27.

2. PROPHET, SERVANT, KING

Other biblical citations in Mark carry potential Christological significance as well. These generally assign Jesus the role corresponding to an Old Testament prophet or king.

a. Isaiah 6:9-10: The Failure-Inducing Prophet

Somewhat paradoxically, the Gospel that begins by casting Jesus in the role of the returning κύριος of Isaiah 40 goes on to assign him the additional role of the prophet of Isaiah 6 — a prophet whose ministry occludes rather than enlightens the people's understanding (Mark 4:10-11; cf. Isa 6:9-10). In Mark, the passage describing a ministry that fails to transform its recipients falls into Jesus's explanation of why he teaches in parables. It thus functions as an interpretive key for his activity, if not his person. In this case, the role he takes up is that of the prophet who announces the work of God to a people whose path to judgment will be sealed through their rejection of the prophet's message.

b. Numbers 27:17; 1 Kings 22:17: Shepherd for the Shepherdless

In Mark's rendition of the feeding of the five thousand, the stage is set by a multitude of people running ahead of Jesus and the disciples to a remote place where the latter were headed by boat (6:32-33). When he disembarks, Mark tells us, Jesus had compassion on the people because they were like sheep without a shepherd (ὅτι ἦσαν ὡς πρόβατα μὴ ἔχοντα ποιμένα), a situation Jesus addresses by teaching them many things (6:34).

The phrase "like sheep without a shepherd" likely echoes one of two scriptural texts.[25] In Numbers 27:17 Moses responds to a divine prediction of his death by imploring God to appoint someone over the congregation, to lead them out and bring them in, so that they may not be like sheep without a shepherd (ὡσεὶ πρόβατα οἷς οὐκ ἔστιν ποιμήν, LXX; כַּצֹּאן אֲשֶׁר אֵין־לָהֶם רֹעֶה, MT). In response, God tells Moses to take Joshua and lay hands on him, transferring some of his majesty to Joshua, so that the people will listen to Joshua as he inquires of God and leads the people in turn (27:18-21). In 1 Kings 22:17

---

25. Each of these reflects Israel's need for a human shepherd, and thus color whether the roles are assigned to God as shepherd or a representative human shepherd. Hays's decision to focus on Ezekiel 34 as a means of ascribing the status of divine shepherd as such to Jesus unduly minimizes both the more direct allusions and the role of the Davidic shepherd in that chapter (*Reading Backwards,* 23-24).

the prophet Micaiah predicts the death of King Ahab of Israel in battle using an identical Hebrew phrase, one that is rendered somewhat differently in the Greek, "like a flock for which there is no shepherd" (ὡς ποίμνιον ᾧ οὐκ ἔστιν ποιμήν). Neither Greek translation is an exact match for Mark, although the use of πρόβατα perhaps draws Mark 6:34 closer to Numbers 27:17 than to 1 Kings 22:17. Each passage anticipates the death of Israel's leader. Moses is not only prophet and lawgiver but also the one who has led the people into battle as directed by God (e.g., Num 21:32-35), thus playing the role of what we might term political leader in addition to his role as prophetic mediator.

In Mark's narrative, the reader comes to Jesus's statement about the people's state immediately after the tale of John's murder at the hands of Herod. In that story, Herod the tetrarch is referred to as king (βασιλεύς) five times (6:14, 22, 25, 26, 27), the only appearances of the word in Mark outside of six references to Jesus in the passion narrative (15:2, 9, 12, 18, 26, 32), with the exception of a general reference to kings in Mark 13:9. In addition, Herod refers to his kingdom (βασιλεία) in his rash oath to his stepdaughter (6:23). With these pieces in place, Herod's weakness as one who must capitulate to a request for John's head because of his guests and his death-dealing, as stylized by the grisly dessert course of a prophet's head on a serving platter, provide a foil for the kingdom of God proclaimed and inaugurated by Jesus. The immediately subsequent feeding story transforms the wilderness into a panoply of banqueting tables (συμπόσια συμπόσια, 6:39). The guests at this feast are not Herod's great ones, tribunes, and first citizens (μεγιστᾶσιν, χιλιάρχοις, πρώτοις, 6:21), but a nameless crowd of shepherdless sheep. And the final course is not a human head on a platter, but a collection of leftovers sufficient for yet another banquet. Thus, the narrator's announcement that Jesus's actions, beginning with his teaching, are the acts of caring for sheep that have no shepherd, points first of all to the notion that Herod is no true king of Israel. Instead, Jesus plays that role through his teaching, tending, and feeding the sheep. Such a reading comports well with the prophetic vision of 1 Kings 22:17, in which Israel is scattered for lack of a king.

Another dynamic may also be in play. Throughout Mark, John the Baptist is linked to Jesus as the latter's forerunner. We saw this above in the discussion of Isaiah 40:3. The theme continues: Jesus proclaims the gospel only after John's arrest (1:14); Herod fears that the work of Jesus signals John's own resurrection (6:14, 16); the connection between John and Jesus recurs in the list of popular explanations of Jesus's identity prior to Peter's confession (8:28); as "Elijah," John's fate anticipates that of the son of man (9:11-13); and a question about where John gets his authority entails an answer about where Jesus, too, gets his authority (11:29-33). It is thus possible that the shepherdless state of the people reflects not only the vacuous nature of Herod's rule, but also the prophetic absence of John after his murder. In this, Jesus might be seen as playing Elisha to John's Elijah in performing a feeding miracle with a surprising abundance of leftovers (2 Kgs 4:42-44), or playing Joshua to John's Moses: the one chosen by God to be a successor and even to embody a measure of the predecessor's majesty or glory (הוד, MT; δόξα, LXX; Num 27:20).

The roles of Moses and Joshua are both prophetic and more broadly executive and military, leading to descriptions of Moses as not only lawgiver and prophet but also king in some early Jewish literature (e.g., Philo, *Mos.* 1.60). Thus, the Old Testament references to Israel being like sheep without a shepherd reflect substantially overlapping concerns, concerns that are met through Jesus's multivalent provision for the people through compassion, teaching, and feeding. In Mark 6:34 we find an Old Testament citation with Christological import: Jesus fills the role of shepherd that is associated with the great prophet Moses (Exod 3:1) and the great king David (1 Sam 16:11; 17:34; Ezek 34:23).[26] The miracle of the feeding of the five thousand thus contextualizes the Jesus who performs the miracle within Israel's tradition of idealized human figures who metaphorically shepherd the people of God.[27]

This shepherding motif is one way in which kings and other leaders of Israel's biblical tradition participate in God's rule over the created order. God is the shepherd of Israel (e.g., Psalm 23; Ezek 34:11-16; Isa 40:11), and yet this shepherding is also entrusted to humans. In Ezekiel 34 the relationship between YHWH and the shepherds is distinguishable and separable: God judges the poor shepherds, and God promises to rescue and gather the sheep, displacing the shepherds with God's own care: "I myself will be the shepherd of my sheep, and I will make them lie down, says the Lord YHWH" (34:15, NRSV, alt.). This divine shepherding and rescue, however, will be mediated by a Davidic king: "I will set up over them one shepherd, my servant David, and he shall feed them: he shall feed them and be their shepherd" (34:23, NRSV). This simultaneous assignment of the shepherd role to both YHWH and David illustrates the necessity of asking not only whether God is at work in a given action, but also what such a divine action will look like "from below." Because idealized human figures, such as Davidic kings, often play roles that mirror the divine, it

---

26. Cf. John Lierman, *The New Testament Moses: Christian Perceptions of Moses and Israel in the Setting of Jewish Religion* (WUNT2 173; Tübingen: Mohr Siebeck, 2004), 108-10.

27. Cf. Roger David Aus, *Feeding the Five Thousand: Studies in the Judaic Background of Mark 6:30-44 Par. and John 6:1-15* (Lanham, MD: University Press of America, 2010), 155-59.

is not enough to say, for instance, that Yнwн is shepherd of the people, so that if a messianic figure is depicted as shepherd then this figure is divine. Such a line of argument has been advanced around the notion that the Gospels depict Jesus's arrival in Jerusalem as Yнwн's prophesied return to Zion.[28] In Mark 6 the feeding narrative unfolds under the rubric of Jesus as shepherd. The care and feeding that Jesus executes evokes the divine provision of Ezekiel 34, where Yнwн promises to feed, make the people lie down in good land, bind up the injured, and strengthen the weak (e.g., vv. 14-16). Thus one might well say that an allusion to Ezekiel 34 is in play as well in Mark 6, and specifically that Israel's God is fulfilling the promise that God will shepherd the flock that is Israel. The means for this shepherding is the presence of the idealized human figure, the Davidic king who plays the shepherding role on the earth.

The notion that Jesus as shepherd conjures up images not only of a prophet-king but also of one who plays the part of Yнwн is an important both/and to hold in hand as we explore one further possible allusion. Dale Allison has suggested that Psalm 23 lies in the background of this particular shepherding story.[29] That psalm begins with the identification of the shepherd as Yнwн, even as the feeding narrative commences with Jesus taking the role of shepherd (Ps 23:1; Mark 6:34). The psalm's shepherd ensures that the psalmist does not suffer lack, and causes the "sheep" to lie down in green pastures (23:2).[30] In Mark 6 Jesus not only feeds the people from apparent nothingness, thereby ensuring that they do not suffer lack, but in a peculiar addition of graphic detail Mark also states that Jesus ordered the people to recline on the green grass (ἐπὶ τῷ χλωρῷ χόρτῳ, v. 39).[31] If such an extended allusion is in play, then it might help explain one of the most perplexing verses in the whole of the Gospel of Mark: in the immediately following episode, Jesus comes walking on the sea to the strained disciples, and "he intended to pass

---

28. N. T. Wright, *Jesus and the Victory of God* (Minneapolis: Fortress, 1996), 615-24, 631-42. Michael F. Bird, "Did Jesus Think He Was God?" in *How God became Jesus: The Real Origins of Belief in Jesus' Divine Nature* (ed. Michael F. Bird; Grand Rapids, MI: Zondervan, 2014), 45-70, redeploys Wright's argument about Jesus embodying Yнwн's return to Zion in order to argue, more directly than Wright does himself, that Jesus is himself the God who is so returning (52-61).

29. Dale C. Allison Jr., "Psalm 23 (22) in Early Christianity: A Suggestion," *IBS* 5 (1983): 132-37.

30. Cf. Bernd Kollmann, "Brot und Fisch bis zum Abwinken (die Speisung Fünftausend): Mk 6,30-44 (ActJoh 93)," in *Kompendium der frühchristlichen Wundererzählungen, Band 1, Die Wunder Jesu* (ed. Susanne Luther and Jörg Röder; Gütersloh: Gütersloher Verlagshaus, 2013), 294-303, here 298.

31. Allison, "Psalm 23," 134.

by them" (ἤθελεν παρελθεῖν αὐτούς, 6:48). It may well be that Mark's Jesus here is looking to "lead [them] upon waters of rest" (ἐπὶ ὕδατος ἀναπαύσεως, Ps 23:2, LXX).[32] That latter episode is tied to the feeding narrative by the editorial comment that the disciples' fear and confusion was generated by their failure to understand about the loaves, their hearts being hardened (Mark 6:52). Jesus who teaches, perhaps thereby leading these sheep in the way of righteousness (Ps 23:3), and who prepares a feast in the wilderness, is in fact playing roles that are assigned to Israel's God in its biblical narrative. And once we add the multiple allusions to the feeding of Israel in the wilderness, such divine roles only increase.

If, however, we point out these connections between Jesus's actions and those of Israel's God in the biblical narrative and conclude from them that Jesus is "somehow being depicted as sharing in the divine identity," we are begging the question of the Christological significance of the story. The question we must answer to arrive at the heart of the Gospels' Christology is not, Do these texts associate or even identify Jesus with YHWH? but instead, What do the identifications of Jesus with YHWH in these texts tell us about the identity of Jesus? The evidence marshaled throughout this study suggests that this identification is a development and application of the manifold possibilities available to early Jewish writers who would see in a messiah figure one who plays various roles of YHWH on the earth. Dale Allison, surveying such shepherding imagery, concludes that eschatological interpretation is in play, a Davidic shepherd who would rule over both Israel and the nations.[33] Jesus as messianic shepherd plays the role of YHWH in feeding people in the wilderness, gathering them, binding them, and finally leading them back to Zion. These claims do not make Jesus YHWH. They fit within the idealized human paradigm in which Jesus is the fulfillment of the expectation that when YHWH so acts, it will be through a human (Davidic) messiah.

c. Zechariah 13:7: The Stricken Shepherd

In surveying the depictions of Jesus as eschatological shepherd, Allison also draws attention to Zechariah's prophecy, "Strike the shepherd, that the sheep may be scattered" (13:7, NRSV), cited in Mark 14:27.[34] In Zechariah 9–14 we find extensive use of sheep and shepherding imagery, including the notion

---

32. This idea was first suggested to me by Hank Tarlton.
33. Allison, "Psalm 23," 136.
34. Allison, "Psalm 23," 136.

that the people wander like sheep who have no shepherd due to the divination and idolatry in the land (10:2). The prophet symbolically enacts the poor
shepherding and the judgment it warrants from God (11:4-17). Judgment on
the shepherds, and on the people more generally, forms the core of Zechariah's
message, though chapter 12 includes a promise of restoration in which "the
feeblest among them on that day shall be like David, and the house of David
shall be like God, like the angel of YHWH, at their head" (v. 8). That moment is
further defined as the day when YHWH "will seek to destroy all the nations that
come against Jerusalem" (v. 9), after which a repentant Jerusalem is cleaned
(13:1-6). In the sweep of Zechariah's prophecy we thus find, as in Mark, an essentially shepherdless people (despite the presence of numerous officeholders
who should be the people's guides and protectors), an anticipation of judgment
on those shepherds and the people more generally, a restoration following
judgment that is marked by an idealized people who are "like David," an idealized Davidic king who is "like God," and these latter two in turn as the earthly
markers of YHWH's own presence to fight on behalf of the people. In addition
to these similarities, the final prophecy in Zechariah 14 is of an eschatological
battle that appears to have cosmic implications (vv. 6-8). Zechariah's rather
blunt association of the eschatological Davidic king being like God is a clear
instance of the idealization of the role of Israel's awaited messiah, even an
identification of that Davidic royal figure with God, but an identification that
in no way amounts to a redefinition of Israel's God as such.

One peculiarity of Mark 14:27 is that Jesus, who plays the role of stricken
shepherd, is not the faithless shepherd of Zechariah's prophecy. It might well
be argued that in both Mark and Zechariah the smiting of the shepherd is
God's doing (cf. Mark 14:35-36; 15:34). Another, significant difference is that
in Zechariah God appears to be the indirect agent, as the divine voice speaks
in the imperative mood (πατάξατε, LXX; הַךְ, MT); in Mark, however, the
person and mood are changed to first-person indicative (πατάξω). With this,
Mark's Gospel more directly involves God in the narrative. And yet the role of
God is not assigned to Jesus. God remains a separate agent who acts on Jesus
(even as this same God acts through Jesus at numerous points in the Gospel).
When Mark deploys the shepherd motif from Zechariah, he does not do so
in such a way as to write Jesus into the role of direct divine overseer. Instead,
he depicts Jesus as the human under-shepherd whom God strikes as part of a
comprehensive program of judgment and restoration of Israel.

Can this paradigm hold up even when broader allusions to Zechariah are
broached? In the chapter subsequent to the one anticipating the stricken shepherd, we find one of two references to the Mount of Olives from the scriptures

of Israel (Zech 14:4; cf. 2 Sam 15:30). Prophesying an eschatological battle, Zechariah says, "Then Yʜᴡʜ will go forth and fight against those nations when he fights on a day of battle. On that day his feet shall stand on the Mount of Olives, which lies before Jerusalem on the east; and the Mount of Olives shall be split in two from east to west by a very wide valley" (14:3-4, NRSV, alt.). The prophecy continues with a proclamation that on that very day Yʜᴡʜ will become king of the whole earth (14:9), a theme that resonates deeply with Jesus's proclamation of the kingdom of God and with the passion narrative's royal motifs. More specifically, as Marcus points out, the anticipation of a "day" when God will become king resonates with the words of Jesus at the Last Supper that he will not drink fruit of the vine until "that day when I drink it new in the kingdom of God" (Mark 14:25).[35] The "blood of the covenant" from Mark 14, moreover, may be drawing on the similar phrase from Zechariah 9:11, where God's remembrance of the blood of the covenant is the cause of captives being set free.[36] Thus, Zechariah 9–14 provides a web of connections with the Markan passion narrative, and Mark 14 in particular, including a possible reference to Jesus playing the role of Yʜᴡʜ by taking his stand on the Mount of Olives. The question then becomes whether such an allusion signals that Mark's Jesus is, after all, representative of a direct divine intervention rather than being the agent mediating Yʜᴡʜ's arrival.

First, I recall the reader's attention to Zechariah 12:8, cited above, which indicates that this eschatological kingship of Yʜᴡʜ can be understood even within the context of Zechariah itself as being mediated by an idealized Davidic king.[37] Second, we have seen enough of Mark's handling of biblical texts by now to know that he is capable of changing their referents to suit his purposes. In Mark's citation of Malachi 3:1 and Isaiah 40:3, pronouns and nouns were changed so that the referent would no longer clearly be God. This should make us exceedingly cautious about assuming that Mark intends for an allusion to be read in its historical-critical originality in order to determine the

---

35. Marcus, *Way of the Lord*, 156.

36. Marcus, *Way of the Lord*, 157.

37. Due to my coverage of Zechariah texts here, I will not explore them again in Matthew's Gospel. However, John Nolland, "The King as Shepherd: The Role of Deutero-Zechariah in Matthew," in *Biblical Interpretation in Early Christian Gospels*, vol. 2, *The Gospel of Matthew* (LNTS 310; ed. T. R. Hatina; London: T&T Clark, 2008), 133-46, arrives at similar conclusions in his study of the First Evangelist: "most of the quotations and allusions from Deutero-Zechariah are to be understood as designed to suggest, and then to bolster, the idea that Jesus, as the king of Zech. 9.9, is the one who is to fulfil all the ideals for the shepherding of God's people" (134).

interpretation of the subsequent passage in which it occurs. Third, Marcus has demonstrated that Zechariah 14:4 was read messianically, and even enacted messianically, by other interpreters.[38] Josephus, for instance, tells of an Egyptian prophet who gathered people to himself on the Mount of Olives, promising to conquer Jerusalem and set himself up as leader of the people (*J. W.* 2.261-63). Mark's invocations of Zechariah are thus best understood as signaling that Jesus is the messianic agent through whom God's reign will be established. The nature of the eschatological battle is in some ways transformed through Jesus's death on the cross, and yet the judgment looming over Jerusalem suggests that the overall plotline of Zechariah 9–14 has not been left too far afield. The transformation effected has been one of assigning the triumphant messianic role to the same shepherd who was stricken by God.[39] Such a transformation embodies the mystery of Mark's Gospel: Jesus is Christ, but fulfills his messianic vocation through rejection, suffering, and death prior to resurrection and glory.

d. Laments of Israel's King

Allusions to biblical antecedents are ripe for the plucking in Mark's passion narrative. Joel Marcus lists fourteen possible allusions to "Psalms of the Righteous Sufferer" in chapters 14–15.[40] Stephen Ahearne-Kroll is somewhat less sanguine about these allusions (and such a title), paring the list down to six allusions: Psalm 40:10 LXX in Mark 14:18; Psalm 41:6, 12; 42:5 LXX in Mark 14:34; Psalm 21:19 LXX in Mark 15:24; Psalm 21:8 LXX in Mark 15:29; Psalm 21:2 LXX in Mark 15:34; and Psalm 68:22 LXX in Mark 15:36.[41]

Once again, we are confronting an area of exegetical inquiry whose full exploration pays rich dividends for the reader of Mark. However, such an exhaustive treatment goes beyond the needs of the current study for one significant reason: in these psalms, and in their employment in the Markan text, the complainant is clearly a human figure (often associated with David in the history of interpretation) who is laying out his case before God. Using Ahearne-Kroll's more abbreviated list, I briefly sketch the use of the lament psalms in Mark's passion narrative, including any possible Christological implications.

38. Marcus, *Way of the Lord*, 156-57, 159.
39. Cf. Marcus, *Way of the Lord*, 162-63.
40. Marcus, *Way of the Lord*, 174-75.
41. Ahearne-Kroll, *Psalms of Lament*, 61-77.

i. Psalm 40:10 LXX: The One Who Shared My Bread

Jesus's prediction of betrayal by one of the twelve is flagged as an allusion to Psalm 41:9 (MT; Ps 41:10, LXX) in the marginal reference of the Nestle-Aland 28: "One of you who eats with me will hand me over" (εἷς ἐξ ὑμῶν παραδώσει με ὁ ἐσθίων μετ᾽ ἐμοῦ, Mark 14:18). The Septuagint reads, "The one who eats my bread has worked a great deception upon me" (ὁ ἐσθίων ἄρτους μου ἐμεγάλυνεν ἐπ᾽ ἐμὲ πτερνισμόν). Thus, there is little precise verbal correlation beyond ὁ ἐσθίων, and the MT is no closer to Mark than the LXX, but the idea of betrayal by an intimate who has not only shared table fellowship but has also been a trusted companion is common to both texts. Importantly, the psalm appeals to God to be the psalmist's defender in the face of such human betrayal: "But you, Lord, have mercy on me and lift me up so that I may repay them" (Ps 40:11, LXX). The allusive force of the psalm scripts Judas into the role of the psalmist's betrayer and Jesus into the Davidic voice of the psalmist. Moreover, as Marcus points out, the superscription εἰς τὸ τέλος (Ps 40:1, LXX) may indicate an eschatological reading of the psalm, thus signaling that Jesus's betrayal is part and parcel with the coming eschatological assize.[42] The "Christology" of this hermeneutic is not one that places Jesus into the role of God, but one that confirms his role as God's chosen agent for whom God's promised presence and deliverance are absent. It may also incorporate Jesus's death into the eschatological labor pangs that lead to the age to come.[43]

ii. Psalms 41–42 LXX: The Saddened Soul

Jesus expresses his anguish in Gethsemane by saying to the disciples, "My soul is deeply grieved, to the point of death" (περίλυπός ἐστιν ἡ ψυχή μου ἕως θανάτου, Mark 14:34). This is widely seen as an allusion to Psalms 42:5, 11 (41:6, 12, LXX); 43:5 (42:5, LXX), originally a single psalm whose refrain reads, "Why are you deeply grieved, soul [ἵνα τί περίλυπος εἶ ψυχή]? And why are you troubling me? Hope upon God, because I will praise him. My God is the salvation of my face." The hope expressed in this refrain is the flip side of the problem that comes into focus over the course of the three stanzas: God has abandoned the psalmist. Excluded from the festal assembly, and God's very presence (42:1-4; 41:1-5, LXX), the psalmist is forgotten by God, mocked by his enemies as

---

42. Marcus, *Way of the Lord*, 177-78.

43. Cf. Dale C. Allison Jr., *The End of the Ages Has Come: An Early Interpretation of the Passion and Resurrection of Jesus* (Philadelphia: Fortress, 1985), 27-39.

one whom God has abandoned (Ps 42:9-10; 41:10-11, LXX). And so the final strophe pleads with God for just vindication, the very presence of God for the purpose of deliverance (43:1-2; 42:1-2, LXX), so that the psalmist might once again come to the altar and sing praises in God's presence (43:4; 42:4, LXX). As Ahearne-Kroll argues, the refrain thus functions as an invocation to the God who has abandoned the psalmist in his time of anguish. While addressing himself, the psalmist also reminds God of God's obligations to God's faithful servant: "by the end of the psalm, because of the direct challenge to God and the conditional vow expressed in the third strophe, the refrain functions as a key part in the overall rhetoric of the psalm in attempting to persuade God to act on behalf of the psalmist."[44]

Mark's allusion to the psalm evokes its sense of abandonment in darker hues than the original. The deep grief of Jesus is not spoken in the midst of a word of encouragement that the time of suffering will soon be over, as we find in the psalm. Instead, it signals that the anguish of Jesus's situation has him on the cusp of death itself (14:34). The heightened intensity of the scene in Gethsemane might well be explained by the more direct role God plays in the affliction of Jesus. While the suffering psalmist presents a subtle case against God for dereliction of duty, Jesus wrestles with God as the one whose will is making the suffering and looming death a necessity (14:36). Weaving the psalm into the scene in Gethsemane, Mark (or his source) has built on the notion of the divine hand being behind Jesus's death (cf. "*I* will strike the shepherd," 14:27) by evoking a matrix of divine abandonment of a faithful servant. In a moment we will turn to Psalm 21 LXX, from which comes the verbiage for Jesus's cry of dereliction in Mark 15:34. We see in Gethsemane that Jesus's abandonment by God has already begun. The prayer for deliverance (14:36) will not be answered until the resurrection.

Thus, the evocation of Psalms 41–42 dramatically underscores a Christological point that could well be made without them: Jesus and God are separate characters in Mark. God plays the role of empowering deliverer; Jesus plays the role of God's idealized human agent, the suffering faithful king.[45] At the crucial juncture of the story, moreover, the fulfillment of Jesus's role demands being abandoned by the God to whom he still calls out as "father" (14:36). The invocation of Psalms 41–42 helps cement the picture of Jesus as a human messiah who plays the role previously filled by righteous predecessors, but in a unique, climactic, and even eschatological manner.

---

44. Ahearne-Kroll, *Psalms of Lament*, 182.
45. Cf. Ahearne-Kroll, *Psalms of Lament*, 186-91.

iii. Psalm 21:2, 8 LXX: Forsaken by God

If the theme of divine abandonment is subtly evoked through allusion to Psalms 41 and 42, it is declared loudly through Jesus's invocation of Psalm 22:1 (21:2, LXX) on the cross, an invocation that Mark translates, ὁ θεός μου ὁ θεός μου, εἰς τί ἐγκατέλιπές με; ("My God my God, why have you abandoned me?" 15:34). These final words of Jesus, spoken almost immediately before his death (15:37), confirm earlier hints that the experience of Psalm 21 is being played out in Jesus's crucifixion and provide a test case for any would-be Markan Christology.

Prior signals that Psalm 21 lies behind the passion narrative include the allusion to verse 19, in which the psalmist's enemies divide his clothing by lot (Mark 15:24). Within the psalm, this image depicts the humiliation the psalmist experiences at the hands of his enemies due to the divine abandonment expressed at the fore. The division of clothing precedes a plea to God to help (Ps 21:20, LXX). Ahearne-Kroll suggests that such a division of clothing indicates that his enemies already take him for dead.[46]

It may also be that the psalm's depiction of his enemies surrounding him and shaking their heads (ἐκίνησαν κεφαλήν) before ridiculing him (Ps 21:8-9, LXX) is echoed in Mark's depiction of Jesus's revilers (ἐβλασφήμουν αὐτὸν κινοῦντες τὰς κεφαλὰς αὐτῶν, 15:29). If so, however, the mockery comes with an important distinction. The psalmist is mocked for trusting in God, and taunted about the Lord not coming to rescue him (Ps 21:9, LXX). Jesus, however, is taunted with jeers that he attempt to act on his own behalf (Mark 15:31-32). This difference encapsulates the failure of the religious authorities in Mark to rightly apprehend the claims of Jesus: twice Jesus's claims to be or act as a uniquely authoritative agent of God have been met with charges of blasphemous adoption of divine prerogatives (2:7; 14:64). While they see Jesus making divine claims about himself, I have argued throughout this book that the reader sees Jesus claiming to be God's agent who has been empowered to so act. Here, too, they mistake the power of salvation: Jesus does not look to save himself, playing the role of God; instead, he has entrusted himself to God.[47] If Mark is alluding to Psalm 21:8, the shift he makes in the enemies' taunts provides another point of confirmation for the thesis of this project: Jesus is the messianic figure who has entrusted himself to God;

---

46. Ahearne-Kroll, *Psalms of Lament*, 200.

47. Against Ahearne-Kroll, *Psalms of Lament*, 203, who suggests that the taunting of Jesus also summons him to have God act on his behalf.

the religious leaders cannot see that Jesus is God's idealized human agent and so mistake his claims as usurpations of divinity. After receiving these taunts, Jesus's character redirects the reader's attention to the true hope for his salvation — the hope that has not materialized — when he utters the cry of dereliction.

The invocations of Psalm 21 confirm the notion that throughout the passion narrative Jesus plays the role of human messiah, the Davidic figure who suffers unjustly because God has not chosen to deliver him from his unjust oppressors.[48] In fact, the psalm entails God in the active agency of those who bring about the psalmist's suffering: "You lead me down into the dust of death" (21:16, LXX).[49] Ahearne-Kroll goes on to say, "Jesus embodies the suffering of David from Psalm 21 not to foreshadow Jesus's vindication at the resurrection, but to express the outrage of Jesus's suffering and God's abandonment in the midst of it."[50] And here we come face to face with what is perhaps the greatest challenge to any would-be divine Christology in Mark: how can it account for Jesus's words from the cross? The scene that develops over the course of chapters 14 and 15 is one in which Jesus is abandoned by God out of divine necessity. The perplexities with which the later Christian tradition has had to grapple as apparent contraindications of Jesus's divine ontology, including Jesus's will differing from the will of the father (14:36) and his being abandoned by God (15:34), are not inherently problematic within Mark's story for that same reason. In Mark, they are, as in the psalms of lament themselves, problematic moments because God is abandoning the righteous human king who has faithfully represented God's reign to the earth. However, they are fully consonant with Mark's idealized human Christology, in which the distinction between Jesus and God as characters in the story is never breached.

iv. Psalm 68:22 LXX: Vinegar to Drink

Psalm 68 LXX is the final song of the suffering righteous I consider here. It is a plea to God for deliverance. Consistent with other such psalms, it confronts God with God's absence in the face of persecution from the hands of

48. Matthew S. Rindge, "Reconfiguring the Akedah and Recasting God: Lament and Divine Abandonment in Mark," *JBL* 130 (2011): 755-74, argues persuasively that divine abandonment, not hope for future deliverance, is the accent sounded by Jesus's cry. This helps underscore the distinction between the characters of Jesus and God that pervade the Gospel.

49. Ahearne-Kroll, *Psalms of Lament*, 200.

50. Ahearne-Kroll, *Psalms of Lament*, 210.

the psalmist's enemies. The superscription affiliates this psalm with David, thus lending a royal overtone to its complaint, and making for an easy appropriation in a context of messianic suffering. The verse to which Mark makes possible allusion reads: "For my food they gave me gall, and for my thirst they gave me sour wine to drink" (ἐπότισάν με ὄξος, Ps 68:22, LXX). In the crucifixion story, this line is evoked after the cry of dereliction when someone fills a sponge with sour wine (ὄξους) and gives it to Jesus to drink (ἐπότιζεν αὐτόν, Mark 15:36).

The effect of the allusion is to once again co-inscribe the story of Jesus with the story of the suffering psalmist: he plays the part of a righteous king of Israel who has been left by God to be persecuted by his enemies. The psalm presents this as a problem that God must resolve, and plays a role in calling God to take such rectifying action.[51] For the purposes of my study, this is a final instance in which Mark demonstrates that Jesus's role is that of idealized human figure, which entails not only the wondrous acts of power on display in Mark 1–8, but also fidelity through suffering and death as predicted and enacted in Mark 8–16. Mark's Jesus is a separate character from God, and the crucifixion scene is an extensive meditation on God's absence from the human messiah, using the psalms of the righteous sufferer as an interpretive key.

v. Conclusion: Jesus's Lamentations in Mark

Despite the brevity of this sketch of the uses of lament psalms in Mark's passion narrative, the exegetical significance of my thesis begins to shine through. When we read Mark's Gospel as a story of an idealized human figure, it allows us to maintain the story's differentiation between the character of Jesus and the character of God in a consistent manner. The role that Mark assigns to Jesus from the lament psalms, including the powerlessness Jesus experiences in the face of the divine plan for his death as well as the betrayal expressed by Jesus in the cry of dereliction, is the role of the human agent whose case is being made to the God who is not playing the role of faithful deliverer. These passages are rich with Christological significance, and that Christological import is found in the depiction of Jesus filling the role of a suffering king of the Jews. Such a Christology might be nuanced in other important ways, such as Marcus's claims that the deployment of these psalms helps paint a picture of Jesus as the eschatological agent whose suffering both signals the near arrival of God's final intervention on behalf of God's people and the fate of those

---

51. Cf. Ahearne-Kroll, *Psalms of Lament*, 211-12.

people (including Mark's community) prior to their own final vindication.[52] Such nuances specify ways in which Jesus is the idealized human figure whose life functions decisively at the turn of the ages.

Additionally, these psalms come together to make the same point I argued with respect to the son of man: all depict an idealized agent of God who, paradoxically, is given over by God into the hands of God's and the agent's enemies. Mark's idea of a suffering messiah is reflected not only in the suffering of the Davidic figure of the psalms, but also in the suffering saints of the Most High who are then vindicated and given an eternal kingdom in Daniel 7. Such coherence lends further weight to the credibility of my thesis.

e. Isaiah 53: The Suffering Servant

In addition to a suffering son of humanity and a suffering righteous king, Mark's passion narrative (and its anticipations) also depict Jesus as a suffering servant, drawing on Isaiah 52:12–53:12. The language of being "handed over" (παραδίδωμι) is used three times in this Isaianic servant song (κύριος παρέδωκεν αὐτόν, "the Lord handed him over," 53:3; παρεδόθη εἰς θάνατον ἡ ψυχὴ αὐτοῦ . . . καὶ διὰ τὰς ἁμαρτίας αὐτῶν παρεδόθη, "his life was handed over to death . . . and on account of their sins he was handed over," 53:12).[53] This language permeates the passion narrative, and passion predictions, as well (Mark 9:31; 10:33; 14:10, 11, 18, 21, 41, 42, 44; 15:1, 10, 15). The silence of Jesus at his trials (14:61; 15:5), while not complete, appears to reflect the servant being silent like a lamb being led to the slaughter or before its shearers (Isa 53:7). Jesus's silence before Pilate leads to the latter's amazement (θαυμάζειν, Mark 15:5), which may well reflect the statement that "the nations will be greatly amazed at him" (θαυμάσονται ἔθνη πολλὰ ἐπ' αὐτῷ, Isa 52:15). Moreover, as Joel Marcus has suggested, the whole Barabbas incident (Mark 15:6-15) might be read as narrating the notion of substitution in which the servant bears the sins of others (Isa 53:6, 12).[54]

Such a list, while perhaps not exhaustive, is sufficient for the purposes of my argument.[55] In playing the role of the "suffering servant," one might argue

---

52. Marcus, *Way of the Lord*, 175-86.

53. Marcus, *Way of the Lord*, 187-88.

54. Marcus, *Way of the Lord*, 188. To this list one might add possible allusions to Isaiah 50:6, which mentions whipping, slapping, and spitting, elements that are picked up in Mark 10:34 and 14:65 (189).

55. For an extensive discussion of the possible influence of Isaiah 53 on Mark 10:45, see Watts, *Isaiah's New Exodus*, 257-87.

that Jesus is being depicted as the culmination of the line of prophets (cf. Mark 12:1-12), or perhaps the embodiment of Israel who is the servant of the Lord.[56] But consistent to the original context, Mark's narrative depicts Jesus as the one who is handed over, and completely identified with the people for whom his life is being given, and is never depicted as the Lord God who stands behind the transactions. Indeed, by embedding such allusions in a narrative that depicts Jesus wrestling vigorously with God against the plan that he is enacting on earth, Mark demonstrates in no uncertain terms that Jesus and God are separate characters.

To my knowledge, there is no significant scholarly argument to the effect that Mark's suffering servant is the embodiment of Isaiah's κύριος. The point I offer in this section, then, should be relatively uncontroversial. But it is no less significant for its broad acceptance because it adds a final piece to the puzzle of Mark's Christology. In this puzzle, Mark consistently depicts Jesus as God's idealized human agent on the earth. It is precisely this consistency in the clearest depictions of Jesus's identity that makes it unlikely that the nods or hints in the direction of divine Christology add the dimension of a preexistent or otherwise divine Christ. Indeed, what the passion narrative shows us in clearest terms is that the Jesus of Mark's story so fully embodies the person of the suffering Davidic king, and of the suffering servant, that he stands entirely on the human side of the divine-human divide, pleading to God for justice, accusing God of abandonment, and being left in the end with only the prophesied hope that the God who is truly Other will raise him from the dead.

B. MATTHEW

As we approach the relationship between Jesus, scripture, and Israel's God in Matthew's Gospel, we are once again treading territory whose borders we have already had occasion to cross. In discussing Jesus as "son of God," we had recourse to biblical precedents in titles for kings and in Isaac's relationship to Abraham. In exploring Jesus as "son of man," we looked to Daniel's vindicated Israel as the backdrop for Matthew's unique exposition of the figure as eschatological king and judge. While delving into Jesus's exercise of authority over all creation, Matthew's affiliation of healing with Jesus's Davidic sonship

---

56. Corporate dynamics of the servant songs might be picked up in the way that John the Baptist and Jesus's disciples are also entailed in being handed over (παραδίωμι; Mark 1:14; 13:9-12) (Marcus, *Way of the Lord*, 193-94).

commanded our attention. When discussing Matthew's birth narrative, we were immediately thrust into interpretation of Jesus's association with David, Abraham, and the Babylonian exile by way of Jesus's genealogy; and we were driven to explore the Christological significance of the virgin birth (Matt 1:18, 23-25; cf. Isa 7:14) and Jesus's birth in Bethlehem (Matt 2:4-6; cf. Mic 5:1-3) as they find explication in Matthew's fulfillment citations.

We thus approach the question of Jesus's relationship to Israel's scriptures and Israel's God with the following data securely in place. First, Matthew introduces his narrative with a genealogy that puts in the reader's hands a Christology in which Jesus is Davidic messiah, who will be offered up like Isaac was, in the time when God is fulfilling God's promise to restore Israel from its Babylonian exile. Second, this eschatological, royal, suffering messianism is consistently embodied in Matthew's son of God and son of man Christology, as each of these Christological facets appropriates important biblical precedents. Third, a preliminary exploration of some of Matthew's formula citations has indicated that through these uniquely Matthean quotations Jesus is cast in the roles of idealized human figures from Israel's scriptures ("Immanuel," a coming Davidic messiah, Israel itself) rather than the unmediated role of God. Fourth, Matthew parts ways with Mark by placing the notion of Jesus as Davidic messiah front and center, assigning such a role to Jesus in a manner consistent with the development of ideas around a "son of David" and, more explicitly, Solomon himself, in the post-exilic period. Thus, Richard Beaton can summarize Matthew's use of scripture as contributing "to Matthew's overall narrative strategy of demonstrating the continuity of God's purposes in the life and ministry of Jesus of Nazareth with the history of the Jewish people."[57] It now remains to be seen if other biblical citations in Matthew continue in this vein of offering readers a multiperspectival vision of Jesus playing the roles of idealized human figures from Israel's scriptures, or if there are glimpses of Jesus playing the role of Israel's God in such a fashion as to identify him as more than God's chosen agent on the earth.

1. FULFILLING THE LAW AND THE PROPHETS

The relationship of Jesus to Israel's scriptures as uniquely cast by Matthew is captured in the Sermon on the Mount when Jesus says, "Do not think that I

---

57. Richard Beaton, *Isaiah's Christ in Matthew's Gospel* (SNTSMS 123; New York: Cambridge University Press, 2002), 18.

have come to abolish the law or the prophets. I have not come to abolish but to fulfill [πληρῶσαι]" (5:17). The formula citations provide a glimpse into how Matthew envisions Jesus fulfilling the prophets and, I argue, Jesus's treatment of scripture in the Sermon on the Mount points toward how he fulfills the law. These two topics, then, will now command our attention, followed by a brief discussion of Jesus's statement that "all the prophets and the law prophesied until John" (11:13).

a. Fulfilling the Prophets: Fulfillment Citations

As mentioned previously, in turning to the fulfillment citations we are picking up threads of previous discussions. Isaiah's "Immanuel" prophecy and Hosea's retrospective "out of Egypt I have called my son" are deployed by Matthew in the fulfillment scheme that provides scriptural interpretation for the life of Jesus, in particular in the stories surrounding the birth narrative.[58] In these examples, Jesus's relationship to scripture lies clearly within the roles of the human agents who participate in Israel's divine drama. This pattern continues: the slaughter of the infants by Herod is said to fulfill Jeremiah 31:15 about Rachel's weeping (Matt 2:16-18). The movement of Jesus's family to Nazareth is said to fulfill the notion (for which no definite scriptural support has been found) of one being called a Nazarene (Matt 2:22-23). In Matthew 4:14 Jesus's relocation to Capernaum is said to fulfill Isaiah's declaration of light shining on those in darkness (Isa 9:1-2, Eng.; 8:23–9:1, MT, LXX).[59] Jesus's healing ministry is said to fulfill Isaiah 53:4, in which the servant "takes our weaknesses and heals our diseases" (Matt 8:17). A similar conjunction of an Isaianic servant song (Isa 42:1-4) and Jesus's healing ministry appears in Matthew 12:15-23.[60] In the following chapter, Jesus's speaking in parables is said to fulfill the words of the psalmist who so speaks (Matt 13:35; Ps 78:2). At the so-called triumphal entry, Matthew cites the text from Zechariah 9:9

---

58. Krister Stendahl, "Quis et Unde: An Analysis of Mt 1–2," in *Interpretation of Matthew* (ed. Graham Stanton; Edinburgh: T&T Clark, 1995), 69-80, tied the early formula citations into the overarching point of Matthew 1–2 as demonstrating who Jesus is and from whence he comes.

59. Cf. Beaton, *Isaiah's Christ*, 97-110, esp. 110, where he draws a conclusion that describes God working through Jesus as "spirit-endowed Messiah."

60. Beaton, *Isaiah's Christ*, 118, concludes that both citations of "servant" passages depict Jesus as one who "identifies with a broken humanity, offering healing and freedom." This is profoundly significant, Christologically, while representing a Christology that does not equate Jesus with God.

that anticipates the king riding on a donkey — even providing an additional colt to make sure that the passage is literally "fulfilled" (Matt 21:1-7). Finally, Judas's betrayal for thirty pieces of silver is said to fulfill the words of Zechariah 11:13 (Matt 27:9).

Throughout, Matthew's narrative appropriates the narrative contours of Israel's story. As I concluded in a previous study of these texts:

> The narrative perspective allows us to see that Jesus did not simply come to embody principles or fulfil prophetic predictions, but to take the story of Israel to himself. Thus, Jesus "fills" the words of the OT scriptures as an actor bringing a new interpretation to the role, and a new conclusion to the story. . . . Matthew is not necessarily looking for patterns of activity, but for moments in a plot that is unfolding for the second time, only now with a different player cast in the role of Israel. . . . Matthew is engaged in a program of intentional, creative reapplication of the OT to a person whom he believes to have breathed new life into the character of Israel.[61]

Recognizing that Jesus plays the role of Israel, rather than God as such, as he and the story unfolding around him embody the scriptural texts assigned through these fulfillment citations, provides us with a crucial piece of evidence for how Jesus is more broadly related to scriptural predecessors in Matthew.[62] Don Senior characterizes the formula quotations by saying, "The formula citations take their place within the full repertoire of how Matthew uses the Old Testament to underwrite the story of Jesus for his community and, at the same time, to provide his community with a new reading of their scriptures in light of the faith in Jesus's identity as the Messiah and Son of God."[63] Senior thus cautions against totalizing the force of this particular group of citations, while drawing attention to their important function as part of a larger whole. That

---

61. J. R. Daniel Kirk, "Conceptualising Fulfilment in Matthew," *TynBul* 59 (2008): 91, 93.

62. It seems to me that Hays's arguments to the contrary, to the effect that Jesus plays the roles of both God and Israel, lean far too much simply on the fact that in some of these passages God is also depicted as deliverer (*Reading Backwards,* 39-43). Surely this is the case — God rescues Israel. But methodologically Hays has offered no clues for how the Gospel reader should know that a different character (i.e., God) than the one directly invoked (such as Israel or Moses) is also playing a role that we should impute to Jesus, or why such an imputation would make Jesus the divine actor per se rather than the agent through whom God is at work.

63. Don Senior, "The Lure of the Formula Citations: Re-assessing Matthew's Use of the Old Testament with the Passion Narrative as a Test Case," in *Scriptures in the Gospels* (BETL 131; ed. Christopher M. Tuckett; Leuven: Leuven University Press, 1997), 89-115, here 115.

function, in turn, is thoroughly Christological. Scripture is reread in light of convictions about Jesus's identity. This is why Jesus's playing the roles of Israel and various representative human figures such as Isaiah's servant and Immanuel provide us with Christological content that is significant for the argument of this book. Jesus is fulfilling Israel's scriptures, not by filling at every turn roles that are the exclusive purview of God, but by filling those roles ascribed to significant human figures of Israel's past, present, or anticipated future. Moreover, since each citation is exclusive to Matthew, these citations provide a glimpse into the particular relationship between the scriptural precedents and the life of Jesus that typifies the First Gospel. In the formula citations, there is no beckoning of the reader to reimagine roles that had previously been reserved for God alone now being filled by Jesus.

b. Fulfilling the Law: The Sermon on the Mount

In the Sermon on the Mount (Matthew 5–7) Jesus inserts himself into the teaching act in a way that Matthew signals is nothing short of astonishing (7:28-29). The concluding pericopes place Jesus, and Jesus's teachings, at the cutting edge of the final judgment: Jesus is the judge to whom people appeal (7:21-22); his knowledge of a person is both salvific (7:23) and inseparable from someone's doing the will of God (7:21). Hearing Jesus's own words and doing them is likened to building a house with a strong foundation (7:24-25); in contrast, hearing Jesus's words and not doing them is likened to building a house on shifting sands (7:26-27). The Sermon on the Mount depicts a Jesus who is situating himself, his role in the story, and his teaching at a unique place in the life of the people of God. The achievement of the Sermon on the Mount is not simply to articulate a thoroughgoing ethics for the people of God, but to make a radical, centralizing claim for Jesus.[64]

The narrated postscript to the sermon indicates that Jesus's distinction lies in the manner (not, we might add, the unique moral content) of his teaching: he teaches as one having authority, something that Matthew contrasts with the scribes' manner of teaching (7:28-29).[65] Although we have no access to scribal teaching as such from the first century, it should be relatively uncontroversial to suggest that a defining marker of scribal knowledge and teaching was the

---

64. Cf. Robert Guelich, The Sermon on the Mount: A Foundation for Understanding (Dallas: Word, 1982), 27; Jack Dean Kingsbury, Matthew as Story (2nd rev. ed.; Minneapolis: Fortress, 1988), 64-65.

65. Cf. Dale C. Allison Jr., The Sermon on the Mount: Inspiring the Moral Imagination (New York: Herder and Herder, 1999), 7-8.

passing on of tradition (cf. Mark 7:3, 5; Josephus, *Ant.* 13.16.2; *m. Avot* 1:1-18). The point in the sermon where Jesus's manner of teaching most sharply, and we might say intentionally, contrasts with one in which traditions are passed along, is in the so-called antitheses (Matt 5:21-48). Here, Jesus contrasts his teaching with what has been spoken before ([ἠκούσατε ὅτι] ἐρρέθη, vv. 21, 27, 31, 33, 38, 43). Moreover, in these same passages we find the most obvious citations of scripture in the sermon. Jesus's own claims to authoritative utterance are captured in the recurring ἐγὼ δὲ λέγω (5:22, 28, 32, 34, 39, 44), ἀμὴν λέγω (5:18, 26; 6:2, 5, 26), and more simply, λέγω (5:20; 6:25, 29).[66] Christology and biblical citation are working hand in hand in the sermon, which purports to depict a Jesus who has come not to abolish the law, but to fulfill (Matt 5:17). Thus Robert Guelich concludes: "Above all else, the Sermon on the Mount makes a *christological* statement . . . the Sermon's christology corresponds to the Gospel's christology, which is primarily a 'fulfillment christology.'"[67]

Dale Allison suggests that the sermon is rightly interpreted against two particular biblical precedents. First, the beatitudes draw the reader to Isaiah 61, suggesting that Jesus is "Isaiah's eschatological prophet."[68] In particular, the blessing on those who mourn (Matt 5:4) echoes the mission of the servant as stated in Isaiah 61:2 that the one anointed with God's spirit will comfort all who mourn, and the blessing on the poor in spirit "is inspired by Isaiah 61:1."[69] Echoes of Isaiah 61 might continue with Jesus's admonition to "rejoice and be glad" (Matt 5:12), as the prophet had said, "My soul will rejoice in the Lord" (Isa 61:2).[70] The notion that Matthew's Jesus is understood in part through an Isaianic servant Christology is affirmed through Jesus's response to John the Baptist in 11:5, in which Jesus takes up Isaiah 61:1's declaration of the blind seeing and the poor having the good news preached to them in his description of his ministry (see also Matt 12:18-21).[71] The beatitudes' cohesion with Isaiah 61 suggests that one important prong of the Christology of the sermon, as that Christology ties Jesus to the scriptures of Israel, is the notion of Jesus as the Isaianic servant. From Isaiah 61, this would indicate that the authority resident in Jesus's proclamations comes from "the spirit of the Lord God" (Isa 61:1) that Jesus received at his baptism, a spiritual anointing that Isaiah 61 directly associates with being sent to "proclaim good news."

66. Cf. Allison, *Sermon on the Mount,* 24.
67. Guelich, *Sermon on the Mount,* 27 (italics original).
68. Allison, *Sermon on the Mount,* 15; Guelich, *Sermon on the Mount,* 27, 97-98, 117-18.
69. Allison, *Sermon on the Mount,* 15-16; Guelich, *Sermon on the Mount,* 71-72.
70. Allison, *Sermon on the Mount,* 16.
71. Allison, *Sermon on the Mount,* 16.

Second, the Sermon on the Mount fits within Matthew's unfolding Moses typology. Dale Allison has convincingly argued that the early chapters of Matthew, in particular, contain a thoroughgoing Moses typology.[72] The announcement of Jesus's birth, Herod's slaughter of the innocents, Jesus's own descent and ascent out of Egypt (including a citation of Hos 11:1, which refers to God's summoning of Israel out of that land), the baptism, and the forty days (cf. "years" for Israel) in the wilderness all echo either the biblical story of Moses or else traditions of interpretation that grew up around it.[73] Thus, when Jesus goes up the mountain and sits in the posture of a teacher before commencing the sermon, we are on firm ground to see Jesus playing the role of Moses on the mountain, giving a new (or "renewed") law to the people. Such a typology creates a strong presupposition in favor of the Christological conclusion Allison draws: "In Matthew's world, 'Moses said' was the equivalent of 'God said.' So to make Jesus one like Moses was a way of saying that, in similar fashion, Jesus's word is God's word. That is, the parallels with Moses are intended to exalt the authority of Jesus, to make him a dispenser of divine revelation."[74]

The unique authority in view, then, would not be that of the unmediated presence of God incarnate, providing a new formulation of the code of conduct required of God's people; instead, it would be the unique authority of another law-giving agent of God who speaks for God rather than simply participating in a stream of interpretation that reflects on the law once given.

Matthew moves immediately from Jesus's statement that he has come not to abolish the law and the prophets, but to fulfill (5:17), and admonition to a righteousness exceeding that of the scribes and Pharisees (5:20) into the so-called antitheses. The reader must thus interpret these statements as indications of continuity between Jesus and the law, while at the same time recognizing that Matthew's Jesus claims a unique place for himself as one who "fulfills" the law. Matthew's reader has already seen through the formula citations how Jesus fulfills the prophets in surprising ways.

The six "antitheses" do not, generally speaking, present antithetical content as Jesus lays his own teaching alongside what came before. Instead, his injunctions typically contain related, complementary, and expanded requirements. The "antithesis," if one exists, is between the law itself, or the tradition of its teaching, as the source of knowledge of God's commands, and Jesus as the arbiter of the divine will. Thus, the first antithesis cites the commandment

---

72. Dale C. Allison Jr., *The New Moses: A Matthean Typology* (Minneapolis: Fortress, 1993).

73. Allison, *Sermon on the Mount*, 17-18.

74. Allison, *Sermon on the Mount*, 19.

"spoken to the ancients" (ἐρρέθη τοῖς ἀρχαίοις) in the Decalogue, "You shall not kill" (Matt 5:21; cf. Exod 20:13; Deut 5:17). Jesus's own command (ἐγὼ δὲ λέγω) warns against anger and demands an active posture of reconciliation toward an estranged sister or brother (Matt 5:22-24). Jesus's injunctions, if obeyed, will see to it that the original command is kept, but more than this it addresses both internal causes of strife and demands that his followers live in a reconciled community. Thus, there is an affirmation of (the goal of) the original command even while the listeners are met with substantively new directives for life together as the people of God. Precisely the same pattern is at work in the second antithesis, where Jesus ups the ante against adultery by prohibiting a lustful look and demands the casting away of offending members of the body (5:27-32). Once again, the original commandment is preserved, and yet Jesus's own word demands a preservation of purity that exceeds what is written.

A general theme of intensification carries through the next four antitheses, even if the precise relationship between the thing that was said (ἐρρέθη) and Jesus's command is not the same throughout. From regulation of how a divorce must occur, Jesus intensifies the implications of divorce and remarriage (5:31-32). Jesus elevates all speech to the level of oath making, such that no special oaths should be or need be taken because every "Yes" or "No" bears the same weight (5:33-37).

Jesus invokes the *lex talionis* only to suggest that the whole notion of a just and fair recompense for wrongs is insufficient for his followers, who should offer more of themselves to those who would take from them or harm them, rather than seeking recompense for themselves from those who do them wrong (5:38-42). Once again, the original law would not be broken, and indeed would be very much preserved, under the regime that Jesus commends, and yet Jesus demands an active, positive engagement toward the neighbor that is not deducible from the commandment itself. In a similar move, and perhaps one that explicates Jesus's reworking of the notion of recompense and revenge, Jesus demands love of not only the neighbor who is defined by kinship and friendship, but also the enemy (5:43-48). The definition of "neighbor" is so expanded as to include enemies, calling for a transformed community that looks more like the God who causes the sun to shine and the rain to fall upon the just and the unjust alike (5:45). Although the command in Leviticus 19:18 to not take vengeance on fellow countrymen (בני עמך) would not be broken by someone keeping Jesus's command, the transformation of those to whom it applies creates a new demand for those who accept Jesus's way of fidelity to God.

The antitheses parallel the formula citations in this respect: in their content they provide new, often unpredictable significance for the biblical passage cited.[75] The biblical predecessor, like a container of meaning, perhaps maintains its shape, but it is filled with new substance. In each instance, the use to which Matthew puts the text is not available to any reader who picks up the verse in question. Instead, there is a genuinely new reading of, and significance to, the text in question as Jesus "fulfills" it, or, perhaps better said, "fills it" with new meaning. Thus, the upshot of the antitheses, as with the formula citations, is to shift the focus from the scriptural precedents themselves to Jesus, the lawgiver through whom they come to the disciples. "It is not the Mosaic law in and of itself that has normative and abiding character for disciples, but the Mosaic law as it has passed through the crucible of Jesus's teaching."[76]

What, then, are the Christological implications for such a refracting of Israel's legal tradition? Jesus is placing himself in a position of final authority as the one who can instruct the people of God. Through the thoroughgoing contrast between "what was said" and his own word, particularly when "what was said" is most often commandments that would have been associated with Moses, Jesus sets himself up as more than an interpreter of the Mosaic tradition. He assumes the role of Moses himself. Such a claim answers both the thoroughgoing Moses typology of which the Sermon on the Mount is a part, and the astonishment of the people who recognize that Jesus teaches as one who has authority rather than as one who participates in a stream of commentary. The authority is, of course, divine authority; however, it is divine authority that, within the story of Matthew, is mediated through the person of Jesus as he plays the role of new Moses. Thus, Guelich's framing of Matthew's Christology as "fulfillment Christology" is apt, even if it leaves us asking the further question, "What does 'fulfillment' mean for Matthew?"[77]

The answer to this question, as we have seen, is that Jesus simultaneously fills up and transforms the biblical texts, providing them with new substance and content based on his life and teaching. Such transformations are salvific (Isa 7:14 in Matt 1:18-25), Christological (Mic 5:2 in Matt 2:2-6, though here the transformation is not so great), Israelite (Hos 11:1 in Matt 2:13-15), Mosaic (the antitheses in Matthew 5), and servant-like (Isa 42:1-4 in Matt 12:23). Throughout, Jesus fulfills, either directly or indirectly, by playing the role of an idealized human figure through whom God is climactically at work in the world. There

75. See Kirk, "Conceptualising."
76. Kingsbury, *Matthew as Story*, 65.
77. Guelich, *Sermon on the Mount*, 27.

is a Christological question with which the reader of Matthew's biblical citations, and the Sermon on the Mount in particular, is confronted. Its answer is not a divine Christology, but a multifaceted, high human Christology. In the Sermon on the Mount, the particular high, human Christology in view is one in which Jesus recapitulates the role of the servant of Isaiah 61 and of Moses, who gave the law that he received directly from God.

c. The Law and the Prophets Are until John

One underlying assumption in Matthew's program is that Jesus fulfills because his ministry represents the beginnings of the eschatological in-breaking of the kingdom of God. This eschatological dynamic helps account for the peculiar ways Matthew uses scripture, inasmuch as his assumption about how the story is in the process of resolving enables him to reread, and reimagine, the prophets. In addition, the notion of God's kingdom coming down from heaven to earth opens the ethical playing field for the heightened injunctions we find in the reread law of the Sermon on the Mount. The significance of eschatology for Matthew's understanding of the law and the prophets comes clearly to the fore in Matthew 11:13 — a passage that not only upholds the general conclusions reached thus far in the current chapter, but that ties together Christological threads we discussed in previous chapters as well. Thus, this final step in my investigation of Matthew's use of "the law and the prophets" will demonstrate that the Christology entailed in Matthew's discussion of law and prophets coheres with the idealized human paradigm that has accounted for his Christology to this point.

Matthew 11:13 reads: "For all the prophets and the law were prophesying until John" (πάντες γὰρ οἱ προφῆται καὶ ὁ νόμος ἕως Ἰωάννου ἐπροφήτευσαν). The first thing to notice is the peculiar assertion that not only the prophets but also the law were prophesying. This signals that Matthew's view of the law is diachronic, pointing to something beyond itself (cf. Paul's similar claim in Rom 3:21). This confirms the perhaps unstated assumption in the previous section, that Matthew's notion of "fulfillment of the law" is not to be understood as "doing everything that the law says," but as a moment of eschatological realization and transformation. The transition point in the story of both the law and the prophets is the time immediately after John the Baptist.

John marks the transition point between the time of anticipation or prophecy and the time of the forcibly advancing kingdom (11:12).[78] The time of the

---

78. See. D. A. Carson, "Do the Prophets and the Law Quit Prophesying before John? A

forcibly advancing kingdom, then, is one way of articulating what the prophets and the law anticipated. This leaves us with the question of what light this passage might shed on the Christological significance of Jesus's statement about the arrival of the age of fulfillment. The broader context of chapter 11 provides us with a few answers.

First, John hears of "the deeds of the Christ" and asks if Jesus is the coming one, or if another should be expected (11:2-3).[79] Jesus responds with a pastiche of allusions to Isaiah: the blind see, the deaf hear, the dead are raised, the poor have the good news preached to them, and those who do not take offense at Jesus are blessed (11:5-6). The conjunction of restored sight and hearing, together with the celebration of the poor, echoes the restoration of Israel prophesied in Isaiah 29:18-19. The amalgam of blind receiving sight, deaf hearing, and lame legs being restored is anticipated in Isaiah 35:5-6, while the resurrection of the dead alludes to Isaiah 26:19. Perhaps more importantly, especially in light of the allusions to Isaiah 61 in the beatitudes, Isaiah 61:1 LXX speaks of both the poor having the gospel preached to them and the blind receiving sight in addition to anticipations of healing and release. If Isaiah 26:19; 29:18-19; and 35:5-6 signal significant metaphors for understanding God's restoration of Israel, Isaiah 61 provides an indication of the means: the spirit of God anoints the servant of God both to proclaim God's favor and to enact it through these deeds of restoration. Thus the first important indication about the Christology of the long-awaited age is that Jesus is the fulfillment of Isaiah's servant.[80]

Inasmuch as our concern is the conjunction of biblical interpretation and Christology, one particular observation by Davies and Allison merits our attention. They suggest, "the verse contains more than a list of miracles: it also supplies a hermeneutical suggestion. Jesus' language directs one to Isaiah and is therefore an invitation to put Jesus' ministry and Isaiah's oracles side by side. Are not the promises of salvation being fulfilled? Is not eschatology in the process of being realized?"[81] The biblical allusions, combined as they are and deployed within Matthew's Gospel, suggest that the "expected one" is

---

Note on Matthew 11:13," in *The Gospels and the Scriptures of Israel* (JSNTSup 104/SSEJC 3; ed. C. A. Evans and W. R. Stegner; Sheffield: Sheffield Academic, 1994), 179-94.

79. W. D. Davies and Dale C. Allison Jr., *A Critical and Exegetical Commentary on the Gospel according to Saint Matthew* (3 vols.; ICC; Edinburgh: T&T Clark, 1991), 2:240, highlight "deeds of the Christ" as a key phrase, demonstrating that its presence helps show the reader that the words and deeds of Jesus are messianic.

80. So also Davies and Allison, *Matthew*, 2:242-43.

81. Davies and Allison, *Matthew*, 2:243.

an idealized human figure, in fulfillment of Isaianic expectation, and not an unmediated visitation by God.

The second clue to the identity of Jesus in respect to the eschatological change of which John is harbinger is found in Jesus's giving voice to the blended citation of Exodus 23:20 and Malachi 3:1 (discussed above in reference to Mark 1:2-4): "Behold, I send my messenger before your face, who will prepare your way before you" (ἰδοὺ ἐγὼ ἀποστέλλω τὸν ἀγγελόν μου πρὸ προσώπου σου, ὃς κατασκευάσει τὴν ὁδόν σου ἔμπροσθέν σου, Matt 11:10). Jesus says that John is this messenger (11:10). Here, Matthew and Luke (7:27) agree against Mark by citing these verses separately from Isaiah 40:3 and in the broader context of discussing John's ministry in the wake of John's query about Jesus. Importantly, however, all three Gospels maintain the change in pronouns from Malachi 3:1, such that the messenger who is spoken of in the third person prepares the way for some unnamed person who is addressed in the second person (πρὸ προσώπου σου), rather than following Malachi 3:1 in which the first-person pronoun is used to indicate that the messenger prepares the way for God (πρὸ προσώπου μου). At this turning of the ages from the time of prophecy to the time of fulfillment, Jesus does come along to play the role of God, in one sense, as he follows the preparatory work of Elijah (cf. 11:14).[82] However, he does so not as God himself, but rather as one who is other than God, such that the divine voice addresses him as "you." To this we should add as well that the first portion of the citation comes from a word spoken to Israel in the wilderness, making the second-person referent the people of God as a whole.

Thus, the application of these biblical texts to Jesus does not invite the reader into a singular understanding of the natures of Jesus and God, but into a recognition that Jesus is the agent of God who brings about the time of fulfillment that God's agent John had anticipated. John was the messenger who prepared for this coming kingdom; Jesus is the one through whom the new kingdom begins to make itself known here and now. As Jesus will go on to claim in the following chapter, if he does mighty acts of power by the spirit of God, then the kingdom of God has come upon his hearers (Matt 12:28). Jesus's relationship to the biblical text fits well within the paradigm in which he is one who comes as God's agent of fulfillment.

Third, Jesus highlights his relationship with John the Baptist, and his own life in the era of fulfillment, by contrasting John's manner of life and the reception it received with his own. The fasting John is accused of being possessed by

---

82. Cf. Davies and Allison, *Matthew*, 2:250.

a demon; the "son of man" eats and drinks and is accused of gluttony, drunkenness, and befriending tax collectors and sinners (11:18-19). This returns us to the nature of Jesus's identity as son of man, and so I refer the reader back to that prior discussion. The important point to underscore now is that study of Matthew's depiction of Jesus's relationship to the scriptures of Israel does not create an isolated set of Christological motifs, but brings us in contact with other significant perspectives on the identity of Jesus. There is a consistency amid the diversity, as Matthew offers numerous avenues to travel for understanding the human figure who represents God as God's specially authorized agent for healing, teaching, ruling, suffering, and saving.

2. GATHERING AND SCATTERING

a. Sheep Receive Their Shepherds

Given Matthew's heightened emphasis on Jesus as Davidic messiah in comparison to Mark, the former's appropriation of ὡς[εἰ] πρόβατα μὴ ἔχοντα ποιμένα (Num 27:17; 1 Kgs 22:17; cf. Mark 6:34, discussed above) is somewhat surprising. Whereas Mark deploys the verse to introduce Jesus as shepherd-teacher (as discussed above), Matthew so situates the verse that it redounds to the disciples. In Matthew 9:36–10:1 the disciples are swept up into the eschatological drama unfolding in the ministry of Jesus, with the result that the biblical allusion finds its resolution in Jesus's followers.

As in Mark, the description of people resembling shepherdless sheep is Jesus's own assessment of them. In the case of Matthew, this statement comes after a summary statement about Jesus's preaching and teaching ministry (9:35). His compassion (ἐσπλαγχνίσθη, 9:36; cf. Mark 6:34) is stirred upon seeing their "harassed and helpless" state (NRSV). As in Mark, the "fulfillment" of the verse toward which the passage finally points is less about the people's state matching that of their biblical forebears and more about Jesus's response to alleviate the situation.

Jesus addresses his disciples using harvest imagery, imagery that, in reference to the gathering of people, is fairly interpreted as carrying eschatological connotations: the harvest is plentiful but the workers are few (Matt 9:37; cf. 3:12; 13:30, 39).[83] We can thus recognize that Matthew's employment of scripture in this passage falls within the same general eschatological framework

---

83. So also Davies and Allison, Matthew, 2:148-49.

as what we have seen from his work so far. As Jesus shifts the metaphor from shepherding to harvest, he expands the people's need from a singular overseer to a multitude of gatherers (οἱ ἐργάται ὀλίγοι, 9:37). In response to this, Jesus involves the disciples in two ways. First, he commands them to "implore the Lord of the harvest so that he will send workers" (δεήθητε οὖν τοῦ κυρίου τοῦ θερισμοῦ ὅπως ἐκβάλῃ ἐργάτας, 9:38). In the invocation of God itself, the disciples participate in addressing the problem of the shepherdless sheep. Second, as this passage immediately flows into the authorizing, empowering, and sending of the twelve apostles (esp. 10:1-5), the reader recognizes that the disciples are the answer to their own prayer. The disciples are empowered as gathering agents of the eschatological harvest.

The way in which the disciples are empowered demonstrates that even the sending out of the twelve is fraught with Christological significance. Jesus himself bestows authority over unclean spirits and for healing every sickness and weakness (10:1) — these latter words echoing the summary of Jesus's ministry from 9:35.[84] Their work as "harvesters" is an extension of Jesus's own work.[85] Such an idea is cemented in the final pericope of the mission discourse in chapter 10, when Jesus says, "Whoever receives you receives me, and whoever receives me receives the one who sent me" (10:40). In the schema I have been developing in this book, Jesus is a man who has been given authority by God to represent God's reign to the world, a reign expressed in authority over spirits and bodies among others. The citation of Numbers 27:17 or 1 Kings 22:17 provides an opportunity for Matthew to signal how God is resolving the problem of a shepherdless people. Matthew is not reticent to apply shepherding imagery to Jesus (cf. 25:32; 26:31),[86] and yet here Jesus shepherds not by taking direct oversight of the mission, but by sending coworkers to aid him in his task. The fulfillment of God's response to the problem of shepherdless people comes as Jesus's ministry is extended through other authorized human agents.

b. Eschatological Divisions

In a manner akin to the final sets of sayings in the Sermon on the Mount, the concluding sections of the mission discourse in Matthew 10 focus on Jesus as the agent who determines a person's eschatological destiny. It "makes Jesus and his proclamation the deciding factors in the coming judgment. . . . Jesus

---

84. So also Davies and Allison, *Matthew,* 2:152-53.
85. Cf. Davies and Allison, *Matthew,* 2:146.
86. Cf. Davies and Allison, *Matthew,* 2:147-48.

is thus not just a revealer but the focus of God's eschatological saving action and the criterion of judgment."[87] First, in Matthew 10:32-33 Jesus states that a person's confession or denial of him before people here on earth will correlate with Jesus's confession or denial of that person before his father in heaven. Thus, Jesus is the agent whose word determines a person's standing before God. In all likelihood, this is an indication of eschatological differentiation among humanity.[88] In the subsequent verses we find Jesus echoing Micah 7:6 as he corrects the notion that he came to cast peace on the earth (Matt 10:34-35). Instead, Jesus says he brings a "sword," a remark he interprets by saying, "For I have come to divide a person against his father and a daughter against her mother and a daughter-in-law against her mother-in-law, and the enemies of a person will be his own household."

The divided house occurs in Micah 7 as part of the prophet's lament. The betrayals by the members of the household come as part of a series of illustrations of the wicked dissolution of society, demonstrating the untrustworthiness of even those whom one might assume to be the most faithful. In contrast, the prophet claims to exercise trust in God for salvation. In early Judaism, the text was interpreted to refer to the eschatological tribulation.[89] Matthew's deployment of the verse shifts the connotations in a somewhat different direction. Here, too, the familial divisions are markers of the faithlessness of some; however, the significant caveat is that fidelity to Jesus itself is the cause of division. In the immediately following verse, Jesus picks up the language of father, mother, (son), and daughter from the Micah citation, claiming that familial love must not exceed love for Jesus: "The one who loves father or mother more than me is not worthy of me; and the one who loves son or daughter more than me is not worthy of me." The prophetic denunciation of the divided house becomes, in Jesus's mouth, a call to a divided house — one in which loyalty to Jesus exceeds love of family.[90]

This is not the first time that Matthew's readers have seen Jesus elevate his own place in a person's life above the strictures of familial obligation. In chapter 8 Jesus rebuffs two potential followers (vv. 18-22). The second of these asks for permission to first bury his father. Jesus replies, "Follow me and leave the dead to bury their own dead" (v. 22). Significantly, these scenes come immediately after a formula citation in which Jesus's healing is said to

87. Davies and Allison, *Matthew*, 2:215.
88. Cf. Davies and Allison, *Matthew*, 2:213.
89. Davies and Allison, *Matthew*, 2:219-220.
90. Davies and Allison, *Matthew*, 2:217.

fulfill the servant song of Isaiah 53 (Matt 8:16-17; cf. Isa 53:4). In this passage, the Christology in which Matthew's Jesus takes precedence over filial piety is a servant Christology.

In Matthew 10 a servant Christology is not so squarely at the fore; however, a suffering messiah Christology is. The series of sayings about who is not worthy of Jesus, begun in verse 37 with repetition of the language of father, mother, and daughter from the Malachi allusion, continues with Jesus's warning about not being willing to suffer and die as his follower: "And the one who does not take his cross and follow behind me is not worthy of me. The one who finds his life will lose it, and the one who loses his life for my sake will find it" (10:38-39). The anticipation of Jesus's crucifixion shapes the content of Jesus's call to discipleship. With the in-breaking of the kingdom of God, fidelity to the way of salvation brokers no compromise. In the Gospel narrative, the way of salvation is the way of Jesus, which is ultimately the way of the cross. The Christology reflected in Matthew's appropriation of Micah 7:6 is a "Christology" in the strong sense of the word: it shows the conviction that Matthew sees Jesus as the eschatological agent of God, commitment to or rejection of whom carries eternal consequences. This Christology is given some further shape by the summons to follow Jesus on the way of the cross, a call that makes clear that Jesus is in view as one who has a peculiar vocation that defines the lives of his followers as well.

Jesus's claim to have authoritative representation before God, and a determining role in eternal matters, is a strong claim to occupy a seat of unique authority in the kingdom of God that he proclaims and enacts. However, it is not inherently a claim to divinity. The notion that humans might serve as proxies for God not only has scriptural precedent (e.g., 1 Sam 8:7; cf. chap. 2 above), it is also a role that Jesus extends to his disciples in the subsequent pericope (Matt 10:40-42).

While there is no clear Christological conclusion intimated in the use of Malachi 7:6, at least in terms of Jesus as a divine or idealized human figure, we do learn that a significant component to Jesus's ministry of division is the totalizing call to follow him on his journey to death. Moreover, we learn that other humans, the disciples, extend the ministry of division by bearing in themselves the same sort of representation that Jesus bears: those who receive the disciples receive both Jesus and the father; anyone who honors God's prophets receives a prophet's reward; anyone who treats "one of the least of these" with kindness in the name of a disciple (not Jesus himself) will have a reward. The notion that Jesus signals a time of eschatological fulfillment, and himself participates in the events surrounding the eschatological assize such as gathering and judgment, both coheres with what we have seen thus far in Matthew's use of Israel's scriptures and reaffirms that an idealized human Christology suffices to explain such roles.

3. SIGNS

a. Greater Than Jonah and Solomon

Matthew 12:38-42 contains sayings of Jesus that I addressed briefly in my discussions of Jesus as son of humanity. In these, Jesus says that Jonah is the only "sign" (σημεῖον) that will be given to this generation, a generation that will be condemned by both the men of Nineveh and the queen of the South due to its failure to respond to the something greater than either Jonah or Solomon.

The "sign of Jonah" commands our attention first. Jesus says that the only sign given will be "the sign of Jonah the prophet" (τὸ σημεῖον Ἰωνᾶ τοῦ προφήτου, 12:39). The designation of Jonah as a "prophet" here is significant. For the reader of Matthew, it recalls Jesus's claim in 5:17 that he has come not to abolish the prophets, but to fulfill. We have already seen that "fulfillment" is something Jesus accomplishes as he and the story unfolding around him enact and transform key moments in the human side of Israel's divine-human drama. The same dynamic is at work as Matthew first applies the Jonah story to Jesus.[91] Citing Jonah 2:1 LXX, Jesus says, "For just as Jonah was in the belly of the sea monster three days and three nights, thus the son of humanity will be in the heart of the earth three days and three nights" (Matt 12:40). What was for Jonah a metaphorical death, or near-death, and deliverance (Jon 2:5-7) will be fulfilled in Jesus's literal death and resurrection. Not only does Jesus claim for himself the role of the human prophet (as opposed to God) from this story, he does so for the purpose of anticipating his death — an experience that does not apply to God. In each of these ways, this first association with Jonah confirms what we found in other son of humanity sayings: Jesus is claiming the role of an idealized human figure rather than a preexistent divinity.

The next two claims Jesus makes could easily fit a divine Christology; however, they can equally well fit an idealized human Christology, and so the decision as to what, in fact, they ramify will largely depend on what a reader

---

91. Although the notion of Jonah being a sign is also present in Luke 11:30-32, Luke does not include Jonah's three days and three nights, nor does he otherwise include a passion-resurrection prediction.

takes from elsewhere to understand Matthew's Jesus. In the cases of both Jonah and Solomon, divinely empowered speech drew appropriate recognition from Gentiles: the Ninevites repented; the queen of the South came to hear wisdom (Matt 12:41-42). And so, Jesus says, these others will rise up in the final judgment against this generation and condemn it because something greater than Jonah and greater than Solomon is here. Interestingly, both Matthew and Luke contain the neuter πλεῖον to refer to the greater thing, rather than the masculine form that we might expect for a self-reference. Davies and Allison point out that for the reader of Matthew such a neuter self-reference for something "greater" has already been used in 12:6 as Jesus refers to himself as greater than the temple.[92] In 12:41 the reference to Jonah's preaching (τὸ κήρυγμα) has suggested itself to some as a possible solution: a greater preaching is present with the person of Jesus.[93] This latter suggestion carries some weight, given that κήρυγμα is the nearest preceding neuter noun and that Jesus specifically identifies Jonah as a prophet. Whether one opts for an oblique, yet direct self-reference, or a more circuitous self-reference by way of "preaching" or the kingdom of God, Matthew's Jesus and his ministry claim a greater place than the heroes of old whose divine endowments were recognized even by the far-off Gentiles.[94]

In itself, then, this passage does not provide much specificity in terms of the Christology of Matthew's Gospel. In relation to the biblical predecessors, Jesus is somehow greater. Specifically, we do learn that Jesus will literalize the death and deliverance from death experienced by Jonah. Other indications of how Jesus is greater are more nebulous. However, without in any way minimizing the diversity of specific hermeneutical methodologies Matthew employs, there is a measure of consistency. For all that the Matthean narrative transforms the scriptural antecedents, as Jesus does here with the Jonah story, the role played never shifts in what we might call an "incarnational" direction. God does not play the role of the human actor, and the human actor takes up the divine

92. Davies and Allison, *Matthew,* 2:358.

93. Reginald H. Fuller, *The Mission and Achievement of Jesus: An Examination of the Presuppositions of New Testament Theology* (London: SCM, 1954), 34-35.

94. Focusing on the version of this couplet of sayings in Luke, Anthony LeDonne, "Greater Than Solomon: Orality, Mnemonics, and Scriptural Narrativization in Luke," in *Biblical Interpretation in Early Christian Gospels,* vol. 3, *The Gospel of Luke* (LNTS 376/SSEJC 16; ed. Thomas R. Hatina; London: T&T Clark, 2010), 96-113, reaches similar conclusions about the way in which the form of the sayings in the Gospels would draw attention to Jesus, reinforcing "the importance of Jesus' ministry and identity, that of a preacher for repentance and the kingdom of God" (112).

role only as specially authorized and empowered representative. Such a role
suffices to explain Jesus's claim here. He is greater as the one whose presence
signals the greater age of the kingdom of God, to which all until John the
Baptist could only testify, about which they could only prophesy (Matt 11:11-15;
cf. discussion above).

b. Isaiah the Prophet

In Matthew's parable chapter (chap. 13), he expands on Mark's allusion to
Isaiah 6:9, indicating that his mysterious parables make his audience the fulfillment of the Isaianic mission to confirm the blindness and deafness of Israel.
Introducing the citation, Jesus says that his speaking in parables is an expression of the economy of the kingdom in which those who have will receive more
and those who do not have will have what is theirs taken away from them (vv.
11-13). Whereas Mark's deployment of the passage and its themes makes Jesus's
own words causative of the impairments (ἵνα, Mark 4:12), Matthew's editing
makes Jesus's ministry demonstrative of the impairments that are already present (ὅτι βλέποντες οὐ βλέπουσιν, Matt 13:13).[95] Jesus, then, plays a somewhat
different role in Matthew than in Mark, disclosing the state of the people who
are "dull of heart" (12:15) rather than inducing it.

Subsequent to the lengthy citation, Jesus pronounces a blessing on his disciples for having eyes that see and ears that hear. Their ability to see is not
simply an existential status, however, but is tied to recognition of what God
is doing in Jesus in that particular, eschatological moment.[96] Thus Jesus goes
on: "many prophets and righteous people desired to see what you see and did
not see, and to hear what you hear, and did not hear" (πολλοὶ προφῆται καὶ
δίκαιοι ἐπεθύμησαν ἰδεῖν ἃ βλέπετε καὶ οὐκ εἶδαν, καὶ ἀκοῦσαι ἃ ἀκούετε καὶ
οὐκ ἤκουσαν, 13:17). This builds on the earlier indications that the prophets
in particular have their telos in Jesus and the events around his ministry. As
Davies and Allison state about this verse, "It is an important witness to the fact
that he believed the powers of the eschatological age to be already present and
accessible to human experience."[97]

Matthew's shaping of this particular prophecy, and of the context within
which it is contained, provide further confirmation that Jesus's ministry draws
to itself the scriptures of Israel due to its nature as the eschatological arrival

95. So also Davies and Allison, *Matthew,* 2:392.
96. Cf. Davies and Allison, *Matthew,* 2:389-90, 394.
97. Davies and Allison, *Matthew,* 2:394.

of the sovereign rule of God. Jesus's part in the fulfillment, in this instance, is somewhat akin to that of Isaiah, as he stands in the place of the prophet whose ministry discloses the apostasy of the people. As eschatological agent, however, his own actions form the substance of what the people are incapable of seeing and hearing.

4. CONCLUSION: MATTHEW'S STORY OF FULFILLMENT

Matthew's biblical citations supply a crucial component to the Gospel's overall story, and to its Christology in particular. Jesus himself is the agent of ful- fillment of both law and prophets. Consistently, this agency is accomplished from below, as Jesus inaugurates the eschatological in-breaking of the reign of God, and brings about anticipations of its final realization. The Christological signals contained in intertextual references and allusions point in the same direction as the previously studied indicators: Jesus is an idealized, specially authorized and empowered, human agent of God's coming kingdom. The par- adigm on offer provides sufficient explanatory power to account for Matthew's biblical citations.

C. LUKE

1. LUKE'S HERMENEUTICAL KEY: THE SUFFERING AND GLORIFIED CHRIST

The Third Evangelist provides two of the most direct statements we have in the Synoptic Gospels about Jesus's relationship to the scriptures of Israel. Twice in his resurrection narratives Jesus confronts dejected disciples with a statement about the scriptural mandate for the messiah's ministry. The expositions given by the resurrected Christ do not invite the reader to understand Jesus as the manifestation of Israel's God, but instead point to the necessity of his death and resurrection.

Jesus's encounter with two men on the road to Emmaus provides the con- text for his first exposition of scripture (24:13-35). These two traveling com- panions are downcast, having hoped that the prophet (προφήτης, v. 19) Jesus, killed at the behest of the Jewish leadership, was going to be the one to redeem Israel (vv. 19-21). Moreover, they are befuddled about reports of an empty tomb and angels saying that he is alive (vv. 23-24). For these two traveling companions, the event of Jesus's death has functioned decisively as a contra-indication to their hopes that Jesus would redeem Israel. This is precisely the misapprehension that Jesus's exposition will seek to correct.

The report of Jesus's response provides one basic rubric for understanding Jesus's relationship to the scriptures of Israel as Luke understands it. "And he said to them, 'O foolish ones and hard of heart to believe upon all that the prophets have said. Were not these things necessary, that the Christ would suffer and enter into his glory?' And beginning from Moses and from all the prophets he interpreted for them, in all the scriptures, the things concerning himself" (vv. 25-27). Jesus's words here are directed at the specific concerns that are weighing on Cleopas and his traveling companion: the event of Jesus's death and the report of his missing body and resurrection. The content of his exposition is that the messiah had to suffer and enter into his glory, the former corresponding with their concern about Jesus's death, the latter corresponding to their befuddlement about the empty tomb report. Twice Luke uses the word πᾶς to indicate the pervasiveness of the biblical content Jesus is expounding: the travelers do not believe all (πᾶσιν) that the prophets have spoken (v. 25), and Jesus interprets for them "in all [πάσαις] the scriptures" the things about himself. When Luke wants to epitomize the way in which Jesus and the scriptures relate, it is their anticipation of his death and resurrection that comes into view. Due to the contrary arguments recently offered by Richard Hays (discussed below), this cannot be emphasized strongly enough: Luke tells the reader the content of Jesus's scriptural exposition, and it pertains to occurrences in the life of Jesus, not a divine identity.[98]

The immediately following story is much to the same effect. Jesus appears to the eleven, along with Cleopas and his traveling companion, and correlates what has happened in the past three days, the prophecies of scripture, and Jesus's own teaching prior to his death. Once again, Luke uses the word πᾶς to underscore the pervasiveness of the claim Jesus makes: "It is necessary that all [πάντα] things written about me in the law of Moses and the prophets and psalms be fulfilled" (24:44). This tripartite division of scripture (law, prophets, psalms) is likely an alternative way of saying "all the scriptures" (v. 27). Verse 44 also provides a rare case in which Luke says that scripture has been fulfilled (δεῖ πληρωθῆναι; cf. 4:21). Once again, the reader is given no direct exposition of biblical texts, but is privy to what Jesus says should be found through such an exercise: "Thus it is written that the Christ suffer and rise from the dead the third day, and that repentance for forgiveness of sins be proclaimed in

98. Hays, *Reading Backwards,* 56-57.

his name to all nations beginning from Jerusalem" (24:46-47). Looking back to the preceding Gospel narrative, it is Jesus as crucified and raised who is anticipated by scripture; looking forward to the story of Acts, it is the mission to the Gentiles that scripture predicts.

Richard Hays looks to the passage containing this clear program, articulated by Jesus, to legitimate his Christological reading of Luke. However, this material actually provides the strongest direct evidence against Hays's thesis that Luke summons the reader to recognize Jesus as divine. Hays begins by rightly suggesting that the statement that things throughout the scriptures concern Jesus issues an invitation of sorts for the reader to go back and rediscover in both Luke's Gospel and "Moses and all the prophets" the truth concerning Jesus.[99] However, he follows this with a paragraph in which he baldly asserts that such an invitation impugns New Testament scholars who find lacking in Luke preexistence, incarnation, or Jesus's identity with God.[100] But such an assertion, along with its accusation that those who so read the Gospel stand in the place of the ignorant Emmaus travelers, can stand only so long as the actual content of Jesus's words is ignored. For not only does Jesus say *that* the scriptures concern himself, he also tells the disciples *how* they concern himself. In both the Emmaus story and the subsequent appearance to the eleven, the content of scripture is specified. And in both the specification is that the messiah has to attain to his glory by way of suffering and death. This is the mystery of the identity of Luke's Jesus (as well as Mark's): not that Jesus is covertly depicted as Israel's God in subtle ways throughout the story, but that Jesus takes his throne as glorified messiah through the shocking road of rejection, suffering, and death.

These two stories of post-resurrection appearances invite the reader to take a retrospective glance, not only at the mission of Jesus but also at the scriptures that preceded him and anticipated his work. In so doing, they provide markers for what the reader might expect in such an exercise. These markers are specifically Christological (they are about ὁ χριστός, vv. 26, 46). The kind of Christ Luke is keen for his readers to discover is not, here, a Christ who is actually in some mysterious sense the God of Israel. Instead, the Christ toward whom he sees the scriptures pointing is the Christ who must suffer and die before being raised to glory. Over the centuries, readers have come away from these stories wishing that Luke had provided actual exegetical content to go along with his claims about what the scriptures say. In my estimation, however, such

99. Hays, *Reading Backwards*, 56.
100. Hays, *Reading Backwards*, 57.

disappointment is unwarranted inasmuch as the sermons in Acts, relayed by the same pen, engage the biblical texts using precisely such a hermeneutic.[101] To these we now turn, before returning to the Gospel of Luke itself.[102]

2. CRUCIFIED AND RISEN ACCORDING TO THE SCRIPTURES: SERMONS IN ACTS

A full study of the Christology of Acts would take the current project far afield. And yet, as the sequel to the Gospel of Luke, and as a book in which the characters of the disciples proceed on their mission with the enlightenment given by the resurrected Jesus and the presence of the Holy Spirit, it provides a helpful vantage point for testing the thesis that the scriptures as Luke interprets them in reference to Jesus carry a Christological, rather than divine, import. The survey below will suffice to demonstrate that Luke interprets scripture through the lens of a Christ who is an idealized human figure.

a. Pentecost: A Resurrected Christ

Peter's programmatic sermon on Pentecost (Acts 2:14-36) anchors my discussion of Acts. It represents the transformed voice of the disciples that they discover after receiving the promised Holy Spirit (cf. 1:4-5, 8), the needful empowerment for faithfully bearing witness to Jesus. Although the disciples in general, and Peter in particular, will remain dynamic characters in the story of Acts, the transformations they undergo largely fall within their understanding and enactment of the mission Jesus has given to them. As we will see over the course of my brief survey of speech material, the Christology articulated by Peter in this speech is persistent across the book. For the purposes of the current section of the study, the speech is especially important inasmuch as it might well be described as little more than a Christological exegesis of three biblical texts.

---

101. Cf. J. Ross Wagner, "Psalm 118 in Luke-Acts: Tracing a Narrative Thread?" in *Early Christian Interpretation of the Scriptures of Israel: Investigations and Proposals* (JSNTSup 148/ SSEJC 5; ed. C. A. Evans and J. A. Sanders; Sheffield: Sheffield Academic, 1997), 154-78, esp. 154-55; also David P. Moessner, "*Two* Lords 'at the Right Hand'? The Psalms and an Intertextual Reading of Peter's Pentecost Speech (Acts 2:14-36)," in *Literary Studies in Luke-Acts* (ed. R. P. Thompson and T. E. Phillips; Macon, GA: Mercer University Press, 1998), 215-32.

102. The procedure of beginning with Acts on my question has precedent in the work of Martin Rese, *Alttestamentliche Motive in der Christologie des Lukas* (Gütersloh: Gerd Mohn, 1969).

The first and longest citation comes as Peter interprets the arrival of the spirit and the disciples' speaking in tongues. Peter says that they are seeing what was spoken of by Joel (Joel 3:1-5, LXX). This citation and its use in the speech can be broken into three parts. First, there is the prophecy of a poured-out spirit who enables all God's servants to prophesy, see visions, and dream dreams — with a special emphasis on prophecy as Luke adds καὶ προφητεύσαν ("and they will prophesy") at the end of verse 18 (Acts 2:17-18). Peter uses this section of the speech to respond to the charge of drunkenness (2:15-16). The scene demonstrates that the apostles are not drunk, but that the last days have arrived with the vindication of God's messiah.[103]

Second, there is a description of cosmic signs in verses 19-20. These signs might be pointing in two directions at once. On the one hand, the prediction of heavenly wonders (τέρατα ἐν τῷ οὐρανῷ) and earthly signs (σημεῖα ἐπὶ τῆς γῆς) might be a description of the spirit's advent. Although blood and smoke are missing, there has been the predicted fire, in this case hovering over the disciples' heads (2:3, 19). On Pentecost itself, however, there has not been solar darkness or a sanguine moon. On the other hand, the speech of Peter subsequent to the citation repeats the vocabulary of Joel, as cited in verse 19, in its description of the life of Jesus: "Jesus of Nazareth, a man attested by God to you by deeds of power, and wonders [τέρασιν], and signs [σημείοις] which God did through him in your midst" (v. 22). Peter thus locates the fulfillment of the second part of the Joel passage in the earthly life of Jesus. The likelihood of such a connection is heightened by the fact that the word σημεῖα has been added to the Joel citation in Acts, not being present in the LXX.[104]

Moreover, in saying that Jesus worked deeds of power (δυνάμεσιν), he echoes the promise made by Jesus that those who receive the spirit will themselves be given power (Luke 24:49; Acts 1:8). For the reader of Luke-Acts, who also knows that Jesus himself was conceived by the spirit's power (Luke 1:35), and baptized by (Luke 3:22), filled with (Luke 4:1), and empowered by (ἐν τῇ δυνάμει, Luke 4:14) the spirit, the promise of the poured-out spirit in Joel 3:1-2 (Acts 2:17-18) is now shown to be true not only for Jesus but also true, subsequently, for the disciples. With this in mind, it is likely that the reader should also recall the darkening of the sun at Jesus's crucifixion (Luke 23:44-45) as the fulfillment of Joel's prophecy of a darkened sun (Acts 2:20).[105]

---

103. Darrell L. Bock, *Proclamation from Prophecy and Pattern: Lucan Old Testament Christology* (JSNTSup 12; Sheffield: JSOT, 1987), 166.

104. Cf. Rese, *Alttestamentliche Motive*, 49.

105. Rese, *Alttestamentliche Motive*, 54.

The citation of Joel is therefore not only interpreting the spirit's arrival on Pentecost, it is doing so in such a way as to draw Pentecost into the narrative of Jesus himself.[106] This Christological concern likely lies behind the length of the Joel citation itself, which could easily have stopped right after the prophecy of the outpoured spirit. As Rese concludes, "Der Zweck der Rede nicht eine Apologie des Pfingstwunders ist. . . . Vielmehr ist nach v 36 die Messianität Jesu das Thema der Rede, das Pfingstwunder nur ihr Anlaß."[107] The reception of the spirit becomes a sort of recapitulation in and for Jesus's followers of the life of Jesus as Peter describes it in verse 22.

The Christology by which Joel is interpreted brings us once again to the clearly articulated, idealized human Christology that claims a special working of God through the human Jesus: Ἰησοῦν τὸν Ναζωραῖον, ἄνδρα ἀποδεδιγμένον ἀπὸ τοῦ θεοῦ. Joel 3:1-5 uses the first-person singular throughout, and Luke inserts λέγει ὁ θεός in Acts 2:17 to make clear that the speaker is God. His description of Jesus's ministry maintains the divine source of the power, signs, and wonders, ascribing these to the character of God and thus derivatively to the character of Jesus. The Christology by which Peter interprets Joel 3:1-5 is, first of all, the idealized human Christology that I demonstrated to be at work above in the chapter on Jesus as Lord of all creation. The mention of the darkened sun in both Joel 3:4 (LXX, cited in Acts 2:20) and in Luke 23:44-45 pushes this one step further, to include Jesus's death.[108] Peter in fact turns to this facet of Jesus's time on earth in verse 23, accusing the crowd of complicity in the handing over of Jesus to death.

As Peter describes Jesus's death, God continues to remain a distinct character in the narrative, as Jesus is the one who is the object (τοῦτον) of God's preordained plan and foreknowledge. This pattern of distinguishing between Jesus and God, with Jesus receiving the agency of the God who is other, continues as Peter moves to the resurrection, indicating God as agent and Jesus as recipient of the divine action (ὃν ὁ θεὸς ἀνέστησεν, "whom God raised," v. 24). Thus, the Christology by which Peter interprets Joel's prophecy is not a Christology of divine ontology, or a Christology of divine incarnation, but a Christology of divine empowerment and divine supervision. The uniqueness

106. For all of these reasons, I disagree with the conclusions of Bock, *Proclamation from Prophecy*, 167, that the language of Joel looks to some future day of the Lord. In particular, Bock misses that Peter's speech does, in fact, provide interpretation of the wonders and signs.

107. Rese, *Alttestamentliche Motive*, 46.

108. Thus Rese, *Alttestamentliche Motive*, 55, rightly concludes that the Joel citation interprets the Pentecost event not as the work of God, directly, but as the work of the crucified who had been exalted.

of Jesus is found in God's working through him in life, death, and resurrection, attesting to God's approval of this uniquely empowered human agent, Jesus of Nazareth. In terms of ontology, Jesus is a man. In terms of deeds of empowerment, God is at work in him.

Third, Luke's citation of Joel ends with "and it will be that whoever calls upon the name of the Lord will be saved" (τὸ ὄνομα κυρίου σωθήσεται, Acts 2:21). An initial point to make is that this verse has the potential to open up the significance of the events beyond Israel itself into a more generalized context (as Paul does in Rom 10:12-13).[109] This possibility remains latent, however, though a reader who knows Jesus's words from the end of Luke 24 might be keyed in to it through his indication that scripture anticipates forgiveness of sins being proclaimed to all nations.

In the context of the speech, the most likely referent for the "Lord" upon whom people may call for salvation is Jesus.[110] In the following sentence, after calling his audience to attention with "hear these words," the first words Peter says are "Jesus of Nazareth." The culminating moment of the speech is Peter's declaration that God has made the crucified Jesus both "Lord and Christ" (καὶ κύριον αὐτὸν καὶ χριστὸν ἐποίησεν, Acts 2:36), and the appropriate response to the speech is to be baptized in "the name of Jesus Christ" (ἐπὶ ὀνόματι Ἰησοῦ Χριστοῦ, 2:38).[111] Moreover, in Peter's speech before the Jewish leadership in chapter 4, he says that Jesus Christ of Nazareth is the only name (ὄνομα) under heaven, given among people, by which it is necessary to be saved (v. 12). Thus, the role played by the Lord God (Yhwh) in Joel 3:5 LXX is played by the Lord Jesus in Acts.

The application to Jesus of scriptural texts in which God's name, Yhwh, is rendered κύριος, provides rich potential for theological reflection as to the possible inherent and preexistent unity between Jesus and God.[112] In Acts 2, however, such latent promise does not come to fruition. Jesus is described not only as a "man attested by God" (ἄνδρα ἀποδεδειγμένον ἀπὸ τοῦ θεοῦ, v. 22) and the one who was crucified but raised by God (vv. 23-24), but also as the

109. A significance ascribed to it by Petr Pokorný, *Theologie der lukanischen Schriften* (Göttingen: Vandenhoeck & Ruprecht, 1998), 50.

110. So also Moessner, "*Two Lords*," 220.

111. Cf. Darrell L. Bock, "Proclamation from Prophecy and Pattern: Luke's Use of the Old Testament for Christology and Mission," in *The Gospels and the Scriptures of Israel* (JSNTSup 104/SSEJC 3; ed. C. A. Evans and W. R. Stegner; Sheffield: Sheffield Academic, 1994), 280-307, here 297.

112. See C. Kavin Rowe, "What Is the Name of the Lord?" *HBT* 22 (2000): 135-73; Rowe, *Early Narrative Christology* (Grand Rapids, MI: Baker Academic, 2009).

fruit of David's loins (ἐκ καρποῦ τῆς ὀσφύος) who has been seated on David's throne through the resurrection (vv. 30-32).[113] This resurrected human Jesus mediates the "promise of the father" (1:4), pouring out the spirit (2:33), and in the end it is the human Jesus, "whom you crucified" (ὅν ὑμεῖς ἐσταυρώσατε, 2:36), whom God has made the resurrected Lord and Christ. The penultimate clause of the sermon (καὶ κύριον αὐτὸν καὶ χριστὸν ἐποίησεν ὁ θεός, 2:36), presents a number of difficulties, not least of which is that in the context of the sermon the time at which this ἐποίησεν takes place seems to clearly be the moment of Jesus's resurrection; however, when taken together, Luke-Acts indicates that Jesus is Lord and Christ even from birth (Luke 2:11).

Kavin Rowe's work on Luke's κύριος Christology provides a way forward. In his analysis of the text of Luke, Rowe points out that Luke's narrative, replete with references to Jesus as κύριος, contains a major gap in this particular appellation. The passion narrative is devoid of the word κύριος from the time of Peter's denial ("Peter remembered the word τοῦ κυρίου," 22:61), throughout the trials and crucifixion, until the narrator says that the women did not find "the body of the Lord Jesus" (τὸ σῶμα τοῦ κυρίου Ἰησοῦ, 24:3).[114] Interestingly, a nearly identical phrase is used when Joseph of Arimathea asks for Jesus's body (τὸ σῶμα τοῦ Ἰησοῦ, 23:52), but the word κύριος is not used of the dead Jesus's body.[115]

Two important conclusions follow. The first is that reusing the most pervasive Christological title from the life of Jesus serves to claim a measure of continuity between the identity of the risen Jesus and the Jesus who ministered on the earth.[116] Addressing the use of the κύριος title for Jesus in Acts 2:36 specifically, as this title as well as χριστός had been used in the angelic announcement in Luke 2:11, Rowe remarks, "God's reversal of the human rejection of Jesus is thus expressed in terms of continuity of identity."[117] Having surveyed extensive Christological material in Luke's Gospel for the current study, the implications of such a conclusion are clear: the idealized human figure who is κύριος throughout the Gospel of Luke is the same human figure who is exalted κύριος in the resurrection. If the final verse of Peter's speech is applying to Jesus the κύριος title from Joel 3:5, the great surprise is not that Luke has so spoken of a human as to include him within the inherent identity of God, but that Luke has spoken of God's role being bestowed upon an ideal-

113. Cf. Rese, *Alttestamentliche Motive*, 54-55.
114. Rowe, *Early Narrative Christology*, 183-84.
115. Rowe, *Early Narrative Christology*, 184.
116. Rowe, *Early Narrative Christology*, 185.
117. Rowe, *Early Narrative Christology*, 195.

ized human "Lord." The name of the "Lord" upon whom the people are to call for salvation is Jesus; thus, the hermeneutic is a Christological hermeneutic in which the prophet speaks of the resurrected Christ. This fulfills the expectation created by Jesus in Luke 24 that the law and the prophets anticipate a Christ who will "suffer and enter his glory" (v. 26) or "suffer and rise again on the third day" (v. 46).

The second important conclusion to draw from the absence of κύριος language in the story of Luke from the trials through the crucifixion and burial is that there is in fact a time in the story when Jesus is, in some sense, not κύριος. The body of Jesus can be buried, but the body of κύριος Ἰησοῦς is not to be found in the tomb. The narrative identity of Jesus includes a span in which God hands Jesus over to the judgment of "not-Lord" and "not-Christ" being rendered by the people. And yet, God reverses this judgment by enthroning Jesus as Lord and Christ. Rowe's observations about the silence of Jesus's identity as κύριος open up the natural reading of the sermon: Jesus's resurrection is, in fact, an enthronement of him as Lord and Christ. This is Jesus's entrance into a heavenly reality of which Jesus's earthly ministry was an anticipation, and from which his death threatened to cut him off. So there is a measure of discontinuity between the earthly Lord and the heavenly, enthroned Lord. The difference Peter declares is not ontological (here I agree with Rowe), but neither is it merely epistemic, making known what was always the case (here I part ways with Rowe's argument). The resurrection entails an enthronement that Jesus had not previously experienced, as the remainder of the sermon, and its biblical exegesis not least of all, makes clear.

A second scriptural citation in the sermon is of Psalm 15:8-11 LXX. Its interpretation is a clear instance of a Christ-event hermeneutic the likes of which Luke's Jesus speaks in the resurrection appearances.[118] Noting the psalm's Davidic ascription (Acts 2:25; Ps 15:1, LXX), Peter contrasts its claims with the life of David. David's body did, in fact, see corruption. Peter claims that the psalm is thus a prophecy about Jesus, whom God delivered from Hades and did not allow to see corruption (Acts 2:30-31).[119] The humanity of Jesus is at the forefront in Peter's argument. The biblical text is interpreted as referring to a human, someone from the loins of David (ἐκ καρποῦ τῆς ὀσφύος αὐτοῦ, 2:30).[120] In verse 31 Peter says that David spoke of the resur-

118. This is close to the conclusion of Bock, *Proclamation from Prophecy*, 180.
119. Moessner, "*Two* Lords," 222-27, argues that the purpose of the citation is not only to signal a biblical precedent for the notion of resurrection, but also to suggest a solidarity between Jesus and David in their suffering.
120. Moessner, "*Two* Lords," 230, ties this to Psalm 109:3b LXX, which diverges substantially

rection of the Christ (περὶ τῆς ἀναστάσεως τοῦ χριστοῦ), which provides us with an important marker that in Luke's Christology the term "Christ" means Davidic messiah as such.[121] In both instances, in coming from David's loins and being resurrected messiah, Jesus answers to the scriptural "prophecy" as an idealized human king. Moreover, the connection between Jesus's resurrection and Jesus's bestowal of the spirit is depicted not as Jesus's disposition of a gift that is inherently his to give, but instead a gift that the father had first given to him (2:33). The heavenly activity of Jesus is not depicted as a return to an inherent or previously held position or possession; instead, it is depicted as a true exaltation of Jesus, to a state he had not occupied before, through his resurrection (2:32-33).[122]

To say this much, however, is not to claim that Luke is working with a "low" Christology or with a Christology in which Jesus is "merely" human in some pejorative sense. This is a truly idealized human Christology.[123] The third citation in the passage is from Psalm 109:1 LXX, εἶπεν ὁ κύριος τῷ κυρίῳ μου· κάθου ἐκ δεξιῶν μου. Peter cites this as a further proof that the psalms were not talking about David, but about someone greater. This depiction of being seated at God's right hand is literalized as a reference to Jesus's heavenly enthronement through his resurrection. "David did not ascend into the heavens" (Acts 2:34), and yet he speaks of one who does. This is not a Christology of preexistent enthronement, but of exaltation through resurrection from the dead. The idea that the Christ, specifically as messiah, must be raised again from the dead, must suffer and enter into his glory, is proclaimed by use of this and the previous biblical text, even as the beginning of the proclamation to all nations has begun.[124] This aligns perfectly with the messianic-activity hermeneutics Jesus articulates in Luke 24.

---

from the MT by reading ἐξεγέννησά σε so that the speaker, David, claims to have begotten the "Lord" of whom he speaks.

121. Rese, *Alttestamentliche Motive*, 122.

122. The challenge for the reader of Luke-Acts is to give due weight to both Jesus's messiahship and lordship during his time on earth (as emphasized, e.g., by Rowe, "What Is the Name of the Lord?" and Rese, *Alttestamentliche Motive*, 57-58), and to the enthronement that happens at the resurrection and not only confirms what Jesus was before, but also transforms the quality of his messianic lordship.

123. This is my explanation of what Bock, *Proclamation from Prophecy*, 184, articulates as demonstration of an equality with God "in both task and name," an equality that is not fully explicated, though Bock appears to want his readers to draw the conclusion that this is a divine Christology (cf. esp. 185-86).

124. The correlation between Luke 24:44-46 and Acts 2:14-36 is highlighted by Moessner, "*Two Lords*," 216.

With the final citation, and its application to Jesus, the full significance of the original Joel quotation becomes clear. "Auf die Anrede Jesu als des Herrn aber zielt die ganze Rede. Denn nun steht es fest, daß es der Name Jesus ist, den man anzurufen hat, um gerettet zu werden."[125] The name of Jesus is the name of the Lord; and Jesus has become that Lord through God's raising him from the dead. Jesus is not, here, the God of Israel, Yнwн as such, but the human Lord who sits enthroned at Yнwн's right hand. Of the three texts cited, only the first has any possibility of offering a divine interpretation of Jesus's identity. However, Luke never waivers in taking instead the path we have been exploring throughout this book: depicting Jesus, now in sustained conversation with the scriptures of Israel, as an idealized human figure. This consistency continues throughout Acts.

b. God Raised Up a Prophet Like Moses

The speech made by Peter and John after healing a beggar outside the temple uses scripture for several purposes. First, it echoes the identity of God as articulated in Exodus 3:6. "'The God of Abraham, and the God of Isaac, and the God of Jacob, the God of our fathers, glorified his son Jesus" (Acts 3:13). The citation is slightly modified, so that rather than reading "the God of your father" (ὁ θεὸς τοῦ πατρός σου, Exod 3:6), it ends in Acts with "the God of our fathers" (ὁ θεὸς τῶν πατέρων ἡμῶν). This citation is important for our current study because its rhetorical function in the speech is to demonstrate continuity between the God of Israel's scriptures and the story of Jesus that the apostles are proclaiming and enacting.[126] In establishing this continuity, however, God is not identified with Jesus as being the same character, but instead as being the God at work in Jesus as the same God who was at work in previous moments of the story.[127]

That first citation comes from Moses's call narrative, a fact that becomes more important as we approach the second scriptural citation. In 3:21 Peter emphasizes that all the things they are proclaiming (past, present, and future) take place as "God spoke through the mouth of his holy prophets from long ago." He then cites Moses's promise that God will raise up a prophet like himself (Acts 3:22-23; cf. Deut 18:15, 18). The most obvious Christolog-

---

125. Rese, *Alttestamentliche Motive,* 62; cf. 126-27.

126. Cf. Rese, *Alttestamentliche Motive,* 69-70.

127. Simon David Butticaz, *L'identité de l'Église dans les Actes des apôtres: De la restauration d'Israël à la conquête universelle* (BZNW 174; Berlin: De Gruyter, 2010), 135; Jacques Schlosser, "Moïse, serviteur du kérygme apostolique d'après Ac 3:22-26," *RevScRel* 61 (1987): 17-31.

ical claim is that Jesus is a prophet like Moses — once again interpreting Jesus within an idealized human category, that of Mosaic prophet.[128] It is possible that, within the context of the speech, "raise up" functions as a double entendre. The verb ἀναστήσει (v. 22) can simply mean "to establish" in the sense of a figure coming to power. However, Luke also uses the verb ἀνίστημι to speak of Jesus's resurrection (e.g., Luke 24:7, 46; Acts 2:24, 32; 13:33, 34). Thus, it is quite possible for a reader to hear in this prophecy a surprising anticipation of Jesus's resurrection.[129] If so, we have another example of Luke's hermeneutical strategy, articulated by the resurrected Jesus in Luke 24, embodied by the disciples. Not only are they reading scripture as anticipating Jesus in some general sense, but as anticipating his death and resurrection in particular.

The third piece of Jesus's hermeneutical program, that repentance for forgiveness of sins be proclaimed in his name to all nations beginning from Jerusalem (Luke 24:47), is reflected in the third scriptural citation of the speech. Peter cites Genesis 22:18/Genesis 26:4 with its promise that in Abraham's seed all the peoples (ἔθνη, LXX; πατριαί, Acts 3:25) of the earth will be blessed.[130] He says that the word comes to them first (echoing Jesus's "beginning from Jerusalem"). In itself, the Christological significance of the citation and application appears to be limited to confirming that the resurrected Jesus is at work through the apostles' ministry.

The final verse of the sermon also reiterates the claim that God raised up Jesus, saying it is "for you first . . . he sent him, blessing each of you with repentance from your sins" (3:26). Once again, there is a possible nod toward Jesus's resurrection, as the disciples' speech presents an actualizing hermeneutic that sees the prophecies concerning Jesus as fulfilled not merely in the past of his death and resurrection, but also in the present of his continuing work through them. The Christological hermeneutic stresses a continuity between God as God is at work in the disciples' story and the God who spoke in the preceding scriptural narrative; however, the way in which that continuity is maintained is not through a direct identification of Jesus with God so as to suggest in some mysterious way that he is that God in what might be called a proto-binitarian sense. Instead, it is through an identification of Jesus as the fulfillment of that God's promises and as the

128. Rese, *Alttestamentliche Motive*, 67-68, highlights how the reader of Acts knows that this is an eschatological prophet, not from Deuteronomy 18:15-19, but only from the usage in the speech.

129. Cf. Butticaz, *L'identité de l'Église*, 135.

130. Cf. Pokorný, *Theologie der lukanischen Schriften*, 50-52.

agent through whom that God is at work to bring all the prophets' words to their promised culmination.[131]

c. Arrayed against the Lord and His Christ

The same dynamics as those surveyed in the previous section are at work in the report of the assembly of believers in Acts 4:23-31. In a first citation, God is addressed in terms that resonate with a number of scriptural passages: ὁ ποιήσας τὸν οὐρανὸν καὶ τὴν γῆν καὶ τὴν θάλασσαν καὶ πάντα τὰ ἐν αὐτοῖς ("the one who made the heavens and the earth and the sea and all that is in them," Acts 4:24; cf. Exod 20:11; Ps 145:6, LXX). This helps establish continuity between the identity of the God of Israel's scriptures and the God of the early church. This God is then said to have spoken through the mouth of the prophet, this time the prophet David (Acts 4:25). The prophet, in turn, articulates a Christological prophecy, Psalm 2:1-2.[132] The psalm's depiction of the rulers and nations rising up against the Lord and against his Christ (κατὰ τοῦ κυρίου καὶ κατὰ τοῦ χριστοῦ αὐτοῦ, Ps 2:2; Acts 4:26) is interpreted as referring to the rising up together, against God's anointed son Jesus, Herod and Pontius Pilate, along with the nations and the peoples of Israel (Acts 4:27).[133] The scripture is interpreted as referring to Jesus's death. This is a Christ-event hermeneutic, in which Jesus plays the part of the Lord God's "Christ," and not a hermeneutic of divine ontology.[134]

d. Israel's Story: Rejecting the Prophets

Stephen's speech in Acts 7 is suffused with allusions to and citations of scripture, as he retells large swaths of Israel's story. By and large, the narrative he tells is not Christological. Rather, it depicts God's persistence in rescuing and

131. The focus here on "promises" bears some affinity with the overall program of Bock, *Proclamation from Prophecy;* however, Bock's hesitance to recognize the hermeneutical force of the Christ event is a significant point of contrast between our conclusions.

132. Rese, *Alttestamentliche Motive,* 94-95.

133. Sam Janse, *"You Are My Son": The Reception History of Psalm 2 in Early Judaism and the Early Church* (Leuven: Peeters, 2009), 90-95; Rese, *Alttestamentliche Motive,* 94-95.

134. Janse, *"You Are My Son,"* 95, concludes: "The confession of Jesus as the Christ is the hermeneutic principle to understand the Scriptures and the confessor's own time." It is worth highlighting at this point that Bock, *Proclamation from Prophecy,* 209, concludes that "the major OT theme" in Acts 2-5 is "Jesus's exaltation despite his rejection." Bock's conclusion maps onto the suggestion I have made that the hermeneutical program of Luke 24 plays out, generally, in the book of Acts.

dwelling with the people despite their continued rejection of God's work. Thus, the climactic moment is not one that directly discloses the identity of Jesus, but one that discloses the identity of the people as being in need of repentance. The assertion that the people persecuted the prophets and killed those sent to them (vv. 51-52) connects Stephen's contemporaries with their ancestors due to the former's complicity in Jesus's death.

e. Like a Lamb Led to Slaughter

The brief episode of Philip with the Ethiopian eunuch includes the latter's reading of Isaiah 57:3, with its description of a lamb being led to slaughter, the cutting off of the servant's life. The passage is not interpreted for the reader, nor does it come as part of a larger speech or prayer.[135] And yet the broad contours of its significance are not difficult to discern. Philip uses this as a starting point to tell the eunuch about Jesus (Acts 8:35). We are bereft of the opportunity Luke might have taken to elaborate on any atonement theology he might hold, and indeed the citation itself may have been so shaped as to avoid atonement theology as such.[136] The passage cited speaks of the servant's death at the beginning and end: ὡς πρόβατον ἐπὶ σφαγὴν ἤχθη . . . αἴρεται ἀπὸ τῆς γῆς ἡ ζωὴ αὐτοῦ (8:32, 33). In discussing these as the scriptural words about Jesus, we are on safe ground to assume that the reader is supposed to heed clues that the scriptures speak of the messiah's suffering and fill in the gaps with a Christ-event hermeneutic. These scriptures speak of the human Jesus going to his death.

f. The Resurrection-Begotten Son

The citation of Psalm 2:7 in Paul's sermon in Antioch is an important flag in the ground of idealized human Christology. We find here one of the clearest indications that language appropriated in later Trinitarian discourse is used in the Lukan narrative to depict Jesus within an idealized human Christology.

The sermon begins with quick overview of Israel's story, culminating in the claim that God fulfilled his promise to bring Israel a savior from this one's (David's) seed (τούτου . . . ἀπὸ τοῦ σπέρματος, Acts 13:23). Once again, God as the one who spoke previously is an important point of continuity between the

---

135. This latter point makes it unique among the scripture citations in Acts, as pointed out by Rese, *Alttestamentliche Motive*, 97.

136. Rese, *Alttestamentliche Motive*, 98-99.

scriptural story and the story of the apostles. And once again, Jesus is depicted as a human figure, from David's human lineage, much as he was described as coming from David's loins previously (2:30), through whom God fulfills the promise.[137]

After telling the story of Jesus's death and resurrection, Paul goes on to claim that Jesus's resurrection is the way in which God fulfilled the second psalm (ὁ θεὸς ἐκπεπλήρωκεν τοῖς τέκνοις αὐτῶν ἡμῖν ἀναστήσας Ἰησοῦν ὡς καὶ ἐν τῷ ψαλμῷ γέγραπται τῷ δευτέρῳ, 13:33). Specifically, the claim is that Jesus became God's son at the resurrection, as Paul goes on to cite, υἱός μου εἶ σύ, ἐγὼ σήμερον γεγέννηκά σε (13:33; cf. Ps 2:7, LXX).[138] Jesus is son of God not in some ontological sense, but in the sense of enthroned Davidic king.[139] Paul goes on to allude to Psalm 15:10, discussed above, reiterating that Jesus did not see corruption, though David did (Acts 13:35-37). Inasmuch as the speech focuses on Jesus as a Davidic figure, it articulates a human Christology.[140] Inasmuch as the speech demonstrates that Jesus is greater than David, here by virtue of his resurrection enthronement, it is an idealized human Christology. It is due to Jesus's peculiarly exalted status that Paul can claim that it is through this person that remission of sins is proclaimed (13:38). This is yet another clear example of the Christ-event hermeneutics that Jesus describes in Luke 24.[141]

The sermon ends with a passage that functions much like Stephen's speech in Acts 7. Paul cites Habukkuk 1:5 as a warning to the people that they not be those who do not believe even if God's great work is disclosed to them. This fits the "paradox" Petr Pokorný sees unfurling in many of the scripture citations in Acts: those who end up believing the story are the Gentiles, and yet what they believe is couched as "die Erfülling der Hoffnung Israels."[142] Such citations demonstrate that Luke is not working woodenly with a Christ-event hermeneutic as such, though he does see even passages about Israel past and

---

137. Rese, *Alttestamentliche Motive,* 87-89, argues that here, too, we have a scriptural reference whose fulfillment is seen in the resurrection of Jesus. However, the link is not entirely direct, so I do not wish to push the point here.

138. Janse, "You Are My Son," 96-102.

139. *Pace,* apparently, Bock, *Proclamation from Prophecy,* 247-49, who appears to see resurrection as a demonstration of an already possessed "incorruptible" nature as son. He achieves this conclusion by muting the birth imagery found in the second half of the verse.

140. Cf. Janse, "You Are My Son," 102: "This means that Jesus is portrayed in the colors of a king."

141. Cf. Rese, *Alttestamentliche Motive,* 90: "Die christologische Bedeutung des Zitats liegt in der Einbeziehung der Auferstehung in den Erweis der Messianität Jesu."

142. Pokorný, *Theologie der lukanischen Schriften,* 51. He refers specifically to Acts 13:35, and then also to Acts 24:15; 26:6-7, and 28:20.

present taking on a special urgency in his own eschatological moment. Despite this diversity, however, what we do not ever see is Luke deploying a divine-Christology hermeneutic in which the continuity between the God of the scriptures and the God of the apostolic preaching is found in Jesus's identity as that God.

g. Nations Stream to the Tent of David

At the Jerusalem council James issues the final decision, citing a passage from Amos 9:11-12 that combines a Davidic Christology with the ingathering of the nations.[143] In the passage God promises to rebuild the tent of David that had fallen (Acts 15:16; Amos 9:11), with the goal that "the rest of the people" (οἱ κατάλοιποι τῶν ἀνθρώπων) might seek the Lord (Acts 15:17; cf. Amos 9:12). The issue at hand for the council concerns the inclusion of Gentiles. This citation links the ingathering of the Gentiles with the reestablishment of the line of David. It thus homes in on the final leg of the Christ-event hermeneutic that Jesus articulates in Luke 24:46-47. By this point in Acts, the reader knows that Jesus, especially through his resurrection, is the raising up of the once destroyed house of David. The ingathering of the nations is a component part of what Jesus says will unfold, as prophesied in scripture, as the story moves from crucifixion, to resurrection, to proclamation in Jerusalem, to proclamation to the nations.[144] Thus, although this passage adds little to our quest to understand the Christological implications of Luke's hermeneutics, it confirms the notion that when speaking of Jesus his is a Christ-event hermeneutic. Indeed, Luke might well include this proclamation to the nations as an extension of that very Christ event.

h. Conclusion: Christological Hermeneutics of Acts

This discussion of the hermeneutics of Acts is far from exhaustive, but is representative. Moreover, it is impressively consistent. Acts regularly deploys a Christ-event hermeneutic that sheds light on Luke's Christology by demonstrating how the death and resurrection of Jesus fulfills biblical expectation; and, most particularly, showing how the resurrection functions as an exaltation of Jesus by which he enters into the lofty status of true heavenly enthronement.

143. Cf. Bock, "Proclamation from Prophecy and Pattern," 303.
144. On the importance of Gentile inclusion and Israelite rejection of Jesus, see Bock, "Proclamation from Prophecy and Pattern," 300-304.

Moreover, although scripture is used regularly to demonstrate the continuity between God in scripture and God in the apostle's proclamation, nowhere is that continuity located in the person of Jesus as such.

I have framed this discussion in terms of the hermeneutical program that Luke's resurrected Jesus lays out in Luke 24 in order to demonstrate what it is that Luke has in mind when he suggests that Jesus's followers should turn to the scriptures to understand Jesus rightly. It is worth pointing out at this juncture that similar summary statements can be found in Acts as well. In Acts 26:22-23, for instance, Paul summarizes what all the prophets have said would come to pass in terms of Christ's suffering, his rising from among the dead, and proclamation being made both to Israel and the nations. This underscores that the range of hermeneutical methods deployed by Luke, generally governed as they are by the Christ event, is not accidental. In Acts, Luke interprets Israel's scriptures as pointers toward a human, Davidic Christ who must suffer and be raised before the message he embodies goes out to the ends of the earth.[145]

The work we have just done in getting hold of Luke's hermeneutics in Acts is in no way inconsequential to the more particular question of the Christological implications of the hermeneutics of the Gospel of Luke itself. In Luke 24 the invitation Luke issues through Jesus is in many ways to look backward: to join the disciples in having their understanding of Jesus's ministry reformed by the conviction that scripture anticipates a certain kind of Christ. The work we have done in Acts argues that Luke's invitation to revisit the Gospel and understand it afresh in light of scripture goes astray if such a revisiting looks for ways in which those scriptures might signal that Jesus is, in some sense visible just beneath the surface, identical with Israel's God. Luke's Jesus articulates a Christ-event hermeneutic, not a divine-ontology hermeneutic, and in Acts we see that such a hermeneutical program is carried out with remarkable consistency. So as we turn back to the Gospel of Luke, we do so with a strong presupposition that the scriptural citations and allusions will paint a picture of Jesus as God's idealized human agent, the Christ whose worldwide embrace will succeed a mission that ends in death.

---

145. Adam Gregerman, "Biblical Prophecy and the Fate of the Nations in Early Jewish and Christian Interpretations of Isaiah," in *"What Does the Scripture Say?" Studies in the Function of Scripture in Early Judaism and Christianity*, vol. 1, *The Synoptic Gospels* (LNTS 469/SSEJC 17; ed. C. A. Evans and H. D. Zacharias; London: T&T Clark, 2012), 212-40, demonstrates how Luke employs the "light to the nations" motif of Second Isaiah in order to undergird the missionary program on display in Luke-Acts.

3. LUKE'S SCRIPTURAL STORY

Luke's birth narrative is replete with scriptural allusions, echoes, and citations. However, having already covered this section of his story in depth in the chapter above on Jesus's birth and resurrection, I will begin my survey in Luke 3.[146] Once again, the survey will have to be somewhat selective, but I trust that the material is nonetheless representative.

a. All Flesh Will See (Luke 3:1-6)

As do all three of the other biblical Evangelists, Luke reflects the early church's use of Isaiah 40:3 to interpret the ministry of John the Baptist. However, while John's Gospel contains only "a voice crying in the wilderness, prepare the way of the Lord" (John 1:23; cf. Isa 40:3a), and while Matthew and Mark both go somewhat further, including as well a slightly altered version of the rest of Isaiah 40:3, "make his paths straight" (Matt 3:3; Mark 1:3), Luke alone extends the citation into Isaiah 40:5. The uniquely Lukan addition reads, "Every valley shall be filled and every mountain and hill brought low, and the crooked will be made straight and the rough places into smooth roads, and all flesh will see the salvation of God" (Luke 3:5-6).

A first important point to note is that Matthew and Luke (Q?) agree with Mark in changing the ultimate words of Isaiah 40:3 from τοῦ θεοῦ ἡμῶν to αὐτοῦ, a move that allows a passage that originally spoke of God as such to be applied to a divine agent without claiming divinity for the latter.[147]

Second, the extended citation appears to have its goal in the final phrase: καὶ ὄψεται πᾶσα σὰρξ τὸ σωτήριον τοῦ θεοῦ. This phrase upholds two important pieces of Lukan theology, both of which are also contained in Simeon's prayer (Luke 2:28-32). First is the Christological point that Jesus is the means by which God's salvation is made known (Simeon says, εἶδον οἱ ὀφθαλμοί μου τὸ σωτήριόν σου, Luke 2:30). Among the Synoptic Gospels, "salvation" is a uniquely Lukan theme, as σωτηρ- roots are absent from both Matthew and Mark. Zechariah's song deploys the root three times, celebrating God's raising a horn of salvation (κέρας σωτηρίας) in the house of David (1:69), which consists

---

146. For a concise overview of scripture, and its Christological connotations, in Luke's first two chapters, see Bock, "Proclamation from Prophecy and Pattern," 284-88. He concludes, in concert with my study in chapter 6 above, "The infancy narrative's fundamental christological category from the Old Testament is that of a regal deliverer, the messiah." See also Rese, *Alttestamentliche Motive*, 140-42.

147. Cf. Joel B. Green, *The Gospel of Luke* (NICNT; Grand Rapids, MI: Eerdmans, 1997), 171.

in salvation from enemies (σωτηρίαν ἐξ ἐχθρῶν ἡμῶν, 1:71), knowledge of which salvation is going to be given to the people Israel by John the Baptist (τοῦ δοῦναι γνῶσιν σωτηρίας τῷ λαῷ, 1:77). The texture of such salvation is complex, to which complexity might be added the use of σωτήρ as a title for God in Mary's song (τῷ θεῷ τῷ σωτῆρί μου, 1:47). It lies beyond the scope of my work here to develop a full-orbed articulation of Luke's soteriology, but the antecedents to Luke 3 provide enough pointers to allow a simple summary, which might go something like this: God is the savior whose salvation comes in the person of Jesus, a Davidic messiah, and consists in forgiveness of sins as well as deliverance from some as-yet unspecified enemies.[148] There is both an inseparable connection between Jesus and God, such that Jesus and Jesus's actions can be identified with the "salvation" wrought by God as "savior," and there is also a differentiation between them such that the identities of Jesus and God remain distinct as one would expect of a figure who is depicted as a Davidic messiah.

The second piece of Lukan theology captured in the Isaiah citation is that of a mission that extends beyond Israel to all humanity: πᾶσα σάρξ will see God's salvation (Luke 3:6; Isa 40:5).[149] In Simeon's prayer, this concern was captured in the expectation that the child will be φῶς εἰς ἀποκάλυψιν ἐθνῶν ("a light for the revelation of the nations," Luke 2:31). Such a worldwide concern, articulated by Israel's prophets, is matched at the beginning of Acts as well, when the phrase πᾶσα σάρξ appears in Peter's citation of Joel at Pentecost (ἐκχεῶ ἀπὸ τοῦ πνεύματός μου ἐπὶ πᾶσαν σάρκα, 2:17; Joel 3:1, LXX). Likely, the primary purpose behind Luke's extension of the Isaiah citation is to include this additional element.[150] By including a hint about the worldwide impact of the salvation event John inaugurates, the citation of Isaiah 40 is broadened so as to fall within the general hermeneutical rubric provided by Jesus in Luke 24:44-47. There, he says that scripture not only anticipates a suffering and raised messiah, but also an extension of "forgiveness of sins" (cf. Luke 3:3) to "all nations" (24:47). Jesus's program does not entirely encapsulate Luke's citation of Isaiah 40:3-5; however, the citation does function Christologically inasmuch as John is preparing for the salvation of God that Jesus is bringing to light. This salvation is plotted within a narrative that Luke believes will culminate in its worldwide proclamation. As Bock notes in his assessment of this passage, "Only Luke notes these points. Christology and mission appear side

---

148. Green, *Luke*, 172, comments both on the need to interpret "salvation" in 3:6 in light of what came before in chapters 1–2 and on the "holistic" picture of salvation there developed.

149. Cf. Green, *Luke*, 172.

150. Cf. Rese, *Alttestamentliche Motive*, 170-71.

by side."[151] This extension of the Isaiah citations falls well within the paradigm of an idealized human figure.

b. Sermon at Nazareth (Luke 4:16-30)

Jesus's sermon at Nazareth is Luke's first narrated appearance of Jesus after his baptism, though the indications are that Luke envisions this coming after a season of highly successful ministry (cf. 4:14-15, 23).[152] Inasmuch as the scripture citation Jesus reads speaks of being anointed by the spirit, we do well to note that the success he has experienced is attributed to Jesus's acting "in the power of the spirit" (ἐν τῇ δυνάμει τοῦ πνεύματος, 4:14), which had previously led Jesus into the wilderness for the temptation scene (4:1) after it had descended upon him at his baptism (3:22).[153]

The context for understanding the Christological implications of Jesus's spirit anointing, as described in his reading from Isaiah 61 in Nazareth, include other references to the spirit's activity in Luke's early chapters as well. The first mention of the spirit in Luke is in the promise that John will be filled with the spirit from his mother's womb (1:15). Elizabeth is filled with the spirit as she greets Mary with a prophetic blessing that demonstrates knowledge of the significance of the baby Mary is carrying (1:41-45). Zechariah is filled with the spirit as he prophesies (ἐπροφήτευσεν, 1:67) about the work of God that is coming to pass beginning with the birth of John. Finally, the spirit not only rests upon Simeon (2:25), but has made a promise to him (2:26), and directs him into the temple (2:27) in a way analogous to its directing of Jesus into the desert. Thus, while Jesus is without a doubt the idealized figure par excellence in Luke's two-part story, his empowerment by the spirit is qualitatively continuous with that of other characters.[154] The prophecy that John, who is filled with the spirit,

---

151. Bock, "Proclamation from Prophecy and Pattern," 288.

152. Pokorný, *Theologie der lukanischen Schriften,* 61, also reads this passage in concert with Jesus's hermeneutical scheme as articulated in Luke 24:44-48, seeing both Christological implications per se play out, and Jesus's claim that scripture anticipates the message going out to the Gentiles.

153. Recognizing this, Bock, "Proclamation from Prophecy and Pattern," 289-90, maintains that the current passage depicts Jesus not only as a prophet but also as a regal messiah. Cf. Robert L. Brawley, *Text to Text Pours Forth Speech: Voices of Scripture in Luke-Acts* (Bloomington: Indiana University Press, 1995), 15-16.

154. Rese, *Alttestamentliche Motive,* 148, points out that Jesus's possession of the spirit is not occasional, but something he has "aufgrund seiner Stellung." This, too, is a parallel between Jesus and John. They play different roles in the drama, but both are roles of spirit-empowered humans.

will go forth in the spirit and power of Elijah (1:17) helps provide the category for such spiritual action: it marks out prophets and prophecy.[155]

In the synagogue in Nazareth Luke's Jesus reads the following from Isaiah: πνεῦμα κυρίου ἐπ' ἐμὲ οὗ ἕνεκεν ἔχρισέν με εὐαγγελίσασθαι πτωχοῖς, ἀπέσταλκέν με κηρύξαι αἰχμαλώτοις ἄφεσιν καὶ τυφλοῖς ἀνάβλεψιν, ἀποστεῖλαι τεθραυσμένους ἐν ἀφέσει, κηρύξαι ἐνιαυτὸν κυρίου δεκτόν ("The spirit of the Lord is upon me, because he has anointed me to preach the good news to the poor, he has sent me to proclaim release to the prisoners and restoration of sight to the blind, to set free the oppressed, to proclaim the year of the Lord's favor," 4:18-19; citing Isa 61:1-2). The Christological significance of the passage is patent, particularly when Jesus comments on the text, "Today, this scripture has been fulfilled in your hearing" (Luke 4:21). The possibility of "fulfillment" is present in the sermon itself for two reasons. First, Jesus has been anointed by the spirit, as the text indicates. Second, Isaiah anticipates an act of proclamation, using such verbs three times (εὐαγγελίσασθαι [once, v. 18] and κηρύξαι [twice, once each in vv. 18, 19]). Jesus is the person, "prophesied" by Isaiah, who is the anointed proclaimer. Up through Jesus's short interpretive comment, and in light of the way that the spirit's presence has been described thus far in the Gospel, all signals point toward a differentiation between the character of Jesus, who is anointed, and the character of the Lord God, who has anointed him. And an ideal reader might well infer that the role for which Jesus had been so anointed was that of prophet.[156]

The story turns in verse 23, for reasons we need not explore fully here. Jesus anticipates a taunt from his countrymen because he has not enacted the kinds of healings in Nazareth that he did in Capernaum. In response to this, Jesus replies, "I tell you that no prophet is an object of favor in his homeland" (οὐδεὶς προφήτης δεκτός ἐστιν ἐν τῇ πατρίδι αὐτοῦ, v. 24). This response confirms the category of "prophet" as the one in which Jesus is functioning in this particular narrative (without in any way undermining the unique role Jesus plays in Luke's understanding of the unfolding era of salvation).[157]

155. Cf. Rese, *Alttestamentliche Motive*, 151-52. In this regard, the citation of Joel 3:1-5 in Luke 2:16-21 is an important parallel: the result of the spirit being poured out on all flesh is that "they will prophesy" (Acts 2:17) — a point Luke underscores by adding it to the biblical text in verse 18: "I will pour out from my spirit and they will prophecy (καὶ προφητεύσουσιν, absent from Joel 3:2, LXX and MT).

156. On Jesus as a prophet who forgives sin, in particular, see Rese, *Alttestamentliche Motive*, 151.

157. Bock, *Proclamation from Prophecy*, 110-11, sees a fusion of the idea that Jesus is prophet and messiah unfolding in this passage.

The notion that Jesus takes his role within the prophetic tradition of Israel is underscored as Jesus elaborates his point by appeal to Elijah's care of a Sidonian widow and Elisha's healing of Naaman the Syrian. Jesus's allusions to these biblical predecessors become further commentary on the age of fulfillment in which Jesus is living: the work of Jesus will also overflow the bounds of Israel, even as that of Elijah and Elisha before him, when he is rejected by his people. Indeed, the prophecy of the prophet's rejection in his own fatherland is itself fulfilled when the people rise up in rage and attempt to throw Jesus off a cliff (v. 29). The second half of the story fills in the narrative of Jesus as anointed prophet: he, like his biblical predecessors, will be rejected with a murderous repudiation, with a strong implication that this will lead to dispersing his ministry beyond his kin and eventually beyond Israel.[158]

Thus, with a series of biblical engagements, this opening salvo of Jesus's public ministry demonstrates the sorts of things that must be fulfilled with regard to Jesus: his anointing and prophetic ministry of proclamation, his repudiation by his people, and then a mission beyond that people. Reading this beginning of Jesus's ministry with the end of Luke's story in mind, we can see how Luke has skillfully crafted the opening frame of Jesus's public ministry to depict a messiah whose ministry will walk the path blazed by prophetic predecessors in Israel's scriptural tradition.

c. Fire from Heaven

In light of Jesus's self-association with Elijah and Elisha, it is perhaps not surprising that the disciples evoke Elijah's raining down of fire from heaven when Jesus is spurned by a Samaritan village (Luke 9:54; cf. 2 Kgs 1:10, 12). In the antecedent story, the Samarian king's attempt to consult with prophets of Baal-zebub generates the conflict (2 Kgs 1:2-3). Luke's Jesus, however, rejects the suggestion that the Samaritans of his own day who have rejected him should pay in a like (or worse) manner than the Samaritans of old who ostensibly rejected Israel's God. Luke's reframing of the potential place of the Samaritans in the story of God's work in the world continues later with the parable of the "good Samaritan" in 10:30-37, and the healing of the lepers, including the thankful Samaritan, in 17:11-19.

This rewriting of the prophet's posture toward an ungrateful Samaria, and

---

158. This is its own recurring motif within Luke-Acts, as Bock, "Proclamation and Prophecy," has indicated as well. It also coalesces nicely with Jesus's words in 24:46 that the gospel must be proclaimed to all nations.

the possible opening it leaves for Samaritan repentance and forgiveness, is part of the important thread of a worldwide mission that runs through Luke's two-part work. Samaria will later be mentioned specifically in Jesus's commission to the eleven at the beginning of Acts (1:8), and in chapter 8 of the latter book the command to evangelize the region is fulfilled by Phillip (vv. 1-14, 25). The extension of the mission beyond Israel to Samaria, with the change in posture it represents toward the foreigner when set alongside 2 Kings 1, is inseparable from the presence of Jesus as God's eschatological agent and coincides with the mission component of Jesus's hermeneutical program as articulated in Luke 24:47. However, the passage otherwise adds little to our understanding of Luke's Christology.

d. The Law and Following Jesus

In two separate passages Luke's Jesus is addressed with the question of what the interlocutor must do to inherit eternal life, and both times Jesus begins by quoting from Torah, but ends by establishing his own role in the life of one who would be faithful to God. The verbal coherence of the interlocutors' questions is striking. In 10:25 the lawyer asks, διδάσκαλε, τί ποιήσας ζωὴν αἰώνιον κληρονομήσω, whereas in 18:18 some bystander (τις) asks, διδάσκαλε ἀγαθέ, τί ποιήσας ζωὴν αἰώνιον κληρονομήσω. The single variation lies in the use of the word ἀγαθέ, which draws Jesus's attention in the latter story. We return to this below.

i. The *Shema*, the Beloved Neighbor, and the Good Samaritan

The opening salvo of Jesus's interaction with the lawyer in 10:25-37 offers little by way of Christological insight. When tested by this interlocutor, Jesus deflects the question back to him, asking what he reads in the law. The lawyer himself offers a not-untypical summary of the Torah by citing the command to love God (Deut 6:5) and the command to love neighbor (Lev 19:18). Jesus affirms this answer ("Do this, and you will live") only to have the man, desiring to justify himself (θέλων δικαιῶσαι ἑαυτόν), ask further, "And who is my neighbor?" To this point, the debate had been carried out on the lawyer's ground. To the initial query Jesus asks what the lawyer reads in the law. Now, however, the conversation shifts as Jesus tells the parable of the good Samaritan.[159]

---

159. Craig A. Evans, "Luke's Good Samaritan and the Chronicler's Good Samaritans," in

The "half dead" man (ἡμιθανῆ, 10:30) creates a conundrum for the story's Jewish characters. Such a person may appear to be dead, or indeed die in the near future, which raises the possibility of contracting corpse impurity.[160] Leviticus 21:1-4 specifies that the priest is not allowed to contract corpse impurity for any but a close family member. The Levite presents a more complicated picture, but he may well be heading up to Jerusalem to serve in the temple and therefore be keeping himself pure for that service. In both cases, one might imagine that these special representatives are not "making a choice" between the regulation for purity and the law of love, but are in fact loving their Israelite neighbors by keeping themselves pure for the work of representing Israel through their roles in the temple system. The Samaritan, under no such constraints, cares for the man by the side of the road.[161]

Jesus's climactic question, "Which of these three, does it appear to you, has been neighbor to the one set upon by bandits?" (10:36), shifts the conversation away from Torah per se. Leviticus 19:18 has a ready-made answer to the lawyer's question, as its first part reads, "You shall not take vengeance or bear any grudge against the sons of your own people," prior to the admonition to love one's neighbor as oneself. The only question would seem to be how one defines the "sons of your own people."[162]

Biblical Interpretation in Early Christian Gospels, vol. 3, *The Gospel of Luke* (LNTS 376/SSEJC 16; ed. Thomas R. Hatina; London: T&T Clark, 2010), 32-42, commends the earlier suggestion of F. S. Spencer that Luke modeled his good Samaritan after those who cared for the Judahites in 2 Chronicles 28:1-5. This additional allusion might signify that Jesus is continuing to teach by reference to scripture; however, it does not otherwise help us discern the Christology entailed in the story, so I will not engage it further.

160. So, rightly, Richard Bauckham, "The Scrupulous Priest and the Good Samaritan: Jesus's Parabolic Interpretation of the Law of Moses," *NTS* 44 (1998): 475-89; cf. Snodgrass, *Stories with Intent*, 348.

161. James L. Kugel, *In Potiphar's House: The Interpretive Life of Biblical Texts* (San Francisco: HarperSanFrancisco, 1990), 214-46, demonstrates how the commandments to not hate one's brother, or take revenge against a fellow countryman, and to love one's neighbor (Lev 19:15-18) created an extensive exegetical tradition in which the restrictive sense of these terms was debated, often in ways that signaled it was not only allowed, but even a sacred duty to hate and take revenge on one's enemies.

162. Christopher N. Chandler, "'Love Your Neighbor as Yourself': (Leviticus 19:18B) in Early Jewish-Christian Exegetical Practice and Missional Formulation," in Evans and Zacharias, *The Synoptic Gospels*, 12-56, demonstrates that a number of interpretations of Leviticus 19:18b in early Judaism interpreted it with reference to its context, which sometimes included a "restrictive interpretation" on the love command in light of the prior command to not hold a grudge against a fellow Jew.

The very act of telling his own parable, rather than redirecting attention back to the law, not only shifts the conversation but also has the potential to shift the locus of authority. Such a shift is embodied in the parable itself in two ways. First, the distinction between the actions of the priest, in particular, and the Samaritan includes the likelihood that the former is being scrupulous in his observance of Torah, while the latter, whose interpretation of Torah would be gravely suspect, is free to care for the injured man. Second, the characters themselves differ in that the priest and the Levite are marked in the Jewish assessment, sociologically, as falling within the people rightly demarcated by Torah, while the Samaritan is not. Thus, in a twofold manner, in both his actions and his identity, the Samaritan is not demarcated or approved by "the law" as the other two characters might be considered to be so.

At the culmination of the parable, Jesus issues his own imperative, "Go and you do likewise" (πορεύου καὶ σὺ ποίει ὁμοίως, 10:37). The interaction that had begun with Jesus being addressed as teacher (διδάσκαλε, 10:25) concludes with Jesus giving instruction. That instruction is not derived from the law, but from Jesus's own story of neighbor love. The story in its entirety, then, not only provides a striking example of what neighbor love should look like, it also depicts Jesus exercising a creative teaching authority that is not directly derivative of the law. Luke is, as always, cautious in his depictions of the relationship between Jesus and scripture, demonstrating continuity even as he depicts Jesus as embodying a climactic time of fulfillment (cf., e.g., 5:36-39, esp. v. 39). But without setting aside the importance of keeping the law for gaining eternal life, he has Jesus offer an authoritative teaching on what such keeping of the law might look like that is not, itself, derived from or based on the law. The Christological weight of the passage is in its demonstration of Jesus as authoritative teacher as Jesus's own story and admonition become the basis for enacting love of neighbor. Moreover, Jesus's story hints at the Lukan concern, already addressed numerous times in this chapter, for the salvation offered in Jesus to flower beyond the borders of ethnic Israel.

ii. The Decalogue and Following Jesus (Luke 18:18-23)

The second instance of Luke's Jesus being confronted with the question of what one must do to inherit eternal life is the story of the rich man (Luke 18:18-23), a pericope that has parallels in both Mark (10:17-22) and Matthew (19:16-22). Luke follows Mark in having the interlocutor address Jesus as διδάσκαλε ἀγαθέ (good teacher, Luke 18:18).[163] Luke then follows Mark verbatim, as Jesus distances himself from the ascription ἀγαθός: τί με λέγεις ἀγαθόν; οὐδεὶς ἀγαθὸς εἰ μὴ εἷς ὁ θεός ("Why do you call me good? No one is good except one — God," Luke 18:19; par. Mark 10:18). The response may intend to allude to the *shema*; however, this is not a foregone conclusion. The Greek version of Deuteronomy 6:4 does contain the words ὁ θεός as well as εἷς, such that God is the common masculine singular referent. Otherwise, however, the parallels are slight: κύριος ὁ θεὸς ἡμῶν κύριος εἷς ἐστιν. In Deuteronomy 6:4 ὁ θεός comes after, not before, εἷς. Moreover, it is the noun κύριος rather than the appellation ὁ θεός that functions as the subject for the predicate nominative εἷς. Whether or not such an allusion is in view, Luke's Jesus follows the Markan precedent in questioning the application of such a divine attribute to Jesus. For the reader, who knows that Jesus is more trustworthy than those who address him, the initial effect is to cordon off the title "good" from what is applicable to Jesus, leaving it instead as a divine appellation. Such a move does not, however, diminish the notion that Jesus is an idealized figure in the Gospel, or even this pericope, as its ensuing developments make clear.

Jesus goes on to tell him what he already knows, citing five of the last six commandments (those pertaining to loving neighbor, Luke 18:20). Learning that the man has kept these, Jesus issues a twofold command: to sell all he has and to come follow Jesus, promising treasure in heaven in return (18:21). This twofold admonition destabilizes the biblical commandments inasmuch as it calls into question not their necessity but rather their sufficiency. Not only does Jesus as διδάσκαλος indicate a necessity that is not deducible from the law itself, he also places himself within what is necessary to inherit life: following Jesus is prerequisite.

Such an inscription of Jesus into the life of those who would so honor God as to be given eternal life underscores the tremendous Christological significance entailed in Jesus's interpretation of the Torah. Functioning within Judaism, Jesus does not stand against the law. However, functioning within Judaism as a messiah figure who is both declaring and demonstrating the way to faithfully enact the identity of the people of God, and as the one who is gathering people for just such a life, Jesus places the requirement of following him at the heart of salvation-ensuring obedience.

---

163. Matthew moves the adjective to the questioner's depiction of the thing that must be done (διδάσκαλε, τί ἀγαθὸν ποιήσω, 19:16), perhaps because his own Christological concerns made him wary of the subsequent distancing of Jesus from "good" that he finds in his Markan source.

In both stories, when Jesus teaches what must be done to gain eternal life, he not only takes up the role of interpreter of Torah, but also inserts fidelity to himself into the requirements delineated.

e. Judgment by the Rejected One

Luke 13:23-30 contains a pericope in which Jesus is asked about the number of the saved. In a multilayered response, Jesus admonishes the people to enter through the narrow door, and expands this into a parable of sorts about the master of the house shutting the gate, after which entry will be impossible. The final word of the master appears to allude to Psalm 6:9: "Get away from me all you who work injustice" (ἀπόστητε ἀπ᾽ἐμοῦ πάντες ἐργάται ἀδικίας, Luke 13:27; cf. ἀπόστητε ἀπ᾽ἐμοῦ πάντες οἱ ἐργαζόμενοι τὴν ἀνομίαν, Ps 6:9, LXX). This is followed by a pronouncement of Jesus that the weeping outside will be great as people stream to the patriarchs from all directions to dine in the kingdom of God (Luke 13:28-29). The pericope ends with Jesus's saying that there are people who are last who will be first and there are people who are first who will be last (13:30).

One peculiarity about this parable is its use of the second-person plural as Jesus describes the future scene. Not only does he admonish the people to work hard to enter through the narrow door (ἀγωνίζεσθε, v. 24), he also continues to address them directly as he tells the story of people being cast out and crying out to the householder: "You will begin [ἄρξησθε] to stand outside and knock" (v. 25); "He will answer you [ὑμῖν]" (v. 25); "Then you will begin [ἄρξεσθε] to say" (v. 26); "there will be weeping . . . when you see [ὄψησθε] Abraham and Isaac and Jacob" (v. 28). Thus, the "parable" is perhaps closer to an illustration deployed in direct teaching.

Recognizing the peculiarities of the parable enables us to see that Jesus, too, is a character in the parable, despite its lack of corresponding first-person singular verbs or pronouns.[164] There are several pointers in this direction. First, the interlocutor who begins this pericope addresses Jesus as κύριε (v. 23), the same title that is used to address the master of the house: κύριε, ἄνοιξον ἡμῖν ("Lord, open up for us," v. 25). Second, the crowd to whom Jesus is speaking says, "We ate before you and drank, and you taught in our streets" (v. 26). Thus, the "master" of this eschatological house of salvation is someone whose physical presence on earth was part of the lives of the audience within the narrative to whom Jesus is speaking.

164. Cf. Green, *Gospel of Luke,* 527-33, esp. 531.

In response to this latter plea for recognition the master, whom we have identified with Jesus, says, "I do not know where you are from, depart from me all you who work injustice." Here is the allusion to Psalm 6:9. The psalm begins with a lengthy cry to God for healing, restoration, and deliverance. It is only in the latter half of verse 8 LXX in this ten-verse psalm that we learn the cause: "because of my enemies" (ἐν πᾶσιν τοῖς ἐχθροῖς μου). Then the psalmist addresses his enemies, commanding them to depart, because the Lord has heard his cry. When Jesus reappropriates the psalm, he is the speaker addressing his Jewish audience, warning them that they are in danger of playing the role of his enemies in contrast to the nations who will hear and gather to the message of forgiveness he brings. Indeed, the subsequent two pericopes highlight that Jesus is heading for Jerusalem, where he will die (Luke 13:33), taking his place in the line of prophets who have so suffered at her hands (13:34-35). As the following two pericopes make clear, Jesus as righteous sufferer will need God to deliver him from a literal death, and not only the threat of death that hovers over the head of the psalmist (Ps 6:5-6, LXX). Such an adoption of the psalm provides yet another instance where Jesus's words about scripture's predictions in Luke 24 find expression in the broader story: the scriptures anticipate a Christ who must suffer and enter his glory (v. 26).

Within the teaching unit of verses 24-30, Jesus combines the roles of housemaster (which is also a role of judge) and of Psalm 6's righteous sufferer. As such, the pericope neatly alludes to a time of rejection by his own people before Jesus, as messiah, takes his place as the Lord and guardian of the great eschatological banquet. Within Luke's narrative, this is a thoroughly messianic prerogative: Jesus moves through death to not only resurrection life but also a glorification and enthronement at God's right hand (Luke 24:26; Acts 2:30-33).[165]

f. Numbered among Transgressors

In a uniquely Lukan pericope embedded in the larger Last Supper narrative, Jesus changes the orders he had previously given his disciples: now they are to take money purse, bag, and sword (Luke 22:35-38). The reason for this apparent volte-face is the looming fulfillment of Isaiah 53:12: "For I tell you that

---

165. A similar anticipation is found in the conversation between Jesus and the bandit on the cross, where recognizing Jesus's innocence and his own need of forgiveness, the bandit asks to be remembered when Jesus comes into his kingdom (Luke 23:40-42) — a request Jesus has the power to grant, or at least affirm, even from the cross (Luke 23:43).

this thing that is written is about to have its completion in me, namely, 'And he was reckoned with the lawless.' For indeed, that which concerns me has its completion" (Luke 22:37). Here the character Jesus clearly indicates that a biblical text refers to him. The "completion" (τελεσθῆναι) is going to be in his death, in which he will be wrongly treated as "lawless" though he is, in fact, innocent (cf. 23:41), and in which he will be strung up alongside two criminals (23:32).¹⁶⁶ This is a clear instance of Jesus's messianic mission being given a necessary (δεῖ) path of suffering in order to be brought to completion. Indeed, if we were to look for a place in which Jesus's words while he was still with his disciples was that the messiah must suffer, as scripture says, prior to entering into his glory (24:44-46), this passage would be one of the clearer instances of such a conversation. Scripture here signals that Jesus as messiah must suffer, not that Jesus as messiah is divine.¹⁶⁷

g. Begging for Death (Luke 23:27-31)

In *The Orthodox Corruption of Scripture,* Bart Ehrman summarizes Luke's atonement theology by saying, "the blood of Jesus produces the church because it brings the cognizance of guilt that leads to repentance."¹⁶⁸ This particular way of bringing "cognizance of guilt," moreover, is specially aimed at Israel, demonstrating that they, too, need the forgiveness that God is offering through Jesus.¹⁶⁹ This concern is reflected in the quasi-parable of the householder in 13:23-30, discussed above: Israel is rejecting Jesus, and this entails some looming judgment. The destruction of Jerusalem itself is anticipated not only in the Olivet Discourse but also in uniquely Lukan passages such as 13:1-5 and 13:6-9. Such themes are reflected in Jesus's words to the weeping women en route to his crucifixion site.

166. Cf. Rese, *Alttestamentliche Motive,* 155-58; Bock, *Proclamation from Prophecy,* 138.

167. It is perhaps worth noting here as well that though Luke cites Isaiah 53:12, he does not develop a substitutionary atonement theology from it or cite portions of Isaiah 53 that would lead inexorably in that direction (cf. Rese, *Alttestamentliche Motive,* 154-64). This helps highlight how the citation reflects Luke's own theological concerns as he skirts the atonement theology suggested by Mark.

168. Bart D. Ehrman, *The Orthodox Corruption of Scripture: The Effect of Early Christological Controversies on the Text of the New Testament* (Oxford: Oxford University Press, 1993), 202.

169. Note, for instance, not only the complaint that the apostles are trying to bring Jesus's blood upon the religious leaders (Acts 5:28), and the language of God's overturning the death of Jesus whom "you" crucified (ὑμεῖς ἐσταυρώσατε) in a speech to the Jewish people on Pentecost (Acts 2:36), but also the absence of any notice of crucifixion in the speech before the (non-Jewish) Athenians on the Areopagus (Acts 17:22-31).

Jesus addresses these women as "daughters of Jerusalem," offering a prophetic warning that perhaps turns on its head Zechariah's word of celebration
("Rejoice greatly, daughter of Zion! Shout, daughter of Jerusalem!" Zech 9:9)
that precedes the prophecy of a donkey-riding king. His warning begins by
telling them to weep for themselves and their children (Luke 23:28), and moves
into anticipating a day when barren women will be considered more blessed
(23:29; cf. Mark 13:17, par. Luke 21:23), itself a possible inversion of Isaiah 54:1's
blessing on the fecundity of the formerly barren woman. Jesus then utters a
prophecy in the words of Hosea: τότε ἄρξονται λέγειν τοῖς ὄρεσιν· πέσετε ἐφ᾽
ἡμᾶς, καὶ τοῖς βουνοῖς· καλύψατε ἡμᾶς ("Then they will begin to say to the
mountains, 'Fall on us,' and to the hills, 'Hide us!'" Luke 23:30; cf. Hos 10:8,
LXX).[170] In Hosea, this is an anticipation of the people's reaction to divine
judgment, a judgment that comes in the guise of the nations being gathered
against them (e.g., 10:10). By reiterating this prophecy with the "daughters of
Jerusalem" as his audience, Luke's Jesus appears to be articulating his anticipation that Jerusalem is going to be ravaged by the Romans. This expectation
was previously made crystal clear in Luke's changing of Mark's cryptic allusion
to the desolating sacrilege (Mark 13:14) to a blunt warning about Jerusalem
being surrounded by armies (Luke 21:20).

In uttering these words from Hosea, then, Jesus plays the role of prophet.
But also like Hosea, Jesus himself becomes a living symbol of the message he
is delivering. The concluding words of the pericope read, "Because if they do
this while the tree is green, what shall be when it is withered?" (Luke 23:31).
Destruction at the hands of the Romans is Jesus's own fate in this scene, thus
signaling that the "they" of whom he speaks refers to the Romans who will
subsequently come to destroy the city. Moreover, in this comparison Jesus
stands firmly within the people of Israel, as a healthy and faithful Israelite.
Thus, in taking up the prophetic words of Hosea, Jesus plays the role of a
prophet, as we have seen previously in our investigations of intertextuality in
Luke, and also stands as an idealized human figure to the extent that he can
be upheld as the picture of health in contrast to the faithlessness he anticipates
in the later generation.[171]

170. The only notable difference between the scriptural *Vorlage* and Luke's rendition is that
Luke switches the words πέσετε and καλύψατε such that the former is spoken to the mountains
rather than the hills, and the latter is spoken to the hills rather than the mountains.

171. I note that here Jesus uses the third person, rather than the second person, in contrast
to his words of warning in 13:23-30 that I addressed above. Also, it may be worth noting here
that though the text presents such words of Jesus as prophecy, from the timeframe of the
Gospel's writing the catastrophic event has already transpired.

h. Into Your Hands

Leading up to the moment of Jesus's death, Luke's passion narrative has introduced a few changes that scale back the intensity of Jesus's suffering. In the scene of Jesus's final prayer before being arrested, Luke's Jesus does not say that he is grieved to the point of death (Luke 22:40-41; cf. Mark 14:34; Matt 26:38); neither does he have Jesus repeat his prayer three times as in the other Synoptic Evangelists (Luke 22:46-47; cf. Mark 14:37-42; Matt 26:40-46). Luke's Jesus also heals the ear of the high priest's servant when he is being arrested (22:50-51). We have already had occasion to comment in this chapter upon Jesus's talking to women on the way to the cross (23:27-31) and his promising of a reunion in paradise with the bandit on the cross (23:43), both of which are unique to Luke. In all, then, Luke presents a suffering Jesus who is in much greater control, and less depths of anguish, than we find in Matthew and Mark. Within this general framework we note the significant absence of the cry of dereliction (Mark 15:34; Matt 27:46) with its attendant misunderstanding about Elijah. Instead, Luke's Jesus utters the words πάτερ, εἰς χεῖράς σου παρατίθεμαι τὸ πνεῦμά μου ("Father, into your hands I commit my spirit," 23:46; cf. Ps 30:6, LXX).

The surface-level differences between this cry and the cry of dereliction are sustained by a closer look at each psalm. "My God, my God, why have you forsaken me?" introduces Psalm 21 (LXX; Ps 22, MT) and is followed by nineteen more verses of lament before turning with a cry for deliverance in verse 20 LXX. By contrast, the word of trust, "into your hands I commit my spirit," is found in the first part of Psalm 30 LXX, in which the Davidic psalmist is celebrating his own trust in God and God's care for him in return.[172] It is only in verse 10 LXX that the psalmist turns to cry out for mercy in language reminiscent of what we saw earlier with reference to Psalm 6. Psalm 30 turns yet again in verse 20 LXX so that it, no less than Psalm 21 LXX, ends with a song of celebration for God's goodness and deliverance.

Following the allusion to Psalm 30:6, Luke reads, τοῦτο δὲ εἰπὼν ἐξέπνευσεν. This shapes the reader's understanding of the psalm as a cry of Jesus inasmuch as the psalm's language of πνεῦμα is captured in Luke's reuse of Mark's verb ἐξέπνευσεν. With this "expiration," the reader sees Jesus entrusting his very life into God's hands as he leaves it behind, perhaps of his own will. In all three Synoptic Gospels, the death of Jesus is punctuated with a psalm of lament, but Luke's choice of Psalm 30:6 shades his Christology in a manner unique to his own portrayal of Jesus. Jesus continues to trust God, and to be in relationship

172. Cf. Bock, *Proclamation from Prophecy*, 147.

with God as "father," to the end. The tension between God's promised deliverance of God's faithful servant and the suffering of Jesus on the cross is not as pronounced, as Luke scales it back through indications that God has not, in fact, left Jesus. Importantly, the final words of Luke's Jesus are words of trust that God as his father will be a good steward, and ultimately restorer, of the life he is handing over. Taken with the promise to the bandit on the cross that they would be together in paradise on that same day, we might well imagine that Luke sees the death of Jesus as, in fact, a spiritual entry into God's presence.

With this citation, Luke's Jesus associates himself with a trusting Davidic figure who will have to cry to God for salvation. Such an association maintains a clear distinction between Jesus and God, as God the father must be the one to steward Jesus's "spirit." Peter's sermon in Acts 2 helps explain that God does, in fact, fulfill this role, by raising the man Jesus from the dead. Thus, in this final foray into Luke's use of the scriptures of Israel, we find again that the hermeneutics are messianic, that they depict a suffering messiah who can hope for rescue from his time of anguish and death, and that in so functioning they map well onto Jesus's reading strategy as outlined twice in Luke 24. In turn, we see no indication that Jesus plays the role of God in some manner that signals to the reader that Jesus is, in fact, the God of Israel.

i. Conclusion: Scripture in Luke's Gospel

This survey has been representative, not exhaustive. The citations of and allusions to scripture studied here have not turned up one hermeneutic that Luke applies woodenly across his Gospel and Acts. However, this foray has shown a remarkable center of gravity around the notion of a suffering and resurrected Christ when issues of Christology are in view.[173] The notion that Luke's scriptural Christology revolves around the suffering, resurrection, and proclamation of Jesus as messiah may find tacit affirmation in the parable of the rich man and Lazarus (Luke 16:19-31), in which Abraham says at the end, "If they do not listen to Moses and the prophets, they will not be persuaded even if someone rises from the dead" (v. 31).[174] Luke's Gospel ties together attention to scripture and belief in resurrection, such that the failure to apprehend the one

173. Bock, "Proclamation from Prophecy and Pattern," 293-94, concludes even more sharply that the regal depiction of Jesus as messiah is never far from view, even if categories of "prophet" or "servant," for instance, also appear. Although I have engaged a wider array of Christological motifs, we share a common conclusion that Luke's intertextual Christology is one that highlights Jesus's role as human messiah.

174. Cf. Pokorný, *Theologie der lukanischen Schriften*, 60.

entails failure to apprehend the other. We have also seen, particularly though not exclusively in Acts, that the scriptural interpretation often points toward the people of God growing to encompass a worldwide people. This pattern is captured in Robert Brawley's summary of the temptation narrative: "Jesus's interpretation of scripture implying a universal benefit exposes as deficient the devil's interpretation of scripture for exclusive benefit. Christology ceases to be Christology for its own sake. Jesus has identity as son of God not for his own sake but for the blessing of all the families of the earth."[175]

Luke's scriptural Christology is most often a functional Christology and, importantly, it never leaves the reader to conclude that Jesus is, in some mysterious way, playing the role of Israel's God in anything other than a mediated fashion. It seems to me that efforts to identify Jesus as the God of Israel through scriptural associations fall short in either their attention to the flow of Luke's narrative, the imprecise language to which they must defer, or both. Both weaknesses are found in Douglas Buckwalter's attempts to articulate a divine Christology in Luke-Acts.[176] Illustrative of the former problem, Buckwalter sees the use of the phrase "spirit of Jesus" to be a telling alteration of the phrase "spirit of God."[177] Jesus's conjunction with God's giving of the spirit is, of course, Christologically significant. However, the nature of the significance is worked out in Peter's sermon at Pentecost, where we read that Jesus received the promise of the spirit, and that this reception accounts for the spirit's outpouring (Acts 2:33). The narrative provides a solution to the riddle that is not to be found by surmising in a more general fashion what the significance of the implied relation between Jesus and God might be. Jesus is not identified with God, or as God, by the transitive property with the spirit as the shared term connecting the two as sharing the same identity. Instead, the exalted Jesus is given the spirit from God to pour out upon his followers.

The problem of slippery language occurs in Buckwalter's discussion of the "name" (ὄνομα), as Acts 2:21 cites Joel 3:5. After quoting someone who says that the name, person, and work of God are inseparably linked to those of Jesus, he concludes that the two are "virtually indistinguishable." And then, two paragraphs later, he claims, "Acts 2:21 represents the first of thirty-two times Luke uses ὄνομα with reference to Jesus's deity."[178] The connection between God and Jesus is a given, but what precisely is its nature? From "inseparable,"

---

175. Brawley, *Text to Text*, 26.

176. H. Douglas Buckwalter, *The Character and Purpose of Luke's Christology* (New York: Cambridge University Press, 1996).

177. Buckwalter, *Character and Purpose*, 181.

178. Buckwalter, *Character and Purpose*, 183.

Buckwalter goes to "indistinguishable" (something that the narrative of Luke-Acts undermines considerably), to a claim that the word ὄνομα refers to Jesus's deity. The rhetoric has outstripped both the exegesis and the argumentation.

In this particular chapter we have not revisited all possible biblical allusions in Luke.[179] One group of texts we had covered previously was those concerning the son of man. It may in fact be that this cluster of texts provides the most direct correspondence to Jesus's hermeneutics of a crucified and then glorified messiah. When the angels speak to the women at the tomb, they say, "Do you not remember how he spoke with you while he was still in Galilee [ἐλάλετε ὑμῖν ἔτι ὢν ἐν τῇ Γαλιλαίᾳ], saying it is necessary for the son of man to be handed over into the hands of sinners and to be crucified and on the third day to rise?" (Luke 24:6-7). And they remembered his words (24:8). The admonition of the angels bears striking verbal resemblance to Jesus's later words, "These are my words which I spoke to you while I was still with you" (ἐλάλησα πρὸς ὑμᾶς ἔτι ὢν σὺν ὑμῖν, 24:44), which he specifies as the scriptures concerning himself being fulfilled, and specifically as scripture anticipating that the Christ must suffer and rise again from the dead on the third day (24:44-46). It may in fact be that the son of man sayings, as I interpreted them above in chapter 3, provide some of the clearest indications that the messiah must suffer and be raised to glory. Such a Christological hermeneutic, in turn, would lend further weight to the claims I advanced there that the son of humanity is, in fact, an idealized human figure within the Synoptic Gospels, and Luke in particular, rather than a divine being.

D. CONCLUSIONS: MESSIANIC HERMENEUTICS

Intertextuality is a key component deployed by the writers of the Synoptic Gospels in the development of their multifaceted Christologies. In this chapter, we have discovered that idealized human Christology is a sufficiently broad category, with a sufficiently high Christology, to encompass the depictions of Jesus that the biblical narratives have helped generate. In no instance have we found that the scriptural texts are being deployed to signal that Jesus is somehow the physical presence of Israel's God in any way other than playing the part of God's climactic and specially empowered representative on earth. The occasional re-

179. I have not explored character types, such as "Abraham," for instance. For a compelling study of Zacchaeus as a "son of Abraham," and attendant implications that Jesus is God's agent who brings salvation, see Andrew E. Arterbury, "Zacchaeus: 'A Son of Abraham'?" in *Biblical Interpretation in Early Christian Gospels*, vol. 3, *The Gospel of Luke* (LNTS 376/SSEJC 16; ed. Thomas R. Hatina; London: T&T Clark, 2010), 18-31.

568

placement of a biblical reference to God with a reference to Jesus is a clear indication of Jesus's special place in God's plan, but it has precedent at Qumran.[180] Jesus does stand in a peculiar relationship to these scriptures precisely because all of the Synoptic Evangelists depict him and his ministry as occupying this climactic place and time in which God's promises of a coming messiah are being brought to fruition. Throughout, however, the God of Israel as the one who stands behind these scriptures, and empowers Jesus, is distinguished from the Jesus about whom they are spoken. This leaves us with yet another consistent piece of the Christological puzzle that we have been striving to put together.

In an essay on Christology and the use of scripture in the early church, Maurice Casey makes important observations about Christological developments and deployments of scripture. First, he recognizes that there is significant Christological development in, for example, the Gospel of Matthew; however, he underscores that the controversies reflected in the texts are not over breaches of Jewish monotheism.[181] He then shows how precisely those controversies rise to the surface in John's Gospel. However, he also points out that even in John Christological exegesis is not used to prove Jesus's deity.[182] Although I do not follow Casey at every point in his developmental schema of early Christology, these observations are keen: the earliest followers of Jesus, even through the writing of John's Gospel, did not use scripture to depict Jesus as God even though they regularly deployed scripture in expression of their Christologies.

The Christologies of the Synoptic Gospels fit the paradigm proposed at the start of this study as idealized human Christologies. The Gospels' deployments of scripture show how Jesus is God's agent at the time of eschatological fulfillment. In conversation with Israel's scriptures, he is the idealized Human One, the suffering Davidic messiah, the new Moses, the ideal Israelite, the embodiment of Israel's story, the bringer of salvation, the linchpin in the arrival of the eschatological drama, the criterion for entering into the age to come. This is an exalted and rich Christology. It is sufficiently broad to encompass the different emphases of the three writers and the various stages of Jesus's career as they each tell the story. And it functions as an idealized human Christology, demonstrating that the scriptural anticipation of a faithful human being who would rightly represent God's reign to the world has arrived at last.

---

180. Esther Eshel, "4Q471B: A Self-Glorification Hymn," *RQ* 17 (1996): 175-203, here 180.

181. Maurice Casey, "Christology and the Legitimating Use of the Old Testament in the New Testament," in *The Old Testament in the New Testament: Essays in Honour of J. L. North* (JSNTSup 189; ed. Steve Moyise; Sheffield: Sheffield Academic, 2000), 42-64, here 52-53.

182. Casey, "Christology," 55-63.

Conclusions: A Man Attested by God

A. JESUS AS IDEALIZED HUMAN FIGURE IN THE SYNOPTIC GOSPELS

After creating an elaborately textured portrait of idealized human figures in early Judaism, I have shown how powerful this category can be for interpreting the Jesus of the Synoptic Gospels. Because of its richness and diversity, it is possible to recognize that it applies to each of the three stories, even while robustly affirming that each Gospel writer develops a unique portrait with distinct accents and emphases. Just as there is no single messianism in early Judaism, so also there is no single idealized human mold in which every depiction of Jesus is cast.

I offered idealized humanity as a paradigm to be tested in reading the Synoptic Tradition. Paradigms are not singular symbols, images, or categories, but wholesale ways of looking at a problem, capable of containing and explaining multiple manifestations of the data under review. Idealized human Christology accounts for Moses typology and Davidic messianism. It can explain exaltation to the right hand of God and receipt of worship. It allows for applying YHWH texts from the Hebrew Bible to eschatological heroes. It permits the most exalted identifications of human figures with God. Idealized human Christology is a wide-ranging paradigm that accounts for Christological claims that reach as high as heaven — without thereby demanding the further inference that the character is thought to be preexistent or an earthly apparition of someone who is, inherently, Israel's God. The exalted place occupied by idealized humans makes it difficult to even articulate what would be entailed in the appearance of a divine being who causes us to reimagine the inherent identity of Israel's God. We might say, for instance, that a figure is an earthly manifestation of the one true God — but then we would be on ground that might be trod by Adamic humanity, Israel, the high priest, or a Davidic king. For scholarship in New

Testament Christology, one important conclusion to be drawn from the rich expanse of possibilities inherent in the depiction of idealized human figures in early Judaism is that we have to be much more precise in what language we use to indicate that a person's being "more than merely human" means, in fact, that he has always shared in the inherent, eternal life and work of God.

The rich potential of idealized human figures to encompass exalted depictions of various heroes creates a range of possibilities that have not been well enough accounted for in some recent studies of the Synoptic Gospels. It is not enough to say that a Gospel writer works with a high Christology, for an idealized human Christology can be exceedingly high. Nor is it enough to say that a Gospel writer works with a divine identity Christology, for idealized human figures are quite frequently identified with God. Even to speak of Jesus's divine sonship is not saying enough to determine the nature of Jesus's character because divine sonship is a status bestowed upon many human figures. Each of these ways of articulating the Christology of the Gospels is necessary. However, none is sufficient. Without further definition, none on its own means that Jesus is somehow being depicted as standing on the divine side of the creator-creation gulf, as being inherently ontologically distinct from his fellows. One thing this study has shown is that much greater precision is needed in articulating the claims to an early, high Christology.

Moreover, the sheer capacity of the idealized human rubric for explaining various embodiments of divine presence and authority raise the bar considerably for those who wish to claim that Jesus stories are depicting him as more than this. Of the various rubrics put forward for identifying Jesus as more than an idealized human (e.g., sitting on God's throne, exercising divine sovereignty over the world, receiving worship, standing in for Yhwh in biblical interpretation), the two that appear to stand after all the dust has settled are (1) a clear sign of preexistence prior to any human embodiment and/or (2) participation with God in creation. It is only when one or both of these are in view that we then need to assess what sort of heavenly being might be entailed. At this point, the traditional debates about angelic Christology, wisdom Christology, and the like would be put back on the table. Even here, however, we must be cautious because some heavenly figures are humans who have been exalted to the heavenly realm and are thus not angelic or divine in the conventional sense.

The arguments for early divine Christology and the argument laid out here stake their claims on the same playing field. Both sides of the argument assume that Jewish commitments to the singularity of God make the Christian modifications of Jewish monotheism a surprising, unpredictable turn (although the existence of other heavenly beings alongside God in much early Jewish literature means that we need to define carefully what we mean by such "monotheism"). This creates a similar posture in that both sides assume that the onus is on those who would argue for the surprising eruption of a divine Christology that would reframe our understanding of the inherent identity of God. Where we differ is that I have recognized that much more can be said about humans without transgressing the boundaries of God's unique divinity, and so have not discovered that the Synoptic Gospels so clearly tell the story of Jesus as the incarnation of the creator God.

My argument is generally in line with that of an older age of scholarship; namely, that in reading the Gospels it is only when we get to John that we have a story of preexistent deity walking the earth in and as the person of Jesus of Nazareth. I am aware of the fact that this raises a significant question about the diffusion and development of preexistence Christology across the early church. If Paul's letters, or those written in his name (which might be the case for Colossians), seem to indicate preexistence, at least at points, what then do we make of Jesus stories written ten, twenty, or thirty years later? The first thing to say is that this question is one to which there might be any number of possible answers, and that the asking of it does not immediately cast doubt on the data that generate it. That is to say, the mere fact that one strand of early Christianity evinces a preexistence Christology does not immediately demand that all subsequent instantiations must similarly reflect the notion that Jesus is divine. It is highly unlikely that the Christology of the early church developed in a linear fashion, such that earlier means more primitive and lower whereas later means the development of a higher, more exalted Christology. Also worth observing is that the divinity or preexistence of Christ is a note that is sounded rarely in Paul's letters, probably not at all in Romans (to take one example), and almost never functions as the fulcrum of an argument. It is thus conceivable that the Gospel stories about Jesus during his time on earth are written without reference to preexistence or divinity but that this does not disclose the full dimensions of the Christology held by the author. The argument might then be made that the readers would understand the divine Christology that peeps through the cracks of the story, but then we are into a circular game of assuming a divine Christology is present somewhere in order to see such in the text.

However, I have shown throughout that such an assumption of divinity is not necessary to make sense of the data of Matthew, Mark, and Luke. The idealized human paradigm suffices for even the most exalted depictions. It is better, then, to allow the Gospels to stand as witnesses to a facet of Jesus's identity that, for whatever reasons, has received short shrift in both recent and more ancient study. This does not mean getting behind the Gospels to the human Jesus who inspired the divine Christ of the stories; it means getting into the Gospels to see the human Jesus who populates their pages.

To see Jesus as an idealized human figure is to identify the manner in which Jesus is identified with God in the Gospels. Throughout, I have argued that Jesus is not being rendered as a divine figure himself; however, this does not in any way mute the larger point that the Christology of the Synoptic Gospels is a thoroughly God-centered Christology.[1] The coinherence of God and Jesus in the Synoptic Gospels is not a point of contention between me and the advocates of early divine Christology. The point of contention resides in the nature and significance of that Christological-theological unity. My argument has been that the cohesion exists in Jesus as the eschatological messiah, through the work of God's spirit, as Jesus embodies God's authority, exercises the rule of the dominion of God, enacts his vocation to be suffering Christ, frames his power and suffering and coming future under the rubric of the Human One, and serves as the subject of scriptural reflection.

B. THE STORIES OF JESUS IN MATTHEW, MARK, AND LUKE

One of the benefits of working with a wide-ranging paradigm such as we have in idealized human Christology is that affirming the explanatory power of the paradigm for accounting for the biblical data leaves ample space for simultaneously affirming the unique ways in which each Gospel writer has articulated his Christology. As the Christologies of Matthew, Mark, and Luke each differ in important ways, so too does the texture of the idealized human Christology that each depicts.

Matthew's Jesus is in many ways most richly woven into the narrative of Israel. Indeed, the opening verses locate Jesus within that narrative, at the culmination of the era of exile, as the son of Abraham (Isaac) who must be offered in sacrifice and son of David who will reign over God's kingdom. Matthew's Jesus embodies the stories, and scriptures, of Israel. His life is like that of a new Moses, authorized to speak directly from God without deference to the already-given scripture or its tradition of interpretation. But if the Christology of any of the Synoptic Gospels stands poised to transcend the mold of idealized human figures and stake a claim to divinity, it is Matthew's. As king

---

1. Cf. Marinus de Jonge, *God's Final Envoy: Early Christology and Jesus' Own View of His Mission* (Grand Rapids, MI: Eerdmans, 1998), 110-12.

of the Jews, as God's son, and as resurrected and enthroned ruler, Matthew's Jesus is worthy of worship. The birth of Jesus means "God is with us," and the resurrection of Jesus allows him to say, "I am with you always." Matthew's Human One sits enthroned as king in the final judgment.

And yet, Matthew's Jesus no less than Mark's dies as one God-forsaken. The authority Jesus has when raised is an authority over heaven and earth that is given to him — not one that is inherently his own. Matthew's Human One is no less human (suffering, dying, being raised by God) for the exalted role he plays at the final judgment. And it appears that he is worthy of worship because he is the son of God, which is to say, the king anointed to rule the world on God's behalf. The primary Christological lenses Matthew deploys are those in which Jesus embodies Israel, its heroes, or its eschatological deliverer. These are the keys to deciphering what the reign of heaven looks like in Matthew. The idealized human paradigm clearly accounts for the lion's share of the Christological data, and suffices to explain the rest as well. However, if there is a Synoptic Gospel whose recounting of Jesus's life might show the insufficiency of the idealized human paradigm for fully encompassing the narrated identity of Jesus, it is Matthew.

The debate about the Christology of the Second Evangelist comes down to this: what is the mystery of Mark? Is the mystery that the Jesus about whom the story speaks is, in a stunning surprise, none other than the God of Israel, YHWH of Isaiah, whose way is prepared by the voice in the wilderness? Or is the mystery, instead, that Jesus who demonstrates supreme messianic authority on the earth nonetheless has to die in order to fully attain his kingship? I have tried to establish throughout that for Mark's Jesus the "secret" of his identity is truly a messianic secret and not a divine secret. The secret of Jesus's divine sonship that structures the narrative is disclosed in his death as king, on behalf of the people. The open claim to be son of man finds a surprising path, privately disclosed to Jesus's followers, of suffering and death prior to resurrection glory. In this authority Jesus exorcises, heals, and rules the created order. The son of man is the Human One who exercises the wide-ranging rule originally envisioned for Adam and then David and Israel. The kingdom of God draws near when Jesus comes on the scene as the human king of the kingdom.[2]

Luke's Jesus is the Christ-Lord at birth who is also enthroned as Lord and Christ at his resurrection. His lordship is enmeshed with God's lordship such that at times it is difficult to tell the two apart. Luke's Jesus loses some of

---

2. Cf. Dan McCartney, "*Ecce Homo:* The Coming of the Kingdom as the Restoration of Human Vicegerency," *WTJ* 56 (1994): 1-21.

the lackluster humanity of Mark's Jesus as Luke excises mention of the son's ignorance of the coming hour and replaces the cry of dereliction with Jesus's entrusting of his spirit to the father. Notwithstanding, this same author qualifies the entirety of Jesus's ministry as that of a man attested to by God. Luke provides the clearest explanation that son of God is a way of referring to Jesus as Davidic king and Christ. He shows that Jesus is son of God in the way that Adam was son of God, and thereby establishes Jesus's adult ministry as unfolding within an Adam Christology, even as the birth narrative hints at the beginning of new creation. Jesus is prophet as Isaiah, Elijah, and Elisha were prophets — and especially as the latter two saw that the blessings of God would transgress the borders of Israel. For Luke, the hermeneutical key to the scriptures of Israel is the Christ event — the messiah must suffer and rise on the third day and repentance be proclaimed to all nations — not a divine identity as such.

Each of these, of course, is a rough sketch of material that is too broad and nuanced to be accurately captured in a single paragraph. However, it is no less faithful for its brevity. The Christologies of Matthew, Mark, and Luke are each unique, and they each can nonetheless be read as variations on the idealized humanity theme. Moreover, they can each be read as telling a story that develops its own idealized human Christology. Such readings capture the narrative developments and structural elements as well as the various depictions of Jesus that unfold on a story-by-story basis. Idealized human Christology is not only theoretically or ideologically possible; it also coheres with the stories told.

C. HUMAN CHRISTOLOGY AND JESUS'S FOLLOWERS

As messiah and "king of the Jews," Jesus is a corporate figure. He acts on behalf of others and creates a new spiritual and social order that they are part of. In all three Synoptic Gospels, the quality of the new order that they experience is inseparable from Jesus's own experience and initiation of it. Jesus does not act in a wholly unique way from all who have come before and after, only to ask his followers to live in accordance with some preexistent standard of morality. What Jesus does as son of God, Human One, and Lord of creation becomes the defining set of features of the community he gathers around himself. The content and quality of his life become the content and quality of the lives of his followers. Having said this, there is always danger of misinterpreting the significance of this shared life, as though it in some way minimizes Jesus's own role in the story or accomplishment as Lord and Christ. But the opposite is true. As Christ and Lord and son of God, Jesus inaugurates the reign of God on the earth in such a way that it becomes possible for others to share in the work that he is doing. Others can be part of the family of God and exercise authority on the earth because Jesus does so first.

Jesus is the son of God who addresses God as *"abba*, father" (Mark 14:36). The familial address is not only reflected in a democratized invocation of God as *abba* in Paul's earlier letters (Gal 4:6; Rom 8:15), it is also embedded in Jesus's instructions on prayer (Matt 6:9; Luke 11:2). If there is some uniqueness to Jesus's familiarity or "familial intimacy" in his address to God, it is nonetheless extended to Jesus's followers. This correlates with the notion that Jesus is in some way re-forming the people of God around himself. Those who are seated around Jesus listening to his instruction are the doers of God's will who qualify as his mother, sister, and brother. In Matthew, the notion of Jesus as sibling to his followers, and hence one of many sons and daughters of God, is particularly acute, as Jesus refers to his disciples as his brothers at his resurrection (28:10). The Sermon on the Mount is also replete with references to God as the father of Jesus's followers (5:16, 45, 48; 6:1, 4, 6, 8, 9, 14, 15, 18, 26, 32; 7:11), and then culminates with one climactic use in which Jesus associates himself uniquely with God as father, as he says that the basis of final salvation is doing the will of *"my* father" (7:21). The sermon itself is delivered to those whom Jesus calls to himself, setting the basis of its familial instruction on an identity the people derive from their following of Jesus.

In the study of Jesus as son of God I argued that the title marked him out both as Christ and as one whose destiny included suffering, death, and resurrection. Recognizing the democratization of the familial language does not mitigate the uniqueness of Jesus's function as messiah. In part, the latter is upheld through Jesus himself being the marker of this familial identity. In addition, Jesus's unique place in the family is upheld through his determination of what life in the family entails. Jesus as son of God is the spirit-possessing authority on the earth and the king whose throne is won by death on the cross. Each of these dynamics is expressed more fully in the son of man sayings, and each of these dynamics constitutes part of the life of Jesus's followers.

Jesus claims, as son of man, to exercise authority on the earth in healing and forgiveness, in royal authority over the stipulations of the law, and in exorcism. Such wide-ranging authority Jesus claims because he is the Human One or, in colloquial parlance, the Man. And Jesus mediates the extension of such functions to his disciples, sending them out to preach, heal, and exorcise. In Matthew's Gospel, in which Jesus exerts the strongest force as a new teacher from God, the final command to Jesus's followers is to make disciples, teaching them to obey what Jesus has commanded. They thereby enact Jesus's authority to establish what conduct is pleasing to God. Jesus's claimed authority to forgive sins finds its way into Christian communities, as they become the houses of prayer where people forgive one another, even in ways that are binding in heaven.

The quintessential, defining act of Jesus as son of God and son of man, the most unique and unrepeatable facet of Jesus's life on earth, is his death on the cross. Nonetheless, here too sharing in Jesus's unique vocation marks the identity of the family of God. Immediately after Mark's first passion prediction, Jesus says that this vocation is not his alone, but must be embraced by anyone who would be his follower. The interweaving of Jesus's fate and that of his disciples continues to come to the fore as the disciples' confused rejection of the passion predictions comes hand in hand with misplaced apprehensions of how they will themselves attain greatness. But Jesus's rejoinder takes them to his forthcoming cruciform baptism and his vocation to be life-giving ransom. They too must so serve.

The extension of Jesus's ministry to other people helps us to understand the Gospel narratives in two directions at once. First, it underscores the necessity within the logic of the narrative for Jesus to be understood as a fully human person (even as he is empowered by the spirit of God). More than this, it requires that Jesus be fully human precisely in those areas where we might be most ready to conclude that a divine identity is on display. As son of God and son of man, as healer and exorcist and miracle-worker, Jesus must be acting as a human or else the connection with his disciples is severed. I have throughout the study put forth the participation of the disciples in any act as a negative criterion: anything they do is disqualified, narratively, from being a signal that Jesus so acting is a pointer toward his divinity. Here I am making the positive point, which is the other side of the same coin. Such sharing demands that Jesus be acting as a human so that other humans can recognize themselves as those either addressed by the promise or commanded to follow suit.

In addition to the connection between Christ and follower aiding us in articulating the Gospels' Christology, it also aids us in understanding the Gospels' ecclesiology or, perhaps, the anthropology of the rescued. Jesus is the spirit-empowered messiah, and his life and teachings demonstrate what the life and teachings of his spirit-empowered followers must be. The Synoptic Gospels are involving stories. The point of Jesus's actions and teachings is not to lead the reader to a state of mental assent to the fact of Jesus's messiahship or preexistent divinity (a crude way of understanding the stated purpose of John's Gospel, perhaps, as stated in 20:31). The faith of these stories involves entrusting oneself to Jesus and in that trust enacting his authority and walking the way of the cross. A fully human Christology, in which there is no hint that Jesus's unique ontology enables his special messianic functions, allows for such an entailing of Jesus's followers in the actions and identity of Jesus.

D. LOCATING JESUS IN THE BIBLICAL NARRATIVE

The bulk of this book has been concerned with issues of literary and historical-critical exegesis. And yet explorations of biblical Christology often derive from theological concerns, and mine is no different. So here I would like to make a couple of theological overtures, suggestions that I hope to develop in subsequent work and that I hope others might develop as well.

Tracing the threads of idealized human figures through Jewish tradition both biblical and post-biblical, and seeing its importance for understanding the character of Jesus in the Gospels, this book lays out some major markers for the place of humanity within the larger biblical narrative. The work on the preceding pages lays bare various threads that can be woven into a holistic appraisal of the necessity of human agency across various strands of both Testaments.

A pervasive assumption across the literature surveyed is that humans are an indispensable part of God's design for executing God's sovereignty on the earth and making God known on it. The idea that humanity is created as a type of theophany, a living idol of God, propels the Priestly literature with its elaborate depictions of tabernacle and temple as mini-cosmos. The notion of rule over the earth runs through P's covenant promises as they anticipate kings. Moses plays the part of God on earth both before Pharaoh directly and before the people and the obstacles they face. He becomes a bearer of not only the divine words but also the divine glory itself in his physical person.

In those threads of the biblical tradition that idealize the Davidic king, he plays the part of God on earth as he rules on God's behalf. In some instances, this is mingled with Priestly representation as well. Standing alongside God, the king not only makes God's power known to the people, but at times receives words of praise in corporate worship. Although the biblical tradition includes the position that desire for a human king means the rejection of God as king over the people, there is a powerful voice suggesting that the very way in which God is king over the people is through the kingship of the Davidides. As Ezekiel 34 has it, God will shepherd the people himself, and David will be the shepherding prince. Human figures are an integral part of the means by which God executes God's power, and by which the God of heaven is made known on the earth. The canonical stories, and engagements with them in post-biblical Judaism, remain deeply committed to the notion that the world gets set to rights through the agency of faithful humans.

At the same time, critical junctures in the story evince humanity's failure: expulsion from the garden, the flood, the cycle of the judges, the divided kingdom, the exile. But God's patience with a people in the face of this history attests to the need for people to enact fidelity to God in order for the world as a whole to be rightly ordered. The Deuteronomist lays this out in graphic detail, signaling that Israel's obedience to the covenant of law will be the basis for the flourishing of the earth, fruitfulness, and peace (e.g., Deut 28:1-14). This is its own embodiment of divine identity (28:10). The servant songs attest to the hope that Israel, or its representative, will become the kind of obedient human that will be able to transform God's disposition toward Israel, and with that change bring about an eschatological age of unity, peace, and flourishing on the earth.

Jesus as the Human One enacts the role of faithful servant of God, one who is devoted to God through suffering and thereafter raised, exalted, and enthroned. This is the story of Daniel's one like a son of man, whose story trades on the creation narrative in which humans come into being in order to rule the beasts of the earth. The Adamic Human One reigns on the earth and then reigns over the earth from his heavenly throne. The son of man is the Human One who fulfills humanity's purpose, enters into primal humanity's physical, God-reflecting glory, and calls his followers into the way of being human that they see on display in him. The Human One embodies in himself and also represents the saints of the Most High.

A faithful king. A faithful people. A faithful servant who endures through suffering. These are the sorts of human roles that the plaintive longing of the post-exilic prophets hope to see filled. If we neglect to develop a broader theology of Jesus as idealized human being, fulfilling the hopes articulated throughout scripture of such a person or such a people, then we are left with a deeply unsatisfying *deus ex machina* ending. We are left with a story that backed itself into a corner, was never able to construct a human character capable of fulfilling the quest that drives the narrative, and thus had to surrender its major plot line in favor of a divine entrance from outside to rescue those trapped within the confines of the unfolding script. Put differently, if God is never able to have a human being faithfully attend to God and execute God's reign on God's behalf (as the story seems committed to throughout), then the story in the end is one in which humanity's (and perhaps Satan's) power to

579

thwart God's purposes for creation are ultimately so much stronger than God's power to set things right that God has to give up, abandon the story line, and intervene directly without such human aid.

The description of a failed, *deus ex machina* plot laid out in the prior paragraph is not intended to be a depiction of the biblical theology we are left with in the works of recent proponents of early high Christology. It is, however, not far from what we find on the ground in the popular theological imagination of Jesus's identity and how that identity functions in the biblical story. There, Jesus's humanity remains something to apologize for, something for him to overcome (or, in which he overcomes) rather than taking its proper place as the most crucial and basic thing that must be said about him.

The mystery we need to return to, if we are to properly understand the claims of the Synoptic Gospels, is that the human Jesus is the Lord who executes the reign of Israel's Lord God. When the kingdom of God draws near this does not mean that God is attaining to some new level of sovereignty over the earth per se, it means that a human is now on the scene who faithfully enacts that reign. The mystery of the Synoptic Gospels is that the Christ who rules all things in God's name came into his throne only by a cruciform path. It is that the human messiah sits literally where his predecessors sat only metaphorically: at the right hand of God, executing God's reign from a heavenly throne. These claims are each, in their own ways, just as radical, if not more radical, than the claim that God himself fulfills each of these roles as incarnate, preexistent son. Each of them constitutes a surprising answer of God to the long-asked question of how redemption would finally take place. And each underscores the absolute narratological necessity of a human being playing the climactic role in the cosmic biblical drama.

E. CONCLUDING THOUGHTS

There was a time in the story of the church when the full humanity of Jesus was dearly held as a bulwark against what was perceived to be alien articulations of the Christian story. Christ is fully human. Christ is not some admixture of divine and human so as to make him a third thing. Nor is the Christ some spiritual element that descends upon the earthly Jesus only to abandon him at the end. Thus, from a Christian theological perspective every point I have made in this book must be true: everything that Jesus is and does he does as a human being, and is demonstrative of his humanness.

This does not mean, of course, that every point I have made is exegetically accurate in the literary or historical sense. Indeed, I have set as my primary conversation partners those who see evidence that the other dogmatically true statement about Jesus is also evinced throughout the Synoptic Gospels: that everything Jesus is and does he is and does as one who is fully God no less than fully human. The purpose of this book has been to offer a reading that shows how the first can be exegetically sound in a historical-critical sense without the second receiving similar affirmation. The paradigm of Jesus as an idealized human figure contains such rich possibilities that nothing of what we see in the Synoptic Gospels demands a divine Christology, and few things point strongly in such a direction.

I have two hopes for this study. First, I hope that the category of idealized human figure takes a sufficiently central place in future discussions that it will to some degree stem the rushing tide of conversation about divine Christology and reclaim some ground for exploring the most important thing that the Synoptic Gospels tell us about Jesus: he is some kind of human Christ. This is both a narratively compelling reading of the stories and a rich category about Jesus's identity that interpreters need not apologize for or set aside hastily in hopes of finding a reading with better payoff. Historically and literarily, I have demonstrated that such an identity for Jesus is plausible, even necessary, for interpreting these texts. More than that, I have shown that it is likely a sufficient category. The task of understanding Jesus in these texts, along with the ways that such a task entails understanding God, the world, Jesus's followers, and salvation, must fully embrace the human Jesus and not think that this dimension of his person is a husk to be beaten off in hopes of discovering within some divine mystery that truly unlocks the story.

Second, I hope that as we develop a willingness to read these stories as concurring testimonies about a man first attested by God that the fruit of the labor will be a revisiting of the theological significance of Jesus as the Human One. This idea antedates the Gospels as it finds expression in Paul's Adam Christology. It postdates the Gospels as it finds expression in Irenaeus's theology of recapitulation. Perhaps post-Reformation Protestantism has simply found a simpler object for its core tenet of "salvation by faith alone" in the Gospel of John's calls to believe that Jesus is messiah and divine son than in the active and involving Jesus of the Synoptic Tradition. In a different vein, when the divine messiah proved too much for modernity it stripped the Synoptic Jesus of his idealized character in order to make him merely human — the wandering cynic sage whose aphorisms speak of wisdom but whose life is no powerful demonstration of the advent of God's reign over bodies and nature no less than minds and hearts. Each posture deprives us of the Jesus who was fully and truly human as he is depicted: as an idealized human who faithfully rules every facet of the world on God's behalf, but only attains to this rule because of his willingness to submit to God even to the point of death on the cross.

Here, a vast field of Christological reflection is ripe for harvest. It includes recasting the cosmic hierarchy such that humans are viewed as having a job of rule "higher" than the job of the angelic servants. It entails recognizing that such authority over spiritual beings casts idealized humanity in the role of dispossessing this world of its oppressive powers. It holds pictures of a human ruler overcoming the dehumanizing forces of nature to extend health and sustenance. And it contains the paradoxical narrative of a cruciform road that brings about such power only through the surrender of it.

The Synoptic Gospels confront us with a human person, and challenge us to apprehend his peculiar identity as he plays a unique role at the eschatological turning of the ages with the advent of the kingdom of God. They narrate for us a human who shares in the identity of God in ways analogous to what idealized human figures are supposed to do throughout the stories of early Judaism. They depict for us someone entrusted with the primal human vocation to rule the world on God's behalf. They show us the story of someone whom we will never know fully until we know him first as a man attested by God.

Bibliography

Achtemeier, Paul. "The Lukan Perspective on the Miracles of Jesus: A Preliminary Sketch." In *Perspectives on Luke-Acts*, edited by Charles H. Talbert, 153-67. Edinburgh: T&T Clark, 1978.

————. "Omne Verbum Sonat: The New Testament and the Oral Environment of Late Western Antiquity." *Journal of Biblical Literature* 109 (1990): 3-27.

Achtemeier, Paul J., Joel B. Green, and Marianne Meye Thompson. *Introducing the New Testament: Its Literature and Theology*. Grand Rapids, MI: Eerdmans, 2001.

Adams, Marilyn McCord. "The Role of Miracles in the Structure of Luke-Acts." In *Hermes and Athena: Biblical Exegesis and Philosophical Theology*, edited by Eleonore Stump and Thomas P. Flint, 235-74. University of Notre Dame Studies in the Philosophy of Religion 7. Notre Dame, IN: University of Notre Dame Press, 1993.

Ahearne-Kroll, Stephen P. *The Psalms of Lament in Mark's Passion: Jesus' Davidic Suffering*. Society for New Testament Studies Monograph Series 142. New York: Cambridge University Press, 2007.

————. "The Scripturally Complex Presentation of Jesus in the Gospel of Mark." In *Portraits of Jesus: Studies in Christology*, edited by Susan E. Myers, 45-68. Wissenschaftliche Untersuchungen zum Neuen Testament 2 321. Tübingen: Mohr Siebeck, 2012.

Aletti, Jean Noël, and Xavier Léon-Dufour, eds. *Les Miracles de Jésus selon le Nouveau Testament*. Paris: Éditions du Seuil, 1977.

Allen, Leslie C. *Psalms 101–150*. Word Biblical Commentary 21. Waco, TX: Word, 1983.

Allison, Dale C., Jr. "The Baptism of Jesus and a New Dead Sea Scroll." *Biblical Archaeology Review* 18 (1992): 58-60.

————. "The Embodiment of God's Will: Jesus in Matthew." In *Seeking the Identity of Jesus: A Pilgrimage*, edited by Beverly Roberts Gaventa and Richard B. Hays, 117-32. Grand Rapids, MI: Eerdmans, 2008.

————. *The End of the Ages Has Come: An Early Interpretation of the Passion and Resurrection of Jesus*. Philadelphia: Fortress, 1985.

————. *The New Moses: A Matthean Typology*. Minneapolis: Fortress, 1993.

————. "Psalm 23 (22) in Early Christianity: A Suggestion." *Irish Biblical Studies* 5 (1983): 132-37.

————. *The Sermon on the Mount: Inspiring the Moral Imagination.* New York: Herder and Herder, 1999.

Anderson, Gary A. *The Genesis of Perfection: Adam and Eve in Jewish and Christian Imagination.* Louisville, KY: Westminster John Knox, 2001.

Angel, Joseph L. *Otherworldly and Eschatological Priesthood in the Dead Sea Scrolls.* Studies on the Texts of the Desert of Judah 86. Leiden: Brill, 2010.

Arterbury, Andrew E. "Zacchaeus: 'A Son of Abraham'?" In *Biblical Interpretation in Early Christian Gospels,* vol. 3, *The Gospel of Luke,* edited by Thomas R. Hatina, 18-31. Library of New Testament Studies 376/Studies in Scripture in Early Judaism and Christianity 16. London: T&T Clark, 2010.

Aune, David E. "*Abba.*" In *International Standard Bible Encyclopedia,* edited by Geoffrey W. Bromiley, 3-4. Vol. 1. Grand Rapids, MI: Eerdmans, 1979.

Aus, Roger David. *Feeding the Five Thousand: Studies in the Judaic Background of Mark 6:30-44 Par. and John 6:1-15.* Lanham, MD: University Press of America, 2010.

Baden, Joel S. *The Promise to the Patriarchs.* Oxford: Oxford University Press, 2013.

Baeck, Leo. *Judaism and Christianity: Essays.* Philadelphia: Jewish Publication Society, 1958.

Bahrani, Zainab. *The Graven Image: Representation in Babylonia and Assyria.* Philadelphia: University of Pennsylvania Press, 2003.

Barker, Margaret. "The High Priest and the Worship of Jesus." In *The Jewish Roots of Christological Monotheism: Papers from the St. Andrews Conference on the Historical Origins of the Worship of Jesus,* edited by Carey C. Newman, James R. Davila, and Gladys S. Lewis, 93-111. Supplements to the Journal for the Study of Judaism 63. Leiden: Brill, 1999.

Barr, James. "'Abbā Isn't 'Daddy.'" *Journal of Theological Studies* 39 (1988): 28-47.

Bauckham, Richard. *Jesus and the God of Israel: God Crucified and Other Studies on the New Testament's Christology of Divine Identity.* Grand Rapids, MI: Eerdmans, 2009.

————. "The Scrupulous Priest and the Good Samaritan: Jesus' Parabolic Interpretation of the Law of Moses." *New Testament Studies* 44 (1998): 475-89.

————. "The Throne of God and the Worship of Jesus." In *The Jewish Roots of Christian Monotheism: Papers from the St. Andrews Conference on the Historical Origins of the Worship of Jesus,* edited by Carey C. Newman, James R. Davila, and Gladys C. Lewis, 42-69. Supplements to the Journal for the Study of Judaism 63. Leiden: Brill, 1989.

Beaton, Richard. *Isaiah's Christ in Matthew's Gospel.* Society for New Testament Studies Monograph Series 123. New York: Cambridge University Press, 2002.

Bekken, Per Jarle. *The Word Is Near You: A Study of Deuteronomy 30:12-14 in Paul's Letter to the Romans in a Jewish Context.* Beihefte zur Zeitschrift für die Neutestamentliche Wissenschaft und die Kunde der ältern Kirche 144. Berlin: De Gruyter, 2007.

Beyerle, Stefan. "'Der mit den Wolken des Himmels Kommt': Untersuchungen zum Traditionsgefüge 'Menschensohn.'" In *Gottessohn und Menschensohn: Exegetische Studien zu zwei Paradigmen biblischer Intertextualität,* edited by Dieter Sänger, 1-52. Biblisch-Theologische Studien 67. Neukirchen-Vluyn: Neukirchener, 2004.

Bietenhard, Hans. *Midrasch Tanḥuma B: R. Tanḥuma über die Tora, genannt Midrasch Jelammedenu.* 2 vols. Bern: Peter Lang, 1982.

Bird, Michael F. "Did Jesus Think He Was God?" In *How God Became Jesus: The Real Origins of Belief in Jesus' Divine Nature — A Response to Bart Ehrman,* edited by Michael F. Bird, 45-70. Grand Rapids, MI: Zondervan, 2014.

———. "Of Gods, Angels, and Men." In *How God Became Jesus: The Real Origins of Belief in Jesus' Divine Nature — A Response to Bart Ehrman,* edited by Michael F. Bird, 22-40. Grand Rapids: Zondervan, 2014.

———, ed. *How God Became Jesus: The Real Origins of Belief in Jesus' Divine Nature — A Response to Bart Ehrman.* Grand Rapids, MI: Zondervan, 2014.

Black, C. Clifton. *Mark.* Abingdon New Testament Commentaries. Nashville: Abingdon, 2011.

Black, Matthew. *The Book of Enoch, Or, I Enoch: A New English Edition with Commentary and Textual Notes.* Studia in Veteris Testamenti Pseudepigrapha 7. Leiden: Brill, 1985.

———. "The Messianism of the Parables of Enoch: Their Date and Contribution to Christological Origins." In *The Messiah: Developments in Earliest Judaism and Christianity,* edited by James H. Charlesworth, 145-68. Minneapolis: Fortress, 1992.

Blackburn, Barry L. "The Miracles of Jesus." In *The Cambridge Companion to Miracles,* edited by Graham H. Twelftree, 113-30. New York: Cambridge University Press, 2011.

———. *Theios Anēr and the Markan Miracle Traditions: A Critique of the Theios Anēr Concept as an Interpretative Background of the Miracle Traditions Used by Mark.* Wissenschaftliche Untersuchungen zum Neuen Testament 2 40. Tübingen: Mohr Siebeck, 1991.

Blomberg, Craig. *Jesus and the Gospels: An Introduction and Survey.* 2nd ed. Nashville: B & H Academic, 2009.

Bock, Darrell L. *Proclamation from Prophecy and Pattern: Lucan Old Testament Christology.* Journal for the Study of the New Testament Supplement Series 129. Sheffield: JSOT, 1987.

———. "Proclamation from Prophecy and Pattern: Luke's Use of the Old Testament for Christology and Mission." In *The Gospels and the Scriptures of Israel,* edited by Craig A. Evans and William Richard Stegner, 280-307. Journal for the Study of the New Testament Supplement Series 104/Studies in Scripture in Early Judaism and Christianity 3. Sheffield: Sheffield Academic, 1994.

Boring, Eugene. "Mark 1:1-15 and the Beginning of the Gospel." *Semeia* 52 (1990): 43-81.

Bornkamm, Günther. "The Stilling of the Storm in Matthew." In *Tradition and Interpretation in Matthew,* edited by Günther Bornkamm, Gerhard Barth, and Heinz Joachim Held, 52-57. Philadelphia: Westminster, 1963.

Borsch, Frederick Houk. *The Son of Man in Myth and History*. Philadelphia: Westminster, 1967.

Böttrich, Christfried. "Konturen des 'Menschensohnes' in äthHen 37–71." In *Gottessohn und Menschensohn: Exegetische Studien zu zwei Paradigmen biblischer Inter- textualität*, edited by Dieter Sänger, 53-90. Biblisch-Theologische Studien 67. Neukirchen-Vluyn: Neukirchener, 2004.

Boyarin, Daniel. "Daniel 7, Intertextuality, and the History of Israel's Cult." *Harvard Theo- logical Review* 105 (2012): 139-62.

————. "How Enoch Can Teach Us about Jesus." *Early Christianity* 2 (2011): 51-76.

————. *The Jewish Gospels: The Story of the Jewish Christ*. New York: New Press, 2012.

Brawley, Robert L. *Text to Text Pours Forth Speech: Voices of Scripture in Luke-Acts*. Bloomington: Indiana University Press, 1995.

Broadhead, Edwin Keith. *Naming Jesus: Titular Christology in the Gospel of Mark*. Journal for the Study of the New Testament Supplement Series 175. Sheffield: Sheffield Academic, 1999.

————. "Reconfiguring Jesus: The Son of Man in Markan Perspective." In *Biblical Interpretation in Early Christian Gospels*, vol. 1, *The Gospel of Mark*, edited by Thomas R. Hatina, 18-30. Library of New Testament Studies 304. London: T&T Clark, 2006.

Brown, Raymond E. *The Birth of the Messiah: A Commentary on the Infancy Narratives in the Gospels of Matthew and Luke*. Anchor Bible Reference Library. New York: Doubleday, 1993.

Brueggemann, Walter. *Theology of the Old Testament: Testimony, Dispute, Advocacy*. Min- neapolis: Fortress, 1997.

Buckwalter, Douglas. *The Character and Purpose of Luke's Christology*. New York: Cam- bridge University Press, 1996.

Bultmann, Rudolf. *The History of the Synoptic Tradition*. Translated by John Marsh. Ox- ford: Blackwell, 1968.

————. *Theology of the New Testament*. Translated by K. Grobel. Waco, TX: Baylor Uni- versity Press, 2007.

Butticaz, Simon David. *L'identité de l'Église dans les Actes des apôtres: De la restauration d'Israël à la conquête universelle*. Beihefte zur Zeitschrift für die Neutestament- liche Wissenschaft und die Kunde der ältern Kirche 174. Berlin: De Gruyter, 2010.

Caragounis, Chrys C. *The Son of Man: Vision and Interpretation*. Wissenschaftliche Un- tersuchungen zum Neuen Testament 38. Tübingen: Mohr Siebeck, 1986.

Carrez, Maurice. "L'héritage de l'Ancien Testament." In *Les Miracles de Jésus selon le Nou- veau Testament*, edited by Jean Noël Aletti and Xavier Léon-Dufour, 45-58. Paris: Éditions du Seuil, 1977.

Carson, D. A. "Do the Prophets and the Law Quit Prophesying before John? A Note on Matthew 11:13." In *The Gospels and the Scriptures of Israel*, edited by Craig A. Evans and William Richard Stegner, 179-94. Journal for the Study of the New Testament

Supplement Series 104/Studies in Scripture in Early Judaism and Christianity 3. Sheffield: Sheffield Academic, 1994.

Casey, Maurice. "Christology and the Legitimating Use of the Old Testament in the New Testament." In *The Old Testament in the New Testament: Essays in Honour of J. L. North,* edited by Steve Moyise, 42-64. Journal for the Study of the New Testament Supplement Series 189. Sheffield: Sheffield Academic, 2000.

———. "Chronology and the Development of Pauline Christology." In *Paul and Paulinism: Essays in Honour of C. K. Barrett,* edited by Morna D. Hooker and S. G. Wilson, 124-34. London: SPCK, 1982.

———. *From Jewish Prophet to Gentile God: The Origins and Development of New Testament Christology.* Cambridge: J. Clarke, 1991.

———. *The Solution to the "Son of Man" Problem.* Library of New Testament Studies 343. London: T&T Clark, 2007.

———. *Son of Man: The Interpretation and Influence of Daniel 7.* London: SPCK, 1979.

———. "Where Wright Is Wrong: A Critical Review of N. T. Wright's Jesus and the Victory of God." *Journal for the Study of the New Testament* 20 (1998): 95-103.

Chandler, Christopher N. "'Love Your Neighbor as Yourself': (Leviticus 19:18B) in Early Jewish-Christian Exegetical Practice and Missional Formulation." In *"What Does the Scripture Say?" Studies in the Function of Scripture in Early Judaism and Christianity,* edited by Craig A. Evans and Danny Zacharias, 12-56. Library of New Testament Studies 469/Studies in Scripture in Early Judaism and Christianity 17. London: T&T Clark, 2012.

Charlesworth, James H., ed. *The Messiah: Developments in Earliest Judaism and Christianity.* Minneapolis: Fortress, 1992.

———, ed. *The Old Testament Pseudepigrapha.* 2 vols. Garden City, NY: Doubleday, 1983-1985.

Chester, Andrew. "High Christology — Whence, When and Why?" *Early Christianity* 2 (2011): 22-50.

Cohen, Shaye J. D. *From the Maccabees to the Mishnah.* Philadelphia: Westminster, 1987.

Cole, Steven William, and Peter Machinist, eds. *Letters from Priests to the Kings Esarhaddon and Assurbanipal.* State Archives of Assyria 13. Helsinki: Helsinki University Press, 1998.

Collins, Adela Yarbro. "The Apocalyptic Son of Man Sayings." In *The Future of Early Christianity,* edited by Birger A. Pearson, 220-28. Minneapolis: Fortress, 1991.

———. "'How on Earth Did Jesus Become God?' A Reply." In *Israel's God and Rebecca's Children: Christology and Community in Early Judaism and Christianity: Essays in Honor of Larry W. Hurtado and Alan F. Segal,* edited by David B. Capes, April D. DeConick, Helen K. Bond, and Troy A. Miller, 55-66. Waco, TX: Baylor University Press, 2007.

———. *Mark: A Commentary.* Hermeneia. Minneapolis: Fortress, 2007.

———. "Mark and His Readers: The Son of God among Greeks and Romans." *Harvard Theological Review* 93 (2000): 85-100.

————. "Mark and His Readers: The Son of God among Jews." *Harvard Theological Review* 92 (1999): 393-408.

Collins, Adela Yarbro, and John J. Collins. *King and Messiah as Son of God: Divine, Human, and Angelic Messianic Figures in Biblical and Related Literature.* Grand Rapids, MI: Eerdmans, 2008.

Collins, John J. *The Apocalyptic Imagination: An Introduction to Jewish Apocalyptic Literature.* 2nd ed. Grand Rapids, MI: Eerdmans, 1998.

————. *Daniel: A Commentary on the Book of Daniel.* Hermeneia. Minneapolis: Fortress, 1993.

————. "Qumran, Apocalypticism, and the New Testament." In *The Dead Sea Scrolls Fifty Years after Their Discovery: Proceedings of the Jerusalem Congress, July 20-25, 1997,* edited by Lawrence H. Schiffman, Emanuel Tov, James C. VanderKam, and Galen Marquis, 133-38. Jerusalem: Israel Exploration Society, 2000.

————. *The Scepter and the Star: Messianism in Light of the Dead Sea Scrolls.* 2nd ed. Grand Rapids, MI: Eerdmans, 2010.

————. "The Son of Man and the Saints of the Most High in the Book of Daniel." *Journal of Biblical Literature* 93 (1974): 50-66.

Collins, John J., and George W. E. Nickelsburg, eds. *Ideal Figures in Ancient Judaism: Profiles and Paradigms.* Chico, CA: Scholars, 1980.

Conzelmann, Hans. *The Theology of St. Luke.* Translated by G. Buswell. New York: Harper & Row, 1961.

Cotter, Wendy. *The Christ of the Miracle Stories: Portrait through Encounter.* Grand Rapids, MI: Baker Academic, 2010.

————. *Miracles in Greco-Roman Antiquity: A Sourcebook.* London: Routledge, 1999.

Craigie, Peter. *Psalms 1–50.* Word Biblical Commentary 19. Waco, TX: Word, 1983.

Crouch, Carly L. "Genesis 1:26-7 as a Statement of Humanity's Divine Parentage." *Journal of Theological Studies* 61 (2010): 1-15.

Crowe, Brandon D. *The Obedient Son: Deuteronomy and Christology in the Gospel of Matthew.* Beihefte zur Zeitschrift für die Neutestamentliche Wissenschaft und die Kunde der ältern Kirche 188. Berlin: De Gruyter, 2012.

Cullmann, Oscar. *The Christology of the New Testament.* Translated by Shirley C. Guthrie and Charles A. M. Hall. Rev. ed. Philadelphia: Westminster, 1963.

Davenport, Gene. "The 'Anointed of the Lord' in Psalms of Solomon 17." In *Ideal Figures in Ancient Judaism: Profiles and Paradigms,* edited by John J. Collins and George W. E. Nickelsburg, 87-92. Society of Biblical Literature Septuagint and Cognate Studies 12. Chico, CA: Scholars, 1980.

Davies, W. D., and Dale C. Allison. *A Critical and Exegetical Commentary on the Gospel according to Saint Matthew: In 3 Volumes.* International Critical Commentary. Edinburgh: T&T Clark, 1997.

Davis, Carl Judson. *The Name and Way of the Lord: Old Testament Themes, New Testament Christology.* Journal for the Study of the New Testament Supplement Series 129. Sheffield: Sheffield Academic, 1996.

Davis, Philip G. "Mark's Christological Paradox." *Journal for the Study of the New Testament* 11 (1989): 3-18.

Dechow, Jens. *Gottessohn und Herrschaft Gottes: Der Theozentrismus des Markusevangeliums.* Wissenschaftliche Monographien zum Alten und Neuen Testament 86. Neukirchen-Vluyn: Neukirchener Verlag, 2000.

Diffey, Daniel S. "The Royal Promise in Genesis: The Often Underestimated Importance of Genesis 17:6, 17:16, and 35:11." *Tyndale Bulletin* 62 (2011): 313-16.

Dodd, C. H. *According to the Scriptures: The Sub-Structure of New Testament Theology.* New York: Scribner, 1953.

———. *The Apostolic Preaching and Its Developments: Three Lectures with an Appendix on Eschatology and History.* New York: Harper & Row, 1964.

Donahue, John R. "Jesus as the Parable of God in the Gospel of Mark." *Interpretation: A Journal of Bible and Theology* 32 (1978): 369-86.

———. "Temple, Trial, and Royal Christology." In *The Passion in Mark: Studies on Mark 14–16,* edited by Werner H. Kelber, 61-78. Philadelphia: Fortress, 1976.

Donaldson, Terence L. "The Vindicated Son: A Narrative Approach to Matthean Christology." In *Contours of Christology in the New Testament,* edited by Richard N. Longenecker, 100-121. Grand Rapids, MI: Eerdmans, 2005.

Douglas, Mary. *Purity and Danger: An Analysis of Concepts of Pollution and Taboo.* New York: Routledge, 1966.

Dunn, James D. G. "'Are You the Messiah?' Is the Crux of Mark 14.61-62 Resolvable?" In *Christology, Controversy, and Community: New Testament Essays in Honour of David R. Catchpole,* edited by David G. Horrell and C. M. Tuckett, 1-22. Boston: Brill, 2000.

———. *Christology in the Making: A New Testament Inquiry into the Origins of the Doctrine of the Incarnation.* 2nd ed. Grand Rapids, MI: Eerdmans, 1996.

———. *Did the First Christians Worship Jesus? The New Testament Evidence.* Louisville, KY: Westminster John Knox, 2010.

———. *Jesus and the Spirit: A Study of the Religious and Charismatic Experience of Jesus and the First Christians as Reflected in the New Testament.* Grand Rapids, MI: Eerdmans, 1997.

———. *Romans 1–8.* Word Biblical Commentary 38a. Dallas: Word, 1988.

Edelstein, Emma J., and Ludwig Edelstein. *Asclepius: A Collection and Interpretation of the Testimonies.* Vol. 2. Baltimore: Johns Hopkins University Press, 1945.

Ehrman, Bart D. *How Jesus Became God: The Exaltation of a Jewish Preacher from Galilee.* San Francisco: HarperOne, 2014.

———. *The Orthodox Corruption of Scripture: The Effect of Early Christological Controversies on the Text of the New Testament.* New York: Oxford University Press, 1993.

Elgvin, Torleif. "Priestly Sages? The Milieus of Origin of 4QMysteries and 4QInstruction." In *Sapiential Perspectives: Wisdom Literature in Light of the Dead Sea Scrolls: Proceedings of the Sixth International Symposium of the Orion Center for the Study of the Dead Sea Scrolls and Associated Literature,* edited by John J. Collins and

Gregory E. Sterling, 67-87. Studies on the Texts of the Desert of Judah 51. Leiden: Brill, 2004.

Ellis, E. Earle. "Deity-Christology in Mark 14:58." In *Jesus of Nazareth, Lord and Christ: Essays on the Historical Jesus and New Testament Christology*, edited by Joel B. Green and Max Turner, 192-203. Grand Rapids, MI: Eerdmans, 1994.

Eshel, Esther. "4Q471B: A Self-Glorification Hymn." *Revue de Qumran* 17 (1996): 175-203.

Evans, Craig A. "Jesus and the Continuing Exile of Israel." In *Jesus and the Restoration of Israel: A Critical Assessment of N. T. Wright's Jesus and the Victory of God*, edited by Carey C. Newman, 77-100. Downers Grove, IL: InterVarsity, 1999.

———. "Luke's Good Samaritan and the Chronicler's Good Samaritans." In *Biblical Interpretation in Early Christian Gospels*, vol. 3, *The Gospel of Luke*, edited by Thomas R. Hatina, 32-42. Library of New Testament Studies 376/Studies in Scripture in Early Judaism and Christianity 16. London: T&T Clark, 2010.

Evans, Craig A., and William Richard Stegner, eds. *The Gospels and the Scriptures of Israel*. Journal for the Study of the New Testament Supplement Series 104/Studies in Scripture in Early Judaism and Christianity 3. Sheffield: Sheffield Academic, 1994.

Evans, Craig A., and Danny Zacharias, eds. *"What Does the Scripture Say?" Studies in the Function of Scripture in Early Judaism and Christianity*, vol. 1, *The Synoptic Gospels*. Library of New Testament Studies 469/Studies in Scripture in Early Judaism and Christianity 17. London: T&T Clark, 2012.

Eve, Eric. *The Jewish Context of Jesus' Miracles*. Journal for the Study of the New Testament Supplement Series 231. London: Sheffield Academic, 2002.

Fitzmyer, Joseph A. *The Gospel according to Luke (I–IX): Introduction, Translation, and Notes*. Anchor Bible 28. New York: Doubleday, 1981.

Fletcher-Louis, Crispin H. T. "4Q374: A Discourse on the Sinai Tradition: The Deification of Moses and Early Christology." *Dead Sea Discoveries* 3 (1996): 236-52.

———. *All the Glory of Adam: Liturgical Anthropology in the Dead Sea Scrolls*. Leiden: Brill, 2002.

———. "The Cosmology of P and Theological Anthropology in the Wisdom of Jesus Ben Sira." In *Of Scribes and Sages: Early Jewish Interpretation and Transmission of Scripture*, vol. 1, *Ancient Versions and Traditions*, edited by Craig A. Evans, 69-113. Studies in Scripture in Early Judaism and Christianity 9/Library of Second Temple Studies 50. London: T&T Clark International, 2004.

———. *Luke-Acts: Angels, Christology, and Soteriology*. Tübingen: Mohr Siebeck, 1997.

Flusser, David. "Melchizedek and the Son of Man." In *Judaism and the Origins of Christianity*. Jerusalem: Magnes, 1988.

———. "Resurrection and Angels in Rabbinic Judaism, Early Christianity, and Qumran." In *The Dead Sea Scrolls Fifty Years after Their Discovery: Proceedings of the Jerusalem Congress, July 20-25, 1997*, edited by Lawrence H. Schiffman, Emanuel Tov, James C. VanderKam, and Galen Marquis, 568-72. Jerusalem: Israel Exploration Society, 2000.

Fossum, Jarl E. *The Image of the Invisible God: Essays on the Influence of Jewish Mysticism on Early Christology*. Novum Testamentum et Orbis Antiquus 30. Göttingen: Vandenhoeck & Ruprecht, 1995.

France, R. T. *The Gospel of Mark: A Commentary on the Greek Text*. New International Greek Testament Commentary. Grand Rapids, MI: Eerdmans, 2002.

————. *The Gospel of Matthew*. New International Commentary on the New Testament. Grand Rapids, MI: Eerdmans, 2007.

Frey, Jörg. "Christology from Jewish Roots." *Early Christianity* 2 (2011): 1-3.

Fuller, Reginald H. *The Foundations of New Testament Christology*. New York: Charles Scribner's Sons, 1965.

————. *The Mission and Achievement of Jesus: An Examination of the Presuppositions of New Testament Theology*. London: SCM, 1954.

Garland, Robert. "Miracles in the Greek and Roman World." In *The Cambridge Companion to Miracles*, edited by Graham H. Twelftree, 75-94. New York: Cambridge University Press, 2011.

Garr, W. Randall. *In His Own Image and Likeness: Humanity, Divinity, and Monotheism*. Culture and History of the Ancient Near East 15. Leiden: Brill, 2003.

Gathercole, Simon J. *The Preexistent Son: Recovering the Christologies of Matthew, Mark, and Luke*. Grand Rapids, MI: Eerdmans, 2006.

————. "The Son of Man in Mark's Gospel." *Expository Times* 115 (2004): 366-72.

————. "What Did the First Christians Think about Jesus?" In *How God Became Jesus: The Real Origins of Belief in Jesus' Divine Nature — A Response to Bart Ehrman*, edited by Michael F. Bird, 94-116. Grand Rapids, MI: Zondervan, 2014.

Gaventa, Beverly Roberts. "Learning and Relearning the Identity of Jesus from Luke-Acts." In *Seeking the Identity of Jesus: A Pilgrimage*, edited by Beverly Roberts Gaventa and Richard B. Hays, 148-65. Grand Rapids, MI: Eerdmans, 2008.

Gaventa, Beverly Roberts, and Richard B. Hays, eds. *Seeking the Identity of Jesus: A Pilgrimage*. Grand Rapids, MI: Eerdmans, 2008.

George, Augustin. "Le Miracle dans l'Oeuvre de Luc." In *Les Miracles de Jésus Selon le Nouveau Testament*, edited by Jean Noël Aletti and Xavier Léon-Dufour, 259-68. Paris: Éditions du Seuil, 1977.

Gerhardsson, Birger. *The Testing of God's Son (Matt. 4: 1-11 & Par.): An Analysis of an Early Christian Midrash*. Translated by J. Toy. Lund: Gleerup, 1966.

Glöckner, Richard. *Neutestamentliche Wundergeschichten und das Lob der Wundertaten Gottes in den Psalmen: Studien zur sprachlichen und theologischen Verwandtschaft zwischen neutestamentlichen Wundergeschichten und Psalmen*. Walberberger Studien der Albertus-Magnus-Akademie. Theologische Reihe 13. Mainz: Matthias-Grünewald-Verlag, 1983.

Goff, Matthew. "Reading Wisdom at Qumran: 4QInstruction and the Hodayot." *Dead Sea Discoveries* 11 (2004): 263-88.

Goldingay, John. *Daniel*. Word Biblical Commentary 30. Dallas: Word, 1989.

————. *Old Testament Theology*, vol. 1, *Israel's Gospel*. Downers Grove, IL: InterVarsity, 2003.

González, Justo L. *Luke*. Belief. Louisville, KY: Westminster John Knox, 2010.

Goodenough, Erwin R. *By Light, Light: The Mystic Gospel of Hellenistic Judaism*. New Haven, CT: Yale University Press, 1935.

Goodwin, Mark J. "Hosea and 'the Son of the Living God' in Matthew 16:16b." *Catholic Biblical Quarterly* 67 (2005): 265-83.

Grabbe, Lester L. "'Better Watch Your Back, Adam': Another Adam and Eve Tradition in Second Temple Judaism." In *New Perspectives on 2 Enoch: No Longer Slavonic Only*, edited by Andrei A. Orlov and Gabriele Boccaccini, 273-82. Studia Judaeo-slavica 4. Leiden: Brill, 2012.

Gradl, Hans-Georg. "Glaube in Seenot (die Stillung des Sturms): Mk 4,35-41 (Lk 8,22-25)." In *Kompendium der frühchristlichen Wundererzählungen*, Band 1, *Die Wunder Jesu*, edited by Susanne Luther and Jörg Röder, 257-65. Munich: Güterlsloher Verlaghaus, 2013.

Graupner, Axel, and Michael Wolter, eds. *Moses in Biblical and Extra-Biblical Traditions*. Beihefte zur Zeitschrift für die Alttestamentliche Wissenschaft 372. Berlin: De Gruyter, 2007.

Green, Joel B. *The Gospel of Luke*. New International Commentary on the New Testament. Grand Rapids, MI: Eerdmans, 1997.

————. *The Theology of the Gospel of Luke*. New York: Cambridge University Press, 1995.

Gregerman, Adam. "Biblical Prophecy and the Fate of the Nations in Early Jewish and Christian Interpretations of Isaiah." In *"What Does the Scripture Say?" Studies in the Function of Scripture in Early Judaism and Christianity*, vol. 1, *The Synoptic Gospels*, edited by Craig A. Evans and Danny Zacharias, 212-40. Library of New Testament Studies 469/Studies in Scripture in Early Judaism and Christianity 17. London: T&T Clark, 2012.

Grelot, Pierre. "Les Miracles de Jésus et la Démonologie Juive." In *Les Miracles de Jésus selon le Nouveau Testament*, edited by Jean Noël Aletti and Xavier Léon-Dufour, 59-72. Paris: Éditions du Seuil, 1977.

Grindheim, Sigurd. *Christology in the Synoptic Gospels: God or God's Servant?* New York: T&T Clark, 2012.

Guelich, Robert A. *The Sermon on the Mount: A Foundation for Understanding*. Waco, TX: Word, 1982.

Gunkel, Hermann. *Elijas, Jahve und Baal*. Tübingen: Mohr, 1906.

Hamerton-Kelly, Robert. *Pre-existence, Wisdom, and the Son of Man: A Study of the Idea of Pre-existence in the New Testament*. New York: Cambridge University Press, 1973.

Hare, Douglas R. A. *The Son of Man Tradition*. Minneapolis: Fortress, 1990.

Hartenstein, Judith. "Jenseits der Komfortzone (Jesu Erscheinen auf dem See): Mt 14:22-33." In *Kompendium der frühchristlichen Wundererzählungen*, Band 1, *Die Wunder Jesu*, edited by Susanne Luther and Jörg Röder, 454-64. Gütersloh: Gütersloher Verlagshaus, 2013.

Hatina, Thomas R. "Embedded Scripture Texts and the Plurality of Meaning." In *Biblical*

Interpretation in Early Christian Gospels, vol. 1, *The Gospel of Mark,* edited by Thomas R. Hatina, 81-99. Library of New Testament Studies 304. New York: T&T Clark, 2006.

—————. "From History to Myth and Back Again: The Historicizing Function of Scripture in Matthew 2." In *Biblical Interpretation in Early Christian Gospels,* vol. 2, *The Gospel of Matthew,* edited by Thomas R. Hatina, 98-118. Library of New Testament Studies 310. London: T&T Clark, 2008.

—————, ed. *Biblical Interpretation in Early Christian Gospels,* vol. 1, *The Gospel of Mark.* Library of New Testament Studies 304. London: T&T Clark, 2006.

—————, ed. *Biblical Interpretation in Early Christian Gospels,* vol. 2, *The Gospel of Matthew.* Library of New Testament Studies 310. London: T&T Clark, 2008.

—————, ed. *Biblical Interpretation in Early Christian Gospels,* vol. 3, *The Gospel of Luke.* Library of New Testament Studies 376/Studies in Scripture in Early Judaism and Christianity 16. London: T&T Clark, 2010.

Hays, Richard B. *Reading Backwards: Figural Christology and the Fourfold Gospel Witness.* Waco, TX: Baylor University Press, 2014.

Hayward, C. T. R. *The Jewish Temple: A Non-biblical Sourcebook.* London: Routledge, 1996.

—————. "Sacrifice and World Order: Some Observations on Ben Sira's Attitude to the Temple Service." In *Sacrifice and Redemption,* edited by Stephen Sykes, 22-34. New York: Cambridge University Press, 1991.

Head, Peter M. *Christology and the Synoptic Problem: An Argument for Markan Priority.* Society for New Testament Studies Monograph Series 94. New York: Cambridge University Press, 1997.

Healy, Mary. *The Gospel of Mark.* Catholic Commentary on Sacred Scripture. Grand Rapids, MI: Baker Academic, 2008.

Heil, John Paul. *Jesus Walking on the Sea: Meaning and Gospel Functions of Matt. 14:22-33, Mark 6:45-52, and John 6:15b-21.* Rome: Biblical Institute, 1981.

Henderson, Suzanne Watts. *Christology and Discipleship in the Gospel of Mark.* Society for New Testament Studies Monograph Series 135. New York: Cambridge University Press, 2006.

Hendrickx, Herman. *The Miracle Stories of the Synoptic Gospels.* San Francisco: Harper & Row, 1987.

Hengel, Martin. *Judaism and Hellenism: Studies in Their Encounter in Palestine during the Early Hellenistic Period.* Philadelphia: Fortress, 1974.

—————. *Studies in Early Christology.* Edinburgh: T&T Clark, 1995.

Herring, Stephen L. *Divine Substitution: Humanity as the Manifestation of Deity in the Hebrew Bible and the Ancient Near East.* Forschungen zur Religion und Literatur des Alten und Neuen Testaments 247. Göttingen: Vandenhoeck & Ruprecht, 2013.

Holladay, Carl R. *Fragments from Hellenistic Jewish Authors,* vol. 2, *Poets.* Society of Biblical Literature Texts and Translations 30. Atlanta: Scholars, 1989.

Hooker, Morna D. *The Son of Man in Mark: A Study of the Background of the Term "Son of Man" and Its Use in St. Mark's Gospel*. Montreal: McGill University Press, 1967.

————. "Is the Son of Man Problem Really Insoluble?" In *Text and Interpretation: Studies in the New Testament Presented to Matthew Black*, edited by Ernest Best and R. M. Wilson, 155-68. New York: Cambridge University Press, 1979.

Horbury, William. *Jewish Messianism and the Cult of Christ*. London: SCM, 1998.

Horst, Pieter W. van der. "Moses' Throne Vision in Ezekiel the Dramatist." *Journal of Jewish Studies* 34 (1983): 21-29.

Huizenga, Leroy A. "Matt 1:1: 'Son of Abraham' as Christological Category." *Horizons in Biblical Theology* 30 (2008): 103-13.

————. *The New Isaac: Tradition and Intertextuality in the Gospel of Matthew*. Supplements to Novum Testamentum 131. Leiden: Brill, 2009.

Hurtado, Larry W. *Lord Jesus Christ: Devotion to Jesus in Earliest Christianity*. Grand Rapids, MI: Eerdmans, 2003.

————. *One God, One Lord: Early Christian Devotion and Ancient Jewish Monotheism*. 2nd ed. New York: Continuum, 1998.

Janse, Sam. *"You Are My Son": The Reception History of Psalm 2 in Early Judaism and the Early Church*. Leuven: Peeters, 2009.

Jeremias, Joachim. *Abba: Studien zur neutestamentlichen Theologie und Zeitgeschichte*. Göttingen: Vandenhoeck & Ruprecht, 1966.

Johannson, Daniel. "The Identity of Jesus in the Gospel of Mark: Past and Present Proposals." *Currents in Biblical Research* 9 (2010): 364-93.

————. "'Who Can Forgive Sins but God Alone?' Human and Angelic Agents, and Divine Forgiveness in Early Judaism." *Journal for the Study of the New Testament* 33 (2011): 351-74.

Jonge, Marinus de. *God's Final Envoy: Early Christology and Jesus' Own View of His Mission*. Grand Rapids, MI: Eerdmans, 1998.

Juel, Donald H. *A Master of Surprise: Mark Interpreted*. Minneapolis: Fortress, 1994.

————. *Messianic Exegesis: Christological Interpretation of the Old Testament in Early Christianity*. Philadelphia: Fortress, 1988.

————. "The Origin of Mark's Christology." In *The Messiah: Developments in Earliest Judaism and Christianity*, edited by James H. Charlesworth, 449-60. Minneapolis: Fortress, 1992.

Kahl, Werner. "Glauben lässt Jesu Wunderkraft heilsam überfließen (die Tochter des Jaïrus und die blutflüssige Frau): Mk 5,21-43." In *Kompendium der frühchristlichen Wundererzählungen*, Band 1, *Die Wunder Jesu*, edited by Susanne Luther and Jörg Röder, 278-93. Munich: Gütersloher Verlaghaus, 2013.

————. *New Testament Miracle Stories in Their Religious-Historical Setting: A Religionsgeschichtliche Comparison from a Structural Perspective*. Forschungen zur Religion und Literatur des Alten und Neuen Testaments 163. Göttingen: Vandenhoeck & Ruprecht, 1994.

Kammler, Hans-Christian. "Sohn Gottes und Kreuz: Die Versuchungsgeschichte Mt 4,1-11 im Kontext des Matthäusevangeliums." *Zeitschrift für Theologie und Kirche* 100 (2003): 163-86.

Kee, Howard Clark. *Miracle in the Early Christian World: A Study in Sociohistorical Method.* New Haven, CT: Yale University Press, 1983.

Keener, Craig S. *The Gospel of Matthew: A Socio-Rhetorical Commentary.* Grand Rapids, MI: Eerdmans, 2009.

Kelber, Werner H. "The Hour of the Son of Man and the Temptation of the Disciples (Mark 14:32-42)." In *The Passion in Mark: Studies on Mark 14–16,* edited by Werner H. Kelber, 41-60. Philadelphia: Fortress, 1976.

Kingsbury, Jack Dean. "The Composition and Christology of Matt 28:16-20." *Journal of Biblical Literature* 93 (1974): 573-84.

———. *Conflict in Mark: Jesus, Authorities, Disciples.* Minneapolis: Fortress, 1989.

———. *Matthew: Structure, Christology, Kingdom.* Philadelphia: Fortress, 1975.

———. *Matthew as Story.* 2nd ed. Minneapolis: Fortress, 1988.

Kingsley, Peter. *Ancient Philosophy, Mystery, and Magic: Empedocles and Pythagorean Tradition.* Oxford: Clarendon, 1995.

Kirk, J. R. Daniel. "Conceptualising Fulfilment in Matthew." *Tyndale Bulletin* 29 (2008): 77-98.

———. "Mark's Son of Man and Paul's Second Adam." *Horizons in Biblical Theology* 37 (2015): 170-95.

———. "Time for Figs, Temple Destruction, and Houses of Prayer in Mark 11:12-25." *Catholic Biblical Quarterly* 74 (2012): 510-28.

———. *Unlocking Romans: Resurrection and the Justification of God.* Grand Rapids, MI: Eerdmans, 2008.

Kirk, J. R. Daniel, and Stephen L. Young. "'I Will Set His Hand to the Sea': Psalm 88:26 LXX and Christology in Mark." *Journal of Biblical Literature* 133 (2014): 333-40.

Kittel, Gerhard. "ἀββᾶ." In *Theological Dictionary of the New Testament,* edited by Gerhard Kittel and Gerhard Friedrich, translated by Geoffrey W. Bromiley, 1:6. Grand Rapids, MI: Eerdmans, 1964.

Knohl, Israel. "Melchizedek: Union of Kingship and Priesthood." In *Text, Thought, and Practice in Qumran and Early Christianity: Proceedings of the Ninth International Symposium of the Orion Center for the Study of the Dead Sea Scrolls and Associated Literature,* edited by Ruth A. Clements and Daniel R. Schwartz, 255-66. Studies on the Texts of the Desert of Judah 84. Leiden: Brill, 2009.

Kollmann, Bernd. "Brot und Fisch bis zum Abwinken (die Speisung Fünftausend): Mk 6,30-44 (ActJoh 93)." In *Kompendium der frühchristlichen Wundererzählungen,* Band 1, *Die Wunder Jesu,* edited by Susanne Luther and Jörg Röder, 294-303. Munich: Gütersloher Verlaghaus, 2013.

Kooten, George H. van. *Paul's Anthropology in Context: The Image of God, Assimilation to God, and Tripartite Man in Ancient Judaism, Ancient Philosophy and Early Christianity.* Wissenschaftliche Untersuchungen zum Neuen Testament 232. Tübingen: Mohr Siebeck, 2008.

Krentz, Edgar. "God in the New Testament." In *Our Naming of God: Problems and Prospects of God-Talk Today,* edited by Carl E. Braaten. Minneapolis: Fortress, 1989.

Kugel, James L. *In Potiphar's House: The Interpretive Life of Biblical Texts.* San Francisco: HarperSanFrancisco, 1990.

———. *Traditions of the Bible: A Guide to the Bible as It Was at the Start of the Common Era.* Cambridge, MA: Harvard University Press, 1998.

Kuhn, Thomas S. *The Structure of Scientific Revolutions.* 3rd ed. Chicago: University of Chicago Press, 1996.

Kümmel, Werner G. "Jesus der Menschensohn?" *Sitzungsberichte der Wissenschaftlichen Gesellschaft an der Johann Wolfgang Goethe-Universität Frankfurt am Main* 20 (1984): 147-88.

Laato, Antti. *A Star Is Rising: The Historical Development of the Old Testament Royal Ideology and the Rise of the Jewish Messianic Expectations.* University of South Florida International Studies in Formative Christianity and Judaism 5. Atlanta: Scholars, 1997.

Lamarche, Paul. "Les Miracles de Jésus selon Marc." In *Les Miracles de Jésus selon le Nouveau Testament,* edited by Jean Noël Aletti and Xavier Léon-Dufour, 213-26. Paris: Éditions du Seuil, 1977.

Lanfranchi, Pierluigi. *L'Exagoge d'Ezéchiel le Tragique.* Leiden: Brill, 2006.

———. "Reminiscences of Ezekiel's *Exagoge* in Philo's *De Vita Mosis.*" In *Moses in Biblical and Extra-Biblical Traditions,* edited by Axel Graupner and Michael Wolter, 144-50. Beihefte zur Zeitschrift für die Neutestamentliche Wissenschaft und die Kunde der ältern Kirche 372. Berlin: De Gruyter, 2007.

LeDonne, Anthony. "Greater Than Solomon: Orality, Mnemonics, and Scriptural Narrativization in Luke." In *Biblical Interpretation in Early Christian Gospels,* vol. 3, *The Gospel of Luke,* edited by Thomas R. Hatina, 96-113. Library of New Testament Studies 376/Studies in Scripture in Early Judaism and Christianity 16. London: T&T Clark, 2010.

———. *The Historiographical Jesus: Memory, Typology, and the Son of David.* Waco, TX: Baylor University Press, 2009.

Lee, Aquila H. I. *From Messiah to Preexistent Son: Jesus' Self-Consciousness and Early Christian Exegesis of Messianic Psalms.* Wissenschaftliche Untersuchungen zum Neuen Testament 192. Tübingen: Mohr Siebeck, 2005.

Légasse, Simon. "Les Miracles de Jésus selon Matthieu." In *Les Miracles de Jésus selon le Nouveau Testament,* edited by Jean Noël Aletti and Xavier Léon-Dufour, 227-47. Paris: Éditions du Seuil, 1977.

Leithart, Peter J. *1 & 2 Kings.* Brazos Theological Commentary on Scripture. Grand Rapids, MI: Brazos, 2006.

Levenson, Jon D. *Creation and the Persistence of Evil: The Jewish Drama of Divine Omnipotence.* Princeton, NJ: Princeton University Press, 1994.

Levison, John R. *Portraits of Adam in Early Judaism: From Sirach to 2 Baruch.* Journal for the Study of the Pseudepigrapha Supplement Series 1. Sheffield: JSOT, 1988.

Lierman, John. *The New Testament Moses: Christian Perceptions of Moses and Israel in the Setting of Jewish Religion.* Wissenschaftliche Untersuchungen zum Neuen Testament 2 173. Tübingen: Mohr Siebeck, 2004.

Lincoln, Andrew T. *Born of a Virgin? Reconceiving Jesus in the Bible, Tradition, and Theology.* Grand Rapids, MI: Eerdmans, 2013.

Litwa, M. David. *Iesus Deus: The Early Christian Depiction of Jesus as a Mediterranean God.* Minneapolis: Fortress, 2014.

————. *We Are Being Transformed: Deification in Paul's Soteriology.* Berlin: De Gruyter, 2012.

Longenecker, Richard N., ed. *Contours of Christology in the New Testament.* Grand Rapids, MI: Eerdmans, 2005.

Luther, Susanne. "Steuersünder mit Angellizenz (Die Zahlung der Tempelsteuer): Mt 17:24-27 (EpAp 5,12f.)." In *Kompendium der frühchristlichen Wundererzählungen,* Band 1, *Die Wunder Jesu,* edited by Suanne Luther and Jörg Röder, 485-93. Gütersloh: Gütersloher Verlagshaus, 2013.

Luther, Susanne, and Jörg Röder, eds. *Kompendium der frühchristlichen Wundererzählungen,* Band 1, *Die Wunder Jesu.* Munich: Gütersloher Verlaghaus, 2013.

Luz, Ulrich. *Matthew 21-28: A Commentary.* Hermeneia. Minneapolis: Fortress, 2005.

Makiello, Phoebe. "Was Moses Considered to Be an Angel by Those at Qumran?" In *Moses in Biblical and Extra-Biblical Traditions,* edited by Axel Graupner and Michael Wolter, 115-27. Beihefte zur Zeitschrift für die Alttestamentliche Wissenschaft 372. Berlin: De Gruyter, 2007.

Malbon, Elizabeth Struthers. *Mark's Jesus: Characterization as Narrative Christology.* Waco, TX: Baylor University Press, 2009.

Malone, Francis. "The End of the Son of Man?" *The Downside Review* 98 (1980): 280-90.

Marcus, Joel. "Authority to Forgive Sins upon the Earth: The *SHEMA* in the Gospel of Mark." In *The Gospels and the Scriptures of Israel,* edited by Craig A. Evans and William R. Daniel Stegner, 196-211. Journal for the Study of the New Testament Supplement Series 104/Studies in Scripture in Early Judaism and Christianity 3. Sheffield: Sheffield Academic, 1994.

————. "Entering into the Kingly Power of God." *Journal of Biblical Literature* 107 (1988): 663-75.

————. *Mark 1-8: A New Translation with Introduction and Commentary.* Anchor Bible 27. New York: Doubleday, 2000.

————. *Mark 8-16: A New Translation with Introduction and Commentary.* Anchor Yale Bible 27A. New Haven, CT: Yale University Press, 2009.

————. "Son of Man as Son of Adam." *Revue Biblique* 110 (2003): 38-61.

————. "Son of Man as Son of Adam: Part II: Exegesis." *Revue Biblique* 110 (2003): 370-86.

————. *The Way of the Lord: Christological Exegesis of the Old Testament in the Gospel of Mark.* Louisville, KY: Westminster John Knox, 1992.

Marshall, I. Howard. *The Gospel of Luke: A Commentary on the Greek Text.* New International Greek Testament Commentary. Grand Rapids: Eerdmans, 1978.

———. *Luke: Historian and Theologian*. Grand Rapids, MI: Baker Academic, 1989.

Martínez, Florentino García, and Eibert J. C. Tigchelaar. *The Dead Sea Scrolls Study Edition*. 2 vols. Grand Rapids, MI: Eerdmans, 1998.

McCartney, Dan. "*Ecce Homo:* The Coming of the Kingdom as the Restoration of Human Vicegerency." *Westminster Theological Journal* 56 (1994): 1-21.

McConville, J. G. *God and Earthly Power: An Old Testament Political Theology, Genesis–Kings*. Library of Hebrew Bible/Old Testament Studies 454. London: T&T Clark, 2006.

McGrath, James F. *The Only True God: Early Christian Monotheism in Its Jewish Context*. Urbana: University of Illinois Press, 2009.

McKim, Donald K. *Westminster Dictionary of Theological Terms*. Louisville, KY: Westminster John Knox, 1996.

Meeks, Wayne A. "Moses as God and King." In *Religions in Antiquity: Essays in Memory of Erwin Ramsdell Goodenough*, edited by Jacob Neusner, 354-71. Studies in the History of Religions 14. Leiden: Brill, 1968.

———. *The Prophet-King: Moses Traditions and the Johannine Christology*. Leiden: Brill, 1967.

Meier, John P. *A Marginal Jew: Rethinking the Historical Jesus*, vol. 2, *Mentor, Message, and Miracles*. Anchor Bible Reference Library. New York: Doubleday, 1994.

———. *The Vision of Matthew: Christ, Church, and Morality in the First Gospel*. New York: Paulist, 1979.

Mettinger, Tryggve N. D. *King and Messiah: The Civil and Sacral Legitimation of the Israelite Kings*. Lund: Gleerup, 1976.

Meyers, Alicia D. "Isaiah 42 and the Characterization of Jesus in Matthew 12:17-21." In *"What Does the Scripture Say?" Studies in the Function of Scripture in Early Judaism and Christianity*, edited by Craig A. Evans and Danny Zacharias, 70-89. Library of New Testament Studies 469/Studies in Scripture in Early Judaism and Christianity 17. Edinburgh: T&T Clark, 2012.

Middleton, J. Richard. *The Liberating Image: The Imago Dei in Genesis 1*. Grand Rapids, MI: Brazos, 2005.

Milik, J. T. "*Melkî-Ṣedeq* et *Melkî-Reša'* dans les anciens éscrits juifs et chrétiens (I)." *Journal of Jewish Studies* 23 (1972): 95-144.

Mills, Mary E. *Human Agents of Cosmic Power in Hellenistic Judaism and the Synoptic Tradition*. Journal for the Study of the New Testament Supplement Series 41. Sheffield: JSOT, 1990.

Moberly, Walter. "How Appropriate Is 'Monotheism' as a Category for Biblical Interpretation?" In *Early Jewish and Christian Monotheism*, edited by Loren T. Stuckenbruck and Wendy E. S. North. Journal for the Study of the New Testament Supplement Series 263. London: T&T Clark, 2004.

Moessner, David P. "*Two* Lords 'at the Right Hand'? The Psalms and an Intertextual Reading of Peter's Pentecost Speech (Acts 2:14-36)." In *Literary Studies in Luke-Acts:*

Essays in Honor of Joseph B. Tyson, edited by Richard P. Thompson and Thomas E. Phillips, 215-32. Macon, GA: Mercer University Press, 1998.

Moss, Candida R. "The Man with the Flow of Power: Porous Bodies in Mark 5:25-34." *Journal of Biblical Literature* 129 (2010): 507-19.

Mowery, Robert L. "Son of God in Roman Imperial Titles and Matthew." *Biblica* 83 (2002): 100-110.

Müller, Peter. "Zwischen dem Gekommenen und dem Kommenden: Intertextuelle Aspekte der Menschensohnaussagen im Markusevangelium." In *Gottessohn und Menschensohn: Exegetische Studien zu zwei Paradigmen biblischer Intertextualität*, edited by Dieter Sänger, 130-57. Biblisch-Theologische Studien 67. Neukirchen-Vluyn: Neukirchener, 2004.

Müller, Ulrich B. "Jesus als der 'Menschensohn.'" In *Gottessohn und Menschensohn: Exegetische Studien zu zwei Paradigmen biblischer Intertextualität*, edited by Dieter Sänger, 91-129. Biblisch-Theologische Studien 67. Neukirchen-Vluyn: Neukirchener, 2004.

Newman, Carey C., James R. Davila, and Gladys S. Lewis, eds. *The Jewish Roots of Christological Monotheism: Papers from the St. Andrews Conference on the Historical Origins of the Worship of Jesus*. Supplements to the Journal for the Study of Judaism 63. Leiden: Brill, 1999.

Nickelsburg, George W. E. *1 Enoch: A Commentary on the Book of 1 Enoch, Chapters 1–36, 81–108*. Hermeneia. Minneapolis: Fortress, 2001.

Nickelsburg, George W. E., and James C. VanderKam. *1 Enoch: The Hermeneia Translation*. Minneapolis: Fortress, 2012.

Nolan, Brian M. *The Royal Son of God: The Christology of Matthew 1–2 in the Setting of the Gospel*. Orbis Biblicus et Orientalis 23. Göttingen: Vandenhoeck & Ruprecht, 1979.

Nolland, John. "The King as Shepherd: The Role of Deutero-Zechariah in Matthew." In *Biblical Interpretation in Early Christian Gospels*, vol. 2, *The Gospel of Matthew*, edited by Thomas R. Hatina. Library of New Testament Studies 310. London: T&T Clark, 2008.

———. "No Son-of-God Christology in Matthew 1.18-25." *Journal for the Study of the New Testament* 62 (1996): 3-12.

North, J. Lionel. "Jesus and Worship, God and Sacrifice." In *Early Jewish and Christian Monotheism*, edited by Loren T. Stuckenbruck and Wendy E. S. North, 186-202. Journal for the Study of the New Testament Supplement Series 263. London: T&T Clark, 2004.

Novaković, Lidija. "Matthew's Atomistic Use of Scripture: Messianic Interpretation of Isaiah 53:4 in Matthew 8:17." In *Biblical Interpretation in Early Christian Gospels*, vol. 2, *The Gospel of Matthew*, edited by Thomas R. Hatina, 147-62. Library of New Testament Studies 310. London: T&T Clark, 2008.

———. *Messiah, the Healer of the Sick: A Study of Jesus as the Son of David in the Gospel of Matthew*. Wissenschaftliche Untersuchungen zum Neuen Testament 170. Tübingen: Mohr Siebeck, 2003.

————. "Miracles in the Second Temple and Early Rabbinic Judaism." In *The Cambridge Companion to Miracles,* edited by Graham H. Twelftree, 95-112. New York: Cambridge University Press, 2011.

Olson, Daniel C. "'Enoch and the Son of Man' Revisited: Further Reflections on the Text and Translation of 1 Enoch 70.1-2." *Journal for the Study of the Pseudepigrapha* 18 (2009): 233-40.

Omerzu, Heike. "Geschichte durch Geschichten. Zur Bedeutung jüdischer Traditionen für die Jesusdarstellung des Markusevangeliums." *Early Christianity* 2 (2011): 77-101.

Otto, Rudolf. *The Kingdom of God and the Son of Man: A Study in the History of Religion.* Translated by Floyd V. Filson and Bertram L. Woolf. Rev. ed. Boston: Starr King, 1943.

Peppard, Michael. *The Son of God in the Roman World: Divine Sonship in Its Social and Political Context.* Oxford: Oxford University Press, 2011.

Perrin, Norman. "The High Priest's Question and Jesus's Answer." In *The Passion in Mark: Studies on Mark 14–16,* edited by Werner H. Kelber, 80-91. Philadelphia: Fortress, 1976.

————. *A Modern Pilgrimage in New Testament Christology.* Philadelphia: Fortress, 1974.

Pesch, Rudolf. *Das Markusevangelium.* Herders Theologischer Kommentar zum Neuen Testament 2. Freiburg: Herder, 1976.

Philostratus. *The Life of Apollonius.* Translated by F. C. Conybeare. Loeb Classical Library. London: Heinemann, 1912.

Pitre, Brant J. *Jesus, the Tribulation, and the End of the Exile: Restoration Eschatology and the Origin of the Atonement.* Tübingen: Mohr Siebeck, 2005.

Plutarch. *The Complete Works,* vol. 3, *Essays and Miscellanies.* Middlesex: Echo Library, 2006.

Pokorný, Petr. *Theologie der Lukanischen Schriften.* Göttingen: Vandenhoeck & Ruprecht, 1996.

Popkes, Enno Edzard. "Antikes Medizinwesen und antike Therapieformen." In *Kompendium der frühchristlichen Wundererzählungen,* Band 1, *Die Wunder Jesu,* edited by Susanne Luther and Jörg Röder, 79-86. Munich: Gütersloher Verlaghaus, 2013.

Porphyry. *Life of Pythagoras.* In *The Pythagorean Sourcebook and Library: An Anthology of Ancient Writings Which Relate to Pythagoras and Pythagorean Philosophy,* edited by David R. Fideler, translated by Kenneth Sylvan Guthrie, 123-36. Grand Rapids, MI: Phanes, 1987.

Porter, J. R. *Moses and Monarchy: A Study in the Biblical Tradition of Moses.* Oxford: Blackwell, 1963.

Portier, William L. *Tradition and Incarnation: Foundations of Christian Theology.* New York: Paulist, 1994.

Puech, Émile. "Immortality and Life after Death." In *The Dead Sea Scrolls Fifty Years after Their Discovery,* edited by Lawrence H. Schiffman, Emmanuel Tov, and James C. VanderKam, 512-20. Jerusalem: Israel Exploration Society, 2000.

————. "Messianism, Resurrection, and Eschatology at Qumran and in the New Testament." In *The Community of the Renewed Covenant,* edited by Eugene C. Ulrich and James C. VanderKam, 235-56. Notre Dame, IN: University of Notre Dame Press, 1994.

———. "Une apocalypse messianique (4Q521)." *Revue de Qumran* 15 (1992): 475-522.

Rainbow, Paul. "Melchizedek as a Messiah at Qumran." *Bulletin for Biblical Research* 7 (1997): 179-94.

Rese, Martin. *Alttestamentliche Motive in der Christologie des Lukas.* Gütersloh: Gerd Mohn, 1969.

Rindge, Matthew S. "Reconfiguring the Akedah and Recasting God: Lament and Divine Abandonment in Mark." *Journal of Biblical Literature* 131 (2012): 755-74.

Ringgren, Helmer. *Israelite Religion.* Philadelphia: Fortress, 1966.

Robbins, Vernon K. *Who Do People Say I Am? Rewriting Gospel in Emerging Christianity.* Grand Rapids, MI: Eerdmans, 2013.

Roberts, J. J. M. "Whose Child Is This? Reflections on the Speaking Voice in Isaiah 9:5." *Harvard Theological Review* 90 (1997): 115-29.

Rodgers, Trent. "The Great Commission as the Climax of Matthew's Mountain Scenes." *Bulletin for Biblical Research* 22 (2012): 383-98.

Rowe, C. Kavin. "Acts 2.36 and the Continuity of Lukan Christology." *New Testament Studies* 53 (2007): 37-56.

———. *Early Narrative Christology: The Lord in the Gospel of Luke.* Grand Rapids, MI: Baker Academic, 2009.

Rowe, Robert D. *God's Kingdom and God's Son: The Background in Mark's Christology from Concepts of Kingship in the Psalms.* Leiden: Brill, 2002.

Rowland, Christopher. "John 1.51, Jewish Apocalyptic and Targumic Tradition." *New Testament Studies* 30 (1984): 498-507.

Salowey, Christina A. "Herakles and Healing Cult in the Peloponnesos." Accessed June 4, 2015. http://www1.hollins.edu/faculty/saloweyca/Saloweytext.htm.

———. "The Peloponnesian Herakles: Cult and Labors." PhD diss., Bryn Mawr College, 1995.

Sanders, E. P. *The Historical Figure of Jesus.* London: Penguin, 1993.

Sanders, Seth. "Old Light on Moses' Shining Face." *Vetus Testamentum* 52 (2002): 400-406.

Sänger, Dieter, ed. *Gottessohn und Menschensohn: Exegetische Studien zu zwei Paradigmen biblischer Intertextualität.* Biblisch-Theologische Studien 67. Neukirchen-Vluyn: Neukirchener, 2004.

Schaberg, Jane. "Daniel 7, 12 and the New Testament Passion-Resurrection Predictions." *New Testament Studies* 31 (1985): 208-22.

Schäfer, Peter. *The Jewish Jesus: How Judaism and Christianity Shaped Each Other.* Princeton, NJ: Princeton University Press, 2012.

Schiffman, Lawrence H. "Messianic Figures and Ideas in the Qumran Scrolls." In *The Messiah: Developments in Earliest Judaism and Christianity,* edited by James H. Charlesworth, 116-29. Minneapolis: Fortress, 1992.

Schlatter, Adolf. *Der Evangelist Matthaus: Seine Sprache, sein Ziel, seine Selbstandigkeit: Ein Kommentar zum ersten Evangelium.* Stuttgart: Calwer, 1948.

Schlosser, Jacques. "Moïse, serviteur du kérygme apostolique d'après Ac 3,22-26." *Revue des Sciences Religieuses* 61 (1987): 17-31.

Schreiner, Thomas R. *New Testament Theology: Magnifying God in Christ.* Grand Rapids, MI: Baker Academic, 2008.

Scott, James M. *Exile: Old Testament, Jewish, and Christian Conceptions.* Supplements to the Journal for the Study of Judaism 56. Leiden: Brill, 1997.

Senior, Don. "The Lure of the Formula Citations: Re-assessing Matthew's Use of the Old Testament with the Passion Narrative as a Test Case." In *The Scriptures in the Gospels,* edited by Christopher M. Tuckett, 89-115. Bibliotheca Ephemeridum Theologicarum Lovaniensium 131. Leuven: Leuven University Press, 1997.

Shaver, Brenda J. "The Prophet Elijah in the Literature of the Second Temple Period: The Growth of a Tradition." PhD diss., University of Chicago, 2001.

Smith, Mark S. *The Priestly Vision of Genesis 1.* Minneapolis: Fortress, 2010.

Snodgrass, Klyne. *Stories with Intent: A Comprehensive Guide to the Parables of Jesus.* Grand Rapids, MI: Eerdmans, 2008.

Sorensen, Eric. *Possession and Exorcism in the New Testament and Early Christianity.* Wissenschaftliche Untersuchungen zum Neuen Testament 2 157. Tübingen: Mohr Siebeck, 2002.

Stackert, Jeffrey. "Mosaic Prophecy and the Deuteronomistic Source of the Torah." In *Deuteronomy in the Pentateuch, Hexateuch, and the Deuteronomistic History,* edited by Konrad Schmid and Raymond F. Person Jr., 47-63. Tübingen: Mohr Siebeck, 2012.

Stanton, Graham. *A Gospel for a New People: Studies in Matthew.* Louisville, KY: Westminster John Knox, 1993.

Stegner, William R. "The Baptism of Jesus: A Story Modeled on the Binding of Isaac." *Biblical Research* 1 (1985): 36-46.

———. "Jesus's Walking on the Water: Mark 6:45-52." In *The Gospels and the Scriptures of Israel,* edited by Craig A. Evans and William R. Stegner, 212-34. Journal for the Study of the New Testament Supplement Series 104/Studies in Scripture in Early Judaism and Christianity 3. Sheffield: Sheffield Academic, 1994.

Stendahl, Krister. "Quis et Unde: An Analysis of Mt 1-2." In *Judentum, Urchristentum, Kirche,* edited by Walther Eltester, 94-105. Beihefte zur Zeitschrift für die Neutestamentliche Wissenschaft und die Kunde der ältern Kirche 26. Berlin: Töpelmann, 1960.

———. *The School of St. Matthew and Its Use of the Old Testament.* 2nd ed. Philadelphia: Fortress, 1968.

Strauss, Mark L. *The Davidic Messiah in Luke-Acts: The Promise and Its Fulfillment in Lukan Christology.* Journal for the Study of the New Testament Supplement Series 110. Sheffield: Sheffield Academic, 1995.

Strecker, Christian. "Mächtig in Wort und Tat (Exorzismus in Kafarnaum): Mk 1,21-28."

In *Kompendium der frühchristlichen Wundererzählungen*, Band 1, *Die Wunder Jesu*, edited by Susanne Luther and Jörg Röder, 205-13. Munich: Güterlsloher Verlaghaus, 2013.

Stuckenbruck, Loren T., and Wendy E. S. North, eds. *Early Jewish and Christian Monotheism*. Journal for the Study of the New Testament Supplement Series 263. London: T&T Clark, 2004.

Subramanian, J. Samuel. *The Synoptic Gospels and the Psalms as Prophecy*. Library of New Testament Studies 351. London: T&T Clark, 2007.

Suetonius. *Gaius Caligula*. In *Lives of the Caesars*. Translated by John Carew Rolfe. Vol. 1. Loeb Classical Library. Cambridge, MA: Harvard University Press, 1959.

Swartley, Willard M. *Israel's Scripture Traditions and the Synoptic Gospels: Story Shaping Story*. Peabody, MA: Hendrickson, 1994.

Talbert, Charles H. "Miraculous Conceptions and Births in Mediterranean Antiquity." In *The Historical Jesus in Context*, edited by Amy-Jill Levine, Dale C. Allison Jr., and John Dominic Crossan, 79-86. Princeton, NJ: Princeton University Press, 2006.

Tate, Marvin E. *Psalms 51–100*. Word Biblical Commentary 20. Waco, TX: Word, 1990.

Thimmes, Pamela Lee. *Studies in the Biblical Sea-Storm Type-Scene: Convention and Invention*. San Francisco: Mellen Research University Press, 1992.

Thompson, Marianne Meye. *The Promise of the Father: Jesus and God in the New Testament*. Louisville, KY: Westminster John Knox, 2000.

Tobin, Thomas H. "Miracles, Magic and Modernity: Comments on the Paper of Marilyn McCord Adams." In *Hermes and Athena: Biblical Exegesis and Philosophical Theology*, edited by Eleonore Stump and Thomas P. Flint, 275-81. Notre Dame, IN: University of Notre Dame Press, 1993.

Trunk, Dieter. *Der Messianische Heiler: Eine redaktions- und religionsgeschichtliche Studie zu den Exorzismen im Matthäusevangelium*. Herders Biblische Studien 3. Freiburg: Herder, 1994.

Tuckett, Christopher. "The Present Son of Man." *Journal for the Study of the New Testament* 14 (1982): 58-81.

Twelftree, Graham H. *Jesus the Exorcist: A Contribution to the Study of the Historical Jesus*. Wissenschaftliche Untersuchungen zum Neuen Testament 2 54. Tübingen: Mohr Siebeck, 1993.

———. "Jesus and Magic in Luke-Acts." In *Jesus and Paul: Global Perspectives in Honor of James D. G. Dunn for His 70th Birthday*, edited by B. J. Oropeza, C. K. Robertson, and Douglas C. Mohrmann, 46-58. Library of New Testament Studies 414. London: T&T Clark, 2009.

———, ed. *The Cambridge Companion to Miracles*. New York: Cambridge University Press, 2011.

Van Egmond, Richard. "The Messianic 'Son of David' in Matthew." *Journal of Greco-Roman Christianity and Judaism* 3 (2006): 41-47.

VanderKam, James C. "Righteous One, Messiah, Chosen One, and Son of Man in 1 Enoch

37-71." In *The Messiah: Developments in Earliest Judaism and Christianity*, edited by James H. Charlesworth, 169-91. Minneapolis: Fortress, 1992.

Vermes, Geza. "The Use of בר נש/בר נשא in Jewish Aramaic." In *An Aramaic Approach to the Gospels and Acts*, edited by Matthew Black, 310-30. 3rd ed. Oxford: Clarendon, 1967.

Verseput, Donald J. "The Role and Meaning of the 'Son of God' Title in Matthew's Gospel." *New Testament Studies* 33 (1987): 532-66.

Von Rad, Gerhard. "Das judäische Königsritual." *Theologische Literaturzeitung* 73 (1947): 211-16.

Wagner, J. Ross. "Psalm 118 in Luke-Acts: Tracing a Narrative Thread?" In *Early Christian Interpretation of the Scriptures of Israel: Investigations and Proposals*, edited by Craig A. Evans and James A. Sanders, 154-78. Journal for the Study of the New Testament Supplement Series 148/Studies in Scripture in Early Judaism and Christianity 5. Sheffield: Sheffield Academic, 1997.

Walck, Leslie W. *The Son of Man in the Parables of Enoch and in Matthew*. Jewish and Christian Texts in Contexts and Related Studies Series 9. London: T&T Clark, 2011.

Watts, Rikki E. *Isaiah's New Exodus in Mark*. Grand Rapids, MI: Baker Academic, 2000.

Weeden, Theodore J. *Mark: Traditions in Conflict*. Minneapolis: Fortress, 1971.

Wenham, Gordon J. *Genesis 1–15*. Word Biblical Commentary 1. Waco, TX: Word, 1987.

Willitts, Joel. *Matthew's Messianic Shepherd-King: In Search of "the Lost Sheep of the House of Israel."* Beihefte zur Zeitschrift für die Neutestamentliche Wissenschaft und die Kunde der ältern Kirche 147. Berlin: De Gruyter, 2007.

Wink, Walter. *The Human Being: Jesus and the Enigma of the Son of the Man*. Minneapolis: Fortress, 2002.

Wise, Michael O., and James D. Tabor. "The Messiah at Qumran." *Biblical Archaeology Review* 18 (1992): 60-65.

Witmer, Amanda. *Jesus, the Galilean Exorcist: His Exorcisms in Social and Political Context*. Library of New Testament Studies 459/Library of Historical Jesus Studies 10. Edinburgh: T&T Clark, 2012.

Woude, A. S. van der. "Melchisedech als himmlische Erlösergestalt in den neugefundenen eschatologischen Midraschim aus Qumran Höle XI." *Oudtestamentische Studiën* 14 (1965): 354-73.

Wright, N. T. *The Climax of the Covenant: Christ and the Law in Pauline Theology*. Minneapolis: Fortress, 1992.

———. *Jesus and the Victory of God*. Christian Origins and the Question of God 2. Minneapolis: Fortress, 1996.

———. *Paul and the Faithfulness of God*. Minneapolis: Fortress, 2013.

Zimmermann, Ruben. "Hinführung." In *Kompendium der frühchristlichen Wundererzählungen*, Band 1, *Die Wunder Jesu*, edited by Susanne Luther and Jörg Röder, 513-25. Gütersloh: Gütersloher Verlagshaus, 2013.

Author Index

Achtemeier, Paul J., 315, 450, 479, 481, 482, 483, 485
Adams, Marilyn McCord, 480, 483, 484
Ahearne-Kroll, Stephen P., 185, 196, 491, 496, 497, 498, 499, 509, 511, 512, 513, 514
Allen, Leslie C., 121
Allison, Dale C., Jr., 213, 246, 247, 253, 284, 294, 295, 302, 314, 315, 333, 346, 360, 362, 365, 370, 373, 375, 382, 383, 384, 386, 390, 434, 435, 443, 444, 458, 459, 505, 506, 510, 520, 521, 522, 526, 527, 528, 529, 530, 533, 534
Anderson, Gary, 48, 60
Angel, Joseph L. 131, 132, 133, 134, 135, 136
Anselm, 12, 40
Arterbury, Andrew E., 568
Aune, David E., 213
Aus, Roger David, 453, 455, 504

Baden, Joel, 55, 56
Baeck, Leo, 269
Bahrani, Zainab, 50, 51
Barker, Margaret, 105, 124, 126, 252
Barr, James, 212
Bauckham, Richard, 2, 14, 17-21, 22, 23, 26, 30, 34, 36, 37, 38, 44, 45, 53, 57, 59, 67, 70, 74, 85, 103, 105, 120, 122, 127, 174, 176, 348, 352, 357, 372, 394, 395, 487, 491, 558
Beaton, Richard, 368, 369, 418, 420, 517, 518
Bekken, Per Jarle, 71, 72
Beyerle, Stefan, 144
Bietenhard, Hans, 176
Bird, Michael F., 12, 310, 505
Black, C. Clifton, 213
Black, Matthew, 147, 151, 153, 154, 265

Blackburn, Barry, 194, 195, 196, 205, 413, 414, 430, 432, 433, 445, 486
Blomberg, Craig, 211
Bock, Darrell, 38, 172, 228, 539, 540, 541, 543, 544, 547, 549, 550, 552, 553, 554, 555, 556, 563, 565, 566
Boring, Eugene, 179
Bornkamm, Günther, 443
Borsch, Frederick H., 276, 278, 293
Böttrich, Christfried, 153
Boyarin, Daniel, 31-33, 142, 147, 148, 149, 157, 261, 262, 263, 269, 272, 279, 292, 318, 319, 336, 338
Brawley, Robert L., 225, 226, 554, 567
Broadhead, Edwin K., 190, 218, 264, 268, 308, 309, 325, 332, 345, 358
Brown, Raymond E., 364, 369, 372, 373, 388, 389, 390, 391, 393, 397, 399, 410, 411
Brueggemann, Walter, 50, 54, 78
Buckwalter, Douglas, 567, 568
Bultmann, Rudolf, 179, 195, 257, 264, 265, 266, 269, 280, 307, 308, 345, 414
Butticaz, Simon David, 545, 546

Carrez, Maurice, 436
Carson, D. A., 525
Casey, Maurice, 28, 138, 173, 175, 265, 291, 292, 297, 302, 303, 342, 356, 362, 490, 569
Chandler, Christopher N., 558
Chester, Andrew, 3, 17
Cohen, Shaye J. D., 44
Collins, Adela Yarbro, 30, 31, 33, 52, 58, 98, 102, 103, 106, 148, 157, 182, 184, 193, 194, 195, 197, 202, 207, 212, 213, 219, 220, 238, 242, 245, 259, 262, 270, 274, 280, 287, 288,

310, 313, 325, 328, 342, 372, 377, 378, 390, 392, 437, 439, 440, 492
Collins, John J., 3, 30, 31, 46, 95, 97, 98, 99, 102, 103, 106, 111, 112, 114, 115, 116, 117, 118, 137, 144, 145, 146, 147, 148, 157, 168, 175, 184, 193, 195, 197, 219, 220, 238, 242, 245, 259, 270, 280, 310, 313, 317, 319, 325, 328, 342, 372, 377, 378, 390, 392, 462
Conzelmann, Hans, 218
Cotter, Wendy, 440, 444, 445, 446, 448, 449, 461, 464, 465, 475
Craigie, Peter C., 99
Crouch, Carly L., 53
Crowe, Brandon D., 240, 241
Cullmann, Oscar, 187, 228, 233, 245, 297, 311

Davenport, Gene, 110, 111, 112, 113, 114
Davies, W. D., 213, 246, 247, 253, 284, 294, 295, 360, 362, 375, 382, 383, 384, 434, 435, 443, 444, 458, 459, 526, 527, 528, 529, 530, 533, 534
Davis, Carl Judson, 122, 123, 138, 490
Davis, Philip G., 179, 180, 199, 287, 297
Dechow, Jens, 439
Dibelius, Martin, 314
Diffey, Daniel S., 55
Dodd, C. H., 491
Donahue, John R., 200, 207, 217, 288, 329
Donaldson, Terrance L., 227
Douglas, Mary, 140
Dunn, James D. G., 14, 27, 192, 196, 197, 213, 238, 256, 270, 308, 309, 323, 342, 373, 391, 411

Ehrman, Bart D., 285, 563
Elgvin, Torleif, 132
Ellis, E. Earle, 273, 322
Eshel, Esther, 135, 136, 169, 569
Evans, Craig A., 362, 557
Evans, C. F., 228
Eve, Eric, 82, 117, 416, 434, 436, 459, 460, 461, 462, 478, 479, 486, 487

Fitzmyer, Joseph A., 115
Fletcher-Louis, Crispin, 15, **34-37**, 61, 62, 64, 66, 68, 86, 121, 122, 124, 125, 126, 127, 128, 130, 132, 133, 137, 138, 139, 169
Flusser, David, 121, 123, 124, 135
Fossum, Jarl E., 77
France, R. T., 183, 213, 295-96

Frey, Jörg, 2
Fuller, Reginald H., 108, 533

Garland, Robert, 445, 464, 465
Garr, Randall, 51, 52, 53, 54, 55, 56, 58, 59, 76
Gathercole, Simon J., **29-31**, 36, 176, 193, 196, 207, 210, 211, 223, 244, 266, 276, 279, 280, 301, 310, 332, 336, 342, 351, 372, 375, 423
Gaventa, Beverly R., 389-90, 395, 406
George, Augustin, 477, 480, 485
Gerhardsson, Birger, 225, 226, 227
Goff, Matthew, 134, 135
Goldingay, John, 49, 50, 52, 54, 140, 142
González, Justo L., 388, 391, 397, 399
Goodenough, Erwin, 83
Goodwin, Mark J., 245, 246
Grabbe, Lester L., 59, 60
Gradl, Hans-Georg, 441
Green, Joel B., 219, 221, 223, 227, 228, 229, 236, 237, 296, 315, 334, 390, 391, 395, 397, 401, 404, 457, 458, 552, 553, 561
Gregerman, Adam, 551
Grelot, Pierre, 426, 431, 433, 438, 460, 478, 485
Grindheim, Sigurd, 21
Guelich, Robert, 520, 521, 524
Gunkel, Hermann, 89

Hamerton-Kelly, Robert, 309
Hare, Douglas R. A., 282, 283, 284, 340, 342, 348, 350, 351
Hartenstein, Judith, 447
Hatina, Thomas R., 189-90, 377
Hays, Richard B., 18, **23-26**, 253, 368, 370, 377, 439, 441, 442, 493, 494, 501, 519, 536, 537
Hayward, C. T. R., 125, 127
Head, Peter M., 250, 252, 377, 419
Healy, Mary, 213
Heil, John Paul, 248, 249, 250, 253, 437, 439
Henderson, Suzanne Watts, 216, 217, 279, 450, 452, 453, 455
Hendrickx, Herman, 422, 423, 424, 439, 442, 462, 472, 477, 480, 481, 483
Hengel, Martin, 13, 14, 305
Herring, Stephen L., 49, 50, 51, 53, 54, 56, 80, 81
Holladay, Carl R., 84
Hooker, Morna D., 267, 268, 276, 277, 278,

286, 288, 299, 305, 307, 310, 312, 314, 324,
325, 329, 336, 355
Horst, Pieter W. van der, 86
Horbury, William, 50
Huizenga, Leroy, 129, 189, 239, 361, 362,
382, 383
Hurtado, Larry, 2, 3, 8, 14, 15, 19, **26-29**, 36,
37, 46-47, 99, 153, 154, 369, 372, 375, 380,
395, 408, 412

Irenaeus, 4, 40

Janse, Sam, 185, 186, 547, 549
Jeremias, Joachim, 212, 213
Johannson, Daniel, 3, 47, 275
Jonge, Martinus de, 573
Juel, Donald H., 179, 185, 200, 201, 270-71,
325

Kahl, Werner, 473, 487
Kammler, Hans-Christian, 225, 240, 369
Kee, Howard Clark, 128, 432, 439, 451, 461,
462, 463, 477, 480
Keener, Craig S., 213
Kelber, Werner H., 315
Kingsbury, Jack Dean, 239, 240, 269, 271,
330, 363, 372, 374, 380, 381, 382, 383, 386,
520, 524
Kingsley, Peter, 445, 464, 465
Kirk, J. R. Daniel, 4, 103, 104, 214, 238, 247,
249, 279, 323, 326, 355, 379, 435, 519, 524
Kittel, Gerhard, 212
Knohl, Israel, 120, 121, 122, 123, 124
Kollmann, Bernd, 453, 505
Kooten, George H. van, 67, 68, 69
Krentz, Edgar, 213
Kugel, James L., 90, 102, 121, 153, 154, 558
Kuhn, Thomas S., 5, 6, 7, 8, 20
Kümmel, Werner G., 265

Laato, Antti, 98
Lamarche, Paul, 472, 473
Lanfranchi, Pierluigi, 84
LeDonne, Anthony, 360, 533
Lee, Acquila H. I., 213
Légasse, Simon, 447, 466
Leithart, Peter, 97
Levenson, Jon D., 102
Levison, John R., 48, 60, 61, 70, 71, 72, 74
Lewis, C. S., x

Lierman, John, 83, 84, 504
Lincoln, Andrew T., 367, 368, 388, 389
Litwa, M. David, 13, 14, 15, 392
Luther, Susanne, 456
Luz, Ulrich, 350, 352, 353

Makiello, Phoebe, 86
Malbon, Elizabeth Struthers, 181, 190, 268,
269, 288, 289, 299, 312, 325
Malone, Francis, 336
Marcus, Joel, 183, 185, 186, 191, 195, 196, 197,
198, 199, 201, 263, 266, 274, 276, 280, 287,
317, 331, 348, 354, 355, 439, 440, 453, 492,
494, 495, 508, 509, 510, 515, 516
Marshall, I. Howard, 54, 220
McCartney, Dan, xi, 1, 47, 273, 415, 443,
460, 574
McConville, J. G., 49, 80, 97, 100
McGrath, James F., 104, 105
McKim, Donald K., 213
Meeks, Wayne A., 82, 83, 84, 176
Middleton, J. Richard, 49, 52, 54
Milik, J. T., 121
Mills, Mary, 78, 84, 416, 421, 422, 424, 484,
485
Moberly, Walter, 2
Moessner, David P., 538, 541, 543, 544
Moss, Candida R., 474
Mowery, Robert L., 257, 258
Müller, Peter, 276, 281, 287, 288, 290, 308,
324, 336
Müller, Ulrich B., 154, 270

Nickelsburg, George W. E., 46, 72, 73, 114,
151, 172
Nolan, Brian M., 360, 374
Nolland, John, 364, 369, 508
North, J. Lionel, 27
Novaković, Lidija, 360, 466, 467, 468, 469,
470, 471, 472

Olson, Daniel C., 153
Omerzu, Heike, 8
Otto, Rudolf, 327

Peppard, Michael, 9, 14, 15, 202, 203, 204,
256, 257
Perrin, Norman, 251, 270, 276, 277, 299,
305, 315, 325, 329
Pesch, Rudolf, 196, 494

Philostratus, 445-46
Pitre, Brant J., 213, 245, 362, 363
Plutarch, 202, 370-71, 391, 392, 393, 465
Pokorný, Petr, 340, 390, 391, 398, 541, 546, 549, 554, 566
Popkes, Enno Edzard, 463, 464
Porphyry, 444, 464
Porter, J. R., 50
Portier, William L., 213
Puech, Émile, 62, 63, 118, 462

Rainbow, Paul, 123
Rese, Martin, 538, 539, 540, 542, 544, 545, 546, 547, 548, 549, 552, 553, 554, 555, 563
Rindge, Matthew S., 189, 513
Ringgren, Helmer, 249
Robbins, Vernon K., 470
Roberts, J. J. M., 98, 105, 106
Rodgers, Trent, 381, 383, 386
Rowe, C. Kavin, 18, **22-23**, 282, 297, 388, 389, 393, 394, 395, 397, 398, 402, 409, 410, 456, 457, 541, 542, 543, 544
Rowe, Robert D., 185, 186, 188, 191, 247, 248, 259
Rowland, Christopher, 77

Salowey, Christina A., 463
Sanders, E. P., 420, 433, 442, 447, 448, 460, 462, 473, 486
Sanders, Seth L., 81
Schaberg, Jane, 336, 337, 355
Schäfer, Peter, 63, 73, 75
Schiffman, Lawrence H., 62, 115
Schlatter, Adolf, 296
Schlosser, Jacques, 545
Schreiner, Thomas R., 411
Scott, James M., 362
Senior, Don, 519
Shaver, Brenda, 88, 89, 90, 91, 94, 95, 117
Smith, Mark S., 48, 49, 50, 50-51, 53, 55, 57, 58, 59, 100, 102, 103, 248, 249
Snodgrass, Klyne, 210, 499, 558
Sorensen, Eric, 416, 418, 419, 420, 425, 438
Stackert, Jeffrey, 79
Stanton, Graham, 296, 361

Stegner, William R., 189, 228, 249, 436
Stendahl, Krister, 364, 376, 377, 494, 518
Strauss, Mark L., 219, 221, 223, 226, 228, 229, 230, 231, 389, 390, 395, 396, 397, 398, 400, 407, 408, 410, 411
Strecker, Christian, 422, 423, 424, 438, 459
Subramanian, J. Samuel, 500
Suetonius, 448
Swartley, Willard M., 489

Tabor, James D., 116, 117
Talbert, Charles H., 370, 371, 373, 391, 392
Tate, Marvin E., 100, 101
Thimmes, Pamela Lee, 433, 438, 447
Thompson, Marianne Meye, 160-61, 315
Tobin, Thomas H., 480
Trunk, Dieter, 417
Tuckett, Christopher, 267, 268, 271, 274, 319, 339, 340, 341, 344, 355
Twelftree, Graham H., 416, 425, 428

Van Egmond, Richard, 360
VanderKam, James C., 151, 153
Vermes, Geza, 265
Verseput, Donald J., 238, 363, 372
Von Rad, Gerhard, 98, 106

Wagner, J. Ross, 538
Walck, Leslie W., 308, 331, 345-46, 348, 352
Walsh, J. T., 89
Watts, Rikki E., 492, 493, 494, 515
Weeden, Theodore J., 484
Wenham, Gordon J., 54
Willitts, Joel, 360
Wink, Walter, 287, 358
Wise, Michael O., 116, 117
Witmer, Amanda, 417, 423, 424
Woude, A. S. van der, 121
Wright, N. T., 9, 45, 552, 238, 273, 288, 362, 505

Young, Stephen L., 103, 104, 249, 435

Zimmermann, Ruben, 481

Subject Index

Aaron, 124, 126, 131, 459
abandonment, 201, 510-11, 512-13, 516, 565, 566, 574, 575
Abaris, 444
abba, 212-14, 576
Abel, 76, 173, 331, 348
abomination of desolation (see "desolating sacrilege")
Abraham, 55, 56, 65, 75-76, 96, 129, 159, 160, 161, 165, 166, 189-90, 197, 224, 226, 239, 359, 361, 364, 365, 375, 376, 378, 382-83, 384, 387, 389, 395, 483, 485, 516, 517, 545, 562, 566, 573
Adam (see also "glory, Adam's," "humanity, primeval"), 20, 35, 37, **47-77**, 77, 80, 82, 84, 125, 126, 130, 133, 134, 158, 172, 173, 178, 184, 199, 214, 218, 221, 223, 224, 226, 231, 234, 236, 240, 241, 258, 259, 263, 277, 288, 293, 298, 348, 358, 364, 389, 391, 393, 400, 408, 412, 570, 574, 575
Adam Christology (see "Christology, Adam")
adoption, 14, 98, 104, 156, 203, 204, 210, 219, 257, 353-56
agency (see "mediator" and "vicegerency")
Ahab, 87, 103, 248, 335, 364, 451, 503
Alexander, 449
alms, 240
angels, 63, 64, 66, 73, 75, 77, 83, 85, 86, 97, 117, 121, 122, 123, 124, 128, 129, 131, 133, 134-35, 135, 137, 139, 142, 144, 150, 152, 155, 156, 157, 158, 164, 165, 168, 169, 174, 211, 218, 220, 233-34, 242, 310, 311, 312, 313, 316, 321, 346, 351, 365, 367, 379, 392, 393,

394, 396, 397, 401, 421, 426, 431, 432, 460, 507, 582
animals (wild), see beasts
anointing, 184, 185, 186, 187, 197, 198, 217, 218, 223, 224, 228, 235, 288, 290, 293, 296, 305, 313, 319, 334, 394, 424, 478, 496, 521, 547, 554, 555, 556, 574
Anselm, 12, 40
Antiochus IV Epiphanes, 143, 144, 145, 146, 147, 150, 319, 320, 337
anthropology, 16, **39-41**, 61, 62, 63
anti-creation, 140, 141, 142, 149, 353, 355, 579
Apollo, 444, 445, 463
Apollonius of Tyana, 445-46, 464
ascension (assumption), 87, 89
Asclepiades, 464
Asclepius, 463-64
atonement, 167
Augustus, 446
authority (see also "sovereignty") 11, 12, 18, 28, 29, 33, 38, 43, 52, 57, 80, 83, 87, 89, 90, 92, 93, 100, 103, 105, 106, 107, 108, 114, 116, 129, 137, 149, 163, 166, 186, 191, 204, 205, 206, 207, 208, 209, 211, 215, 216, 217, 226, 234, 236, 246, 249, 253, 255, 258, 263, 265, 268, 269, **272-297**, 298, 301, 304, 305, 306, 307, 310, 314, 317, 318, 319, 320, 321, 322, 323, 324, 326, 330, 332, 335, 336, 339-40, 345, 346, 349, 353, 354, 355, 357, 358, 380-81, 383, 385, 402, 403, 412, 413, 414, 415, 420, **421-25**, 427, 428, 429, 433, 436, 438, 339-40, 442, 449, 452, 460, 461, 473, 474, 475, 483, 496, 501, 503-4, 520, 522, 524, 529, 559, 571, 573, 574, 576, 577

Baal, 32, 88-89, 148, 261
Babylon, 316
baptism (*see* "water, cleansing")
Bartimaeus, 466, 468, 476-77, 497, 499
beasts, 49, 71, 74, 101, 107, 140, 141, 142, 143,
144, 147, 331, 353
Beelzebub (Beelzebul) (*see* "Satan")
Beelzebul controversy, 187, 206, 208, 209,
215, 283-86, 345-46, 418-20, 423, 427, 431,
468
Beliar (*see* "Satan")
beloved son, 189-90, 192, 194, 197, 198, 210,
211, 324, 326, 327, 382, 499
betray ("hand over"), 251, 315, 337, 344, 345,
406, 427, 510, 515
blasphemy, 29, 177, 209, 268, 269, **273-281**,
282, **283-86**, 322, 329-30, 333, 500-501, 512
bread (*see* "feeding")

Caesar (*see* "emperor")
Caesarea Philippi, 242, 272, 298
Canaanite woman (*see* "Syrophoenician
woman")
centurion, 199, 201, 202, 256, 257
chaos, 49, 69, 80, 89, 96, 102, 103, 109, 125,
141, 142, 249, 250, 259, 433, 435, 439, 441-
42, 443, 454, 459
Christ (*see* "messiah")
Christology
Adam, x, 4, 40, 221, 223-24, 229, 231, 277,
288, 292, 293, 334, 358, 390-93, 400,
574, 575, 579, 581
angelic (angelomorphic), 6, 8, 20, 34, 35,
36, 37, 45, 57, 61, 62, 66, 70, 73-74, 86,
130, 131, 571
development, 10, 13
diversity, 7
divine, 3, 4, 5, 6, 7, 9, 16, 20, 21, 23, 23-24,
27, 32-33, 34, 35-36, 37, 38, 42, 43, 45,
70, 77, 103, 113, 119, 137, 148, 153, 174,
175, 177, 193, 194, 197, 207, 212, 215, 217,
221, 246, 250, 251, 252, 254, 261, 262,
273, 278, 279, 299, 316, 322, 343, 352,
357, 374, 388, 394, 397, 405, 408, 434,
435, 441-42, 447, 454, 457-58, 494, 501,
513, 537, 540, 550, 567-68, 572, 581, 582
early high, xi, 1-2, 3, 5, 6, 7, **16-38**, 37, 42,
110, 153, 373, 571, 580
high, 4, 22, 47, 204, 343, 349, 372, 394,
420, 453, 459, 486, 525, 568, 570, 571

low, 3, 22, 25, 47, 486, 544
royal, 28, 46, 47, 178, 182, 184, 185, 186,
187, 193, 199, 200, 201, 202, 204, 207,
208, 209, 210, 211, 214, 215, 217, 218,
219, 224, 234, 235-36, 243, 247, 248,
251, 252, 255, 256, 258, 259, 275, 276,
287, 288, 293, 324-25, 349, 358, 374, 375,
380-81, 383, 407-8, 412, 417, **418-21**,
425, 432, 450, 486, 508, 517, 554, 576
circumcision, 229
clean, 140
Cleopas, 535-36
cloud, 148, 191, 192, 193, 196, 198, 201, 220,
262, 268, 271, 308, 317-18, 325, 327, 350
cock, white 465
commissioning, 31, 216, 228, 241, 375, 381,
427, 457-58
community (people of God), 109, 113, 118,
124, 129, 133, 139, 141, 142, 143, 144, 145,
146, 147, 150-51, 156, 157, 158, **158-73**, 185,
199, 214-17, 231, 246, 260, 279, 281, 305,
318, 380, 384, 385, 386, 387, 523, 560,
575-78, 579
Coronis, 463
corpse impurity, 558
council, divine, 29, 34, 47, 63, 69, 119, 131,
135-36, 147, 148, 149,163, 234, 244, 383
creation, 12, 18, 21, 47, 48, 53, 55, 56-57, 58,
59, 60, 61, 65, 68-69, 80, 96, 97, 100, 101,
102, 104, 107, 108, 109, 114, 118, 125, 126,
127, 128, 129, 137, 140, 141, 144, 149, 152,
165, 169, 172, 175, 220, 221, 224, 277, 291,
353, 356, 357, 358, 364, 371, 373, 391-93,
397, 399, 400, 410, 547, 571, 579, 580
cup, 188, 213, 303

D (Deuteronomist; Deuteronomistic
history), 231
David, king (Davidic kingship), 61, 63, 67,
73, 96, 97-98, 102-4, 105-6, 107-8, 109,
109-110, 110-11, 112, 113, 116, 119, 120, 123,
125, 156, 158, 160, 164-65, 175, 178, 184,
187, 190, 199, 207, 208, 213, 214, 218, 219,
220, 221, 224, 226, 231, 235, 236, 243,
247, 248, 250, 253, 255-56, 258, 260, 270,
287-90, 292, 293, 294, 298, 301, 328, 333,
334, 339, 348, 355, 359, 361, 362, 363, 364,
369-70, 373, 375, 376, 377, 378, 382-83,
387, **387-401**, 405, 407-8, 409, 411, 412,
414, 416, 417, **418-21**, 423, 431, 432, 433,

435, 440, 441, 442, 446, 452, 454, **466-72**, 476-77, 481, 483, 496-99, 504, 505, 506, 507, 508, 509, 510, 513, 514, 516-17, 528, 541-42, 543-44, 544-45, 547, 548-49, 550, 551, 552, 566, 569, 570, 573, 574, 575, 578-79
Demeter, 193
demigod, 220
demons (unclean spirits), 129, 165, 166, 187, **205-9**, 218, **228**, 233, 259, 415, 421-23, 424, 425, 431, 432, 438, 441, 460, 461, 467, 470, 471, 472, 474, 477, 478-79, 484, 486, 487, 495, 527-28, 529
Deuteronomist (*see* "D")
desolating sacrilege ("abomination of desolation"), 320, 321, 326, 564
disciples/discipleship, **41**, 215, 216, 217, 240, 241, 243, 258, 262, 266, 267, 283, 295, 297, 300, 301, 303, 304, 305, 306-7, 311, 331, 340, 381-82, 387, 425-30, 432, 442-43, 449-50, 452, 456-57, 474, 475-76, 477, 483-85, 497, 528-29, **575-78**, 581
 authoritative, 208, 209, 215-16, 234, 262, 278, 283, 301, 302, 305, 306, 318, 453, 471-72, 474, 484-85, 528, 529, 531, 576-77, 578
 derivative 41, 188, 191, 208, 209, 212, 214-17, 218, 234, 237, 240, 241, 243, 254, 258, 266, 267, 278, 300, 301, 303, 304, 305, 306-7, 309, 315, 318, 321, 322, 327-28, 331, 339, 340, 348, 349, 381-82, 385, 425-30, 453, 454, 471-72, 483-85, 528, 529, 531, **575-78**
 suffering, 41, 188, 191, 212, 217, 240, 266, 267, 289, 300, 301, 302, 303, 304, 305, 307, 313, 314, 315, 318, 328, 331, 341, 349, 477, 497, 531, 577, 578
divine council (*see* "council, divine")
divine identity (identification with God), 2, 3, 6, 6-7, 8, 10-11, 12, 17, 18, 19, 21, 22, 23, 25, 27, 30, 33, 34, 36, 37, 38, 42, 44, 53, 73, 78, 81, 84, 88, 96, 98-99, 100, 103, 106, 115, 119, 120, 122, 124, 125, 127, 131, 137, 151, 152, 155, 156, 157, 158, 162-63, 164, 167, 168, 169, 172, 173, 175-76, 183, 223, 244, 246, 248, 249, 251, 253, 259, 296, 327, 352, 354, 369, 372, 393, 394, 396, 405, 412, 425, 434, 469, 494, 495, 501, 506, 536, 537, 542, 546, 551, 567, 570, 573, 579, 582
 in Mark, 18, 193, 495-95, 574

divine name (Yнwн), 18, 19, 35, 47, 108, 117, 122, 123, 126, 134, 136, 137-38, 152, 155, 162, 163, 182, 292, 357, 491-92. 499, 500, 545, 567-68, 570, 574
divine power, 48, 49, 56, 57, 58, 78, 79, 80, 86, 87, 89, 92, 96, 99, 100, 102, 104, 106, 107, 108, 109, 116, 119, 120, 121, 123, 125, 126, 139, 141, 144, 149, 162, 168-72, 175, 185, 186, 194, 204, 206, 216, 220, 246, 248, 249, 250, 259, 309, 316, 328, 329, 331, 384, 392, 400, 409, 410, 427, 428, 429, 433, 434, 439, 440, 449, 453, 454, 456, 473, 484, 487, 491, 499, 539, 540-41, 546, 569, 578-79
divine warrior (*see* divine power)
divinization (deification), 36, 61, 64, 81, 82, 83, 84, 86, 99-100, 105, 106, 109, 121, 130, 135, 139, 196, 302, 372, 463-64, 498
Dorcas, 485
dove, 184, 193, 203-4

Eden, 59, 63, 129, 134
eighth day, 229
El, 32, 148, 261
elders, 209, 211, 255, 326
Eleazar (first century CE), 417
Eleazar (high priest), 452
elect (election), 65, 85, 97, 110, 159, 160, 162, 165, 172, 203, 231, 238, 293, 298, 397
Elijah, **87-91**, 91-92, 93, 93-96, 96, 173, 180, 192, 196, 201, 202, 230, 243, 335, 363, 389, 426, 436, 459, 461, 480, 481, 492-93, 503-4, 527, 555, 556, 565, 575
Elisha, **91-93**, 96, 436, 455, 456, 459, 461-62, 483, 504, 556, 575
Elizabeth, 393-95, 396, 397, 554
Empedocles, 444
emperor (also "Caesar"), 202, 203, 257
enemy, 170, 186, 187, 214, 229, 240, 248, 249, 304, 313, 340, 421, 432, 439, 512, 514, 515, 523, 553, 562
Enoch, 35, 153, 155, 158, 173, 175, 316
enthronement, 178, 184-85, 198, 202, 203-4, 217, 221, 256, 287, 309, 311, 317, 319, 322-31, 328, 329, 333, 336, 346, 347, 352, 353, 357, 358, 375, 380, 381, 383, 385, 387, 402, 405, 407, 408, 409, 410, 412, 418, 427, 485, 496, 497, 498, 501, 543, 544, 545, 549, 550, 562, 571, 574, 576, 579, 580
Epimenides, 444

eschatology, 11, 23, 35, 40, 47, 61, 62, 63, 64,
69, 70, 71, 73, 74, 82, 90-91, 94, 95, 96,
115, 116, 117, 118, 123, 128, 129, 133, 137, 138,
139, 151, 153, 157, 165, 191, 211, 213, 214, 215,
222, 235, 236, 242-43, 254, 255, 264, 265,
267, 269, 279, 280, 281, 284, 285, 302, 305,
308, 309, 314, 320, 321, 326, 327-28, 329,
331, 341, 345, 346, 347, 353, 356, 358, 359,
363, 367, 373, 375, 379, 384, 385, 408, 412,
421, 423, 425, 430, 431, 432-33, 443, 452,
454, 456, 462, 470, 471, 482, 486, 487,
495, 506, 507, 510, 512, 514-15, 521, 525,
526, 527, 528, 529, 529-32, 534, 535, 550,
557, 561, 569, 573, 579, 582
Eve, 74, 130, 155
exaltation, 28, 62, 65, 65, 77, 84, 100, 122,
123, 130, 132, 133, 134, 135, 136, 145, 146,
150, 152, 153, 155, 156, 158, 188, 194, 195,
196, 198, 201, 202, 204, 236, 244, 263, 264,
268, 270, 272, 285, 308, 309, 310, 316, 317,
320, 322, 325, 327, 328, 329, 332, 333, 336,
338, 339, 346, 347, 351, 356, 357, 375, 380,
387, 388, 402, 404, 405, 407, 408, 409,
410, 412, 413, 414, 430, 458, 463, 485, 496,
497, 498, 544, 550, 562, 570, 574, 579, 580
exodus, 77, 79, 80, 81, 159, 160, 161, 162, 166,
198, 208, 229, 230, 232, 239, 452, 459, 518,
522
exile, 163, 164, 245, 360, 362-63, 366, 367,
376, 377, 378, 517, 573
exorcism, 41, 97, 109, 129, 184, 187, 205, 207,
209, 217, 228, 241, 272, 277-78, 281, 298,
414, 415-433, 438, 440, 442, 454, 457, 460,
467, 470, 472, 473, 474, 477, 478-79, 486,
576, 577, 582

faith, faithfulness, 79, 138, 160, 200, 227,
228, 231, 241, 250, 252, 285, 309, 321, 328,
337, 338, 339, 341, 351, 358, 377, 399, 400,
428, 441, 473-74, 519, 523, 530, 557, 564,
566, 569, 578-79, 580
faithless, faithlessness, 428, 473-74, 564
family, 187, 212, 214-17, 221-22, 234, 237, 240-
41, 254, 255, 258, 305, 315, 345, 352, 380,
384, 385, 474, 530-31, 576, 577
fasting, 209, 240
feeding, 41, 92, 93, 96, 160, 166, 217, 225-26,
272, 287, 294, 298, 404, 433, 437, 450-56,
459-60, 462, 503-6
fig tree, 298, 350

firstborn, 64, 76, 104, 133, 135, 155, 159, 160,
165, 229
forgiveness of sins, 12, 18, 29, 33, 35-36, 214,
215, 240, 241, 265, 273-81, 281-83, 284,
285, 286, 293, 324, 365, 366, 367, 381, 387,
396, 400, 404, 405, 422, 457, 458, 460,
473, 523, 536, 541, 546, 549, 553, 555, 562,
563, 576, 577
fruitfulness, 49, 54, 55, 56, 107, 579
fulfillment, 230, 235, 236, 237, 238, 239, 243,
250, 321, 367, 370, 376-78, 387, 395, 396,
400, 401, 403, 407, 409-10, 420, 481, 517-
28, 532, 535, 536, 539, 544, 545, 546, 549,
555, 556, 559, 562-63, 569
functional divinity, 33, 86, 87, 148, 203, 262-
63, 398, 409

Gaius (Caligula), 448
gather, 41, 107, 114, 152, 157, 187, 290, 298,
362, 363, 378, 431, 458, 528
genealogy, 221, 223-24
genius, 203
Gethsemane, 212, 303, 315, 510-12
glory, 67, 68, 77, 94, 109, 112, 119, 124-25,
128, 131, 133, 134, 135, 136, 139, 151, 152, 153,
155, 163, 191, 192, 193, 194, 195, 196, 198,
199, 200, 201, 211, 212, 218, 227, 234, 240,
259, 263, 267, 280, 289, 298, 302, 303, 304,
307-13, 314, 320, 330, 338, 340, 347, 348,
351, 354, 355, 357, 358, 363, 377, 398, 400,
402, 403, 407, 483, 504, 545, 562, 563,
568, 574
Adam's, 51-52, 59-60, 61, 62, 63, 64, 67,
68, 69, 70, 74, 75, 77, 125, 133, 135, 199,
312, 579
God's, 22, 47, 51-52, 58, 59, 61, 63, 64, 67,
68, 69, 70, 75, 76, 77, 80, 81, 86, 96,
101, 109, 112, 113, 119, 126, 127, 128, 129,
130. 131, 132, 134, 135, 139, 152, 156, 163,
171, 190, 193, 194, 196, 199, 229, 230,
231, 259, 267, 280, 298, 307-13, 328,
330, 338, 347, 356, 396, 574, 578
God as literary character, 12, 23, 24, 37, 38,
179, 183, 184, 185, 189, 191, 192, 193, 194,
197, 209, 211, 218, 223, 224, 231, 233, 283,
389, 395, 410, 494-95, 499, 501, 507, 511,
513, 514, 516, 519, 540, 545, 547-548, 548-
49, 551, 555, 569
Great Commission, 241, 380-85

hand over (*see* "betray")

hearts, hard, 159, 164, 165, 403, 449-50, 454, 536

healing, 41, 92, 95, 107, 114, 160, 187, 220, 228, 265, 267, 272, 283, 286, 288, 298, 345, 371, 419, 426, 427, 438, 444, 445, 446, **460-86**, 487, 518, 526, 528, 529, 565, 576, 577

henotheism, 34

Hercules, 463

hermeneutics, 40-41

Herod Antipas, 335, 419, 426, 450-51, 452, 454, 503-4, 547

Herod the Great, 252, 374, 377, 378, 518, 522

Herodias, 450

historical Jesus, 9, 12, 261, 264, 307, 338, 573

holy ones, 32, 117, 129, 131, 133, 134, 135, 142-43, 146, 147, 149-50, 152, 167, 172, 205, 231, 233, 277, 319, 320, 321, 336, 337-38, 339, 462, 472, 579

Human One (*see* "son of man")

humanity, primeval, 47-77, 54, 61, 62, 63, 64, 65, 70, 71, 72, 74, 77, 78, 236, 277, 281, 291, 292, 353, 358, 391, 412, 459, 460, 582

"I am" (ἐγώ εἰμι), 200, 209, 246, 251, 299, 315, 325, 334, 404, 434

"I have come" sayings, 30-31, 280, 342

idealized human figures, 1, 2, **3-4**, 6, 7, 8, 11, 20, 21, 22, 24, 26-27, 29, 31, 35, 36, 39, 41, 42, 43, 44-45, **45**, 46, 47, 50, 51, 53, 54, 55, 56, 58, 59, 60, 62, 64, 66, 71, 73, 74, 77, 81, 84, 86, 87, 88, 89, 99, 102, 103, 106, 108, 117, 120, 121, 122, 126, 127-28, 130, 137, 139, 141, 147, 150-51, 153, 155, 158, 159, 164, 165, 167, 173-76, 178, 182, 186, 194, 196, 197, 199, 201, 204, 206, 207, 208, 209, 212, 216, 217, 218, 219, 222, 225, 226, 227, 228, 230, 233, 236, 240, 242, 246, 250, 253, 254, 258, 259, 262, 263, 265, 272, 273, 277, 278, 282, 286, 287, 292, 296, 297, 299, 300, 301, 304-5, 311, 312, 322, 339, 341, 342-43, 346, 349, 353, 354, 356, 357, 358, 361, 364, 369, 372-73, 375-76, 277-78, 379, 381, 383, 386, 387, 390, 393, 395, 396, 400, 401, 402, 406, 409, 410, 412, 414, 416, 420, 421, 426, 427-28, 429, 430, 433, 434, 435, 441, 442, 447-48, 454, 455, 459, 460, 466, 468, 471, 473, 477, 479, 480, 485, 486, 487, 488, 489, 490, 495, 498, 506, 507, 513, 514, 515, 516, 517, 524, 526-27, 531-32, 532, 535, 538, 540, 542-43, 544, 545, 548, 549, 554, 560, 564, 568, **570-73**, 578-80, 581, 582

image of God, 4, 20, 35, 47, 49, 50, 51, 52, 53, 54, 59, 63, 68, 70, 72, 73, 74, 75, 76, 77, 80, 101, 126, 161, 223, 247, 259

Immanuel, 359, 367, 368-69, 385-87

implied author, 15, 202, 386-87

incarnation, 195, 220, 297, 309, 346, 359, 364-65, 368, 369, 373, 396, 537, 540, 572

instruction (teaching, law), 83, 91, 113, 133, 136, 137, 138, 205, 215-16, 217, 237, 243, 255, 272, 278, 280, 286, 294, 295, 323, 331-32, 347, 400, 418, 421, 422, 423, 438, 451, 452-53, 461, 473, 503, 506, 518, 520-28, 557-61, 573, 576-77, 579

intimacy, 213

Irenaeus, 4, 40, 581

Isaac, 83, 129, 159, 189-90, 197, 239, 361-63, 382, 383, 485, 516, 545, 561, 573

Isaiah, **534-35**, 575

Israel, 7, 8, 10, 11, 12, 22, 32, 35, 55, 56, 61, 64-65, 67, 68, 72, 73, 76, 82, 94, 114, 133, 139, 142, 143, 144, 147, 148, 149, **158-63**, 168, 169, 172, 178, 184, 185, 208, 214, 223, 224, 225, 226, 227, 231, 236, 237, 240, 245, 246, 247, 261, 263, 277, 281, 289, 298, 301, 311, 318, 334, 339, 347, 353, 354, 356, 360, 375, 377, 378, 381, 389, 400, 412, 427, 451, 452, 516, 517, 519, 520, 522, 524, 526, 527, 534, 547, 548, 549, 551, 555, 557, 558, 559, 562, 563-64, 569, 570, 573, 574, 575, 579

J (Jahwist), 79

Jacob, 77, 159, 485, 545, 561

James the son of Zebedee, 188, 302-3

Jerusalem, 102, 109, 111, 172, 183, 209, 230, 272, 288, 289, 290, 298, 303, 314, 321, 323, 563-64

Jesus as literary character, 12, 23, 24, 37, 38, 39, 183, 209-14, 263, 266, 304, 308, 325, 327, 328, 389, 393-95, 403, 409, 410, 428, 486, 494-95, 496, 499, 501, 507, 511, 513, 514, 516, 519, 540, 545, 555, 561, 565, 569

Johannine Jesus, x, 16, 177, 232, 242-44, 262, 297, 299, 305, 322, 389, 407, 412, 569, 581

John the Baptist, 182, 183, 186, 201, 222, 223, 224, 238-39, 242, 243, 274, 275, 277, 279, 324, 341, 381, 384, 388-89, 393, 396, 426,

432, 450-51, 455, 469-70, 481, 482, 492, 495, 503, 521, 525-28, 534, 553, 554-55
John the son of Zebedee, 188, 302-3, 429, 457, 545
Jonah, 343-44, 532-33
Joseph, 364, 365
Joshua, 81, 90, 103, 249, 435-36, 446, 451-52, 454, 502, 504
jubilee, 362, 366, 367
Judas, 315, 344, 519
judge, 184, 308, 311, 331, 348, 351, 352, 385, 402, 421, 431, 432, 452, 458, 520, 574
judgment, 33, 76, 85, 93, 95, 114, 116, 120, 122, 123, 130, 138, 143, 147, 148, 149, 150, 151, 152, 153, 157, 168, 169, 170, 175, 178, 186, 205, 210, 214, 222-23, 224, 231, 239, 262, 267, 280, 285, 299, 307, 310, 311, 316, 322, 324, 326, 327, 330, 331, 336, 346, 347, 350, 351-52, 353, 357, 366, 367, 381, 386, 418, 423, 430, 431, 432, 470, 507, 520, 529-30, 533, 563, 564, 569, 574
Julius Caesar, 446

keys, 306
king (kingship), 52, 53, 55, 56, 58, 59, 61, 78, 80, 85, **96-120**, 105-6, 106-8, 109, 110-11, 127, 128, 142, 143, 149, 172, 173, 178, 180, 184, 185, 186, 190, 198, 199, 202, 207, 208, 209, 215, 216, 217, 219, 221, 224, 234, 235, 236, 242, 247, 248, 250, 252, 253, 255, 256, 259, 277, 281, 296, 304, 307, 324, 325, 332, 334, 347, 348, 352, 353, 358, **360-79**, 385, 394, 400, 414, 415, 417, 425, 430, 431, 433, 440, 449, 450-51, 452, 459-60, 466, 468, 469, 495, 503, 508, 511, 514, 516, 518-19, 533, 544, 574, 575, 579
    God as, 99-100, 102, 105, 106, 109, 120, 122, 123, 369, 507
kingdom (of God), xii, 41, 63, 65, 98, 111, 115, 144, 147, 148, 149-50, 178, 179, 185, 186, 187, 207, 209, 215, 216, 217, 226, 227, 234, 243, 272, 274, 304, 305, 306, 308, 319, 321, 329, 331, 332, 336, 347, 349, 351, 357, 358, 366-67, 390, 420, 425, 427, 429, 431, 439, 440, 442, 450, 455, 468, 482, 483, 484, 486, 500, 503, 508, 509, 525-26, 527, 531, 534, 535, 561, 573, 574, 576, 580, 581, 582

lament, 213

last supper, 230, 274, 303, 562-63
law (see "instruction")
lawlessness, 241, 563
Lazarus, 566
leper, leprosy, 427, 457, 461-62, 470, 842-83
Levi, 129
Levite, 558
liberation (see "salvation")
likeness of God, 50, 51, 52, 53, 54, 59, 66, 67, 68, 75, 76, 81, 84, 87, 96, 105, 119, 126, 248, 259
Lord, 183, 208, 210, 223, 241, 251, 282, 285, 288, 289, 292, 296, 297, 315, 328, 329, 338-39, 393-95, 397, 399, 400, 402-3, 404, 405, 408, 409, 410, 411, 412, 431, 457, 460, 466, 469, 480, 481, 482, 485-86, **491-501**, 516, 541-43, 561-62, 574, 575, 576, 580
    as divine title, x, 22-23, 23, 28, 38, 388-89, 393, 397, 405, 560
love, 164, 523, 530, 557-59

magi, 252, **374-76**, 469
Marduk, 52
Mark-Q overlaps, 222
martyr, 190, 191, 192, 263, 339, 362
Mary, 218, 220, 222, 224, 389-93, 395, 474, 553, 554
mediator (mediation), 73, 78, 79, 81, 87, 88, 89, 92, 112, 117, 118, 131, 132, 151, 153, 161, 163, 164, 168, 173, 175, 197, 208, 212, 215, 217, 223, 227, 234, 237, 247, 248, 272, 281, 282, 284, 296, 298, 311, 315-16, 326, 329, 342, 351, 353, 365, 366, 367, 369, 387, 397, 423, 435-36, 442, 453, 456, 457, 458, 459, 460-62, 467, 473, 480, 485, 490, 491, 492, 499, 501, 508-9, 510, 512, 517, 522, 529, 540, 541, 544, 546, 552, 557, 567, 569, 579
Melchizedek, 117, **120-24**, 173, 254, 331, 366-67, 390, 490
messiah ("Christ"), 3, 72, 114, 115, 116, 123, 130, 151, 156, 158, 178, 179, 181, 223, 228, 233, 235-36, 244, 247, 250, 251, 253, 255, 277, 281, 287, 288, 289, 290, 292, 298, 299, 304, 306, 309, 315, 324, 325, 328, 329, 333, 334, 338, 343, 360, 374, 377, 381, 395, 397, 398, 399, 400, 402, 403-5, 408, 409, 410, 412, 419, 425, 426, 433, 435, 440, 447, 452, 456, 458, 459, 462, 466-72, 473, 475, 476, 479, 481, 485, 486, 492, 496, 499, 509, 513, 514, 519, 526, 537, 539, 540, 541, 542,

543-44, 547, 551, 553, 555, 562, 563, 566, 569, 570, 573, 574, 575, 576, 581

suffering, 25, 32, 39, 41, 150, 178, 179, 180, 181, 182, 188, 189, 190, 191, 192, 193, 194, 195, 197, 198, **199-204**, 207, 210, 211, 212, 213, 214, 217, 218, 228, 230, 234, 235, 239, 240, 242, 255, 256, 260, 263, 264, 265, 266, 267, 269, 270, 272, 280, 288, 289, 297, **298-307**, 307, 308, 309, 312, 313, 315, 318, 320, 321, 322, 328, 329, 330, 331, 334-39, 340, 341, 342, 344, 349, 352-53, 354, 356, 357, 358, 361-62, 363, 375, 382-83, 387, 402, 403, 404, 407, 413, 443, 458, 475, 476, 497, 498, 499, 501, 509-15, 515-16, 517, 528, 531, 535-37, 541, 543, 544, 547, 548, 551, 553, 562-63, 565-66, 568, 573, 574, 575, 576, 577, 579, 580

messianic secret, 187, 189, 191, 206, 207, 232, 299, 325, 472, 574

Metatron, 155

Michael, 144, 173

Michaiah, 451, 503

mind-reading (*see* "thoughts, knowledge of")

miracles (signs), 241, 283, 298, 350, 406, 414, 438, 453, 455, 457, 470, 532, 539, 540

monolatry, 101

monotheism, Jewish, 2, 9, 10-11, 17-18, 26, 28, 37, 44, 45, 66-67, 75, 77, 82, 84, 99, 110, 119, 124, 139, 173-74, 175, 256, 356, 414, 500-501, 569, 571-72

Moses, 20, 22, 27, 35, 50, **77-87**, 89-90, 91, 92, 103, 125, 126, 128, 130, 131, 134, 138, 152, 159, 160, 162, 168, 173, 196, 197, 198, 199, 208, 229, 230, 243, 244, 249, 311-12, 352, 365-66, 377, 378, 381, 382, 383, 386, 387, 403, 435-36, 446, 450, 451-52, 453, 454, 455, 459, 481, 502, 503, 504, 522, 524, 525, 536, 537, 545-47, 569, 570, 573, 578
as God, 78, 79, 80-81, 82, 86, 87, 100

Naaman the Syrian, 461-62, 483, 556

nations (gentiles), 11, 47, 56, 65, 69, 72, 77, 86, 96, 98, 99, 101, 107, 109, 111, 112, 114, 117, 118, 119, 139, 140, 142, 147, 149, 150, 151, 157, 161, 162, 163, 172, 224, 289, 326, 350, 358, 366, 375, 381, 383, 384, 387, 400, 404, 418, 458, 533, 537, 541, 544, 546, 547,

549, 550, 551, 553, 555, 557, 559, 562, 567, 575

nature, authority over, 87, 88, 89, 92, 93, 94, 96, 116, 117, 414, **433-60**, 460, 464-65, 486, 582

Nazirite, 389

Nebuchadnezzar, 337

new creation, 62, 72, 118, 220, 221, 229, 305, 355, 358, 364, 410, 575

Noah, 72, 165, 350, 460

numen, 203

oaths, 295

obeisance, 28, 30, 71, 85, 89, 96, 100, 101, 114, 179, 200, 207, 208, 226, 246, 251, 252, 374, 376, 380, 387, 447, 449, 458, 469, 574

overshadow, 220

P (priestly writer) 54, 56, 96, 125, 127, 140, 247, 440, 578

parousia, 194, 264, 265, 266, 268, 269, 272, 284, 297, 298, **307-334**, **345-53**, 355, 358, 431

passion prediction, 188, 191, 194, 195, 197, 210, 264, 265, 266, 267, **298-307**, 308, 309, 312-13, 337, 338, 357, 401, 402, 403, 515, 577

Passover, 159, 230

paterfamilias, 203

Paul, the apostle, 4, 10, 13, 177-78, 389, 424-25, 429-30, 572

peace, 170, 171

Peter, Simon, 1, 39, 180, 181, 188, 190, 191, 192, 193, 194, 197, 200, 207, 220, 228, 229, 233, 236, 242, 244, 245, 250, 251, 252, 255, 266, 272, 283, 287, 288, 289, 298, 299, 300, 302, 305-7, 312, 325, 333, 406-9, 413, 426, 449, 456, 457, 459, 475, 478, 479, 484, 485, 496, 499, 503, 538-45, 566

Peter's mother-in-law, 228, 472, 477

Pharisees, 238, 254, 287, 295, 382, 401, 454, 482, 522

Philip, 429, 548, 557

Pilate, 200, 547

Plato, 370-71, 392

portents, cosmic, 202

Poseidon, 448

prayer, 72, 79, 83, 172, 209, 212, 214, 230, 240, 279, 315, 326, 565, 576

preaching, 41

preexistence, 4, 16, 23, 25, 26, 29, 30, 35, 39, 82, 93, 96, 102, 113, 129, 148, 153-54, 156, 158, 172, 175, 177, 182, 190, 195, 197, 202, 203, 206, 207, 210, 211, 212, 215, 217, 225, 231-32, 242, 256, 262, 273, 279, 287, 297, 299, 305, 308, 309, 316, 319, 320, 321, 322, 329, 332, 342, 343, 346, 348, 356, 373, 516, 537, 544, 571 572, 577, 580

presence, personal (at physical distance), 93, 96, 384-87

priest (priesthood), 35, 46, 47, 52, 53, 69, **120-139**, 146, 168, 173, 175, 182, 200, 201, 209, 211, 245, 296, 299, 322, 323, 324, 326, 469, 490, 558-59, 570

proclamation, 95, 117, 118, 122, 179, 186, 217, 218, 243, 258, 274, 300, 324, 387, 425, 426, 429, 458, 462, 470, 471, 480, 484, 521, 526, 533, 550, 551, 555, 566, 575

prophet, 46, **77-96**, 173, 184, 211, 230, 235, 241, 242, 296, 298, 323, 324, 327, 341, 342, 343, 367, 378, 387, 403, 423, 426, 455, 461-62, 480, 481, 487, 491, 502, 503, 516, 518, 521, 525-28, 532, 534, 535, 537, 539, 543, 545-47, 548, 553, 554-56, 562, 563, 564, 566

Pyrrhus, 465

Pythagoras, 444-46, 464-65

Q, 27, 222, 354

ransom, 212, 303-4, 577

readers, 179, 180, 181, 182, 183, 184, 195, 200, 201, 202, 206, 211, 245, 259, 266, 271, 275, 278, 283, 289, 299, 306, 318, 325, 330, 332, 346, 347, 359, 361, 362, 386-87, 388-89, 397, 399, 403, 419, 426, 437, 457, 458, 472, 501, 536, 539, 548, 550, 560

    Greco-Roman, 9, **13-15**, 21, 193, 194, 202-4, 256-58, 370-72, 373, 391-92, 444-46, 463-66

rebuke, 181, 206, 207, 228

recapitulation, 4, 227, 581

redemption (*see* "salvation")

reign of God (*see* "kingdom of God")

rejection, 181, 210, 211, 212, 294, 297, 298-307, 314, 315, 340, 341, 341, 342, 345, 352-53, 443, 502, 556, 562, 577

rending, 180, 181, 184, 192, 199, 202, 256, 315

repentance, 25, 183, 224, 238-39, 278, 285, 343, 383, 387, 404, 405, 426, 457, 507, 533, 536, 546, 548, 557, 563, 575

representation, 178, 231, 232, 241, 247, 248, 272, 277, 338-39, 349, 352, 369, 377, 390, 394, 396, 397, 398, 399, 411, 416, 421, 427, 429, 434, 462, 483, 493, 501, 506, 527, 531, 546, 574, 575

reputation, 159, 162-63

resurrection (resuscitation), 74, 75, 87, 90, 92, 93, 94, 95, 96, 117, 151, 192, 194, 195, 197, 204, 211, 212, 221, 234, 235, 252, 256, 266, 267, 285, 286, **298-307**, 308, 309, 310, 312, 313, 316, 320, 321, 322, 327, 328, 329, 330, 332, 333, 337, 343, 344, 346, 351, 357, 358, 372, **379-85**, 387, **401-411**, 418, 427, 445, 458, 462, 465, 470, 471, 480-81, 482, 486, 503, 509, 513, 516, 526, 532, 533, 535-37, 540, 541-42, 543, 544, 545, 546, 549, 550, 551, 553, 562, 566-67, 568, 574, 575, 576, 579

revelation, 194, 206, 210, 232, 233, 234, 242, 244, 245, 253, 329, 358, 374, 406, 409, 450, 457, 497, 522, 553, 579

right hand of God (*see* "exaltation")

righteousness (obedience, virtue), 71, 77, 83, 84, 99, 111, 113, 120, 162, 164, 165, 166, 167, 169, 171, 187, 213-14, 215, 222, 226, 239, 240, 241, 289, 290, 398, 520

rule (*see* "sovereignty")

Sabbath, 65, 126, 143, 165, 228, 286-293, 294-97, 319, 357, 381, 472, 478, 479, 495

Sadducees, 238, 382

salvation (redemption), 101, 107, 116, 122, 123, 144, 157, 160, 168, 171, 208, 227, 228, 229, 231, 239, 249, 253, 285, 302, 305, 309, 310, 314, 315, 321, 329, 330, 342, 358, 365, 366, 367, 369, 373, 376, 387, 395, 396, 397, 398, 400, 404, 411, 414, 429, 433, 436, 443, 446, 452, 454, 466, 481, 511, 512, 520, 524, 526, 531, 535-36, 541, 543, 552-53, 560, 561-62, 565, 566, 569, 574, 581

Samaritan (Samaria), 483, 556-57, 557-59

Sarah, 365, 389

Satan, 129, 165, 166, 186, 187, 192, 208, 226, 227, 228, 233, 234, 293, 300, 301, 303, 358, 359, 366, 381, 415, 420, 424, 427, 433, 460, 467, 468, 478, 484, 567

scribes, 201, 208, 209, 211, 214, 255, 273, 274, 275, 277, 278, 281, 286, 295, 299, 310, 323, 326, 340, 346, 422, 442, 469, 500-501, 520, 522

sending, 210
Serapis, 465
Sermon on the Mount, 240-41, 294
servant (service, servanthood), 37, 57, 66,
    67, 85, 94, 303, 304, 310, 322, 395, 418,
    429, 468, 471, 485, 515-16, 518, 520, 521,
    524, 525, 526, 530-31, 548, 577, 579
Seth, 54, 74, 223
shema, 44
shepherd, 106-8, 114, 243, 312, 374, 377, 396,
    450, 451-54, **502-6**, **506-9**, **528-29**, 578
Simeon, 398-99, 552, 554
Simon, son of Onias, 124, 125
sinners, 295, 341, 342, 344, 385, 401, 457, 528
Socrates, 448
solidarity, 184, 238-39
Solomon, 20, 60-61, 96, **104-5**, 109-110, 187,
    207, 208, 220, 343, 376, 416, 417, 470-71,
    517, 532, 533
son (children) of God, 14, 27, 29, 31, 38, 49,
    53-55, 64, 69, 76, 97, 98, 104, 106, 109, 115,
    119, 120, 129, 133, 135, 155, 157, **158-61**, 164-
    65, 166, **177-260**, 214-17, 268, 270, 271,
    287, 288, 290, 300, 303, 305, 306, 309, 312,
    324, 333, 334, 348, 357, 359, 361, 363, 365,
    372, 373, 377, 378, 382, 383, 384, 385, 387,
    390, 392, 393, 395, 399-400, 409-10, 411,
    413-14, 418, 420, 421, 423, 425, 430, 434,
    435, 440, 441, 442, 447, 449, 454, 459,
    463, 468, 469, 470, 472, 474, 478, 499,
    511, 516, 517, 519, 523, 545, 547, 549, 566,
    567, 570, 575, 576, 577
son of man, 20, 27, 29, 30, 31, 32-33, 38, 46,
    139-58, 180, 181, 188, 191, 192, 194, 195,
    196, 200, 201, 210, 211, 213, 214, 217, 235,
    254, 255, 256, 260, **261-358**, 359, 381, 385,
    401-2, 403, 411, 414, 415, 421, 422, 423,
    431, 442, 443, 460, 473, 474, 476, 498, 515,
    516, 517, 528, 532, 568, 569, 573, 574, 575,
    576, 577, 579, 581
sovereignty, 18, 19, 21, 22, 42, 48, 50, 52-53,
    55, 57, 58, 60, 61, 66, 67, 69, 70-71, 72, 74,
    75, 76, 77, 78, 79, 80, 82, 83, 84, 85, 86, 88,
    89, 92, 96, 99, 100, 101, 103, 104, 105, 107,
    108, 109, 116, 118, 121, 128, 129, 130, 141,
    144, 147, 149, 150, 151, 155, 165, 166, 169,
    170, 171, 172, 174, 178, 186, 203, 205, 206,
    207, 208, 209, 216, 217, 234, 236, 246, 248,
    249, 253, 259, 262, 263, 265, 268-69, 272,
    276, 277, 278, 280, 287, 288, 290, 293, 294,

295, 296, 297, 298, 304, 305, 306, 307, 309,
    313, 317, 318, 319, 322, 323, 336, 346, 349,
    355, 356, 357, 358, 371, 375, 380-81, 385,
    414, 435, 436, 442, 450, 528, 535, 570, 573,
    578, 580, 582
speech, authoritative (*see also* proclama-
    tion), 47, 52, 78, 80, 81, 82, 87, 88, 92, 93,
    94, 96, 294, 520, 522, 524, 533, 568, 573,
    576
spirit, 91, 92, 96, 112, 118, 120, 129, 164, 167,
    180, 202, 203, 404, 406, 521, 565, 567, 575
    of God, 40, 41, 62, 64, 66, 68, 69, 92, 97,
    120, 164, 167, 180, 184, 185, 186, 187,
    190, 192, 205, 206, 207, 209, 212, 216,
    220, 221, 222, 223, 224, 225, 228, 233,
    234, 235, 236, 275, 276, 277, 278, 280-
    81, 283, 284, 288, 290, 293, 329, 355,
    364, 370, 371, 372, 373, 381, 384, 386,
    388, 390, 393, 398, 400, 405, 410, 413,
    414, 418, 420, 423, 427, 428, 458, 459,
    468, 478, 487, 496, 518, 521, 526, 527,
    538, 539, 540, 542, 544, 554-55, 567, 573,
    576, 577
unclean (*see* "demons")
Stephen, 547-48, 549
strong man, 208, 234
sun, 49, 76, 102, 104, 124, 128, 137, 154, 199,
    202, 225, 315, 347
Syrophoenician (Canaanite) woman, 421,
    454-55, 468

tax collectors, 295, 341, 342, 482
Teacher of Righteousness, 138, 182, 490
teaching (*see* "instruction")
Tell Fakhariyeh, 52
temple, 126, 132, 145, 146, 180, 214, 221, 273,
    279, 290, 294, 295, 296, 314, 320, 321, 323,
    324-25, 326, 327, 329, 333, 398, 399-400,
    458, 533, 554, 558
    clearing, 209
    curtain, 180, 181, 315
temptation **225-28**, 382, 383, 567
theophany, 51, 55, 56, 58, 69, 76, 81, 86, 89,
    126, 161, 169, 247, 393, 433, 439, 457-58,
    578
theios anēr, 414
Theudas, 103, 198, 249, 436, 447, 454
three days, 25, 125, 211, 309, 327, 330, 337,
    343, 401, 532, 536, 543, 568, 575
throne, 19, 33, 42, 47, 50, 60, 74, 75, 76, 77,

84-85, 87, 96, 99, 104-5, 106, 109, 114, 118, 130, 131, 132, 136, 142, 147, 148, 149, 151, 152, 153, 156, 175, 198, 210, 219, 220, 248, 255, 262, 272, 311, 346, 347, 348, 349, 351, 352, 357, 571, 576, 579
thoughts, knowledge of, 111, 112, 151, 223, 275, 277, 281, 289-90
Tiberius, 448
Torah, 161, 241, 243-44, 386
transcendence, Jesus's, 29
transfiguration, 75, 80, 179, **191-99**, 202, 204, 210, 220, **229-32**, 233, 312, 313, 318, 335, 347, 457
translation into heaven, 153
trial, Jesus's, 181, 235-36, 268, 315, 322-31, 332-33
tribulation, 211, 213, 301, 302, 305, **314-22**, 326, 327, 329, 331, 345, 349, 358, 363, 443, 530

Vespasian, 465
vicegerency, xi, 1, 3, 4, 11, 12, 20, 22, 39, 40, 48, 49, 50, 52, 53, 56, 57, 58, 59, 60, 61, 63, 66, 70, 71, 72, 76, 77, 78, 79, 80, 84-85, 86, 87-88, 92, 94, 96, 99, 100, 101, 102, 103, 105, 111, 112, 113, 114, 115, 116, 117, 118, 119, 119, 121, 126, 129, 141, 142, 144, 147, 149, 150, 151, 152, 157, 163, 164, 168, 172, 184, 185, 198, 203, 204, 205, 206, 208, 209, 215, 217, 219, 223, 224, 228, 234, 236-37, 248, 249, 250, 253, 254, 258, 259, 263, 268-69, 272, 274, 275, 276, 277, 278, 279, 280, 281, 282, 283, 284, 285, 286, 289, 292, 293, 295, 297, 298, 311, 314, 317, 319, 330, 332, 339, 347, 348, 351, 353, 354, 355, 356, 357, 358, 375, 377, 380-81, 385, 389, 397, 399, 400, 403, 408, 409, 411, 414, 415, 420, 422, 423, 427, 429, 430, 433, 436, 440, 441, 442, 443, 446, 449, 459, 460, 462, 480, 484, 486, 494-95, 499, 506, 509, 512, 513, 528,

529, 535, 540-41, 557, 569, 571, 573, 574, 578-79, 580, 582
virgin, 220, 238, **363-73**, 376, 517, 518, 539
virtue (*see* "righteousness")
visitation, divine, 92

water, 100, 142
  authority over (walking on), 11, 18, 19, 27, 43, 79, 87, 89-90, 91, 92, 93, 96, 103, 104, 118, **246-53**, 257, 259, 272, **433-50**, 460
  cleansing (baptism), 62, 64, 129, 167, 179, 181, **182-90**, 192, 193, 197, 202, 203, 204, 205, 206, 209, 210, 221, 222-23, 224, 232, 238-39, 256, 274, 278, 293, 303, 319, 324, 334, 372, 381-83, 384, 385, 390, 410, 418, 423, 425, 459, 482, 521, 522, 539, 541, 554, 577
widow of Nain, 480-81
wilderness, 12, 101, 162, 186, 225, 226, 227, 451, 493, 522, 527, 574
wisdom, 21, 48, 60, 68, 127, 128, 132, 139, 151, 152, 161-62, 173, 184, 233, 234, 289, 290, 313, 337, 341, 371, 398, 400, 440, 473, 571
word (*see* "speech, authoritative")
worship, 18, 19, 20, 21, 22, 23, 26, 27, 28, 42, 46-47, 47, 70-71, 72, 73, 74, 77, 85, 86, 87, 96, 98, 99-100, 101, 104-5, 109-110, 114, 118-19, 120, 127, 128, 139, 151, 152, 153, 159, 166, 170, 172, 174, 207, 226, 227, 252, 357, 359, **374-76**, 387, 469, 483, 570, 571, 574, 578

Xerxes, 440, 448

Yhwh, Yahweh (*see* "divine name")

Zacchaeus, 342
Zechariah, 395-96, 397, 481, 552, 554
Zeus, 320

Ancient Sources Index

OLD TESTAMENT

Genesis

1	37, 47, 48, 49, 50, 51, 52, 53, 56, 57, 58, 61, 65, 66, 68, 70, 71, 76, 77, 80, 104, 128, 137, 140, 141, 142, 150-51, 224, 247, 354
1–2	136, 354
1:1–2:4	125
1:2	69, 118, 221, 224, 390
1:9	137
1:11-12	140
1:18	49
1:20	55
1:21	140
1:24-25	140
1:26	21, 50, 52, 53, 68, 119, 391
1:26-27	322, 353
1:26-28	40, 49, 51, 52, 53, 54, 55, 61, 67, 75, 96-97, 98, 99, 101, 126, 142, 224
1:26-30	277
1:27	50, 391
1:28	49, 52, 55
1:29-30	353
2	68, 71
2–3	48, 68
2:1	127
2:2-3	291
2:4	360
2:7	71, 224
3:22	97
5:1	360
5:1-2	54
5:1-3	53, 223, 391
5:3	54
8:17	55
9:1	55
9:6	54
9:7	55
12:3	65, 161
14:18	120, 121, 123
17:2	229
17:6	55, 96-97, 224
17:16	96-97, 224
17:20	55
22	190
22:1	189
22:2	239
22:11	189
22:12	189, 239
22:15	189
22:16	189
22:17	97
22:18	546
26:4	546
28:3	55
28:14	65
32:12	97
35:11	55, 224
41:38	184
47:27	55

Exodus

1:7	55
1:8-10	366
2:24-25	159
3:1	452, 504
3:6	545
3:8	79
3:20	79
3:21	79
4:12	79
4:15	78
4:16	78, 82
4:21	79
4:21-23	159
4:22-23	55, 166
4:23	133
6:7	79
6:26	79
6:27	79
7:1	78, 82, 86, 198
7:17	79
7:20b	79
7:25	79
8:5-6	79
8:8	79
8:12-13	79
8:16	79
8:19	79
12:12	80
13:11-16	229
13:16	229
14	249, 436
14:14	79
14:16	79, 103, 249, 435
14:21	79, 249

14:27	103	6:3	389	32:5	159
14:31	79	6:23-26	81	32:6	159
15:11	136	6:23-27	131	32:9	159
20:5	101	6:25	152	32:10-11	159
20:8-11	291	11:16-29	92	32:13-14	159
20:11	547	11:16-30	184	32:15-17	159
20:13	523	18:20	132	32:18	98, 159
20:18-19	81	21:32-35	503	32:27	159
22:29-31	229	23:7	184	32:36-42	159
23:20	91, 492-93, 527	24:17	128	33:16-17	58
24:1	196	27:16-17	451		
24:16	196	27:16-23	451	**Joshua**	
25-31	125, 128	27:17	451, 502-6, 528,	3:7	249, 435
26:33	132		529	3:7-4:19	103
28:3	184	27:18	184	4:14	81, 382
28:6	120	27:18-21	502		
29:37	132	27:18-23	81, 92	**Judges**	
31:3	184	27:20	452, 504	3:10	184
31:10	132	27:21	452	6:34	184
32-34	80	33:52	50		
32:1	81			**1 Samuel**	
32:7	80-81	**Deuteronomy**		1:19	376
33:18	311	4:6-7	161-62	8:4-9	102
33:22	89	4:7	162	8:7	531
34	80	4:32-38	162	10:1-10	184
34:1-8	311	4:37	231	13:14	97
34:8-9	89	5:9	101	15:25	376
34:29	230	5:17	523	15:31	376
34:29-30	196	5:31	83	16:8-10	231
34:29-34	152	6:4	560	16:11	504
34:29-35	80, 128, 312	6:4-5	500-501	16:11-12	452
34:29	80	6:5	557	16:13	97, 112, 288
34:30	81, 230	6:10-12	227	16:13-16	184
34:33-35	81	6:13	226, 374	16:13-23	441
34:34	230	6:16	227	16:14-23	97
34:35	230	7:7	231	16:23	187, 416
39-40	126	8:3	226	17:15	452
		8:5	226	17:28	452
Leviticus		9:9	89	17:34	504
11:3-8	140	10:15	231	22:2	187
11:9-12	140	10:16	164	23:13-29	452
19:15-18	558	10:20	226, 374	24:1	452
19:18	500, 523, 557, 558	10:36	164	24:9	376
19:18b	558	14:12	231	24:25	452
19:19	140	15:2	366	25:23	376
21:1-4	558	17:18-20	222	26:1-3	452
25:13	366	18:15	81, 197, 545		
		18:18	91, 545	**2 Samuel**	
Numbers		28:1-14	579	1:2	376
3:12-13	133	28:10	579		

6:12-14	120	1:10	88, 556	**Job**	
6:21	63, 231	1:12	88, 556	33:4	221
7	97, 102, 104, 115,	2	91	38:7	124
	247, 390, 400	2:9	91	40:9-10	59
7:8	63	2:10	91		
7:11-16	97	2:12	91	**Psalms**	
7:12	219	2:13-14	436	2	97, 98-99, 100,
7:12-14	323	2:14-15	91-92		104, 106, 115, 152,
7:12-16	219	2:19-22	92, 436		161, 163, 184-85,
7:13	219, 325	2:23-25	92		186, 190, 219, 247,
7:14	53, 55, 97, 98, 164,	3:11-20	92		290, 408, 549
	226	3:13-20	436	2:1-2	547
7:16	97	4:1-7	92	2:2	99, 151, 547
8:18	120	4:8-37	92	2:5-6	99
12:20	376	4:11-37	117	2:6	185
14:17	97	4:18-37	436	2:7	53, 55, 98, 185, 223,
15:30	508	4:38-41	92		409-10, 548-49
16:18	231	4:42-44	92, 436, 455, 504	2:7-9	99
		5:1-19	461	2:8	381
1 Kings		5:7	461	2:9	111
3:14	97	5:8	461-62	2:10-12	99
3:22	97	5:14	92	6	562, 565
4:20	97	5:15	93, 462	6:4-5 (6:5-6 LXX)	562
6:16	132	5:26	93, 386	6:7 (6:8 LXX)	562
8:16	231	6:1-7	93, 436	6:8 (6:9 LXX)	561,
8:27	399	6:14-23	93		562
11:6	97	6:25–7:20	436	7:8-9	122
15:11	97	9:7	82	7:9	366
17:1	87	11:18	50	8	58-59, 65, 126, 142
17:1-7	116	13:20-21	117	8:1	312
17:8-24	480	13:21	93	8:3	469
17:9-24	92	14:3	97	8:5	62, 312
17:17-24	117, 461	16:2	97	8:6	51, 59
17:22	461	17:13	82	16 (15 LXX)	407,
17:24	87, 92, 461, 480	17:23	82		423
18:24	88	18:3	97	16:1 (15:1 LXX)	543
18:36	88	21:10	82	16:8-11 (15:8-11 LXX)	543
19:1-2	335	24:2	82	16:10 (15:10 LXX)	205,
19:8	89				278, 407, 423, 549
19:9	89	**1 Chronicles**		18:15-16	439
19:11	89	16:27	58	21:5	58-59, 259
19:13	89	17:14	98	22 (21 LXX)	255-56,
19:15-21	91	22:2-5	325		512-13, 565
19:16	91	28:5	123	22:1 (21:2 LXX)	509,
22:17	451, 502-6, 528,	29:20	104, 105, 252, 376		512, 565
	529	29:22	63	22:7 (21:8 LXX)	509, 512
		29:23	105, 123, 252	22:7-8 (21:8-9 LXX)	512
2 Kings				22:8 (21:9 LXX)	512
1	557	**2 Chronicles**		22:15 (21:16 LXX)	513
1:2-3	556	4:22	132		

22:18 (21:19 LXX) 509, 512
22:19 (21:20 LXX) 512, 565
22:28 77
23 453, 504, 505-6
23:1 505
23:2 454, 505, 506
29:3 439, 443, 506
29:4 58
31 (30 LXX) 565
31:5 (30:6 LXX) 565
31:9 (30:10 LXX) 565
31:19 (30:20 LXX) 565
33:6 221
41:1 (40:1 LXX) 510
41:9 (40:10 LXX) 509, 510
41:10 (40:11 LXX) 510
42 214
42–43 (41–42 LXX) 510-12
42:1-4 (41:1-5 LXX) 510
42:5 (41:6 LXX) 212, 509, 510
42:9-10 (41:10-11 LXX) 511
42:11 (41:12 LXX) 212, 509, 510
43:1-2 (42:1-2 LXX) 511
43:4 (42:4 LXX) 511
43:5 (42:5 LXX) 509, 510
45 99-100, 104, 106, 376
45:3 259
45:4 58, 99
45:5 58, 99
45:6 99, 123
47:2 77
51:11 112
65:7 439, 443
69 (68 LXX) 513
69:21 (68:22 LXX) 509, 513-14
72 100-102, 107
72:1-2 100
72:6-7 100
72:9 100
72:9-11 100
72:11 100, 101

72:12 101
72:13 101
72:14 101
72:17 101, 102, 153-154
74:13 439
77:16 439
78:2 518
82 244
82:1 122, 366
89 97, 100, 102-4, 116, 125, 160, 247-50, 253, 290, 408, 435, 441, 442, 447, 454
89:1-4 102
89:3-4 247
89:5 248
89:5-18 102
89:6 248
89:8 248
89:9 103, 249, 435
89:9-10 439, 441
89:10 103, 248
89:13 103, 248
89:14 103
89:19-37 102
89:21 248
89:22 103
89:23 248
89:23-27 441
89:24 103, 248
89:25 103, 104, 249, 250, 435, 436, 439, 441, 454
89:26 55, 435
89:26-27 104, 247
89:27 248
89:30-33 104
89:35-36 247, 248
89:36-37 104
89:38-42 102
89:43-44 247
90:16 58
91 227
91:12 227
96:6 58
104:1 58
104:30 221
105:16 277
110 325, 408
110:1 (109:1 LXX) 121, 123, 149, 325, 328, 339, 389, 407, 491-92, 496-99, 501, 544-45
110:1-6 348
110:2 149
110:3b (109:3b LXX) 543
110:4 120, 121, 123, 149
110:5-6 149
118 210
118:22-23 499-500
118:26 499-500
132:11 348
145:12 58
146:6 (145:6 LXX) 547

Isaiah
1:4 277
5 326
5:19 277
6 244
6:1-4 457
6:1-10 457
6:5 457
6:7 457
6:8-9 30
6:8-10 457
6:9 534
6:9-10 234, 475, 502
7:14 365, 367-70, 517, 518, 524
7:15-16 368
9 105
9:1-2 518
9:5 123
9:6 99, 370
9:6-7 97, 105-106
11 101, 184
11:1-9 355
11:10 468
13 315, 350
13:3 316
13:4 316
13:6 316
13:7 316
13:10 316, 349
13:11 316
13:11-13 316
13:21 100
14:13-14 136

17:7	277	59:20	163	20:7-8	162
26:19	526	60:1	128	20:8	162
29:18-19	526	60:1-3	163	20:9	162
30:11	277	60:6	163	20:14	162-63
34	315, 350	60:9	277	20:22	162-63
35:5-6	526	60:12	163	28	59-60
37:23	277	60:14	163	34	106-8, 451, 502,
40	362, 502	61	95, 122, 123, 163,		504, 505, 578
40:3	18, 183, 491-96,		521, 525, 526, 554	34:4	107
	501, 508, 527, 552	61:1	490, 521, 526	34:10	107
40:3a	552	61:1-2	117, 555	34:11-16	102, 107, 453,
40:3-5	552, 553	61:2	121, 122, 521		504
40:5	552, 553	62:10	493	34:13-15	107
40:11	504	63:11-14	160	34:14-16	505
40:17	69	63:15	277	34:15	504
40:23	69	63:15-16	160	34:23	107, 504
40:25	277	64:1	181	34:23-24	107, 453
41:1	184	64:8-12	160	34:24	63, 102
41:20	277	66:18-21	112	34:25	107
42:1-4	418, 467, 468, 471,	66:18	112	34:26-27	107
	518, 524			34:28	107
42:4	468	**Jeremiah**		34:30	370
42:6-7	114	1:7	30	36:20	163
42:7	117	3:4	160	37:25	63
42:8	112, 311	3:19	160	41:4	132
42:19	114	5:21	475	44:15	69
43:5	370	7:11	326		
43:14	277	23:56	123	**Daniel**	
43:19	452	31:9	160	3:35	278
45:15-17	23	31:15	378, 518	4:31	337
48:11	63, 311	31:32	378	7	29, 32, 38, 139, 141,
49:6	94	50:39	100		142, 144, 146, 148,
49:7	277				149, 157, 261, 269,
50:6	515	**Ezekiel**			273, 276, 277, 281,
52:7	123, 367	1:5	50		292, 301, 313, 318,
52:12–53:12	515-16	1:10	50		319, 321, 322, 326,
52:15	515	1:13	50		328, 329, 331, 336,
53	563	1:16	50		338, 339, 344, 345,
53:4	471, 518, 531	1:22	50		348, 350, 353-54,
53:6	515	1:26	50		355, 357
53:7	515	1:26-28	50	7:4	141, 353
53:12	515, 562-63, 563	1:28	50, 68, 124, 126	7:5	353
54:1	564	3:1	30	7:6	141, 353
55:5	163, 277	3:4	30	7:8	141, 145, 353
56:4-7	163	7:20	50	7:9	142
56:7	326	8:2	50	7:9-10	147
56:8–59:21	163	10:1	50	7:11	147
57:3	548	10:10	50	7:12	141, 147
57:14	493	10:21	50	7:13	269, 270, 271, 277,
58:9-12	455	10:22	50		313, 317, 318, 325,

	339, 349, 498
7:13-14	141, 147, 263
7:14	139, 142, 147, 149, 155, 156, 158, 276, 317, 348, 385
7:17	142
7:17-18	142, 263
7:18	142-43, 149, 167, 263, 319, 336
7:21	141, 145, 146-47, 150, 319, 321
7:21-22	314, 336
7:22	149-50, 319
7:23-27	142, 263
7:24	143
7:25	141, 143, 150, 274, 319, 321, 336, 337
7:25-26	314
7:26-27	147
7:27	143, 147, 150, 172, 263, 319, 336, 348
8	145, 146, 321
8:9-12	145
8:10-12	145
8:10	146
8:24	143
8:25	146
9	146, 321
9:25	123
9:25-26	145-46
9:27	320
10–12	321
11–12	144, 320, 321, 337, 338
11:31	320
11:36	144, 145
11:45	144, 320
12	146
12:1	144, 145, 320, 321
12:3	75, 195, 196, 313
12:11	320

Hosea

1:10	165
2:1	245, 246
5:14	138, 490
6:6	245, 294-95
10:8	564
10:10	564

11:1	160, 166, 237-38, 245, 377, 378, 518, 522, 524
11:2	160
11:3-4	160
11:9	377

Joel

2:28-32	539-43
2:32	137
3 (MT, LXX)	406
3:1 (MT, LXX)	184, 553
3:1-2 (MT, LXX)	91, 539
3:1-5 (MT, LXX)	539-43
3:4 (MT, LXX)	540
3:5 (MT, LXX)	541, 542, 567

Amos

5:26	50
9:11	116, 550
9:11-12	550
9:11-15	452
9:12	550

Jonah

| 2:1 | 532 |
| 2:5-7 | 532 |

Micah

3:8	184
5	108, 377, 396
5:1-3	517
5:2	108, 396, 517
5:4	108
5:4-5	377
5:13	376-77
7	530
7:6	530, 531

Habakkuk

1:5	549
2:4	490
2:4b	138
3:3	277

Zechariah

3	244
9–14	506-7, 508, 509
9:9	508, 518-19, 564

9:11	508
10:2	507
11:4-17	507
11:13	519
12	109
12:7	109
12:8	109, 507, 508
12:9	109, 507
13:1-6	507
13:7	506-7
14:3-4	508
14:4	507-9
14:6-8	507
14:9	508

Malachi

1:6	160
3:1	91, 182, 183, 335, 389, 492-96, 508, 527
4:4	91
4:5	93, 335, 492
4:5-6	90-91, 389
4:6	95

APOCRYPHA & PSEUDEPIGRAPHA

2 Baruch

| 21:4 | 221 |

1 Enoch

1:1	231
1:8	231
5:7-8	231
25:5	231
38:2-3	231
38:4	231
39:6	231
45:5	231
46:2	154
46:3	154
46:5	152
46:6	152
47	314
48:2	154
48:2-3	153
48:5	151

48:10	151, 152
49:2	151
49:3	151
51	151-52
51:3	151
51:3-4	152
52:4	151
58:1-3	231
60:10	154
61:8	152
61:8-9	152
61:10	152, 158
62:5	152, 154
62:6	152
62:7	154
62:9	151, 152, 154
62:14	154
63:11	154
69:26	154
69:27	154, 348
69:29	154
70:1	154
70:4	231
71	153, 158
71:14	153,154, 158
71:17	154
85-90	72
85:3	72, 172
90:6-27	314
90:9	114
90:10	114
90:20	114, 331
90:28-29	325
90:30	172
90:37	72, 172
93:1	231

2 Enoch

71	122

3 Enoch

4	155

4 Ezra

7:28	156
7:28-29	157
12:32	156
13:8-12	157
13:12-13	157

13:29-32	157
13:38	157
13:52	156
14:9	156

Exagogue of Ezekiel the Tragedian

68-76	198
68-89	452
70-82	84-85
81	85
85	85
85-86	85

Jubilees

1:7-18	164
1:17	370
1:23	164
1:24	164
1:24-25	164
2:17-20	165
2:18	165
2:20	133, 165
2:21	165
2:28	165
2:30	165
2:31	165
10:1-14	460
10:7-14	165
11:14-24	166
11:18-22	166
11:23-24	166
12:20	165
18:18-19	361
31	129-30
31:14	129-30, 138
31:15	130
48:9-19	166

Judith

8:26	361
16:14	221

Letter of Aristeas

99	138

Life of Adam and Eve
Vita

13:1-3	73, 207

14:1-2	73, 207
14:3	73
37-38	74

Apocalypse

10-11	74
10:3	74
11:1	74
24:4	74

1 Maccabees

1:54	320
2:58	94
4:46	82
14:41	82

2 Maccabees

9:8-10	136

Psalms of Solomon

2:31	313
3:12	313
17	110-11
17:1	110-11, 293
17:3	111
17:3-4	293
17:4	111, 113
17:5-20	111
17:21	111, 113, 293, 400
17:21-26	289-90
17:22	114
17:22-24	290
17:22-25	111
17:23	111
17:24	111
17:25	111, 112, 275
17:26	111, 114
17:26-27	111
17:27	111, 114, 400
17:29	111
17:29-31	111
17:29-32	112
17:30	111, 114
17:31	112, 400
17:32	111, 112, 113, 233, 400
17:34	113, 293, 400
17:36	111
17:37	111, 112, 290, 400
17:40	111

17:40-41	111	13:3	76	V, 8-12	62-63
17:42	113	13:5	76	V, 16-17	63, 69
17:43	233-34	13:6	76	V, 19	63, 69
17:43-45	111	13:7	76	V, 23	63
17:46	113, 293, 400	13:10	76	IX, 27	64
18:4	400			XI, 3	63
18:7	400	**Testament of Levi**		XII, 5	63
18:7-8	233	3:3-8	129	XII, 30-32	64
		16:3-5	128	XIV, 11-13	63, 69, 234
Sirach		18	128	XIV, 15-16	63
23:9	277	18:3	128	XVI, 4	63
24	125, 127	18:5	128		
24:13	127	18:6-7	128-29, 190	**1QM**	
24:14	127	18:8	129	III-IV	168-72
45:7-8	124	18:10	129	X	169
45:8	124	18:12	129	X, 8-9	169
47:11	348			XI	114
48	94	**Tobit**		XII, 1	169
48:2	94	14:5	325		
48:3	94, 116			**1QS**	
48:4	94	**Wisdom of Solomon**		II-III	167
48:5	94	2:18	166	III, 3-8	167
48:10	94	4:15	167	III, 7-8	167
49:16	125	5:17-20	61	III, 11-12	167
50	124, 125, 127, 137, 138	7:7	184	III, 20-22	168
50:1	125	9:1-3	61	IV	62, 133
50:3-4	125	9:2-4	60	IV, 7-8	62, 69
50:5-7	124	9:3	61	IV, 7-26	199
50:5-8	125	9:5	61	IV, 23	69
50:7b	126	9:7	166	IV, 20-26	62
50:9-10	126	10-11	175	IV, 21	62
50:10	127	10:1-2	60	IV, 25	62
50:11	124	10:17	167	V, 5-6	168
50:11-13	126	12:15-18	61	V, 9	168
50:12	126, 127	16:10	166	V, 12-13	168
50:14-21	126	16:26	166	IX, 11	31, 130
50:19	127	18:1	166	XI, 7-9	168
50:21	128	18:4	166		
		18:5	166	**1QSa**	
Testament of Abraham		18:13	166	II, 11-22	130
8:5	348				
11	75			**1QSb**	
11-13	331	**QUMRAN**		IV, 25	131
11:4	75			IV, 27	131
11:9	75	**1QapGen**			
12-13	76	19-20	478	**1QpHab**	
12:4	76, 348			VII, 1-2	490
12:5	76	**1QH**[a]		VIII, 1-3	138, 182
12:5-13:6	348	IV, 15	62		

4Q167
2, 2 — 138, 182, 490

4Q174
1 I, 2 — 116
1 I, 7-9 — 116
1 I, 10-11 — 186
1 I, 13 — 116, 186

4Q216
VII, 11 — 64, 133

4Q246 (Aramaic Apocalypse)
II, 1 — 115, 248, 390
II, 1-3 — 115
II, 1-5 — 186
II, 4 — 115
II, 4-9 — 115
II, 5 — 115, 390
II, 7-9 — 248
II, 8 — 115
II, 9 — 390

CD
XII, 23 — 130
XX, 1 — 130

CD-A
III, 20 — 69
III, 18-IV, 4 — 69

4Q287
frag. 1-2 — 66
frag. 2, 7 — 66
frag. 2, 9 — 66, 69
frag. 3 — 65
frag. 3-5 — 66
frag. 4 — 65, 69
frag. 5, 13 — 65

4Q252
V, 3 — 31

4Q369
1 II, 1 — 155
1 II, 3 — 155
1 II, 7 — 155

4Q374
2 II, 6 — 86
2 II, 8 — 86
2 II, 9-10 — 86

4Q381
frag. 1, 8 — 37, 66, 234
frag. 1, 11 — 37, 66
frag. 15 — 103
frag. 76-77, 14-16 — 67

4Q400
1 I, 3 — 131
1 I, 6 — 131-32
1 I, 15 — 132

4Q401
frag. 11, 3 — 124

4Q418
frag. 81 — 132
frag. 81, 1 — 133, 134
frag. 81, 3 — 132, 134
frag. 81, 4 — 132
frag. 81, 4-5 — 133
frag. 81, 5 — 133
frag. 81, 11-14 — 134

4Q421
7 I, 10-12 — 135
7 I, 11 — 136
7 I, 11-12 — 135-36

4Q471b
1-3 — 135
4 — 136
5 — 135
7 — 135

4Q491c
1, 5 — 136
1, 8 — 136

4Q504
frag. 1-2, 3 — 68-69
frag. 1-2, 4 — 69
frag. 8 — 37

4Q521
2 I — 415
2 II, 2 — 117
2 II, 7 — 117, 118
2 II, 8 — 118
2 II, 11-12 — 95, 117
2 III — 95
2 III, 1 — 118

4Q541
9 I, 2 — 137
9 I, 3-5 — 137
9 I, 5 — 137

4Q558
4 — 95
5 — 95

11Q5
27, 2 — 199

11QMelchizedek
II, 4-6 — 366
II, 6 — 122, 182, 366, 490
II, 6-8 — 366
II, 10 — 366
II, 10-11 — 366
II, 13 — 122-23, 331, 366
II, 23-24 — 123

11QPs^a
XXVII, 9-10 — 416

JOSEPHUS

War
1.1 — 143
2.258-63 — 452
2.261-63 — 509

Antiquities
2.205 — 366
2.211 — 365
2.213 — 365
2.215 — 366
2.216 — 366
2.284-87 — 435
2.347-48 — 449

4.326	90	1.155	82
6.11	417	1.155-56	436
8.45	187, 207, 417, 470, 471	1.155-58	198, 452
8.46-49	417	1.156	82
8.47	417	1.158	82
8.327	461	2.64	72
12.5	143		
13.16.2	521		
19.6	449		
20.97	103, 198, 249, 436, 447, 454		

PHILO

Embassy to Gaius

144-45	446

Legum allegoriae

1.88-89	71

De opificio mundi

83-88	70
83	70-71
88	71
134	71
136	71
140	71

De praemiis et poenis

89-91	71
125	72

Quod omnis probus liber sit

43	83

De sacrificiis Abelis et Caini

5	83
8	83
10	83, 90

De somniis

164-65	83-84

De vita Mosis

1.60	504

NEW TESTAMENT

Matthew

1	250, 419
1:1	240, 243, 360, 361, 466
1:1-17	360-63, 378
1:3	364
1:5	364
1:6	364
1:11	245, 470
1:12	245, 470
1:16	364
1:17	245
1:18	364, 517
1:18-25	363-73, 524
1:19	365
1:20	364
1:20-21	365, 367-68
1:21	239
1:23	296, 359, 367, 369, 517
1:23-25	517
2:1	374
2:2	252, 374, 447, 469
2:2-6	524
2:3	374
2:4	374, 377
2:4-6	517
2:6	374, 396
2:8	252
2:9	374
2:11	29-30, 252, 447, 469
2:13-15	524
2:15	237-38, 240, 245, 377, 518
2:16	378
2:16-18	366, 518
2:20	378
2:22-23	518
3:2	238, 274

3:3	552
3:6	238
3:7	238
3:8	240
3:9	382
3:11	238, 384
3:11-12	222, 239, 432
3:12	528
3:14	183, 238
3:15	238
3:16	382
3:17	239, 240
4:1	384
4:1-11	347
4:3	240
4:6	240
4:8	381
4:8-10	415
4:10	374
4:12	382
4:14	518
4:17	427, 432
4:23	471-72
4:23-25	460
4:24	419
5–7	241, 382, 520
5:1	240, 347
5:4	521
5:9	240
5:11	341
5:11-12	240
5:12	521
5:16	240, 241, 244, 576
5:17	517-18, 521, 522, 532
5:18	521
5:20	521, 522
5:21	521, 523
5:21-48	521
5:22	521
5:22-24	380, 523
5:26	521
5:27	521
5:27-32	523
5:28	521
5:31	521
5:31-32	523
5:32	521
5:33	521
5:33-37	523

5:34	521
5:38	521
5:38-42	523
5:39	521
5:43	521
5:43-48	241, 523
5:44	521
5:45	240, 523, 576
5:48	240, 576
6:1	240, 576
6:2	521
6:4	240, 576
6:5	521
6:6	240, 576
6:8	240, 576
6:9	240, 384, 576
6:11	240
6:13	240, 347
6:14	240, 254, 576
6:14-15	241, 254
6:15	240, 576
6:18	240, 576
6:25	521
6:25-34	241
6:26	241, 521, 576
6:29	521
6:32	241, 576
7:3-5	380
7:7-11	241
7:11	576
7:21	241, 431, 576
7:21-22	520
7:21-23	431
7:21-27	332, 353
7:23	241, 520
7:24	241, 347, 384
7:24-25	520
7:24-27	431
7:26-27	520
7:28-29	94, 520
8-9	466
8:2	252, 374
8:16-17	530-31
8:17	471, 518
8:18	442
8:18-22	340, 437, 530
8:19	340
8:19-20	442
8:20	281, 340, 345, 352-53

8:21	442
8:22	530
8:23	442, 443
8:23-27	433-36, 436-44
8:24	443
8:25	443
8:27	436, 443
8:28-34	421
8:29	421, 430, 432
9:1-8	281-82
9:4	282
9:6	282, 286, 345, 385
9:8	273, 275, 280, 282, 306, 385, 479
9:9	295
9:11	295
9:12	295
9:13	245, 295
9:18	252, 374
9:27	466, 467
9:27-31	466
9:27-34	468
9:28	466
9:29	466
9:32-34	467
9:35	460, 467, 472, 529
9:36	243
9:36–10:1	528
9:37	528, 529
9:38	529
10	347, 531
10:1	416, 460, 529
10:1-5	529
10:5-8	471
10:6	427
10:7	427
10:8	427, 460
10:17	345
10:17-18	345
10:19-20	284
10:20	384
10:21	345, 427
10:22	427
10:23	345
10:25	346, 427
10:32-33	284, 530
10:34-35	530
10:37	531
10:38-39	531
10:40	529

10:40-41	427
10:40-42	531
11:2	243, 470
11:2-3	470, 526
11:2-6	242, 469-70
11:3	242-43
11:4-5	242
11:4-6	470, 471
11:5	521
11:5-6	526
11:6	254
11:7-15	243
11:8-19	30
11:10	470, 527
11:11-15	534
11:12	525
11:13	518, 525
11:14	335, 527
11:16-19	243
11:18-19	280, 341, 528
11:19	293-94, 341, 342, 352-53
11:20	470
11:21	470
11:23	470
11:25	469, 470
11:27	242, 245
11:28-30	386
12:1	294
12:1-8	293-96
12:3	294
12:4	294
12:5-6	294
12:6	533
12:7	245, 294
12:8	296
12:9	469
12:15	419, 460, 534
12:15-16	467
12:15-23	467, 518
12:15-32	418
12:17	468
12:17-21	467
12:18	384, 468
12:18-20	418
12:18-21	521
12:18-28	384
12:19	468
12:21	418, 468
12:22	419, 460, 467

12:22-32	347	15:22	420-21, 468	23:10	255
12:23	419, 467, 524	15:24	427	23:17	295
12:23-24	469	15:25	374	23:19	295
12:24	420, 468	15:28	468	23:21	295
12:24-31	467	15:30	460	23:22	295
12:26-28	468	16:13	306, 308	23:34	30
12:28	431, 468, 527	16:13-20	459	24	349
12:31	284	16:13-28	333	24-25	351
12:32	283, 284	16:15-17	244-46, 255	24:3	349
12:38-42	532-34	16:16	245, 306, 372, 447	24:5	251
12:39	343, 532	16:17	233, 245, 447	24:7	349
12:40	343, 532	16:18-19	275	24:27	349
12:41	443, 533	16:21	306, 308, 337, 343	24:30	94, 350
12:41-42	533	16:24-28	331	24:32-36	350
12:42	417, 471	16:27	331, 431	24:36	255
12:43-45	417	16:28	308, 332	24:37	349, 350
12:46-50	380	17:12	335	24:39	349, 350
12:50	384	17:14-20	415	24:42	350
13	254, 534	17:23	337	24:44	351
13:11-13	534	17:24	458	25:31-46	431
13:13	534	17:24-27	456, 458-59	25:31	151, 351, 385
13:17	534	17:26	459	25:32	351, 529
13:19	346, 347	17:27	459	25:34	34, 385, 431
13:23-30	561-62	18:15-21	380	25:35	385
13:27	561	18:18-20	386	25:35-36	352
13:30	528	18:20	380, 385, 386	25:36	385
13:35	518	18:35	254	25:40	352, 384, 385
13:36-43	346	19:16	560	25:41	351-52, 432
13:37	346	19:16-22	559	25:42-43	352
13:37-38	346	19:18	151	25:45	352
13:38	346	19:22	460	26	344
13:39	528	19:28	94, 262, 311, 331,	26:2	344
13:41	195, 332, 346, 347,		333, 347, 349, 352	26:22	251
	431	20:19	337	26:24	344
13:43	347	20:20	374	26:25	251
13:58	474	20:21	332	26:28	274
14:13	455	20:29-34	468-69	26:31	529
14:14	455, 460	21:1-7	519	26:36	255
14:22-33	246-53, 433-36,	21:12-13	469	26:38	565
	446	21:14	469	26:39	435
14:26	251	21:15	469	26:40-46	565
14:27	251	21:15-17	470	26:45	344
14:28	251	21:16	469	26:64	333, 381
14:30-31	250	21:16-17	469	27:9	519
14:33	28, 257, 372, 374,	21:24	460	27:40	255
	443, 447, 469	22:44	499	27:42-43	255
15:3-9	254	23:3	255	27:43	257
15:12	254	23:7-8	384	27:46	565
15:12-14	254	23:8-12	255	27:54	256, 257
15:13	254	23:9	255	27:63	401

28:6	401	1:21-23	421	2:28	267, 272, 291, 332,
28:7	379, 380	1:21-27	94, 429		415, 495
28:8-10	379	1:21-28	187, 205, 421, 438,	3:1-6	187, 454
28:9	28, 374		452, 473	3:7-8	187
28:10	380, 381, 576	1:21-2:12	421	3:7-12	460
28:12	216-17	1:22	205, 207, 209, 277,	3:10	187, 206
28:16	382		278, 279, 422, 438	3:10-12	472
28:16-20	383	1:22-28	278, 472	3:11	187, 205, 206, 207,
28:17	28, 252, 374	1:23-28	228		208, 233, 415, 424,
28:18	276, 310, 332, 333,	1:24	167, 205, 277, 299,		440
	346, 375, 380		423, 432	3:11-12	208, 413, 474
28:19	347, 384	1:25	438	3:12	206, 299
28:20	93, 241, 296, 359,	1:27	205, 207, 209, 277,	3:13-15	215, 216
	384		279, 415, 422, 423,	3:13-19	187
			438, 440	3:14-15	278, 453
Mark		1:29-31	228, 472	3:15	41, 208, 279, 416,
1	276	1:29-34	187		425, 426
1-8	293, 297, 301, 302,	1:32-34	187, 228, 472	3:20-21	215
	514	1:34	438, 460	3:20-30	208
1:1	181, 182, 184, 185,	1:39	187, 415, 471-72	3:20-35	473
	186, 192, 200, 289,	1:39-44	273	3:22	276
	299, 325, 475, 495	1:40-45	187, 462	3:22-30	187, 208, 209, 416
1:1-8:30	272	2	298, 307, 319, 331	3:23	192
1:2	183, 335, 492	2:1-5a	422	3:23-26	300
1:2-3	18, 24, 182-83, 184	2:1-12	187, 214-15, 265,	3:23-27	303
1:2-4	201, 527		273-81, 422, 438,	3:23-30	415
1:3	183, 552		452, 460	3:26	192
1:4	274	2:1-3:6	286, 422	3:27	208
1:4-6	192	2:5	273, 473	3:28	284
1:5	183	2:6	275	3:28-29	330
1:6	492	2:6-7	269, 500	3:28-30	269, 293
1:7	274	2:6-10	209	3:29	284
1:7-8	222, 432, 495	2:7	18, 268, 273, 500-	3:29-30	423
1:8	205, 275		501, 512	3:31-35	187, 215
1:9	183	2:8	275	3:33	215
1:10	184, 192, 199	2:10	29, 265, 267, 272,	3:33-35	474
1:11	179, 181, 184, 185,		276, 279, 291, 319,	3:34	215
	186, 189, 192, 199,		324, 331, 415, 473	3:34-35	187, 305, 315
	440	2:10c-12	422	3:35	215
1:12	205	2:12	210, 286, 479	4	436
1:12-13	186, 208	2:13-17	187	4:1	437
1:13	101, 192, 300	2:17	290, 295	4:1-34	216, 437
1:14	495, 503	2:23	287	4:1-41	452
1:14-15	207, 432	2:23-28	286-93	4:10-11	502
1:15	183, 186, 319, 495	2:24	287	4:10-13	437
1:16-20	187	2:25	287, 294	4:12	475, 534
1:16-3:6	277	2:25-26	496	4:15	192, 208, 300
1:17	41, 300, 301	2:26	287	4:35	437
1:17-18	215	2:27	290, 291, 338	4:35-41	433, 439
1:21-22	421	2:27-28	287	4:36	437, 443

4:37	443	6:32-33	502-6	8:32	197, 298, 300, 475
4:38	443	6:33	451	8:32-34	300
4:39	438	6:34	452, 502, 504, 505,	8:33	192, 208, 300
4:40-41	437		528	8:34	41, 215, 266, 267,
4:41	18, 413, 436, 438-	6:34b	455		301, 302, 317-18
	39, 440	6:37	41, 453	8:34-37	267
5	436, 473	6:39	451, 503, 505	8:34-38	314, 321
5:4	208	6:39-44	452	8:34–9:1	191, 331
5:6-7	205, 208	6:41	41, 453	8:35	267, 302, 310, 330
5:7	207, 208, 233, 415,	6:42	454	8:36	302
	430	6:45-52	433-36	8:37	302
5:19	208	6:48	505-6	8:38	194, 196, 266, 267,
5:19-20	495	6:50	18		307, 310, 311, 314,
5:20	208	6:51-52	450		329, 331, 338, 358,
5:21-24	472	6:52	437, 450, 454, 506		431
5:30	474	6:53-56	460	9	298, 302, 304
5:34	473	7:3	521	9:1	332
5:35-43	472	7:5	521	9:2	191, 196
5:36	473	7:24-30	454	9:2-7	94
5:39	299	7:26	454	9:2-8	75, 92, 113
5:43	413, 472	7:28	454	9:4	192, 196
6	436, 437, 450-55,	7:30	468	9:5	197
	473	7:36	299	9:7	179, 192, 196, 197,
6:1	473	8	298, 302, 304, 313,		318
6:1-52	450-55		436	9:9	192, 195, 312, 338
6:2	473	8–16	301, 302, 514	9:11	335
6:3	473, 474	8:1-3	454	9:11-13	192, 201, 492, 495,
6:5	473, 474	8:1-10	453-54		503
6:6	473, 474	8:11	41	9:12	192, 335, 337, 338
6:7	208, 209, 215, 278,	8:15	454	9:13	335
	279, 416, 426, 453,	8:17	454	9:14-27	415, 475-76
	474	8:18	475	9:14-29	209, 298, 428
6:7-13	216	8:22-26	496	9:19	428
6:8	474	8:22–10:52	289	9:22	428
6:12	41	8:23-24	475	9:23	428
6:12-13	216, 426, 453, 460	8:24	476	9:24	473
6:13	208, 279	8:25	475	9:29	428-29
6:14	426, 503	8:27	194, 266	9:30	475
6:14-16	413	8:27-30	191, 272, 497	9:30-37	304
6:15	426	8:27-33	188, 197, 475	9:31	272, 308, 337, 338,
6:15-16	335	8:27–9:13	191, 192, 194		476, 515
6:16	503	8:28	266, 335, 426, 503	9:33-37	475
6:21	450, 503	8:29	181, 288, 299, 426,	9:35	304
6:22	450, 503		475	9:36-37	304
6:23	450, 503	8:30	207	9:37	476
6:25	450, 503	8:31	192, 194, 211, 266,	9:38	429
6:26	450, 503		267, 272, 298, 299,	9:38-39	209
6:27	450, 503		307, 308, 309, 335,	9:39-40	429
6:28	450-51		337, 338, 343, 476	10	298, 302, 304, 475
6:31	450, 451	8:31-33	181, 191, 287	10:1	419

10:13-16	475	12:25	75	14:25	508
10:17-22	559	12:29-30	495, 500	14:27	506-9, 511
10:18	18, 560	12:32	500	14:34	212, 213, 315, 509,
10:31	305	12:33	500		510, 511, 565
10:32-45	497	12:34	500, 501	14:35	213
10:33	272, 310, 337, 338,	12:35-37	288-90, 476,	14:35-36	507
	476, 515		496-99	14:36	188, 213, 303, 435,
10:34	308, 337, 515	12:36	325, 328, 329, 497,		501, 511, 513, 576
10:35-45	475		498, 499	14:37-38	315
10:37	188, 302, 407	12:36-37	498	14:37-42	565
10:41	303	12:37	18, 289	14:41	337, 344, 515
10:41-45	188	12:40	310	14:42	515
10:42-45	451	13	290, 313, 314, 319,	14:44	515
10:43	303		321, 326, 327, 345,	14:53	299
10:44	303		346	14:55	323
10:45	272, 303, 306, 338,	13:1-2	323	14:55-61	322
	515	13:1-4	314, 320	14:56	323
10:46-48	466	13:2	315	14:57	323
10:46-52	298, 476	13:6	315, 325	14:58	315, 323
10:47	496	13:9	315, 326, 503	14:59	323
10:47-48	288, 496	13:11	284	14:60	324
10:52	476, 497	13:12	315	14:60-64	188
11	475	13:14	320, 564	14:61	182, 200, 245, 268,
11:3	495	13:14-20	314, 320		270, 324, 515
11:9	495, 499	13:17	564	14:61-62	266, 299, 325,
11:10	288	13:19	320		328, 329, 497
11:12-14	298	13:20	331	14:62	18, 195, 200, 201,
11:12-23	314	13:24	315		209, 267, 268, 287,
11:12-25	290	13:24-25	349		299, 315, 317, 322-
11:15-17	323	13:24b	316		31, 327, 332, 338,
11:18	209, 323, 326	13:26	195, 271, 317, 318,		355, 498
11:20-24	298		325, 327, 329, 331,	14:64	310, 512
11:23-25	279		349, 355	14:65	515
11:25	214, 215	13:26-27	211, 349	15:1	515
11:27	326	13:28-32	350	15:2	200, 503
11:27-28	209	13:30-31	211	15:5	515
11:27-33	18	13:32	211, 212	15:6-15	515
11:28	279, 323-24, 326	13:34	279	15:9	200, 503
11:29	279	13:35	350	15:10	515
11:29-30	279	13:36	315	15:12	200, 503
11:29-33	503-4	13:37	315	15:15	515
11:30	324	14-15	321, 509, 513	15:18	200, 503
11:33	279	14:3-9	199	15:19	208
12:1-12	209-211, 314, 324,	14:8-9	289	15:24	509, 512
	499, 516	14:10	515	15:26	200, 503
12:6	210	14:11	515	15:27	189, 302-3
12:8-11	499	14:18	509, 510, 515	15:29	509, 512
12:9	495	14:21	335, 344, 515	15:29-30	269, 330
12:10-11	210, 495, 499	14:23	303	15:31-32	2, 512
12:12	326	14:24	188	15:32	325, 503

15:33	315	2:10	397	4:24	555
15:33-39	183	2:11	397, 398, 457, 542	4:25	479
15:34	310, 501, 507, 509,	2:15	397	4:25-27	556
	511, 512, 513, 565	2:25	554	4:26	479, 480
15:36	201, 202, 509, 514	2:25-27	398	4:27	483
15:37	201, 202, 512	2:26	398, 400, 554	4:29	556
15:38	199, 202, 315	2:27	554	4:31-37	296
15:39	179, 188, 199, 201,	2:28-32	552	4:33-37	228
	257	2:30	398	4:34	432, 438
15:61-62	181	2:31	553	4:35	438, 477
16	275	2:32	398, 400	4:36	415, 439
		2:34-35	398	4:38-39	228
Luke		2:40	399	4:39	477
1–2	400, 407	2:41-51	221	4:40	460, 478
1:1	387	2:41-52	399	4:40-41	228, 478
1:6	388	2:41	221	4:41	424, 477, 478, 479
1:13-17	388	2:43	221	5:4-7	457
1:15	92, 388, 389, 554	2:47	399	5:4-11	456-58
1:16	388	2:48	221, 399	5:5	456
1:17	388, 389, 555	2:49	221, 399	5:8	457, 458
1:20	230	3:1-6	552-54	5:10a	457
1:23	389	3:3	274, 553	5:10b	457
1:31-35	115	3:5-6	552	5:15	460, 478
1:32	218, 219	3:6	553	5:17	282
1:32-33	219, 226, 389-90	3:15	223	5:17-26	282-83
1:33	219	3:15-16	222, 223	5:22	223
1:34	220, 224, 390	3:15-17	223	5:24	341
1:35	218, 220, 392, 539	3:15-18	432	5:25	283
1:36-37	393	3:16	222	5:26	283, 286
1:41-45	393, 554	3:22	92, 223, 232, 334,	5:30-32	457
1:43	393, 457		539, 554	5:36-39	559
1:45	393-94	3:23-38	223, 250	5:39	559
1:47	553	3:27-31	360	6:1	296
1:54	395	3:38	54, 221, 334, 391	6:1-5	296-97
1:55	395	4:1	539, 554	6:5	297, 341
1:67	554	4:3	225, 333	6:17-19	478
1:68	397, 404, 481	4:3-13	334	6:18	478
1:69	395, 397, 398, 481,	4:4	225	6:18-19	419
	552	4:8	226	6:22	341
1:70	395	4:9	225, 333	6:23	341
1:70-71	395	4:12	227	6:26	341
1:70-73	481	4:14	539, 554	6:35	234
1:71	395, 553	4:14-15	554	7:12-16	92
1:72	395	4:16-30	554	7:13	480
1:76	396, 457	4:18	555	7:16	480-81
1:77	396, 553	4:18-19	555	7:18-35	481
1:78	396, 481	4:18-21	235	7:19	482
1:78-79	396	4:19	555	7:21	460
2:4	396	4:21	230, 536, 555	7:22	482
2:9	312	4:23	554, 555	7:22-23	482

7:27	527	10:21-24	232	17:17-18	483
7:27-28	482	10:21	232, 234	17:21	483
7:29-30	482	10:22	232, 242	17:22	349
7:31-35	482	10:25	557, 559	17:22-35	349
7:33	351	10:25-37	557	17:24	350
7:33-34	30, 280	10:29	234	17:26	350
7:33-35	341	10:30	558	17:27	350
7:34	342	10:30-37	556	17:30	350
7:35	341	10:36	558	18:8	351
7:36-50	457	10:37	559	18:9-14	457
8:2	460	11:2	576	18:18	557, 560
8:19-21	437	11:13	234	18:18-23	559-61
8:22	437, 480	11:20	431	18:19	560
8:22-25	433-36, 436-44	11:21	234	18:33	337
8:24	438, 457	11:24-26	417	19:1-10	457
8:25	436, 439	11:29	343	19:7	342
8:26-39	479	11:30-32	532	19:10	342, 351
8:28	430	12:8-9	284	20:42	499
8:31	431	12:8-10	285	21:20	564
8:39	480	12:10	283, 284, 333	21:23	564
8:45	457	12:11-12	284	21:27	38
9:1	416, 460	12:40	351	21:29-33	350
9:1-2	483	13:1-5	563	21:36	351
9:1-6	483	13:6-9	563	22:16	230, 233
9:6	460, 484	13:10-16	478	22:22	344
9:11	460	13:11	460	22:27	306
9:22	337, 343	13:12	478	22:28-30	348-49
9:26	431	13:13	479	22:30	311
9:27	332	13:16	460, 478	22:35-38	562
9:28	229	13:23	561	22:37	562-63
9:29	230	13:23-30	563, 564	22:40	565
9:31	230	13:24	561	22:42	435
9:33	457	13:24-30	562		22:46-47
9:35	230-31	13:25	561	22:48	344
9:42	477	13:26	561	22:50-51	565
9:47	223	13:28	561	22:61	402, 542
9:49	457	13:28-29	561	22:63-71	333
9:54	556	13:30	561	22:65	333
9:57	340	13:33	562	22:66-71	235
9:57-60	340	13:34-35	562	22:67	333
9:58	340	15:1-32	457	22:68	333
10:1-12	483	15:11-32	234	22:69	333
10:8	484	16:19-31	566	22:70	333-34
10:9	427, 460	16:31	566	22:71	334
10:16	427	17	350	23:2	236, 334
10:17	234, 427, 484	17:11-19	556	23:25	285
10:17-20	483	17:12-19	482	23:27-31	563-64, 565
10:18	29, 234, 432	17:13	457	23:28	563, 564
10:18-19	484	17:14	482	23:29	564
10:19	427, 428	17:15-16	483	23:30	564

23:31	564
23:32	563
23:34	285
23:36	285
23:39	285
23:40-42	562
23:41	563
23:43	562, 565
23:44-45	539, 540
23:46	565-66
23:47	334
23:52	542
24	407, 541, 544, 549, 551, 566
24:3	403, 542
24:6	401
24:6-7	568
24:7	332, 337, 546
24:7-8	401
24:8	568
24:13-35	403, 535
24:19	404, 535
24:19-21	535
24:20	403-4
24:21	404
24:23	403-4
24:23-24	535
24:25	536
24:25-26	234
24:25-27	24-25, 404, 536
24:26	404, 407, 537, 543, 562
24:26-27	403
24:27	536
24:30	233
24:36-49	25, 403
24:37-43	404
24:38-43	233
24:39	310, 407
24:44	230, 387, 401, 536, 468
24:44-46	544, 563, 468
24:44-47	553
24:44-48	554
24:44-53	458
24:46	234, 337, 407, 458, 537, 543, 546
24:46-47	387, 404, 537, 550
24:47	546, 553, 557
24:48	405

24:49	405, 458, 539
24:52	28, 458
John	
1:1	177
1:6	31
1:12	177
1:21	82
1:23	552
2:19-21	323
5:17	177
5:18	177
10:18	500
11:52	177
12:34	266
17:5	322
18:5-6	251
20:21	281
20:22	92
20:23	215, 275, 280
20:31	577
Acts	
1:4	542
1:4-5	538
1:8	220, 538, 539, 557
2	236, 402, 405-11, 479, 484, 566
2:1-39	92, 236
2:3	539
2:4	217
2:14-36	538, 544
2:15-16	539
2:16-21	414
2:16-24	539-43
2:17	540, 553
2:17-18	539
2:19	414, 484, 539
2:19-20	539
2:20	539, 540
2:21	108, 137, 541, 567
2:22	1, 12, 283, 285, 406, 414, 479, 480-81, 483, 484, 539, 540, 541
2:22-24	285
2:23	406, 407, 540
2:23-24	541
2:24	540, 546
2:25	108, 407, 543

2:25-28	205
2:27-38	458
2:30	407, 452, 543, 549
2:30-31	543
2:30-32	542
2:30-33	562
2:31	407, 543-44
2:32	407, 546
2:32-33	544
2:32-36	303
2:33	458, 485, 542, 544, 567
2:34	108, 544
2:34-36	499
2:35-36	285
2:36	108, 285, 408, 409, 485, 540, 541, 542, 563
2:38	457
2:38-41	285
2:39	108
2:43	484
2:43-47	484
3:6	485
3:13	285, 395, 485, 545
3:14-20	285
3:17-21	284
3:19	457
3:21	545
3:22	546
3:22-23	545
3:22-26	481
3:25	546
3:26	285, 458, 546
4:12	541
4:23-31	547
4:24	547
4:25	547
4:26	547
4:27	547
4:30	484
5:12	484
5:12-16	484
5:15	220
5:16	429
5:28	563
5:31	333, 457
6:8	484
7	285, 547, 549
7:51-52	548

7:55-56	333	5	355	**Revelation**		
7:56	266	5:2	312	11:1-12	327	
8:1-14	557	5:17	432	11:12	317	
8:6-7	484	6:3-5	188	21:3	370	
8:7	429	8:15	212, 576			
8:13	484	8:21	312			
8:25	557	8:29	178, 214	**TARGUMS**		
8:25-39	548	8:29-30	312			
8:32	548	8:32	189	**Fragmentary Targum**	77	
8:33	548	10:9	108			
8:35	548	10:12-13	541	**Targum Pseudo-**		
9:32-35	485	10:13	108, 137	**Jonathan**	77	
9:35	485					
9:36-43	485	**1 Corinthians**		**Targum Neofiti**	77	
9:42	485	5:3	386			
10:38	478	5:3-4	93			
13:22	548	5:4	386	**MISHNAH**		
13:23	548	6:2-3	311, 322, 331, 432			
13:27-31	284	6:3	421	*Avot*		
13:33	409, 546, 549	12:13	384	1:1-18	521	
13:34	546	15	355	3:3	386	
13:35	549	15:20	178			
13:35-37	549	15:20-28	381	*Ta'anit*		
13:38	549	15:25	499	3.8	447	
13:47	398	15:28	178			
15:13-21	550					
15:16	550	**Galatians**		**OTHER RABBINIC**		
15:17	550	3:26-27	177, 384	**TEXTS**		
16:16	429	3:29	384			
16:17	429, 430	4:6	212, 576	*Genesis Rabbah*		
17:22-31	563			34:14	331	
17:29-31	224	**Philippians**				
17:31	285, 351	2:9	108	*Pesiqta Rabbati*		
19:11	430			36:1	104, 250, 436	
19:11-17	430	**Colossians**				
19:12	430	1	16	*Pesiqta de Rab Kahana*		
19:13-15	425	1:15	72	76a	117	
19:13-16	430	2:5	93, 386			
19:15	206			*Tanḥuma Bemidbar*		
19:17	430	**1 Thessalonians**		3:15	176	
24:15	549	4:14	322			
26:6-7	549					
26:22-23	551	**Hebrews**		**GRECO-ROMAN**		
28:20	549	1:13	407, 499	**LITERATURE**		
28:23-28	234	5:6-10	122			
		6:20	122	**Aelius Aristides**		
Romans		7:1	122	*Heracles*		
1:3-4	221	7:10-17	122	40.11	463	
1:4	381, 410	8:5	244	40.12	463	
3:21	525					

Dio Cassius
Roman History
59.17.11 — 449

Dio Chrysostom
De regno 3
30 — 448
31 — 448

Dionysius of Halicarnassus
Roman Antiquities
1.76-77 — 370

Empedocles
Fragments
111 — 464-65

Homer
Hymns
16.1-4 — 463

Iliad
2.729-33 — 464

Plato
Republic
407 — 463-64

Plutarch
Alexander
3 — 370

Numa
4.4 — 371
4.4-8 — 371

Parallel Lives: Pyrrhus
3.4 — 465

Romulus
2 — 370

Symposium
8.1 — 370-71

Tacitus
Histories
4.81-82 — 465